SAP PRESS e-books

Print or e-book, Kindle or iPad, workplace or airplane: Choose where and how to read your SAP PRESS books! You can now get all our titles as e-books, too:

▶ By download and online access
▶ For all popular devices
▶ And, of course, DRM-free

Convinced? Then go to **www.sap-press.com** and get your e-book today.

SAP® BusinessObjects™ Web Intelligence

 PRESS

SAP PRESS is a joint initiative of SAP and Galileo Press. The know-how offered by SAP specialists combined with the expertise of the Galileo Press publishing house offers the reader expert books in the field. SAP PRESS features first-hand information and expert advice, and provides useful skills for professional decision-making.

SAP PRESS offers a variety of books on technical and business-related topics for the SAP user. For further information, please visit our website: *www.sap-press.com*.

Greg Myers and Eric Vallo
SAP BusinessObjects BI System Administration (2nd edition)
2014, approx. 550 pp., hardcover
ISBN 978-1-4932-1000-8

Haun, Hickman, Loden, Wells
Implementing SAP HANA
2013, 837 pp., hardcover
ISBN 978-1-59229-856-3

Christian Ah-Soon and Peter Snowdon
Getting Started with SAP Lumira
2014, approx. 565 pp., hardcover
ISBN 978-1-4932-1033-6

Ah-Soon, Mazoué, Vezzosi
Universe Design with SAP BusinessObjects:
The Comprehensive Guide
2014, 729 pp., hardcover
ISBN 978-1-59229-901-0

Jim Brogden, Heather Sinkwitz, Dallas Marks, Gabriel Orthous

SAP® BusinessObjects™ Web Intelligence

The Comprehensive Guide

Galileo Press

Bonn • Boston

Galileo Press is named after the Italian physicist, mathematician, and philosopher Galileo Galilei (1564–1642). He is known as one of the founders of modern science and an advocate of our contemporary, heliocentric worldview. His words *Eppur si muove* (And yet it moves) have become legendary. The Galileo Press logo depicts Jupiter orbited by the four Galilean moons, which were discovered by Galileo in 1610.

Editor Sarah Frazier
Acquisitions Editor Kelly Grace Weaver
Copyeditor Julie McNamee
Cover Design Graham Geary
Photo Credit Shutterstock.com/96795922/© Triff
Layout Design Vera Brauner
Production Graham Geary
Typesetting SatzPro, Krefeld (Germany)
Printed and bound in the United States of America, on paper from sustainable sources

ISBN 978-1-4932-1057-2
© 2014 by Galileo Press Inc., Boston (MA)
3rd edition 2014

Library of Congress Cataloging-in-Publication Data
Brogden, Jim, 1972-
SAP businessobjects web intelligence : the comprehensive / Jim Brogden, Heather Sinkwitz, Dallas Marks,
Gabriel Orthous. -- [third edition].
pages cm
Includes index.
ISBN 978-1-4932-1057-2 (print) -- ISBN 1-4932-1057-2 (print) -- ISBN 978-1-4932-1058-9 (ebook) --
ISBN 978-1-4932-1059-6
(print and ebook) 1. BusinessObjects. 2. Business intelligence--Data processing. 3. Management information systems.
I. Title.
HD38.7.B717 2014
658.4'038028553--dc23
2014025884

Contents at a Glance

Dear Reader,

To create a comprehensive guide, you need a comprehensive team. With two previous editions under their belts, these seasoned co-authors have once again banded together and delivered an updated version to follow the release of WebI 4.1. Offering a foundation for one of the industry's most powerful business intelligence reporting tools, this book presents not only an informative guide into SAP BusinessObjects Web Intelligence, but the culminating knowledge and experience of experts in the field.

So, how do you make a core design product of SAP look sexy a third time around? Jim Brogden was up to the task. A man of wit and incredible leadership skills, Jim encouraged the team with everything from Braveheart-esque speeches to Harry Potter "chosen one" references. Despite busy careers and schedules, Jim, along with Heather Sinkwitz, Dallas Marks, and Gabriel Orthous, pulled together and delivered. You now hold their combined efforts in the palms of your hands—or mouse!

I'm confident that this resource will provide vital insights as you explore the capabilities and landscape of SAP BusinessObjects Web Intelligence. Your comments and suggestions are the most useful tools to help us make our books the best they can be; we encourage you to visit our website at *www.sap-press.com* and share your feedback.

Thank you for purchasing a book from SAP PRESS!

Sarah Frazier
Editor, SAP PRESS

Galileo Press
Boston, MA

sarah.frazier@galileo-press.com
www.sap-press.com

Contents

Acknowledgments

I'd like to begin by thanking the publishing team at Galileo Press—Kelly Weaver, Emily Nicholls, and Sarah Frazier for all their assistance and direction throughout the development process of this edition. And a big thanks to Jon Kent for working so tirelessly on past Web Intelligence books.

I'd also like to express sincere appreciation to Olivier Duvelleroy, Gregory Botticchio, Frank Prabel, and Eric Vallo for their technical assistance and guidance.

Finally, I'd like to give many thanks to my lovely and enduring wife, Christi, for her constant support, and for sacrificing countless evenings out while I worked on this edition. And a special thanks to my boys, Jamie and Hunter, for providing the motivation to work hard every day.

Jim Brogden

I have had the pleasure of working with so many inspiring, innovative people during my career in this industry, whose passion and energy continuously motivates me as I journey through new adventures and challenges. The number of colleagues, friends, and family who provide my foundation, my support, my inspiration, and my passion are too many to mention, but it does not diminish their incredible roles and the amount of gratitude I hold for them – thank you to each of you! I want to a make special mention of my new Trax family and fabulous team members, whose spirit and support is inspiring. Finally, I want to thank my family and friends for their kind words, support, and understanding while I worked on this book, especially my beautiful boys, Zen and Max.

Heather Callebaut Sinkwitz

I'd like to thank my wife, Kristin, and my children, Emily, Catherine, and Benjamin, for their patient love and support during the development of this book.

Dallas Marks

I would like to extend my greatest gratitude to the people who have supported me throughout my career as a Business Intelligence professional. First, I'd like to thank my wife, Adriana, and our kids for always believing in me and allowing my "side projects."

Additionally, I would like to thank my mother and father, Martha and Juan, for building an environment where I could shine. With their undivided support, I was able to overcome the odds and learn the value of education and hard work. In the words of Juanito, *"Para atrás ni para echar impulso."*

Last, I would like to thank my mentor and colleague, Louise Kulczewski. She has helped me understand and focus on important aspects of my BI career. For example, six years ago she taught me the "NYC Rule" for report creation, which states: "Create a report and leave it lying in the middle of New York City. If someone picks it up, would they know what it is? Or how to use it?" With Louise's encouragement, I've been able to grow as a BI professional and take on multiple challenges. She is truly a Level-5 leader, and I'm lucky to call myself her friend.

Gabriel Orthous

Foreword

When I first saw BusinessObjects in 1991, it ran on Windows 2.1, and was quite impressive. Then, the BusinessObjects Full Client 3.0 version was released with a fully graphical drag-and-drop user interface, and I was blown away. So far ahead of anything else, in what was called the "Decision Support space" at that time, this version functioned as a client server solution, running on the desktop in either standalone, offline, or connected to a server repository online.

The mid-90s saw a move towards web browser-based solutions, with Business-Objects releasing both a thin client version of the Full Client known as ZABO (Zero Administration Business Objects), and a brand new web-based version known as Web Intelligence. At that time, Web Intelligence only had about half the functionality of the BusinessObjects Full Client tool, and very little user adoption. However, with each subsequent release of BusinessObjects, more capabilities and functionalities were added, and user adoption steadily increased.

With the acquisition of Crystal Decisions in 2003, and the adoption of the Crystal Enterprise platform (known as XI), Web Intelligence became the first Business-Objects tool to be ported to the new platform ahead of the Full Client tool (later renamed Desktop Intelligence). With the release of BusinessObjects XI R2 and XI 3, cool new functions were added to Web Intelligence. This included a Rich Client version that provided the offline capability that so many BusinessObjects users utilized.

Web Intelligence quickly became the BusinessObjects tool of choice, due to its seamless combining of versatile business intelligence query and analysis with rich report creation and formatting capabilities. As the BusinessObjects suite became the most widely used and popular business intelligence solution around the world, Web Intelligence clearly stood out as the flagship product, remaining so to this day.

The last five years have seen even more usage of Web Intelligence than ever before, providing powerful business intelligence insight for organizations everywhere.

One of the premier reference resources to both drive and support that increased usage has been this book. This third edition brings a further update to the latest functionality in Web Intelligence 4.1 SP 3, which includes one of my favorite features—freezing headers. Yes, I know this has existed in Excel for a long time, but it is just cool to have it in Web Intelligence now, alongside all those other super neat features.

This book has become the Bible for Web Intelligence users everywhere, and it is easy to see why. With everything you need in one place, it goes beyond the standard documentation and tutorials available with the product itself. It has also become popular as a reference guide and support aide in Web Intelligence classes.

Recently, I saw a demonstration of an integrated location intelligence solution for pharmaceutical sales representatives. With this they could track patient diagnoses and drugs prescribed across hospitals around the USA. The map was completely interactive, as well as integrated with the data, so you could see the diagnoses and drugs by state, county, zip code, city, and distance, from any location. This also fed into a dynamic heat map which, in turn, was connected to drillable graphs and tables with colored threshold alerts. It looked like a state-of-the-art data visualization dashboard and it was simply stunning. It was Web Intelligence at the top of its game.

So how do you create a Web Intelligence application like that?

Well, start with this book and the rest will come easy.

I have had the honor to meet all of the authors of this book and have had the privilege to work as a colleague with one of them. They are all truly Web Intelligence gurus who have gained that status from working extensively with the product in real world situations. Their experience has been forged through living and breathing Web Intelligence and their combined knowledge and insights have been condensed into the pages of this book.

Web Intelligence has earned its status as the premium Business Intelligence tool in the marketplace today. Use this book and go forth to continue to "webify the world"!

Paul Grill
CEO of InfoSol Inc.

The release of the SAP BusinessObjects BI 4.0 platform brought with it countless improvements to the enterprise suite and a complete overhaul to SAP BusinessObjects Web Intelligence. Continuing with the momentum gained from the 4.0 release, SAP BusinessObjects BI 4.1 further strengthens the SAP BusinessObjects product line with many useful enhancements.

1 Introduction to SAP BusinessObjects Web Intelligence 4.1

The industry's most powerful business intelligence ad hoc query and analysis reporting tool received a major facelift with version 4.0 and built on that new foundation with SAP BusinessObjects BI 4.1. The completely redesigned user interface gives business users the ability to create even more persuasive and engaging analysis documents than before. SAP BusinessObjects Web Intelligence 4.1 (which we'll refer to as Web Intelligence) now comes with a powerful charting engine for a much-improved presentation of data, metrics, and analytics. These new visual attributes provide users with the capability to create powerful dashboard/report hybrids known as *dashports*.

Web Intelligence 4.1 delivers an ideal self-service reporting experience with the capability to query SAP InfoCubes using SAP Business Explorer (SAP BEx) queries, use SAP BusinessObjects Analysis workspaces for multidimensional reports, access traditional relational databases through SAP BusinessObjects universes, and connect to SAP's revolutionary high-performance analytical appliance SAP HANA.

Web Intelligence provides business users with the tools to make better decisions and offer deeper insight into company data. The major benefits include the ability to drill, pivot, chart, track changes, publish, schedule, and share business information online and within a single online portal. The combination of an enhanced Report Panel, seamless connectivity to an extensive list of data sources, and the capability to contain vast amounts of data makes Web Intelligence the premier tool of choice for analyzing data.

This chapter introduces you to the key features and core functionality of the Web Intelligence reporting tool. We'll also discuss the steps for setting up the report viewing properties, introduce the reporting analysis environments, and describe the basics of viewing and saving reports.

1.1 Features of Web Intelligence

Web Intelligence has been known for many years by report developers as "WebI" (pronounced "webby"). It's best known as a highly intuitive, web-based query and analysis tool that provides business users with the capability to create and modify queries without having to write a single line of SQL.

Because Web Intelligence reduces the complexity of report building, business users have unprecedented opportunities to analyze and leverage company information. Self-service business intelligence has become a reality in Web Intelligence 4.1, which boasts an enhanced Report Panel designed for more intuitive report development, and data interaction. Reporting documents are published and shared through the BI Launch Pad portal, a convenient and efficient way of distributing reports to users across the enterprise.

The architecture of SAP BusinessObjects BI 4.1 lets Web Intelligence reports operate purely within a web browser. This delivery style significantly reduces deployment costs, making it easier for companies of all sizes to use the SAP BusinessObjects reporting suite. Web Intelligence plays a very important role in extending analysis across the enterprise and to a large audience of casual users, power users, and executives. This means that report viewers of every skill level can easily leverage Web Intelligence to interact with and analyze data on a frequent basis to solve business problems.

Key Strengths of Web Intelligence 4.1

- Improved charting engine for a standardized data visualization experience across SAP BusinessObjects BI 4.x reporting tools
- Ribbon-style controls for comfortable and intuitive interaction
- Ability to build multidimensional queries and analyze hierarchical data sets sourced from SAP BEx queries, SAP BusinessObjects Analysis workspaces, and Online Analytical Processing (OLAP) universes

---

- New chart types, including tag cloud chart, polar bubble and scatter charts, pie with variable slice depth, box plot chart, tree map chart, and heat map
- Ability to generate SQL without knowledge of underlying data structures
- Ability to develop and analyze reports in a zero-client online portal structure
- Self-service access to company data for business users
- Ability to merge dimensions of multiple data providers for more robust reports
- Drill-down functionality in reports
- Extensive set of out-of-the-box report section functions
- Ease-of-use in creating analytical documents with a variety of chart types
- Integration with Microsoft Office via SAP BusinessObjects Live Office
- Easy access to SAP InfoCubes through SAP BEx queries
- Use of web services, text files, and Microsoft Excel spreadsheets as data sources
- Capability to copy queries, variables, tables, and charts from one document to another
- Enhanced reporting styles and new charting features
- Ability to add hyperlinks and element links to report objects

In the following sections, we'll discuss the core product functionality of Web Intelligence, including its six primary functions (query, report, analyze, share, customize, and integrate).

1.1.1 Core Product Functionality

The primary function of Web Intelligence 4.1 is two-fold: to provide the capability to query a set of data without any knowledge of the SQL language, and to interactively analyze data to further restrict, expand, and modify the way information is displayed and delivered. After data is retrieved, formatting can be easily applied to present results in a variety of customized formats.

The data retrieved with Web Intelligence 4.1 is displayed in the report section by using report element templates. The available templates include data tables, charts, and freehand cells designed to meet a wide variety of reporting requirements. After your query has been refreshed, and the results are returned, you can easily visualize the data by inserting report elements and result objects into your reports.

You can quickly organize reports by inserting breaks to group the data and by applying block-level or report-level filters with just a few clicks of the mouse.

Notice the extensive set of shortcut icons that assist with frequently used customizations. These icons are located at the top of the screen in the Web Intelligence design mode and are grouped into three toolbars.

When you're ready to share your work, you can easily publish your documents to the BI Launch Pad. Users across the enterprise will then have the opportunity to view and interact with your reports by logging on to the BI Launch Pad through a web browser without any installation requirements.

Extended interaction is available to users by right-clicking on a report or report element for on-the-fly modification and customization in design mode.

Let's consider the primary Web Intelligence functions:

▶ **Query**
Building queries in Web Intelligence 4.1 is much easier than in previous versions of this software. In Web Intelligence 4.1, you have the capability to connect to an SAP BEx query as a data source, connect to an Analysis View as a data source, or include multiple universes within the same document. In addition, you can quickly and graphically generate complex SQL statements within the Web Intelligence Query Panel that contain subqueries and unions (referred to as combined queries).

Now in 4.1 Service Pack 3 (SP3), Excel spreadsheets can be used as a data source for Web Intelligence in both the BI Launch Pad and in Web Intelligence Rich Client.

▶ **Report**
Over the course of this book, you'll learn to create everything from simple reports to complex analysis documents with multiple report tabs. You can unlock the full potential of Web Intelligence 4.1 by using the built-in editing and formatting features available for presenting data quickly and accurately. Reporting with Web Intelligence is also very flexible and intuitive. Never again will your reporting solution cause the bottleneck in your BI solution.

▶ **Analyze**
You'll learn how to use drill filters, report filters, block filters, and built-in report functions to provide detailed, laser-targeted analyses. You'll discover the extensive list of report functions and contexts available for creating precise variables and formulas.

Web Intelligence 4.1 enables you to provide deep analysis, deliver valuable analytical reports to the user community, and become a more insightful analyst and subject matter expert (SME) with your clients' data. You can perform on-the-fly modifications to reports with an extensive set of options available when you right-click on a report in design mode.

▶ **Share**

You'll be able to publish your Web Intelligence report documents to the BI Launch Pad portal for collaborative analysis. The documents can then be scheduled to execute the generated SQL statements and distribute the reports to enterprise user inboxes or through external email.

BI Launch Pad delivers Web Intelligence reports within the default folder structure or within a folder-like structure known as categories. Reporting documents can also be delivered in the BI workspace (previously known as Dashboard Builder).

You can distribute reports to the mobile devices of your workforce with SAP BusinessObjects Mobile. Mobile integration is a powerful feature of SAP BusinessObjects BI 4.1.

▶ **Customize**

Have you ever wanted to create professional Web Intelligence report dashboards that are customized to fit the color and style of your client? Build fresh, innovative, interactive, and data-rich documents that meet any organization's style requirements while also delivering powerful BI.

▶ **Integrate**

You'll discover the capabilities of integrating a variety of data sources such as SAP BW with Web Intelligence 4.1. For dashboard integration, you can generate web services for use as consumable data sources by other SAP products, such as SAP BusinessObjects Dashboards.

These six areas describe the capabilities of Web Intelligence and are the focus of this book.

1.1.2 Web Intelligence Offline

Operating remotely gives users greater flexibility and the freedom to work offline and outside the BI Launch Pad. Offline mode, also known as standalone mode, is possible with the client tool called Web Intelligence Rich Client.

This portable version of Web Intelligence provides report developers with the capability to disconnect from the Central Management Server (CMS) and work outside the BI Launch Pad. Web Intelligence Rich Client also lets you use a local data source; for example, you can import an Excel spreadsheet or text file as a local data source to create Web Intelligence documents.

Figure 1.1 shows the initial screen you see when you launch Web Intelligence Rich Client 4.1. Your options are split into two categories: NEW DOCUMENT and OPEN DOCUMENT.

In the NEW DOCUMENT box, you can choose from creating a report sourced from UNIVERSE, EXCEL, BEX, ANALYSIS VIEW, TEXT, or WEB SERVICES. The OPEN DOCUMENT box allows you to quickly reopen recent documents.

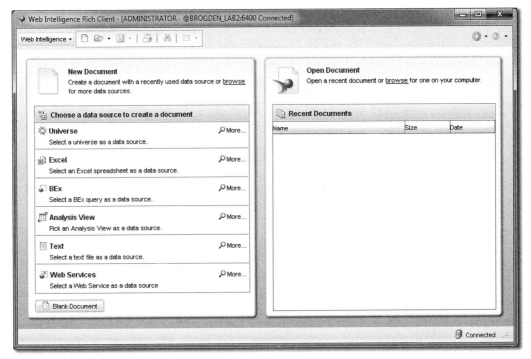

Figure 1.1 Web Intelligence Rich Client 4.1 Initial Screen

Web Intelligence Rich Client is one of nine client tools available in SAP Business-Objects BI 4.1 that can be installed on a user's computer. See Chapter 21 for a closer look at the Web Intelligence Rich Client tool.

1.1.3   SAP BusinessObjects BI 4.1 Client Tools

Figure 1.2 shows the full list of SAP BusinessObjects BI 4.1 client tools. The highlighted tool, Web Intelligence Rich Client, can be launched to connect to the SAP BusinessObjects BI 4.1 system or can be used in standalone mode.

Other valuable SAP BusinessObjects BI 4.1 client tools include the Information Design Tool, Query as a Web Service Designer, Report Conversion Tool, Translation Management Tool, Universe Design Tool, and Widgets.

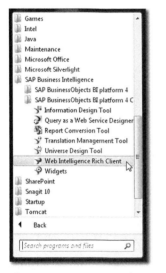

Figure 1.2 SAP BusinessObjects BI 4.1 Client Tools

If Web Intelligence Rich Client doesn't already exist on your computer, you can install it by going to the VIEW or MODIFY section located in the WEB INTELLIGENCE settings on the PREFERENCES page. Click INSTALLATION REQUIRED, which is located to the right of the desktop selection to begin the installation.

Each client tool is mutually exclusive, and the tools provide completely different functionalities. Most business users will need only the tools used for accessing data, such as Web Intelligence Rich Client and Query as a Web Service Designer.

1.1.4   Web Intelligence and the Microcube

After a query has been refreshed in Web Intelligence, the data is stored in memory in an unseen microcube. A *microcube* is a data storage structure existing within each report to store the query results behind the scenes. Users can present any combination of the data with any type of data block or chart type while also providing the ability to drill down and apply report-level or block-level filters.

By storing the result data of each document for the last query that was successfully executed, the microcube allows you to analyze data using different dimensions in separate report tabs and report blocks while revealing only the data that you request. Until the data becomes visible in a report, it remains stored behind the scenes in the microcube. The style, format, and presentation of the data remain the decision of report designers to most effectively display data to solve business problems.

1.2   Reading Web Intelligence Reports

The BI Launch Pad is the centralized web portal designed to provide access to all of your BI content, securely and within a single platform. The BI Launch Pad lets you create, modify, save, share, and analyze valuable company data from a single location and within a browser.

SAP BusinessObjects BI 4.1 will help you enable business users to make better informed decisions. The built-in structures of Web Intelligence work seamlessly within the BI Launch Pad, providing the capability to analyze data with ease.

Web Intelligence allows users to conveniently create and modify reports through an Internet browser or by working locally with Web Intelligence Rich Client with standalone and disconnected capabilities.

Working in offline mode allows report developers to disconnect from the CMS and work locally with saved Web Intelligence documents rather than through a browser. This functionality facilitates the frequently requested task of saving and editing Web Intelligence documents outside of the BI Launch Pad portal.

> **Note**
>
> Web Intelligence 4.1 refers to viewing reports as *reading* and to editing or modifying reports as *designing*. We'll describe these slight changes in the latest version in more detail in later chapters.

Figure 1.3 shows a custom-formatted Web Intelligence report with Element Link filters being read in a browser within the BI Launch Pad.

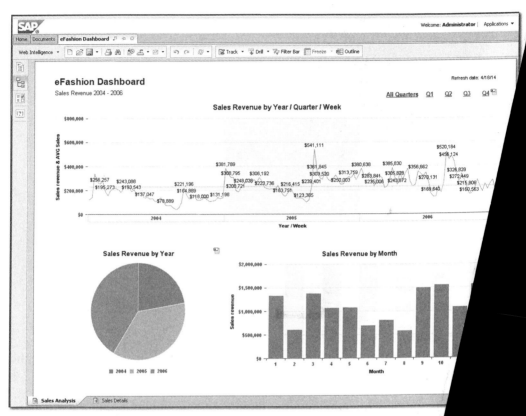

Figure 1.3 Web Intelligence 4.1 Report in the BI Launch Pad

Most report consumers will need only to read or view reports; designing re is generally left to power users and report developers. While reading re users will have the opportunity to drill, filter, and export results to PDF or files.

1.3 Adjusting Web Intelligence Preferences

A number of configurable settings are available to enhance the user e when reading and interacting with Web Intelligence reports in the BI L

To adjust settings for reading and designing reporting documents, begin by clicking on the PREFERENCES link located in the upper-right corner of the BI Launch Pad (see Figure 1.4).

Click to set or adjust Web Intelligence preferences.

...es Link in the BI Launch Pad

...r security permissions, the PREFERENCES page allows you to ...ral settings and the default settings for viewing/reading and ...reporting documents.

...e Web Intelligence preferences that you can adjust locally in ...ddition to these Web Intelligence preferences, you can adjust ...other preference groups with settings in the BI Launch Pad:

...E PASSWORD

...ZONE

...OR OLAP

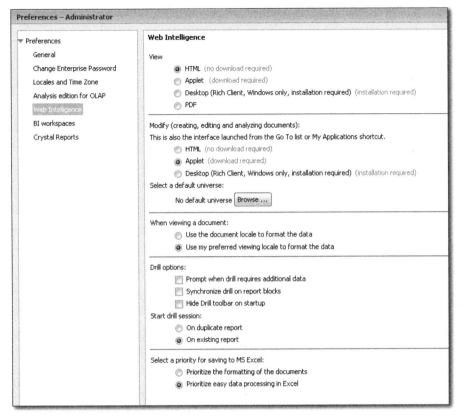

Figure 1.5 Web Intelligence Preferences

Web Intelligence settings consist of the following:

▶ VIEW

▶ MODIFY

▶ SELECT A DEFAULT UNIVERSE (OPTIONAL)

▶ WHEN VIEWING A DOCUMENT

▶ DRILL OPTIONS

▶ START DRILL SESSION

▶ SELECT A PRIORITY FOR SAVING TO MS EXCEL

Let's explore these settings further.

1.3.1   Setting the View and Modify Selection Types

Depending on whether you're a casual user who needs only to read and print reports or a report designer who requires access to the Query Panel, the selections made to view and modify reports play an important role in the features that will be available to you.

Let's examine the selection types available for both VIEW and MODIFY:

▶ HTML (NO DOWNLOAD REQUIRED)
The HTML setting provides a fully functional HTML panel that allows users to read and design reporting documents with all of the features in the REPORT PANEL. The biggest advantage of using the web setting to read and design documents is the ability to link to a document. This feature is covered in detail in Chapter 15. Extensive improvements have been made with this viewer, and it now contains 99% of the functionality in the Applet (Java) viewer.

▶ APPLET (DOWNLOAD REQUIRED)
The APPLET setting is the selection used for creating queries with Web Intelligence in the BI Launch Pad and advanced interactive reports by using the Java plug-in. This setting was once used almost exclusively by power users and advanced report consumers, but now in SAP BusinessObjects BI 4.1, the HTML viewer has become the preferred viewer type by many report developers.

The disadvantage to this setting is that linking to another document isn't available, and the full OpenDocument syntax is required to link to another published report, document, or dashboard.

▶ DESKTOP (RICH CLIENT, WINDOWS ONLY, INSTALLATION REQUIRED)
This selection is used to automatically launch Web Intelligence Rich Client when reports are viewed or modified.

▶ PDF
The PDF option is unique to the VIEW preference list and has very little interactive functionality. The primary feature of this viewing format is to open the Web Intelligence report in a PDF for easy distribution. After the document opens, you can print or save the PDF report. PDF reports can be easily shared with users across the enterprise, emailed, posted to an FTP site, or published to the SAP BusinessObjects BI 4.1 platform.

There is one setting that is unique to the MODIFY list and that's the ability to browse for a default universe. This feature is available so a specific universe can be assigned as the default universe for when new reports are created.

The next set of properties describes how to set the viewing locale and time zone for reports and the BI Launch Pad. This feature is an important descriptive value, showing accurate times for when reports were last saved and refreshed.

1.3.2 Locale When Viewing a Document

When viewing a Web Intelligence document, the data can be formatted by either the document locale or preferred viewing locale. To set the preferred viewing locale to be different from the default browser locale, follow these steps:

1. Click the USE MY PREFERRED VIEWING LOCALE TO FORMAT THE DATA option under the WEB INTELLIGENCE preferences.

2. Select the LOCALES AND TIME ZONE preferences section, which is shown in Figure 1.6.

3. Change the PRODUCT LOCALE setting to either USE BROWSER LOCALE or ENGLISH.

4. Choose the PREFERRED VIEWING LOCALE from more than 130 locale options.

5. Select a CURRENT TIME ZONE or use the selection LOCAL TO WEB SERVER.

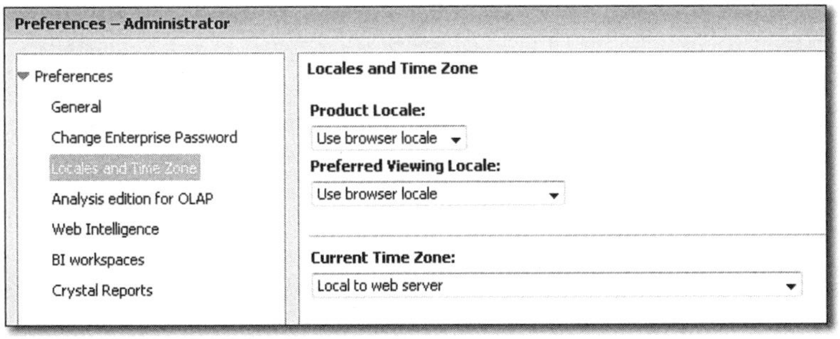

Figure 1.6 Locales and Time Zone Preferences

1.3.3 Drill Option Preferences

In addition to providing drill filters in drill mode, many data tables and charts let you drill down with a single click. This type of drilling is available when drill mode is activated, and the dimension objects have been added to a hierarchy in the universe.

As shown in Figure 1.7, three settings are available for selection under DRILL OPTIONS when setting WEB INTELLIGENCE preferences:

▶ PROMPT WHEN DRILL REQUIRES ADDITIONAL DATA

▶ SYNCHRONIZE DRILL ON REPORT BLOCKS

▶ HIDE DRILL TOOLBAR ON STARTUP

Any combination of these settings can be selected. We recommend that you select PROMPT WHEN DRILL REQUIRES ADDITIONAL DATA and SYNCHRONIZE DRILL ON REPORT BLOCKS. You can also show or hide the drill toolbar when opening a report.

You also have the choice of defining where a drill session starts: ON DUPLICATE REPORT or ON EXISTING REPORT. The default selection is ON EXISTING REPORT.

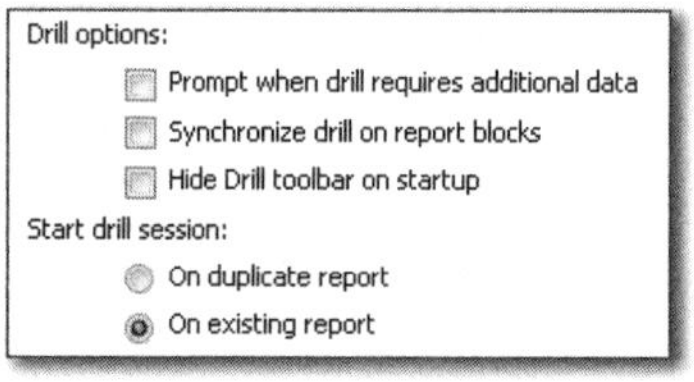

Figure 1.7 Drill Options Settings and Drill Session Start Type

1.3.4 Saving to Microsoft Excel Priority

The final setting in Web Intelligence preferences is to assign the priority for saving reports to Excel: either the formatting of the documents or easy data processing in Excel (the default setting).

> **Note**
>
> Be sure to click the SAVE button or the SAVE & CLOSE button in the lower-right corner of the PREFERENCES window to complete your changes. Refresh your browser to ensure that all preference changes are enabled and integrated into your session.

Adjusting the Web Intelligence preferences based on your needs ensures that you optimize the features for viewing, modifying, and creating reports. Let's explore the reporting and analysis environments next.

1.4   The HTML Viewer versus the Applet (Java) Viewer

As Web Intelligence continues to evolve, the two viewer types available to users become more and more similar. It wasn't long ago that the HTML viewer, previously known as the Web viewer, had minimal functionality, and the Applet (Java) viewer was reserved for power users. But thanks to the efforts of the Web Intelligence product development team, users now have two full-featured viewer types to choose from.

The Applet viewer, previously known as the Rich Internet Application (RIA) viewer, requires the installation of the Java Runtime Environment plug-in and maintains a functional advantage over the HTML viewer, but by the slimmest of margins. Originally touted as the viewer of choice for advanced report designers, its fraternal twin, the HTML viewer, now has 99% of the same functionality and an almost indiscernible appearance.

Because the HTML viewer doesn't rely on a third-party plug-in, many users find it easier to maintain and faster at delivering reports than using the Applet viewer. This was the case with Web Intelligence in version 4.0 and 4.1, but not in 4.1 SP3. Your voices were heard, and the product development team has delivered an Applet viewer that now allows you to open reports much faster than previously in the 4.x releases.

In many ways, both viewers are now practically equal. However, because of the speed in opening a report and connecting related reports through Document Linking, the advantage goes to the HTML viewer, while the Applet viewer maintains a functional advantage over the HTML viewer by delivering conditional formatting and custom number formatting.

The next section will introduce you to the concept of zero-client versus thin-client report creation and delivery with Web Intelligence.

1.5   Web Intelligence Reporting and Analysis Environments

Web Intelligence reports are created by, and delivered to, business users in either a zero-client or thin-client method, with the primary method of delivery being zero-client. To begin working with Web Intelligence, reporting documents are accessed either through a web browser after logging on to the BI Launch Pad, or by opening the locally installed Web Intelligence Rich Client tool.

1.5.1 Zero-Client Online Analysis

You don't have to install SAP BusinessObjects BI 4.1 software to experience the benefits of Web Intelligence. With just a web browser, you can log on to the BI Launch Pad to view, create, edit, analyze, schedule, or interact with Web Intelligence reporting documents. All of the functions, tools, and data delivery elements are at your fingertips with just a few clicks and proper credentials to access the SAP BusinessObjects BI platform.

1.5.2 Thin-Client Development

Since the addition of the Web Intelligence Rich Client, analysis has been extended to power users who need to analyze data when disconnected from the CMS or SAP Enterprise Portal. When you are connected to the CMS, you can export or publish documents directly to the enterprise system for online analysis. Once published, reports created in Web Intelligence Rich Client are easily shared with other enterprise users through standard group security permissions.

The next section describes display modes for viewing reports.

1.6 Report Display Modes

Web Intelligence reports can be viewed in the BI Launch Pad with two different display modes: PAGE and QUICK DISPLAY (see Figure 1.8). PAGE mode allows you to view the report the way it fits onto a printed page while also providing the capability of drilling into the data. QUICK DISPLAY mode is used primarily for reports intended for analysis but not for printing.

Each mode displays data differently, and you can easily toggle back and forth between modes as necessary by following these steps:

1. Enter design mode by clicking on DESIGN in the upper-right corner.
2. Select the PAGE SETUP tab from the primary REPORT PANEL tab set.
3. Select the DISPLAY tab from the third group of subordinate tabs.

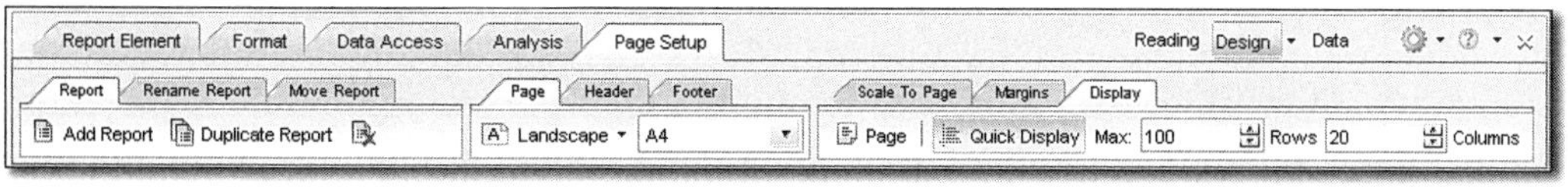

Figure 1.8 View Modes Available in Web Intelligence

Web Intelligence documents can be saved to the repository of the CMS by clicking on SAVE As from the SAVE menu.

1.6.1 Saving in the Applet Viewer

To save the report outside of the enterprise platform (in the Applet viewer), follow these steps:

1. Select SAVE As (see Figure 1.9) after clicking on the SAVE icon, and then select either DESKTOP, DOCUMENTS, or COMPUTER as the export location.

2. When exporting the data outside the enterprise, choose one of the following file types: XLS, XLSX, or PDF.

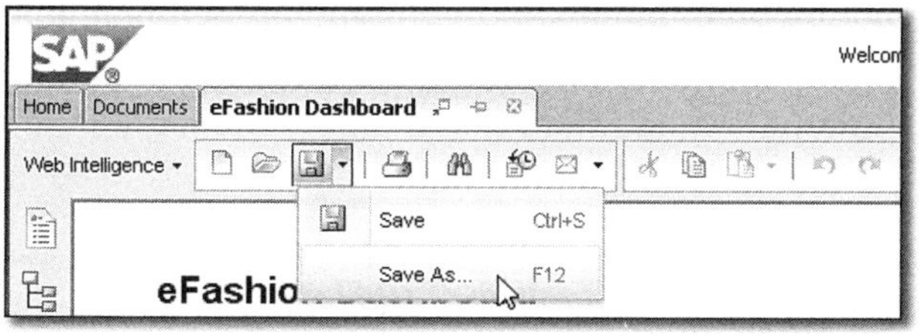

Figure 1.9 Save a Web Intelligence Document in the Applet Viewer

By clicking on SAVE, you overwrite the existing version. Depending on your rights, you can update Web Intelligence documents that reside in the folder structure within the BI Launch Pad. When working in a production environment, the best workflow is to save documents to your MY DOCUMENTS area if you'd like to make changes to the query or one of the REPORT tabs.

1.6.2 Saving in the HTML Viewer

To save the report outside of the enterprise platform (in the HTML viewer) select the EXPORT icon, and then select one of the following export types (see Figure 1.10):

- EXPORT DOCUMENT AS
- EXPORT CURRENT REPORT AS
  - PDF
  - EXCEL 2007
  - EXCEL
  - CSV ARCHIVE
  - TEXT
- EXPORT DATA TO CSV

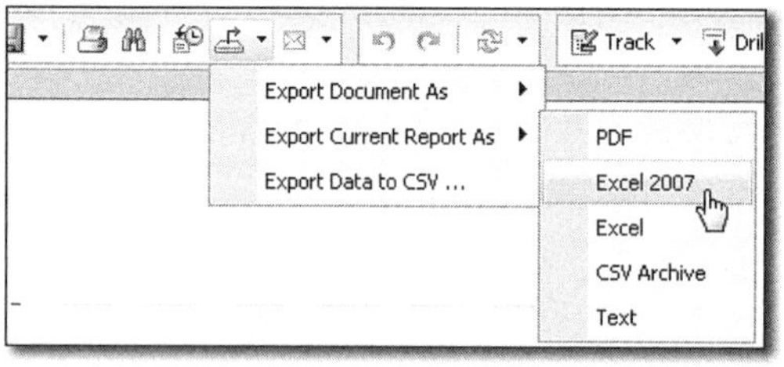

Figure 1.10 Exporting a Document from the HTML Viewer

1.7 Summary

Web Intelligence provides an extensive set of mature features that combine complex query building with detailed analytical reporting capabilities. This best-in-class reporting tool introduced in 1997 has evolved to become the standard ad hoc analysis and reporting tool for many businesses around the world. With version 4.1, you can easily source reports from SAP BEx queries, Analysis Views, and patented semantic layer universes.

The core functionality of Web Intelligence contains an extensive list of valuable data analysis features. Report building becomes much easier for business users because they can develop complex queries visually without knowledge of the underlying SQL. The ability to query multiple data sources within the same document and link the results by merging dimensions is an extremely valuable analytical report development feature.

Web Intelligence reports can be easily viewed and analyzed by using only a web browser connected to the BI Launch Pad. Reporting documents can be shared with selected users across the enterprise and then scheduled to be refreshed and delivered to a user inbox or external email address.

You can take analysis offline with Web Intelligence Rich Client. Report developers can now save Web Intelligence documents locally and analyze data without being connected to the CMS. With all of the functional capabilities delivered within Web Intelligence 4.1, SAP has completely replaced its predecessor reporting tool, which was known in previous versions as Desktop Intelligence. In SAP BusinessObjects BI 4.1, Desktop Intelligence has been retired, and existing reports from a previous version need to be converted to Web Intelligence to be viewed in 4.1. See Appendix A for a checklist that describes the nine steps of report conversion.

The next chapter describes the new additions introduced to Web Intelligence in SAP BusinessObjects BI 4.1 up through SP3. SAP BusinessObjects BI 4.1 includes many new features to improve productivity and the user experience.

The user experience continues to improve with every release and service pack in SAP BusinessObjects 4.x. Make the biggest impact with Web Intelligence by taking advantage of the latest enhancements introduced in SAP BusinessObjects BI 4.1 Service Pack 3 (SP3).

2   What's New in Web Intelligence 4.1?

SAP BusinessObjects BI 4.1 is the latest major release in the SAP BusinessObjects BI 4.x platform. This release is an important step in the SAP BusinessObjects lifecycle as it strengthens the product line with numerous updates, enhancements of existing features, and the introduction of new capabilities. Ever since the introduction of the SAP BusinessObjects BI 4.0 platform, and the retirement of Desktop Intelligence (DeskI), SAP BusinessObjects Web Intelligence (which we'll refer to as Web Intelligence or WebI) has been under the microscope for feature comparisons with DeskI. Although WebI is more powerful than DeskI in many ways, there was still a small feature gap in the SAP BusinessObjects BI 4.0 release of Web Intelligence. This gap got even smaller with the release of SAP BusinessObjects BI 4.1.

Functionality, such as custom grouping—once only available in DeskI—was introduced in Web Intelligence. In addition, core capability enhancements continued to be added to Web Intelligence. Those enhancements include features such as custom color palettes, freeze headers and column rows, connectivity options with SAP HANA, user experience improvements made to the HTML viewer, and performance improvements in the Applet viewer.

This chapter covers the new enhancements introduced in SAP BusinessObjects BI 4.1 up to SP3, which is the latest service pack at the time of publishing.

Two notable new features in Web Intelligence in SAP BusinessObjects BI 4.1 include the custom grouping option and the ability to freeze headers in table report elements. These new features will be discussed in detail in the coming sections, but we'll start our coverage of the latest enhancements introduced in SAP

BusinessObjects BI 4.1 SP3 with functional improvements relating to the break-through in-memory data platform—SAP HANA.

2.1 SAP HANA Variable Support in SAP BusinessObjects BI 4.1 SP3

Universes based on an SAP HANA source that contains variables and input parameters are now supported in Web Intelligence in SAP BusinessObjects BI 4.1 SP3. This new capability provides developers with options needed for producing more specific reporting documents and leveraging the in-memory and real-time capabilities of the SAP HANA columnar database.

Input parameters from SAP HANA sources are mapped to prompted query filters in the Query Panel in Web Intelligence. When reports are refreshed, you'll be prompted to enter or select values that will filter the results being retrieved by your query. This is an important new addition because it limits the amount of data being returned by your queries, reduces the amount of data returned to the Web Intelligence microcube, and makes it easier for users to focus on specific subsets of data.

Additional user-defined prompted filters can also be added to the QUERY FILTERS pane to further restrict the data being returned. In these situations, you should first run the report with the SAP HANA input parameters to make note of the prompt texts from each input parameter. This step can potentially prevent the duplication of prompts and help you synchronize the prompt texts when combining with multiple queries.

2.1.1 Support of Query Stripping

Query stripping is a query performance improvement technique that was once available only to OLAP universes and data sources. Now in SAP BusinessObjects BI 4.1 SP3, this technique can also be applied to any relational universe, including SAP HANA universes. This feature provides another method for improving query performance by stripping out all objects from the query that are not directly or indirectly being used in the Report Panel.

This feature provides significant query improvements to queries based on SAP Business Warehouse (SAP BW) queries and is enabled by default at the universe layer when connected to nonrelational sources. But when the source is a relational database management system (RDBMS), a few settings must be manually enabled first.

2.1.2 Enabling Query Stripping

Three options must be enabled to turn on query stripping. In addition, in each report, there are two places that must be manually selected in order to enable query stripping. These settings are also required when creating Web Intelligence documents sourced from SAP BW or SAP Business Explorer (SAP BEx) sources.

Query stripping must be enabled at the following levels:

▸ Universe level

▸ Query level

▸ Document level

Enabling Query Stripping at the Universe Level

The third location that must be enabled is completed in the Information Design Tool and in the business layer.

Open the QUERY OPTIONS tab in the business layer and check the ALLOW QUERY STRIPPING option. Be sure to save the changes and then publish it to the SAP BusinessObjects BI platform repository. For query stripping to be applied in reports sourced from relational universes, this step must be completed first.

Enabling Query Stripping at the Query Level

To enable query stripping at the query level, begin by opening the QUERY PANEL, and then editing the QUERY PROPERTIES. Check ENABLE QUERY STRIPPING and then click OK. This option is displayed in Figure 2.1.

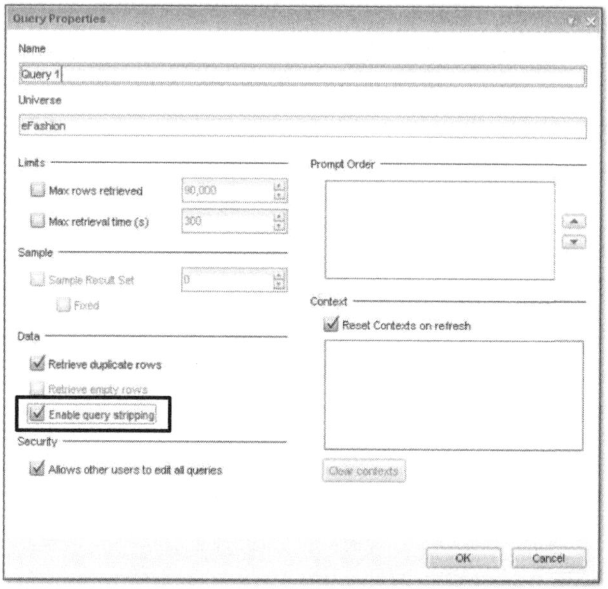

Figure 2.1 Enable Query Stripping at the Query Level

Enabling Query Stripping at the Document Level

To enable query stripping at the document level, return to the Report Panel. Next, click the PROPERTIES tab followed by the document selection, as shown in Figure 2.2.

Figure 2.2 Properties Tab and Link to the Document Summary Window

Check the ENABLE QUERY STRIPPING option in the DOCUMENT SUMMARY window (see Figure 2.3).

With query stripping enabled in all three areas, the SQL script generated by Web Intelligence will be modified each time an object is either added or removed from a report element in the Report Panel. Each time an object has been removed or added to a report element, the query should be refreshed again to apply the query stripping feature to the SQL generation engine.

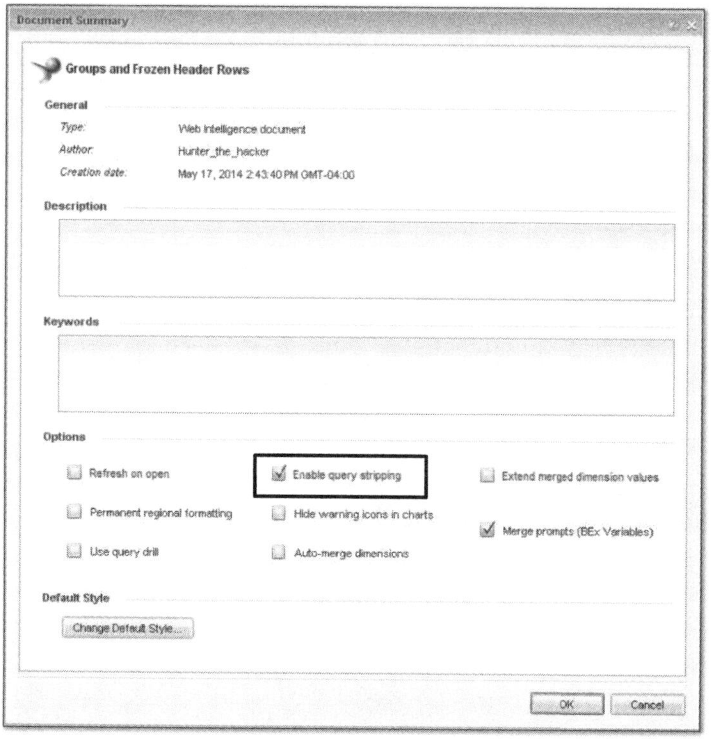

Figure 2.3 Enabling Query Stripping at the Document Level

2.2 Freeze Header Rows and Left Columns

Analyzing large data sets in Web Intelligence just got easier with the FREEZE HEADER ROWS and FREEZE LEFT COLUMNS options available when reading a report. Large data sets can now be analyzed easier with this new feature. As you scroll through rows of results, the header will remain visible. In the past, an analyst might have to review several hundred rows of data and then lose track of the column names in the process. This is no longer a problem when you enable the new FREEZE HEADER ROWS and FREEZE LEFT COLUMNS settings.

2.2.1 Freeze Rules

The FREEZE HEADER ROWS feature is one of the few that cannot be enabled in design mode. This option was designed specifically to improve the user experience and exclusively for analysis purposes of users. To this point, freezing headers and left columns can only be enabled when viewing a report in reading mode.

There are only two requirements for enabling freeze headers:

▶ View the report in reading mode.

▶ Select a data table.

Even in reading mode, the FREEZE option will be disabled until either a table header or the table values are selected.

Figure 2.4 shows the FREEZE icon in the toolbar while it's disabled. In this image, the report is only being viewed, and no data tables have been selected.

City+	Quarter	Quantity sold	Margin	Sales revenue
Group 1	Q1	20,601	$1,230,077	$3,197,164
Group 1	Q2	17,242	$1,189,519	$2,854,778
Group 1	Q3	20,376	$985,482	$2,892,638

Figure 2.4 Freeze Option in the Toolbar without a Table Selected

2.2.2 Enabling Freeze Settings

Clicking anywhere in the table will enable and make clickable the FREEZE icon in the reporting toolbar in reading mode. Clicking FREEZE will set the FREEZE HEADER ROWS option to the on position. Clicking it a second time will turn it off. With a row or column in a table selected, click the small down arrow to examine the additional FREEZE options. From here, you'll be able to turn the FREEZE HEADER ROWS option to either on or off (checked or unchecked) and also to enable FREEZE LEFT COLUMNS. You'll have the option to freeze up to the first five columns in a table with this feature enabled. Figure 2.5 shows these options.

FREEZING LEFT COLUMNS is a very useful feature when analyzing reports with a large number of columns. As you scroll to the right to view the values in each column, columns 1 through 5 can be configured to display at all times for easier analysis. This feature helps by displaying up to the first five dimensional columns to provide contexts to columns being analyzed that in earlier versions would have been out of view.

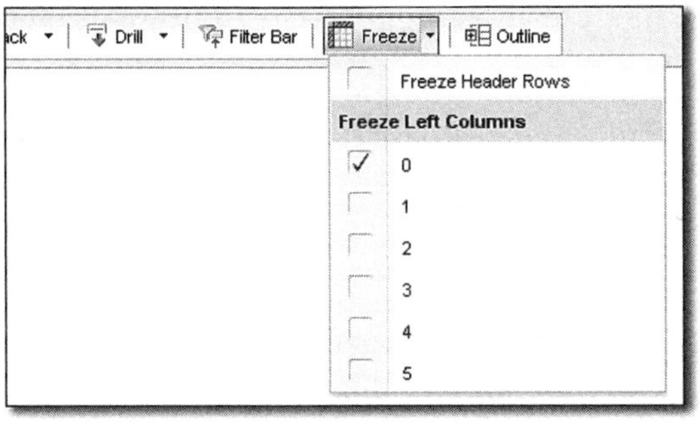

Figure 2.5 Freezing Header Rows and Left Columns

Figure 2.6 shows a small table with FREEZE HEADER ROWS enabled.

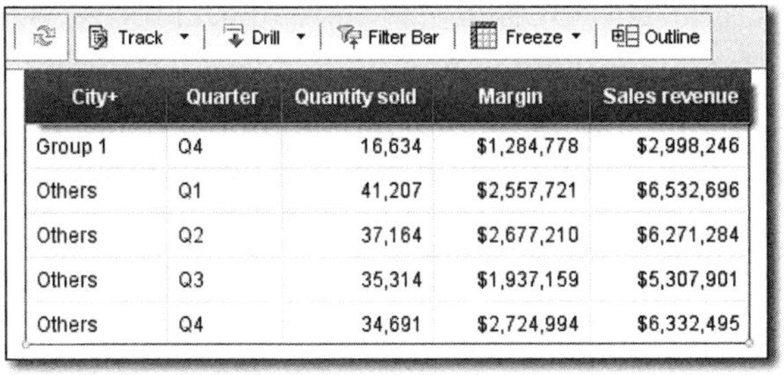

City+	Quarter	Quantity sold	Margin	Sales revenue
Group 1	Q4	16,634	$1,284,778	$2,998,246
Others	Q1	41,207	$2,557,721	$6,532,696
Others	Q2	37,164	$2,677,210	$6,271,284
Others	Q3	35,314	$1,937,159	$5,307,901
Others	Q4	34,691	$2,724,994	$6,332,495

Figure 2.6 Scrolling through a Report with Freeze Header Rows Enabled

Freezing one left column is shown in Figure 2.7, while a report is scrolled to the right. Frozen columns are easily identified with a subtle shadow on the right edge.

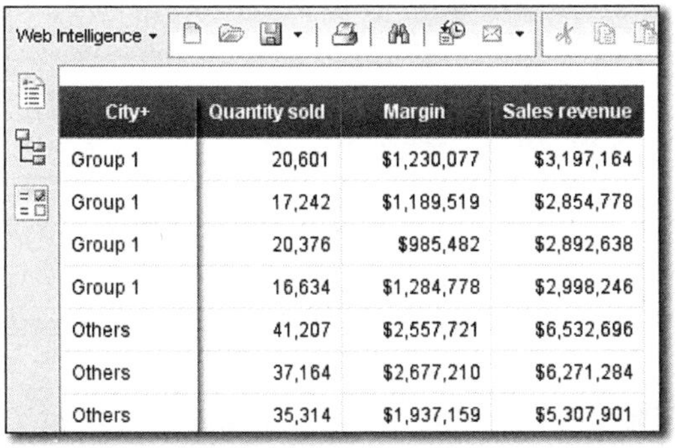

City+	Quantity sold	Margin	Sales revenue
Group 1	20,601	$1,230,077	$3,197,164
Group 1	17,242	$1,189,519	$2,854,778
Group 1	20,376	$985,482	$2,892,638
Group 1	16,634	$1,284,778	$2,998,246
Others	41,207	$2,557,721	$6,532,696
Others	37,164	$2,677,210	$6,271,284
Others	35,314	$1,937,159	$5,307,901

Figure 2.7 Scrolling through a Report with a Frozen Column

Next we'll talk about another useful new enhancement in the 4.1 release of Web Intelligence—the group feature.

2.3   Custom Grouping

One of the top new features introduced in SAP BusinessObjects BI 4.1 is the capability to create custom groups of dimensional values. Previously only available in DeskI, this simple but extremely powerful feature was one of the most requested functions by Web Intelligence report developers.

Up to this point, you would have had to write compound IF statements in a formula or variable to accomplish custom grouping. And, depending on the number of conditions, this methodology could become a lengthy and manual process. But now in SAP BusinessObjects BI 4.1, custom groupings can be created with ease.

> **Note**
>
> You must be working within a data table to create a new custom grouping.

Figure 2.8 shows the GROUP function located in the primary ANALYSIS tab and DISPLAY subtab. The CITY object is selected from a vertical table and then the GROUP function becomes enabled. Grouping must be added while in design mode.

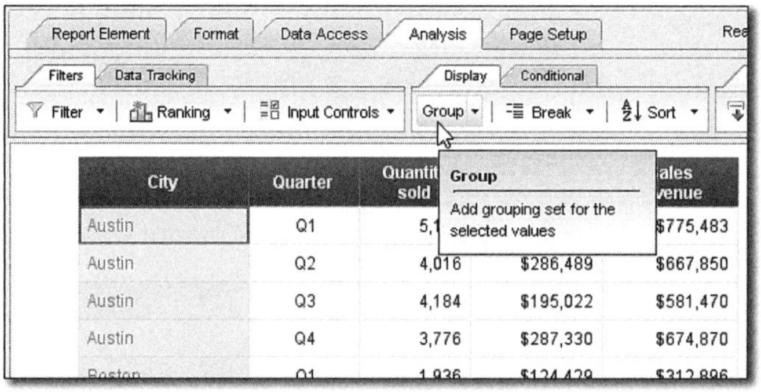

Figure 2.8 Creating a New Custom Group Based on a Dimension Object

> **Note**
>
> A dimensional object must be selected from a REPORT ELEMENT data table before the GROUP function will become enabled.

After selecting a dimensional object and clicking the GROUP function, the MANAGE GROUPS window, as shown in Figure 2.9, will appear. This is where you can select a custom set of values and add them to the same group.

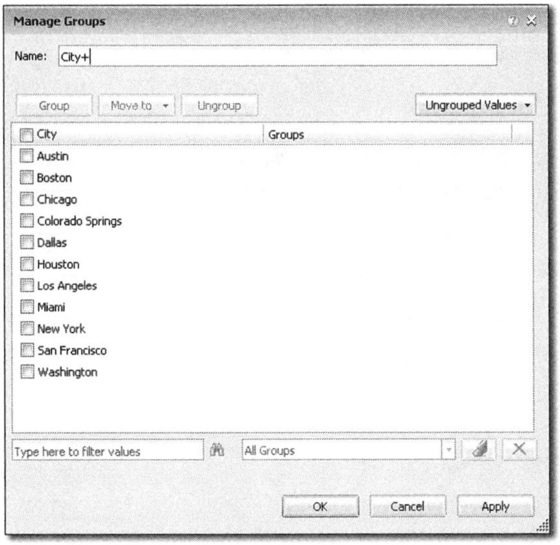

Figure 2.9 Managing Custom Groups

2.3.1   Steps for Creating Custom Groups

There are the two basic ways to create custom groups:

▸ Select all dimensional values, and then uncheck the unneeded values.
▸ Select only the values that should be assembled into the same group.

After the desired combination of values has been selected, click the GROUP button to assign them to a group. By default, the NEW GROUP name will be the first value selected followed by a + symbol. This name can be easily changed to something more meaningful.

Figure 2.10 shows the NEW GROUP window with the default name of the group being added. Change the name to a word or phrase that will clearly describe the collection of values to your users. Click on OK to confirm and proceed.

After a new group has been created, the group name will be displayed along with all the other values available in the dimension object. This helps you identify the remaining values that haven't been assigned to a group (see Figure 2.11).

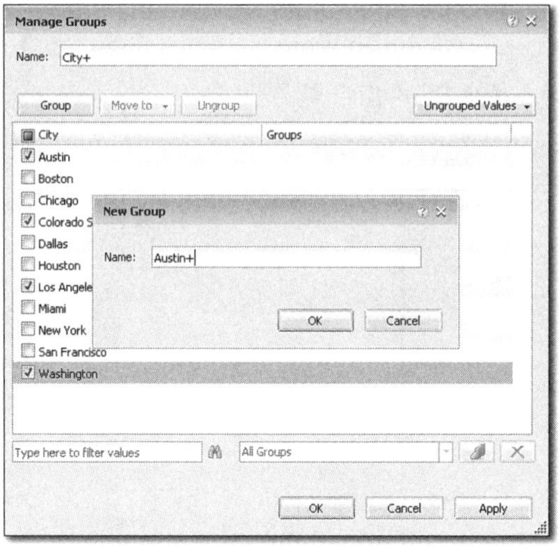

Figure 2.10 Naming a New Custom Group

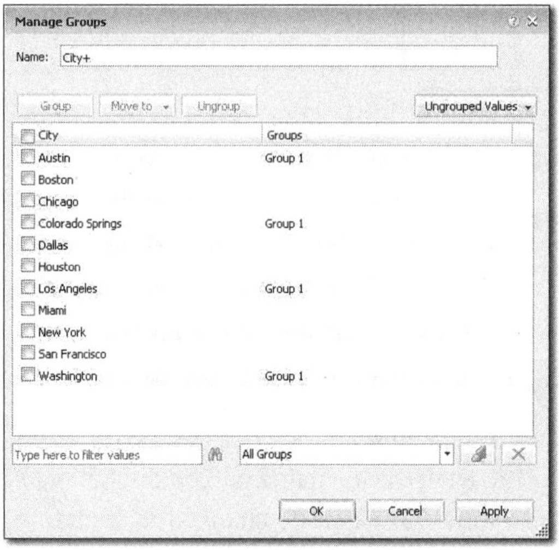

Figure 2.11 Dimension Objects with Custom Groups Listed

You'll have three options after setting up your first group:

- ▶ Create additional groups for values that have not been assigned to a group.
- ▶ Leave the values as they are so individual dimensional values can be compared to the new custom group(s).
- ▶ Assign the remaining values to an OTHERS group.

The final option listed here is done by first clicking the Ungrouped Values button in the Manage Groups window.

The next step is to select the Automatically grouped option, as displayed in Figure 2.12. You are then prompted to enter a group name for the remaining values. The default name of "Others" can be changed to a more meaningful word or phrase.

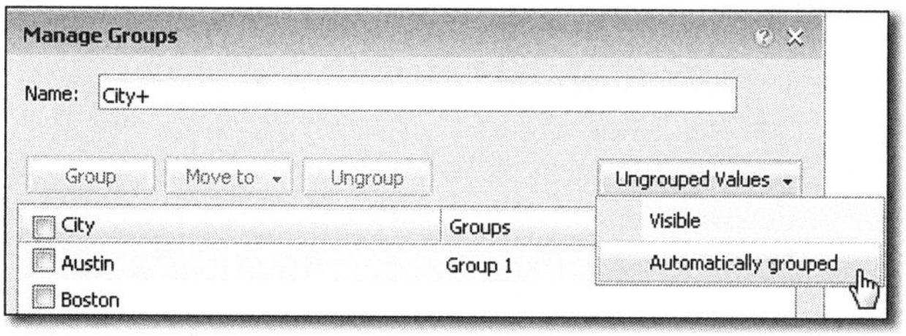

Figure 2.12 Assigning Ungrouped Values to be Automatically Grouped

Now all values will have a group name associated with them. Figure 2.13 shows all of the City objects with a group name assigned to them. By default, a plus symbol is added to the object name that's used in a new custom group. A new variable is added with a name such as City+. This can be overwritten in the Manage Groups window and replaced with a more preferred variable name.

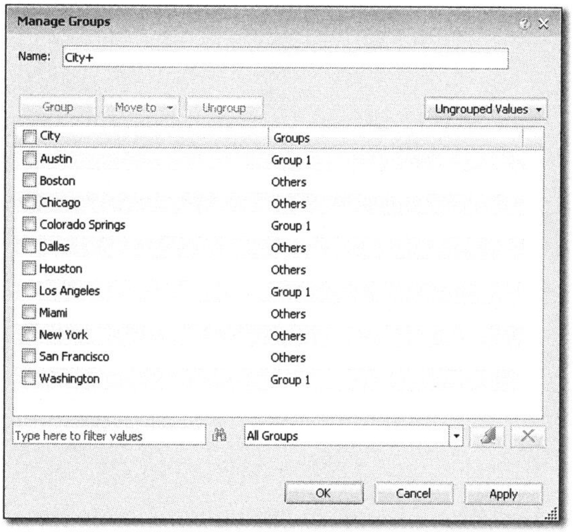

Figure 2.13 All Values with a Group Name Assigned

2.3.2 Custom Group Values in a Table

After creating your new group(s), you'll see the group names as column values in your data table. This can help you aggregate values to fit custom business requirements and even create custom hierarchies by combining groups with breaks. Figure 2.14 shows the table with the new group added.

City+	Quarter	Quantity sold	Margin	Sales revenue
Group 1	Q1	20,601	$1,230,077	$3,197,164
Group 1	Q2	17,242	$1,189,519	$2,854,778
Group 1	Q3	20,376	$985,482	$2,892,638
Group 1	Q4	16,634	$1,284,778	$2,998,246
Others	Q1	41,207	$2,557,721	$6,532,696
Others	Q2	37,164	$2,677,210	$6,271,284

Figure 2.14 Custom Group Values in the Data Table

After a group has been created, you can click a grouped object, click the down arrow beside the GROUP icon in the ANALYSIS/DISPLAY tabs, and choose any of the following options (see Figure 2.15):

▶ MOVE TO GROUP
Click on a specific value to assign it to a different group.

▶ UNGROUP
Return the grouped dimension to its original state.

▶ RENAME GROUP
Change the group name of the value selected.

▶ UNGROUPED VALUES
Toggle between making the ungrouped values either VISIBLE or AUTOMATICALLY GROUPED.

▶ MANAGE GROUPS
Launch the MANAGE GROUPS window so you can regroup dimensional values.

This menu is pictured in Figure 2.15.

Next, we'll talk about the improvements for merging dimensions in SAP Business-Objects BI 4.1.

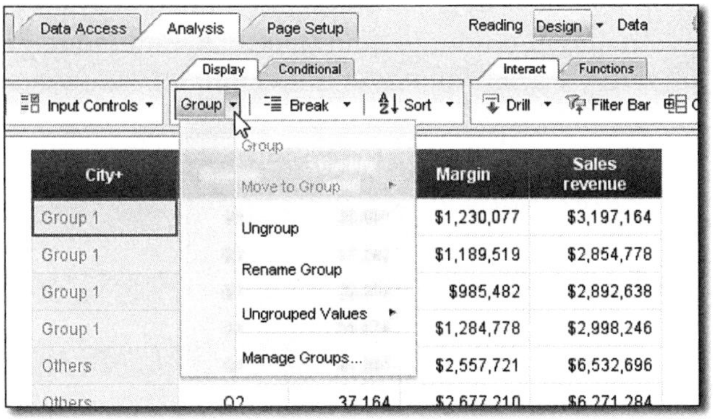

Figure 2.15 Interacting with an Existing Custom Group

2.4   Merged Dimension Improvements

Merging dimensional objects from multiple queries received a much needed upgrade in SAP BusinessObjects BI 4.1. Now when new queries are added to existing documents, objects can easily be merged to existing merged objects.

Following are the three new features related to merging dimensions in SAP BusinessObjects BI 4.1, which make a big difference to developers that work with queries from multiple data sources and hierarchical data:

▸ Adding an object from a new query to an existing merged object

▸ Removing an object from a merged object

▸ Merging objects with hierarchies

2.4.1   Adding an Object to an Existing Merge

When a new query is added to a document that already has merged objects, you can now add an object from the new query to an existing merged dimension object. Figure 2.16 shows a sample of the available objects from a document with three queries that contains a merged dimension for the YEAR object created from only two of the queries.

To add the YEAR object from QUERY 3 to the MERGED DIMENSIONS instance of YEAR, select YEAR in QUERY 3 and YEAR from the MERGED DIMENSIONS class, and then right-click.

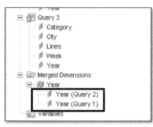

Figure 2.16 Merged Dimension for the Year Object from Two Queries

Next, select ADD TO MERGE (see Figure 2.17).

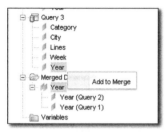

Figure 2.17 Adding an Object to an Existing Merged Dimension

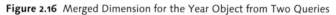
Tip

If your document contains multiple data sources, change the ARRANGED BY option located at the bottom of the AVAILABLE OBJECTS pane from ALPHABETIC ORDER to QUERY. This object listing type makes it easier to locate the object instances needed.

After selecting ADD TO MERGE, the MERGED DIMENSIONS instance of the YEAR object will show that it was created from all three instances of the object, as shown in Figure 2.18.

Figure 2.18 Merged Dimension Object Added

2.4.2 Removing an Object from a Merged Dimension Instance

To remove an object that has been merged, right-click on the object and select REMOVE FROM MERGE (see Figure 2.19).

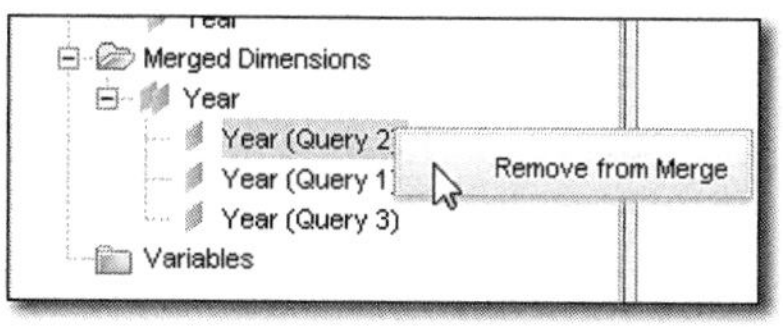

Figure 2.19 Removing an Object from a Merged Dimension

2.4.3 Merging Objects with Hierarchies

Merging objects from queries with hierarchies provides results in the following scenarios:

▶ Objects merged from queries with the same hierarchy maintain the full hierarchy.

▶ Objects merged from hierarchical queries with flat dimensions keep the hierarchy intact, but the object from the flat query will become a member of the top level.

▶ Objects merged from two different hierarchies will merge members from both sources, which are copied with each parent to maintain accuracy.

In the next section, we'll discuss a few usability improvements in 4.1 SP3.

2.5 Usability Improvements

The new enhancements introduced to Web Intelligence in SAP BusinessObjects BI 4.1 make for a better overall user and developer experience. Many of these features are easy to implement but make a big difference with common tasks such as filtering tables and charts, formatting different areas in the Report Panel, and ease of use when interacting with the Query Panel.

These types of improvements continue to improve productivity for both report consumers and developers. The first section we'll cover discusses improvements made to input controls.

2.5.1 New Input Control Features

Two new features were added to input controls that increase development times in multi-tabbed reports and also provide new options that better meet business requirements when filtering reports.

A common workflow for report developers is to make duplicate copies of existing report tabs to serve as starting points for new reports. This is especially the case when reports have been carefully created with several report elements, relative positioning has been applied, styles and colors have been wisely chosen, and filtering has been added. With much of the time-consuming work already completed, developers can make duplicate reports and then edit them. This may include assigning different objects to charts, turning charts into tables, turning tables into charts, and so forth. Previously, one feature would not copy over when duplicate reports were created. Now in the updated SAP BusinessObjects BI 4.1, however, duplicating a report copies any existing input controls into the new report.

Filtering that Meets Business Requirements

Depending on the dimension and business context, some objects can't be aggregated together. In these cases, individual values must be analyzed alone, because it doesn't make sense to analyze all values. Up to this point in Web Intelligence, input controls included an ALL VALUES selection by default for dimensional filtering.

Now in SAP BusinessObjects BI 4.1, there's a new a new property for removing all values called ALLOW SELECTION OF ALL VALUES, as shown in Figure 2.20.

To remove all values from appearing in the input control, just uncheck this entry. By disabling this option, you'll be required to select a default value before the input control can be finalized. Use the ellipsis icon beside the DEFAULT VALUE(S) property, shown in Figure 2.21, to view a list of values for the dimension in the input control. Select OK to enable the new control.

When report consumers begin viewing the report in reading mode, they must select at least one dimensional value, but they won't have an ALL VALUES option to select (see Figure 2.22).

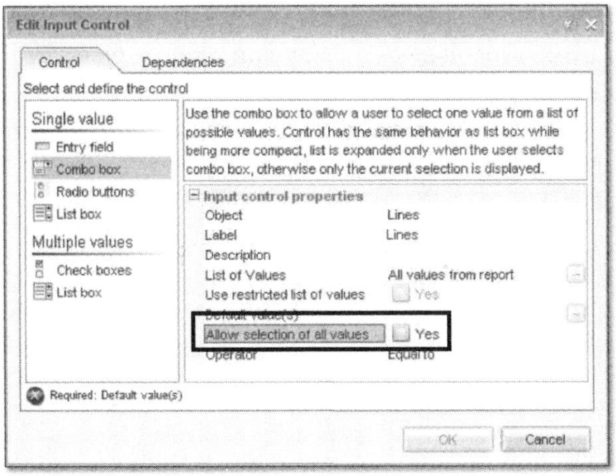

Figure 2.20 Input Control Property with Allow Selection of All Values Option

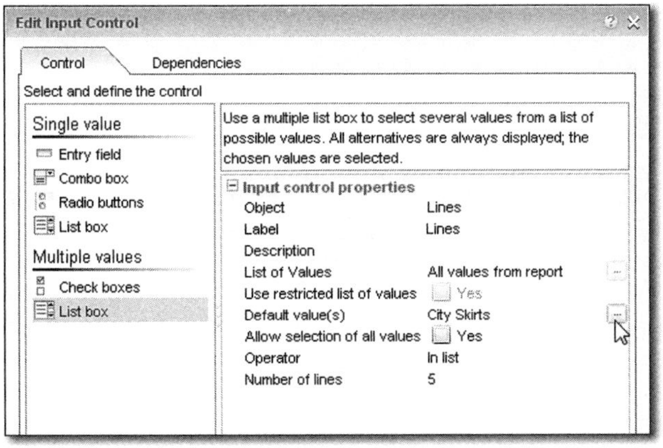

Figure 2.21 Selecting a Default Value for Input Control

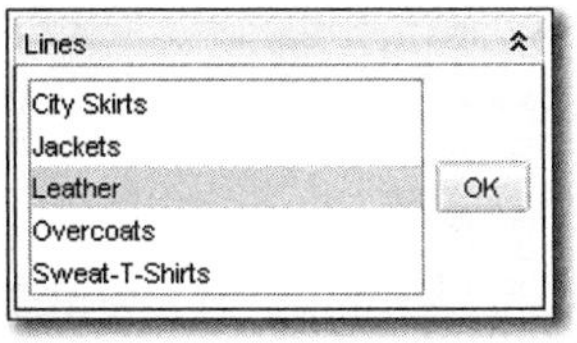

Figure 2.22 Interacting with an Input Control in Reading Mode

2.5.2 Improved Header and Footer Property Access

Another simple new feature is the capability to quickly and directly modify the properties of the report header and report footer by right-clicking on the header or footer and selecting either FORMAT HEADER or FORMAT FOOTER (see Figure 2.23).

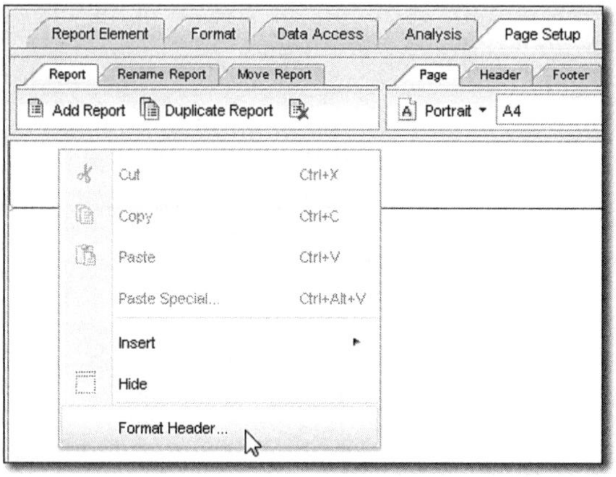

Figure 2.23 Right-Click Menu of the Report Header

By clicking this entry, a FORMAT HEADER window will open with the following options specifically available for formatting the report header:

▶ BORDER
Use this category to apply a border to any side of the header or footer with varying style and thickness.

▶ APPEARANCE
This is an ideal area for adding a company logo to the report. It's entered as a BACKGROUND IMAGE. To add a logo, select the IMAGE FROM FILE option in the PATTERN section, and then browse locally to upload the image (see Figure 2.24). After selecting an image, you can set specific properties for displaying the logo appropriately on the report as listed here:

  ▷ DISPLAY
    – NORMAL – STRETCH – TILE – HORIZONTAL TILE – VERTICAL TILE
  ▷ POSITION
    – LEFT – CENTER – RIGHT
    – TOP – CENTER – BOTTOM

▶ LAYOUT

This category includes a checkbox for showing/hiding the header or footer and also provides a height value selector in case you want to set the height to a specific value.

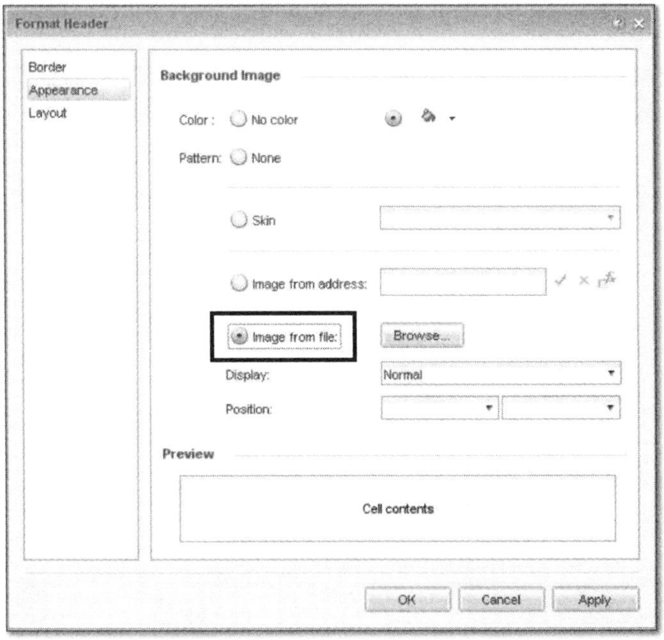

Figure 2.24 Selecting a Background Image in the Format Header Window

2.5.3 Formula Editor Enhancements

For report developers who frequently write detailed and complex formulas, a new feature has been added to the Formula Editor to help with explicit value selection. This new operator is a handy addition when writing formulas that require multiple entries or lengthy entries. It also removes some of the manual involvement by allowing values to be selected rather than typed, thus reducing the potential spelling errors.

To begin using the new Values operator, enter the Formula Editor to write a new formula or edit an existing one.

Using the Dynamic Values Operator

Follow these steps:

1. Write or edit a formula in the Formula Editor.

2. Select an object from the list of available objects.

3. Add an operator to the formula.

4. With the object still selected in the AVAILABLE OBJECTS list, double-click the VAL-UES operator, as shown in Figure 2.25.

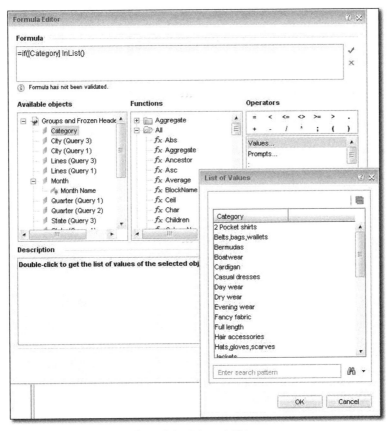

Figure 2.25 Viewing the Values of the Selected Object

5. A LIST OF VALUES window opens for the associated object.

6. Select one or more objects from the list (see Figure 2.26).

7. Click OK to add the values to the formula, as shown in Figure 2.27.

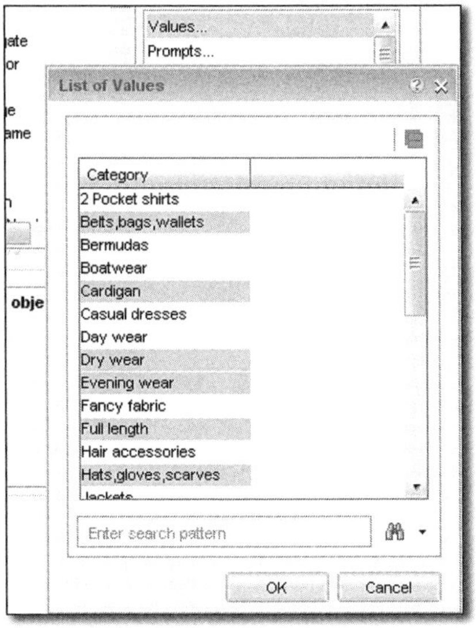

Figure 2.26 Selecting Values to be Added to a Formula

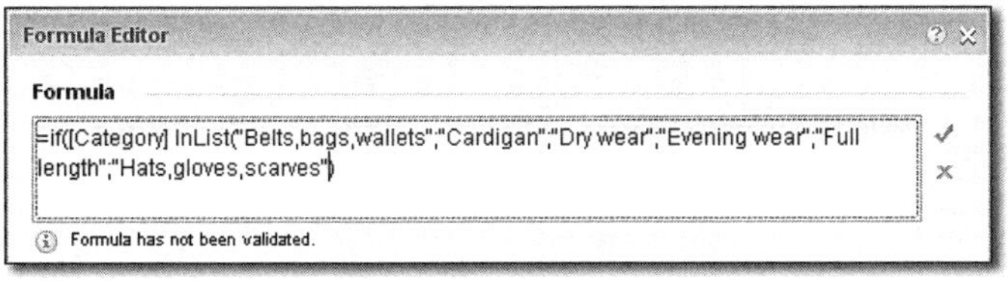

Figure 2.27 Values Added to the Formula

Next, we'll talk about the improvements made for interacting with queries.

2.5.4 Query Editing and Refreshing Updates

In SAP BusinessObjects BI 4.0, when a document was refreshed that contained multiple queries, all of the queries had to be refreshed at the same time. Now in SAP BusinessObjects BI 4.1, however, documents that contain multiple queries can either be refreshed all at once or individually.

From the REPORT PANEL, in design mode, click the DATA ACCESS tab, and then locate the REFRESH icon within the DATA PROVIDERS subtab. Now when you click the small down arrow immediately to the right of the REFRESH icon, you can select a query from the list and only that query will be refreshed (see Figure 2.28).

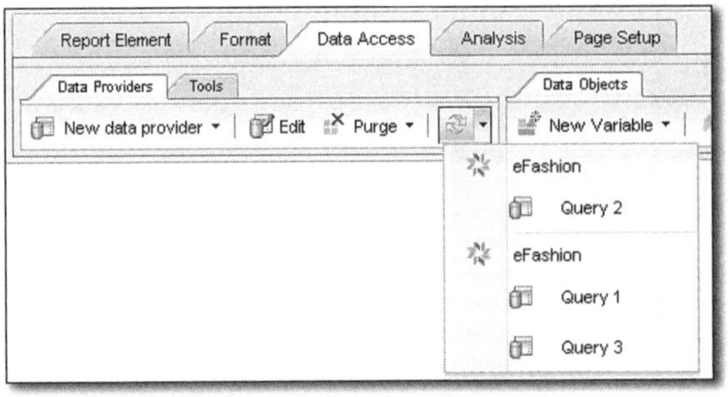

Figure 2.28 Refreshing a Single Query from the Report Panel

Refreshing Single Queries from the Query Panel

The same option is also available while working in the Query Panel. When creating or editing queries in the Query Panel, click the down arrow located immediately to the right of the RUN QUERIES button. This selection will show all of the queries within the document, and you can select a single query to be refreshed (see Figure 2.29).

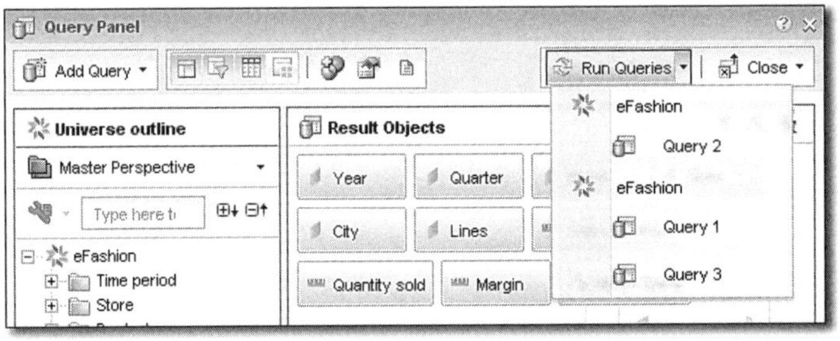

Figure 2.29 Selecting Single Queries from the Query Panel

Note

To refresh all queries in the document, click the RUN QUERIES button.

Editing Queries

Getting to the Query Panel is also easier in SAP BusinessObjects BI 4.1. A new EDIT QUERY icon (see Figure 2.30) has been added that provides access to the Query Panel, regardless of which tab you're currently viewing. The only requirement is that you're in design mode.

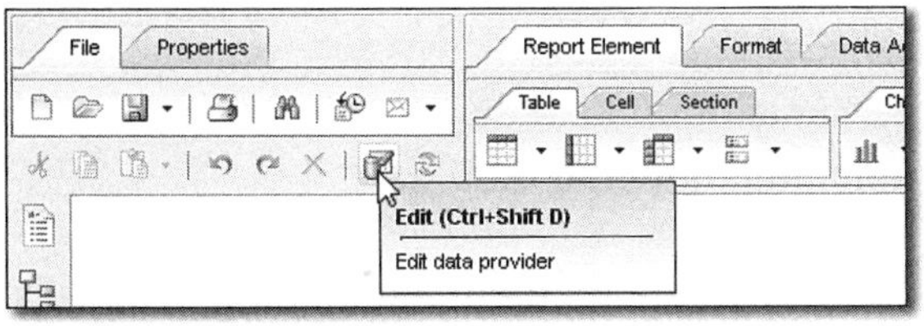

Figure 2.30 Edit Query Icon

Now that you've discovered the new features related to accessing the Query Panel and refreshing individual queries, let's discuss the latest capabilities for applying custom color palettes to charts for producing reports that meet any company's color and style requirements.

2.6 Customizing Color Properties

Now in SAP BusinessObjects BI 4.1, developers have the flexibility of modifying chart colors with a variety of techniques. These new methods give developers the tools to produce consistent and precisely color-coded reports. In addition, administrators now have the capability to define global chart palettes and modify the default styles used in reports. These new capabilities provide unprecedented customization and visualization options for Web Intelligence.

First, let's discuss the custom color palettes available for all chart types.

2.6.1 Custom Color Palettes

In each color palette, there are 32 total colors with 8 primary colors (see Figure 2.31; full color screenshots are available in the e-book).

From the CREATE PALETTE window, you can generate a new combination of colors based purely on their appearance or from specific color codes to create precise and easily repeatable color settings.

Perform the following steps to begin creating a custom palette:

1. Select an existing chart on your report.

2. Locate the CHART STYLE subtab on the primary FORMAT tab.

3. Expand the PALETTE STYLE dropdown list, then scroll down, and select CUSTOM (see Figure 2.32).

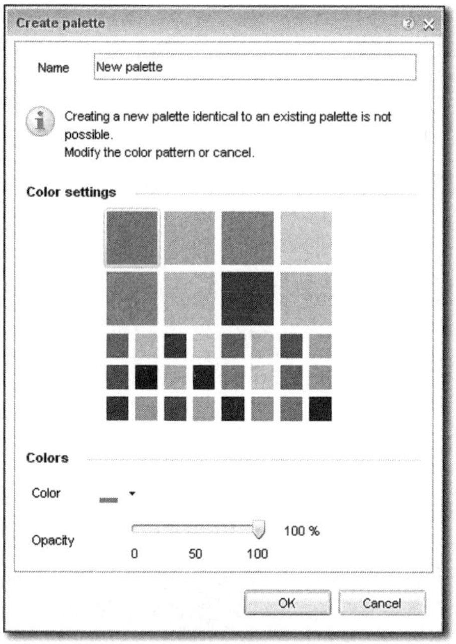

Figure 2.31 Adjusting Colors in a Custom Color Palette

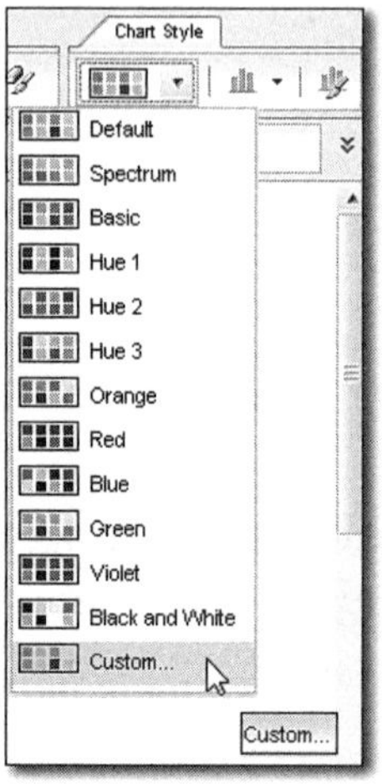

Figure 2.32 Creating a Custom Color Palette

Clicking CUSTOM launches the MANAGE PALETTES window, as shown in Figure 2.33. After this window opens, click NEW in the CUSTOM section to begin creating a new custom palette.

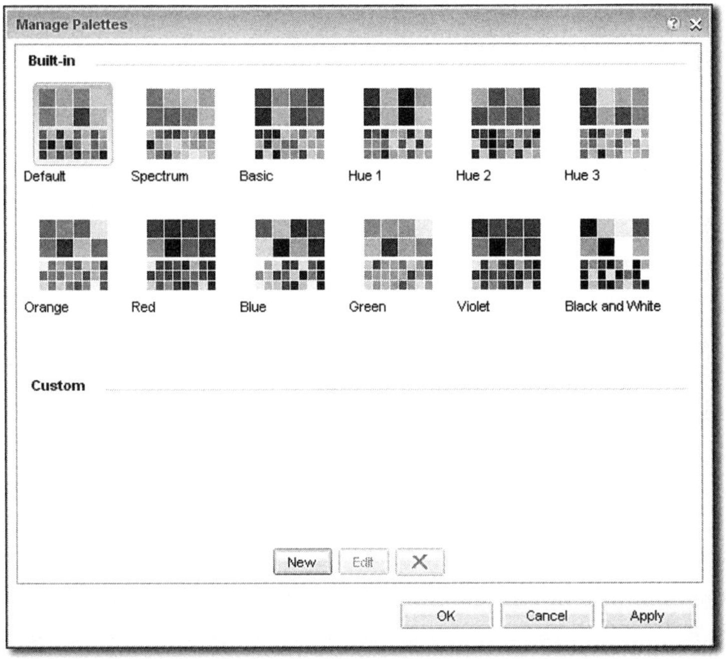

Figure 2.33 Creating a New Custom Palette

2.6.2 Creating a New Custom Color Palette

Begin assigning new colors by clicking one of the existing color boxes located in the COLOR SETTINGS area. Next, click the color picker to assign a new color to the placeholder box selected.

Select MORE COLORS under the default list of choices to make your color selection by code, as shown in Figure 2.34.

By selecting MORE COLORS, you'll launch the CUSTOM COLOR window that can be used for choosing precise colors from these five color definition choices, which appear as tabs in Figure 2.35:

▶ SWATCHES

▶ HSV

▶ HSL

▶ RGB

▶ CMYK

69

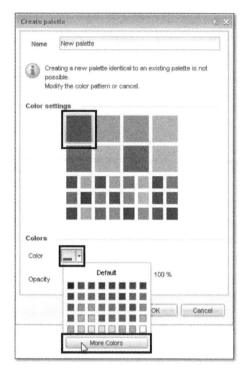

Figure 2.34 Selecting Custom Colors for Your New Custom Palette

The CREATE PALETTE window also provides an OPACITY option to further modify colors assigned to each color setting. Use this property to soften selected colors and give a level of transparency from 0 to 100%.

In Figure 2.35, which shows the CMYK tab, notice how many options are available for selecting a color. Begin by selecting CYAN, MAGENTA, or YELLOW to use as a base color. Then you'll have several choices for fine-tuning your selection:

▶ Use the crosshairs in the color area selector.

▶ Adjust the tint in the vertical color adjustor.

▶ Use the sliders to increase or decrease the weight of a color element.

▶ Use specific numbers to define the color.

▶ The three previous tabs, HSV, HSL, and RGB, provide this same functionality.

Next we'll talk about how to override palette colors with new colors to a data series in a chart.

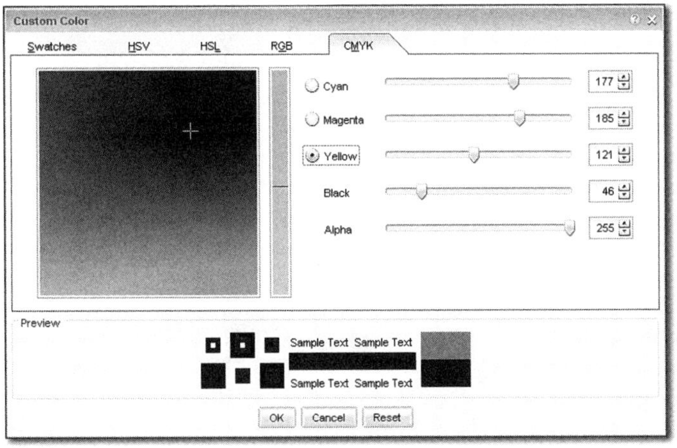

Figure 2.35 shows the Custom Color Selector with the CMYK tab options.

Figure 2.35 Custom Color Selector Options in the CMYK Tab

2.6.3 Formatting Data Series Colors

Two options are available for overriding palette colors in a chart. Both are applied in design mode, and both require you to select a charted data series. This can be a pie slice, data point on a line chart, bar on a bar chart, or column on a column chart.

The first method is accomplished by selecting a data series and then changing the background color by using the icon in the FORMAT tab. For example, Figure 2.36 shows where the 2004 values are being changed to supersede the colors in the palette.

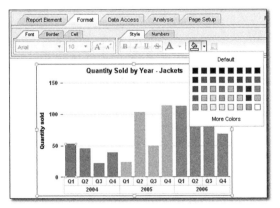

Figure 2.36 Overriding Palette Colors

Format Data Series Option

The next option, new with SAP BusinessObjects BI 4.1, provides the ability to add additional formatting for a single data series. This option is available by right-clicking on a charted element (bar, column, pie slice, etc.) and then selecting FORMAT DATA SERIES (see Figure 2.37).

Figure 2.37 Right-Click Menu after Selecting a Chart Element

The FORMAT DATA SERIES window provides a few different features, all of which will apply only to the series selected (see Figure 2.38).

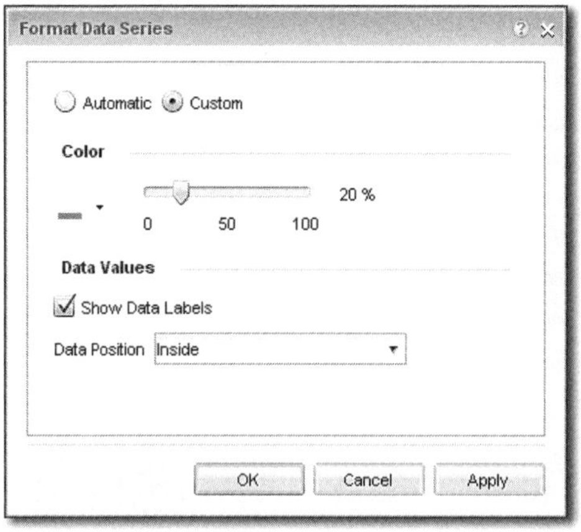

Figure 2.38 Format Data Series Options

To get started, you'll need to select the CUSTOM option. By default, the AUTOMATIC option is selected with all of the adjustable properties disabled. Clicking CUSTOM will enable the following properties:

▶ COLOR

  ▷ COLOR picker icon is used to open the CUSTOM COLOR window discussed in the previous step.

  ▷ OPACITY slider is used to select an opacity effect from 0% (transparent) to 100% (opaque).

▶ DATA VALUES

  ▷ SHOW DATA LABELS checkbox

  ▷ DATA POSITION

Figure 2.39 shows the chart modified by changes made to the first data series with the settings adjusted in Figure 2.38.

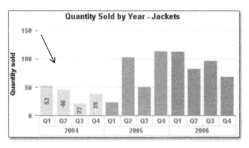

Figure 2.39 Changes to a Chart after Formatting a Data Series

2.6.4 Defining Global Chart Palettes

From a global perspective, administrators now have the opportunity to define a corporate palette that can be used by all users and will become the default palette for all new charts. This is accomplished by editing the color codes in the *VisualizationConfig.template.xml* file. In a simple Windows Server installation, this file is found in the following location:

C:\Program Files (x86)\SAP BusinessObjects\SAP BusinessObjects Enterprise XI 4.0\images

There are 32 color values assigned with RGB codes in the file. Edit any of the codes, then save the file as both *VisualizationConfig.xml* and *VisualizationConfig.template.xml,* and restart your web server.

Do not modify the palette ID from the default: `<PALETTE ID="corporate">`.

> **Note**
>
> This is an administrative task and should only be attempted by experienced administrators in a test or development environment before attempting in production. Also, a backup copy of the *VisualizationConfig.template.xml* file should be made in case you need to revert back to the original.

2.6.5 Modifying Default Styles

Another task available to administrators is the capability to modify the default styles in Web Intelligence by editing the *WebIDefaultStyleSheet.css* file. In a standard Windows Server installation of SAP BusinessObjects BI 4.1, the file is found in the following location:

C:\Program Files (x86)\SAP BusinessObjects\SAP BusinessObjects Enterprise XI 4.0\images

With this file, style elements can be modified to produce a very specific and extensive collection of formatted properties. Experience with Cascading Style Sheets (CSS) is required to edit this file.

2.7 Using Excel as a Data Source in the BI Launch Pad

Have you ever wanted to use a Microsoft Excel file as the data source to build a Web Intelligence report? Now you can in SAP BusinessObjects BI 4.1 SP2 forward.

With a Microsoft Excel spreadsheet as a data source, you can take advantage of the extensive data display capabilities and filtering options in Web Intelligence and then share your document with users across the enterprise in the SAP BusinessObjects BI 4.1 platform.

Reports using Excel as a data source can be created in the following interfaces:

▶ In the BI Launch Pad using the Applet viewer (as shown in Figure 2.40)

▶ Web Intelligence Rich Client

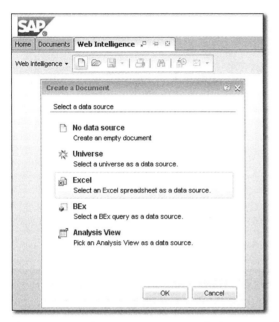

Figure 2.40 Excel as a Data Source – Inside the BI Launch Pad

The primary requirement for creating a document sourced from Excel is to publish the Excel file(s) to the SAP BusinessObjects BI platform to be used as the data source.

Follow these steps to publish an Excel file to the platform:

1. Log on to the BI Launch Pad, and go to the DOCUMENTS tab.

2. Select the folder to save the Excel file to.

3. Click the NEW option, and select LOCAL DOCUMENT (Figure 2.41).

4. Browse to the Excel file to be published.

5. Revise the title, add a description, and add keywords (optional settings).

6. Click ADD to proceed.

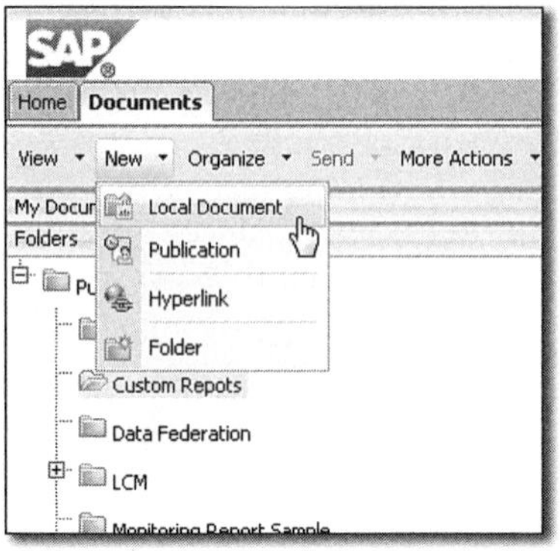

Figure 2.41 Add Excel Files to the SAP BusinessObjects BI Platform as New Local Documents

Now that you've added an Excel file to the SAP BusinessObjects BI platform, you can use it as a data source for creating a Web Intelligence report.

2.7.1 Creating Queries from Excel Files

When creating a new Web Intelligence document or adding a new query to an existing document, select EXCEL when prompted to select a data source. Then navigate to the folder that you published the file to, and select the spreadsheet to be used as the source.

After selecting the Excel file, you're taken to a CUSTOM DATA PROVIDER – EXCEL window, as shown in Figure 2.42. Use this window to make a few property elections for the file that you're about to use:

▶ SHEET NAME
Choose the worksheet that you want to use as your source if the source Excel file contains multiple tabs.

▶ FIELD SELECTION
Choose from ALL FIELDS, RANGE DEFINITION, and RANGE NAME.

▶ FIRST ROW CONTAINS COLUMN NAMES
This is checked and enabled by default.

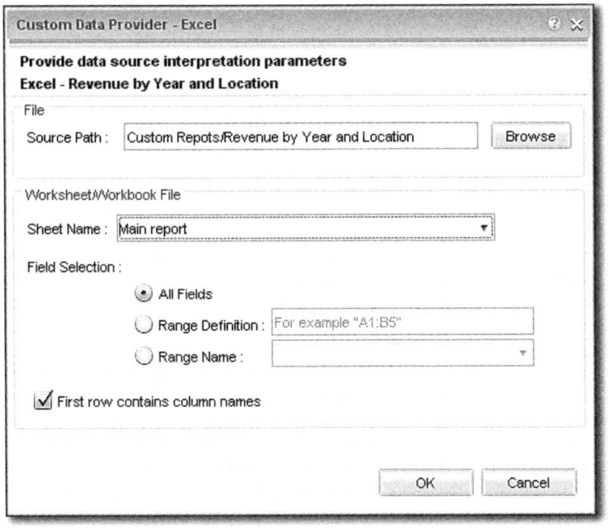

Figure 2.42 Custom Data Provider – Excel

Selecting OK takes you to an abbreviated Query Panel. This window provides the following information and is displayed in Figure 2.43:

▶ RESULT OBJECTS

▶ DATA SAMPLES

▶ OBJECT PROPERTIES

  ▶ Modifiable name of each object

  ▶ Qualification (dimension or measure)

  ▶ Data type (if the type is a measure, the aggregate function is also displayed)

▶ QUERY PROPERTIES

  ▶ Query name

  ▶ Source path

  ▶ REFRESHABLE checkbox (enabled by default)

▶ EDIT SETTINGS
  This button provides the option of switching sheet names.

▶ Click RUN QUERY to view the results in the Report Panel.

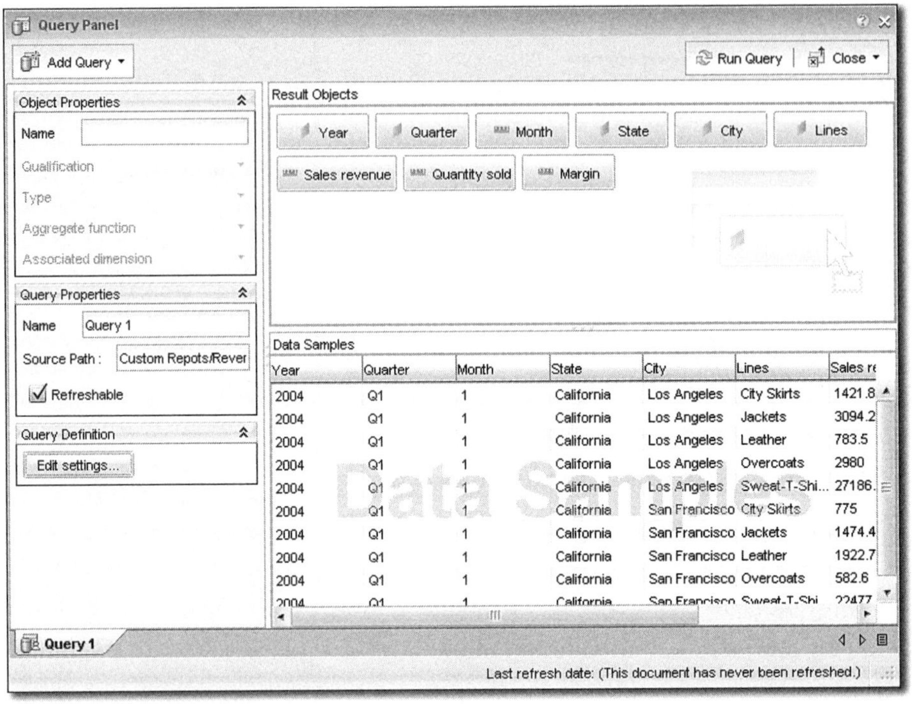

Figure 2.43 Query Panel for Excel-Based Data Sources

You're now ready to take advantage of all the features provided in the Report Panel. When you're ready, save the new reporting document to the SAP Business-Objects BI platform, and share it with other users.

Now that we've discussed how to create a report from an Excel file, let's talk about updating the Excel file and report(s) that are using it as a source.

2.7.2 Updating Published Excel Files

To update a spreadsheet on the SAP BusinessObjects BI platform, right-click on the file, and then select ORGANIZE followed by REPLACE FILE as shown in Figure 2.44.

After clicking REPLACE FILE, you'll be prompted to browse for the replacement Excel file. Select the updated file, and then click the REPLACE button to proceed. Just confirm the replacement by clicking OK on the popup, as shown in Figure 2.45.

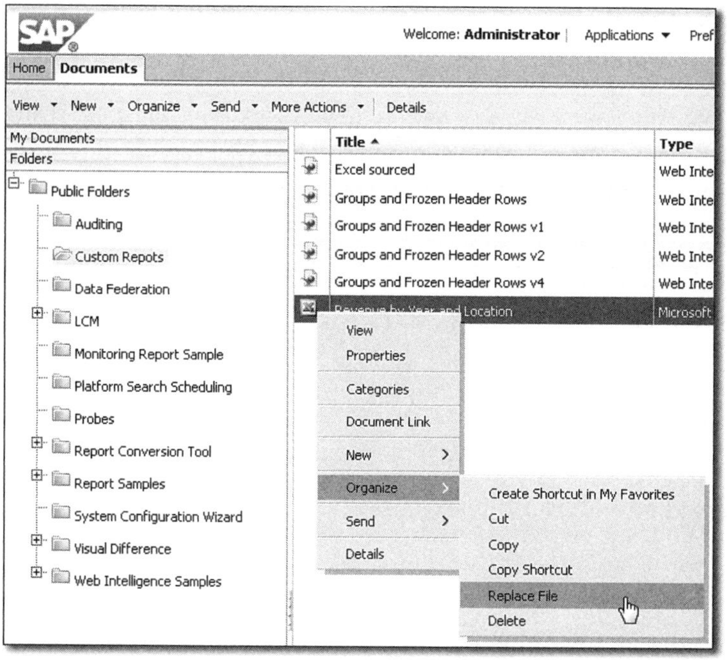

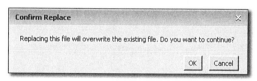

Figure 2.44 Replacing Published Excel Files

Figure 2.45 Confirming the Replacement of an Excel File in the BI Launch Pad

2.7.3   Refreshable Queries Based on Excel

To see the updated changes in Web Intelligence report(s), open any document that uses the updated Excel file as a source and click REFRESH. The data in the updated version of the spreadsheet will now be in your report(s).

> **Note**
>
> Web Intelligence documents that use Excel files as a data source must be refreshed before any updated data in the file is retrieved by Web Intelligence.

2.8 Charting Enhancements

Since the advanced charting engine was introduced in Web Intelligence with the release of SAP BusinessObjects BI 4.0, report developers have been creating reporting documents with more charts than ever before. Because of this newfound popularity in visually displaying data, the product development team continues to provide useful improvements with every release and service pack.

In this section, we'll describe the following new charting features in SAP BusinessObjects BI 4.1 up to SP3:

▸ Format data series

▸ Series color options

▸ New waterfall chart properties

▸ Modify individual line widths in a line chart

2.8.1 Format Data Series

Formatting a data series is most useful when a chart is created with two dimension objects assigned to it. When only a single dimensional object has been assigned to a chart and the data series is formatted, the formatting will apply to the entire chart.

2.8.2 Series Color Options

Another new feature in SAP BusinessObjects BI 4.1 that applies to formatting the data series in a chart is the SERIES COLOR option. This feature is useful when the dimensional values in a chart frequently changes through filtering or query refreshes, and users prefer to have the same color applied to the same value.

To permanently assign a color to a dimension, right-click on a charted column, row, line, or slice, and select SERIES COLORS • SET AS DEFAULT COLORS (see Figure 2.46). This option freezes the color in the palette to the charted dimension.

If the DEFAULT COLORS option has been enabled, and you want to return it to the default, disable it by selecting the CLEAR COLOR ASSIGNMENT option that's also available in the SERIES COLORS options.

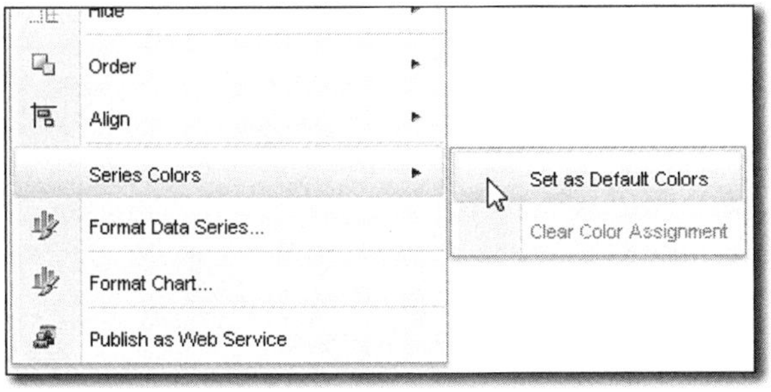

Figure 2.46 Setting Default Colors to Dimension Objects in a Chart

2.8.3　New Waterfall Chart Properties

Waterfall charts provide a useful way of visualizing the cumulative effect of sequential values and illustrating the impact of a measure across a dimensional category. Displaying the totals, or end result, as a charted column, is now an option in a waterfall chart. This feature is enabled by selecting the CALCULATE AND SHOW THE TOTAL option located in the GENERAL category of the FORMAT CHART window.

These other options added to the waterfall chart in SAP BusinessObjects BI 4.1 are helpful for displaying key elements in the waterfall as well:

► START VALUE COLOR

► TOTAL VALUE COLOR

► NEGATIVE VALUE COLOR

► POSITIVE VALUE COLOR

► REFERENCE LINE

Change the default color settings from AUTOMATIC to FIXED VALUE to make the results in the waterfall easier to interpret. The biggest positive and negative impacts on the overall totals are spotted more easily with custom color changes. Figure 2.47 shows these properties located in the PALETTE AND STYLE category.

To add a reference line that connects each value in a waterfall chart, enter the FORMAT CHART window of a waterfall chart, and select the PLOT AREA category. There, check the REFERENCE LINE setting as shown in Figure 2.48.

Figure 2.49 shows a waterfall chart with all of the settings modified that are listed previously, including the reference line and data values.

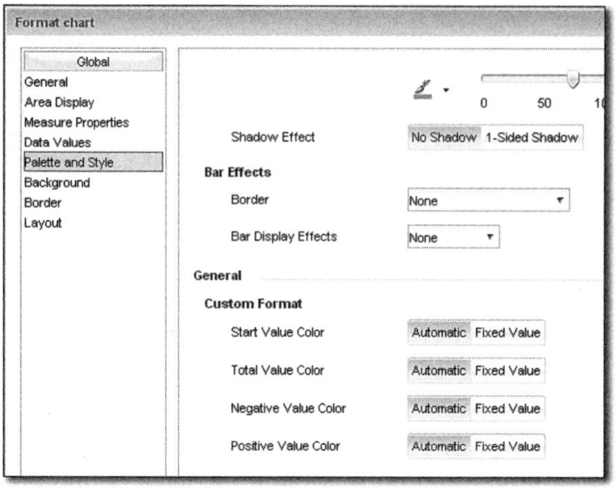

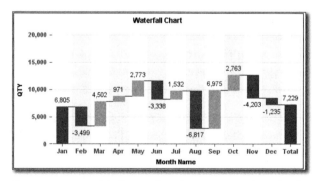

Figure 2.47 Custom Color Formatting Options in a Waterfall Chart

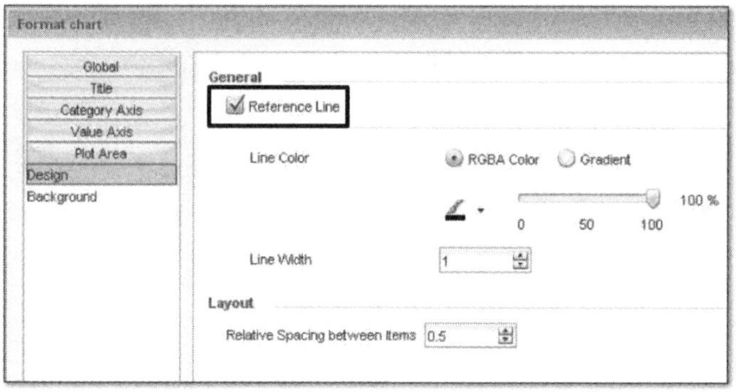

Figure 2.48 Adding a Reference Line to a Waterfall Chart

Figure 2.49 Waterfall Chart with Reference Line and Fixed Value Colors

2.8.4 Individual Line Widths in Line Chart

Line charts have a new feature in SAP BusinessObjects BI 4.1 that allows for the widths of individually charted lines to be increased. This is a simple, but helpful feature because it allows developers to create line charts that give more weight to a certain measure.

To increase the width of a line, begin by selecting a charted data point in a line chart. Next, right-click on the data point, and then select the FORMAT DATA SERIES option. The options window that opens will include a LINE WIDTH setting as shown in Figure 2.50.

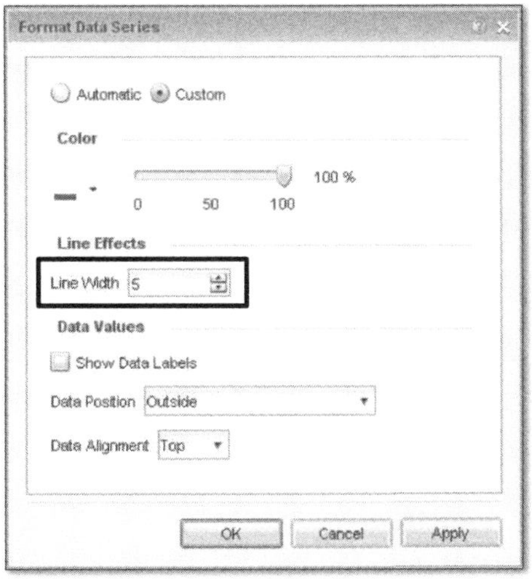

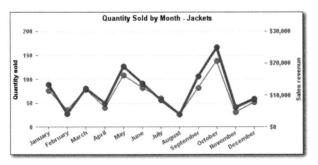

Figure 2.50 Line Width Option in a Line Chart

The result of this new option produces a line chart, like that shown in Figure 2.51.

Figure 2.51 Line Chart with a Modified Line Width

Next, we'll discuss a few new features for formatting measures in tables that are in the form of currency and a new predefined cell for displaying user responses to prompted filters.

2.9   Report Formatting Improvements

For report developers and business users who work with financial data, it's a very common need to show the correct currency format in a report. Now there's an icon where the following currency types can be applied with a single click:

▶ Dollar

▶ Euro

▶ Yen

Just select a row or column in a data table, and click the CURRENCY icon located in the FORMAT tab and NUMBERS subtab (see Figure 2.52).

Figure 2.52 Currency Symbol Icon

For columns or rows presenting data in percentages, there is a new PERCENT icon located immediately to the right of the CURRENCY icon.

Predefined Cell for Prompts

To dynamically display users' responses to prompted query filters, there's a new predefined cell. This feature is ideal for report titles, subtitles, headings, or descriptive texts that provide the complete context of the data being analyzed.

Follow these steps to add this new predefined cell to a report:

1. Select the REPORT ELEMENT tab, and then select the CELL subtab.

2. Click the PRE-DEFINED button to view all of the predefined cells, as shown in Figure 2.53.

3. Click the PROMPT option.

4. Select the prompted value to be added to the report.

5. Choose a location on the report canvas to place the new cell.

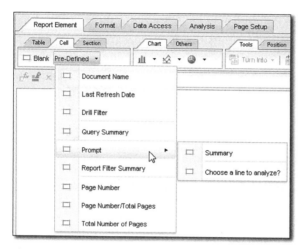

Figure 2.53 Adding a Predefined Cell for the User Response from a Prompted Filter

The formula added will include the `UserResponse()` function. After adding the cell to the report canvas, click it to view the formula in the formula bar. You can then copy the formula generated and paste it into any number of places, including chart titles, report headers, or column headings.

2.10 Summary

Web Intelligence continues to receive notable enhancements with every new release and service pack. Now that SAP HANA variables and input parameters are interpreted by Web Intelligence as prompted filters, the combination of these two products form a winning technical combination that cannot be matched. As the product development team continues to implement improvements, many based on crowd-sourced requests contributed through SAP's Idea Place website (*ideas.sap.com*), the industry's leading query and analysis reporting tool continues to separate itself from competing tools.

SAP BusinessObjects BI 4.1 brought improvements to both SAP HANA connectivity and SAP BW variable management, and better usability for hierarchies in SAP

BEx sourced reports, including more capabilities with merging objects of hierarchies for multiconnected reports. Support of optional parameters from SAP ERP sources, query stripping in relational sources, and easier access to the Query Panel provide even more capabilities for accessing data.

The popularity of SAP BusinessObjects has extended around the globe and has been met by new globalization enhancements that provide a growing list of supported languages in SAP BusinessObjects BI 4.1. Now with bidirectional language support for RightToLeft (RTL) readability and in a mirrored interface, Arabic and Hebrew users can take advantage of the growing list of analytical features in Web Intelligence.

With all these new features being introduced with every release, report developers can't help but be excited about what's to come.

In the next chapter, we'll talk about creating new Web Intelligence documents and queries in the Query Panel.

Create queries graphically with the highly intuitive and enhanced Query Panel in SAP BusinessObjects Web Intelligence 4.x. Use the Result Objects pane and Query Filters pane to access the data you need from universes, SAP BEx queries, Analysis Views, web services, Excel files, and text files, and then create and share powerful analysis documents with business users.

3   Creating New Documents and Queries

The Query Panel in Web Intelligence provides business users with an intuitive interface for retrieving and filtering data. Much more than a simple tool for querying relational data sources, Web Intelligence 4.1 lets you connect directly to SAP Business Explorer (SAP BEx) queries and Analysis Views (a user-defined subset of multidimensional OLAP data sources from Analysis workspaces).

Queries are created graphically as objects (database fields) and are inserted into the Result Objects pane on the Query Panel. This collection of objects is translated into the `Select` section of the generated SQL statement, and the `where` clause gets its information from the objects included in the Query Filters pane. Query filters can be hard-coded conditions created in the universe or dimension objects inserted into the Query Filters pane with manually assigned values.

After a query has completed successfully, the retrieved data is stored within each document in an unseen *microcube*. At this point, the data is ready to be formatted and presented in a report.

This chapter takes you through every aspect of creating a Web Intelligence 4.1 document from within the BI Launch Pad portal and outlines the different query types available. With Web Intelligence Rich Client, a standalone version of the tool, users are provided with the capability to access a *local data source* by connecting to Excel files, text files, or even web services.

A common purpose for accessing local data sources is to use existing Excel files to create documents with all of the powerful filtering and visualization features available in Web Intelligence 4.1.

3.1 Creating a Web Intelligence 4.1 Document

The portal interface in SAP BusinessObjects BI 4.1 provides two ways to launch the Web Intelligence query and analysis tool in the BI Launch Pad. After logging on to the BI Launch Pad and going to the HOME tab, you'll notice a column on the right-hand side of the page with six application shortcuts. These links are beneath the MY APPLICATIONS heading.

Figure 3.1 shows the shortcut icons for these six applications in the BI Launch Pad:

▶ MODULE

▶ ANALYSIS EDITION FOR OLAP

▶ INFORMATION STEWARD

▶ CRYSTAL REPORTS FOR ENTERPRISE

▶ BI WORKSPACE

▶ WEB INTELLIGENCE

Click on the bottom icon in the list to begin creating a Web Intelligence document.

An alternate method of launching Web Intelligence from within the BI Launch Pad is by clicking on the APPLICATIONS link located in the top menu of the page. Links to the same six applications as previously described will appear but in a different order.

Figure 3.2 shows the result of clicking on the APPLICATIONS menu link and selecting WEB INTELLIGENCE from the list provided.

Web Intelligence opens to a blank screen with all of the shortcut icons disabled except for two choices:

▶ Create a new document ([Ctrl]+[N])

▶ Open (retrieve) a document from the server ([Ctrl]+[O])

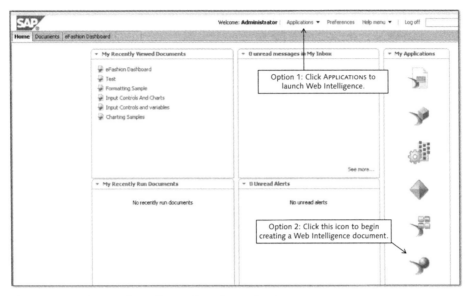

Figure 3.1 Launching Web Intelligence from My Applications

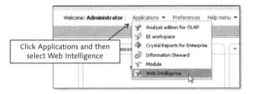

Figure 3.2 Launching Web Intelligence from the Applications Menu Link

From the WEB INTELLIGENCE tab itself, you have additional options to interact with the document by clicking on one of three small icons located beside the document name. This is where you can enlarge the screen by opening the document in a new window or simply close the Web Intelligence application. There are three clickable icon options on the WEB INTELLIGENCE tab:

▶ OPEN IN A NEW WINDOW

▶ PIN (OR UNPIN) THIS TAB

▶ CLOSE

Figure 3.3 shows the options available after launching the Web Intelligence application and before a document is created or opened.

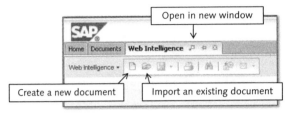

Figure 3.3 Options Available before Creating or Opening a Document

Click on the BLANK DOCUMENT icon to create a new Web Intelligence document. You'll have four data source options (UNIVERSE, BEX, EXCEL, and ANALYSIS VIEW) when working from within the BI Launch Pad and a fifth option for NO DATA SOURCE. The option to create Web Intelligence documents sourced from Excel files was introduced in SAP BusinessObjects BI 4.1.

The option to create Web Intelligence documents sourced directly from an SAP BEx query or Analysis View is a feature introduced in SAP BusinessObjects BI 4.0. Access to these two data sources greatly expands the reach of Web Intelligence; it allows users working in an SAP Business Warehouse (SAP BW) environment with existing hierarchical SAP BEx queries to leverage the strengths of the Web Intelligence product and extensive Report Panel capabilities.

Figure 3.4 shows the data sources available for creating a new document when using the Applet viewer.

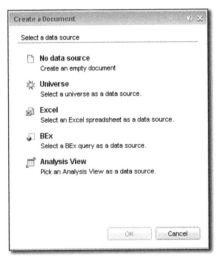

Figure 3.4 Selecting a Data Source for Creating a New Document in the Applet Viewer

Figure 3.5 shows the data sources available when creating a new report while working in the HTML viewer. Notice that the only data source type available in the HTML viewer is UNIVERSE.

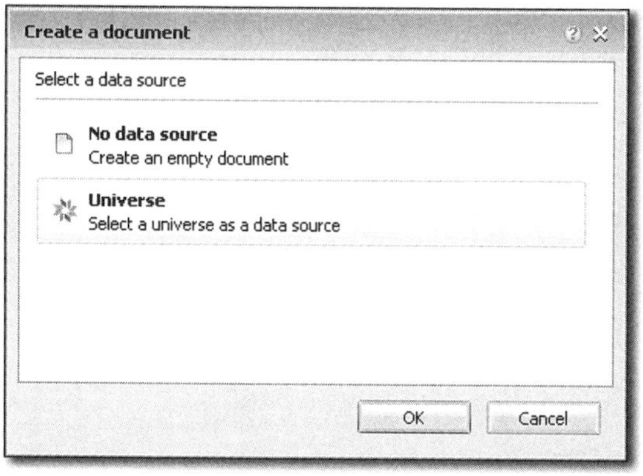

Figure 3.5 Selecting a Data Source for Creating a New Document in the HTML Viewer

Let's explore each of these data sources.

3.1.1   Universe as a Data Source

The patented SAP BusinessObjects semantic layer known as the universe remains the primary method for connecting reporting documents to traditional data warehouses and relational databases. SAP BusinessObjects BI 4.0 introduced the Information Design Tool to allow universes to be created from multiple sources; it also changed the name of the tool previously known as Designer to the Universe Design Tool.

But little has changed from a user's perspective when it comes to connecting to a universe to query a database. Database fields, known in the universe as objects, are used in the Query Panel to retrieve data and to restrict the results to return only the information needed.

After selecting UNIVERSE as the data source for a new document, you're presented with a list of available universes that you have permission to access. Click on a universe in the list, and click on SELECT to proceed. Figure 3.6 shows an example list of available universes that can be used as a data source.

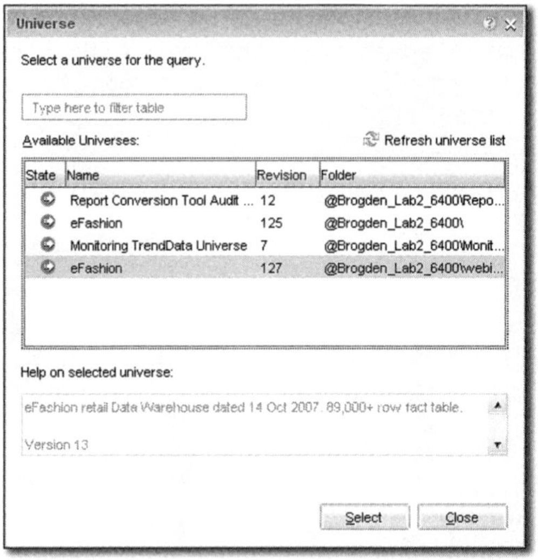

Figure 3.6 Available Universes

After you make your universe selection, the Web Intelligence tool will be launched and opened to the QUERY PANEL. Before you can begin analyzing information and creating reports, you need to retrieve information from your data source. The Query Panel is your window for accessing that data.

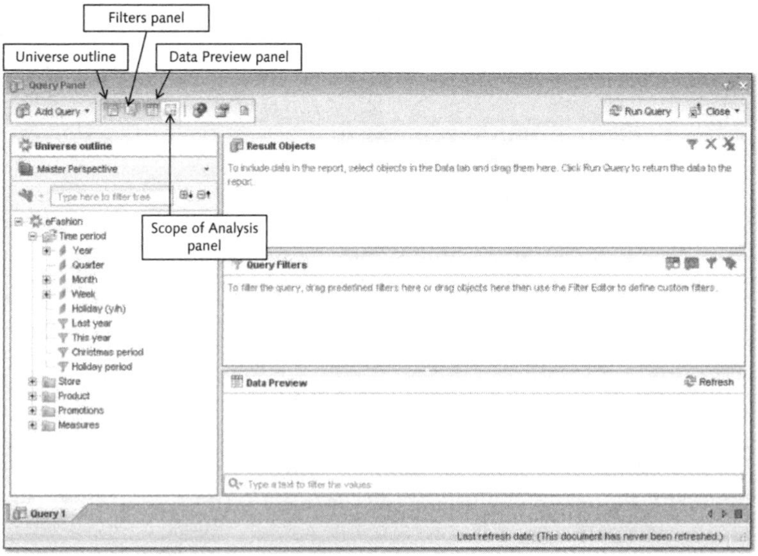

Figure 3.7 Query Panel in Web Intelligence 4.1

Figure 3.7 shows the Query Panel and the shortcut icons for toggling four of the five primary panes within the Query Panel to the on or off position. The Query Panel will be described further in Section 3.2.

Another option is to use an SAP BEx query as a data source.

3.1.2 Direct Connection to an SAP BEx Query

One of the most exciting new enhancements to Web Intelligence in version 4.0 was the ability to connect directly to a SAP BEx query. This feature has continued to evolve and improve in SAP BusinessObjects BI 4.1 as it allows SAP BW customers to use Web Intelligence while also being able to view and interact with hierarchical data created by an SAP BEx query.

To begin the process of connecting to an SAP BEx query with Web Intelligence, you need to create a new OLAP connection that uses the *SAP BI Consumer Services (BICS) client* and then releases each SAP BEx query to be used as a data source for Web Intelligence.

Releasing SAP BEx Queries to Be Accessed by Web Intelligence

To make your SAP BEx queries accessible to Web Intelligence, you need to release each query for external access in the BEx Query Designer. In the Properties section, locate Release for OLE DB and OLAP and then check the Allow External Access to this Query box beneath it. This setting certifies an SAP BEx query for external use and allows it to be consumed by the Web Intelligence application in SAP BusinessObjects BI 4.1.

Creating an OLAP Connection

To create a connection that allows Web Intelligence to connect to a hierarchical SAP BEx query, open the Universe Design Tool and create a new OLAP connection. This method of connectivity lets you access SAP BEx queries directly without going through the universe layer.

After logging on to the Universe Design Tool, select File • New • OLAP Connection, as shown in Figure 3.8.

You should give your new OLAP connection an identifiable resource name to be selected in reporting documents when connecting directly to an SAP BEx query. We also recommend that you add a description of the resource; this can be very helpful in environments with multiple resources.

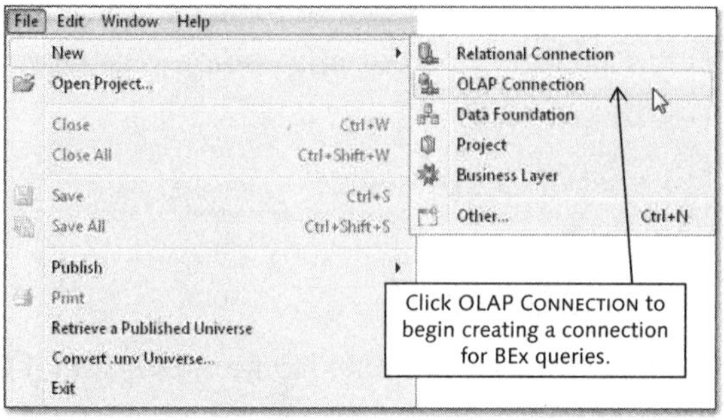

Figure 3.8 Creating an OLAP Connection in the Universe Design Tool

Figure 3.9 shows the screen for creating a resource name and description.

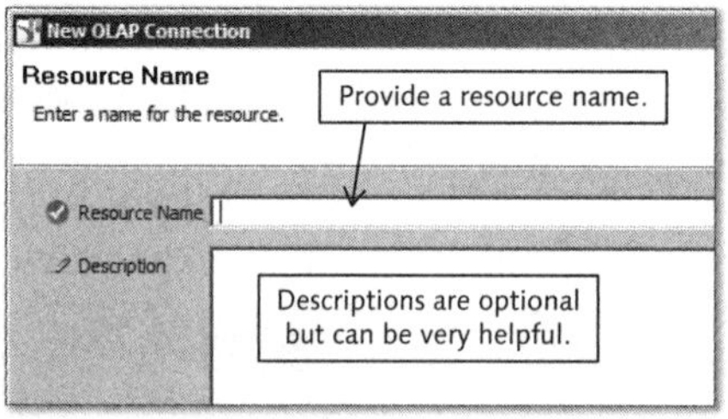

Figure 3.9 Creating a Resource Name and Description for a New OLAP Connection

After entering a resource name, click on NEXT to proceed, and then select the SAP BICS CLIENT network layer listed under SAP NETWEAVER BI 7.x.

Figure 3.10 shows the OLAP MIDDLEWARE DRIVER SELECTION window displayed when you choose your OLAP driver. Depending on the databases and drivers available to you, it's important to note that OLAP connections can be made to other multidimensional database vendors such as Microsoft and Oracle.

Figure 3.11 shows the list of parameters needed to make a successful connection to the SAP BICS Client and SAP NetWeaver BI 7.x. In addition to a username and password, you need to know the following properties to log on:

▶ CLIENT (number)

▶ SYSTEM ID

▶ APPLICATION SERVER NAME and SYSTEM NUMBER or MESSAGE SERVER NAME and GROUP NAME

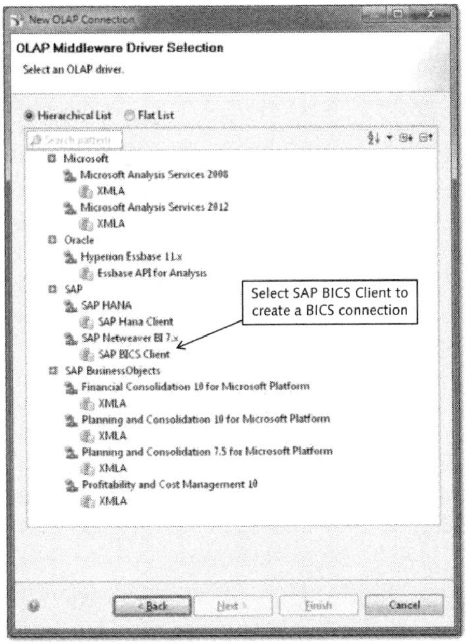

Figure 3.10 Creating the SAP BICS Client as the OLAP Middleware Driver Selection

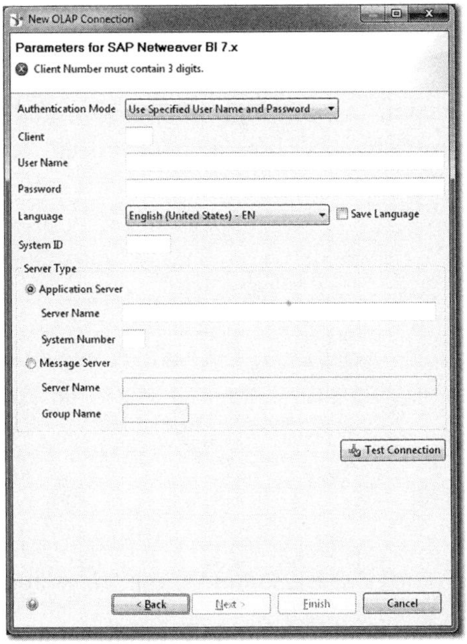

Figure 3.11 Parameters for Connecting to SAP NetWeaver BI 7.x

The final step is to select a cube from the list of available choices in the INFOAREA or FAVORITES folder. You can also create connections to several multidimensional data vendors.

After making your cube selection, click on NEXT to define the repository where the connection will be published. Figure 3.12 shows the CUBE SELECTION window used when creating a new OLAP connection.

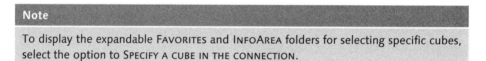

Figure 3.12 Cube Selection Window for Creating a New OLAP Connection

> **Note**
>
> To display the expandable FAVORITES and INFOAREA folders for selecting specific cubes, select the option to SPECIFY A CUBE IN THE CONNECTION.

Click on FINISH to publish the new connection to your repository. Figure 3.13 shows the message that appears after successfully publishing a new connection.

Figure 3.13 OLAP Connection Published Successfully

Next we'll examine using Analysis Views as a data source.

3.1.3   Analysis Views as a Data Source

Analysis Views are created to give users access to a subset of data derived from an *Analysis workspace* and a multidimensional data set. This new capability provides a means of accessing a specific arrangement of cube data within the Web Intelligence application and outside of the Analysis workspace.

Using Analysis Workspaces to Create Analysis Views

Many hierarchical dimensions and measures can be included in an Analysis workspace to solve complex business problems and provide very detailed information. However, many users see the vast amounts of data in a cube as overwhelming and difficult to use.

The addition of Analysis Views solves this problem by allowing a specified set of dimensions and measures to be viewed and analyzed in Web Intelligence. This new data source lets users leverage the benefits of working in Web Intelligence while also getting the value of interacting with data that originated from a multidimensional cube.

To begin creating Analysis Views, connect to a multidimensional data source in SAP BusinessObjects Analysis, OLAP edition, as shown in Figure 3.14.

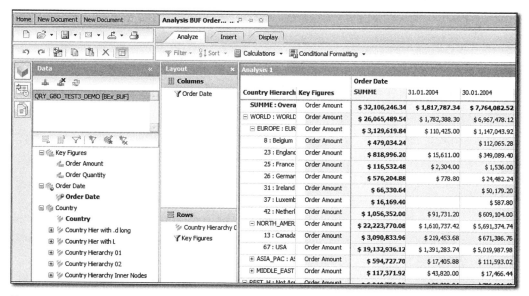

Figure 3.14 Viewing a Cube in SAP BusinessObjects Analysis, OLAP Edition

Creating an Analysis View

You can add columns and rows to the workspace to create an arrangement of dimensions and measures to share with other business users within Web Intelligence 4.1 or SAP Crystal Reports for Enterprise. Recall that the three primary data sources available for creating reporting documents with version 4.1 are universes, SAP BEx queries, and Analysis Views with a fourth option for Excel.

Figure 3.15 shows a multidimensional workspace in SAP BusinessObjects Analysis, OLAP edition, with the EXPORT icon selected.

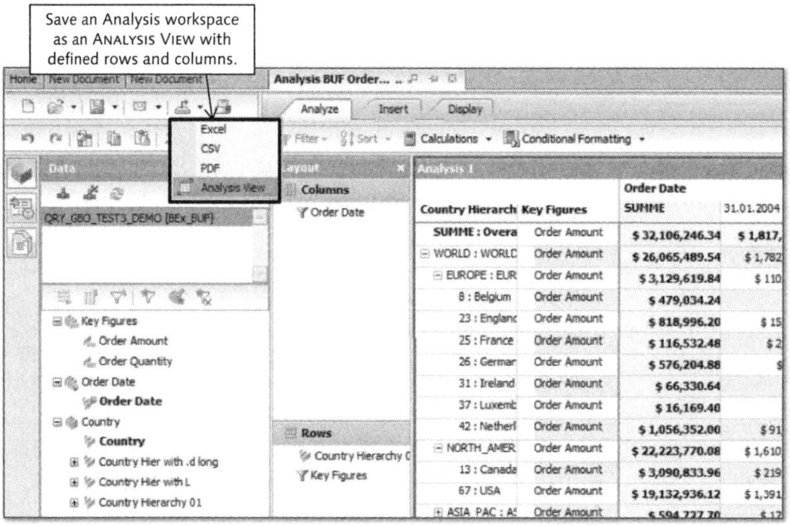

Figure 3.15 Generating an Analysis View from an SAP BusinessObjects Analysis, OLAP Edition Workspace

To save the grouping of column and row objects in a view to be accessed by Web Intelligence 4.1 or SAP Crystal Reports, with EXPORT selected, click on ANALYSIS VIEW from the list of choices.

When publishing an Analysis View to the SAP BusinessObjects BI 4.1 repository, you should select a folder with the appropriate group and user permissions. Secure distribution is an important consideration when publishing content because information should be made accessible only to the intended group of users.

Typical reasons for creating and publishing Analysis Views generally relate to the requirement of providing users with appropriate and relevant information in a format that is easy to use in Web Intelligence or SAP Crystal Reports.

Figure 3.16 shows the window provided when saving an Analysis View to the repository. Select an appropriate folder to save the object to, provide a name for the new Analysis View, and then click on SAVE to publish.

After an Analysis View has been published, users can open it with Web Intelligence to quickly analyze and interact with the data and use the extensive functional capabilities in the Report Panel such as charting, drilling, and filtering.

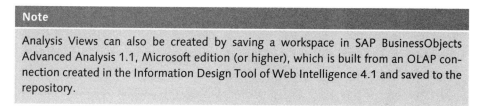

Figure 3.16 Saving an Analysis View to the Folder Structure in the Repository

---

Note

Analysis Views can also be created by saving a workspace in SAP BusinessObjects Advanced Analysis 1.1, Microsoft edition (or higher), which is built from an OLAP connection created in the Information Design Tool of Web Intelligence 4.1 and saved to the repository.

More users can take advantage of the rich feature set in Web Intelligence 4.1 with the option to create reports sourced from Analysis Views. The next section introduces the Query Panel and describes the panes used for retrieving data.

3.2 The Query Panel in Web Intelligence 4.1

The Query Panel in Web Intelligence 4.1 provides an intuitive interface for selecting objects and retrieving results from universes, SAP BEx queries, Analysis Views, web services, Excel files, and text files.

Figure 3.17 shows a glimpse of the full QUERY PANEL at the beginning of the query-building process after you have selected a universe as the data source.

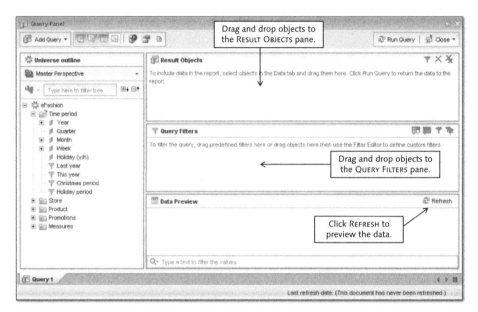

Figure 3.17 Navigating the Web Intelligence Query Panel

The Query Panel consists of five major sections:

▶ UNIVERSE OUTLINE
Contains the objects available in the universe or SAP BEx query in the connected data source.

▶ RESULT OBJECTS
Retrieves data from the database when you drag and drop objects from the UNIVERSE OUTLINE pane to this pane to begin creating a query.

▶ QUERY FILTERS
Restricts the results returned from the data source.

▶ SCOPE OF ANALYSIS

Shows the hierarchy and drill path of the objects in the universe.

▶ DATA PREVIEW

Displays a preview of the result set based on the objects included in the RESULT OBJECTS pane.

Note

The SCOPE OF ANALYSIS and DATA PREVIEW panes can't be displayed at the same time. Toggle between these sections by using the shortcut icons in the upper-left corner of the Query Panel.

3.2.1 Universe Outline Pane

The UNIVERSE OUTLINE pane is located on the left side of the document and shows you the database fields or objects that can be retrieved or used to filter the query. This pane allows objects to be displayed in two different groupings. You can switch between these two perspectives to see objects categorized by class or sorted by navigation paths. Figure 3.18 shows the two perspective selections for viewing objects in the universe outline.

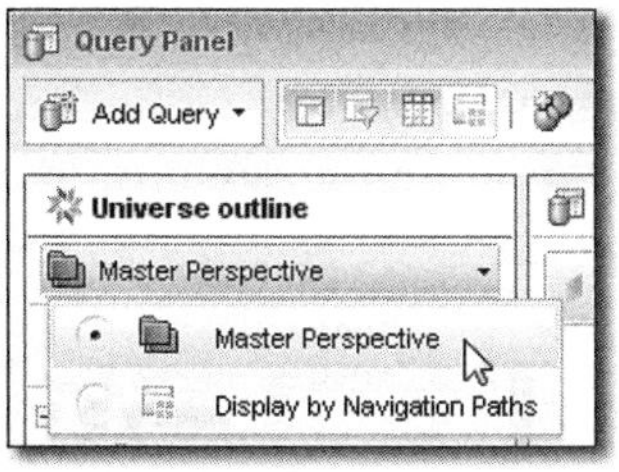

Figure 3.18 Perspectives for Viewing Objects in the Universe Outline

The purpose of the UNIVERSE OUTLINE pane is to provide the list of objects available in the connected data source to be used as result objects or filters in the query. This pane contains the classes and objects that were previously set up in the universe or SAP BEx query used as the source. The terminology used for object aliasing in universe design begins to play an important role in the Query Panel when deciding which objects to include in the query.

3.2.2 Query Properties

Query properties are used to set properties for eight different categories in the current query. You can access the properties by clicking on the QUERY PROPERTIES icon located at the top of the Query Panel.

The first property to be updated is the query name. This setting becomes very useful when multiple queries are added to a single Web Intelligence document. Let's examine the eight query properties shown in Figure 3.19:

▶ NAME
This property allows you to revise the name of any query in the document or Query Panel.

▶ UNIVERSE
This property is read only and displays the name of the current universe.

▶ LIMITS
You can apply the MAX ROWS RETRIEVED and MAX RETRIEVAL TIME(S) settings to restrict the result size and retrieval duration of the query by clicking on the checkbox beside the desired setting and then revising the associated number to your preference.

▶ SAMPLE
Sampling enables you to retrieve a fixed or random sample of the data when querying databases that support it. Random sampling is applied by default unless FIXED is selected. Sampling is disabled if your database doesn't support sampling.

▶ DATA
This property provides the option to retrieve duplicate rows or unique rows when refreshing. Both settings are unchecked by default.

▶ SECURITY
This section provides the option to allow other users to edit all queries and is

checked by default. If unchecked, only the report developer can make revisions to the current document.

▶ PROMPT ORDER

This section allows you to change the order of the prompts if multiple prompted filter objects exist in the QUERY FILTERS pane.

▶ CONTEXT

This setting provides the option to reset contexts upon refreshing (unchecked by default). A checkbox is provided to clear contexts before the next refresh.

Tip

Choosing to display the objects by hierarchies gives you an opportunity to see the relationship of the dimension objects in the universe. This is useful when setting up drillable report filters with cascading values.

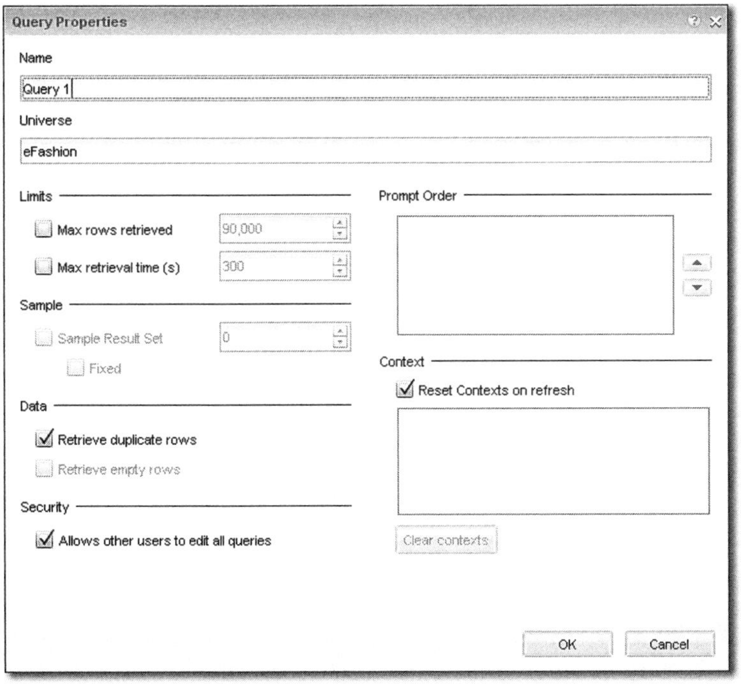

Figure 3.19 Query Properties

Understanding the properties available in the Query Panel is important for effectively producing queries with a desired outcome, such as limiting the number of rows retrieved by a query or defining the order of prompted filters. The next section describes how you can add new queries and edit existing queries.

3.3   Adding and Editing Queries

Queries are easily created in Web Intelligence 4.1 by performing the first or both of the following actions:

▶ Adding data objects to the RESULT OBJECTS pane

▶ Adding custom or predefined filters to the QUERY FILTERS pane to restrict the data being returned (optional)

Objects can be moved to these panes by dragging them from the UNIVERSE OUTLINE and dropping them into the desired pane. The same result can be accomplished by double-clicking on objects in the UNIVERSE OUTLINE.

> **Tip**
>
> When double-clicking on an object predefined as a condition, the object will be inserted into the QUERY FILTERS pane only.

The combination of result objects and query filters produces an SQL statement used to access data from universes. The next section describes how this SQL script can be viewed and edited.

3.3.1   Evaluating Generated SQL Script

After a query has been created, you have the opportunity to review and edit the query script generated by the Query Panel. You can view the SQL script generated from the query by clicking on the VIEW SCRIPT shortcut icon at the top of the Query Panel. Two options are available in the Query Script viewer to either view or edit the query script:

▶ Use the query script generated by your query.

▶ Use custom query script.

The script becomes editable when you select the USE CUSTOM QUERY SCRIPT option. The QUERY SCRIPT window now includes numbered rows to assist in reading and editing the syntax of the query.

Tip

The Report Panel is displayed after a query has been refreshed. To return to editing the query, switch to design mode, click on the DATA ACCESS tab, select the DATA PROVIDERS tab, and then click on EDIT QUERY.

Figure 3.20 shows the options available when viewing the script of the query. The default selection is the USE THE QUERY SCRIPT GENERATED BY YOUR QUERY radio button.

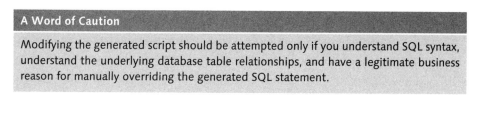

Figure 3.20 View Query Script Generated by the Query Panel

Click on the USE CUSTOM QUERY SCRIPT radio button to make changes to the generated script.

A Word of Caution

Modifying the generated script should be attempted only if you understand SQL syntax, understand the underlying database table relationships, and have a legitimate business reason for manually overriding the generated SQL statement.

When the Select section of the generated SQL statement is modified, the number of objects, data types of result objects, and the order of the data types must match the items in the RESULT OBJECTS section.

When the USE CUSTOM QUERY SCRIPT option is selected, the grayed-out script becomes modifiable. Editing the script will enable the UNDO button located at the bottom of the QUERY SCRIPT VIEWER screen. You can also copy the script for use outside of the document. This is helpful if you need to paste the SQL statement into another window to edit it or email it to a colleague.

A VALIDATE button is also present when modifying the original script. This is a very handy feature that protects you from submitting a custom SQL statement to the database that contains errors.

Restricting the Modification of Generated SQL

From an administrative perspective, the rights to view SQL and edit the query script can be denied in the Central Management Console (CMC) by modifying the included rights of an access level.

Locate the application collection and the Web Intelligence type for a full list of specific modifiable rights in the CMC. The name of the right is listed as QUERY SCRIPT–ENABLE VIEWING (SQL, MDX...).

Every Web Intelligence document can contain data sourced from multiple queries with varying source types. The following section explains how new queries are added and how the results can be used within the reporting document.

3.3.2 Adding Queries and New Data Providers

New queries can be added to documents that are made up of result objects that have absolutely nothing in common with the result objects in the existing query. This is common if reporting requirements present elements from both unrelated data sets on the same report or within the same document.

There are three ways to add new queries and new data providers in an existing document, two of which are found in the Report Panel. The first option is by clicking the NEW DATA PROVIDER function, available on the DATA ACCESS tab in the Report Panel while in design mode (see Figure 3.21).

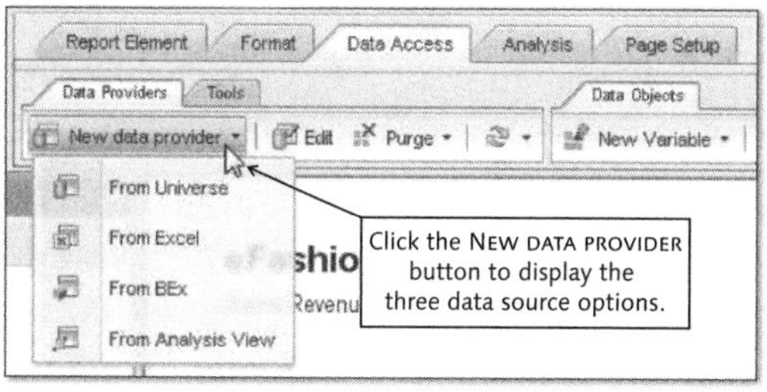

Figure 3.21 Adding a New Data Provider from the Report Panel

New to SAP BusinessObjects BI 4.1 is the EDIT DATA PROVIDER icon located on the main toolbar, and just above the side panel (see Figure 3.22).

Figure 3.22 The New Edit Data Provider Icon in SAP BusinessObjects BI 4.1

The final option is the ADD QUERY button available in the upper-left corner of the QUERY PANEL, as shown in Figure 3.23.

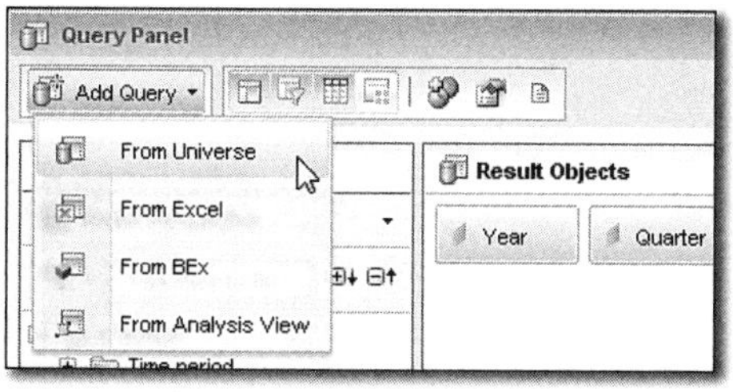

Figure 3.23 Adding a New Query from the Query Panel

Figure 3.21 and Figure 3.22 show the data sources that are available while adding a NEW DATA PROVIDER from the Report Panel and while working within the BI Launch Pad. The same data sources are available when the ADD QUERY button is clicked from within the Query Panel.

Including New Result Data

After a new query has been added to a Web Intelligence 4.1 document and the query is refreshed for the first time, you're prompted to choose how the new results are to be displayed. Figure 3.24 shows the three available choices described here:

▶ INSERT A TABLE IN A NEW REPORT

This selection adds the results from the new query to a new REPORT tab (default selection).

▶ INSERT A TABLE IN THE CURRENT REPORT

A data table containing the results from the new query will be added to the previously existing report.

▶ INCLUDE THE RESULT OBJECTS IN THE DOCUMENT WITHOUT GENERATING A TABLE

This selection includes the data in the microcube but doesn't add it to a report.

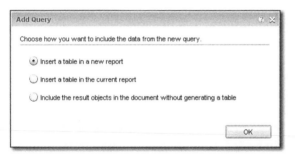

Figure 3.24 Choosing How Data from the New Query Is Displayed

Data Synchronization Properties

Web Intelligence can merge your dimensions automatically if the AUTO-MERGE DIMENSIONS checkbox is checked in the document properties accessed through the PROPERTIES tab in the Report Panel. Click on the DOCUMENT link to launch the DOCUMENT SUMMARY window displayed in Figure 3.25.

Document Summary Options

The DOCUMENT SUMMARY window contains a couple of very important property settings to enhance the effectiveness of particular reports. The most commonly used options include REFRESH ON OPEN for prompted reports, AUTO-MERGE DIMENSIONS for queries with multiple data sources, and ENABLE QUERY STRIPPING to improve performance when connecting to SAP BEx queries or OLAP universes. Figure 3.25 shows the DOCUMENT SUMMARY options accessed through the PROP-ERTIES tab in the Report Panel.

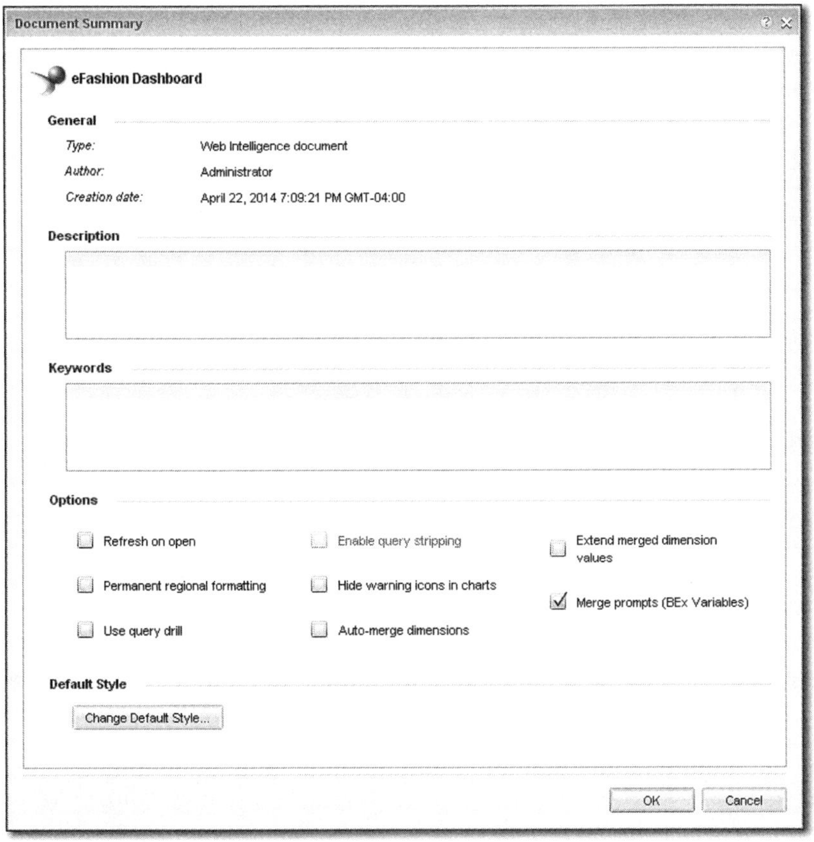

Figure 3.25 Document Summary Options

Let's examine each of these DOCUMENT SUMMARY options:

▶ REFRESH ON OPEN
This option forces the query to be refreshed when the report is opened. This feature is useful in prompted reports and when the data is restricted to the user logged on to the BI Launch Pad.

▶ PERMANENT REGIONAL FORMATTING
This option permanently sets the locale or regional formatting of the document.

▶ USE QUERY DRILL

This option modifies the underlying query when drilling down or drilling up in a report. Dimensions are added or removed to the RESULT OBJECTS section of the query, and query filters are added dynamically based on the drill selection. The scope of analysis is also modified dynamically. The query drill feature is most commonly used when reports contain aggregate measures calculated at the database level.

▶ ENABLE QUERY STRIPPING

This feature allows SAP BEx queries to be generated with only the objects used in the Report Panel. You can now also apply query stripping to reports sourced from relational universes when the option to ALLOW QUERY STRIPPING is applied in the Information Design Tool followed by checking the ENABLE QUERY STRIPPING option in a Web Intelligence report.

▶ HIDE WARNING ICONS IN CHARTS

This feature hides general warnings that could potentially appear in the upper-left corner of a chart.

▶ AUTO-MERGE DIMENSIONS

This option automatically merges dimensions when more than one query is added to the document that contains objects with the same name, same data type, and from the same universe.

▶ EXTEND MERGED DIMENSION VALUES

This selection shows all of the data in a report that contains synchronized or merged dimension objects, not just the values relating to the merged objects.

▶ MERGE PROMPTS (BEx VARIABLES)

This selection is useful when multiple SAP BEx queries are in a single WebI document. Identical prompts appearing in each query are synchronized and only show the prompt a single time to the user.

3.3.3 Setting Up a Combined Query

The idea behind combined queries is to return a single set of data, that would otherwise be impossible to retrieve, with a single query. Combined queries are created in the Query Panel and merged at the database level to compare the rows in one query to the rows retrieved by an additional query.

The returned values can be displayed in one of three different relationship types:

▸ **Union**
Includes the rows from both queries.

▸ **Intersection**
Includes the rows common to both queries.

▸ **Minus**
Includes the rows from the first query minus the rows from the second query.

Combined Query Requirements

These are the two primary rules for creating a combined query:
▸ Result objects in each query must contain the same number of objects, or the query won't refresh.
▸ The order of the objects in both queries must have matching data types. If the data types don't match, then the query won't refresh.

Unions

Unions are most commonly used when you are attempting to build a result set with incompatible objects that can't be included in the same block in a report, due to database or universe configurations.

In many cases, all of the result objects will be exactly the same in both queries (except for minor differences in result objects or query filters). The results from both queries are pushed to the database to complete the merging, and a single set of results is returned.

The first query in a union is created like any other query. To add a union query, you need to click on the ADD A COMBINED QUERY shortcut icon located in the Query Panel in design mode (see Figure 3.26).

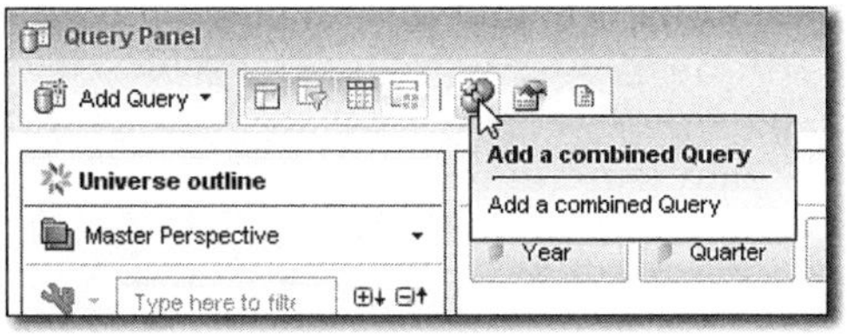

Figure 3.26 Adding a Combined Query to Create a Query Union

After a combined query has been added, QUERY 1 changes names to become COM-BINED QUERY 1, and a COMBINED QUERY 2 is inserted. You can toggle back and forth from these two queries by clicking on the buttons that include the new query names, located in the lower half of the UNIVERSE OUTLINE.

Tip
The default combined query type is union. To change from union to intersection or minus, double-click on UNION in the QUERY MANAGER pane located to the left of the combined query names (as shown in Figure 3.27).

Figure 3.27 shows the Universe outline after a combined query is inserted.

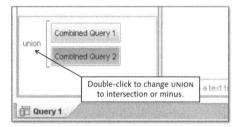

Figure 3.27 Combined Query Added to the Universe Outline

Intersection

You can add intersections when you want to produce a combined query that returns only the values that appear in both queries. The purpose of this type of query is to cut away any nonintersecting data.

Minus

You can use the minus combined query to remove everything in the results of the first query from the results of the second query. The purpose of this type of combined query is to find the results in the first query that aren't in the results of the second.

Remove a Combined Query

To remove a combined query, drag the unneeded COMBINED QUERY button to the UNIVERSE OUTLINE section that includes the classes and objects.

Now that we've discussed the basics of adding and editing queries, the next section describes how to create queries sourced from SAP BEx queries.

3.4 Creating SAP BEx Queries

Direct access to SAP BEx queries was one of the key enhancements to Web Intelligence 4.0, and it continues to increase the popularity of Web Intelligence in SAP BusinessObjects BI 4.1. This new capability allows SAP BW customers to leverage their existing SAP BEx queries as a data source for building Web Intelligence documents.

Setting up connectivity to SAP BEx queries was discussed in Section 3.1.2; this section focuses on creating a Web Intelligence document based on an SAP BEx query used as data source. When an SAP BEx query is used as the source, objects placed in the RESULT OBJECTS pane will have new hierarchical capabilities in the Query Panel.

To get started using SAP BEx as a data source, create a new query or document in Web Intelligence, and select BEx as the data source, as shown in Figure 3.28.

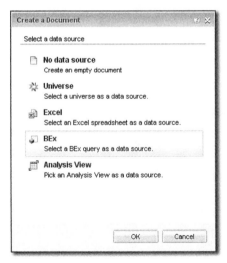

Figure 3.28 Selecting BEx as the Data Source for a New Document

After selecting BEx as your new data source, you're prompted to choose the SAP BEx query from a list of certified queries displayed within your preconfigured connections. Expand the CONNECTIONS to display available queries, as shown in Figure 3.29.

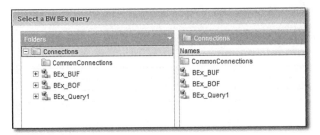

Figure 3.29 Available Connections When Selecting an SAP BEx Query

After you expand the CONNECTION containing the required query, select the query from the right side of the panel, and click on OK to proceed. Figure 3.30 shows examples of two SAP BEx queries that can be selected as the data source.

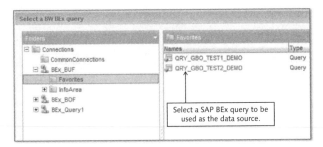

Figure 3.30 Selecting an SAP BEx Query

When an SAP BEx query is selected as the data source for a Web Intelligence 4.1 document, the Query Panel contains very different functionality than when sourced from a universe. The RESULT OBJECTS pane takes on a whole new set of capabilities and allows users to drill into hierarchical member data within the SAP BEx query. Figure 3.31 shows a query sourced from an SAP BEx query with a single object added to the RESULT OBJECTS pane.

To interact with hierarchical objects, select the icon located immediately to the right of the object name after it has been added to the RESULT OBJECTS pane. This will launch the MEMBER SELECTOR pane, allowing you to expand, collapse, and check any of the member values to retrieve exactly the information you need.

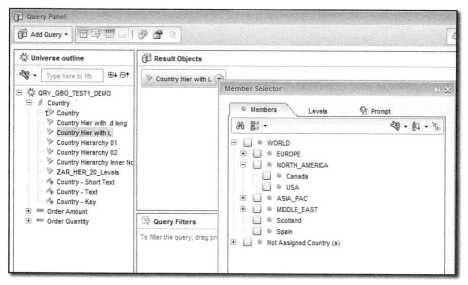

Figure 3.31 Viewing the Member Selector Pane of an SAP BEx Result Object

You can also right-click on a specific member to launch additional capabilities. The following options are displayed in Figure 3.32:

▶ SELF
Selects only the member.

▶ CHILDREN
Selects only the child members of the selected member.

▶ DESCENDANTS
Selects all descendants of the selected member.

▶ DESCENDANTS UNTIL NAMED LEVEL
Returns all descendants through a specified level.

▶ DESCENDANTS UNTIL
Returns all descendants until reaching a chosen value.

The MEMBER SELECTOR lets you navigate through the hierarchies with a LEVELS tab, which displays the number of levels within the selected hierarchical object and allows you to select a specific level for analysis. All levels — or any combination of the available levels — can be chosen.

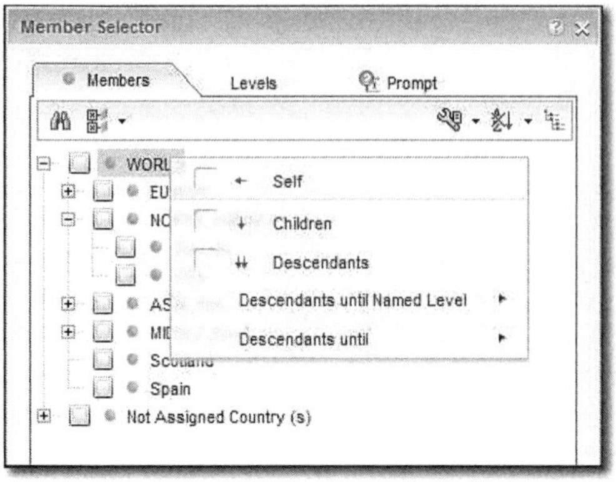

Figure 3.32 Right-Click Options Available within the Member Selector

Hierarchical data will be returned to the Report Panel for intuitive and logical navigation of the multitiered data structures. Expandable and collapsible data blocks are available in the Report Panel specifically designed for hierarchical interaction for reports originating from SAP BEx query data sources.

The MEMBER SELECTOR window allows you to perform in-place filtering rather than requiring additional steps and the QUERY FILTERS pane. However, query filters can still be used as long they contain objects not in the RESULT OBJECTS pane. Figure 3.33 shows the LEVELS tab selected and how to enable levels.

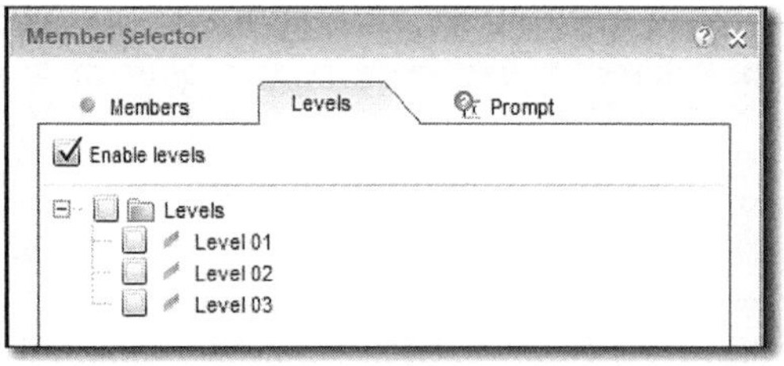

Figure 3.33 Levels of a Selected Member in Result Objects

SAP BEx member prompting is also available to provide a form of guided analysis. Use the PROMPT tab shown in Figure 3.34 to enable prompting and ask users for input when reading reports. Users can be prompted to select specific members or levels in a hierarchical structure for selective analysis. This setting saves time and helps users get directly to the information they need and at the right level of detail.

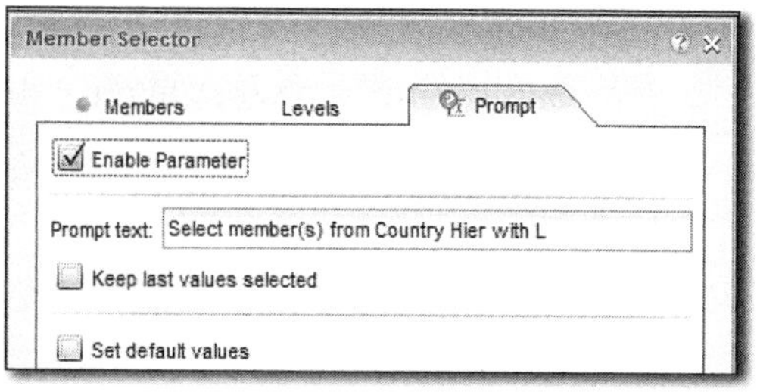

Figure 3.34 Prompt Tab of a Selected Member

The capability to create reporting documents directly connected to SAP BEx queries gives SAP BW customers the same reporting features as customers accessing relational databases connected with universes.

The next sections discuss the features available for restricting the amount of data returned in a query by using filters.

3.5   Query Filters

Query filters are used to generate the `Where` clause for the SQL script that is submitted to the data source. These objects work very closely with the Result Objects pane to provide a simple and intuitive interface for retrieving and restricting data from the data source.

Query filters allow you to minimize the amount of data returned from the query by restricting the results to specific criteria. For example, you can add the Month dimension to the Query Filters pane and set it to July, and then add the Year dimension and set it to 2014. Doing this will retrieve all the values for the objects included in the Result Objects pane for July 2014. Query filters offer you the following benefits:

▶ Ability to return only the data you need to fulfill reporting requirements
▶ Ability to restrict confidential data from being displayed in reports or being returned to the microcube
▶ Ability to retrieve manageable result sets that can be exported to Excel, exported as a PDF, or printed

Filters are identified by two major categories: predefined filters (or conditions) and custom filters.

3.5.1 Predefined Filters

Predefined filters are created by a developer or administrator and saved in the universe as *conditions*. These predefined conditions are easily recognizable in the Query Panel because a yellow filter icon appears to the left of the condition name.

An example of a very simple predefined filter is the This Year condition predefined in the demo eFashion universe. The following line of code was added to the Where section in the properties of the condition to create the filter:

```
Calendar_year_lookup.Yr = '2006'
```

A more accurate and user-friendly name for this object would be Year 2006 rather than This Year to minimize any potential confusion in the future.

Predefined filters are created in the universe and can contain a variety of complex SQL formulas. By creating predefined filters, users can easily and intuitively constrain their queries to return specific data sets without having to create their own filters.

Condition Segments

Universe developers can create conditions containing any of the following segments:

- **Case statements**
  Provide If/Else/Then logic to a condition or object.
- **And/or logic**
  Multiple filters can be applied within a single condition.
- **In list**
  Allows a condition to be created for many items in a list.

3.5.2 Custom Filters

Custom filters are conditions created by report developers. These types of filters are created when dimension objects are dragged and dropped into the QUERY FILTERS pane, an operator is chosen, and a value is entered or selected.

After a dimension object has been added to the QUERY FILTERS pane, you can choose how to set up the filter. This includes modifying the operator and assignment type, and configuring the filter properties.

A dimension object can be set up as a filter with one of the following five types:

▶ CONSTANT
Manually enters a custom value.

▶ VALUE(S) FROM LIST
Provides a list of values for one or more selections.

▶ PROMPT
Prompts the user to enter or select a value when the query is refreshed.

▶ OBJECT FROM THIS QUERY
Provides the capability to select a predefined object or variable as the dimension value (although you can't use the In List or Not In List operators).

▶ RESULT FROM ANOTHER QUERY
Allows filters to be created using a result object retrieved by a different query within the same document.

The default operator when a dimension is added to the QUERY FILTERS pane is In List, and the default assignment type is Constant.

The operators available when creating a condition are as follows:

▶ IN list
Retrieves the data for one or more selected or entered values.

Example: City IN ('Austin','Boston','Chicago','Dallas')

▶ NOT IN list
Restricts the query from returning data for one or more selected or entered values.

Example: City NOT IN ('Austin','Boston','Chicago','Dallas')

▶ = (equal to)
Obtains data equal to a selected or entered value.

Example: Lines = Sweaters

▶ <> (not equal to)
Obtains data not equal to a selected or entered value.

Example: Lines <> Jackets

▶ > (greater than)
Retrieves only the data greater than an entered value.

Example: Sales revenue > 1500

▶ > = (greater than or equal to)
Retrieves only the data greater than or equal to a selected or entered value.

Example: `Sales revenue >= 1500`

▶ < (less than)
Retrieves only the data less than a selected or entered value.

Example: `Sales revenue < 1500`

▶ < = (less than or equal to)
Retrieves only the data less than or equal to a selected or entered value.

Example: `Sales revenue <= 1500`

▶ `BETWEEN`
Retrieves only the data between two values.

Example: `Sales revenue BETWEEN 1500 and 2000`

▶ `NOT BETWEEN`
Retrieves only the data not between two values.

Example: `Sales revenue NOT BETWEEN 1500 and 2000`

▶ `IS NULL`
Retrieves only the values that don't have data (i.e., have a null value).

Example: `Lines IS NULL`

▶ `IS NOT NULL`
Retrieves only the values that have data.

Example: `Lines IS NOT NULL`

▶ `Matches pattern`
Retrieves the data that matches the pattern of a selected or entered value. This operator is translated as `Like` when the SQL script is generated. In the example, rows for all objects where the lines begin with S will be returned:

Example: `Lines Matches pattern 'S%'`

Note

The wild card character (%) is used to represent an indefinite number of characters. The underscore symbol (_) is used to represent a single character. An example of using three underscore wild card characters is a formula written as `City = 'Bos___'` used with the `Matches pattern` operator. The result returns Boston.

▶ Different from pattern

Retrieves the data that doesn't match the pattern of a selected or entered value. This operator is translated as Not Like when the SQL script is generated. The following example returns all the rows where the value in the lines object does not begin with S:

Example: Lines Different from pattern 'S%'

▶ Both

Retrieves data that corresponds to two values; if the Both filter is used with a dimension object, an intersection is generated.

▶ Except

Retrieves the data for other values in the dimension while restricting a selected or entered value; a minus query is generated when this operator is used.

3.5.3 Quick Filters

Quick filters are created when you select a dimensional object from the Result Objects pane and click on the Filter icon located in the upper-right corner of the pane. This procedure opens the Add Quick Filter dialog box, where you can quickly define the new condition or filter.

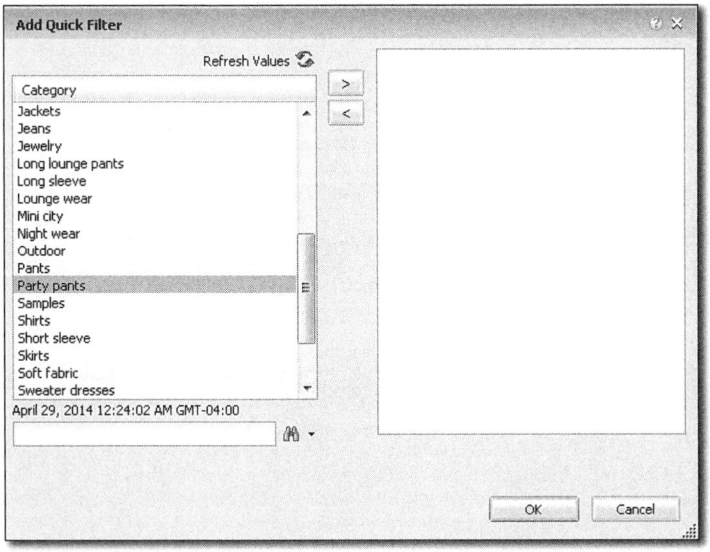

Figure 3.35 Adding a Quick Filter to a Result Object

Figure 3.35 shows the ADD QUICK FILTER dialog box that opens when a quick filter is added for the LINES object. The operator is set to Equal To if a single value is selected, but if multiple values are selected from the displayed values, the operator will be set to In List. You can modify the operator of the object after the new filter has been created and added to the QUERY FILTERS pane.

3.5.4 Subqueries

Subqueries are used in Web Intelligence to produce a query within a query. This type of document is used when the primary query needs to be filtered by the inner query or subquery. When a query containing a subquery is refreshed, the subquery runs first and then returns the values to be filtered in the main query. This type of query is used when the main query needs to be filtered by a value that isn't known at the time of refresh.

Figure 3.36 shows how you can add a subquery to an existing filter by simply clicking on the ADD SUBQUERY button in the upper-right corner of the QUERY FILTERS pane.

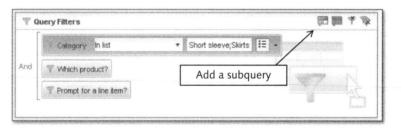

Figure 3.36 Inserting a Subquery into the Query Filters Pane

After adding a subquery to your document, you'll need to drag predefined filters or custom-defined object filters into the new SUBQUERY FILTER window to create the "query within a query" effect.

> **Note**
>
> It's worth noting that subqueries can only be added while working within the Applet viewer. Even though the HTML viewer has grown significantly since version 4.0, this is one of the few areas where the Applet viewer still has an advantage.

An example scenario for using a subquery is the requirement to return all cities within two selected states. This is accomplished with the following steps:

1. Create a query from the eFashion universe, and then add the City object to the RESULT OBJECTS pane.

2. Select the City object in the RESULT OBJECTS pane.

3. Click on the ADD A SUBQUERY button in the QUERY PANEL to create a subquery for the City object.

4. Drag the STATE object into the SUBQUERY pane of the City object.

5. Set the STATE operator to IN LIST.

6. Select VALUE(S) FROM LIST for the STATE filter, and then move NEW YORK and CALIFORNIA to the SELECTED VALUE(S) frame.

7. Run the query.

The results returned will include only cities within California and Texas. Figure 3.37 shows the CITY and STATE subquery used in the example.

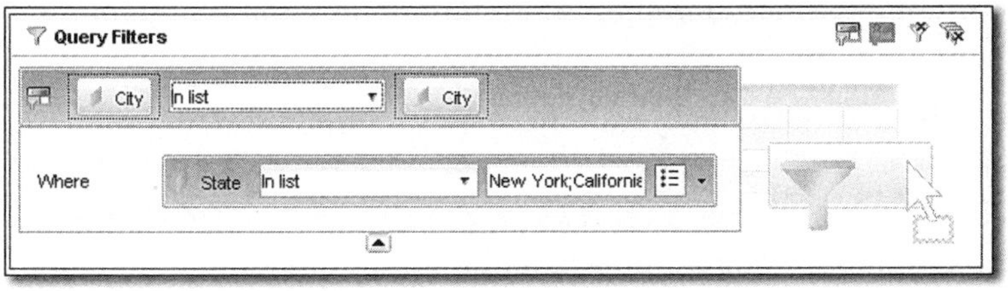

Figure 3.37 Subquery Example for City and State

3.5.5 Nested Conditions

Query filter conditions can be grouped by using AND and OR to perform extended business logic with conditions.

Figure 3.38 shows a QUERY FILTERS pane with four predefined and grouped conditions. These conditions are grouped to provide a more customized filtering technique. Rather than just dragging all four conditions into the pane, they are added as condition pairs or groups.

You can group filters by following these steps:

1. Drop an object or predefined condition to the very bottom of the condition that you want to group it with.
2. By default, the objects will appear in an AND group.
3. If OR is required, double-click on the new AND group operator, and the group operator will become OR.

The example in Figure 3.38 will return only the values associated with last year's Christmas period or the holiday period for this year.

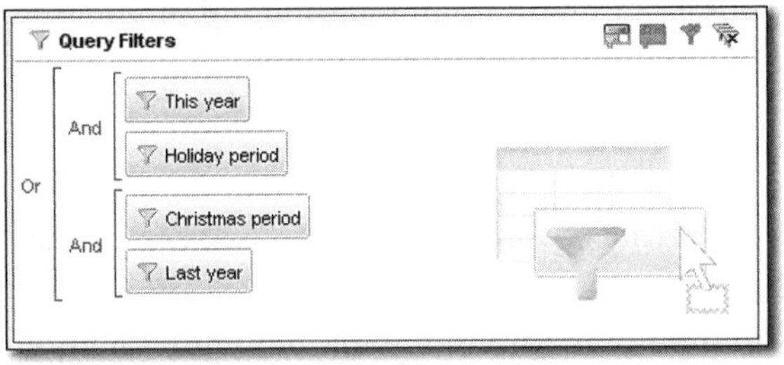

Figure 3.38 Nested Predefined Query Filter Conditions

Query filters minimize or completely eliminate returning unnecessary information. You can apply a combination of custom and predefined filters that accurately restricts information. You can also add prompted filters to documents that require user input when opening or refreshing reports.

3.6 Prompted Queries

Prompted queries require report consumers to make selections before a Web Intelligence document is opened. This is achieved by following two steps:

1. Create prompted query filters.
2. Set the document to REFRESH ON OPEN.

3.6.1 Saving a Report to Refresh on Open

To save a report so that it refreshes on open, follow these steps:

1. Edit the report in design mode in the REPORT PANEL.

2. Select the PROPERTIES tab located in the upper-left corner of the REPORT PANEL, and then select the DOCUMENT link.

3. Check the REFRESH ON OPEN selection under OPTION as described in Section 3.3.2. Click on OK to accept.

Alternatively, you can set a document to be refreshed on open while saving a Web Intelligence document by following these steps:

1. Click on SAVE AS while either reading or designing a report.

2. When the PUBLISH A DOCUMENT TO THE SERVER window appears, click on the ADVANCED button beside the report name.

3. Check the REFRESH ON OPEN box, select a folder to save the document to, and then click on SAVE.

Figure 3.39 shows how to force a document to be refreshed when it's opened when saving a report while using the Applet viewer in SAP BusinessObjects BI 4.1.

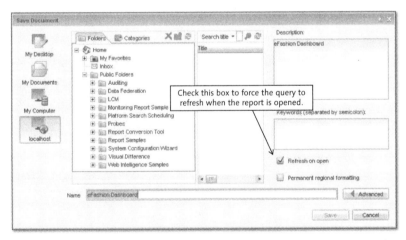

Figure 3.39 Saving a Document while in the Applet Viewer and Forcing It to Refresh when Opened

3.6.2 Creating a Prompted Filter

To create a prompted filter, follow these steps:

1. Click on the PROPERTIES button located to the right of the filter object to reveal five filter condition types.

2. Select PROMPT as the condition type.

3. Click on the PROMPT PROPERTIES button located immediately to the left to set up the properties for the prompted condition.

4. Figure 3.40 shows the SAVE AS window when saving a Web Intelligence document in SAP BusinessObjects BI 4.1 while using the HTML viewer.

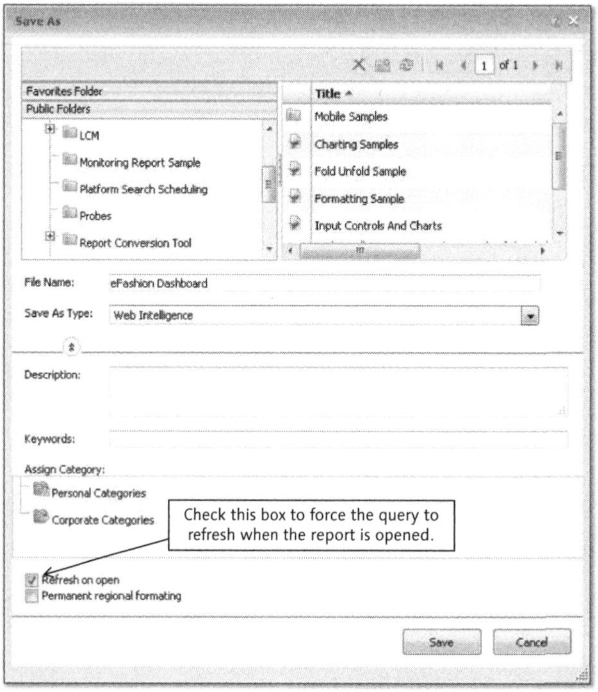

Figure 3.40 Save a Web Intelligence Document to Refresh on Open when Working in the HTML Viewer

3.6.3   Setting Prompt Properties

Let's look at modifiable prompt properties. The available parameter properties for a prompted filter are shown in Figure 3.41:

▶ PROMPT TEXT
This text box lets report developers create customized and appropriate messages for business users when they are prompted to enter or select values. This property is important because it can be used when creating hyperlinks.

▶ PROMPT WITH LIST OF VALUES

This property provides the user with a distinct list of values for the prompted dimension.

▶ KEEP LAST VALUE(S) SELECTED

This property lets the user maintain the values of the previous refresh. This setting shouldn't be selected when the data being queried is of a sensitive nature.

▶ SELECT ONLY FROM LIST

This property prohibits users from entering values and requires that they select only from the list of values.

▶ OPTIONAL PROMPT

This property is used to set the prompt to be optional.

▶ SET DEFAULT VALUE(S)

This property lets the user enter one or more default values.

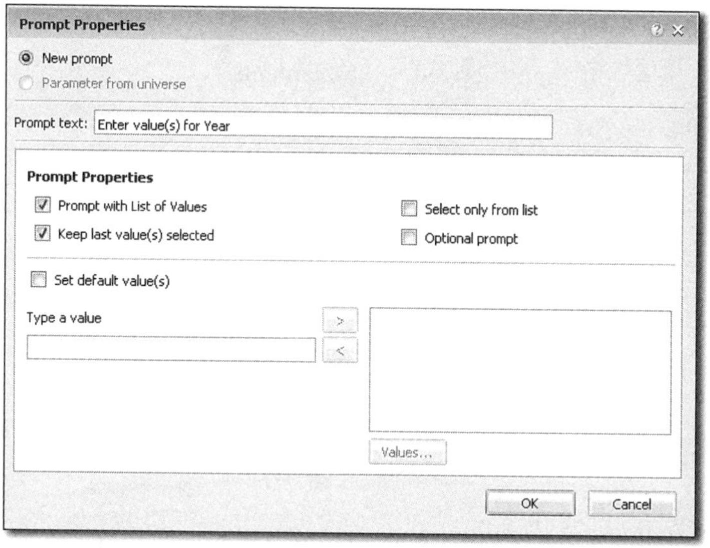

Figure 3.41 Prompt Filter Properties

3.7   Summary

You can use the highly intuitive Query Panel in Web Intelligence for self-service access to company data from just about any type of data source. Ad hoc report building is painless with the extensive set of query features available for business users in the zero-client web-based version of Web Intelligence 4.1.

The Web Intelligence Query Panel offers users the following strengths:

▶ Offers intuitive self-service access to company data

▶ Graphically generates SQL scripts from universe objects

▶ Interacts with dimension members sourced from SAP BEx queries

▶ Accesses data sourced from Analysis workspaces with Analysis Views

▶ Provides an easy-to-learn drag-and-drop web-based interface

▶ Retrieves data from multiple data sources into a single document

▶ Merges dimensions to combine results from different sources

▶ Makes more than 15 different condition types available when filtering objects

▶ Produces combined queries: union, intersection, minus

▶ Creates query-within-a-query results with subqueries

▶ Uses custom SQL by modifying generated SQL statements

▶ Applies condition groupings with AND and OR

▶ Limits the query retrieval time and row counts with query properties

▶ Prompts users for input when reports are refreshed when opened

▶ Adds quick filters for speed and accuracy

▶ Sources documents from web services, Excel files, and text files

Using the drag-and-drop interface of the Query Panel, you can create queries to graphically transform prebuilt universe objects into analytical reports. The objects added to the RESULT OBJECTS pane and QUERY FILTER pane generate script to access data sources without users having to write a single line of code.

Report developers of all experience levels benefit from the ease of use of Web Intelligence. You can also take your queries even deeper by retrieving data from multiple data sources. Once only available in Desktop Intelligence, dimensions from different data sources can now be merged within the same document to provide a robust set of data for analytical report building.

Also, with just a few clicks of the mouse, you can create complex documents with combined queries and subqueries by modifying generated SQL statements. Precise results are returned by constraining values at the database level with a rich set of operators for query filtering. You can group your conditions in nested pairings with the AND and OR operators for more complex filtering.

You can learn to control your row counts by limiting the maximum number of rows retrieved by a query. Your DBAs will appreciate the reduced stress on the database when you set a maximum retrieval time on your queries.

Several features make Web Intelligence 4.1 the best-in-class query and analysis solution for any data warehouse, data mart, or business intelligence reporting environment: the combination of an extensive set of query features, an intuitive web-based report development interface, access to cube data through Analysis Views, and the capability to connect directly to SAP BEx queries.

Now that we've discussed creating queries and retrieving data from universes, SAP BEx queries, and Analysis Views, Chapter 4 discusses how information is displayed in the Report Panel in Web Intelligence 4.1.

Web Intelligence 4.x reports are used to analyze, present, and interact with highly formatted data, which enables accurate and more informed decisions. You can use drill filters, input controls, charts, Available Objects tables, block filters, and a lengthy set of report functions to produce highly customized reports. Additionally, with a powerful charting engine, Web Intelligence users are able to consume rich graphical reports.

4   Creating a Report in Web Intelligence 4.1

Using Web Intelligence 4.1 reports, you can view, analyze, and share company data in a secure, customized, and drillable web-based delivery format. Reports are saved to the file repository server and delivered to the end user using the BI Launch Pad (the SAP BusinessObjects BI 4.1 reporting portal).

Web Intelligence enables you to present company data in your reports by adding data blocks and charts to the Report Panel via several provided report templates. You can group data by adding multiple sections and breaks to produce analytical documents by including sorts and drill filters.

After creating a Web Intelligence reporting document, users can quickly share their findings with other users across the enterprise by saving reports in the file repository and folder structure storage area accessed with BI Launch Pad. Depending on permissions, users are either granted or denied access to view, schedule, or even edit documents while working within the BI Launch Pad.

The application also enables users to identify significant values by including *conditional formatting* in reports. Conditional formatting can be applied to many columns in a report, assigned to every column or row in an Available Objects table, or applied to single columns and headers of Available Objects table reporting elements. You can easily identify and track data changes by activating *data tracking*.

Web Intelligence also allows users to create precisely designed reports with the aid of a *report grid* and *snap to grid* functionality. In addition, you can maintain defined formatting and object placement relationships by assigning *relative position* attributes to report elements.

Due in part to the broad set of features available in the Web Intelligence Report Panel, report developers can produce highly customized free-form presentations for better insight into company data.

Let's begin our discussion of report creation in Web Intelligence 4.1 by describing the different panels available to report developers, introducing the various sections in the Applet viewer, and then taking you through the process of presenting data in a report.

The Web Intelligence Report Panel is available in four different formatting tool types for view mode, that is, HTML, APPLET (Java), DESKTOP (RICH CLIENT), and PDF, and in three tool types for modify mode, that is, HTML, APPLET (Java), and DESKTOP (RICH CLIENT). These options are shown in Figure 4.1. You can select the tools to use by clicking on PREFERENCES in the BI Launch Pad and then choosing a Web Intelligence view tool or modify tool.

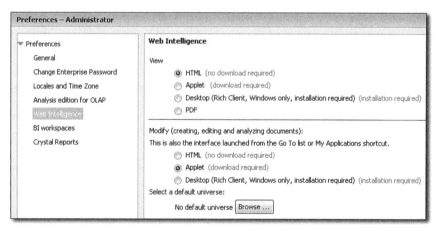

Figure 4.1 Web Intelligence 4.1 Preferences

4.1 Adding Data to Report Elements

Data is added to reports by adding result objects or variables to any of the report elements such as a table, chart, or cell.

Follow these steps to add a report element to the document pane of a Web Intelligence report after your query has been refreshed:

1. Click on DESIGN. All document editing must be done in design mode rather than reading mode.
2. Select the REPORT ELEMENT tab from the ribbon toolbar.
3. Select the TABLE subtab, and then select the data table to be added.
4. Choose a location on the report canvas, and click to insert the data table type selected, as shown in Figure 4.2.

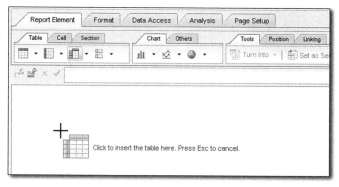

Figure 4.2 Drag and Drop "Define Cross Table" to Canvas

> **Note**
>
> You can build the report elements without actually seeing the data by viewing the structure of the document pane, which is very useful when working with large sets of data. You can toggle between STRUCTURE ONLY and WITH DATA by using shortcut keys Ctrl+2 and Ctrl+3.

4.1.1 Populating a Cross Table

Table objects are the basic elements in reports; the following steps guide you through adding a cross table (crosstab) to a report. There are two methods for assigning objects to a report element.

Dragging and Dropping Objects onto a Table

The first method is accomplished by dragging a result object from the AVAILABLE OBJECTS tab in the side panel and then dropping it into the appropriate section in the cross table. Figure 4.3 shows the [Sales revenue] measure object being added to a cross table.

Figure 4.3 Drag and Drop "Sales Revenue Measure" to Crosstab

Assigning Data to Report Elements

The second method for assigning objects to a data table or chart is by right-clicking on a report element and selecting ASSIGN DATA. Figure 4.4 shows the menu presented when right-clicking on a crosstab.

Note

The ASSIGN DATA option for connecting result objects and variables to report elements is available for both charts and data tables. Figure 4.5 shows the ASSIGN DATA window for connecting data to a crosstab.

Figure 4.4 Right-Clicking on a Crosstab to Assign Data

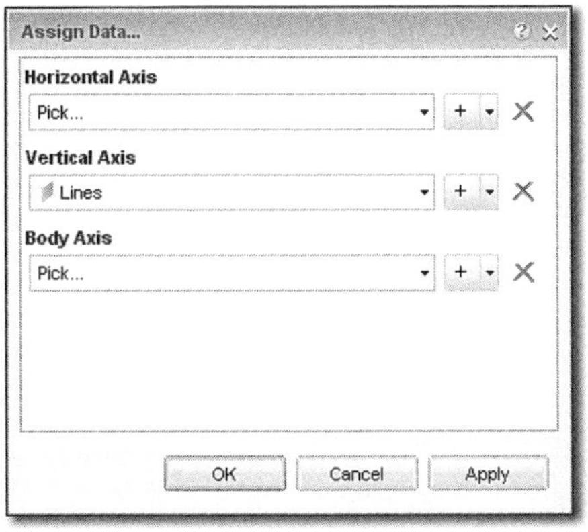

Figure 4.5 Assign Data Window When Connecting Objects to a Crosstab

4.1.2 Populating a Chart

Charts can be populated with data objects very similarly to the way data tables are created. To get started with the editing and chart building process, be sure that you're in design mode. Drag and drop dimension objects and measure objects from the AVAILABLE OBJECTS tab from the side panel onto the chart. Objects can be dropped anywhere on the chart; the engine will know where to assign dimension and measure objects.

You will instantly see charted values after at least one dimension and one measure has been dropped onto the chart. If you're in design/structure only mode, return to design/with data to see the data populated in the charts and tables.

Note

A chart must include at least one dimension object and one measure object, while a data table can contain a single object.

The next section discusses how you can use sections and breaks to enhance the readability and functionality of a report.

4.2 Sections and Breaks

Grouping data in Web Intelligence is accomplished by setting sections for dimension objects or applying breaks to columns displayed in tables. *Sections* are used to group data into visually separated segments. *Breaks* provide the capability to quickly insert subtotals into Available Objects tables.

You can add multiple sections to a single report; subsequently added sections display data in subsections. One restriction of a section is that it can't be a measure object.

4.2.1 Setting a Section

Figure 4.6 shows the City object in a vertical table being set as a section.

To add a section to a report, follow these steps:

1. Use an existing data table containing result objects. After you have inserted a table into your report and populated it with result objects, identify an object to set as the section.
2. Right-click on the object, and select SET AS SECTION. This will split the rows into groups based on the values of the dimension defined as the section.

Figure 4.6 Setting the City Object as a Section

After you've set an object as a section, it will be removed from the table and added as a table header. The remaining values in the table will be separated by the values of the dimension section.

Figure 4.7 shows the outcome of setting the `City` result object column in the data table to a section. The `City` object has been added as a block header, and the object is no longer a column in the table.

Austin

Quarter	Sales revenue	Quantity sold	Margin
Q1	$775,483	5,102	$291,469
Q2	$667,850	4,016	$286,489
Q3	$581,470	4,184	$195,022
Q4	$674,870	3,776	$287,330

Boston

Quarter	Sales revenue	Quantity sold	Margin
Q1	$312,896	1,936	$124,429
Q2	$291,431	1,647	$126,060
Q3	$249,529	1,623	$87,385
Q4	$429,850	2,470	$173,810

Figure 4.7 City Dimension Object Set as a Section

137

After you've added the section you can also add additional report elements to that section. The values in any additional elements are grouped by the same values in the section heading.

To view the size of a section(s) and structure of a report, click on the DESIGN arrow and select STRUCTURE ONLY (also accessible using shortcut keys Ctrl+3). View the report structure to resize the height of the section.

Figure 4.8 shows the structure view of the report that contains the section you added in the previous step.

Figure 4.8 Structure Only View of a Report

Formatting Sections

To apply formatting to a section in a report, right-click anywhere in the section while in design with data mode and select FORMAT SECTION from the list of options. From the FORMAT SECTION window, you can apply various settings including the following:

▶ HIDE WHEN EMPTY

▶ HIDE WHEN FOLLOWING FORMULA IS TRUE

▶ BACKGROUND COLORS AND IMAGES

▶ VERTICAL PROPERTIES:

  ▶ START ON A NEW PAGE

  ▶ REPEAT ON EVERY PAGE

  ▶ AVOID PAGE BREAK

> **Note**
>
> An important setting that is often difficult to locate is the MINIMUM TOP OFFSET section setting. For a report that contains at least two pages and a section, this setting should always be changed manually to 0.00, or the first page of your report will have a gap above the first sectioned value.

Accessing the Minimum Top Offset Setting

To access the Minimum Top Offset setting, follow these steps:

1. Right-click on a section.

2. Select FORMAT SECTION.

3. Select the LAYOUT category.

4. Update the MINIMUM TOP OFFSET function to 0.00.

This setting is pictured in Figure 4.9.

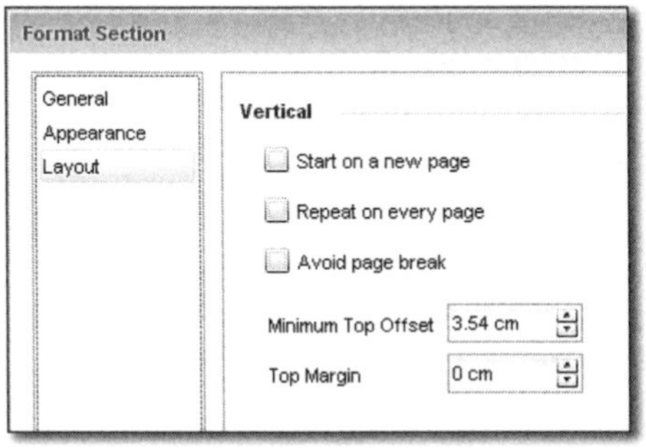

Figure 4.9 Locating the Minimum Top Offset Section Setting

4.2.2 Grouping Data with Breaks

Another way of grouping table data in a Web Intelligence report is by using breaks. Breaks are similar to sections, except that when you add them, they don't include block headings. When you add a break, a new set of break properties becomes available for customization.

To edit the properties of a break right-click on the column that includes the break, and then locate the MANAGE BREAKS option under BREAKS.

Figure 4.10 shows the break properties available when designing a report.

After a section or break has been created on a table, you can unfold and fold a data table to toggle between viewing detailed and aggregated data.

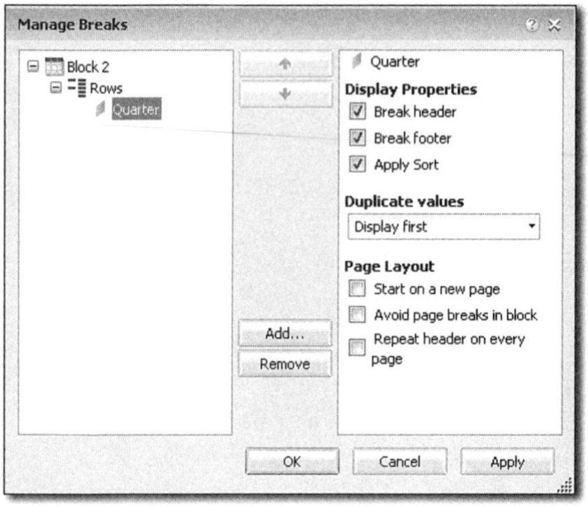

Figure 4.10 Managing Break Properties

4.3 Outline Navigation

The outline feature adds collapsing and expanding "sections" on the left side of the Report Panel. Figure 4.11 shows a collapsed outline in a table with defined sections.

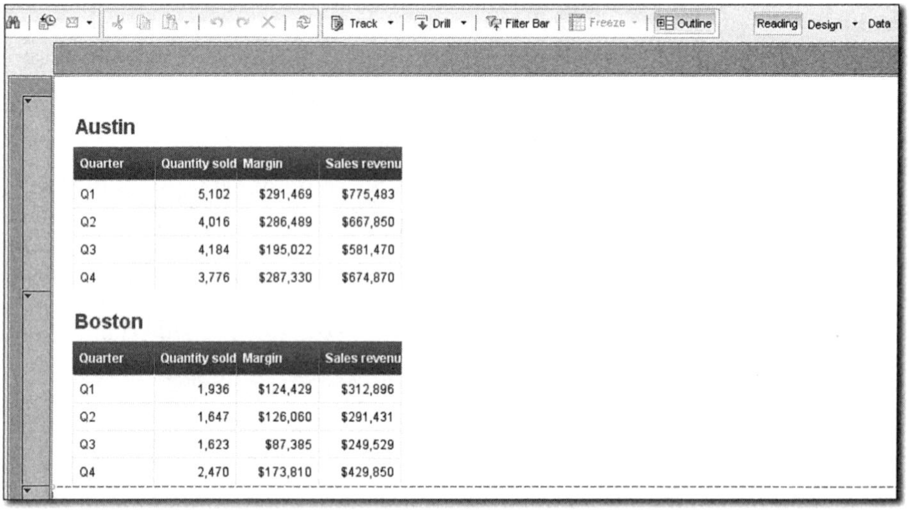

Figure 4.11 Show/Hide Outline from the Interact Menu

The outline feature adds a layer of interactivity to your SAP BusinessObjects BI 4.1 reports because users have a choice of whether to show or not to show detailed information. This allows for increased "real estate" on the canvas because all reports can start in the summarized view, and you can choose whether or not to expand to see the details.

Page navigation has also been improved in SAP BusinessObjects BI 4.1. Now all reports have a navigation icon that lets the user know whether additional pages exist in each direction. Figure 4.12 shows the PAGE NAVIGATION icon located in the lower-right corner of each Web Intelligence report. When additional columns or rows are present in a report, this icon provides easy access to the data not currently on the screen.

Figure 4.12 Page Navigation

The following section describes how to insert sorting and ranking into a report.

4.4   Enhanced Sorting and Ranking

Sorting and ranking are two simple techniques that increase report readability by displaying the most significant information to report consumers in the shortest amount of time. In just a couple of clicks, columns can be sorted, or the rows in a table can be ranked to display the top 10 sales revenues by the dimension of your choice. Both functions are available to report consumers in design mode. Let's begin by examining sorting.

4.4.1   Sorting

Sorting can be applied to tables or charts in a report and to either dimension objects or measures. Sorting is always applied within breaks and sections. Figure 4.13 shows the SORT menu options available in the toolbar menu under the ANALYSIS/DISPLAY tabs.

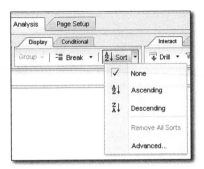

Figure 4.13 Sort from the Toolbar Menu under Analysis/Display

Four sort types are available to you while viewing a report in BI Launch Pad or when editing a Web Intelligence document:

▶ NONE
Natural sorting occurs based on the type of data in the columns.

▶ ASCENDING
Sorting begins with the smallest value at the top (e.g., A, B, C, or 2, 4, 6).

▶ DESCENDING
Sorting ends with the smallest value at the top (e.g., C, B, A, or 6, 4, 2).

▶ CUSTOM
Sorting is defined by the user; it often applies to character names but doesn't apply to measures. It is accessible via MANAGE SORTS in the menu options.

Sorting data in charts or tables allows users to quickly access data points in alphabetical or numerical order.

Applying Sorting

To apply sorting within a table, follow these steps:

1. Select the column or result object to be sorted.

2. Select the SORT option in the ANALYSIS/DISPLAY tabs.

3. Select the sort type.

4. Select NONE to remove applied sorting and return to default.

To apply sorting within a chart, follow these steps:

1. Click on DESIGN/STRUCTURE ONLY located on the main toolbar to switch from data view to structure only view.

2. Click on the object in the chart to be sorted.

3. Select the SORT option on the ANALYSIS/DISPLAY tabs.

4. Select the sort type.

5. Click on DESIGN/WITH DATA to return to see the sort selected.

6. Return to the structure view, and add, remove, or edit an existing sort.

7. Click on the SORT icon again to remove the sort.

Custom Sorting

Custom sorting is available only for dimension objects and while editing a document in the Report Panel.

When you select custom sorting, the dimension values of the object will be displayed in natural or descending order. You can re-sort the item values by selecting values individually and clicking on the up or down arrows until the values are in the order that you prefer.

An example of this sorting is when a month name object sorts alphabetically rather than chronologically. For months to appear in chronological order, you need to create a custom sort to reorder the values. If you have data only through June, then July through December values won't appear in the list.

This is when you need to include *temporary values*. Enter the month names from July to December, add them to the existing list, and then order them chronologically rather than alphabetically. This will keep the month data sorted correctly for all future refreshes.

Figure 4.14 shows an Available Objects table with the month abbreviation field. The only way to sort the months correctly is to apply a custom sort.

	California	Colorado	DC	Florida	Illinois	New York	Texas
April	$666,321	$191,846	$275,751	$158,363	$278,195	$617,851	$901,464
August	$339,651	$86,830	$119,664	$84,942	$114,890	$288,166	$475,473
December	$616,205	$171,163	$234,192	$174,343	$230,092	$592,567	$835,928
February	$410,620	$126,135	$177,509	$104,562	$174,747	$400,589	$619,780
January	$692,714	$193,912	$278,756	$215,327	$375,172	$836,078	$1,125,918
July	$515,407	$144,586	$201,581	$129,514	$180,673	$652,721	$667,380
June	$420,305	$128,635	$177,787	$136,504	$209,522	$591,598	$634,289
March	$796,347	$205,635	$310,557	$195,799	$296,490	$750,448	$1,129,872
May	$673,522	$179,595	$252,909	$195,131	$362,877	$818,641	$963,523
November	$504,464	$143,069	$221,179	$131,686	$207,226	$566,677	$736,391
October	$768,555	$209,508	$341,052	$179,634	$277,572	$735,190	$1,024,197
September	$1,075,459	$279,361	$371,014	$173,354	$315,203	$731,694	$1,003,450

Figure 4.14 Default or Natural Sorting Applied to the Month Abbreviation

Custom Sort Dialog Box

Figure 4.15 shows the CUSTOM SORT dialog box used to sort the month name abbreviations. Click on the values in the provided list box, and then use the arrows to the right to move them up or down the list.

The left side of the CUSTOM SORT screen allows you to add temporary values for items that don't currently appear within the list of values.

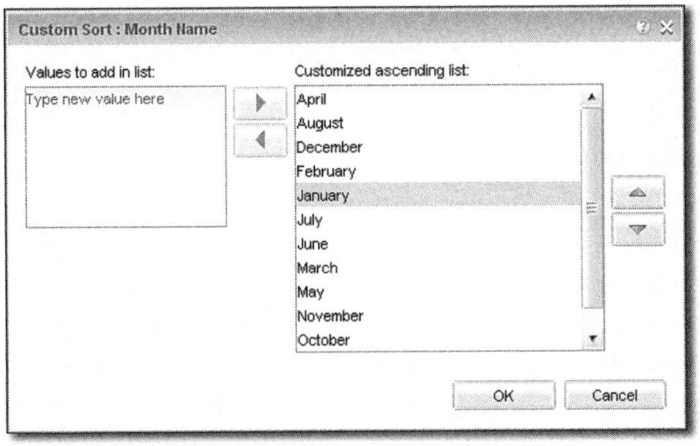

Figure 4.15 Custom Sorting

Remove Custom Sort Value

If a custom sort has been added but needs to be removed, click on the temporary value in the list of values to enable the DELETE CUSTOM SORT button. Click on the button to permanently remove the custom value from the list.

Figure 4.16 shows sorting being set on a measure within a data table and within a section.

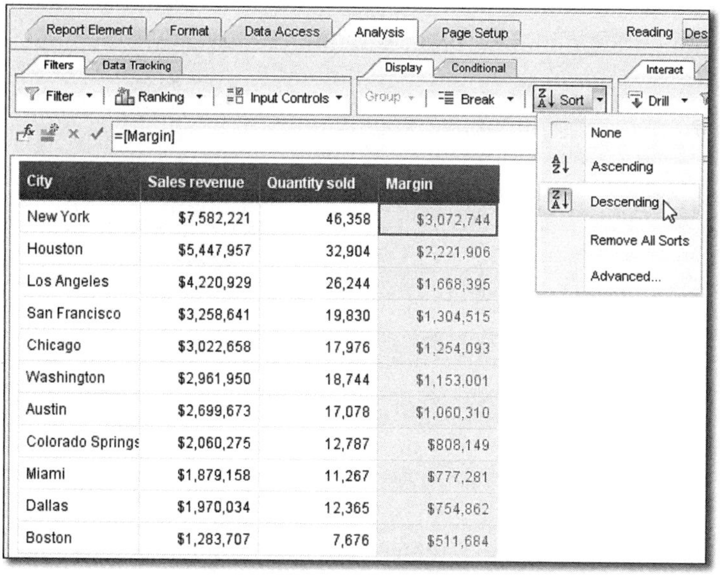

Figure 4.16 Margin Sorted in Descending Order

> **Note**
>
> Notice that custom sorting isn't an option when sorting on a measure object. Custom sorting is only available for dimension objects.

Enhanced Sorting

Sorting in charts and data tables is a very common requirement when analyzing data in reports. Now in SAP BusinessObjects BI 4.1, chart sorting has been enhanced to provide users with even more flexibility when displaying data visually in reports.

Sorting can become a necessary function when displaying data from two or more measures or dimensional objects. The Region Color feature, available when assigning data to charts, provides this capability by allowing charts to be created that display two dimensional values for a single measure. Depending on the values being charted, this combination of measures and dimensions can be difficult to interpret. To ease the complexity of displaying and analyzing this type information, the sort feature now allows you to sort by dimension, measure, or by the dimensional value selected in the Region Color section.

Figure 4.17 shows the SORT menu with a column chart selected that contains two dimension objects and a single measure object.

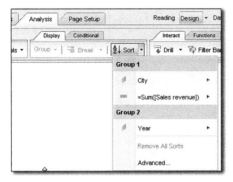

Figure 4.17 Sorting by Group

In Figure 4.17, the Year object is being used in the Region Color section while the City object is the primary Category Axis object. With this feature, you can apply sorts to dimensions in both groups and also to any measure object in the chart. Figure 4.18 shows a chart being sorted by two dimensions from separate groups: City and Year.

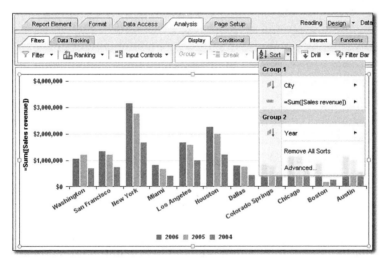

Figure 4.18 Sorting a Chart by Two Dimensions

Multigroup charting displays information in a compound format and is ideal when the number of values in both dimension objects is relatively small.

Custom Sorting

To create a custom sort, click on the small downward arrow to the right of the SORT function, and then select the MANAGE SORTS option. This menu provides additional options for customizing sorts on the selected chart. The following options are available in the MANAGE SORTS window:

▶ Revise the priority of sorts if more than one sort has been added.

▶ Modify the direction or order of a chart between ascending or descending.

▶ Add a new object to be sorted, or remove an existing sort.

▶ Define a custom order to sort an object.

▶ Reset an existing custom sort object back to ascending or descending.

Sorting in a Cross Table (Crosstab)

Compound sorting isn't reserved for charts only. Cross table report elements can also contain multiple sorts applied to the dimension objects in both the columns and rows in the table.

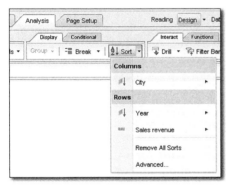

Figure 4.19 Applying Sorts to a Crosstab

Figure 4.19 shows the sort options that are available when a cross table is selected, the City object is assigned to the horizontal axis, and the Year object is assigned to the vertical axis. You can apply sorting to objects in the COLUMNS and

Rows sections. Use the MANAGE SORTS option to set up custom sorting on either object.

Like sorting, ranking also helps the report consumer access the most significant information.

4.4.2 Ranking

Ranking is used to display the top or bottom number of objects within a block. Values are ranked by dimensions and are based on measures of several different types and calculation modes:

▶ TOP/BOTTOM
Select TOP, BOTTOM, or both, and then use the up and down arrows or text box to set number of values.

▶ BASED ON
Select a measure to use for ranking.

▶ RANKED BY (optional)
This selected dimension object is used by the ranking to create the top or bottom values.

▶ CALCULATION MODE:

 ▶ COUNT: This mode returns the top or bottom n records of the BASED ON selection.

 ▶ PERCENTAGE: This mode returns the top or bottom $n\%$ of records of the total number of records and the BASED ON selection.

 ▶ CUMULATIVE SUM: This mode returns the top or bottom records for the cumulative sum of the measure selected and (optionally) the BASED ON selection; doesn't exceed n.

 ▶ CUMULATIVE PERCENTAGE: This mode returns the top or bottom records for the cumulative sum of the measure selected and (optionally) the BASED ON selection; doesn't exceed $n\%$.

Ranking takes precedence over any sorts previously set up in a report block.

Note

Web Intelligence includes *tied rankings*, which means that if you want to display the top 10 values, and 3 records have the same value, 13 records will appear in the top 10 list.

To add a ranking, follow these steps:

1. Modify your Web Intelligence document. (Ranking can be applied only in design mode.)

2. Select a table or chart to be ranked.

3. Click on the RANKING button located on the reporting toolbar on the ANALYSIS tab and FILTERS subtab.

4. Select the RANKING PROPERTIES in the RANKING dialog box.

Two options—EDIT RANKING and REMOVE RANKING—will be available if a ranking has already been added to a report element, because only one ranking can be added to a report element.

Figure 4.20 shows the RANKING dialog box opened when ADD RANKING or EDIT RANKING is selected. This dialog box allows you to configure the ranking properties by checking the TOP, BOTTOM, or both ranking property types followed by selecting the BASED ON, RANKED BY, or CALCULATION MODE to create or edit a ranking.

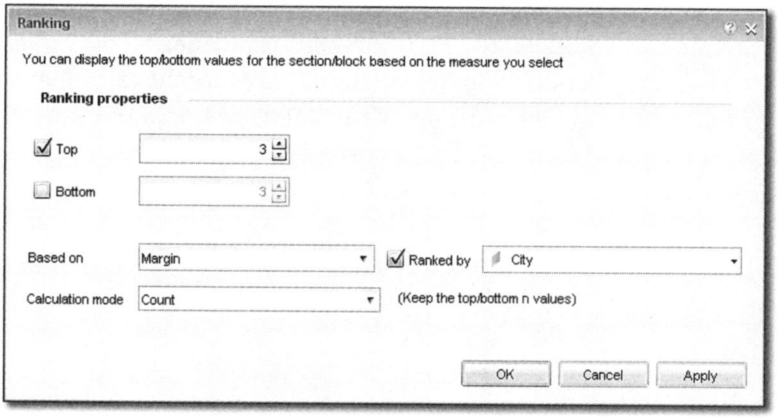

Figure 4.20 Ranking Dialog Box for a Crosstab

The next section discusses conditional formatting rules and how they can be used to alert report consumers about important conditional elements in Web Intelligence reports.

4.5   Conditional Formatting

Web Intelligence reports use conditional formatting rules (previously known as alerters) to highlight values that meet a specified set of criteria. When a set of criteria has been met, values can be displayed with customized formatting. This includes the capability to modify the following areas:

▶ **Text**
Font, type, size, color, underline, strikethrough

▶ **Background**
Color, skin, image from URL, image from file

▶ **Border**
One or more sides, border size, color

> **Note**
>
> Because of the capability to add a background image in a conditional formatting rule, reports can be designed to function as scorecards and display trend icon images based on a value's relation to a target value or threshold.

Figure 4.21 shows the New Rule button for conditional formatting on the ribbon toolbar. It's worth noting that only the Applet viewer provides the capability of adding a new conditional rule. Even though the HTML viewer in SAP Business-Objects BI 4.1 has improved tremendously compared to SAP BusinessObjects BI 4.0, this feature is still only available in the Applet viewer.

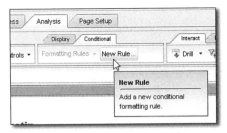

Figure 4.21 New Conditional Rule Button on the Ribbon Toolbar

The following are some of the limits when applying conditional formatting in a report:

- ▶ Up to 30 conditional formatting rules can be applied to a single Web Intelligence reporting document.
- ▶ Conditional formatting can be applied to a maximum of 20 different rows or columns in a table report element.
- ▶ Up to 10 different alerts can be applied to a single column.
- ▶ A single conditional formatting can contain up to 6 conditions.

Clicking the NEW RULE button will launch the FORMATTING RULE EDITOR window, which is shown in Figure 4.22. From this window, modify the following settings to set up the criteria for the new conditional format rule:

- ▶ NAME
  Give the conditional rule a descriptive and unique name; this is important if you have many rules. The default value in this field is "Conditional Format."
- ▶ DESCRIPTION
  Enter a clear description of what each conditional rule will perform.
- ▶ FILTERED OBJECT OR CELL
  Select the field or result object to be evaluated.
- ▶ OPERATOR
  Select the operator to be used (e.g., EQUAL TO, GREATER THAN, etc.).

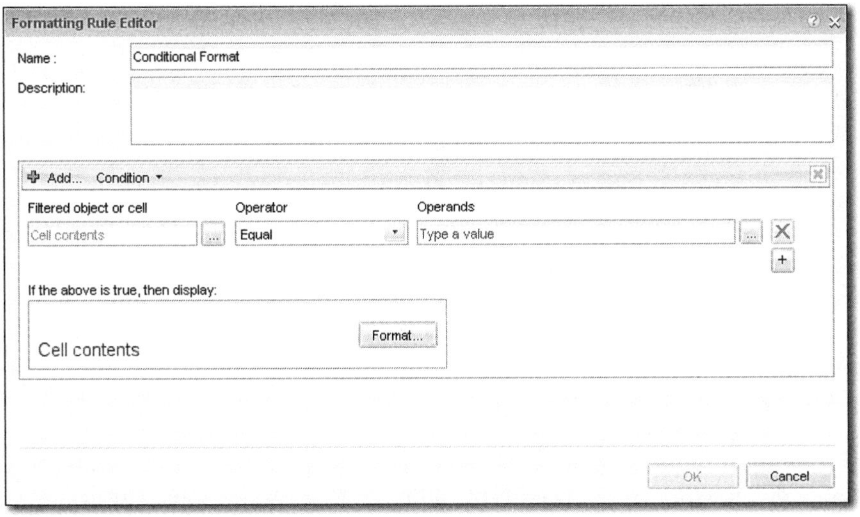

Figure 4.22 Formatting Rules Editor

▶ OPERANDS
Enter a value to represent the target or threshold to trigger the conditional format.

After configuring these five settings, click on the FORMAT button to launch the FORMATTING RULES DISPLAY window used to define the visual attributes of the new rule (see Figure 4.23).

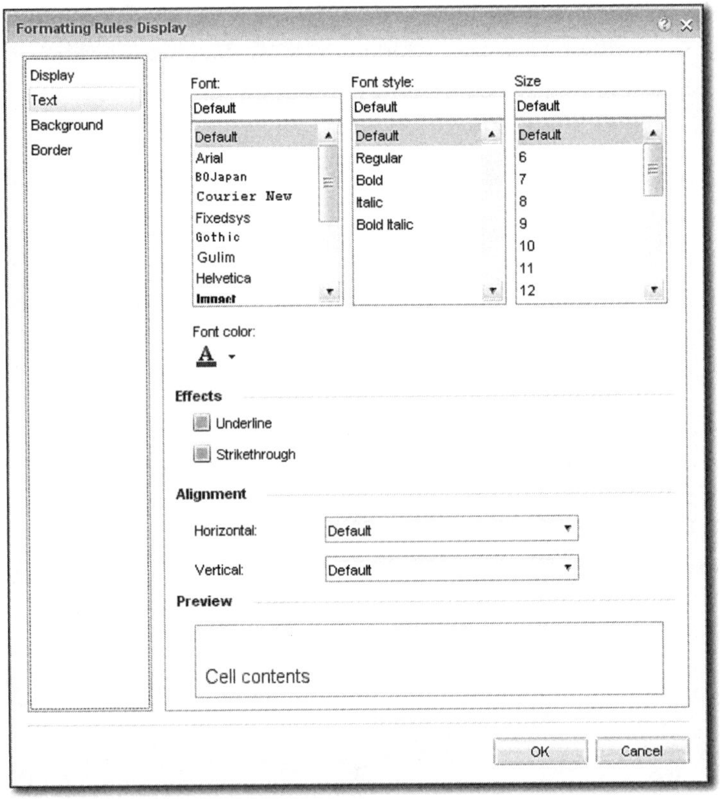

Figure 4.23 Formatting Rules Display

From this window, revise the following items to create the criteria for the conditional display:

▶ TEXT
Change the default font size and font color. Default color is already selected to red, but you can choose another color by clicking on the down arrow and selecting from the color palette.

▶ BACKGROUND

Choose colors, patterns, or images to apply to the cell background.

▶ BORDER

Choose any style for the cell border to accentuate the cell.

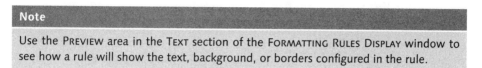

Note

Use the PREVIEW area in the TEXT section of the FORMATTING RULES DISPLAY window to see how a rule will show the text, background, or borders configured in the rule.

After you've created a new conditional formatting rule, select a column or table heading, and then click on the FORMATTING RULES icon on the ribbon toolbar under the ANALYSIS/CONDITIONAL tabs. All available conditional formatting will have an open checkbox located to the left of the conditional formatting name.

Check the rule that you want to apply to the selected column, and click on OK. Figure 4.24 shows a conditional formatting rule being applied with these three steps:

1. Select the column to apply the conditional formatting to.

2. Click on the FORMATTING RULES icon.

3. Check the conditional format(s) to be applied to the selected column(s).

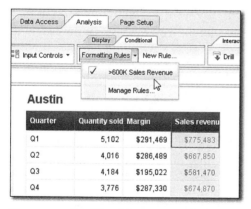

Figure 4.24 Conditional Formatting Rules Applied to a Column in a Table

The next section explains how to modify report headers and footers and describes the method for including background images in reports.

4.6   Headers, Footers, and Background Images

The header and footer sections in a Web Intelligence document can be hidden or displayed depending on your preference or business requirements.

To toggle the Header on or off, begin by entering design mode, and then click the primary Page Setup tab. Next, select either the Header or Footer subtabs. Notice that the Show button will either be on or off. Figure 4.25 shows the Show Header icon with the header enabled and the header height at 1.4 cm.

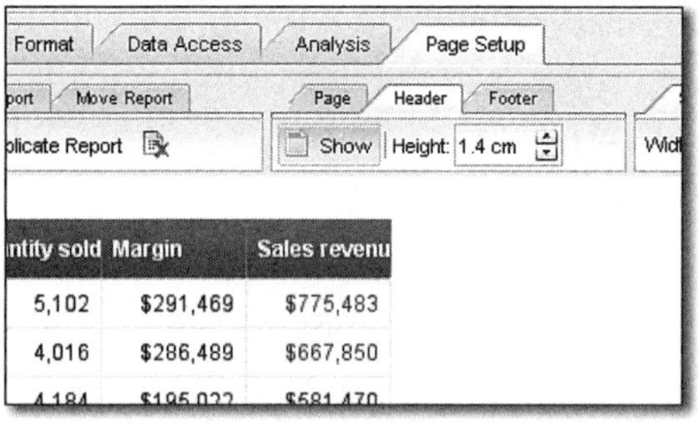

Figure 4.25 Report Header Set as Visible in a Report

If the page header and footer have both been removed from a report, and you need to add them back in, follow these steps:

1. Click on the Page Setup • Header tab on the ribbon toolbar.

2. Click on the Show button to turn the header on. You can also set the height of the header in this step.

3. Click on the Page Setup • Footer tab on the ribbon toolbar.

4. Click on the Show button to turn the footer on. You can also set the height of the footer in this step.

Quite often, report developers need to include background images or company logos in Web Intelligence reporting documents. You can easily do this by following just a few steps:

1. Go to the Report Elements • Cell tab on the ribbon toolbar. Drag the Blank icon onto the canvas.

2. After the blank cell has been added, right-click on the cell, select Format Cell, and choose Appearance in the Format Cell window. You can also click on the

APPEARANCE icon under FORMAT/STYLE on the ribbon toolbar. Figure 4.26 shows the properties available for the blank cell under APPEARANCE.

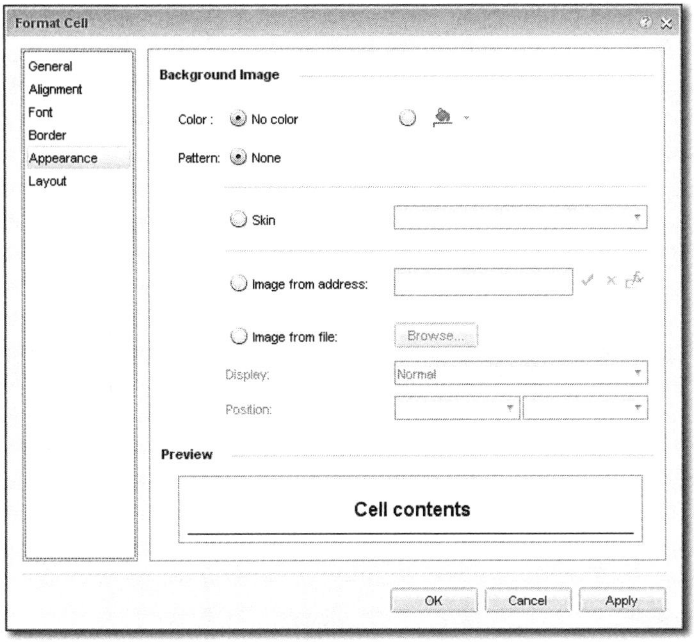

Figure 4.26 Format Cell Appearance

The BACKGROUND IMAGE dialog box opens to provide four options under PATTERN (see Figure 4.27):

▶ NONE
Default selection.

▶ SKIN
Shows five predefined photos.

▶ IMAGE FROM ADDRESS
Opens a dialog box for manual URL entry.

▶ IMAGE FROM FILE
Enables browsing to locate and select a local image.

You can create background images with the following file types: PNG, BMP, GIF, JPG, or JPEG.

Images are presented with five different display types:

▶ Normal

▶ Stretch (not supported in HTML)

▶ Tile

▶ Horizontal Tile

▶ Vertical Tile

The position of the images can be displayed in any of these combinations:

▶ Top, Center, Bottom

▶ Left, Center, Right

Note

When images are selected as background images in a blank cell element, the recommended display selection should be set as the Stretch setting. This selection will resize the image to scale when the cell size is either increased or decreased.

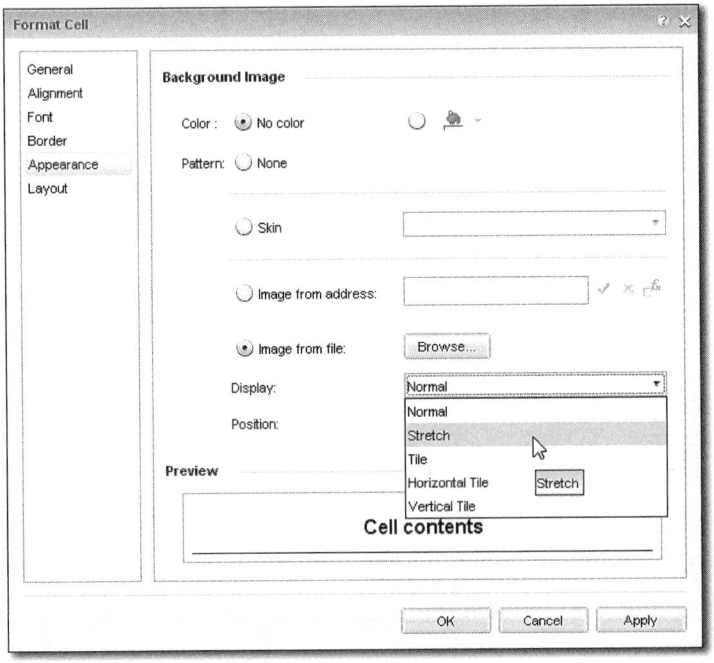

Figure 4.27 Display Image Options Dialog Box

Headers, footers, and background images can be used to add context to Web Intelligence reports. Report headers and footers can contain document names, company logos, or page numbers. Images can be useful to illustrate concepts. Choosing the right placement for images and creating a consistent look and feel is imperative in achieving strong usability for report consumers.

4.7   Summary

Reports in Web Intelligence 4.1 are created for viewing, analyzing, and sharing company data in a secure, customized, and drillable web-based delivery format. You can create reports by using the result objects and report elements, and by setting properties in the tabs provided in the side panel. Reports are physically presented in the document pane and easily enhanced with the extensive list of shortcut icons in five provided toolbars.

Web Intelligence allows you to present multiple reports within a single reporting document that contains a variety of data visualization component types. You also have the ability to create drillable and highly formatted reports that include sections, breaks, sorting, ranking, and report filters to produce effective analytical documents.

Changes in report data can be easily identified when data tracking is enabled and when detailed conditional formatting has been created.

SAP BusinessObjects BI 4.1 provides a full spectrum of reporting components for displaying data. These include Available Objects tables, freehand cells, scorecarding capabilities through the use of conditional formatting, and more than 25 different types of charts.

The Report Panel provides a highly intuitive development canvas that allows business users to create, edit, and share reports with ease.

Chapter 5 describes how to navigate the Web Intelligence reporting interface and explains the SAP BusinessObjects BI 4.x ribbon-based toolbar. This is important because the Web Intelligence 4.x interface has changed from previous releases of the SAP BusinessObjects product. A bit of familiarization is necessary to get used to all the icons and their placements; however, you'll find that the grouping of icons is much more intuitive because it's based on their functional areas.

The updated, streamlined interface in Web Intelligence 4.x is easy to use for both report developers and consumers. Use the ribbon toolbar for faster and more intuitive access to icons based on various functional areas. Design, analyze, and share reports to effectively solve business issues.

5 The Web Intelligence 4.1 Report Panel

This chapter begins by exploring the Web Intelligence 4.1 Report Panel, the robust reporting interface that allows report designers to create dynamic data presentations and visualizations. The reporting interface in Web Intelligence 4.x positions all icons on an enhanced toolbar in tabs grouped by functional areas for logical and effective development. The updated side panel replaces the Report Manager from XI 3.1 and allows for easy access to useful areas such as Available Objects, Document Summary, Report Map, and Input Controls. The newly designed reporting interface also positions a robust status bar at the bottom of the report page that allows you to easily refresh reports, enable tracking, and navigate pages.

5.1 The Web Intelligence 4.1 Reporting Interface

The reporting interface in Web Intelligence 4.1 has two main interface options—READING and DESIGN—to accommodate different types of user interaction within a report. The reading mode has been exclusively designed for report consumers who only need to view and drill into a report rather than edit it. The design mode provides many more capabilities and gives power users and report developers a full spectrum of creation and editing options.

In Figure 5.1, the REPORT PANEL is shown in design mode and within the Applet viewer. Pictured is the report canvas with four basic chart types and the five tabs used to quickly access reporting functions when creating or modifying Web Intelligence reports. Within these tabs, you'll find a well-organized collection of icons available for intuitive interaction and configuration of report elements and data.

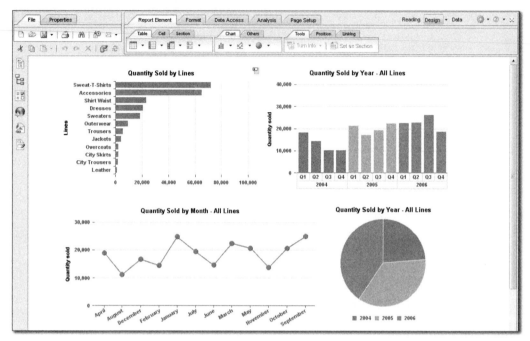

Figure 5.1 The Web Intelligence Report Panel in Design Mode

Figure 5.2 shows the streamlined appearance of the REPORT PANEL in reading mode.

Navigate between these interface options by toggling between the READING and DESIGN buttons located in the upper-right corner of the panel.

A useful option in the reporting toolbar is STRUCTURE ONLY, found in the DESIGN menu and shown in Figure 5.3.

If you're using the HTML viewer, you'll have easy access to all of the interface options by right-clicking on the top bar and selecting APPLICATION MODE, as shown in Figure 5.4.

The EDITING option corresponds to the DESIGN • WITH DATA selection while the SHOW STRUCTURE option goes with to DESIGN • WITH STRUCTURE selection.

Figure 5.2 The Web Intelligence Report Panel in Reading Mode

Figure 5.3 Design Button Allows Access to Structure Only Mode

Figure 5.4 Application Mode Menu in the HTML Viewer

Now that you're familiar with the view modes in SAP BusinessObjects BI 4.1, the next section describes the ribbon-style toolbar and the functions located within it.

5.2 Reporting Toolbars

The formatting toolbar in Web Intelligence is similar to the Microsoft Office ribbon-style toolbars that you're probably already familiar with. This method of configuring properties allows for easier access to report formatting icons. The toolbar becomes very useful when configuring charts and tables, customizing report features, modifying data access settings, and adding analytical features to reports. Figure 5.5 shows the formatting toolbar in design mode. Whether you're updating a horizontal table, vertical table, cross table, form, or freestanding cell, the ribbon toolbar allows you to instantly revise the format of entire columns with only a couple clicks.

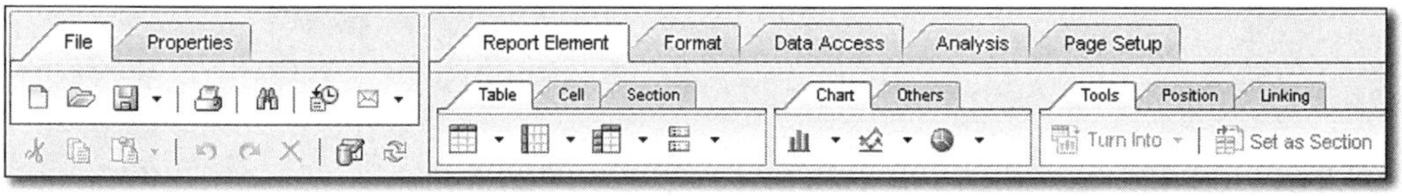

Figure 5.5 Formatting Toolbar in Design Mode

> **Note**
>
> The reading mode toolbar is different from the design mode toolbar. They were designed to execute separate functions and to be more in line with the needs of report consumers and report designers. The reading mode toolbar is much more streamlined for optimal viewing and filtering capabilities.

There are some slight differences in the functions available in the toolbar between the Applet viewer and HTML viewer.

The ribbon toolbar in design mode contains five primary tabs, each providing categorized functions and shortcut icons. We'll start by describing the report property tabs, located on the left side of the report page and only available in design mode, while providing a detailed description of each tab's individual function.

Overview of the Function Tabs in Design Mode

Following are the function tabs in design mode:

▶ FILE
  Located on the left side of the window, this tab is used for adding new reports,

opening existing documents, saving, printing, exporting, and sending reports to other users.

▶ PROPERTIES
This tab allows you to view and revise document and application properties with three primary menu options:

  ▶ VIEW: Quick access to viewing or hiding the various toolbars.

  ▶ DOCUMENT: Launches the DOCUMENT SUMMARY properties window.

  ▶ APPLICATION: Change the measurement unit preferences: CM or INCHES.

▶ REPORT ELEMENT
This tab delivers report elements for displaying data.

▶ FORMAT
This tab delivers a large number of formatting properties.

▶ DATA ACCESS
With this tab, you can add new data providers, edit existing ones, or add new variables to a reporting document.

▶ ANALYSIS
With this tab, you can create filters, input controls, enable data tracking, add conditional formatting, and much more.

▶ PAGE SETUP
This tab contains all page formatting options in one location.

Let's explore the functions and options available in each tab.

Report Property Tab – File

Figure 5.6 shows the FILE tab and its associated icons:

Figure 5.6 File Tab

▶ NEW
This icon is used to create a new document.

► OPEN

This icon allows you to access previously saved Web Intelligence documents.

► SAVE

This icon is used to save reports with SAVE, SAVE AS, or SAVE TO ENTERPRISE options.

► PRINT

This icon provides one-click report printing by transforming the report into a PDF file.

► FIND

This icon allows you to search report data with the FIND toolbar.

► HISTORY

If this report has been previously scheduled, the report instances will be available through this icon.

► EXPORT

(HTML viewer only) With this icon, save a document locally as a PDF, XLSX, XLS, CSV, or text file.

► SEND TO

Use this icon to send the report to an email address, another SAP BusinessObjects user, or an FTP server. Note that the SAP BusinessObjects administrator is required to configure plug-ins on the server to use the email distribution functionality.

► UNDO/REDO

These icons let you undo or redo previous actions.

► CUT/COPY/PASTE

These icons let you cut, copy, and paste any report element, including charts and tables.

► DELETE

Use this icon to delete selected components.

► EDIT DATA PROVIDER

New in SAP BusinessObjects BI 4.1, this icon provides quick access to the Query Panel for query editing.

► REFRESH

This icon allows for new data to be brought into the report. Being able to refresh data is a primary function when generating reports.

Report Property Tab – Properties

Figure 5.7 shows the VIEW menu of the PROPERTIES tab. The following options can be found within the PROPERTIES tab:

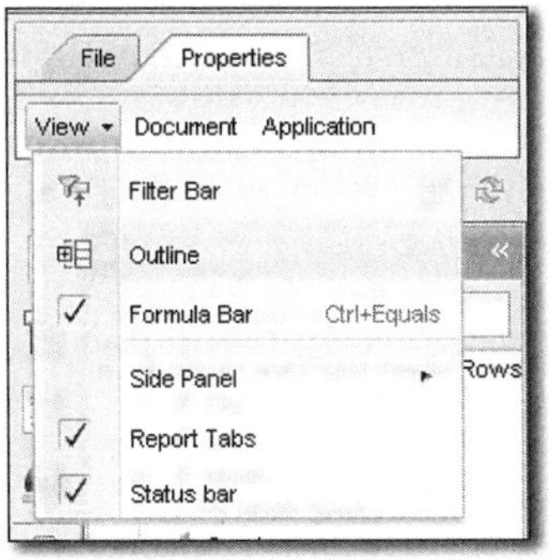

Figure 5.7 Properties Tab

▶ VIEW

Allows report developers to access the FILTER BAR, OUTLINE (also known as FOLD/UNFOLD), FORMULA BAR, and SIDE PANEL (or LEFT PANE). Additionally, you can toggle the REPORT TABS and STATUS BAR on and off using their respective checkboxes.

▶ DOCUMENT

Provides a summary of configurable document properties, including type, author, description of the document, and creation date. Configurable options include the following:

  ▶ DESCRIPTION

  ▶ KEYWORDS

  ▶ REFRESH ON OPEN

  ▶ PERMANENT REGIONAL FORMATTING

  ▶ USE QUERY DRILL

  ▶ ENABLE QUERY STRIPPING: Can be applied to relational universe-based reports when ALLOW QUERY STRIPPING has been enabled in the Information Design Tool and ENABLE QUERY STRIPPING has also been enabled in the DOCUMENT SUMMARY section of each report.

  ▶ HIDE WARNING ICONS IN CHARTS

  ▶ AUTO-MERGE DIMENSIONS

▶ EXTEND MERGED DIMENSION VALUES

▶ MERGE PROMPTS (BEX VARIABLES)

▶ APPLICATION
Allows developers to set the measurement units to display in either centimeters or inches. In the Applet viewer only, you can also enable the SHOW GRID and SNAP TO GRID options here.

Report Element Tab

Figure 5.8 shows the REPORT ELEMENT tab and its associated icons. This is the first primary tab used for displaying data on the report canvas.

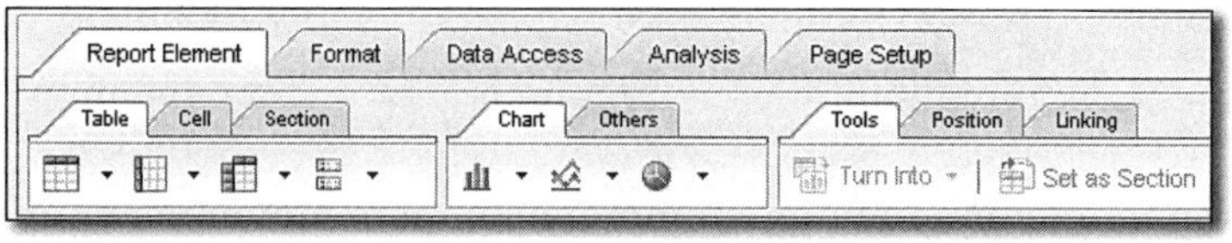

Figure 5.8 Report Element Tab

First let's examine the tabs under the REPORT ELEMENT tab section by section:

▶ TABLE

  ▶ VERTICAL TABLE: Displays header cells at the top of the table.

  ▶ HORIZONTAL TABLE: Displays header cells to the left of the table.

  ▶ CROSS TABLE or CROSSTAB: Displays dimensions across the top and along the left side of the table while displaying measures in the body of the table.

  ▶ FORM: Displays categorized dimension descriptions or mailing addresses.

▶ CELL

  ▶ BLANK CELLS: Used for custom headings or subheadings or to display information that should appear in an Available Objects table.

  ▶ PREDEFINED: Predefined single value containing metadata about report.

▶ SECTION

  ▶ INSERT SECTION: Allows report developers to insert a section using available objects.

▶ CHART (chart types are examined in Chapter 7)

- COLUMN: Graphically presents values in vertical or horizontal charts (available column charts: stacked column, 100% stacked column, dual axis column, dual axis column and line, and 3D column).

- LINE: Displays data graphically with connected data points (available line charts: vertical/horizontal mixed, vertical/horizontal stacked, vertical/horizontal percent, 3D line, 3D surface, dual axis line, and surface).

- PIE: Displays data as a percentage of the whole with pie slices (available pie charts: pie with variable slice depth, donut, 3D pie, and 3D donut).

- OTHERS

  - BAR: Graphically represents horizontal bar charts (available bar charts: vertical/horizontal stacked bar, 100% stacked bar, vertical/horizontal grouped, vertical/horizontal perfect, vertical/horizontal bar and line, and 3D bar).

  - POINT CHART: Includes scatter plot, bubble chart, and more point charts.

  - MORE: Includes box plot, radar chart, tree map, heat map, and tag cloud.

- TOOLS

  - TURN INTO: Transforms selected object into a different type table or chart.

  - SET AS SECTION: Allows report developers to insert a section using selected object.

- POSITION

  - ORDER

  - ALIGN

- LINKING

  - ADD HYPERLINK

  - LINK TO DOCUMENT: (HTML viewer only)

  - ADD ELEMENT LINK

- TABLE LAYOUT
  Appears only when a data table on the report canvas has been selected.

  - BREAK

  - INSERT

  - HEADER: Lets you show table headers. Useful when break headers have been added to the report.

  - FOOTER

- ▶ BEHAVIORS
  - ▷ HIDE
  - ▷ PAGE BREAK
  - ▷ REPEAT: Allows tables, headers, or breaks to repeat on every page.

Format (or Formatting) Tab

Figure 5.9 shows the FORMAT tab (or FORMATTING tab as it's called in the HTML viewer) and its associated icons:

- ▶ FONT
- ▶ BORDER
- ▶ CELL
- ▶ STYLE
- ▶ NUMBERS
  One-click currency conversion was added in SAP BusinessObjects BI 4.1.
- ▶ ALIGNMENT
  - ▷ WRAP TEXT: Allows a word wrap style of formatting to be applied to the selected column or columns so that a carriage return takes place within the cell rather than extending the value horizontally.
- ▶ SIZE
- ▶ PADDING
- ▶ TOOLS
  - ▷ FORMAT PAINTER: Applies formatting. Quickly copy the format of an existing cell or column and apply it to an additional cell or column by first selecting a cell that contains the preferred formatting, clicking on the FORMAT PAINTER icon, and then clicking on the text to which you would like to apply the formatting.
  - ▷ FORMATTING: Displays all formatting options for the selected report element.
  - ▷ CLEAR FORMAT: Resets all formatting to the default formats.
  - ▷ CHART STYLE: Will be hidden unless a chart element appearing on the report canvas has been selected.

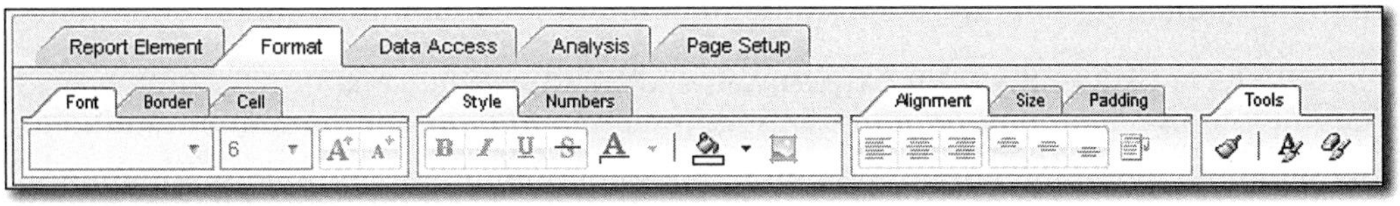

Figure 5.9 Format Tab

Data Access Tab

Figure 5.10 shows the DATA ACCESS tab and its associated icons:

▶ DATA PROVIDERS

  ▶ NEW DATA PROVIDER: Adds a new query to the existing document.

  ▶ EDIT: Returns to the Query Panel to edit a query.

  ▶ PURGE: Purges report data. This is important when publishing reports to the file repository with restricted data. You can purge all data from all data providers or choose an individual data provider to purge.

  ▶ REFRESH: Submits the query to the data source to retrieve the most recent data.

▶ TOOLS (Applet viewer only)

  ▶ CHANGE SOURCE

  ▶ EXPORT DATA

▶ DATA OBJECTS

  ▶ NEW VARIABLE

  ▶ MERGE

Figure 5.10 Data Access Tab

Analysis Tab

Figure 5.11 shows the ANALYSIS tab and its associated icons:

▶ FILTERS

   ▶ FILTER

   ▶ RANKING

   ▶ INPUT CONTROLS

▶ DATA TRACKING
Prompts you to set the reference point for data tracking. A variety of data tracking options are available when tracking has been enabled. These options include font formatting for dimension insertions and deletions, detail changes, and increased/decreased values for measures.

▶ DISPLAY

   ▶ GROUP: (new in SAP BusinessObjects BI 4.1)

   ▶ BREAK

   ▶ SORT

▶ CONDITIONAL

   ▶ FORMATTING RULES

   ▶ NEW RULE: (Applet viewer only)

▶ INTERACT

   ▶ DRILL: Used to enable drill mode. It also provides a drill pane to drop result objects for simple report filtering. Drill mode allows report consumers to drill up or drill down the drill path for deeper and quicker analysis.

   ▶ FILTER BAR

   ▶ OUTLINE

▶ FUNCTIONS

   ▶ SUM

   ▶ COUNT

   ▶ MORE: Includes avergage, min, max, and percentage.

   ▶ FORMULA BAR

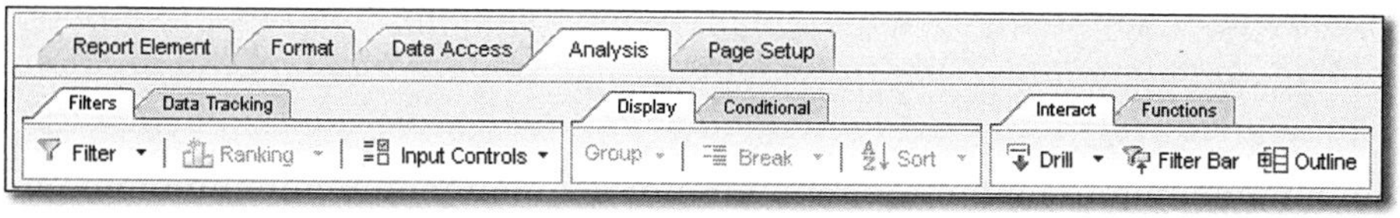

Figure 5.11 Analysis Tab

Page Setup Tab

Figure 5.12 shows the PAGE SETUP tab and its associated icons:

- ▶ REPORT
  - ▶ ADD REPORT
  - ▶ DUPLICATE
  - ▶ DELETE
- ▶ RENAME REPORT
- ▶ MOVE REPORT
  - ▶ MOVE LEFT
  - ▶ MOVE RIGHT
- ▶ PAGE
  - ▶ PAGE ORIENTATION (landscape or portrait)
  - ▶ PAGE FORMAT (A4, Letter, Legal, etc.)
- ▶ HEADER
  - ▶ SHOW BUTTON
  - ▶ PAGE HEADER HEIGHT
- ▶ FOOTER
  - ▶ SHOW BUTTON
  - ▶ PAGE FOOTER HEIGHT
- ▶ SCALE TO PAGE
  - ▶ WIDTH
  - ▶ HEIGHT
  - ▶ SCALE

- ▶ MARGINS
  - ▶ TOP MARGIN
  - ▶ BOTTOM MARGIN
  - ▶ LEFT MARGIN
  - ▶ RIGHT MARGIN
- ▶ DISPLAY
  - ▶ PAGE MODE
  - ▶ QUICK DISPLAY
  - ▶ ROWS
  - ▶ COLUMNS

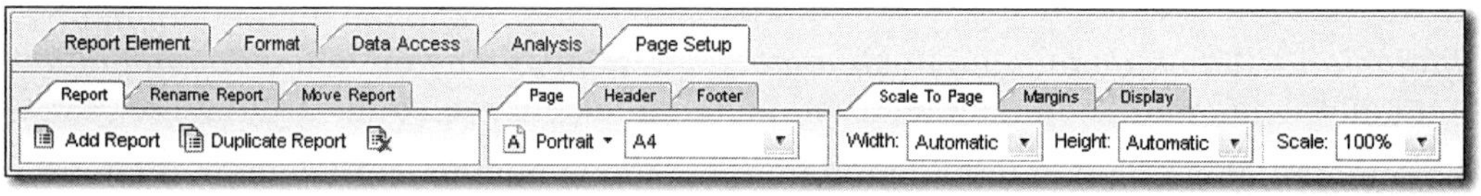

Figure 5.12 Page Setup Tab

The ribbon-based toolbar in Web Intelligence 4.1 is a robust interface that allows users to quickly access all functions related to creating reports. The next section describes the usability of the side panel (or left pane), which also provides main functions necessary for report maintenance and creation.

5.3 The Side Panel

The *side panel* (previously known as the left pane) contains icon tabs that give additional information and is required for creating Web Intelligence reporting documents. This panel also plays a critical role in editing existing documents. Figure 5.13 shows the first tab of the side panel, which is DOCUMENT SUMMARY.

The side panel, which can be displayed in normal or minimized mode, is different for reading mode, design mode, and data mode. Let's examine each of these now:

- ▶ **Reading mode**
  - ▶ DOCUMENT SUMMARY: This tab includes information about the report, such as author, date created description, keywords, last refreshed, last modified

date, last modified by, duration of previous refresh, document options, data options, and parameters. This metadata about the report is useful for the administrator because it shows who has created and refreshed the document. Additionally, it shows the duration of previous refresh records, that is, the number of seconds the report took to refresh on the previous refresh. (Note that if never run, this value will be zero.)

▶ REPORT MAP (or NAVIGATION MAP): This tab provides a linked list of the reports and section values within each report in the document.

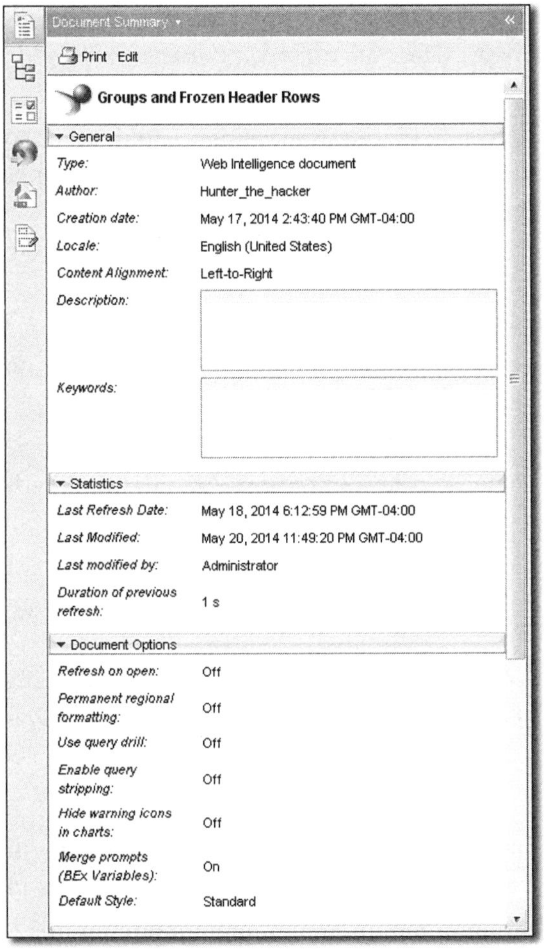

Figure 5.13 Side Panel – Document Summary

▶ INPUT CONTROLS: This tab allows report users to identify whether any components have been used to filter report data using input controls. The user can select a map of all input controls already saved on the document, choose to reset the values of saved input controls, or both.

▶ USER PROMPT INPUT: Displays prompt filters that exist in the Query Panel. Users can access this area to quickly change filters and refresh queries.

▶ **Design mode**

▶ DOCUMENT SUMMARY: This tab includes the same information types as described earlier for reading mode.

▶ REPORT MAP (or NAVIGATION MAP): This tab provides a linked list of the reports and section values within each report in the document.

▶ INPUT CONTROLS: This tab allows both report developers and users to include a variety of components to filter report data. The report designer can create new input controls by clicking on the NEW button under the INPUT CONTROLS tab. Users can select values from any input controls in the report or reset the values to their default settings.

▶ WEB SERVICE PUBLISHER (Applet viewer only): This tab allows the report designer to create web services using existing components or blocks from Web Intelligence reports.

▶ AVAILABLE OBJECTS: This tab contains the fields included in the RESULT OBJECTS pane in the Query Panel and locally created formulas and variables. All objects in this tab are available to be displayed in reports.

▶ USER PROMPT INPUT (HTML viewer only): Displays prompt filters that exist in the Query Panel. Users can access this area to quickly change filters and refresh queries.

▶ DOCUMENT STRUCTURES AND FILTERS: DOCUMENT STRUCTURES provides a detailed listing of all objects existing within the document. The FILTERS icon shows when a filter has been applied to a report element or data block.

▶ **Data mode (Applet viewer only)**

▶ DATA: This tab contains the fields included in the RESULT OBJECTS pane in the Query Panel and locally created formulas and variables. All objects in the AVAILABLE OBJECTS tab are available to be displayed in reports.

Figure 5.14 shows the result objects from the Query Panel in the AVAILABLE OBJECTS tab. The data for the fields displayed in the AVAILABLE OBJECTS tab has been retrieved from the database and exists within the document's microcube.

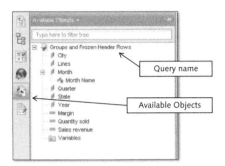

Figure 5.14 Available Objects

Click on the DOCUMENT SUMMARY tab in either reading mode or design mode. To reveal the report information, click on EDIT to update fields such as DESCRIPTION or KEYWORDS. The REFRESH ON OPEN option is used to prompt users for input each time a report is opened and also refreshed.

In the next section, we'll discuss the various features of the Report Panel—the area of the report used for displaying data.

5.4   Report Panel

The Report Panel or report canvas is where report elements are placed when you create Web Intelligence reports. This is the primary section in the Report Panel and is the section used for displaying data.

The report canvas or document pane consists of three sections:

▶ Report header (optional)
▶ Report body
▶ Report footer (optional)

Tip
When a query is refreshed for the first time, the result objects will appear in the document pane in a report titled REPORT 1. All result objects will also appear in the side

panel. For all subsequent refreshes after the initial refresh, the side panel will be updated with the latest list of result objects, but the objects appearing on the document pane won't change unless revised manually by the report developer.

The three report tabs in a single report are shown in Figure 5.15.

Figure 5.15 Three Report Tabs

Report tab names can be easily adjusted by right-clicking on the tab names. To rename, insert, duplicate, or delete report tabs, use these methods:

1. Right-click on the report name tab located in the lower left of the report.

2. Select RENAME to change the name of the report tab.

3. Select ADD REPORT to add a new report tab.

4. Select DUPLICATE to make a duplicate copy of the current report.

5. Select DELETE REPORT to remove the current report tab.

Figure 5.16 shows the actions available when you right-click on the report name tab located at the lower left of the document pane. The MOVE REPORT option is enabled only when two or more reports exist within the document.

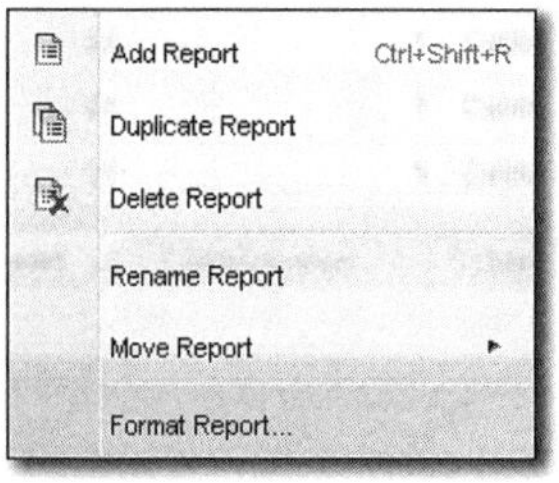

Figure 5.16 Actions Available When Right-Clicking on the Report Tab

Data Tracking

Activating data tracking from the status bar is a recent addition to Web Intelligence and has become a valuable analysis feature. To activate data tracking in a report, click on the TRACK function located in the ANALYSIS tab and DATA TRACKING subtab. You'll immediately be prompted to set the reference point to begin tracking data returned by your queries.

Another method for activating data tracking is to click the TRACK CHANGES option located in the status that appears directly beneath the report canvas on the bottom border of the browser.

Page Features

The page navigation tools are located on the status bar (see Figure 5.17) and allow you to scroll from the current page being viewed to the next page, last page, previous page, and first page. The page navigation options also come with two icons to toggle between the page modes of the report.

The following is a description of the two modes for viewing reports (see their icons in Figure 5.17):

▶ QUICK DISPLAY MODE
   This is the default display mode and provides the most ideal screen space for analyzing data. The maximum displayed vertical and horizontal records can be adjusted in the PROPERTIES tab to modify the default settings.

▶ PAGE MODE
   This mode displays reports as they would appear if printed or exported to PDF. This mode is commonly selected in dashboard reports.

The zoom options on the status bar allow you to increase the zoom of the page from a minimum of 10% to a maximum of 200%. There is also an option to zoom to PAGE WIDTH or WHOLE PAGE (also known as SCALE TO PAGE). This feature is located in the PAGE SETUP tab.

The REFRESH icon is also available on the status bar and found in the lower-right corner of your browser. The refresh function allows new data to be retrieved from a data source and inserted into the report. Figure 5.17 shows the REFRESH button and the last time the report was refreshed.

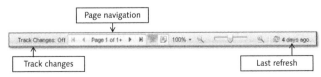

Figure 5.17 Page Navigation on the Status Bar

Formula Bar

The formula bar provides quick access to the definition of an object in a table or cell. You can save time by revising object definitions in the formula bar rather than always editing variables and formulas in the variable editor.

To access the bar, right-click on the main ribbon bar, and then select FORMULA BAR to toggle the formula bar on and off.

Note

The formula bar is accessible only in design mode. Figure 5.18 shows the menu to access the formula bar.

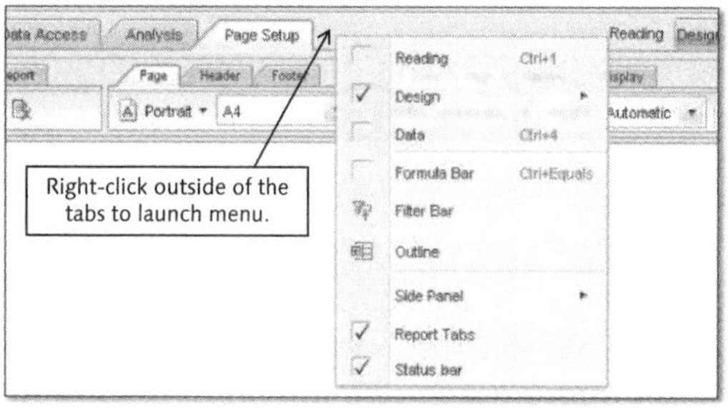

Figure 5.18 Menu to Access the Formula Bar

The formula bar can also be expanded to allow report developers to see more code on the screen. Figure 5.19 shows the formula bar expanded by using the double up arrows.

Figure 5.19 Formula Bar Expanded

5.5   Report Property Categories

Five major report element formatting types are available in the Web Intelligence ribbon toolbar:

▶ REPORT ELEMENT
▶ FORMATTING

▶ DATA ACCESS

▶ ANALYSIS

▶ PAGE SETUP

These functional areas make it easy for you to identify which category to select when looking for a particular function. We'll discuss each of these areas in detail in the coming sections.

5.5.1 Report Elements

The REPORT ELEMENT tab on the ribbon toolbar offers many shortcuts to the most frequently used objects in a report: tables, charts, and predefined cells. When a report element is selected on the Report Panel, you'll see that the REPORT ELEMENT tab on the toolbar displays specific icons for the type of element selected. Figure 5.20 shows two additional tabs (TABLE LAYOUT and BEHAVIORS) containing icons to format a table when a table object has been selected.

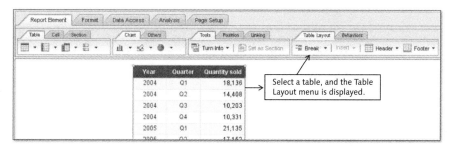

Figure 5.20 Selecting a Table Displays Additional Tabs on the Report Element Toolbar

Report elements allow report developers to add data to the canvas and create robust visualizations for users. You can quickly convert an existing table to a chart or convert an existing dimension column into a section. Follow these steps to convert a table into a bar chart:

1. Select an existing table from the canvas.

2. Select the TOOL tab on the REPORTS ELEMENT toolbar.

3. Select the TURN INTO icon, and then select BAR CHART.

179

The table has been converted into a bar chart. Note that there are two tabs added to the REPORT ELEMENT tab on the toolbar. If a chart is selected, then CHART STYLE and CELL BEHAVIOR appear on the toolbar.

Relative Position and Object Alignment

Proper element alignment and relative positioning will improve the overall attractiveness and effectiveness of your reports. When business users view reports that contain charts and data tables aligned in unusual ways, the reports aren't usually as convincing as well-designed and properly formatted reporting documents.

Use the alignment functions to format the placement of report elements and the RELATIVE POSITION feature to maintain consistent spacing and alignment when one or more blocks or report elements exist on a report.

Figure 5.21 shows the alignment types available when two or more report elements are selected:

▶ ALIGN LEFT

▶ ALIGN CENTER

▶ ALIGN RIGHT

▶ ALIGN TOP

▶ ALIGN MIDDLE

▶ ALIGN BOTTOM

▶ RELATIVE POSITION

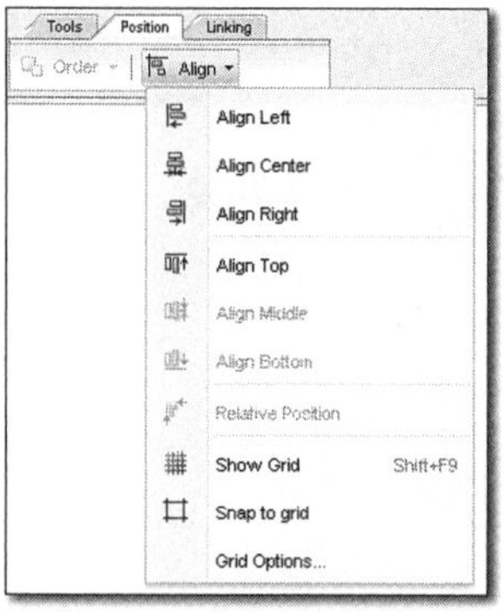

Figure 5.21 Align Types from the Position Tab under the Report Element Tab

The RELATIVE POSITION setting allows two report elements to be tied together and spaced by a selected number of pixels (inches).

To set up relative positioning, select a secondary report element, and then select RELATIVE POSITION from the ALIGN icon under the POSITION tab. Figure 5.22 shows the RELATIVE POSITION properties of a table in a report.

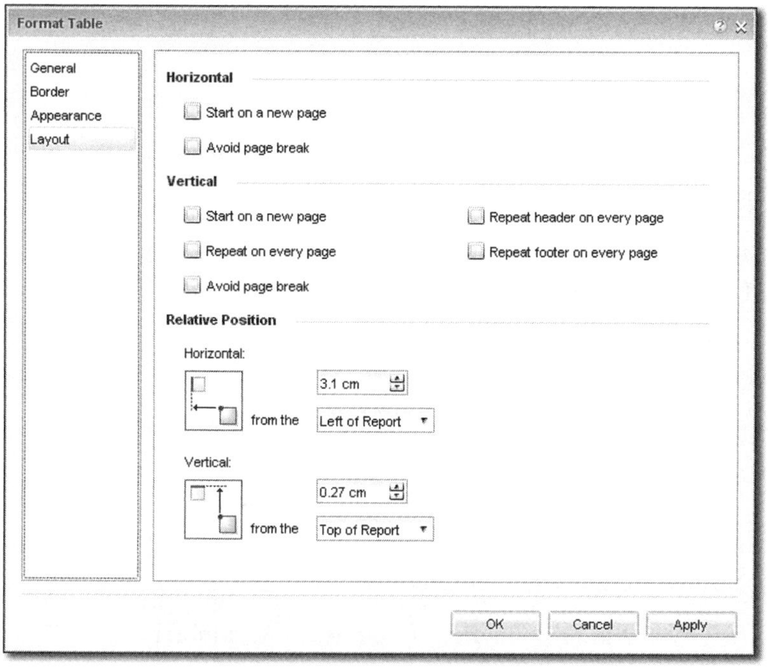

Figure 5.22 Relative Position Properties for a Table

Follow these steps to assign a position to a chart or table within a report:

1. Select LEFT EDGE, RIGHT EDGE, or NONE from the first box at the top, and then select TOP SIDE OF, BOTTOM SIDE OF, or NONE from the bottom setting.

2. Select the object(s) to assign the relative distance to.

3. Choose the relative distance for both the top section and the bottom section.

Relative positioning of charts and data tables gives report developers the flexibility to present data in a similar format when the amount of data being reported fluctuates as filters and input control values are selected and reselected.

5.5.2 Formatting

The FORMAT tab on the ribbon toolbar gives report developers many formatting functions, such as font size, styles, borders, alignment, and much more. The TOOLS tab allows report developers to copy the format of previously produced components onto new components. Figure 5.23 shows the FONT, STYLE, ALIGNMENT, and TOOLS tab icons under the FORMAT tab.

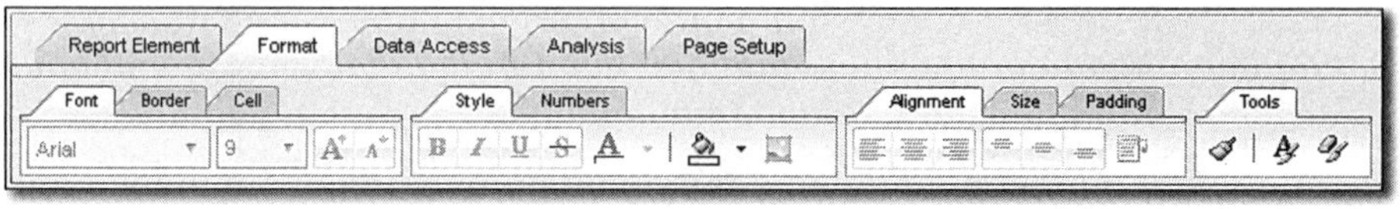

Figure 5.23 Format Toolbar

Under the TOOLS tab, there are three icons that help report developers tremendously when duplicating report elements:

▶ FORMAT PAINTER
Allows for duplicating formatting from one object and applying it to another object.

▶ FORMATTING
Displays all formatting options for the selected report element.

▶ CLEAR FORMAT
Resets all formatting to the default formats.

Follow these steps to duplicate formatting from one cell to another:

1. Move the DOCUMENT NAME predefined cell from the REPORT ELEMENTS • CELL tabs onto the canvas.

2. Select the newly added cell by clicking on it.

3. Select the FORMAT tab and, under the STYLE tab, select ITALIC and UNDERLINE. Then change the text color to red.

4. Place the LAST REFRESHED DATE predefined cell from the REPORT ELEMENTS • CELL tabs onto the canvas.

5. Select FORMAT PAINTER from the FORMATTING • TOOLS tabs, and apply the DOCUMENT NAME cell format to the LAST REFRESHED DATE cell. Figure 5.24 shows a column selected in a vertical table and the FORMAT PAINTER icon selected.

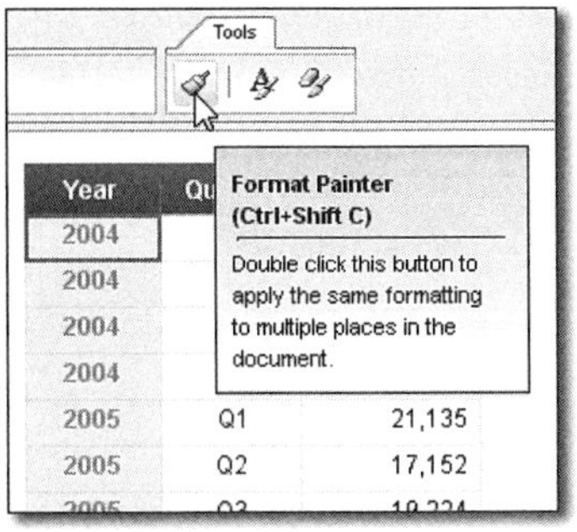

Figure 5.24 Applying Formatting from One Cell to Another

> **Note**
>
> You can copy and duplicate cell formats to any type of objects. You can also duplicate table and chart formats. Formatting report elements provides a consistent appearance for ease of use.

5.5.3 Data Access

The Data Access tab on the ribbon toolbar offers functions for managing data providers, creating new variables, and merging dimensions from multiple data sources.

Whether your data comes from a centralized universe or simply from an Excel file, it's important to understand when to refresh, purge, or redefine data providers. Figure 5.25 shows the Purge icons under the Data Access tab.

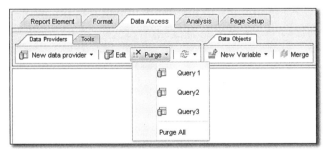

Figure 5.25 Refresh and Purge Icons under the Data Access Tab

By restricting the amount of data returned from a data source, report developers can manage the query performance in the report while constructing it. A good way to achieve this is by understanding how much data is needed per data provider. When multiple data providers are generated for a particular report, developers may choose to refresh or purge individual data providers to increase the performance of the report.

Follow these steps to purge the results from an individual data provider:

1. Create two data providers, and refresh all data.
2. Click on the PURGE dropdown arrow.
3. Select the first data provider to purge.

You'll now have data from only the second data provider. Figure 5.25 shows the PURGE button options when you click the dropdown arrow.

Reports with highly secure data should be purged before they're published to the SAP BusinessObjects BI platform. Users with the appropriate permissions will be able to refresh the reports and retrieve the results. Users without the necessary permissions won't be able to see the data because the reports were published after the results were purged.

It's also important to purge the results when publishing prompted reports to the SAP BusinessObjects BI platform. Saving reports with data will eventually take a toll on the server.

5.5.4 Analysis

The ANALYSIS tab on the ribbon toolbar offers functions for interacting with the report data. Filtering, ranking, input controls, grouping, breaks, sorts, drilling, outline, and functions provide a robust way to interact with report elements, and they're all available within this tab.

By using a combination of these analysis functions, you'll be able to customize and filter report data to meet business requirements and greatly enhance the user experience. By applying detailed customizations in a report, you can create a reporting solution that can be easily consumed by users at different levels in the organization. Figure 5.26 shows the expanded MORE button under the FUNCTIONS subtab of the primary ANALYSIS tab to apply basic calculations on measure columns in tables.

These predefined functions are AVERAGE, MIN, MAX, and PERCENTAGE.

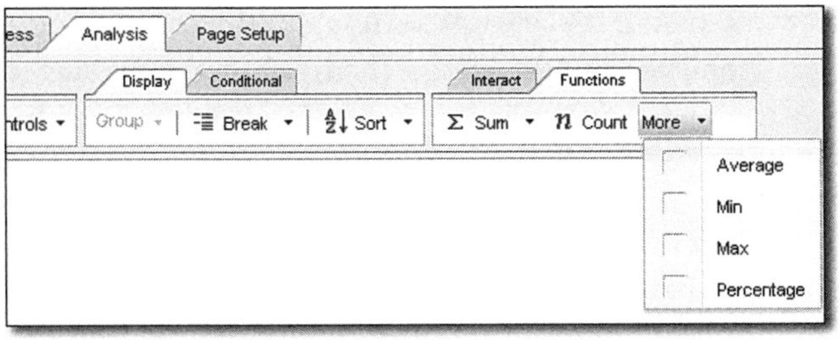

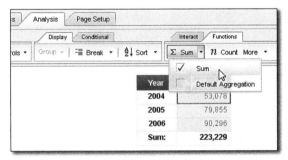

Figure 5.26 Expanded More Button under the Functions Tab

Follow these steps to create an aggregated value in a data table:

1. Create a table with a numeric measure object column.

2. Select the column to apply the sum to.

3. Click on SUM under the FUNCTION tab, and then check SUM.

A new row appears at the end of the table with the column summed up, as shown in Figure 5.27.

Figure 5.27 Sum Table Column

5.5.5 Page Setup and Layouts

Page margins in a Web Intelligence report can be modified to fit business requirements or standards. The default margins in a report are as follows:

- Top margin: 0.79 inches or 2 cm
- Bottom margin: 0.79 inches or 2 cm
- Left margin: 0.79 inches or 2 cm
- Right margin: 0.79 inches or 2 cm

You can adjust the margins by accessing the MARGINS subtab in the primary PAGE SETUP tab. Locate the margin properties, and then use the up or down arrows to change the size.

The changes take effect when you click off of the size adjustment arrows. Figure 5.28 shows the margins properties and highlights the top margin adjustment arrows for modifying the margin sizes.

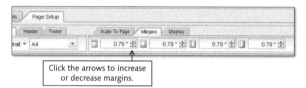

Figure 5.28 Adjusting Page Margins

Report property categories are functional groupings for formatting icons based on their functional area. These groupings in tab format make it easier for the report designer to access the needed functions.

5.6   Summary

Web Intelligence 4.1 provides a full spectrum of reporting components as well as a full line of functions to format every element to a customized look and feel. Users and report developers can now access several different formatting tools from multiple ways. This includes toolbars, right-click menus, the side panel, and the status bar. An example of the multiple ways of performing a function is the REFRESH button. This feature can be found in three different locations: the status bar, the DATA ACCESS/DATA PROVIDERS subtab on the ribbon toolbar, or the reading mode toolbar.

Chapter 6 describes how to display data in tables in a Web Intelligence report. Tables are powerful reporting elements and the primary method for delivering data to users. They can also be quickly and precisely formatted by using the icons located on the new ribbon toolbar.

The features in Web Intelligence 4.1 display data and transform business information into analytical and data-rich reports. You can strategically group, break, and position data tables and freehand cells in the Report Panel to convey information to the user in the most meaningful way.

6 Displaying Data with Tables

You can display data in Web Intelligence 4.1 by inserting result objects into 4 different data table types and 26 different chart types. These are known in Web Intelligence as report elements.

This chapter focuses on presenting data using the four report element tables and the blank cells located on the ribbon toolbar. We'll discuss charts in detail in Chapter 7 and Chapter 8.

Figure 6.1 shows the tables available in the REPORT PANEL used by Web Intelligence to display data. The four table types are HORIZONTAL TABLE, VERTICAL TABLE, CROSS TAB (or cross table), and FORM. Each table contains an extensive set of properties that can be modified to allow for detailed reporting customizations.

After you refresh a query for the first time in a new document, the full list of result objects is displayed in a vertical table in the Report Panel by default. Any subsequent refreshes that include additions to the RESULT OBJECTS pane in the Query Panel won't automatically include the additional fields in the report, but the result objects will appear in the AVAILABLE OBJECTS tab on the left side panel in the report. These objects can be easily added to new or existing report elements by dragging them from the AVAILABLE OBJECTS pane and then dropping them onto charts or cells in a data table.

> **Tip**
>
> The AVAILABLE OBJECTS tab is used to maintain the list of result objects and variables available to be added to report element tables and charts. These objects can be sorted alphabetically or by query.

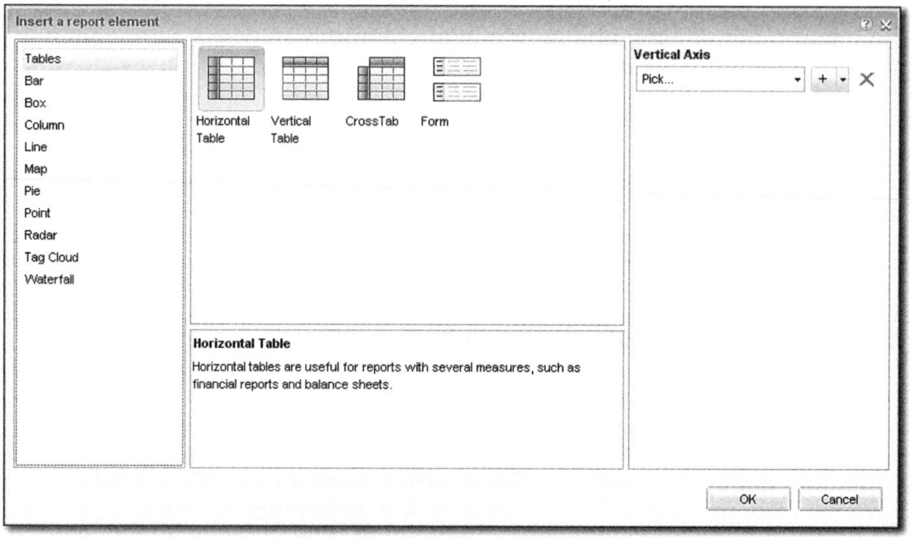

Figure 6.1 Tables Available for Displaying Data

Figure 6.2 shows the default appearance of data as it appears in the Report Panel when five result objects are added to the Query Panel in the initial refresh of a document.

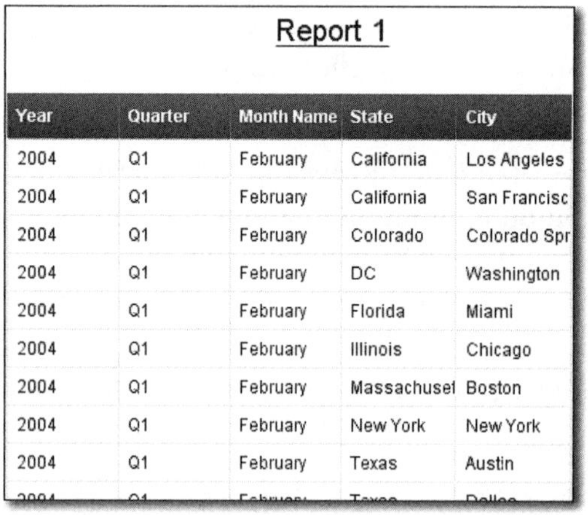

Report 1

Year	Quarter	Month Name	State	City
2004	Q1	February	California	Los Angeles
2004	Q1	February	California	San Francisc
2004	Q1	February	Colorado	Colorado Spr
2004	Q1	February	DC	Washington
2004	Q1	February	Florida	Miami
2004	Q1	February	Illinois	Chicago
2004	Q1	February	Massachuset	Boston
2004	Q1	February	New York	New York
2004	Q1	February	Texas	Austin

Figure 6.2 Default Display in the Report Panel

After running a query for the first time, a report will be created by default with a blank cell report element and will be given the underlined title "Report 1" to make it easy to locate.

You can add formulas and result objects to the report title to provide a dynamic title based on user interactions. An example of a dynamic report title can be created by using one of the following formulas:

▶ `=DrillFilters (" / ")`

▶ `=If(Count([City])=1;[City];"All "+Count([City])+" Cities")`

> **Note**
>
> Both example formulas require objects to be added to the report filter toolbar. The second formula requires the CITY object to be added to the report filter.

Chapter 12 will focus on writing formulas and variables to solve business problems. This chapter offers many examples and syntax explanations to give you the tools to create your own set of valuable and creative calculations.

So, let's first examine how to effectively use tables to convey data to the reader.

6.1   Using Tables

Tables are the Web Intelligence 4.1 reporting components used to present data to business users. Tables provide many customizable properties to help you quickly format and design useful reports and display the data in a style that best fits your requirements.

Figure 6.3 shows options available in the TABLE LAYOUT subtab when you click on an existing table. This subtab is found in the primary REPORT ELEMENT tab.

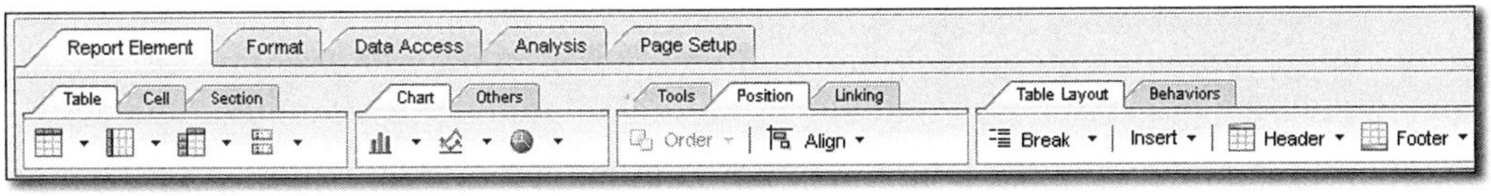

Figure 6.3 Table Layout Subtab under the Report Element Tab

These properties are available in two primary categories, which are represented as tabs:

▶ TABLE LAYOUT

  ▸ BREAK: Allows for the adding and removal of breaks.

▸ INSERT: Allows for inserting rows above, below, left, or right of the position of the cursor on an active table.

▸ HEADER: Toggles the table header on and off.

▸ FOOTER: Toggles the table footer on and off.

▸ BEHAVIORS

▸ HIDE: Hides the selected dimension or the entire table.

▸ PAGE BREAK: Inserts a page break to avoid a page break.

▸ REPEAT: Allows repeating table on every page and for repeating of selected columns or rows.

6.1.1 Add Report Elements While Designing Reports

To add a report element to a report, simply drag an element from the TABLE or CHART subtabs under the REPORT ELEMENT tab and drop it onto the Report Panel. The option to add data tables or charts while viewing reports is very useful to ad hoc report consumers and developers, but it must be done in design mode.

Figure 6.4 shows the shortcut icons used to access the different types of data tables that can be included in the main Report Panel.

Note

While designing a report, you can right-click anywhere on the Report Panel or report canvas and click on INSERT from the menu to add a specific data table type or chart from the list of choices.

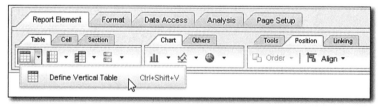

Figure 6.4 Shortcut Icons to Add Report Elements

After selecting a table from the REPORT ELEMENT tab, choose a general location on the report canvas to place it. Adding an empty table to your report is just a starting point for custom report creation. You can always move the table to a more precise location at any point in the editing/designing process.

Figure 6.5 shows a vertical table being placed on a report.

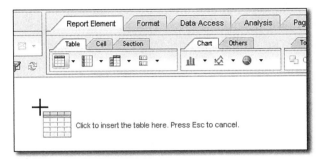

Figure 6.5 Vertical Table Report Element Being Added to a Report

After a table has been added, you can begin assigning result objects to the table by clicking on the AVAILABLE OBJECTS tab on the side panel and then dragging available objects and dropping them onto the table element recently added.

Another workflow for adding objects to a table is to right-click on the report element and select ASSIGN DATA. This method is perhaps the easiest and fastest way to assign objects to a table or chart.

Figure 6.6 shows the `State` result object being added to an empty cross table while designing a report.

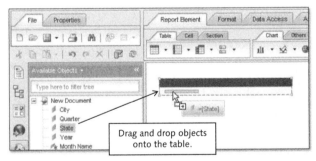

Figure 6.6 Dragging and Dropping the State Object to Add It to a Vertical Table

Note
With SAP BusinessObjects BI 4.1, you must be in design mode to add objects to tables and charts. Reading mode is for viewing only.

6.1.2 Manage Table Properties

Every table has an extensive list of properties to allow for modification and customization. Figure 6.7 shows the properties associated with a vertical table. In addition to table properties, specific elements within tables can be modified.

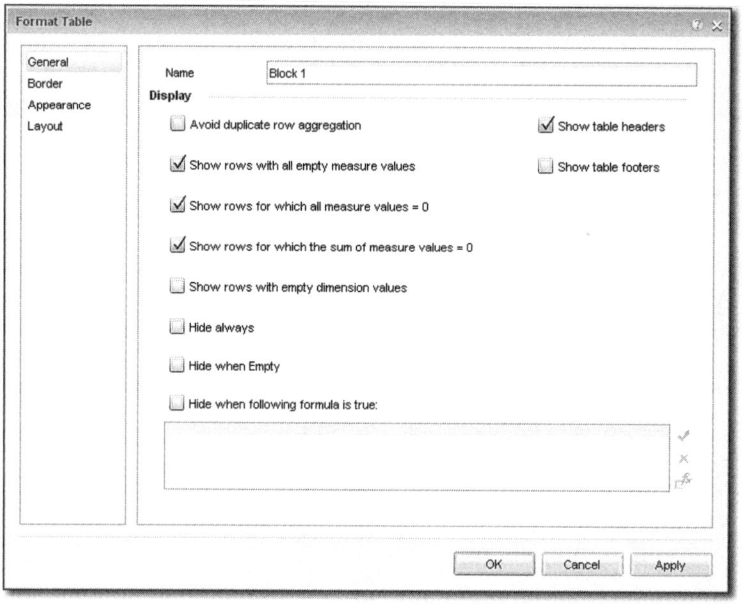

Figure 6.7 General Properties of a Vertical Table

To access table properties, right-click on the table element, and then select FORMAT TABLE.

General Property

The GENERAL property pane contains a NAME setting that allows you to rename the selected block. Figure 6.7 shows the name as "Block 1." Click on the name to replace the default name with a new name of your choice.

> **Tip**
>
> If relative positioning will be included in your reports, it's a best practice to rename your table and chart blocks with a descriptive or meaningful name. Because Web Intelligence provides a default name for all objects, setting up relative positioning can become confusing without descriptive or meaningful names assigned to each object or block.

Border Property

The BORDER property pane allows you to modify many border aspects of a table. You can add a border using the STYLE subtab within the primary FORMAT tab or by right-clicking to select the BORDER grouping in the FORMAT TABLE window. You can specify a border style, thickness, and color for the table border. Figure 6.8 shows the properties that can be specified for table borders.

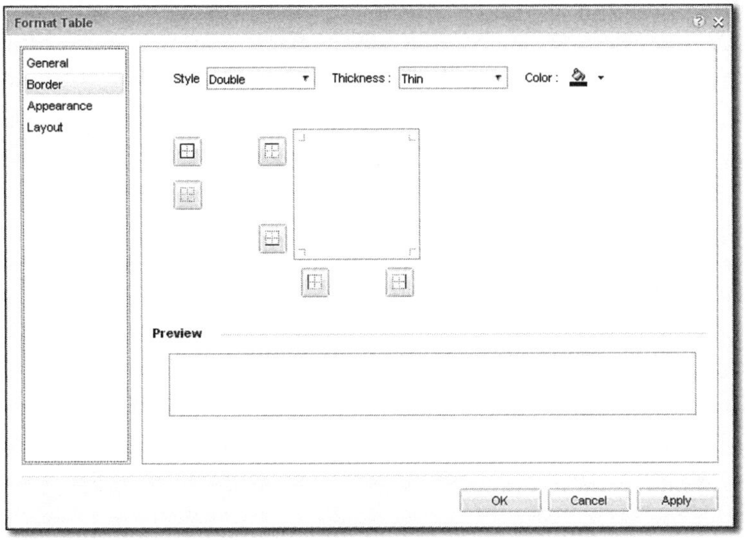

Figure 6.8 Border Properties of a Vertical Table

Appearance Property

The APPEARANCE property pane allows you to modify many visual aspects of a table. Figure 6.9 shows the properties that can be adjusted for table appearances.

▶ BACKGROUND IMAGE

 ▶ COLOR: Changes the background color of headers, rows, columns, or cell spacing if the spacing is set to 1 pixel or greater.

 ▶ PATTERN: Applies one of these four background images to a selected table section:

  – NONE.

  – SKIN: CURVE, SAP BUSINESSOBJECTS, DOTS, DRAFT, FINAL COPY.

- IMAGE FROM ADDRESS: Prompts you to choose display and position of image after entering URL.

- IMAGE FROM FILE: Prompts you to browse for a local or network image.

▶ SPACING AND PADDING
Changes the space format of the cells by modifying the following settings:

  ▶ HORIZONTAL: Modifies the cell spacing of a table (default spacing value set at 0 inches).

  ▶ VERTICAL: Modifies the cell spacing of a table (default spacing value set at 0 inches).

▶ ALTERNATE COLOR
Adjusts the frequency and color of the alternate row or column coloring.

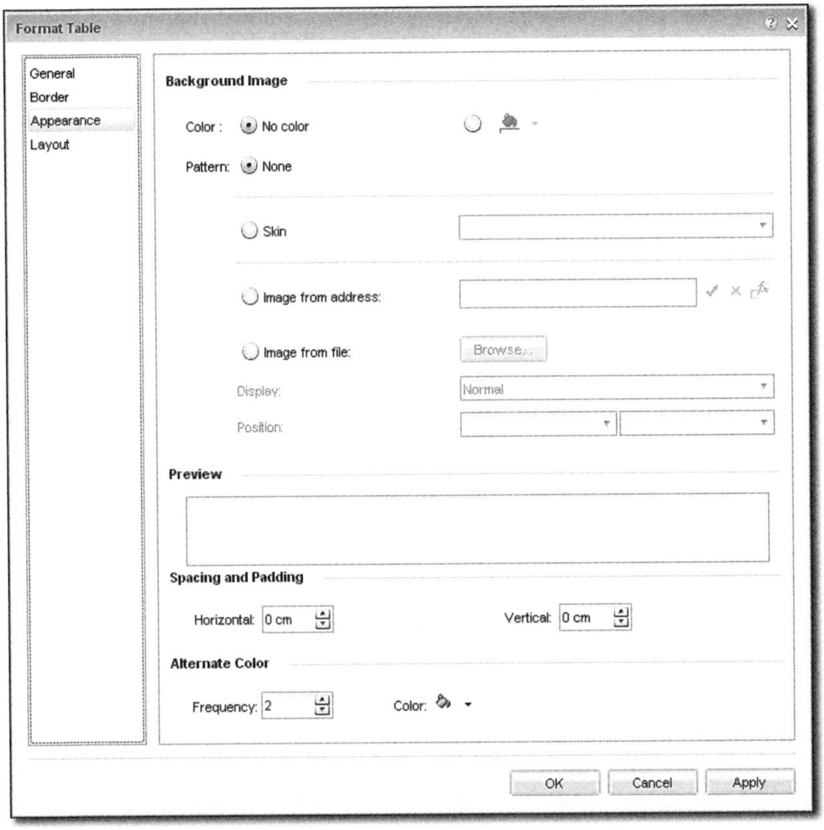

Figure 6.9 Appearance Properties of a Vertical Table

Layout Property

The LAYOUT property pane allows you to assign a variety of positioning settings to report elements in a report. Figure 6.10 shows the properties that can be specified for table layouts. Following is a complete list of page layout properties for both a horizontal and vertical table layout:

▶ START ON A NEW PAGE
Sets the block to start on a new page.

▶ AVOID PAGE BREAK
Fits the table on one page where possible.

▶ REPEAT ON EVERY PAGE
Sets the cell to repeat on every new page.

▶ REPEAT HEADER ON EVERY PAGE
Repeats the table header on every page.

▶ REPEAT FOOTER ON EVERY PAGE
Repeats the table footer on every page.

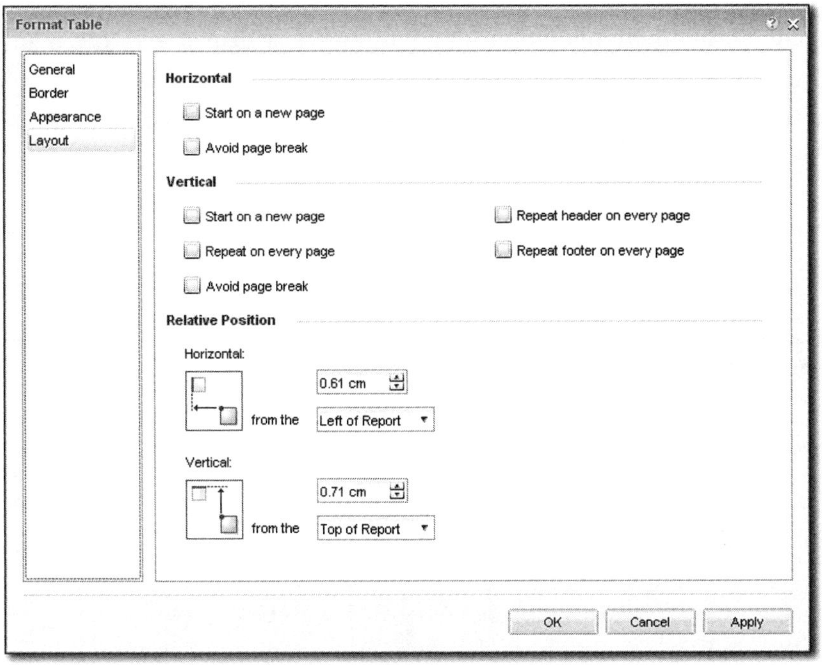

Figure 6.10 Layout Properties of Vertical and Horizontal Tables

You can assign the upper-left corner of a table, chart, or cell to another block by choosing two settings in the RELATIVE POSITION section of the LAYOUT screen: the left edge and the top edge.

6.1.3 Grouping

One of the top new features introduced in SAP BusinessObjects BI 4.1 is the capability to create custom groups of dimensional values. Previously only available in Desktop Intelligence, this simple, but extremely powerful, feature is one of the most requested functions by Web Intelligence report developers.

Up to this point, you would have had to write compound IF statements in a formula or variable to accomplish custom grouping. And depending on the number of conditions, this methodology could become a lengthy and manual process. But now in SAP BusinessObjects BI 4.1, custom groupings can be created with ease.

The reason that grouping is featured in this chapter on displaying data with tables is because you must be working within a data table in order to create a new custom grouping.

Figure 6.11 shows the GROUP function located in the primary ANALYSIS tab and DISPLAY subtab. In the image, the City object is selected from a vertical table and then the GROUP function becomes enabled. As with all other changes, grouping must be added while in design mode.

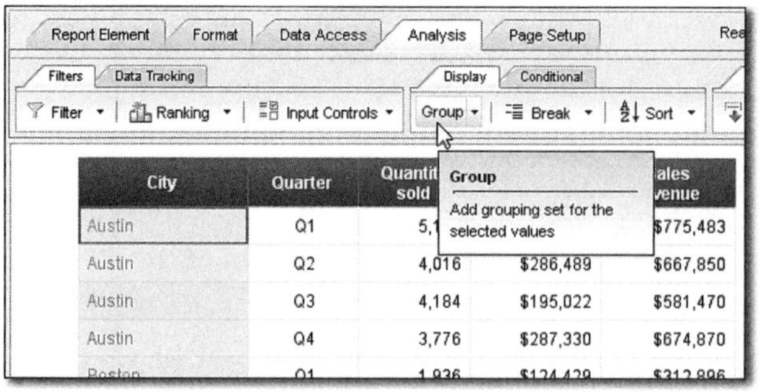

Figure 6.11 Creating a New Custom Group Based on a Dimension Object

> **Note**
>
> A dimensional object must be selected from a report element data table before the GROUP function will become enabled.

After selecting a dimensional object and clicking the GROUP function, the MANAGE GROUPS window, as shown in Figure 6.12, will appear. This is where you'll have an opportunity to select a custom set of values and add them to the same group.

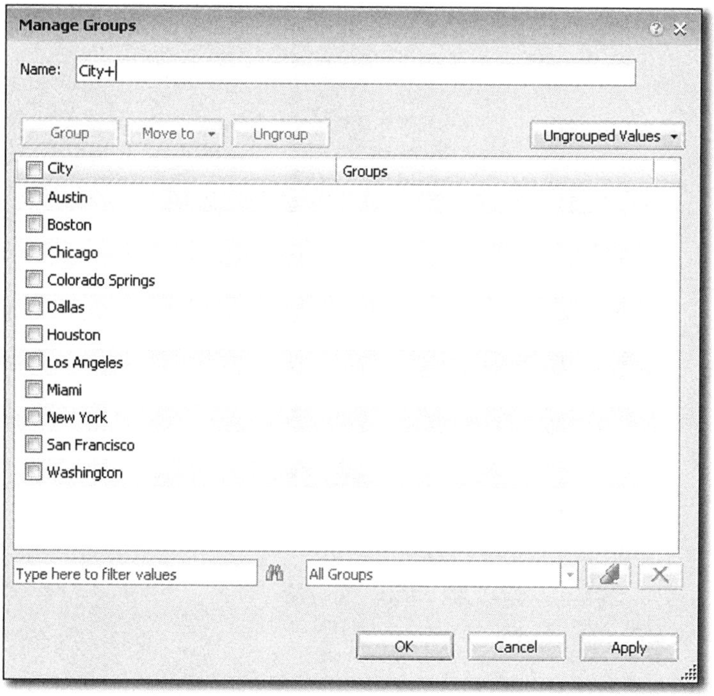

Figure 6.12 Managing Custom Groups

Steps for Creating Custom Groups

The following are the two basic ways to create custom groups:

▶ Select all dimensional values, and then uncheck the unneeded values.

▶ Select only the values that should be assembled into the same group.

After the desired combination of values has been selected, click the GROUP button to assign them to a group. By default, the NEW GROUP name will be the first value selected followed by a + symbol. This name can be easily changed to something more meaningful.

Figure 6.13 shows the New Group window with the default name of the group being added. Change the name to a word or phrase that will clearly describe the collection of values to your users. Click OK to confirm and proceed.

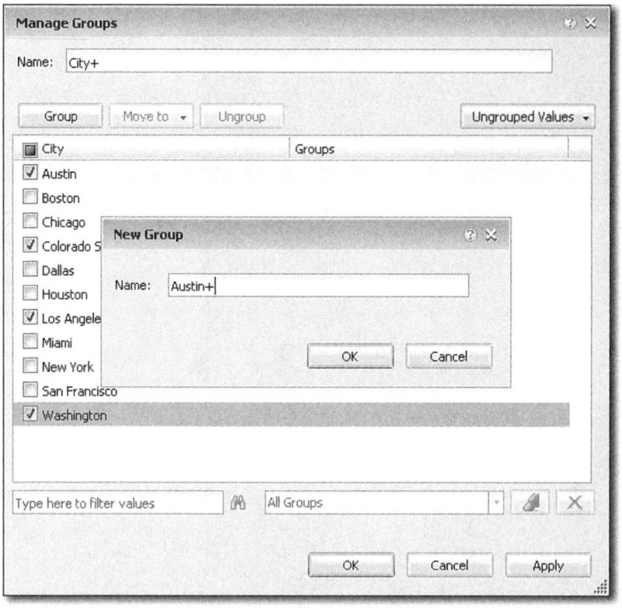

Figure 6.13 Naming a New Custom Group

After a new group has been created, the group name will be displayed along with all the other values available in the dimension object. This helps you to identify the remaining values that have not been assigned to a group, as shown in Figure 6.14.

Note

After setting up the first group, you have three options:

▶ Create additional groups for values that have not been assigned to a group.
▶ Leave the values as they are so individual dimensional values can be compared to the new custom group(s).
▶ Assign the remaining values to an Others group.

The final option just listed, assigning the remaining values to an Others group, is done by first clicking the Ungrouped Values button in the Manage Groups window.

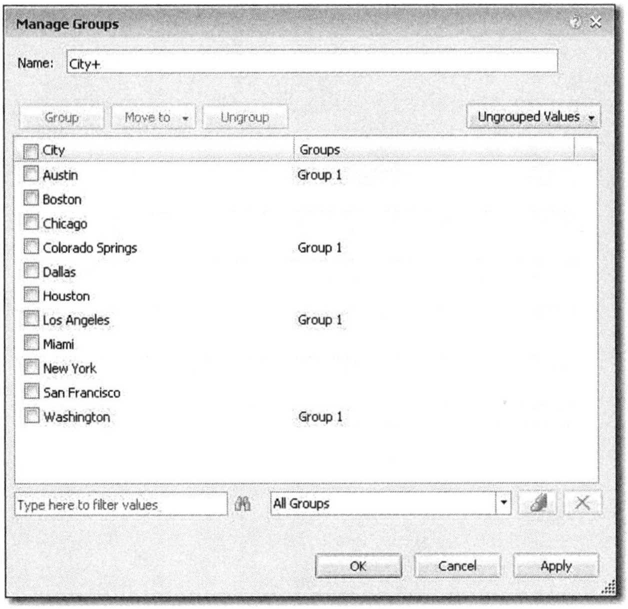

Figure 6.14 Dimension Objects with Custom Groups Listed

The next step is to select the AUTOMATICALLY GROUPED option, as displayed in Figure 6.15. Selecting this choice will prompt you to enter a group name for the remaining values. The default name of "Others" can be changed to a more meaningful word or phrase.

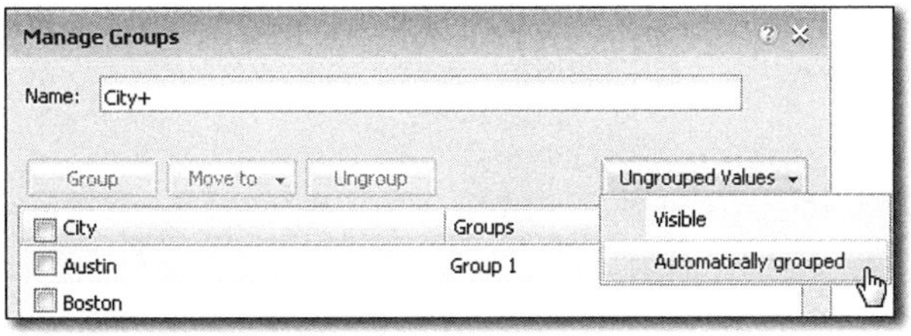

Figure 6.15 Assigning Ungrouped Values to be Automatically Grouped

Now all values will have a group name associated to them. Figure 6.16 shows all of the City objects with a group name assigned to them.

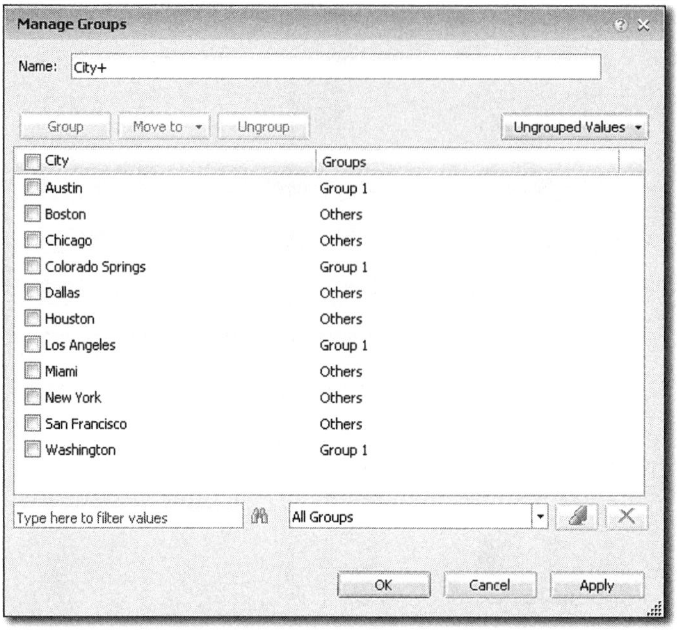

Figure 6.16 All Values with a Group Name Assigned

Custom Group Values in a Table

After creating your new group(s), you'll see the group names as column values in your data table. This can help you aggregate values to fit custom business requirements and even create custom hierarchies by combining groups with breaks. Figure 6.17 shows the table with the new group added.

City+	Quarter	Quantity sold	Margin	Sales revenue
Group 1	Q1	20,601	$1,230,077	$3,197,164
Group 1	Q2	17,242	$1,189,519	$2,854,778
Group 1	Q3	20,376	$985,482	$2,892,638
Group 1	Q4	16,634	$1,284,778	$2,998,246
Others	Q1	41,207	$2,557,721	$6,532,696
Others	Q2	37,164	$2,677,210	$6,271,284

Figure 6.17 Custom Group Values in the Data Table

After a group has been created, you can perform any of the following tasks:

▶ MOVE TO GROUP
Click a specific value to assign it to a different group.

▶ UNGROUP
Return the grouped dimension to its original state.

▶ RENAME THE SELECTED GROUP
Change the group name of the value selected.

▶ UNGROUPED VALUES
Toggle between making the ungrouped values either VISIBLE or AUTOMATICALLY GROUPED.

▶ MANAGE GROUPS
Launch the MANAGE GROUPS window so you can regroup dimensional values.

These options are available by clicking on a grouped object and then clicking the small down arrow beside the GROUP icon in the ANALYSIS/DISPLAY tabs (see Figure 6.18).

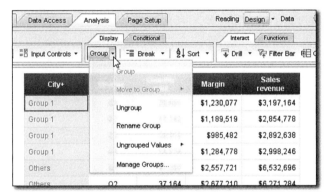

Figure 6.18 Interacting with an Existing Custom Group

Next we'll discuss another new SAP BusinessObjects BI 4.1 feature: freezing header rows and columns.

6.1.4 Freezing Header Rows and Columns

With the primary strength of Web Intelligence being its ability to handle large data sets and crunch results in highly analytical reports, freezing headers has been a much requested feature for several years. The wait is over—now in SAP BusinessObjects BI 4.1—freezing header rows and columns is a default feature.

Freezing headers is helpful because it keeps the header of a data table visible as you scroll through a report to review results. In the past, an analyst might be reviewing results with several hundred rows of data and then lose track of the column names. This is no longer a problem when you enable the new FREEZE HEADER ROWS and FREEZE LEFT COLUMNS settings.

Enabling Freeze

Freezing headers is one of the few features that isn't enabled while in design mode; this option can only be enabled when reading a report.

There are only two requirements for enabling freeze headers:

▶ View the report in reading mode.
▶ Select a data table.

Even in reading mode, the FREEZE option will be disabled until either a table header or the table values are selected. Figure 6.19 shows the FREEZE icon in the toolbar while it's disabled.

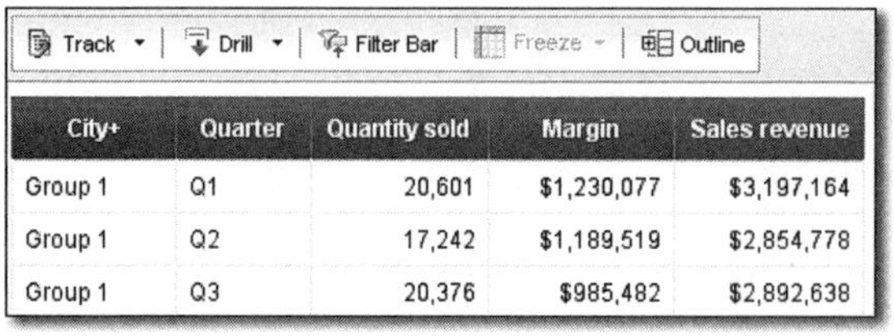

Figure 6.19 Disabled Freeze Icon

Clicking anywhere in the table will enable the FREEZE icon to make it clickable. Clicking FREEZE will set the FREEZE HEADER ROWS option to on. Clicking it a second time will turn it off.

With a row or column in a table selected, click the small downward arrow to examine the additional Freeze options. From here, you'll be able to turn the FREEZE HEADER ROWS option to either on or off (checked or unchecked) and also to enable FREEZE LEFT COLUMNS. You'll have the option to freeze up to the first five columns in a table with this feature enabled. Figure 6.20 shows these options.

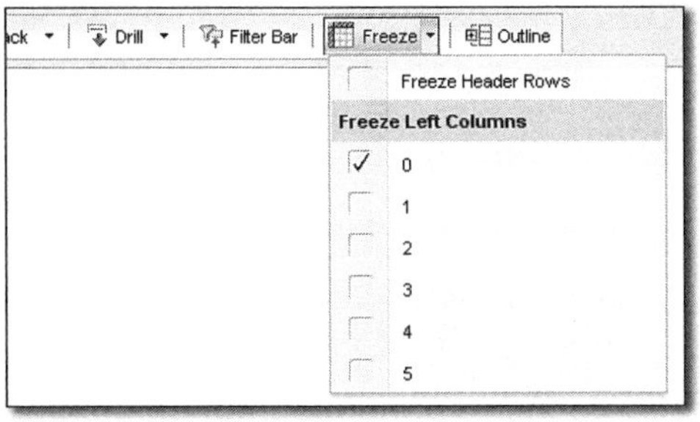

Figure 6.20 Freeze Options

Freezing columns is a very useful feature when analyzing reports with a large number of columns. As you scroll to the right to view the values in each additional column, the first five columns can be configured to display at all times, making analysis easier.

Figure 6.21 shows a small table with FREEZE HEADER ROWS enabled.

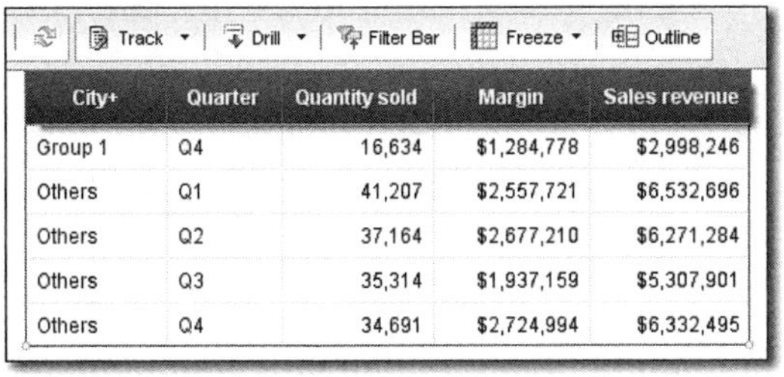

City+	Quarter	Quantity sold	Margin	Sales revenue
Group 1	Q4	16,634	$1,284,778	$2,998,246
Others	Q1	41,207	$2,557,721	$6,532,696
Others	Q2	37,164	$2,677,210	$6,271,284
Others	Q3	35,314	$1,937,159	$5,307,901
Others	Q4	34,691	$2,724,994	$6,332,495

Figure 6.21 Scrolling through a Report with Freeze Header Rows Enabled

Freezing one left column is shown in Figure 6.22 while a report is scrolled to the right. Frozen columns are easily identified with a subtle shadow on the right edge.

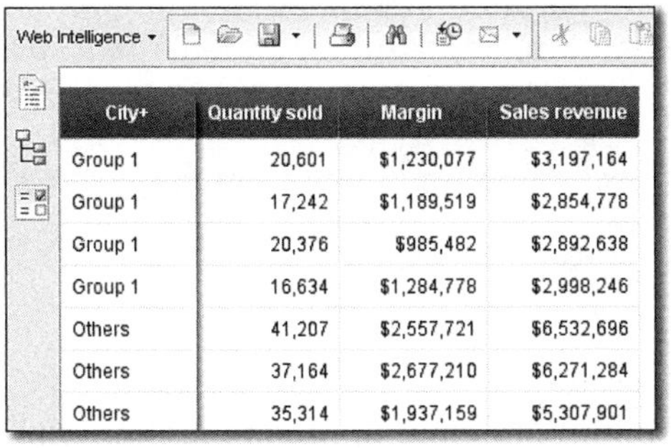

City+	Quantity sold	Margin	Sales revenue
Group 1	20,601	$1,230,077	$3,197,164
Group 1	17,242	$1,189,519	$2,854,778
Group 1	20,376	$985,482	$2,892,638
Group 1	16,634	$1,284,778	$2,998,246
Others	41,207	$2,557,721	$6,532,696
Others	37,164	$2,677,210	$6,271,284
Others	35,314	$1,937,159	$5,307,901

Figure 6.22 Scrolling through a Report with a Frozen Column

The next section discusses the types of data tables available for you to use in the Report Panel of a Web Intelligence reporting document.

6.2   Table Types

Four table types are available in Web Intelligence SAP BusinessObjects BI 4.1:

▶ HORIZONTAL TABLE
Header cells are listed on the left of the table.

▶ VERTICAL TABLE
Header cells are listed on the top of the table.

▶ CROSS TABLE
Dimensions are listed across the top and along the left side of the table. Measures are displayed in the body as a cross-section of the charted dimensions. These are also known as crosstabs.

▶ FORM TABLE
These tables are commonly used to display small groups of related information such as addresses or employee information.

Let's take a look at each table type.

6.2.1   Horizontal Table

Figure 6.23 shows a horizontal table populated with five result objects: State, City, Sales revenue, Quantity sold, and Margin.

State	California	California	Colorado	DC	Florida	Illinois
City	Los Angeles	San Francisco	Colorado Springs	Washington	Miami	Chicago
Sales revenue	$4,220,929	$3,258,641	$2,060,275	$2,961,950	$1,879,158	$3,022,658
Quantity sold	26,244	19,830	12,787	18,744	11,267	17,976
Margin	$1,668,395	$1,304,515	$808,149	$1,153,001	$777,281	$1,254,093

Figure 6.23 Horizontal Table Populated with Five Result Objects

6.2.2   Vertical Table

The vertical table and the cross table are the most commonly used tables. Figure 6.24 displays a vertical table populated with the same result objects as in Figure 6.23.

Note

You can easily add vertical tables to a report by selecting multiple result objects in the AVAILABLE OBJECTS tab and then dragging and dropping them onto the Report Panel.

State	City	Sales revenue	Quantity sold	Margin
California	Los Angeles	$4,220,929	26,244	$1,668,395
California	San Francisco	$3,258,641	19,830	$1,304,515
Colorado	Colorado Springs	$2,060,275	12,787	$808,149
DC	Washington	$2,961,950	18,744	$1,153,001
Florida	Miami	$1,879,158	11,267	$777,281
Illinois	Chicago	$3,022,658	17,976	$1,254,093
Massachusetts	Boston	$1,283,707	7,676	$511,684
New York	New York	$7,582,221	46,358	$3,072,744

Figure 6.24 Vertical Table Populated with Five Result Objects

6.2.3 Cross Table

Figure 6.25 shows a cross table with two dimension objects and a measure.

	California	Colorado	DC	Florida	New York
Accessories	$1,869,006	$565,625	$841,711	$524,750	$2,248,134
City Skirts	$74,934	$17,537	$24,245	$16,804	$80,192
City Trousers	$48,184	$12,977	$20,933	$13,811	$75,984
Dresses	$555,253	$160,249	$220,425	$151,545	$660,168
Jackets	$152,835	$27,371	$51,814	$28,203	$138,313
Leather	$73,189	$14,916	$14,340	$6,664	$24,232
Outerwear	$200,696	$52,644	$81,257	$57,855	$306,859
Overcoats	$81,364	$24,386	$31,208	$16,348	$111,569
Shirt Waist	$824,658	$195,711	$368,226	$178,024	$771,176
Sweaters	$502,669	$157,155	$180,686	$151,992	$695,291
Sweat-T-Shirts	$2,788,298	$773,185	$1,006,242	$716,471	$2,330,098
Trousers	$308,484	$58,521	$120,864	$16,691	$140,204

Figure 6.25 Cross Table with Two Dimension Objects and a Measure

Figure 6.26 shows a cross table that contains the same fields as in Figure 6.25, but the dimension objects across the top and along the left side of the table have switched positions to provide the user a different perspective when analyzing the data.

Cross tables are often referred to as *pivot tables* because of their ability to pivot or switch the dimension objects from the top and left sides of the table.

Swap the dimensions to pivot the table

	Accessories	City Skirts	City Trousers	Dresses	Jackets
California	$1,862,006	$74,934	$48,184	$555,253	$152,835
Colorado	$565,625	$17,537	$12,977	$160,249	$27,371
DC	$841,711	$24,245	$20,933	$220,425	$51,814
Florida	$524,750	$16,804	$13,811	$151,545	$28,203
Illinois	$914,886	$16,709	$20,890	$203,858	$54,477
Massachusetts	$104,874	$11,453	$7,912	$142,857	$23,847
New York	$2,248,134	$80,192	$75,984	$660,168	$138,313
Texas	$2,845,561	$105,901	$84,044	$821,267	$200,447

Figure 6.26 Cross Table Displayed with Five Result Objects

6.2.4 Form Table

A form table is most commonly used to display information relating to customers, employees, addresses, or other sets of closely related fields and objects. It is recommended that you add a dimension object at the top of the form table with detail objects added beneath the related dimension item.

Figure 6.27 shows where to drop an object in a form table so it appears as the second dimension in the table.

Year	2004
Quarter	Q1
Year	=[Quantity sold]
Quarter	Q2

Figure 6.27 Object Added to an Existing Form Table

Figure 6.28 shows the finished result of the action displayed in Figure 6.27.

Year	2004
Quarter	Q1
Quantity sold	18,136

Year	2004
Quarter	Q2
Quantity sold	14,408

Figure 6.28 Form Table Displayed with Three Result Objects

The next section discusses the process of converting or turning existing report elements into different display types. You can turn charts into cross tables or vice versa in just a few clicks.

6.3 Converting Table Formats and Types

Tables can be quickly converted to other table types or report element types by right-clicking on a table and selecting TURN INTO. Figure 6.29 shows a vertical table selected and the right-click menu displayed.

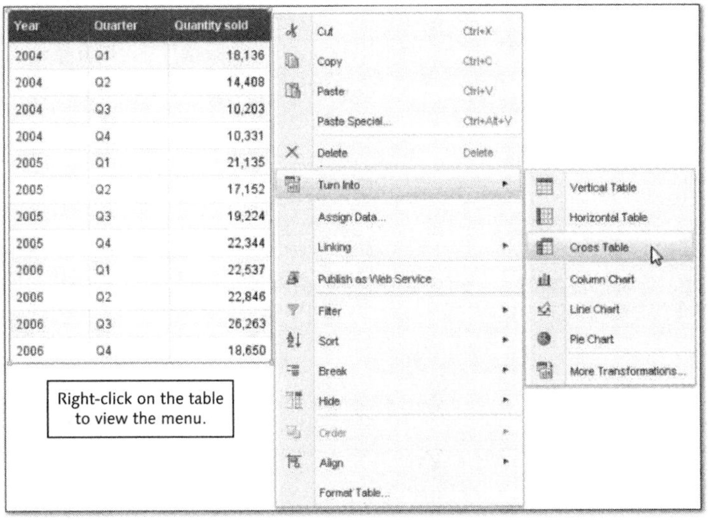

Figure 6.29 Right-Click Menu with a Table Selected

Note

To copy and paste a report element, right-click on the table or chart, and click on COPY. Then right-click in the REPORT PANEL, and click on PASTE.

The commonly used procedure of pressing [Ctrl]+[C] followed by [Ctrl]+[V] can also be used to copy and paste report elements in the Report Panel.

When a report is in design mode and TURN INTO is selected by right-clicking on a table or chart, a MORE TRANSFORMATIONS option will be displayed to provide users with more report element choices outside of the six types listed. This option allows you to change the data table to any table or chart with one more click.

Figure 6.30 shows the TURN INTO window that is used to convert the current report element to a different element or component type. This option is available when MORE TRANSFORMATIONS is selected.

The current report element type is selected by default, and a visual representation of the element type appears, as shown in Figure 6.30.

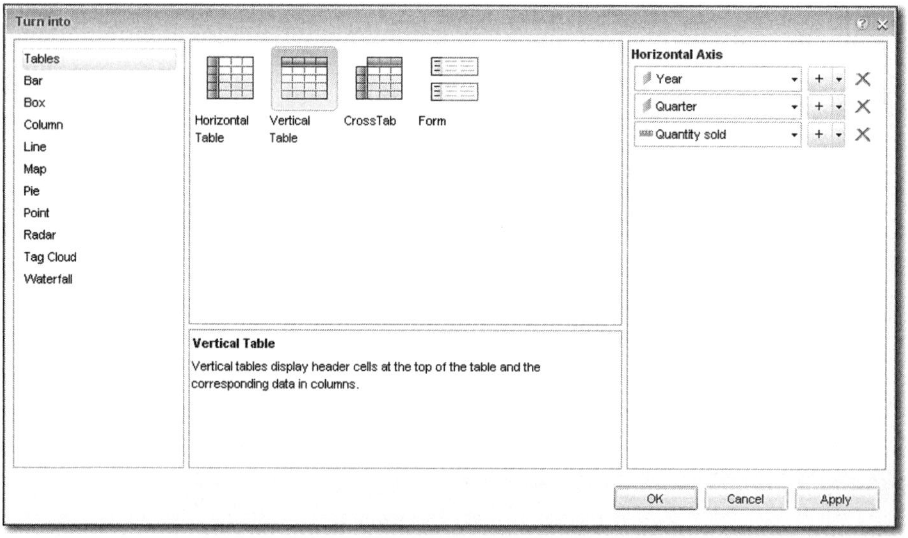

Figure 6.30 Turn Into Window for More Transformations

The next section discusses the use of single blank cells in a report.

6.4   Blank and Predefined Cells

Blank and predefined cells are flexible report elements that can be used for a variety of purposes. These cells can be placed anywhere in the report canvas and can be used for many functional reasons such as displaying informational text, last refreshed dates, and listing drill filter selections and values.

6.4.1   Blank Cells

Blank cells, as shown in Figure 6.31, can be used to enhance reports by providing many different descriptive pieces of information. Examples of common uses for blank cells include adding them to display headings, subheadings, instructions, contact information, refresh dates, text labels, single values, formulas, or calculations.

Figure 6.31 Blank Cell Element Provided in the Report Element Tab

Insert the blank cell report element to strategically place text labels, headings, or other custom values in a report to provide a better context for report consumers. With the blank cell element, you also have the capability to create hyperlinks to other reporting documents, link to an SAP BusinessObjects Dashboards flash object, or link to a website.

Chapter 15 will go into more detail about hyperlinking in reports.

6.4.2   Predefined Cells

The following nine predefined cells are available in the CELL subtab under the primary REPORT ELEMENT tab. You can use these cells to insert a specific element of information into a report by inserting the object into the report canvas:

▶ DOCUMENT NAME

Displays the name of the Web Intelligence document. The `DocumentName ()` formula is used in this object.

▶ LAST REFRESH DATE

Object used to display the last refresh date of the query in a Web Intelligence document. If two or more queries exist in the document, a DATA PROVIDER window will prompt you to select the query to identify the last refresh. The `LastExecutionDate ()` formula is used in this object.

▶ DRILL FILTER

A single cell object containing the `DrillFilters ()` function. This function becomes useful when dynamic headings or subheadings are required to display the dimensional selections made by users when objects are added to the report filter toolbar.

▶ QUERY SUMMARY

Provides many details relating to the query or queries in the document, including query name, universe name, last refresh date, execution duration, number of rows retrieved, and result objects returned. The `Query Summary ()` function is used in this object.

▶ PROMPT

   ▶ SUMMARY: Displays the details of prompted filters. The `PromptSummary ()` function is used in this object.

   ▶ PROMPTED RESPONSES: When prompts are added in the Query Panel, answers to the prompts can be easily grabbed now in SAP BusinessObjects BI 4.1 with this new feature that translates to `UserResponse("prompt text")`.

▶ REPORT FILTER SUMMARY

Provides details on the filters used in the Report Panel of a document. The function `ReportFilterSummary ()` is used in this object.

▶ PAGE NUMBER

Uses the function `Page ()` to display the page number.

▶ PAGE NUMBER/TOTAL PAGES

This cell uses the following functions concatenated together to display the current page number followed by the total number of pages in the document: `Page()+"/"+NumberOfPages ()`. The end result will be displayed as 1/16 for page 1 of 15. This formula can be modified to display Page 1 of 16 rather than 1/16 by using the following formula: `="Page "+Page()+" of "+NumberOfPages()`.

▶ TOTAL NUMBER OF PAGES

Displays the total number of pages in a report. The function `NumberOfPages ()` is used in this object.

Figure 6.32 shows all available predefined cells that you can drag and drop onto the report canvas.

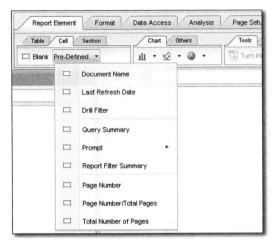

Figure 6.32 Predefined Cells in the Ribbon Toolbar under the Report Element Tab

6.5 Summary

Tables are the components used by Web Intelligence to visually deliver data in a reporting document. Remember that you can use four different types of tables to present table data, and you can adjust properties settings to modify every aspect of a table report element. And now in SAP BusinessObjects BI 4.1, you can quickly and easily add custom groupings to your data tables, freeze header rows, and freeze left columns.

Tables offer the convenience of quickly adding result objects and variables to a report to view data returned from your queries. Table data can be grouped into sections or include breaks to create visually separate groups—all with a single table report element. Enable users to quickly convert table objects into charts with as few as two clicks, and use blank or predefined cells to enhance reports to display single value calculations, dynamic headings, hyperlinks, and page numbers.

Chapter 7 will provide an in-depth discussion of displaying data with charts and describe all of the features in the powerful charting engine of SAP BusinessObjects BI 4.1.

You can graphically display business data in Web Intelligence 4.1 reports from 26 different chart types available in 10 different categories. By adding charts to sections, you can visually present business data in multiple chart instances by using only a single object.

7 Displaying Data with Charts

Web Intelligence received a major upgrade in version 4.0 with a new charting engine that provided notably enhanced visual and functional capabilities. The powerful charting capabilities continues in SAP BusinessObjects BI 4.1 with a new chart type, custom color palettes, and new formatting properties for adding custom touches to your charts. Each chart type includes an extensive set of adjustable properties for designing reports that meet any business requirement and display standard.

You can quickly make a visual impact with reports by using one or more of the 26 chart elements to present information. Charts complement data in reports by allowing users to discover data trends graphically, identify issues, and pinpoint outliers at a glance. By using the most appropriate chart for each unique business scenario, you can build powerful reporting applications. Figure 7.1 shows the different report element categories in the left-hand panel, along with the seven column chart types available.

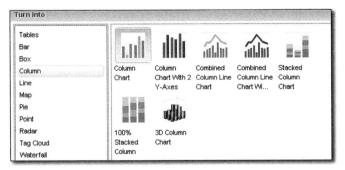

Figure 7.1 Categories of Chart Type Report Elements

In addition to displaying data, charts can function as clickable and interactive objects with the new *element linking* feature delivered in SAP BusinessObjects BI 4.0, or by enabling *drill*. The drill feature provides the capability for charts or data tables to dynamically navigate up or down a dimensional hierarchy setup at the universe level and reveal details at different levels.

Let's first examine how to add chart elements to a report.

7.1   Adding Charts to a Report

You can use two basic methods to add charts to a report, both of which are only available while working in design mode or while you are editing a report.

The first method is accessed by clicking on the REPORT ELEMENT tab in the REPORT PANEL and then choosing either the CHART or OTHERS subtab, depending on the chart category required. Figure 7.2 shows these tabs with the CHART tab selected.

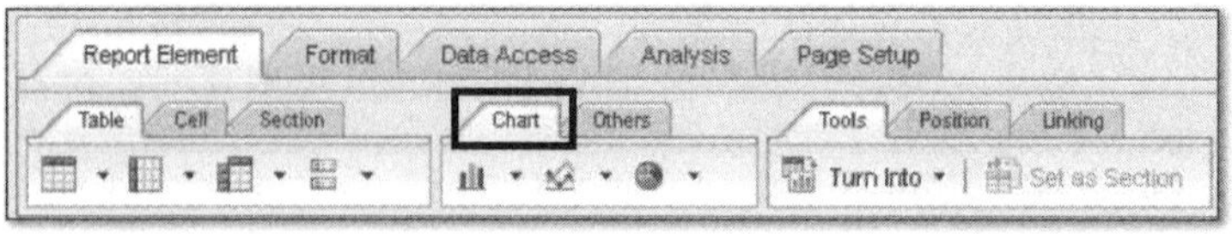

Figure 7.2 Adding Common Chart Components from the Report Element Tab

The three most commonly used chart categories are available from within the CHART tab. From this tab, you can quickly add any of 12 different types of column, line, and pie charts to your reports. Additionally, there are options for selecting MORE COLUMN CHARTS, MORE LINE CHARTS, and MORE PIE CHARTS by clicking the down arrow to the right of each chart category, as pictured in Figure 7.3. Clicking MORE COLUMN CHARTS will reveal all seven of column chart types.

Select the OTHERS tab to add bar charts, point charts, or a noncategorized chart type to your report canvas. Figure 7.4 indicates how to access these chart types with the OTHERS tab selected.

Click on the small down arrow located immediately to the right of each chart category to display several specific chart types within the selected category. The following section describes each of these chart types.

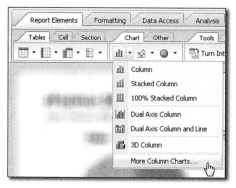

Figure 7.3 Column Chart Options

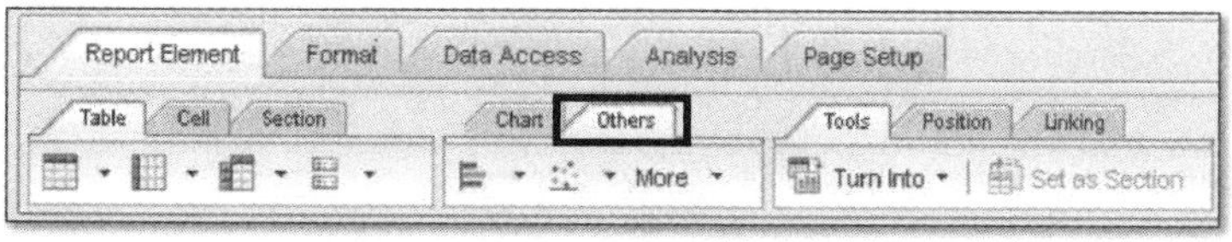

Figure 7.4 Adding Chart Components from the Others Tab

Another way to add charts to a report is by right-clicking on a report canvas. From the right-click menu, mouse over INSERT to view several report elements that can be easily added. This option provides a quick way of inserting a new section, data table, chart, or other type of report element into a report.

Figure 7.5 shows the right-click menu and the choices available after hovering over INSERT. After you make your selection from the list of available choices, you are guided to pick an area on the report canvas to place the element. Click on INSERT A REPORT ELEMENT to view a menu containing every type of report element.

Figure 7.6 shows the INSERT A REPORT ELEMENT window that provides easy access to every chart type or data table grouped into functional report element categories. Select a report element category from the menu to display the available chart types associated with the selection.

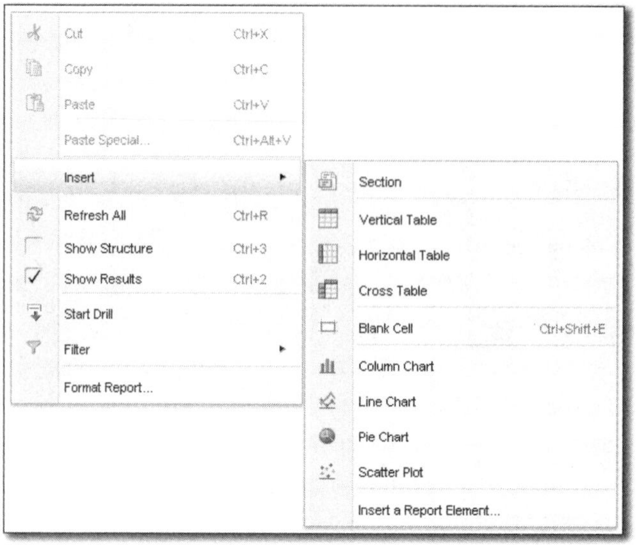

Figure 7.5 Right-Clicking on a Report Canvas and Then Hovering Over Insert

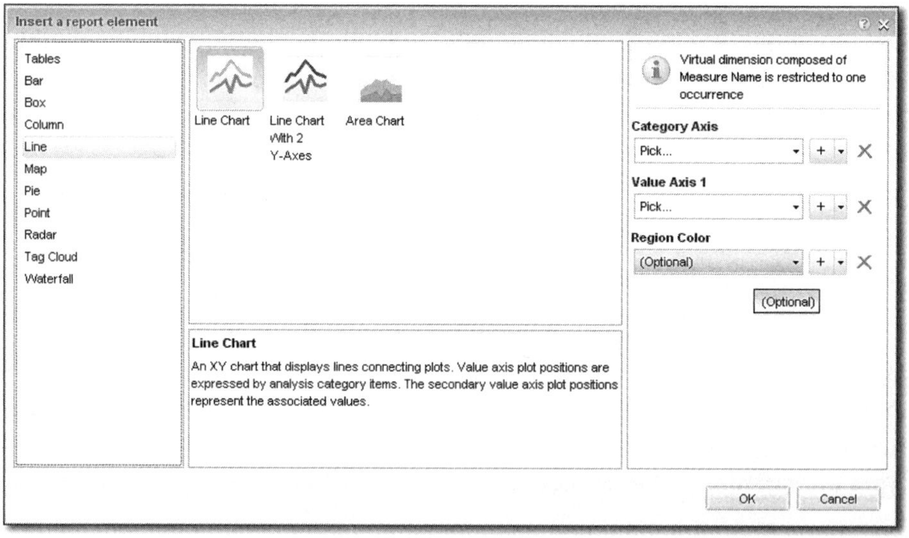

Figure 7.6 Inserting a Report Element

Notice that the tools used for assigning data values to the selected report element are listed on the right side of the window. These tools deliver three basic functions:

▶ **Select an object**
Select from any of the available objects in the document. This includes objects retrieved by a query or variables created locally.

▶ **Add an additional object**
Click on the plus (+) symbol or downward arrow symbol to insert, hide, edit, or select a number format of a numerical object.

▶ **Remove an object**
Click on the X symbol to remove any optional object.

Now that we've covered how to add a chart to a report, let's shift our attention to differentiating between the various types of charts that are available to you.

7.2 Chart Types

A single Web Intelligence report can contain any combination of report elements, and several different charts can appear on the same report. The variety of chart types available provides report designers with the tools needed to create highly customized reporting documents that target the unique needs of displaying complex data while also meeting user requirements. This could mean creating reports with row counts in the hundreds of thousands, building interactive and visual reports that function similarly to dashboards, or a combination of both.

Figure 7.7 shows a report that provides a visual alternative to data tables by displaying data in four different types of charts. The extensive set of editable properties for each chart type in SAP BusinessObjects BI 4.1 now makes it possible for designers to customize reports to fit any color scheme or style requirements.

Each chart type provides several different modifiable properties for adjusting the area display, data values, palette and style, background, border, and layout.

Additionally, you can make several modifications to the category axis, value axis, plot area, legend, title, and global features of a bar, column, or line chart. These properties are described in Section 7.3.

Sections and Charts

When sections are added to a report, charts containing the section object will break by the section and appear as multiple charts.

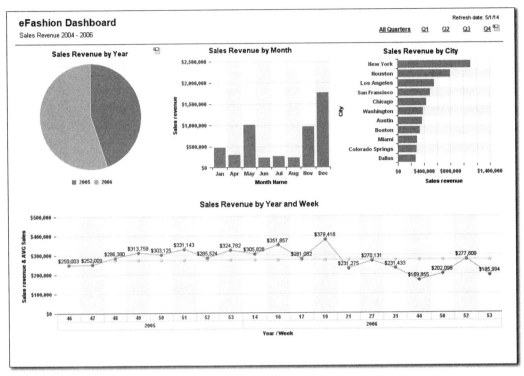

Figure 7.7 Four Charts Types in a Single Report

7.2.1 Column Charts

Column charts display data vertically and are available in seven different types, including dual axis value, combined, stacked, 3D, and basic columnar style. The following is the complete list of column chart types as they're described in the Web Intelligence 4.1 Report Panel:

▶ COLUMN CHART
A chart constructed of vertically oriented rectangular bars. The heights of the rectangles are proportional to the values associated to different category items.

▶ COLUMN CHART WITH 2 Y-AXES
A column chart with two value axes. It allows a part of a data series to be plotted against one axis and a part of the data series to be plotted against the other axis.

▶ COMBINED COLUMN LINE CHART
A chart displaying a combination of a column chart and a line chart. The chart types share the same value axis.

▶ COMBINED COLUMN LINE CHART WITH 2-AXES
A chart displaying a combination of a column chart and a line chart. The chart types have their own value axis.

▶ STACKED COLUMN CHART
A chart constructed of vertically oriented and stacked colored rectangular bars. The heights of the rectangles are proportional to the values associated to different category items. Rectangles are colored according to legend entries.

▶ 100% STACKED COLUMN CHART
A 100% stacked column chart with data displayed as parts of a whole (as percentages). A whole is a column, and a series is a subdivision of the column.

▶ 3D COLUMN CHART
An XYZ column chart. The secondary category axis represents an additional analysis category item.

Column Charts

Column charts, which compare dimensional values from at least one measure and dimension object, are the most commonly used chart types for this task. With the new charting engine introduced in Web Intelligence 4.1, these chart types include more than 200 adjustable properties for customizing chart objects to fit into any visual style.

In fact, 3D column charts allow the same type of comparisons but with a different visual effect. Although 3D chart types are less commonly used than standard column charts, they still provide a useful alternative for communicating results. With a 3D chart, an optional secondary value can be included to visually compare results. Figure 7.8 shows a standard column chart and a 3D column chart with a secondary measure value on the same axis.

Charts are populated with data after they've been added to the report canvas. After you've added the chart, right-click on a chart, and then select ASSIGN DATA from the menu of available choices. Begin assigning dimension or detail objects to the CATEGORY AXIS section and measure objects to the VALUE AXIS section.

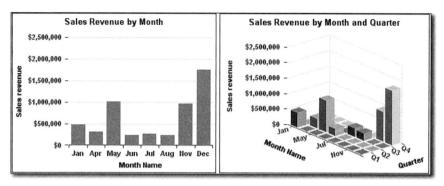

Figure 7.8 Column Chart and 3D Column Chart

Figure 7.9 shows the ASSIGN DATA window used to connect data objects to chart elements. You can assign multiple dimensions and measures to a single chart element, and you can change the column color using the REGION COLOR option.

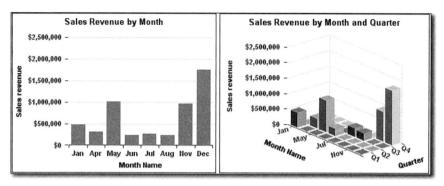

Figure 7.9 Assigning Data to Chart Elements

Dual Value Axes Column Charts

Report designers have several options for displaying multiple measure objects within a single chart. Multiple measures can be displayed in charts on the same axis, but if they have a significantly different factor, they should be displayed on a different axis for readability. Dual value axes chart types are available to handle this requirement.

Figure 7.10 shows a column chart with 2 Y-axes and a combined column line chart with 2 Y-axes. Though both charts display the `Margin` and `Sales revenue` object data, only the version on the right includes a line chart to differentiate the values.

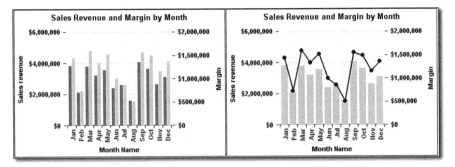

Figure 7.10 Displaying Data in Dual Value Axes Charts

Stacked Column Charts

Stacked column charts are also used to display values from two or more measure objects simultaneously. These chart types should include measure objects representing individual parts of a whole. The 100% stacked column charts also display values as part of a whole but with a 100% scale. Each column in a 100% stacked column chart represents the total value, while the stacked items are the individual parts. Figure 7.11 shows a stacked column chart and a 100% stacked column chart that both contain the `Margin` and `Sales revenue` objects charted by month. You can mouse over each charted data element to view the dimensional description and value of the item. This feature exists for every chart type and is beneficial to users when analyzing data subsets. When drill is enabled, the charted columns and category axis values can be used to navigate up and down the hierarchy of dimensional objects as preconfigured in the universe.

> **Note**
>
> When drill is enabled, mouse-over information for charted measures is displayed. This information is replaced with a statement indicating what will occur if the column is clicked. The message displayed on mouse-over with drill enabled will generally read, *drill up to <dimension object name> or drill down to <dimension object name>*.
>
> You must disable drill to view the charted values on mouse-over.

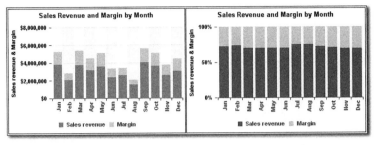

Figure 7.11 Stacked Column Chart and 100% Stacked Column Chart

One requirement of the stacked column chart is to include at least two measure objects and a dimension or detail object. Without a second measure object, the chart will function as a standard column chart.

The 100% stacked column chart also requires at least two measure objects. With only a single measure object, every column would convert to 100%.

Using Column Charts

Column charts are useful when comparing values of single dimensional objects or into dimensional groups for a greater depth of analysis.

The following are a few key advantages of using column charts to display data:

▶ Quickly identify the highest value by spotting the tallest column

▶ Quickly identify the lowest value by spotting the smallest column

▶ Easily compare column sizes

A second dimension object can also be added to a stacked column chart. Visual groupings in the category axis are created when a second dimension object is added. Figure 7.12 shows a stacked column chart with two measures and two dimensions while hovering over the charted revenue value for March.

Figure 7.12 Stacked Column Chart with Two Dimensions and Two Measures

7.2.2   Line Charts

Line charts are primarily used to measure performance over a period of time. When you measure values using line charts, you can quickly identify upward and downward trends over time intervals, reoccurring patterns, and spikes of proportionally high and low values.

Line charts allow users to pinpoint patterns and quickly identify points in time when significant trends start, end, and peak. One method that can be used to easily identify when trends are significant is to add a variable to a line chart that calculates the average of a measure being charted. By adding this additional object, movement of data above or below the average is easily detected. This method of analysis provides an additional visual indicator for the user and helps demonstrate exactly when a measure began trending above or below an average and whether the trend is worthy of further investigation.

Line Chart Types

The following are the three line charts, as described in Web Intelligence 4.1:

▶ LINE CHART
An XY chart that displays lines connecting plots. Value axis plot positions are expressed by analysis category items. The secondary value axis plot positions represent the associated values.

▶ LINE CHART WITH 2 Y-AXES
An XY chart with two axes displaying lines connecting plots. Category axis plot positions signify analysis category items. The value axis plot positions, on both axes represent the associated values.

▶ AREA CHART
An XY chart that displays a surface made up of a connection of plots.

Let's examine each of these now.

Line Chart Types

Standard line charts are the primary component used to display data trends over intervals of time. Use a *line chart with 2 Y-axes* to display the correlative trend of two measures across a specified period of time. These chart types are used when the values are related but are of a significantly different factor.

In Figure 7.13, a standard line chart is presented along with a line chart with dual axes. In the dual axes example, the monthly correlation of the MARGIN and SALES REVENUE measures is displayed. Because the factors of these two measures aren't significantly different, the standard line chart is the most ideal selection.

Figure 7.13 Standard Line Chart and a Line Chart with Dual Axes

Key Applications of Line Charts

► Display data across time.
► Analyze patterns in interval data.
► Identify data shifts in trend data.
► Recognize seasonal cycles.
► Pinpoint high and low spikes in the data.

Area Charts

Area charts—previously known as surface charts—are used to provide a visual representation of data made up of connection plots. These chart types are used in similar scenarios as line charts and display a series of data points connected by a line with the area filled in below the line. Area charts and line charts are the only chart categories intended to display contiguous data.

Web Intelligence 4.1 provides a large number of adjustable properties to modify the appearance of charts. Within these properties is the capability to modify the *region type* of a chart type. You can access this setting by right-clicking on a chart and selecting FORMAT CHART. Locate the GLOBAL property group, and select REGION TYPE. From this window, you can change the type to bars, lines, or surfaces. Select SURFACES as the region type to convert it to an area display. In Figure

7.14, the first area chart shows the Sales Revenue object set to Surfaces, and the Margin object set to Bars. The second chart shows the region type set as Surfaces for both measure objects.

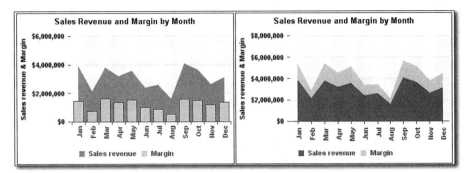

Figure 7.14 Surface Chart and Line Chart with Dual Axes with Surface Region

7.2.3 Pie Charts

Pie charts are used to show dimensional values as a proportion of the whole data set. The pie or donut represents the sum total of a measure, while each slice represents the individual parts that are added together to become the whole.

Only one dimension can exist in a pie chart, and values can't represent over 100% of the measure being evaluated. These are the three chart types available in Web Intelligence 4.1, followed by their descriptions as they appear in the Report Panel:

▶ **Pie chart**
A circular chart made up of sectors. The area of the circle represents a whole, and the sectors of the circle represent the parts of a whole.

▶ **Pie with variable slice depth**
A circular chart made up of sectors. The area of the circle represents a whole,

and the sectors of the circle represent the parts of a whole. The sectors may have some depth expressing a third value.

- **Donut chart**
  A chart similar to a pie chart, but it is ring shaped.

Let's expand on these further.

Pie and Donut Charts

Pie charts are useful when displaying values as proportions of the whole. Data values in pie charts are displayed in slices for each dimension object value and interpreted as a percentage of the whole. Properties can be configured to display several descriptive data labels, including the value, label, percentage, or a combination of two labels. The data label position can be assigned to appear either inside or outside the pie, and the label layout can be positioned on the side of the pie or in a circular layout.

Other attributes can also be enabled or configured, including the following: 3D look, color palette adjustments, textures, light and shadow effects, background color assignment, and border assignments.

Figure 7.15 shows a standard pie chart followed by a donut chart, with both charts displaying the same measure and dimension object.

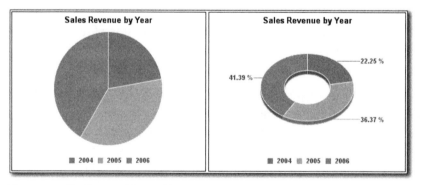

Figure 7.15 Pie Chart and Donut Chart

The donut chart in the example has 3D enabled and displays the percent value of each slice. These values are configured by right-clicking on the chart object and selecting FORMAT CHART. Many of the configurable appearance settings are located within the GLOBAL properties group.

Pie with Variable Slice Depth

A new type of pie chart was introduced in Web Intelligence 4.0 that allows report designers to communicate two values within a single pie chart. This component provides a depth dimension to pie charts and displays values from a second measure through exploding pie slices.

The chart pictured in Figure 7.16 shows values from the Sales revenue and Quantity sold measures in a variable slice depth pie chart by yearly values.

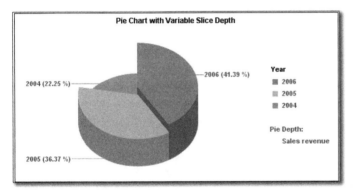

Figure 7.16 Pie Chart with Variable Slice Depth

In the figure, the size of each dimensional slice represents each year's sales revenue as a percentage of the whole group of all three years being reviewed. The depth dimension in the pie chart illustrates the quantity sold by year. It's easy to see a correlation between the two measures when both measures are represented in the same chart.

Charting in Business Reports

When you use variable slice depth pie charts in reports, make sure that the results can be easily interpreted by the intended audience. Misrepresented or misinterpreted data can lead to costly mistakes and potentially catastrophic situations. Always create thoroughly labeled report elements that describe the measures, dimensions, and context of the information being presented. Formula-driven title labels, legends, category values, and data labels should be used when appropriate to thoroughly communicate information to report consumers.

7.2.4 Point Charts

Use scatter charts to plot the values of two variables and to display the correlation in the style of linear regression. Bubble charts display values similar to scatter charts but with varying sizes of bubbles to represent the values of a third variable. Other types of point charts include polar scatter and polar bubble charts; both of these chart types are used to display data points with a radial axis and an angular axis on a circular charting canvas rather than a standard rectangular canvas. Values are spread over 360 degrees, and data points are plotted between two numbers and then located within bands defined by the second variable.

Polar bubble charts go a step further than polar charts because they display a third value and present the bubbles in varying sizes. The following are the four types of point charts, as described in Web Intelligence 4.1:

- **Scatter plot**
  An XY chart displaying plots. Plots are positioned with coordinates given by a pair of values. Each plot may have colored symbols representing the analysis category item associated with the values.

- **Bubble chart**
  A two-dimensional chart of points representing a collection of data. Extra variables are represented by the size of the points.

- **Polar scatter chart**
  A chart with one radial axis and one angular axis, where each data point is represented with a symbol. Similar to a bubble chart, but without the sizing of points.

- **Polar bubble chart**
  A two-dimensional chart with one radial axis and one angular axis of points representing a collection of data. Extra variables are represented by the size of the points.

Scatter Charts

Scatter charts are used to display the correlation between two measure objects. Depending on the relationship of the charted values, trends can be easily observed that illustrate the strength or weakness in the correlation of the variables used to plot the data points. Many analysts view scatter charts as one of the best components for visualizing data and locating trouble areas to investigate further.

Positive trends are observed when the plotted data points ascend on both the X- and Y axes, moving from the lower-left corner of the chart to the upper-right corner. This type of trend is pictured in Figure 7.17. The example shows a linear or straight line trend that proves when QUANTITY SOLD increases, the SALES REVENUE also increases. Even though a trend is observed in the plotted points, you can still identify outliers. The screenshot shows that when the plotted values from July are compared to those from November, Sales revenue was lower in July while the Quantity sold was much higher.

Figure 7.17 Scatter Chart with a Positive Trend Correlating Sales Revenue and Quantity Sold

These findings provide valuable insight into potential revenue issues that deserve additional research. The result of the findings could uncover problems that have caused decreased profits.

Negative trends are observed when one set of data increases while the other decreases. In these scenarios, the plotted data points move in an organized fashion from the upper-left corner of the chart toward the lower-right corner.

If no pattern is observed among the plotted data points, then no relationship exists for the charted variables.

Bubble Charts

Bubble charts produce results very similar to those of scatter charts but with one addition—the potential to add a third variable to the chart to represent the data in bubble sizes. If patterns are observed in the plotted bubbles, then a relationship exists for the variables being charted.

Figure 7.18 shows a bubble chart with the same information displayed in the scatter chart shown in Figure 7.17 but with the addition of increasing bubble sizes to represent the values of a third measure. You can enhance the appearance of the bubbles by making adjustments to several configurable properties available in the FORMAT CHART window. Many of the visual settings can be found when editing settings in the PALETTE AND STYLE section located in the GLOBAL chart settings.

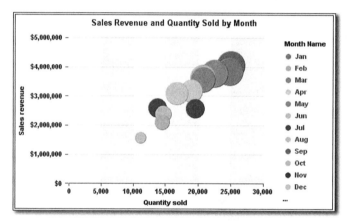

Figure 7.18 Bubble Charts Displaying the Correlation of Two Measures

Polar Charts

Polar charts display a series of values grouped by a dimensional result object on a 360-degree circle. Values are measured by their lengths from the center of the chart. The farther the point is away from the center, the larger the value.

Figure 7.19 shows a polar scatter chart with SALES REVENUE and QUANTITY SOLD values plotted by region. The chart plots the values on the 360-degree canvas by the amount of quantity sold and within multiple sales revenue bands on the circular background.

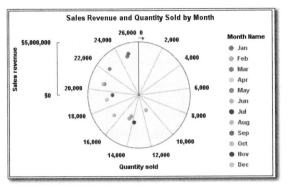

Figure 7.19 Polar Scatter Chart with Two Measures Plotted

Figure 7.20 shows the same values charted on a polar bubble chart but with a third measure added. The polar bubble chart displays bubble sizes based on the relative size of the values in the `Margin` object.

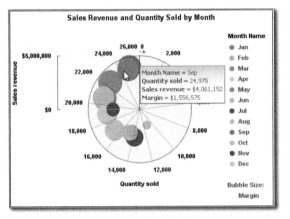

Figure 7.20 Polar Bubble Chart with Three Measures Plotted

7.2.5 Bar Charts

Bar charts produce an effect similar to that of column charts but display information in horizontal bars rather than vertical columns.

You can use bar charts in reports to compare dimensional information with values from at least one measure and dimension object. These chart types are commonly used to present dimensional values so they can be read easier. Figure 7.21

shows a bar chart with the SALES REVENUE measure presented by the LINES dimension. Hover over a bar to see the exact measurement values.

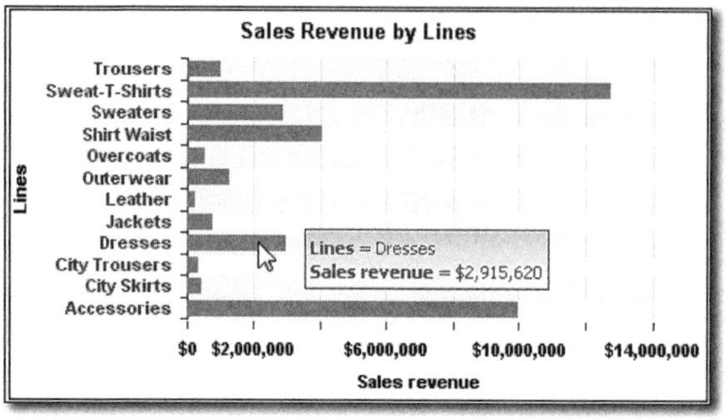

Figure 7.21 Bar Chart

The following bar charts are available for your use:

▶ **Bar chart**
A chart constructed of horizontally oriented rectangular bars. In bar charts, the heights of the rectangles are proportional to the values associated to different category items.

▶ **Horizontal bar chart**
A horizontal bar chart that displays data as a series of bars. It is best used for representing three series of data, where each series is represented by a color stacked in a single bar.

▶ **100% stacked bar**
A stacked bar chart with data displayed as parts of a whole (as percentages). A whole is a bar, and a series is a subdivision of the bar.

When adding stacked bar charts to reports, include at least two measure objects and at least one dimension or detail object. Without a second measure object, the chart will function as a standard bar chart.

The 100% stacked bar chart requires at least two measure objects. With only a single measure object, every column would convert to 100%. You can use this type of chart to present measures as a percent of whole values by a dimension. Figure 7.22 shows two stacked bar charts.

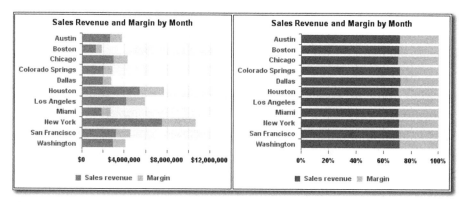

Figure 7.22 Stacked Bar and 100% Stacked Bar Chart

7.2.6 Other Chart Types

Six additional chart types within Web Intelligence 4.1 provide report designers with even more options for displaying data:

▶ **Box plot**
A box plot chart is a graphical display of a five-number summary based on the distribution of a data set: the maximum, the minimum, the first quartile, the third quartile, and the median. It can also show abnormal values called outliers.

▶ **Radar**
A radar chart (also known as a spider chart) displays several axes starting from a unique origin and with a common scale. Each axis represents an analysis category item. Plots are directly placed on an axis according to the associated values. Plots can be linked by lines.

▶ **Tree map**
This chart displays values within nested rectangles that can be colored. The levels of nesting correspond to the level of hierarchical breakdown. The size of the rectangles and their color both express a set of values.

▶ **Heat map**
This chart displays values that are represented by colors in a map using a category axis and optionally a second category axis. The colors of the rectangles are determined by a measure value.

▶ **Tag cloud**
A mono-dimensional visualization representing data as words where the word font size represents its relative weight in the data set.

▶ **Waterfall**
A chart of vertical bars for which each bar starts at the level of the previous one with the goal of showing the cumulative effect of the values of a measure. This type of chart allows you to represent the successive variations of a measure or to show the positive and negative contributions of a measure along the different category items

Let's examine each of these further.

Box Plot and Radar Charts

Box plot charts are used to show the distribution of data ranges for a dimension object into five primary groupings. Each chart will also contain a category dimension to axis value. These charts show the following elements of information in a single graphic:

▶ **Maximum**
The highest value in the chart, excluding outliers.

▶ **First (or upper) quartile**
In the chart, 25% percent of the values are greater than this value.

▶ **Median**
The middle of the data set in the chart.

▶ **Third (or lower) quartile**
In the chart, 75% percent of the values are greater than this value.

▶ **Minimum**
The lowest value in the chart, excluding outliers.

Outliers are displayed in dots and plotted either above the maximum or below the minimum markings. These values can be hidden by checking the HIDE OUTLIERS options located in the PLOT AREA section available when formatting the chart. Figure 7.23 shows the different segments of a charted box plot. Figure 7.24 shows a box plot chart showing the yearly value ranges for values within the Quarter object used as the primary category axis dimension and compares it to a radar chart.

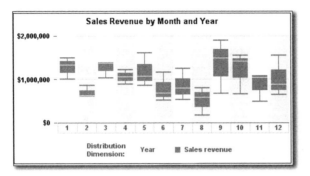

Figure 7.23 Box Plot Ranges

Radar charts are used to quickly convey the "big picture" of one or more variables through a dimensional object. The primary benefit of radar charts is that they allow the user to analyze several different factors related to a single item. The points closest to the center of the axis indicate low values, while the charted points near the edge indicate high values. The right side of Figure 7.24 shows a radar chart displaying Sales revenue and Margin values by region.

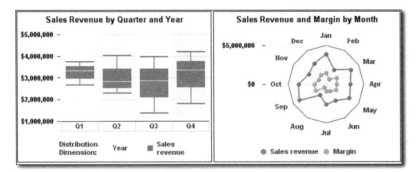

Figure 7.24 Box Plot Chart and Radar Chart

Tree and Heat Map

Tree maps are used for displaying hierarchical data to allow users to quickly identify unexpected patterns, exceptions, and significant factors. Data values are then displayed in rectangular areas of varying sizes, color, and position. Figure 7.25 shows a tree map chart with Sales revenue values charted by Category. You can mouse over the rectangles to show a tooltip that includes the dimension and measure values of the rectangle on the tree.

Heat map charts also display data in rectangular shapes but with a slightly different way of using color. The box style of charted values is also different in the heat map compared to the tree map. Heat maps let you display data from one or more dimensional category axis values and a single measure object; you can add a secondary category axis value when assigning data to a chart.

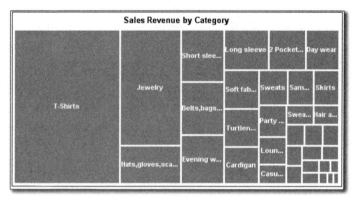

Figure 7.25 Tree Map for Sales Revenue by Category

Tag Cloud

The tag cloud chart is a report element that was first introduced to Web Intelligence in SAP BusinessObjects BI 4.0. This component displays data values by using only the text data in a dimension or detail object. The size of each dimensional value is determined by the associated measure object.

When assigning data to the component, the TAG NAME setting is used to associate a dimension object, and the TAG WEIGHT setting is where the measure object is assigned. Objects used in the TAG NAME should contain values made up of either single words or very short phrases for clearly displaying results. The purpose of the component is to quickly show the prominence of specific terms. Figure 7.26 shows a tag cloud component created using the `Category` object and `Sales revenue` object.

A creative and functional use of this component is to anchor an element link to it for passing values to other report elements on the same report canvas.

Figure 7.26 Tag Cloud Chart

Waterfall Chart

Waterfall charts have historically been used for displaying the cumulative effect of sequential values and illustrating the impact of a measure across a dimensional category. This chart type was new to the Web Intelligence chart repertoire, beginning in Feature Pack 3 in SAP BusinessObjects BI 4.0.

It's customary to include the total values when creating a waterfall chart because many users analyzing data with this type of chart will want to know how the final values relate to the start. The option to include totals as a charted bar is available through a setting in the FORMAT CHART window.

Figure 7.27 shows a simple waterfall chart that displays the impact of the QTY object by month for an entire year.

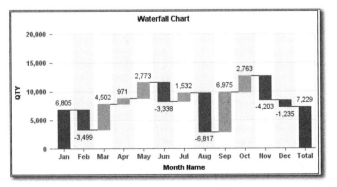

Figure 7.27 Waterfall Chart with a Total Bar and Reference Lines Enabled

237

After launching the FORMAT CHART window, select the GENERAL category found in the GLOBAL property grouping, and then scroll down to the CALCULATE AND SHOW THE TOTAL checkbox. Figure 7.28 shows the setting used to add the total value to the waterfall chart.

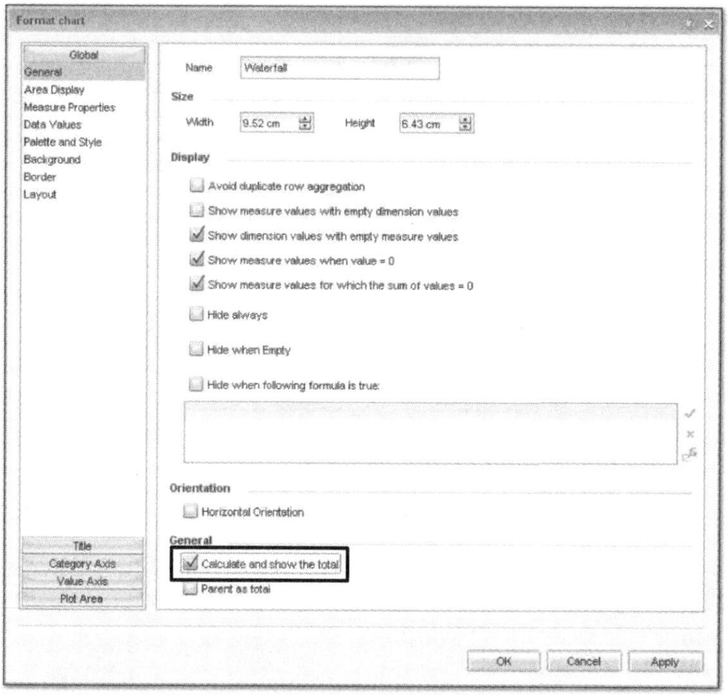

Figure 7.28 Enabling the Totals Bar on the Waterfall Chart

To make the biggest visual impact with a waterfall chart, SAP BusinessObjects BI 4.1 introduced a few helpful settings for displaying key elements:

- START VALUE COLOR
- TOTAL VALUE COLOR
- NEGATIVE VALUE COLOR
- POSITIVE VALUE COLOR

By changing the default setting of these value colors from automatic to a fixed value, report consumers will have an easier time interpreting the results in the chart. These settings make it much easier to locate which dimensions had the biggest positive and negative impacts on the overall totals. Figure 7.29 shows these properties located in the PALETTE AND STYLE category.

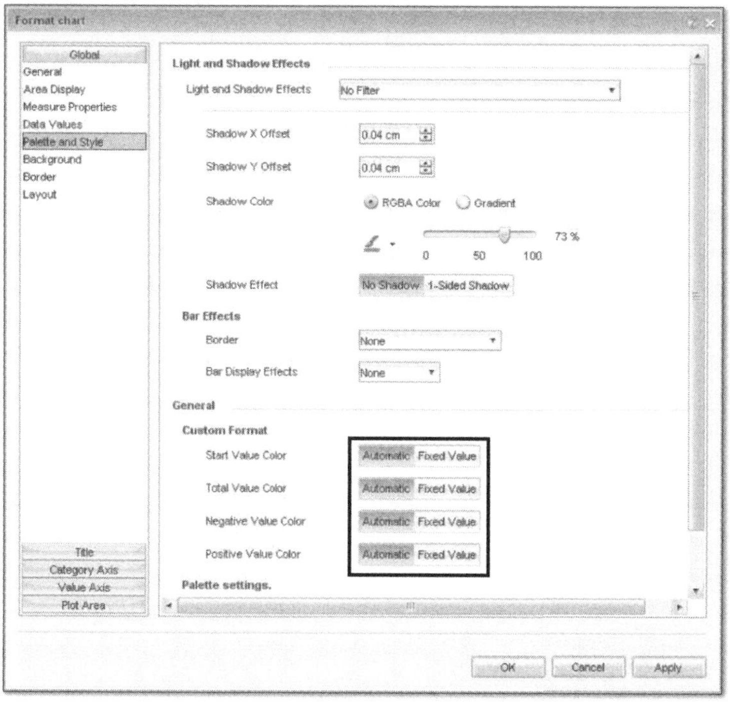

Figure 7.29 Setting Custom Value Colors in a Waterfall Chart

Converting Chart Types

You can easily convert charts into data tables or other chart types by right-clicking on a chart object while in design mode and selecting TURN INTO. This method of converting an existing chart or table provides seven choices: VERTICAL TABLE, HORIZONTAL TABLE, CROSS TABLE, COLUMN CHART, LINE CHART, PIE CHART, and MORE TRANSFORMATIONS. Select the MORE TRANSFORMATIONS option to launch a window that gives you the opportunity to convert the existing chart to any chart group, and then choose from any of the 26 chart types or 4 data table types.

Now that we've examined the various types of charts at your disposal, let's transition to the properties that govern those charts.

7.3 Chart Properties

Chart properties in Web Intelligence 4.1 have been dramatically improved over pre-SAP BusinessObjects BI 4.0 versions of the product. With more than 200 different properties available, report designers have more choices than ever to create highly customized and formatted charts and reports. Each chart type contains its own set of properties for displaying data values, changing the presentation effect and style, and applying formatting to titles, legends, and axis values.

To begin customizing the format of a chart, enter design mode and then right-click on the chart to be edited. With the menu displayed, click on FORMAT CHART to launch the chart editor and begin making changes to the properties and attributes. Chart properties are grouped into the following major categories for logical access:

▶ GLOBAL

▶ TITLE

▶ LEGEND

▶ CATEGORY AXIS

▶ VALUE AXIS

▶ PLOT AREA

Figure 7.30 displays the categories of a column chart. Here, the global properties are listed, and the other five property categories are minimized at the bottom left of the figure.

Each category contains specific properties that can be modified to change the style and visual presentation. To access the individual properties, click on the category groupings located on the left side of the format editor.

You can modify individual properties by selecting the subgroup of each property category and then manipulating the specific options on the right side of the editor. Property subgroups provide an even more detailed collection of properties. Each chart type varies slightly by the number of properties available to each type. Following is a description of the property categories for a column chart:

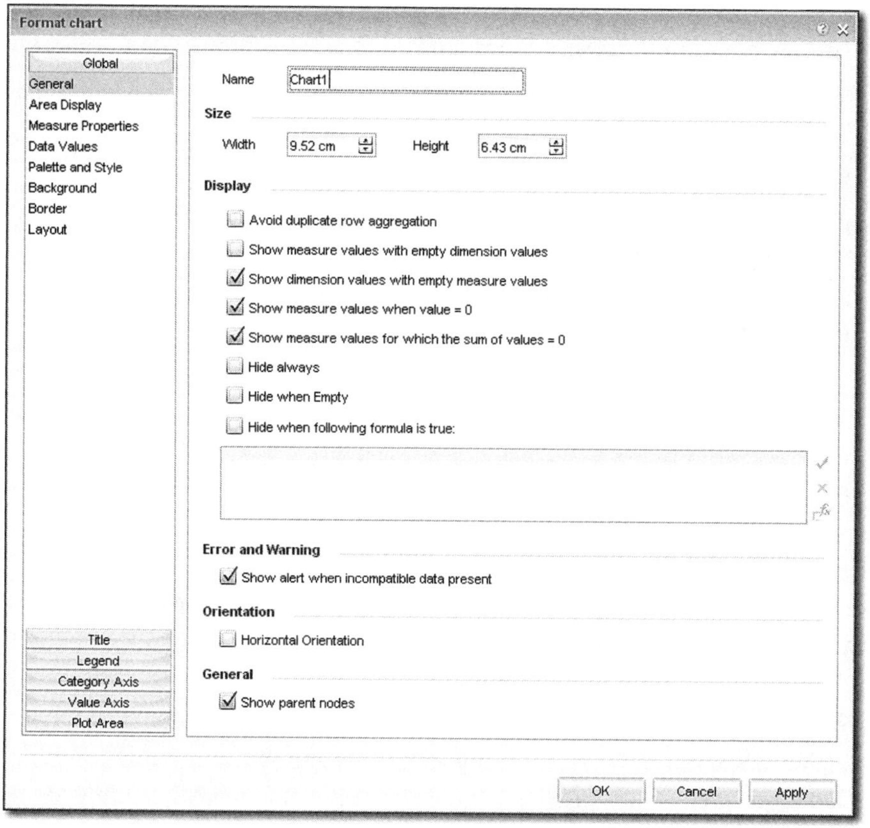

Figure 7.30 General and Global Properties of a Column Chart

▶ GLOBAL

Use the GLOBAL category to revise properties that apply to the entire chart. Eight subgroups are available within the GLOBAL category:

▷ GENERAL: Edit the name and size of the chart and enable settings to hide the chart dynamically with a formula.

▷ AREA DISPLAY: Enable or disable a chart title and edit the title label. Use the formula editor to create a dynamic title. Also change the visibility of chart axes, legends, and data values.

▷ MEASURE PROPERTIES: Change the region type from bars, lines, and surfaces.

▷ DATA VALUES: Check DATA LABEL DISPLAYING MODES to display the values being charted. Customize the data type being displayed, data position, orientation, and font properties.

▶ PALETTE AND STYLE: Make visual changes by setting the 3D look, color palette, marker symbols, bar effects, and light and shadow effects. This subgroup of properties provides several advanced capabilities to generate highly customized chart objects.

▶ BACKGROUND: Assign the background color to be RGBA color or gradient.

▶ BORDER: Assign the style, thickness, color, and border type.

▶ LAYOUT: Enable or disable layout properties such as starting on a new page, avoiding page break, repeating on every page, and assigning the relative position to other report elements on the canvas.

▶ TITLE

Use this property category to apply a dynamic or static title, and edit the layout spacing, orientation, location, layout width, layout height, font properties, and border and background choices.

▶ LEGEND

Use this property category to modify properties associated with the legend values or title of the legend. These properties include making it visible and choosing symbol size, layout location, spacing, orientation, text and font properties, and border and background settings.

▶ CATEGORY AXIS

Use this property category to apply visual settings to axis values. Settings include hiding or displaying the category axis itself and adjusting axis orientation, reverse order on axis, color options, and font properties.

▶ VALUE AXIS

Use this property category to hide the axis, change the stacking type, modify the scaling method, adjust the layout and orientation, provide changes to color options, edit font properties, and assign a number format.

▶ PLOT AREA

Use this property category to make the following adjustments to the plot area settings: invert superimposition order of series, spacing within and between groups, grid and background style, color, and lighting.

Useful Chart Properties

With more than 200 adjustable properties, some of the most significant properties can be difficult to locate. Don't overlook these properties when creating charts that engage users and display information in meaningful, actionable and insightful ways:

▶ GLOBAL • PALETTE AND STYLE

   ▶ 3D LOOK DEPTH: 3D LOOK—Enhances the visual display of the report element to produce a 3D effect.

   ▶ BAR DISPLAY EFFECTS: Adjusts the width and brightness in addition to adding volume effects to applicable chart types.

   ▶ LIGHT AND SHADOW EFFECTS: REAL LIGHTING AND COMPLEX SHADOWS—Creates the illusion of subtle light with shadows behind the charted values.

   ▶ LINE EFFECTS: LINE WIDTH—Adds thickness to a line to produce a fuller visual impact.

   ▶ LINE EFFECTS: SPLINE LINE—Produces lines with smoothed curves at the data point locations (also known as a smoothing spline).

▶ PLOT AREA • BACKGROUND

   ▶ GRID AND BACKGROUND: STRIPED BACKGROUND.

▶ CATEGORY AXIS • DESIGN

   ▶ LAYOUT: REVERSE ORDER ON THE CATEGORY AXIS AND SHOW LABELS.

Figure 7.31 shows the same basic line chart twice, but several properties have been adjusted on the right. These adjustments include increasing the line size and symbol width, checking the SPLINE LINE option in the LINE DISPLAY EFFECTS section, and applying a subtle striped background to the plot area.

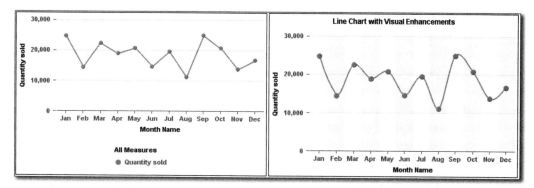

Figure 7.31 Basic Line Chart with and without Property Changes

243

Many other modifiable properties are available when right-clicking on an existing chart:

▶ CUT

Remove a chart from a report. PASTE becomes enabled after CUT has been selected.

▶ COPY

Select COPY to begin the copy/paste process of duplicating a chart or data table (you must use this method to copy instead of the commonly used $\boxed{\text{Ctrl}}$+$\boxed{\text{C}}$ command).

▶ DELETE

Remove a chart from a report.

▶ TURN INTO

Switch the existing report element to another chart type or data table.

▶ ASSIGN DATA

Assign the dimension, detail, or measure objects to the chart.

▶ LINKING

Add hyperlinks or element links to other report elements.

▶ START DRILL

Enable simple filtering to constrain information on reports.

▶ FILTER

Add a new filter to the selected chart, or add a new input control.

▶ SORT

Select MANAGE SORTS to define a new sort to apply to the object.

▶ HIDE

Hide the object, enable the chart to hide when empty, or select HIDE WHEN to create a formula and force the object to only be displayed when the criteria defined in the formula is met.

▶ ORDER

Layer objects, including bring to front, send to back, bring forward, and send backward.

▶ ALIGN

Select two or more objects to align the objects by left, center, right, top, middle, and bottom (also available are RELATIVE POSITION, SHOW GRID, SNAP TO GRID, and GRID SETTINGS options).

▶ FORMAT CHART
Launch the extensive chart formatting editor.

▶ PUBLISH AS WEB SERVICE
Launch the PUBLISH CONTENT window to generate a web service from the values in the selected object, and use web services as a data source for SAP Business-Objects Dashboards. This option is only available from within the Applet viewer.

These are just a few of the options that can be used to improve the way data is delivered in custom charts. Next, we'll describe the various ways to quickly format a chart without entering the formatting window.

7.4   Zone Formatting

Zone formatting gives report designers the capability to modify every aspect of a chart by using the tools provided in the FORMAT tab. The original and more comprehensive method of applying visual changes to charts requires entering the FORMAT CHART window to apply property changes. There, you can make properties and formatting changes to adjust the existing settings within the chart. Properties are categorized into several functional groupings for a complete collection of adjusting settings in one panel.

> **Note**
>
> Other than changing the colors of a chart, zone formatting can only be accomplished while working within the Applet viewer.

In addition to the functionality provided in the FORMAT CHART window, zone formatting allows report designers to make changes instantly to a chart zone with only a single click. Make these property adjustments by selecting a bar, column, or line in a chart and then using the various options located in the FORMAT tab.

The following chart zones and properties can be modified using the properties available in the FORMAT tab:

▶ CHART TITLE
Font, border, style, alignment

▶ CHART
Border, background color, size

▶ VALUE AXIS
Font, style, numbers

▶ CATEGORY AXIS
Font, style

▶ AXIS LABELS
Font, border, style

▶ LEGEND
Background color

▶ LEGEND TITLE
Font, border, style, alignment

This new time-saving feature lets you modify charts quicker than ever before.

7.5 Summary

When you have access to 26 different chart types and more than 200 modifiable properties, visually presenting data to users can range from being a simple method to quickly displaying data or highly customized user experience. The chart types include 7 column charts, 3 bar charts, 3 line charts, 4 point charts, and 3 pie charts. In addition, 6 additional chart types are available for displaying data in a less traditional form with types such as a tree map, heat map, box plot, radar chart, waterfall chart, and tag cloud.

Report designers have never had more choices for the customization of reports than with the features available in Web Intelligence 4.1. You can alter charts to include volume effects, a 3D appearance, and several adjustable light and shadowing effects. In addition to formatting reports and reporting elements, you can convert individual charts into other chart types or data tables with as few as three clicks, create a dynamic chart title with formula capabilities, and apply custom formatting to every axis category and title.

Chapter 8 goes a step further and discusses many advanced topics concerning charting.

With the charting engine in Web Intelligence in SAP BusinessObjects BI 4.1, you can produce visual reports that vividly illustrate the data being displayed. Explore the extensive chart properties to create highly customized reports that generate the maximum impact for each unique scenario.

8 Making an Impact with Charts

Web Intelligence is known for its ability to retrieve high volumes of data and produce detailed analytical reports. After data is returned to the Report Panel, analysis is enhanced through the use of features such as simple filters, drilling, and input controls. Now in SAP BusinessObjects BI 4.1, charting can also be included in the list of powerful devices available at your fingertips for clearly displaying information and emphasizing important values. The charting engine first introduced in SAP BusinessObjects BI 4.0 upgrades the tool's capabilities to present information in 26 different customizable and visually engaging chart components. Each chart type provides properties to configure the finest of details, with many charts offering over 200 adjustable settings.

Charts also provide an intuitive method for drilling into results and guiding users to details at lower levels or aggregating up to higher levels in a hierarchy. Navigation can be synchronized when more than one chart is displayed in a report, and both contain hierarchical dimension values and when drilling has been enabled.

Displaying hierarchical data in charts is possible for data sourced from either multidimensional or relational data sources. Options are provided to produce visual groupings when more than one dimension object is added to a chart and display multilevel analysis within a single graphic.

This chapter covers all these topics and provides examples to help you make an appropriate visual impact with charts based on the data requirements and audience expectations.

8.1   Properties That Enhance the Display of Data

Whether you're using bar charts, column charts, or scatter charts to display data, the number of available configurable properties varies for each chart type. Properties range from making simple font changes in chart titles to enabling a 3D look and applying complex shadows in the Light and Shadow Effects setting in the global Palette and Style property category to maximize the visual impression of data.

These steps explain how you can begin modifying chart properties:

1. Enter design mode.

2. Right-click on the chart to be edited.

3. Select FORMAT CHART.

Before making changes to the visual presentation of a chart, be sure that you understand the business reason behind every modification. Visual changes configured simply to add flair or contrast may be useful in some scenarios but will not be well received in every business setting. In fact, there are several things you should consider when planning and making visual changes to charts:

▶ The users' expectations

▶ The client's visual standards

▶ Graphics and colors that enrich the communication of results

▶ Clear display of data that is not confusing and does not misrepresent

▶ Color scheme (colors should not provide meaning because up to 10% of users are color-blind)

Remember that visual attributes should be used to enhance the data being presented rather than distract users or detract from the content being displayed. Information should be easy to read and understand, not confusing or misleading.

Report element placement is also very important when presenting information with charts. Layouts should be well aligned and precisely placed on the report canvas. Consumer confidence is greatly diminished when report elements are misaligned, have inconsistent sizes, or are created with erratic color schemes. You can use the width and height adjustment options in the FORMAT tab and the SIZE subtab to make precise adjustments to chart element widths and heights.

To align two or more charts, hold down the Ctrl key, and select all the charts that need to be aligned. Then right-click and select ALIGN. Alignment options include align left, center, right, or top, middle, bottom.

Modifying Chart Properties

The FORMAT CHART window in Web Intelligence 4.1 provides a tremendous number of options for configuring charts. With just a few adjustments, standard reports with charts can be elevated to visually stunning reports, scorecards, dashboards, or report/dashboard hybrids known as dashports. Let's explore the configurable options available in the FORMAT CHART window that can be used to change the appearance of a chart. Every chart type contains several unique options that are specific to that chart type, as well as several settings that can apply to all chart types.

The settings described here present the options available in a column chart.

Global Configurable Options

▶ GENERAL
Use this category to rename the chart, adjust the width and height of the entire report element, and assign up to eight different display options, including settings that show measure or dimension values when empty. From here, you can also show error and warning icons when chart drivers encounter incorrect data values and whether you can change the axis orientation when configuring a bar or column chart.

▶ AREA DISPLAY
Use this category to add a dynamic title label with a formula and also to select a location (top, bottom, left, or right) to display the chart title. Other options include the ability to show or hide category axis labels, values, title, data values displayed on the charted shape, and legend details.

▶ MEASURE PROPERTIES
Use this category to quickly switch the chart type to bars, lines, or surfaces.

▶ DATA VALUES
Check the DATA LABEL DISPLAYING MODE option to display data values on the charted shapes and to configure the appearance of the following data labels:

▸ DATA TYPE: Choose from displaying the data by value, label, or percent.

▸ DATA POSITION: Select the position to display the data label.

In a column chart, change the orientation from vertical to horizontal for ideal readability. Configure a variety of font properties, including font size, border size, border color, spacing, and background color.

▶ PALETTE AND STYLE

Enhance your chart with depth and color, and apply other effects (as shown in Figure 8.1):

▸ DEPTH: 2D look or 3D look

▸ PALETTE: 12 different palette combinations that come out of the box plus the option to include a custom palette, or use the slider to adjust the transparency effect from 0 to 100% for opaque to invisible.

▸ CHART SERIES STYLE

  – BAR DISPLAY EFFECTS: NONE, VOLUME, GRADIENT, GLOSSY, CYLINDER, or LIGHT GLOSSY.

  – LIGHT AND SHADOW EFFECTS: NO FILTER, SIMPLE LIGHTING, SIMPLE SHADOWS, SIMPLE LIGHTING AND SHADOWS, REAL LIGHTING, COMPLEX SHADOWS, REAL LIGHTING AND COMPLEX SHADOWS, and IMAGE EMBOSSED WITH LIGHTING AND COMPLEX SHADOWS.

After you select a LIGHT AND SHADOW EFFECT from the GLOBAL • PALETTE AND STYLE grouping, you have five additional options that enable additional customization and precise adjustments. Figure 8.1 shows the modifiable options available when you select REAL LIGHTING AND COMPLEX SHADOWS:

▸ LIGHT POWER: Define ranges from –1.00 to 1.00.

▸ SHADOW X OFFSET: Allowable range: 0 to 0.52 cm.

▸ SHADOW Y OFFSET: Allowable range: 0 to 0.52 cm.

▸ FILTER PASS COUNT: Define the complexity of the effect; set from 1 to 9.

▸ FILTER WINDOW SIZE: Determine the smoothness of the shade; set from 1 to 9.

▸ SHADOW COLOR: Choose between RGBA COLOR and GRADIENT.

▶ BACKGROUND

Choose between RGBA COLOR and GRADIENT.

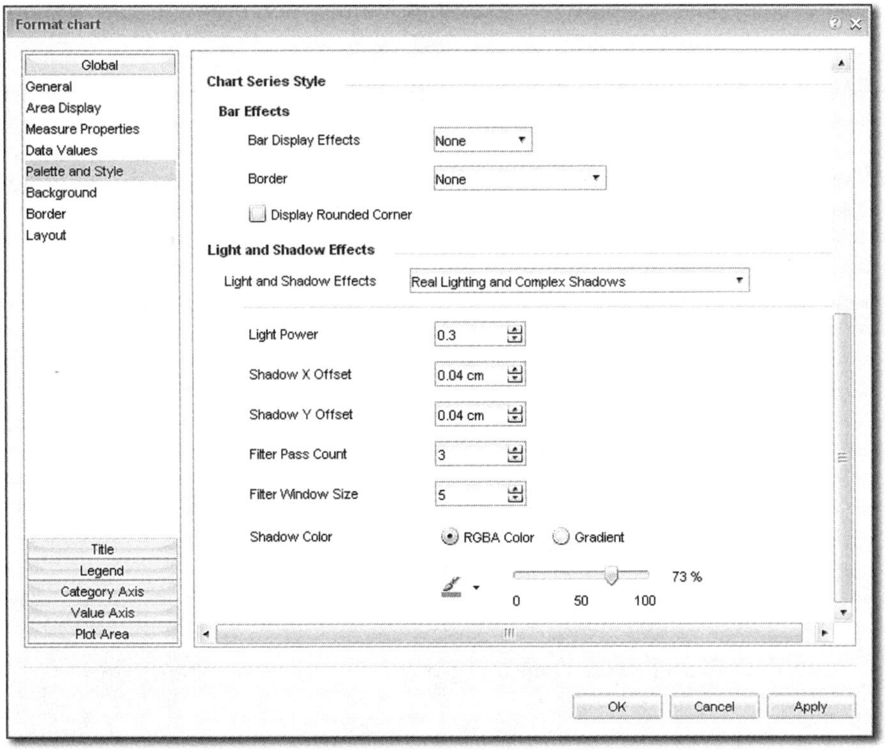

Figure 8.1 Palette and Style Options on the Global Category for a Column Chart

▶ BORDER
Select a border style, thickness, color, and border area.

▶ LAYOUT

  ▶ START ON A PAGE: Enable/disable.

  ▶ AVOID PAGE BREAK: Enable/disable.

  ▶ RELATIVE POSITION: Set the element's location relative to another object.

Title Category Options

▶ DESIGN

  ▶ GENERAL: Display/hide the title and configure the title label.

- ▸ Layout: Select the layout location of the title (top, bottom, left, right), and select the orientation and spacing of the title.
- ▸ Text: Define font properties, and set a text policy to wrap, truncate, or choose to not wrap long titles.
- ▸ Border and Background: Choose a border size (None, Thin, Medium, Thick), border color, and background color.

Legend Category Options

▸ Design

- ▸ Visible: Set the legend to be visible or not visible (checkbox option).
- ▸ Layout: Select the location of the legend (top, bottom, left, right).
- ▸ Group by Dimension: Enable/disable.
- ▸ Spacing: Options range from 0 to 8.
- ▸ Orientation: Automatic or vertical lettering.
- ▸ Symbol Size: Options range from 4 to 32.
- ▸ Text: Define font properties and set a text policy to wrap, truncate, or choose to not wrap long titles.
- ▸ Border and Background: Choose a border size (None, Thin, Medium, Thick), border color, and background color.

▸ Legend Title

- ▸ Visible: Set the legend to be visible or not visible (checkbox option).
- ▸ Title Label: Display an automatic title or create a custom title.
- ▸ Layout: Define the spacing and orientation.
- ▸ Text: Define font properties and set a text policy to wrap, truncate, or choose to not wrap long titles.
- ▸ Border and Background: Choose a border size (None, Thin, Medium, Thick), border color, and background color.

Category Axis Options

▸ Design

- ▸ Visible: Display/hide the category axis (checkbox option).

- ► Layout: Enable/disable the following options:
  - – Display Axis
  - – Reverse Order on the Category Axis
  - – Continuous Axis Layout
  - – Show Labels
  - – Adjust Layout: Define the width and height to Automatic, Fixed, or Proportional.
  - – Display Staggered Axis Labels: Choose Wrap, Truncate, or No Wrap.
- ► Color Options: Choose from RGBA Color or Gradient for the Axis Color, Grid Color, and Grid Background Color.
- ► Text: Define font settings.
- ► Title
  - ► Visible: Enable/disable the category axis label, and choose a title label type between an Automatic or Custom title (optionally apply a label separator).
  - ► Layout: Revise the title spaces within allowable range from 0 to 8.
  - ► Text: Configure font settings.
  - ► Border and Background: Define the border size, color, and background color.

Value Axis Options

- ► Design
  - ► Visible: Display/hide the value axis (checkbox option).
  - ► Stacking: Unstacked, Stacked, Globally Stacked Chart, Scaling, and Layout. Also use this option to include a Region Color when assigning data to a chart.
  - ► Scaling: Choose the origin in range from Always or Automatic, and define axis scaling from Linear or Logarithmic. Also use this option to set a minimum and maximum value to the chart and set a unit scale factor that ranges from 0 to 24.
  - ► Layout: Enable/disable the display axis, show labels, adjust layout, and display staggered axis labels.

  ▶ COLOR OPTIONS: Set the axis color to either RGBA COLOR or GRADIENT,

  ▶ TEXT: Define font settings.

▶ TITLE

  ▶ GENERAL: Enable/disable the axis title.

  ▶ LAYOUT: Revise the title spaces within the allowable range from 0 to 8.

  ▶ TEXT: Configure font settings.

  ▶ BORDER AND BACKGROUND: Define the border size, color, and background color.

Plot Area Options

▶ DESIGN:

  ▶ Enable/disable the INVERT SUPERIMPOSITION ORDER OF SERIES setting, and set the SPACING WITHIN GROUPS and SPACING BETWEEN GROUPS within a range from –1.00 to 1.00.

▶ BACKGROUND

  ▶ GRID AND BACKGROUND: Set the background of a chart to be either a plain background or a striped background, and make specific color changes to the following:

    – BACKGROUND COLOR

    – CATEGORY AXIS GRID COLOR

    – VALUE AXIS GRID COLOR

  Additionally, the option to show or hide a dashed line is presented in the section.

Careful configuration of chart properties can make a significant difference in the way data is displayed when presented to users.

8.2   Drilling in Reports with Multiple Charts

Two or more charts commonly appear on a report canvas, so it's crucial that the information remain accurate after drilling occurs. As users begin to drill into charted values and analyze data at a finer granularity, the current dimension value is replaced by the next dimension in the hierarchy setup at the universe level. To further extend drilling capabilities, you need to increase the scope level in the SCOPE OF ANALYSIS pane in the Query Panel to the needed level.

When multiple charts or tables on the same report canvas contain the same dimensional value, drilling can be synchronized between the components when only one value is selected.

To enable synchronized drilling, click on the PREFERENCES link in the BI Launch Pad, and then select WEB INTELLIGENCE from the list of preference categories. Scroll down to the DRILL OPTIONS section, and check the SYNCHRONIZE DRILL ON REPORT BLOCKS checkbox, as shown in Figure 8.2.

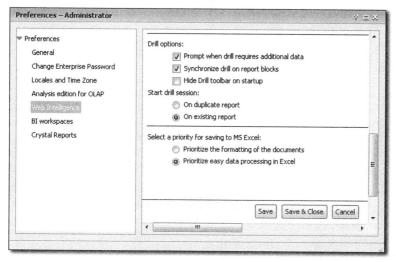

Figure 8.2 Synchronize Drill on Report Blocks Setting

You may want to disable synchronized drilling in some situations, such as when you prefer that other charts or data tables on the canvas remain intact until clicked.

When a charted value is selected while drilling is enabled, the dimension object of the value selected is added to the filter bar, and the value is selected. By adding the object to the filter bar, every element in the report will be filtered by the value selected, regardless of whether synchronized drilling has been enabled.

8.3 Hierarchical Charting with Relational Data

Displaying multiple dimensions in a single chart can be achieved in Web Intelligence, whether connected to a relational data source or a multidimensional cube. In Web Intelligence 4.1, right-click on a chart; then, while in design mode, select ASSIGN DATA. You can add several dimensions to the Category Axis. Figure 8.3 shows a bar chart built with two dimension objects.

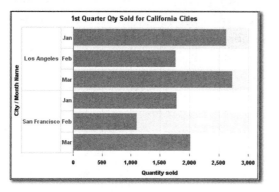

Figure 8.3 Multiple Dimensions Displayed in a Column Chart

Although you can add several additional dimension objects to the Category Axis, you might not be able to display more than three dimensions. This depends on the size of the chart itself and the amount of data in each dimension. As Figure 8.4 shows, you can add more than one object to the REGION COLOR section when assigning data to the chart object.

Figure 8.4 Assigning Multiple Dimension Objects to a Column Chart

Multiple dimension values are displayed in nested clusters to communicate the hierarchical groupings of the data in the chart. These axis values are clickable when drilling is enabled, which allows for seamless navigation up and down a hierarchy. When you hover over a column, bar, pie slice, or label, tooltips appear and provide the direction of the current drill option.

8.4 Reports Functioning as Dashboards

Web Intelligence lets users retrieve more than 100,000 rows of data and produce detailed analytical reports. With SAP BusinessObjects BI 4.1, you can also present data visually with interactive charting components and in a style that resembles a dashboard.

Several new features in SAP BusinessObjects BI 4.1 can be used together to create a dashboard experience inside a Web Intelligence report. The following are eight features that can be used to present data interactively and in a dashboard or score-card format:

▶ **Element linking**
Use the element linking feature to pass values from one chart component to other dependency components on the same report tab. This feature allows for interactivity between components, even when hierarchies have not been set up at the universe level.

▶ **Drill**
Use the drill feature to perform in-place drilling to analyze dimensional values at different levels. This feature is aided by the SCOPE OF ANALYSIS pane and hierarchies set up in the universe.

▶ **Hide**
Use the HIDE and HIDE WHEN features to produce dynamic visibility. You can write a formula to show or hide a chart or other report element when specific conditions are met. This feature allows for layers of components to be used in a single report and then only be displayed when data conditions are met. These conditions can be the result of simple filter selections, element link selections, drill values, or data retrieved from the data source.

▶ **Scale to Page**
The FIT TO PAGE functionality popularized in Desktop Intelligence has been included in Web Intelligence as SCALE TO PAGE. This feature is accessed by

going to the primary PAGE SETUP tab and then locating the SCALE TO PAGE subtab in the third subtab group. Figure 8.5 shows the options available for scaling a report page:

▶ WIDTH: The default selection is AUTOMATIC and can be changed from 1 to 9 pages.

▶ HEIGHT: The default selection is AUTOMATIC and can be changed from 1 to 9 pages.

▶ SCALE: The scale can be changed from 10% to 400% of the current report.

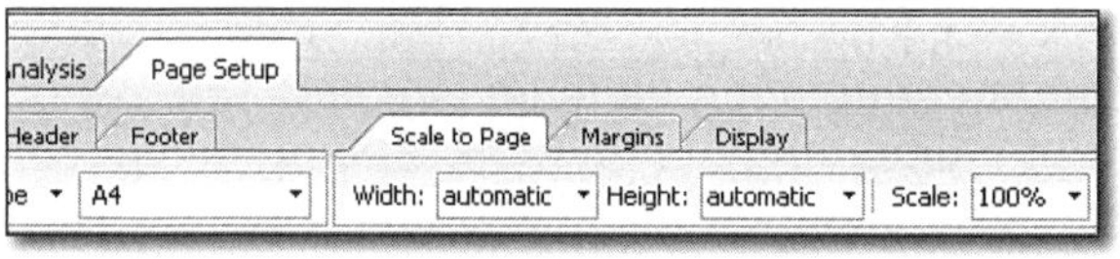

Figure 8.5 Scale to Page Tab

The functionality provided in the SCALE TO PAGE tab works best when used in conjunction with the PAGE MODE selection on the DISPLAY tab. These two choices are displayed in Figure 8.6.

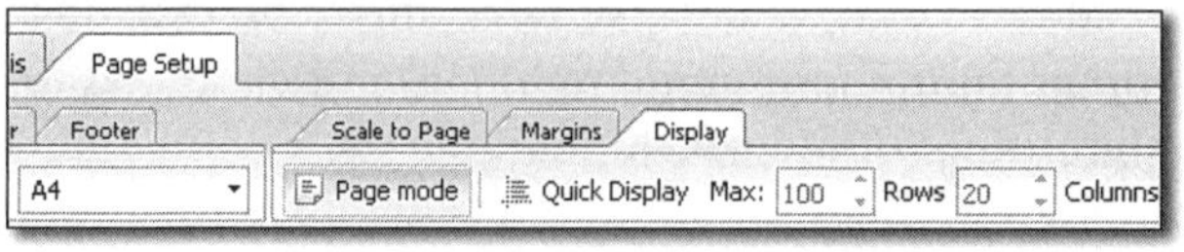

Figure 8.6 Toggling between the Display Formats: Page and Quick Display

You have two options for the display mode, both found in the DISPLAY tab. The first option, PAGE, is used when a report needs to be analyzed on a single screen or printed report. You should use this setting when creating a Web Intelligence dashboard or exporting to PDF. The second option, QUICK DISPLAY, is used primarily for analysis or exporting to Excel.

▶ **New charting engine**
The charting engine introduced to Web Intelligence in SAP BusinessObjects BI 4.0 has profoundly improved the data visualization capabilities of the product. Charts can be designed to include flashy styles with complex lighting or be displayed in a conservative and minimalistic format to present data in a style free of unwanted shadows.

▶ **Input Controls**
The Input Control tools were introduced in Service Pack 2 (SP2) in SAP BusinessObjects Enterprise XI 3.1, and they continue to offer interactive filtering capabilities to Web Intelligence in version 4.1. Use this feature to give users more choices for slicing, dicing, filtering, and analyzing data.

▶ **Conditional formatting**
Known in previous versions as *alerters*, the conditional formatting tools allow specific values to be easily identified in data tables when property changes are conditionally applied to values that meet the outlined criteria. Formatting changes are displayed in real time as users explore reporting documents using filters, element links, and input controls. With conditional formatting, reports can be transformed from simple rows and columns to highly informative scorecards with visual indicators to help you manage your business and drive change.

▶ **Additional report tabs for extensive data analysis**
This feature amplifies Web Intelligence to become both a data visualization tool and data analysis reporting tool. By having both capabilities within the same tool, a single document can contain multiple data sources, several dashboards, report/dashboard hybrids or dashports, and also analytical reports containing many thousand records.

You can reach new heights with your reports by combining the features outlined in this section. Scaling the report to fit to a single page, including drilling, Input Controls, and the Hide When feature, along with uniquely customized charts, can go a long way in engaging users and delivering actionable information to them in the most effective format possible.

8.5   Formatting Tips

With more than 200 potential configuration options available for most chart types, it may seem difficult to select areas that provide the greatest impact. This section shows a few of the settings that can be easily changed to make a significant impression and produce increased readability.

8.5.1   Measure Formatting

To properly present a measure in a chart, you'll need to assign the most appropriate number format to the measure, or the chart won't be adequately communicating results to the user. The window for setting this format is accessed by right-clicking on a chart and selecting ASSIGN DATA.

From the ASSIGN DATA window, dimension objects are assigned to appear in the CATEGORY AXIS and measure objects in the VALUE AXIS sections. Click on the plus (+) symbol located to the right of the object selected to add a second object to the chart.

To configure the number format of a measure object, click on the small down arrow located immediately to the right of the plus (+) symbol. Clicking on this arrow will display up to nine different options, depending on the number of objects already assigned to the chart, as shown in Figure 8.7. Click on FORMAT NUMBER to assign a specific format to the measure object.

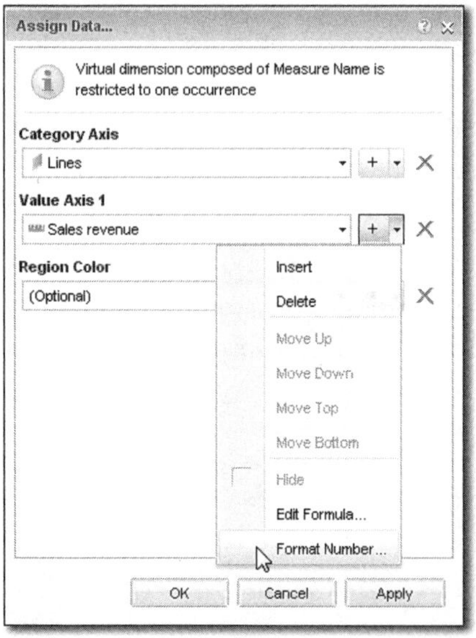

Figure 8.7 Formatting the Number of the Value Axis Measure Object

The FORMAT NUMBER window lets you choose from 40 preset number formats displayed in six different format groupings. There's also a CUSTOM group that allows you to create your own format. Note that custom formatting is only available in the Applet viewer. And for formatting money measures, the CURRENCY grouping received an update in SAP BusinessObjects BI 4.1. There are now six currency formats preset for display values in Euro and Yen.

Figure 8.8 shows the FORMAT NUMBER window and the format groupings available in the Applet viewer. To set a format, select a grouping from the left side of the window, and then click on your preferred format on the right side of the window.

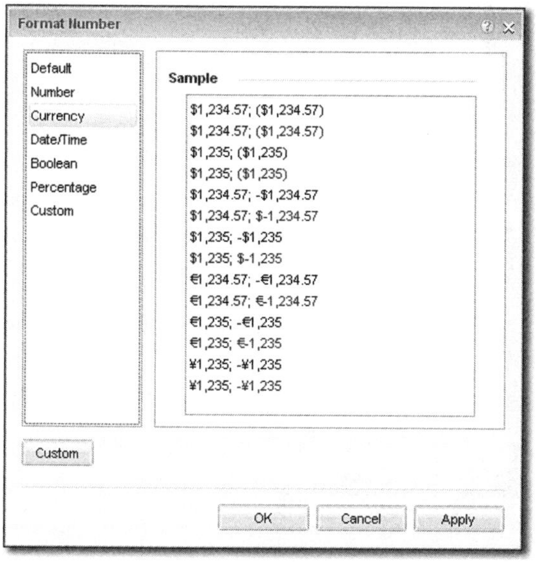

Figure 8.8 Formatting the Number of a Measure Object in a Chart

If the specific format you need isn't found in the list of choices on the right, click on the CUSTOM button to create your own format.

8.5.2 Region Color and Value Axis Stacking

If you'd like each column in a column chart to be displayed with a different color, add a dimension object to the REGION COLOR section when assigning data to a chart. The same dimension object added to the CATEGORY AXIS section can be used, or a completely different object can be selected.

This setting is optional and is used to visually display groupings within the charted values. Figure 8.9 shows the State object assigned to a chart that already contains STATE in the CATEGORY AXIS.

This methodology provides a different color for each state value in the chart.

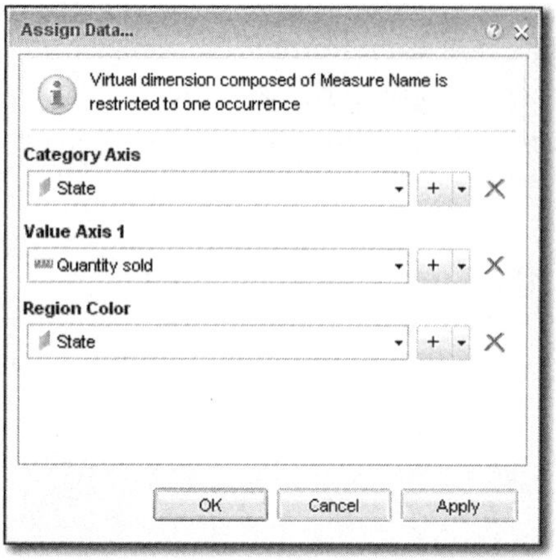

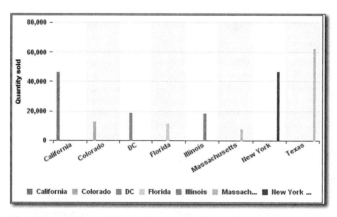

Figure 8.9 Assigning a Region Color to a Chart

Assigning a region color object to a column chart will display the columns in very thin bars, as shown in Figure 8.10. This result may be acceptable in some scenarios, but it's more likely that users will expect to see the columns in a standard width.

Figure 8.10 Column Chart with a Region Color Object Assigned

To display the columns with a wider width, enter the FORMAT CHART window, and revise the STACKING option in the VALUE AXIS grouping.

The default setting is UNSTACKED. By changing the STACKING selection to either STACKED CHART or GLOBALLY STACKED CHART, the option of converting the chart to a 100% STACKED CHART becomes enabled.

Leave the 100% STACKED CHART option unchecked unless your chart contains at least two measures and you'd like to show their correlation. To see the column chart with wider bars, just select STACKED CHART, and click OK, as shown in Figure 8.11.

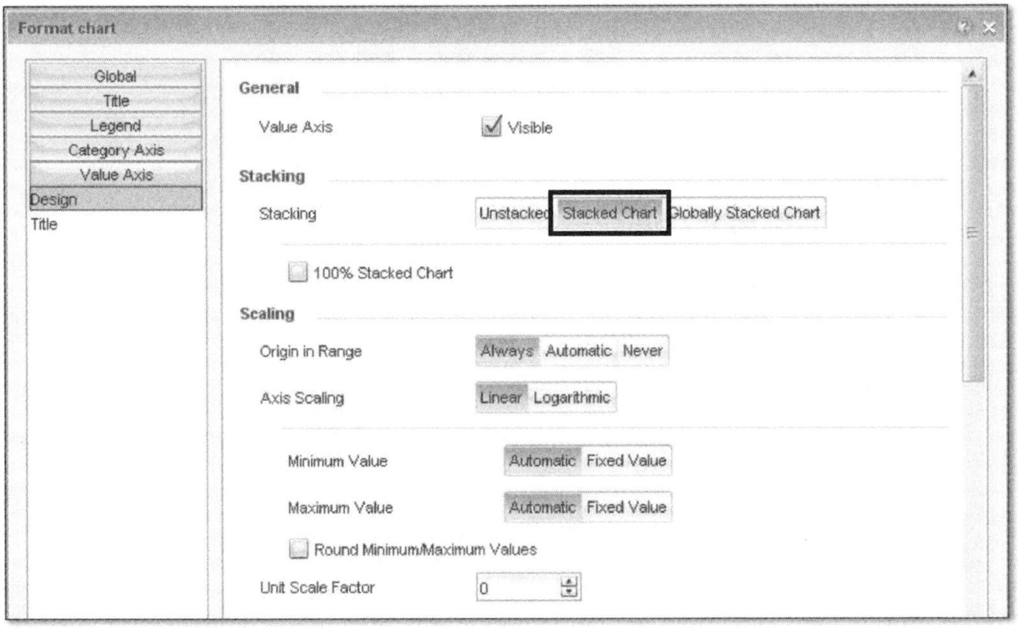

Figure 8.11 Stacking Options

Columns will be presented in a standard width when either STACKED CHART or GLOBALLY STACKED CHART is selected as the STACKING option. This setting is useful because it increases the readability of the data presented in the chart.

Figure 8.12 shows the same chart previously displayed in Figure 8.10, with the only difference being that STACKED CHART was selected as the stacking option, as shown in Figure 8.11. Any dimension object or variable existing in the document can be added to the REGION COLOR section to create visual groupings by color.

Next, we'll discuss how to create charts using a customized collection of colors.

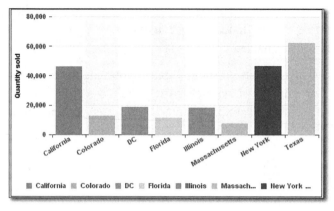

Figure 8.12 Column Chart with Stacked Chart Option Selected

8.6   Custom Color Enhancements

As described in Chapter 2, SAP BusinessObjects BI 4.1 provides the ability to create custom color palettes. This great new feature gives developers the flexibility to build charts and reporting documents that use precise color codes, which is often a requirement in many businesses and corporations. Chart colors can now be consistent, accurate, and in line with the required color standards at any organization.

In each color palette, there are 32 total colors with 8 primary colors, as displayed in Figure 8.13.

From the CREATE PALETTE window, you can create a new combination of colors based purely on their appearance, or you can use color codes to create precise and repeatable variations.

Perform the following steps to begin creating a custom palette:

1. Select an existing chart on your report.
2. Locate the CHART STYLE subtab found on the primary FORMAT tab.
3. Expand the PALETTE STYLE dropdown, and then scroll down and select CUSTOM (see Figure 8.14).

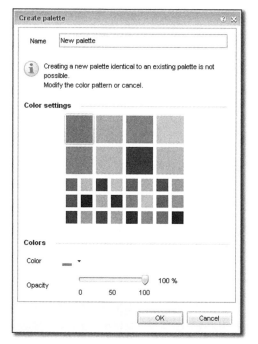

Figure 8.13 Adjusting Colors in a Custom Color Palette

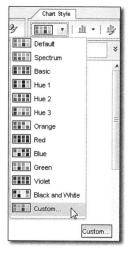

Figure 8.14 Creating a Custom Color Palette

4. In the MANAGE PALETTES window, click NEW in the CUSTOM section to begin creating a new custom palette as shown in Figure 8.15.

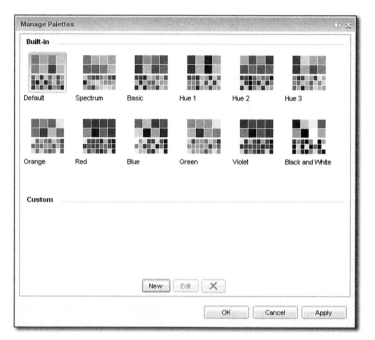

Figure 8.15 Creating a New Custom Palette

5. Begin setting the colors by clicking one of the existing colors located in the COLOR SETTINGS area, and then click the color picker selector. Select MORE COLORS under the default list of choices to make your color selection by code (see Figure 8.16).

6. By selecting MORE COLORS, you'll launch the CUSTOM COLOR window. This window provides five different ways of choosing a color: SWATCHES, HSV, HSL, RGB, and CMYK.

The next several screenshots show each of the custom color windows used for choosing colors in the most accurate and repeatable method. Figure 8.17 shows the CUSTOM COLOR window and the number of choices available on the SWATCHES tab.

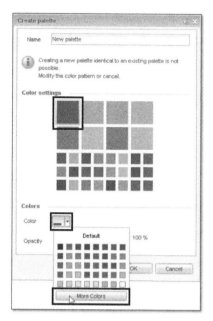

Figure 8.16 Selecting Custom Colors for Your New Custom Palette

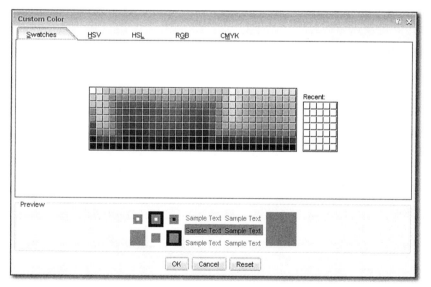

Figure 8.17 Custom Color Choices – Swatches

7. In each of the next four color choice tabs, you can select colors using any of these methods:

   ▶ Clicking in the color picker square

   ▶ Changing the color by tint in the vertical gradient

   ▶ Using sliders to manually adjust specific color elements

   ▶ Changing the Hex color code

   ▶ Modifying the numeric value of color elements such as the following:

     – HUE

     – SATURATION

     – VALUE

     – LIGHTNESS

     – TRANSPARENCY

     – RED/GREEN/BLUE (RGB)

     – ALPHA

     – CYAN/MAGENTA/YELLOW/BLACK (CMYK)

Figure 8.18 through Figure 8.21 show the various options available for adjusting and defining colors on the other tabs in the CUSTOM COLOR window. The following is a description of how adjustments are made in each CUSTOM COLOR selection type:

▶ SWATCHES
Choose from 288 predefined color choices.

▶ HSV
Color codes are generated by adjusting colors by HUE, SATURATION, and VALUE. The level of TRANSPARENCY is also selectable (see Figure 8.18).

▶ HSL
Generate color codes based on HUE, SATURATION, LIGHTNESS, and TRANSPARENCY (see Figure 8.19).

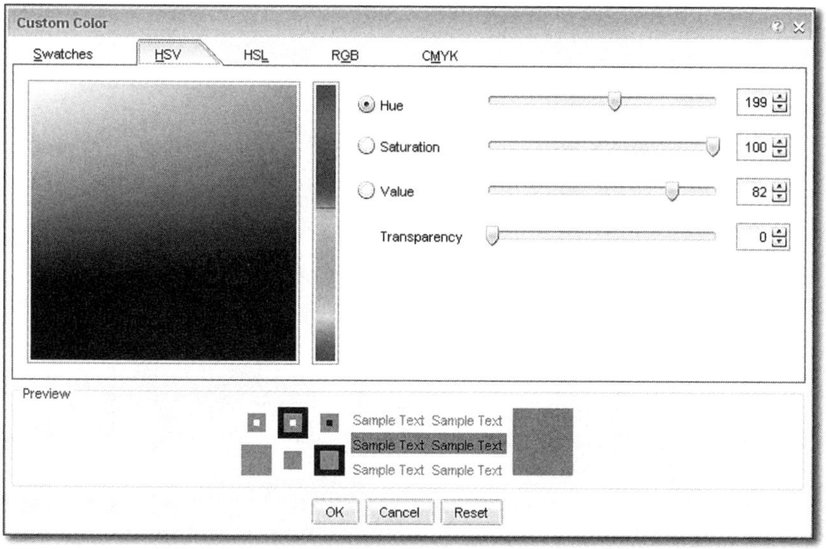

Figure 8.18 Custom Color Choices – HSV

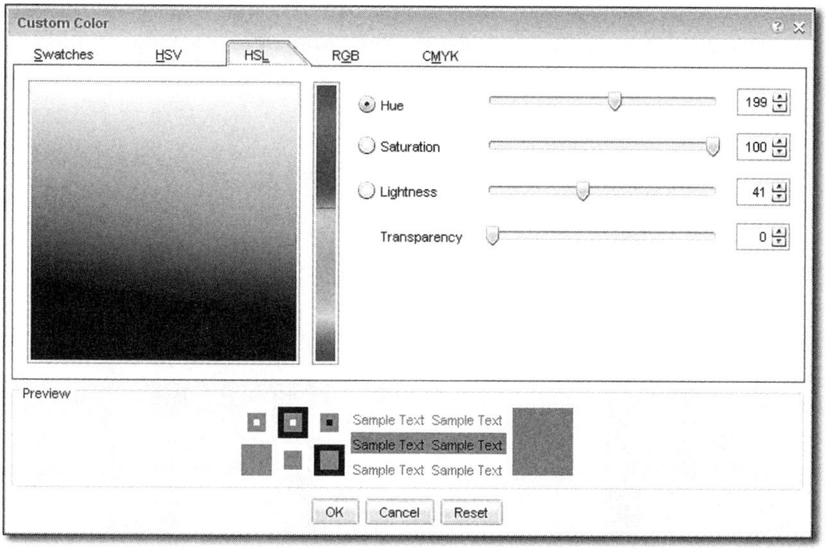

Figure 8.19 Custom Color Choices – HSL

▶ RGB

Define the levels of RED, BLUE, and GREEN in a color (see Figure 8.20).

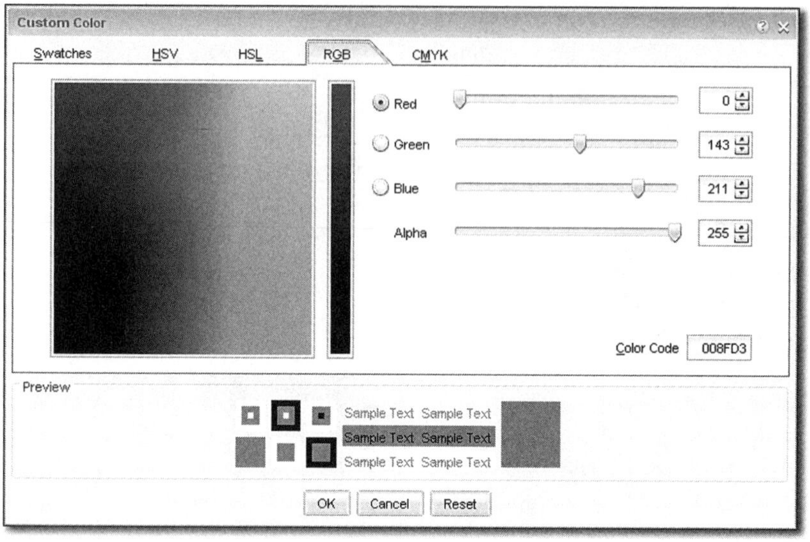

Figure 8.20 Custom Color Choices – RGB

▶ CMYK

Create a precise color by using traditional CYAN, MAGENTA, YELLOW, and BLACK color levels. ALPHA represents the level of transparency in this color selection category (see Figure 8.21).

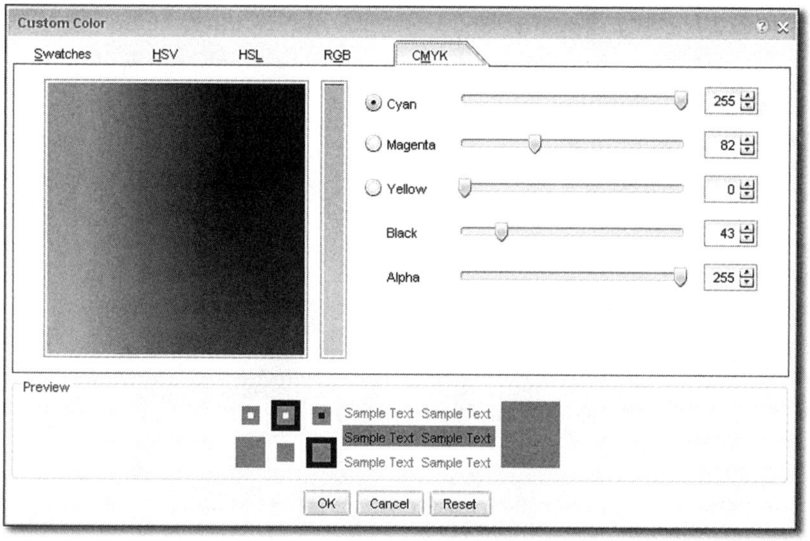

Figure 8.21 Custom Color Choices – CMYK

8.7 Summary

Charting in Web Intelligence 4.1 has been elevated to include improved linking and a boardroom-quality appearance. With an extensive array of configurable properties, charts can include changes to more than 200 different attributes. You can use the full list of provided features to produce highly effective and visual reporting documents that function as dashboards and scorecards while also delivering the data volumes that only Web Intelligence can cleanly consume.

Data analysis is improved by making adjustments to visual settings such as number formats in charts and the stacked chart option when assigning a region color to a chart. The next chapter describes the various report properties and tools available for creating precisely formatted reports.

Web Intelligence 4.1 contains specific metadata about reports, providing report users with a quick and accessible way to modify and interact with them. You can use the various tools and properties in Web Intelligence 4.1 to produce highly configured reports that most effectively communicate information.

9   Report Properties, Tools, and Formatting

This chapter describes the various properties that can be modified in Web Intelligence 4.1 to increase the readability and usability of reporting documents. The new robust reporting interface in version 4.1 gives users quick access to a report's metadata through the tools located in the side panel. The side panel in the Report Panel contains five sections in design mode, three in reading mode, and one in data mode. Each section delivers useful and relevant information to users for the report viewing scenario. The following sections outline all of the functional capabilities delivered in the side panel of the Report Panel.

9.1   Formatting Report Properties

The new reporting interface in Web Intelligence 4.1 allows for dynamic formatting of report properties while working in design mode. This section explains the ways to access report properties and how to most effectively display reports for different types of report consumers.

The side panel (formerly called the left pane) of the Report Panel was introduced in Chapter 5, and this chapter expands on that introduction by describing all of the functionality available in the side panel. This side panel plays a critical role in editing existing documents and creating new reports. Notably, it's different for reading mode, design mode, and data mode, so you'll notice that some functionality is not available when viewing a report in reading mode. The differentiation between capabilities in the reading and design modes provides greater control to power users and report developers in design mode. Reading mode provides a cleaner interface designed specifically for report consumers who need only to view, analyze, filter, and export report data.

Table 9.1 shows the side panel properties available in each mode.

Reading Mode	Design Mode	Data Mode
▶ DOCUMENT SUMMARY	▶ DOCUMENT SUMMARY	▶ DATA
▶ REPORT MAP	▶ REPORT MAP	
▶ INPUT CONTROLS	▶ INPUT CONTROLS	
	▶ WEB SERVICE PUBLISHER	
	▶ AVAILABLE OBJECTS	
	▶ DOCUMENT STRUCTURES AND FILTERS	

Table 9.1 Side Panel Properties Listed by Mode

When expanded, the side panel provides report developers with access to available objects, an area for creating new input controls, access to the web service publisher, and a display of report metadata in the DOCUMENT SUMMARY, as shown in Figure 9.1.

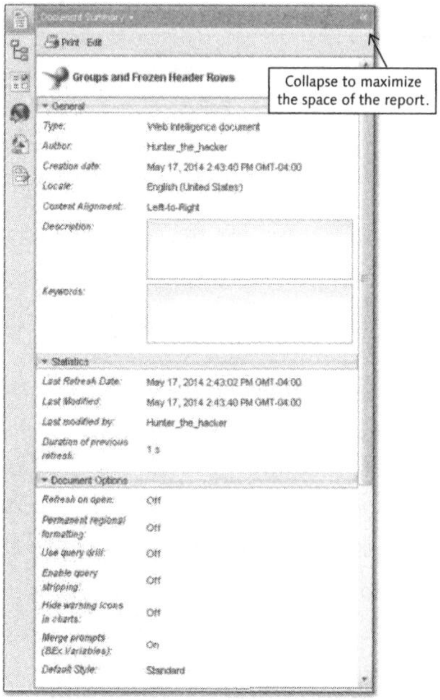

Figure 9.1 Document Summary Details in the Side Panel

The following sections outline the functional options available in the side panel tabs.

9.2   Document Summary

The DOCUMENT SUMMARY tab includes information about the report. These values are listed here:

- ▶ Author
- ▶ Creation date
- ▶ Locale
- ▶ Content alignment direction
- ▶ Description
- ▶ Keywords
- ▶ Last refresh date
- ▶ Last modified date
- ▶ Last modified by
- ▶ Duration of previous refresh
- ▶ Several document and data options

This report metadata is useful for administrators to see who has created and refreshed published documents. The DURATION OF PREVIOUS REFRESH setting is helpful to users when refreshing queries. The amount of time the query took to refresh in its last run is used to provide an estimated wait time when the query is refreshed again. If the query has never been run, then this value will be zero.

The following buttons and fields are relevant to the DOCUMENT SUMMARY tab:

- ▶ PRINT
  Sends the document properties to the printer.
- ▶ EDIT (design mode only)
  Allows the report developer to update the GENERAL section with metadata about the report. It's important to be specific when entering a description and key words that accurately describe the report. The KEYWORDS section is used to quickly locate relevant report data by using the search option in the BI Launch

Pad. Figure 9.2 shows the properties available in the DOCUMENT SUMMARY window.

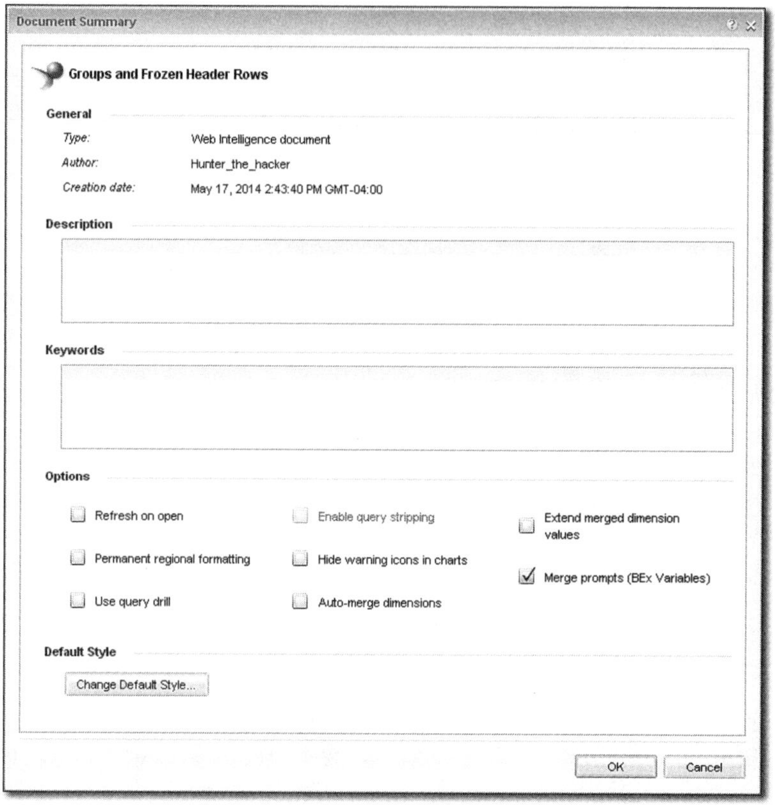

Figure 9.2 Document Summary

▶ GENERAL section
Provides a description of the type of document, author, and creation date. This window also displays descriptions and key words assigned to the report. Click on EDIT at the top of the DOCUMENT SUMMARY tab to enter new values or make changes to existing information in the DESCRIPTION or KEYWORDS sections.

▶ STATISTICS
Provides the following elements of information:

  ▶ LAST REFRESH DATE

  ▶ LAST MODIFIED

- LAST MODIFIED BY

- DURATION OF PREVIOUS REFRESH (in seconds)

- DOCUMENT OPTIONS

  Indicates the on or off status of the following six report parameters and describes the DEFAULT STYLE:

  - REFRESH ON OPEN

  - PERMANENT REGIONAL FORMATTING

  - USE QUERY DRILL

  - ENABLE QUERY STRIPPING

  - HIDE WARNING ICONS IN CHARTS

  - MERGE PROMPTS (BEx VARIABLES):

- DATA OPTIONS

  Three options are displayed in this section:

  - DATA TRACKING

  - AUTO-MERGE DIMENSIONS

  - EXTEND MERGED DIMENSION VALUE

  Whether the options have been enabled or disabled in the current report, all three are listed as either ON or OFF, and the latter two can be turned on in the OPTIONS section when editing the DOCUMENT SUMMARY.

  Data tracking is enabled by navigating to the ANALYSIS tab located above the Report Panel, and then selecting the DATA TRACKING subtab located in the ribbon toolbar. Click on TRACK to choose the tracking method to be applied.

- PARAMETERS

  Provides prompt name(s) as well as key dates saved with the report.

The DOCUMENT SUMMARY tab provides a significant amount of descriptive report information, including the last refresh time. This information can be used by report designers to troubleshoot any potential performance issues when queries are refreshed.

By identifying queries with lengthy refresh times, developers can focus on improving retrieval times and the user experience.

9.3   Report Map

The REPORT MAP tab provides a list of the reports and section values within each report and provides navigation to all of the reports in the document. Figure 9.3 shows a REPORT MAP with two report tabs and all sections associated with the first report tab.

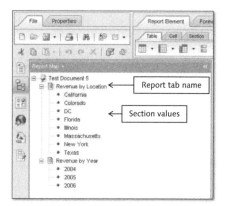

Figure 9.3 Report Map

9.4   Input Controls

This tab allows users to slice, dice, and interact with data while reading a report. This set of features is designed for filtering reports and is easily accomplished by setting up individual controls from the INPUT CONTROLS tab in the side panel.

In design mode, options include adding new input controls and viewing a detailed list of all objects on the current report with the map selection. A RESET button is available to quickly clear all input control selections.

New input control filters can only be added while in design mode, while the MAP and RESET options are available in both design mode and reading mode. Follow these steps to create a new input control:

1. Enter design mode, and select the INPUT CONTROLS tab from the side panel.

2. Click on the NEW button at the top to add a new input control.

3. Select the object or variable to use as the source of the control, and click on NEXT.

4. Choose the preferred control type and make modifications to the input control properties. Click on NEXT to proceed.

5. Assign report elements to accept the filter value of the input control, and click on FINISH.

The input control map outlines all input controls created for the report. Each input control is assigned a report element at time of creation. The map view allows report users to see all of the dependencies of each input control. This option toggles to either on or off. To get out of map view, just reclick MAP to toggle to the off position.

Figure 9.4 shows the map view for all objects on a report. Input controls and their dependencies are easily identified.

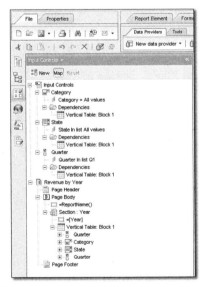

Figure 9.4 Map View for All Input Controls

The RESET button resets all updated input controls to their original defaulted values. Use this button when a series of selections have been made, and you'd like to return all of the filters back to their defaults.

Input controls are one of the most powerful filtering tools you can add to a report to encourage interactivity for report users. This functionality allows users to slice or filter data in a report using retrieved dimensions, measures, or variables. Although the maximum number of input controls is 30 per report, we recommend that each report contain between 2 and 10 input controls depending on the report's requirements because reports with more than 10 input controls can become convoluted and confusing to interpret. Whenever possible, you should revise the input control label to include a name using appropriate business terminology and descriptive terms that fully describe the context of the filter.

Depending on the qualification of the object used in the input control, this powerful interactivity tool can create input controls with the following control types:

- Single-value selections
  - Entry field
  - Combo box
  - Radio buttons
  - List box
  - Calendar
  - Entry field
  - Spinner
  - Simple slider
- Multiple selections
  - Checkbox
  - List box
  - Double slider

Each control type created from a dimension or detail object contains the following configurable settings:

- LABEL
- DESCRIPTION
- LIST OF VALUES

▶ DEFAULT VALUES

▶ ALLOW SELECTION OF ALL VALUES checkbox (new in SAP BusinessObjects BI 4.1)

▶ OPERATOR

This functionality allows for customized user interaction. You'll need to ensure that the label name and description are descriptive enough for the user to understand how to use input controls. Figure 9.5 shows the input control properties for a combo box control named STATE.

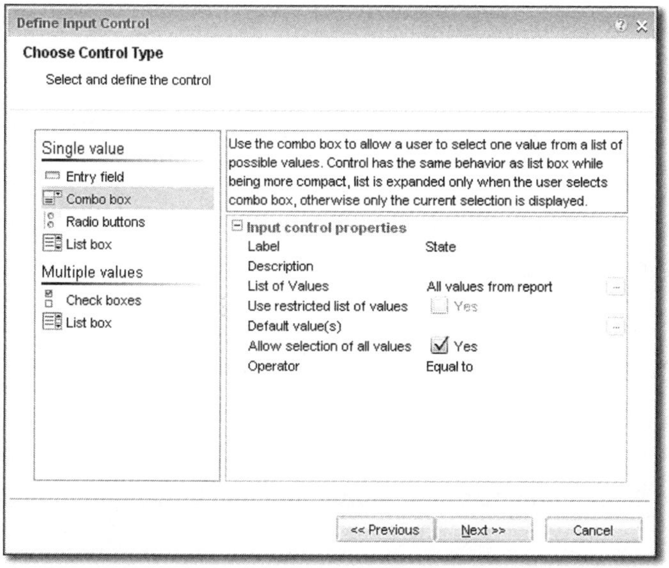

Figure 9.5 Input Control Based on the State Object

> **Note**
>
> Input controls segment or filter data at the report level, while prompted filters restrict data at the query level. The right mix of filters is based on user requirements, balancing query performance, and providing the optimal user experience.

You can edit existing input controls in design mode by clicking on the wrench icon available on the right side of the header bar. Four icons appear when you hover over the header bar of an input control:

▶ EDIT

▶ HIGHLIGHT DEPENDENCIES

▶ REMOVE

▶ COLLAPSE OR EXPAND

Figure 9.6 shows the icons that appear when hovering over an input control title in design mode.

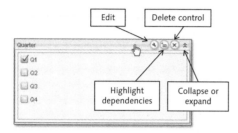

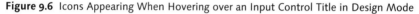

Figure 9.6 Icons Appearing When Hovering over an Input Control Title in Design Mode

9.5 Web Services Publisher

This tab allows the report designer to create web services using existing components or blocks from Web Intelligence reports. Figure 9.7 shows the Web Service Publisher with a Web Service Definition Language (WSDL) for REVENUE_STATE_LINES.

Let's examine some of the important options here:

▶ MANAGE SERVERS
This button is used to add a web services host to the current document. If you're planning to connect to a web service created by Query as a Web Service, use this tool to retrieve the host name. After adding the host name in the provided text box, the URL is automatically generated.

▶ WEB SERVICES PUBLISHER
This tab's options are accessed by icons:

   ▶ VIEWS: Allows the designer to view created WSDL by the following three options (additionally, an option is presented in the VIEW menu to show web services by query):

      – VIEW BY WEB SERVICE

      – VIEW BY DOCUMENT AND WEB SERVICE

      – VIEW BY DOCUMENT AND BLOCK

▶ DELETE: Deletes a selected web service.

▶ EDIT: Launches the Publish Content wizard to edit an existing web service.

▶ RENAME: Renames a web service group.

▶ REFRESH: Refreshes a web service group.

▶ TEST: Tests the input request and server response for a web service group.

▶ IMPORT WEB SERVICE QUERY: Displays the web services properties of the query and enables the IMPORT WEB SERVICE QUERY option (available only when the SHOW WEB SERVICES CONTENT option in the VIEW menu is checked).

▶ SEARCH: Searches for existing web services (this is one reason that WSDL names and descriptions should be descriptive in nature).

Figure 9.7 Web Service Publisher

▶ WEB SERVICES PROPERTIES

  ▶ WSDL URL: Shows the URL associated with the selected web service query and is also used to connect to data in SAP BusinessObjects Dashboards.

   – Example syntax of the WSDL URL is: `http://Brogden_Lab2:8080/dsws-bobje/qaawsservices/biws?WSDL=1&cuid=ASVq8sMDg_BHiIAv7r0PEa0`

Follow these steps to create a new web service:

1. Right-click on an existing table or chart.

2. Select PUBLISH AS WEB SERVICE.

3. The Publish Content wizard is launched. Click on NEXT to proceed.

4. Click on NEXT on the IDENTIFY DUPLICATE CONTENT window.

5. Enter a descriptive name and (optionally) a description, and then click on NEXT, as shown in Figure 9.8.

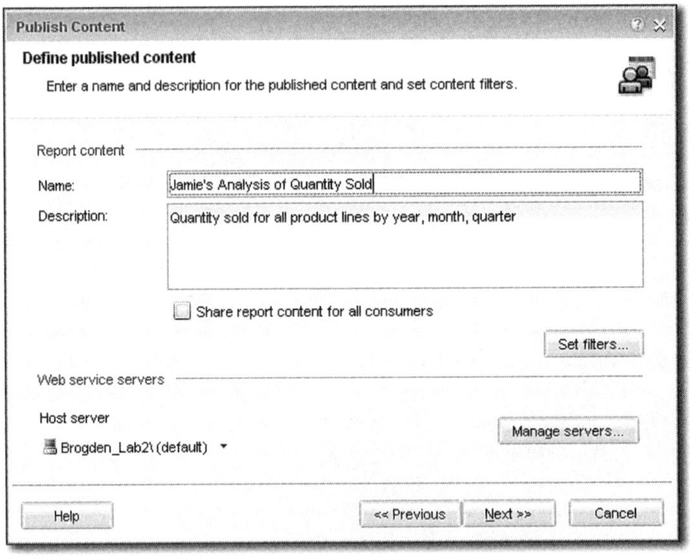

Figure 9.8 Defining a New WSDL Name and Description

6. Click on the CREATE button shown in Figure 9.9.

7. Give the new web service a name with no spaces.

8. Add a DESCRIPTION for the web service, and click on FINISH.

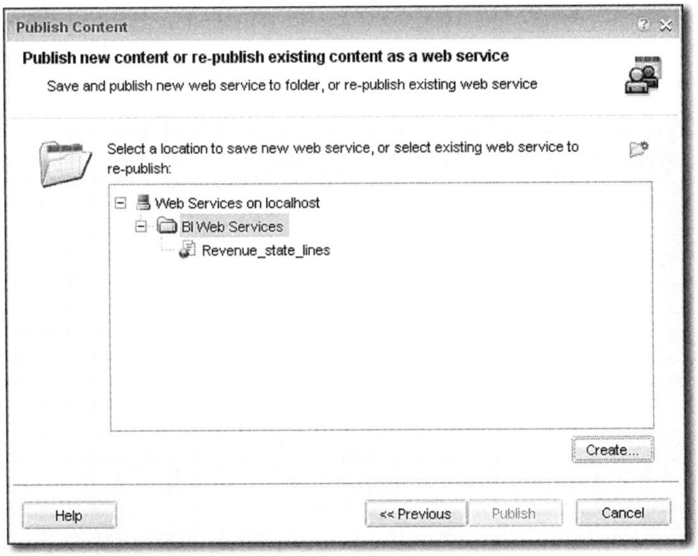

Figure 9.9 Publishing Content as a Web Service

9.6 Available Objects (Design Mode Only)

After you add a data provider and retrieve data from your source, you'll find all of the result objects available for report consumption in the AVAILABLE OBJECTS tab. The AVAILABLE OBJECTS tab contains the following sections and is only available in design mode:

▶ FILTER BAR
Filters objects by name.

▶ LIST OF AVAILABLE OBJECTS
Displays all of the report's result objects, including locally created variables.

▶ Arranged by option and located at the bottom of the window, these sections provide two options for viewing objects:

　▶ ALPHABETICAL ORDER: Arranges the available objects in alphabetical order.

　▶ QUERY: Displays all available objects by query name.

Report developers can drag and drop any available object onto the report canvas or assign them to report elements. Figure 9.10 shows three objects being dropped together onto the report canvas.

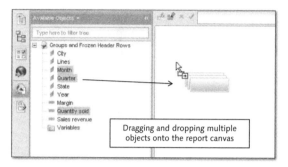

Figure 9.10 Drag and Drop from Available Objects

9.7 Document Structures and Filters

This tab provides a detailed listing of all objects existing within the document and is only available in design mode. Use the DOCUMENT STRUCTURES AND FILTERS tab to access the following:

▶ FILTER button
Shows/hides filters that exist on report elements and data blocks within the report.

▶ AXIS button
Toggles on and off the report axis found in charts and data tables.

▶ Report structure elements
Displays the document structure by report tabs.

All report level filters are assigned by a funnel-shaped icon; other report elements also have distinctive icons. It's important to name report elements appropriately in order to easily identify them in this view. Figure 9.11 shows document structure and filters.

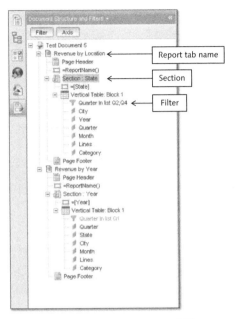

Figure 9.11 Document Structure and Filters

9.8   Data

The DATA tab is only available when data mode is selected. To enter this option, click on the DATA button in the upper-right corner of the report immediately to the right of the option to enter design mode. This tab shows all data providers and available objects, including dimensions, measures, details, and variables.

The following elements are available in the DATA tab:

▶ FILTER BAR
   Filters objects by name.

▶ EXPAND and COLLAPSE buttons
   Expand and collapse data sources (queries).

▶ Data source and variables list
   Displays all queries generated for the report as well as associated variables (you can edit variables by right-clicking on a variable name and selecting EDIT).

Figure 9.12 shows the DATA tab, including query name and associated query properties.

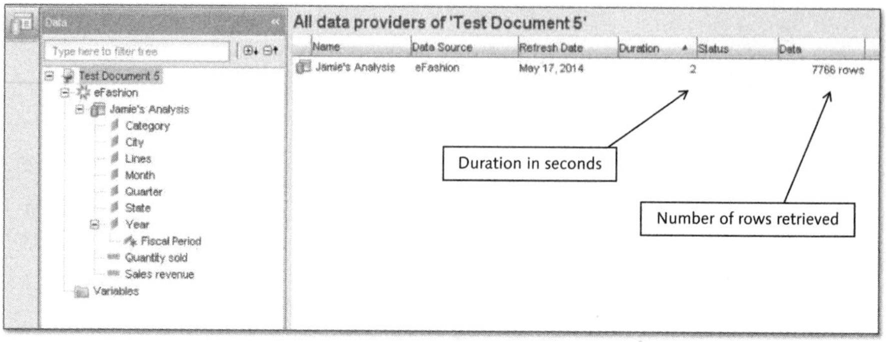

Figure 9.12 Data Tab with Query Information

The purpose of the data mode is to view specific elements of metadata about the data sources in a report. This metadata includes query names, data sources, refresh dates, duration of queries, and the number of rows retrieved.

Figure 9.13 shows actual data retrieved for the query when selecting the query name.

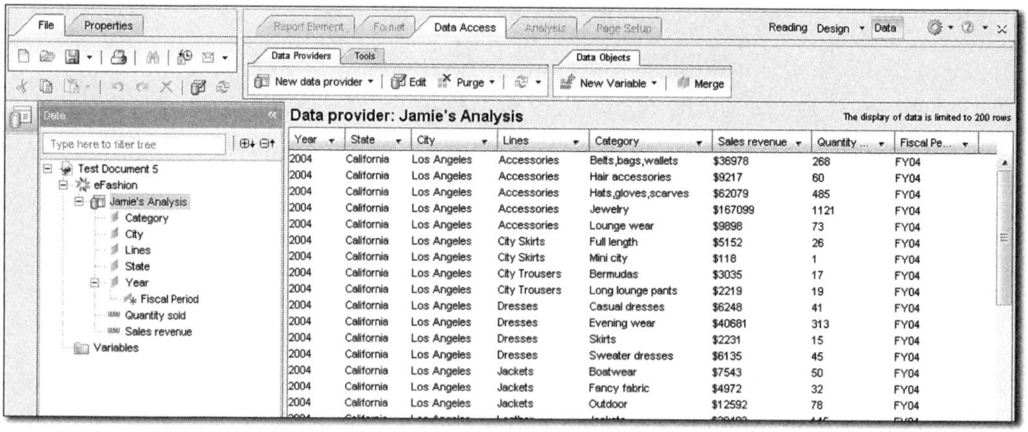

Figure 9.13 Data Provider with Data

To view the values returned within a single object, just enter data mode, and then select an object from your list of the available objects list. This includes objects retrieved by your queries and also locally created variables. Figure 9.14 shows the data values for the City object retrieved in the JAMIE'S ANALYSIS query.

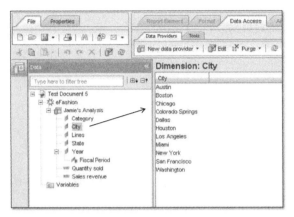

Figure 9.14 Data Values in the City Object

Next, we'll look at how to configure report properties to help maintain a defined standard for reporting and add a consistent look and feel to your reporting documents.

9.9   Style Sheet Modification

Report designers now have the capability to create reports that contain a consistent set of style features across multiple reporting documents. This feature allows report designers to change the default style of a Web Intelligence 4.1 report by importing a customized style sheet or Cascading Style Sheet (CSS) file.

Users can also export all of the existing formats created in a report to a new, unique style sheet. This is a very powerful feature because it gives report designers the freedom to modify a wide variety of visual settings through the multi-tabbed toolbar, and then save all of those settings into a single CSS file that can be applied to other reports.

To change the default style of a report, click on the PROPERTIES tab while in design mode, and then select the DOCUMENT button shown in Figure 9.15.

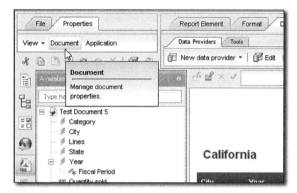

Figure 9.15 Opening the Document Properties

Changing the Default Style

Located in the lower-left corner of the DOCUMENT PROPERTIES window is a new category listed as DEFAULT STYLE. Within this category is a single CHANGE DEFAULT STYLE button. Click on this button to import a new CSS file or export the existing formatting settings to a new CSS file.

Figure 9.16 shows the DOCUMENT SUMMARY window. Notice the CHANGE DEFAULT STYLE option located in the lower-left corner of the DOCUMENT SUMMARY. Click this button to import a different style (and CSS file), export the current style, or reset the current style in the report to the default style.

After clicking on the CHANGE DEFAULT STYLE button, the DEFAULT STYLE window appears with the following three options (Figure 9.17):

▶ IMPORT STYLE

▶ EXPORT STYLE

▶ RESET STANDARD DEFAULT STYLE

Clicking on IMPORT STYLE allows you to search for a local CSS file to assign to the current Web Intelligence reporting document. Clicking on EXPORT STYLE gives you the option to save the formatting within the current document to a new CSS file that can be used in other reports.

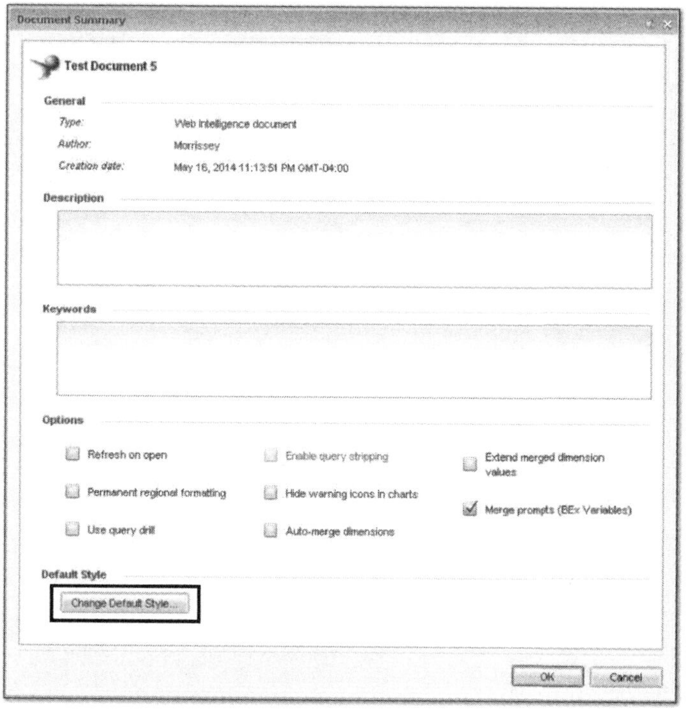

Figure 9.16 Changing the Default Style of a Report

Figure 9.17 Importing, Exporting, and Resetting a Default Style

Be sure to choose an appropriate name and location when saving a new CSS file. The file can also be shared with other users or be published to a shared directory on a network.

After you've exported a reporting style as a local CSS file, you can begin making edits to the file outside of Web Intelligence and then reimport it into the current report or any other Web Intelligence report in SAP BusinessObjects BI 4.1.

Open the CSS file with your preferred file editor, such as Notepad or WordPad. The following is just a sample of the settings that can be edited in the CSS file:

- Font-family
- Font-size
- Color
- Font-weight-bold
- H-Spacing
- V-Spacing
- Page-records-horizontal
- Page-records-vertical
- Page-format-dimension-width
- Page-format-dimension-height
- Page-format-margin-top
- Page-format-margin-left
- Page-format-margin-bottom
- Page-format-margin-right
- Background-color
- Background-fill
- Background type
- Text-v-align
- Text-align
- Min-width
- Min-height

Formatting is grouped into several functional sections that match the structure of a report. The following is a sample of the formatting groups that contain editable formatting sections:

▶ **General settings**

   ▶ Font-family

   ▶ Font-size

   ▶ Font-color

   ▶ Font-weight

   ▶ Default-date-h-align

▶ **Report and Areas**

   ▶ Page body section

   ▶ Page header

   ▶ Page footer

   ▶ Settings for sections

▶ **Tables and Forms**

   ▶ Settings for a table

   ▶ Settings for a form

▶ **Charts**

   ▶ Not supported in CSS attributes

▶ **Columns and Rows**

   ▶ Column width default size and break separator

   ▶ Row height default size and break separator

▶ **Cells**

   ▶ Several cell attributes for the various sections in a report. A few of the possibilities include changing the default attributes in the following areas: page header, page footer, page body, cell in a section, and summary cells.

▶ **Table Cells**

   ▶ Various cell attributes of formats within a table

Global standards can be created by system administrators by editing the *WebiDefaultStyleSheet.css* file located on the server. Always make a backup copy of this file before making any changes in case you need to revert back to the default CSS settings.

A few of the key reasons to update the *WebiDefaultStyleSheet.css* file is to standardize on import data display formats and to also include a company logo on every report with consistent size and placement on the report.

> **Note**
>
> Chart colors are managed globally in the *VisualizationConfig.template.xml* file located at *C:\Program Files (x86)\SAP BusinessObjects\SAP BusinessObjects Enterprise XI 4.0\images* in a Windows Server deployment.
>
> A corporate color palette can be defined by editing any or all of the 32 colors in this file. Colors in this file are defined in 4 color defining strengths: red (R), green (G), blue (B), and the level of transparency (A). An example color definition is <COLOR A="**255**" B="**125**" G="**125**" R="**0**"/>.

Standardizing on a collection of settings defined in a CSS file provides for a more consistent presentation of reports and a more cohesive overall reporting solution. This feature also saves report developers a significant amount of time compared to working in previous versions that require making configuration changes to individual reports to attain visual consistency.

9.10 Summary

Web Intelligence 4.1 provides a full spectrum of reporting properties, tools, and formatting. The side panel in the Report Panel offers easy-to-access tools for reports designers and users to find metadata information about reports. It's important to keep report properties up to date with detailed and relevant descriptions so that users can understand the context of the report's content.

Additionally, the side panel allows for robust user interaction by using input controls. Input controls can be created against dimensions, measures, or variables, and they allow the report user to filter data and change parameters in real time.

Lastly, options such as web services allow advanced developers to leverage the speed and security of Web Intelligence to consume data from external applications delivered through a web service.

Next, Chapter 10 takes a deep dive into filtering data in both the Query Panel and Report Panel. Now that you've learned how to navigate a report's metadata and properties, you'll learn how to filter data in a report to make reports more meaningful for users.

Web Intelligence 4.1 provides several different ways to filter data and present specific information for answering business questions. Whether you are restricting data in the Query Panel or filtering results in the Report Panel, you have many options for displaying detailed and accurate company information.

10 Filtering Data in the Query Panel and Report Panel

Filtering and restricting data produces reporting documents that provide business users with pertinent and contextually relevant information. You can restrict the amount of information returned to your report by applying query filters in the Query Panel. Query filters translate to the where clause of the generated SQL statement and help you minimize the amount of information returned to the microcube in a Web Intelligence 4.1 document.

After running or refreshing a query in a Web Intelligence document and retrieving data, you can filter your results to produce reports with data tables and charts containing subsets of the data returned.

Several different types of filters can be applied to reports and report elements, including the types found in the filter bar, filters applied directly to specific report elements, input control filters, and conditionally hidden report elements.

This chapter covers these data filtering methods and offers screenshots to help explain how each method is accomplished in Web Intelligence 4.1.

10.1 Filtering in the Query Panel

Query filtering restricts the amount of information retrieved from a data provider when a query is refreshed. Query filtering is achieved by including any of three filter types when creating a query:

- ▶ **Predefined filters**
  Filter objects created in the universe.

- ▶ **User-defined filters**
  Filters defined in the Query Panel.

- ▶ **Prompted filters**
  Filter objects that prompt users for input.

Let's examine each of these more closely.

10.1.1 Predefined Filters

Predefined filters are objects that have been previously set up in the universe. These filter types are symbolized with a yellow funnel icon and contain SQL syntax that assigns a value to an object or contains a formula to calculate the value.

Figure 10.1 shows four predefined filters in a query sourced from the eFashion universe. This example shows how predefined filter objects appear to users in the QUERY PANEL of a Web Intelligence 4.1 document. These filter objects are often aliased with descriptive terms that easily communicate the function of the filter to business users for intuitive report filtering.

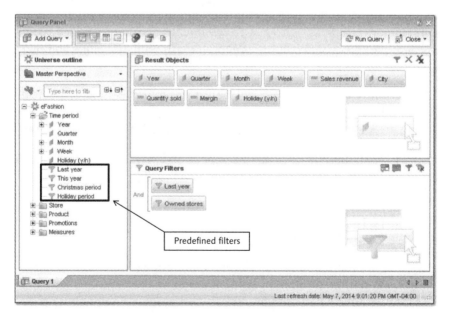

Figure 10.1 Identifying Predefined Filters in the Query Panel

A predefined filter generally contains the assignment of a specific value or set of values and also a description. Figure 10.2 shows the filter object definition for the Christmas period object in the eFashion universe while editing the properties of the object in the Universe Design Tool of SAP BusinessObjects BI 4.1 SP3.

The key element in a predefined filter is the WHERE section in the filter definition. Figure 10.2 sets the WHERE section of the CHRISTMAS PERIOD filter for the CALENDAR_YEAR_LOOKUP.WEEK_IN_YEAR to be between week number 46 and 53. Whenever this object is used in a query, the data returned will have occurred within this weekly time frame.

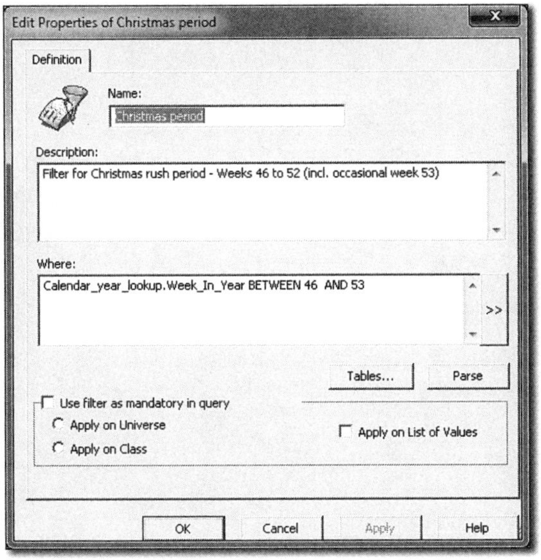

Figure 10.2 Properties of the Predefined Christmas Period Filter Object

The DESCRIPTION field of a filter object plays an important role because it communicates additional information about the object to the user when creating a query.

Mouse over a predefined filter in the QUERY PANEL to see the filter's description. Figure 10.3 shows the description of the Christmas period object that appears when you hover over it in the QUERY PANEL.

In many cases, predefined filters need to be applied by default to every query created from a specific universe. This can be accomplished by checking the USE FILTER AS MANDATORY IN QUERY option when creating or editing the filter object properties in the Universe Design Tool (see Figure 10.4).

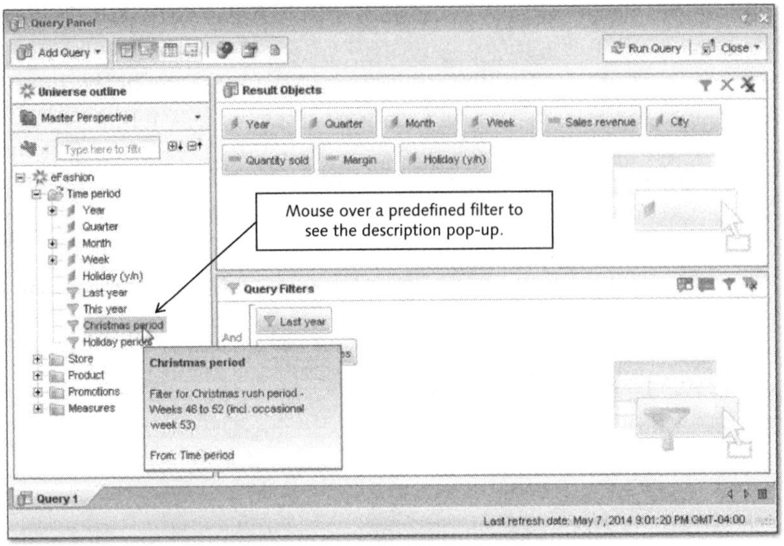

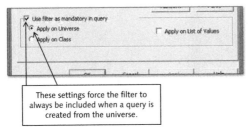

Figure 10.3 Predefined Filter Descriptions

Figure 10.4 Applying Filter as Mandatory Query

As a universe designer, you'll have the opportunity to set a predefined filter to be applied on either the entire universe or the class where the filter is saved. These options become enabled when the USE FILTER AS MANDATORY IN QUERY checkbox is checked.

A single predefined filter can either include the assignment of values to multiple objects or contain a variety of complex formulas. By adding a predefined filter to a Web Intelligence query, you ensure that the data returned to the microcube will be restricted by the conditions defined in the filter.

When creating a predefined filter object, make sure that you name the object with a term or short phrase that clearly describes the purpose of the filter with terminology known by the user community and anticipated audience.

10.1.2 User-Defined Filters

User-defined filters are created in the Query Panel by adding dimension, detail, or measure objects to the QUERY FILTERS pane. Objects are added to the QUERY FILTERS pane by dragging them from the universe outline and dropping them in the QUERY FILTERS pane.

After adding an object to the QUERY FILTERS pane, you need to select an operator for the object. By default, the operator assigned by Web Intelligence is In List. Change the operator by clicking on the small down arrow located immediately to the right of the existing operator. Figure 10.5 shows the Quarter object after it has been added to the QUERY FILTERS pane.

After an operator has been selected, click on the icon to the right of the input box to select the assignment type.

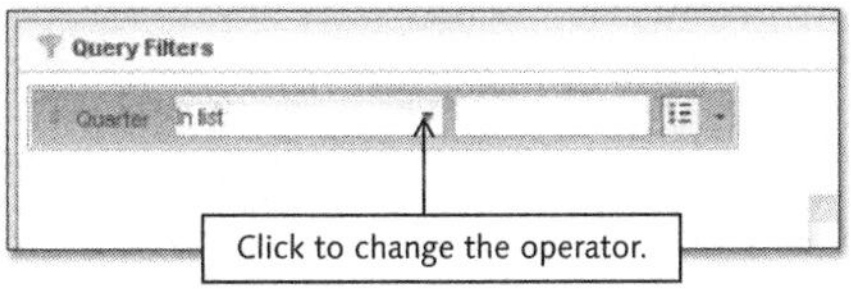

Figure 10.5 Viewing a Dimension Object in the Query Filters Pane

The following operators are available for creating filters with detail, dimension, or measure objects:

▶ In list

▶ Not in list

▶ Equal to

▶ Not Equal to

▶ Greater than

▶ Greater than or Equal to

▶ Less than

▶ Less than or Equal to

► Between

► Not Between

► Is null

► Is not null

► Matches pattern

► Different from pattern

► Both

► Except

Figure 10.6 shows the assignment type choices available in Web Intelligence 4.1 when creating a user-defined filter. The default assignment type selection is CONSTANT.

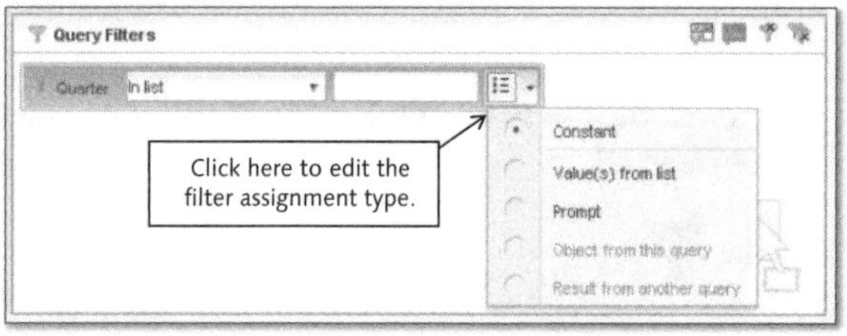

Figure 10.6 User-Defined Filter Assignment Types

The following are filter assignment types:

► CONSTANT
Allows the user to type a constant value.

► VALUE(S) FROM LIST
Launches the LIST OF VALUES dialog box to select one or more values from a distinct list of values for the selected object.

► PROMPT
Prompts for user input when a query is refreshed.

► OBJECT FROM THIS QUERY
Selects from the available objects and variables (not enabled when the IN LIST or the NOT IN LIST operator is selected).

► RESULTS FROM ANOTHER QUERY
Selects a value from a different query within the same document.

When a measure object is added to the QUERY FILTERS pane, a small calculator icon appears inside the value box. This icon is used to launch a calculator panel and provide users with the capability to add a specific number without using their keyboard. Figure 10.7 shows this calculator panel with a measure object.

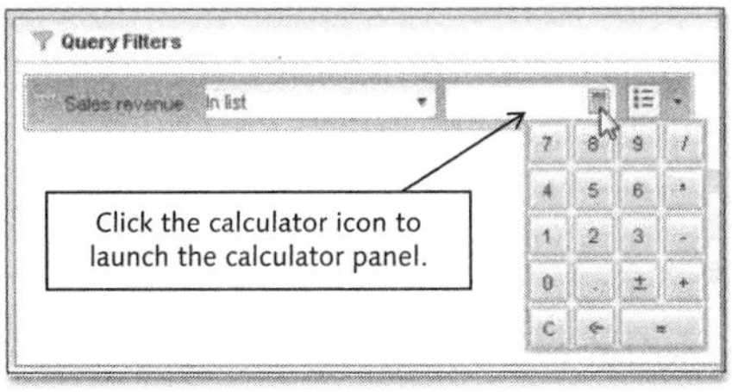

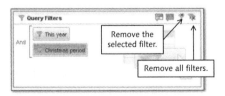

Figure 10.7 Calculator Panel in the Measure Filter

Remove Filter Objects from the Query Filters Pane

To remove filter objects, choose any of these methods:

▸ Select the filter and press Backspace.

▸ Drag the filter from the QUERY FILTERS pane, and drop it in the UNIVERSE OUTLINE panel.

▸ Select the filter, and then click on the X in the upper-right corner of the pane.

▸ Click on the REMOVE ALL button in the upper-right corner of the pane.

Figure 10.8 shows the icons located in the upper-right corner of the QUERY FILTERS pane. Use these icons to remove a single filter or to remove the entire set of query filters. You'll be prompted with a dialog box asking, ARE YOU SURE YOU WANT TO DELETE ALL FILTERS?

If you click on YES, all of the filters will be removed without an option to undo the changes.

Figure 10.8 Removing One or All Filters

10.1.3   Value(s) from List

When Value(s) from list is selected as the filter assignment type, a full distinct list of the values that belong to the object being filtered will be displayed.

Lists of values (LOVs) are either enabled or disabled when the objects are created in the universe. Custom LOVs can also be created in the universe to provide cascading prompted filtering to report consumers.

To select values from the LIST OF VALUES dialog box, follow these steps:

1. Select VALUES from the list of distinct values to be included.

2. Click on the > button to add the values to the SELECTED VALUE(S) box.

3. Click on OK to accept.

10.1.4   Prompted Filters

Use prompted filters to require report consumers to provide input when refreshing a report. The user's response will be passed into the where clause when the SQL statement is generated.

When a Web Intelligence 4.1 reporting document is saved with the document property option REFRESH ON OPEN selected, and the document includes prompted filters, users will be required to answer the prompt(s) as the report opens.

If PROMPT is selected as the filter's assignment type, a PROMPT PROPERTIES icon will be displayed to provide options for configuring the prompt (see Figure 10.9).

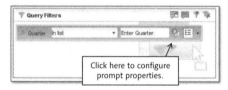

Figure 10.9 Locating the Prompt Properties Icon

Prompt Filter Properties

When a prompted filter object is included in a query, report developers have the opportunity to revise a variety of properties for each filter object.

Figure 10.10 shows the PROMPT PROPERTIES window that is launched when you define a prompt. The following are the associated properties:

▶ PROMPT TEXT
A prompt text is added by default. This property is important if the document and filter will receive values passed to it with a hyperlink. This will be discussed in detail in Chapter 15.

▶ PROMPT WITH LIST OF VALUES
This property displays a distinct LOV for the object being filtered.

▶ KEEP LAST VALUES SELECTED
This property defaults to the last value selected.

▶ SELECT ONLY FROM LIST
This property requires the selection to be made only from the provided LOV rather than allowing freehand entry.

▶ OPTIONAL PROMPT
This property permits the prompt to be optional rather than required.

▶ SET DEFAULT VALUES
This property allows a default value to be added to the filter.

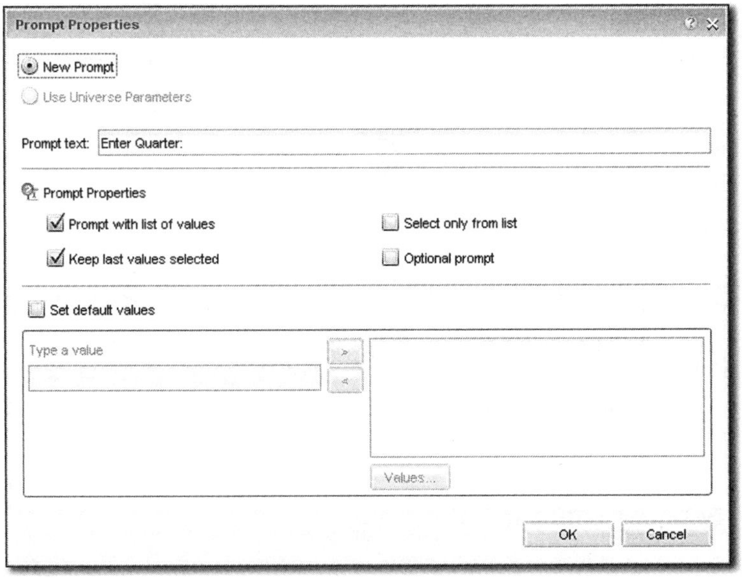

Figure 10.10 Prompt Dialog Box for Configuring Prompted Filters

The next section describes the process of applying several different types of filtering in the REPORT PANEL.

10.2   Filtering in the Report Panel

Report filtering provides business users with the capability to display a small subset of data in a report rather than everything returned from the query and stored locally within the microcube.

It's very common for business requirements to call for Web Intelligence reports that contain charts for specific values in a data set along with additional charts or data table elements that display diverse divisions of the values. This type of functionality is possible in Web Intelligence 4.1 by applying different report filters to each element (chart, table, or section) within a report.

When values are filtered in a report, the data is hidden only from the user and remains within the microcube for use in other report tabs within the document. This way, business users can insert new report tabs and set up new filters without affecting other reports in the same document.

Filtering report data can be achieved by performing the following actions:

▸ Adding simple filters to entire reports by assigning values to objects on the filter bar

▸ Adding filters to specific elements in a report by assigning values to objects in the Report Filter Panel

▸ Interacting with report data by using input controls

> **Note**
>
> This chapter is written in the context of reading and designing reports with the RICH INTERNET APPLICATION preference setting for viewing and modifying reports. This setting can be selected from the Web Intelligence preferences assigned in the BI Launch Pad.

10.2.1   Simple Filtering with the Filter Bar

Simple report filters are easily added to a reporting document by clicking on the FILTER BAR button in the reporting toolbar while in design mode.

The ideal method of adding simple report filters entails the following three steps:

1. Enter design mode.

2. Select the ANALYSIS tab.

3. Click on the FILTER BAR button located on the INTERACT subtab.

Figure 10.11 shows the FILTER BAR button on a report in design mode. Enabling the filter bar lets you drop objects onto the bar for simple report filtering.

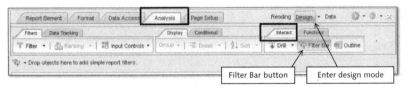

Figure 10.11 Enabling the Filter Bar in Design Mode

Even though the FILTER BAR button is present in reading mode, simple filters can only be added while in design mode. This toggle is primarily used in reading mode to turn off simple report filters. Figure 10.12 shows the filter bar with objects added for filtering.

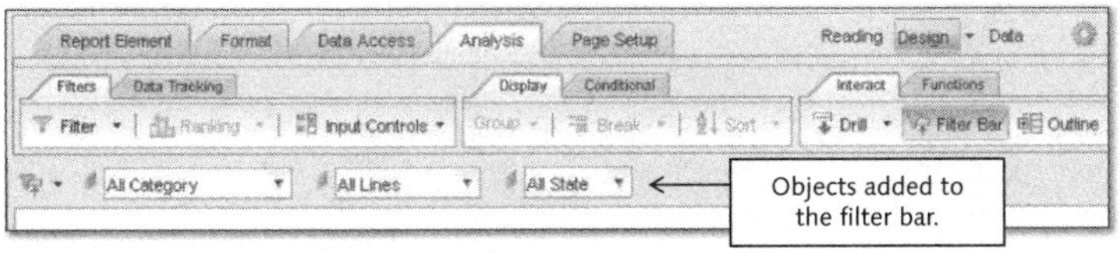

Figure 10.12 Report Filter Bar with Objects Added

Simple report filters are added by dragging and dropping result objects onto the filter bar. Distinct LOVs will be displayed in dropdown components and provide a flexible method of filtering the entire report.

Simple filtering can be toggled on or off by selecting the REPORT FILTER TOOLBAR icon located on the default toolbar.

10.2.2 Report Element Filters

Report element filters in Web Intelligence 4.1 can be added to single data blocks, charts, sections, or to entire reports. This type of filtering is applied to reports while in design mode only.

Follow these steps to add a filter to a specific report element:

1. Right-click on the element, and select FILTER from the list of choices.

2. Select ADD FILTER to launch the REPORT FILTER window.

3. From the FILTER MAP pane in the REPORT FILTER window, select the report element to assign the new filter to, and click on ADD FILTER.

4. Choose from the list of available objects to begin creating the filter.

5. Select the operator for the filter.

6. Assign or enter a value, and then click on OK.

Figure 10.13 shows the menu displayed when right-clicking on a report element.

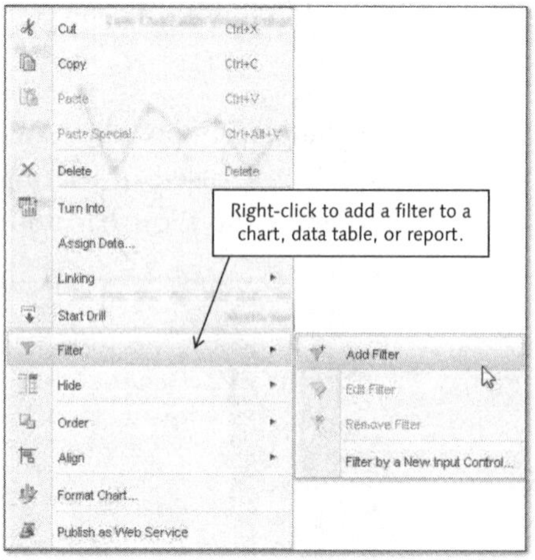

Figure 10.13 Adding a Filter to a Report Element

Choosing ADD FILTER allows you to place a filter on the element selected or switch to another element on the current REPORT PANEL. From this menu, you'll also have the opportunity to edit or remove existing filters or to add a new input control filter.

Every element (chart, table, section, or report) on the Report Panel can be assigned one or more unique filters for the creation of highly customized reports.

The REPORT FILTER window introduced in Web Intelligence 4.0 lets you assign filters to every element on the Report Panel without having to right-click on each element individually. Select the element from the FILTER MAP pane that you'd like to assign the filter to, and then click on ADD FILTER.

Notice that charts, data blocks, sections, and even entire reports are displayed in the FILTER MAP pane for easy configuration of filters (see Figure 10.14).

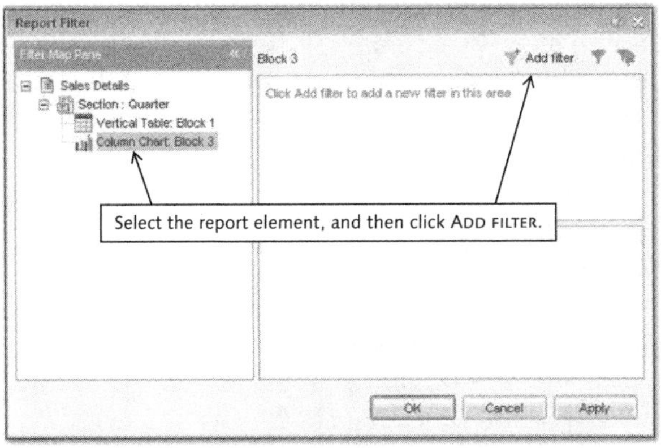

Figure 10.14 Report Filter Window and the Filter Map Pane

After you select ADD FILTER, the list of objects available in the existing report will be displayed. Select an object and click on OK to proceed with creating the filter.

Figure 10.15 shows the AVAILABLE OBJECTS window as it appears when adding a report filter. This window will display all objects retrieved from your query and also existing variables created within the report.

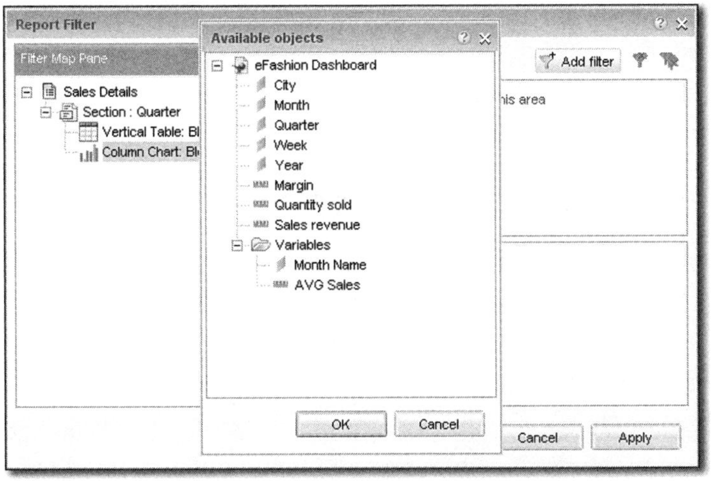

Figure 10.15 Available Objects for Creating a Report Filter

After selecting a dimension or measure and clicking on OK, you can select an operator for the filter. The default operator is IN LIST, which allows for multiple selections to be made from a distinct list of values.

Twelve different operators are available for this type of filtering. Figure 10.16 shows a chart element with a single filter assigned to it. In this example, the City object has been selected along with the In list operator. The list of available state values is displayed at the bottom of the screen.

Double-click on or select values followed by clicking on the > symbol to assign a value to the filter. Click on APPLY, and click OK to accept.

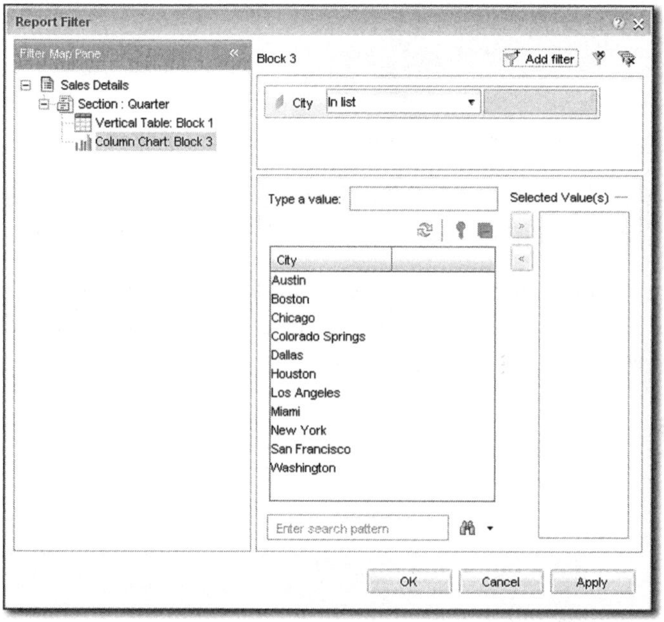

Figure 10.16 Assigning an Operator to a Chart Filter

In the next section, we'll cover how to use input controls to control data results.

10.2.3 Filtering with Input Controls

Input controls provide users with the flexibility to interact with and analyze report data in several different ways. You can choose from four different components for filtering single-value dimension objects or two components for multiple-value dimension filtering.

Similar to report element filters, input controls can be assigned to charts, tables, sections, or entire reports. They must be created while in design mode.

To create an input control, enter design mode, and right-click on a report element. Then click on FILTER • FILTER BY A NEW INPUT CONTROL. Figure 10.17 shows a portion of the menu displayed when you right-click on a report element with FILTER selected.

Figure 10.17 Adding a New Input Control When Right-Clicking on a Report Element

Another way to add a new input control is by clicking on the ANALYSIS tab, the FILTERS subtab, and then INPUT CONTROLS. This method of adding a new input control is also available only in design mode and is shown in Figure 10.18.

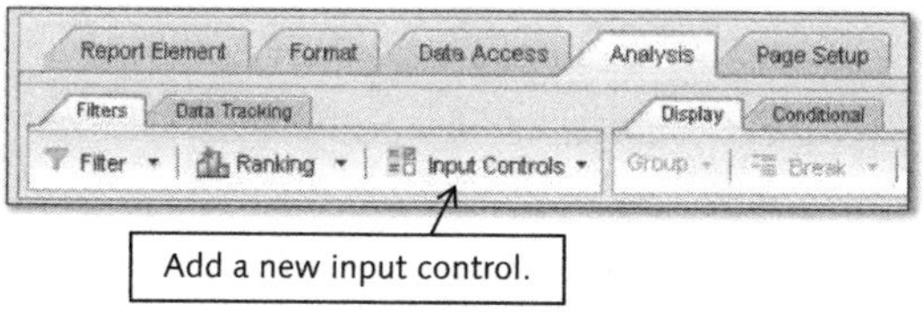

Figure 10.18 Adding a New Input Control from the Toolbar

After selecting FILTER BY A NEW INPUT CONTROL, the DEFINE INPUT CONTROL window will appear and prompt you to select a report object as the basis for the new input control filter. The objects can be arranged alphabetically or by query. This option is helpful when filtering reports sourced from multiple data sources.

You may also want to create input controls with objects existing in the selected block (chart or data table). This is accomplished by checking the INCLUDE OBJECTS FROM SELECTED BLOCK ONLY box at the bottom of the window. Figure 10.19 shows these options at the bottom of the DEFINE INPUT CONTROL box.

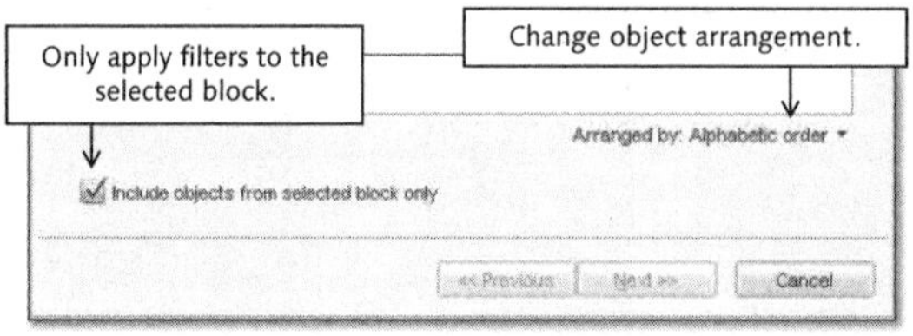

Figure 10.19 Properties When Defining a New Input Control

Figure 10.20 shows the types of input controls available for single-value and multiple-value dimension objects. This figure also shows the ALLOW SELECTION OF ALL VALUES option new to Web Intelligence in SAP BusinessObjects BI 4.1 SPs.

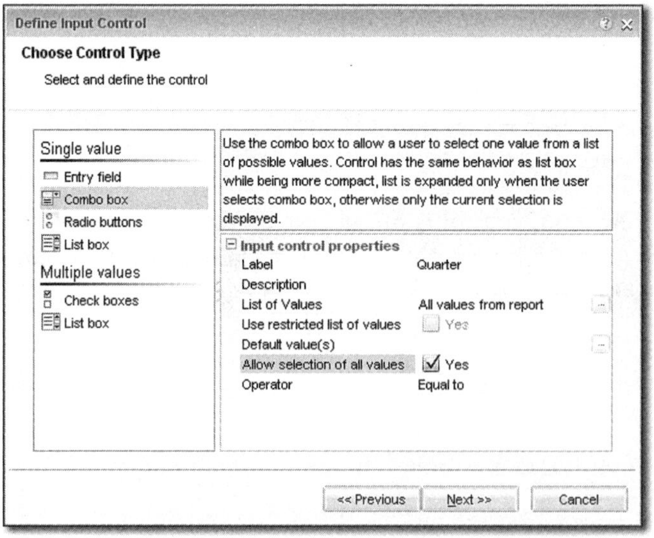

Figure 10.20 Input Control Properties for a Dimension Object

> **Note**
>
> One new feature in SAP BusinessObjects BI 4.1 SP3 worth noting is the ALLOW SELECTION OF ALL VALUES option, which is checked by default. Uncheck this selection to remove ALL VALUES from being displayed in the INPUT CONTROLS box. This setting forces the input control to always have at least one value selected. Because of its requirement, a default value is required after unchecking the ALLOW SELECTION OF ALL VALUES option.

The following input control properties are single-value control types for dimension objects:

▶ ENTRY FIELD
Allows for user input without a consistency check.

▶ COMBO BOX
Allows users to select from a list of possible values with the selected value being displayed in the box.

▶ RADIO BUTTONS
Enables users to select from a list of possible values (the selected value is displayed as checked).

▶ LIST BOX
Enables users to make several selections from a list of possible values.

The following input control properties are multiple-value control types for dimension objects:

▶ CHECKBOXES
Provide users with the ability to make several selections from a list of possible values (the selected values are shown as checked).

▶ LIST BOX
Provides users with the ability to make several selections from a list of possible values.

Except for the entry field control type, each input control type comes with several modifiable properties. The following input control properties for dimension objects can make a big difference in terms of how data is returned and how the control is presented to users:

► LABEL

This property is the revisable name of the input control. The default entry is the object name.

► DESCRIPTION

This is an optional area for entering a full description of the input control filter. We recommend that you add a complete description of the input control, including the blocks it's assigned to and the business meaning of the filter.

► LIST OF VALUES

This property allows for a custom or restricted list of available values to be used. This is a good practice for creating regulated reports that allow users to view and interact only with limited values.

► USE RESTRICTED LIST OF VALUES

This property is used in combination with the LIST OF VALUES property when a custom list of values has been selected.

► ALLOW SELECTION OF ALL VALUES

Checked by default to show all values with the input control being created.

► DEFAULT VALUE(S)

This property lets you select a default value.

► OPERATOR

This property provides you with the following six operators for filtering data:

  ► EQUAL TO

  ► NOT EQUAL TO

  ► LESS THAN

  ► LESS THAN OR EQUAL TO

  ► GREATER THAN

  ► GREATER THAN OR EQUAL TO

► NUMBER OF LINES

This property allows designers to set the number values that will be displayed when the input control is viewed. The default setting is 5.

After choosing the control type, the next step is to assign it to report elements.

Assigning Dependencies to Input Controls

After selecting the control type and configuring the properties of the control, you need to assign the control filter to elements on the report. Click on NEXT on the CHOOSE CONTROL TYPE window to proceed to the ASSIGN REPORT ELEMENTS window (see Figure 10.21). This is where report elements are selected to have the new input control filter assigned.

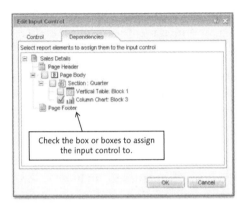

Figure 10.21 Assigning Report Element Dependencies in an Input Control

Available elements to assign the input control filters to include the report page body, sections, charts, and data tables. The boxes indicate that the elements can be selected and explicitly assigned to the input control filter.

When a top-level box is selected (e.g., the report page body or section), all elements nested within that object will be checked by default and grayed-out. To uncheck a specific child element, you need to uncheck the top-level element and then explicitly check the box of the element(s) requiring the input control assignment.

Adding Input Controls on Measure Objects

Because measures and dimensions need to be filtered differently, defining input controls on measure objects is accomplished with a different set of control types and properties. Several control types are available for filtering numerical values rather than descriptive data.

The following are single-value control types:

▶ ENTRY FIELD
Allows for user input without a consistency check.

▶ SPINNER
Allows users to enter or adjust values with arrows.

▶ SIMPLE SLIDER
Provides users with a slider component to select values between a defined interval (requires a minimum, maximum, and increment value at time of creation).

The double slider is a multiple-value control type that provides users with two sliders for selecting and changing a range of values. This functionality lets users focus on specific data elements that fall within a range defined by the position of the sliders. It requires a minimum and maximum value to be defined when the control is created and also requires an increment value at the time of creation.

Figure 10.22 shows the available control types and properties for an input control created with a measure object.

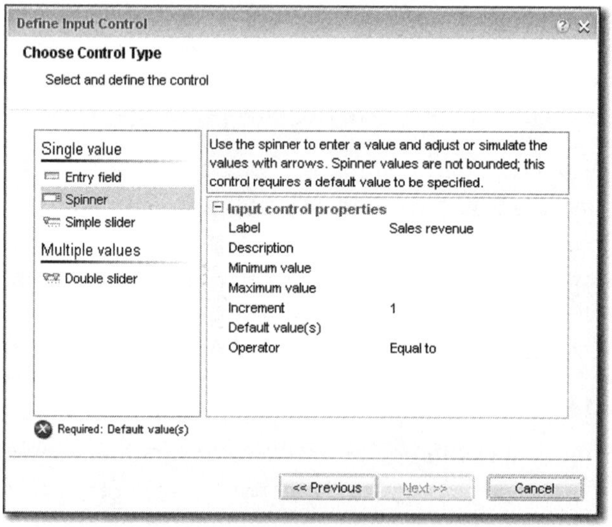

Figure 10.22 Adding a New Input Control on a Measure Object

Properties of Input Controls Created with Measure Objects

It's important to know that the minimum and maximum values must be set on the spinner, simple slider, and double slider input controls. The filter operator is also adjustable, allowing you to change the default EQUAL to operator if the input control requires a different operator such as LESS THAN or GREATER THAN.

After you've created one or more input controls, it's time to save your document to the BI Launch Pad and share your report with other users to begin exploring and analyzing the results.

Interacting with Input Controls

Users can interact with input controls while reading reports without a need for editing or working in design mode. By default, input controls are located on the left side of the Report Panel.

Report data updates instantly as users interact with input control values, thus providing a fluid analysis experience. Figure 10.23 shows a report with two input controls viewed in reading mode.

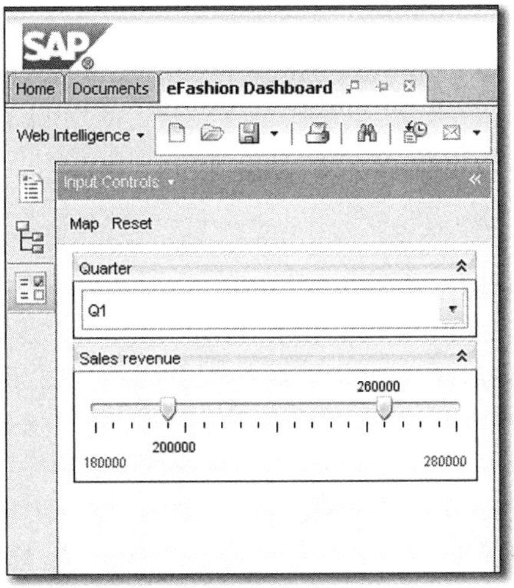

Figure 10.23 Input Controls Displayed While in Reading Mode

Editing or Removing an Input Control

To edit the properties of an existing input control, begin by entering design mode and then locating the input control to be updated. With appropriate permissions, you'll be able to edit and remove any input control existing within the report.

Mouse over the input control title of the control to be modified to display three shortcut icons previously not visible. These icons allow you to easily edit, show dependencies, or delete the control (see Figure 10.24).

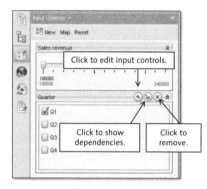

Figure 10.24 Editing or Removing an Input Control

Editing an input control will return you to the window used to define the control and its properties during creation. From this screen, you can change the filter's dependencies, modify its properties, or even change the control type.

10.3   Conditionally Hiding Report Elements

Conditionally hiding report elements is a type of report filtering similar to the dynamic visibility feature available in SAP BusinessObjects Dashboards. This type of conditional formatting provides designers with the capability of creating reports that resemble and function as dashboards in many ways. This includes adding layers of components onto a single report and then triggering the appropriate components to be displayed based on the result of custom formulas. It may also mean hiding report elements when they are empty.

There are two ways to conditionally hide report elements; both are enabled when in design mode. Figure 10.25 shows the menu that appears when you right-click on a report element. Click on HIDE • HIDE WHEN... to write a formula to allow for conditional visibility.

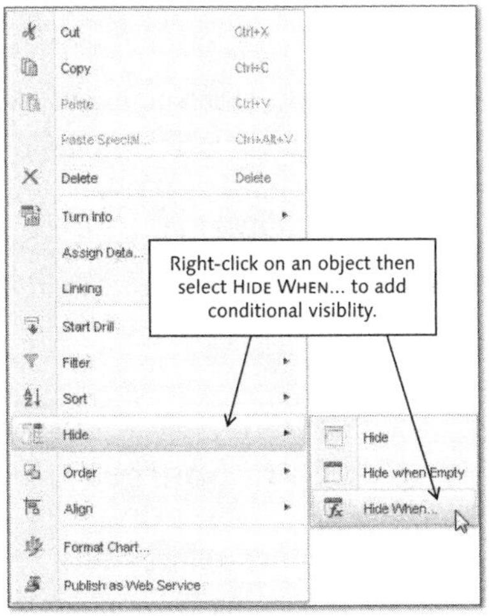

Figure 10.25 Setting Conditional Visibility with the Hide When Feature

Another method for selecting HIDE WHEN... is to right-click on a report element and then click on FORMAT TABLE. Both methods will take you to the GENERAL tab of the FORMAT CHART window (shown in Figure 10.26, along with the area to enable the HIDE WHEN feature).

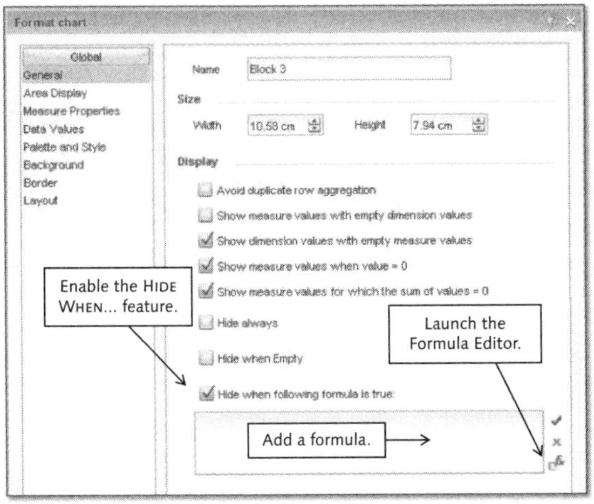

Figure 10.26 Configuring the Hide When Feature

The HIDE menu is available to any chart type, data table, or section within a report. A common reason for enabling HIDE WHEN conditional formatting is to display different customized charts based on the number of dimensions being viewed.

As users begin to analyze refined data sets by drilling into results through the use of the filter bar and input controls, the number of dimensions that meet the criteria will shrink significantly, which changes the way the data is displayed. For robust reporting documents that resemble the functionality of dashboards, use the HIDE WHEN feature to display appropriate report elements that match the amount of data being viewed at any given time.

10.4   Hierarchical Navigation with SAP BW Data Sources

Web Intelligence allows you to display and interact with hierarchical data retrieved from SAP Business Explorer (SAP BEx) queries with components ideally suited for viewing multidimensional data. Data tables in Web Intelligence take on a whole new appearance with hierarchical data, and they provide the capability to filter, expand, and collapse hierarchy members to view data at more granular levels.

After you've connected to an SAP BEx query, select members from one or more levels by dragging a hierarchy to the RESULT OBJECTS pane in the QUERY PANEL. Specific members can also be selected from different levels to create a customized view of the data.

Figure 10.27 shows the MEMBER SELECTOR window displayed when selecting members of a hierarchy in the RESULT OBJECTS screen in the QUERY PANEL.

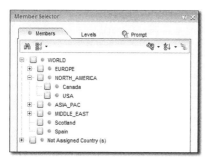

Figure 10.27 Selecting Values from a Hierarchy with the Member Selector

Figure 10.28 shows the LEVELS tab in the MEMBER SELECTOR window, which you can use to access a member through a selected level. Check ENABLE LEVELS to make level-based selections. All member values will be returned through the selected level because levels cannot be skipped using the level-based selection method.

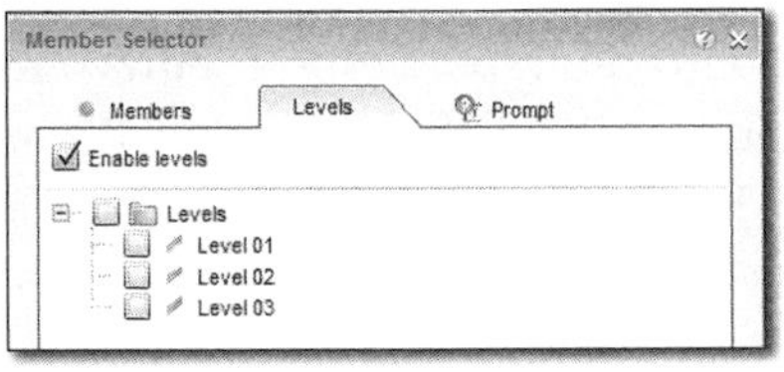

Figure 10.28 Selecting Levels in a Hierarchy

Navigating Hierarchical Data in the Report Panel

Hierarchical data is analyzed in the Report Panel with expandable and collapsible member values. Figure 10.29 shows a hierarchy retrieved from an SAP BEx query and aggregated at the highest level. Click on the plus (+) symbol beside the member to expand and view the children in the second level of the hierarchy.

Country Hier with L	Order Amount	Order Quantity
⊞ WORLD	242,431,244.6	266,818

Figure 10.29 Hierarchical Data Aggregated at the Highest Level

For deeper analysis, continue to expand the child values to view all descendants in a hierarchy. Figure 10.30 shows values from three different levels.

Country Hier with L	Order Amount	Order Quantity
⊟ WORLD	242,431,244.6	266,818
⊞ EUROPE	25,977,635.54	31,009
⊟ NORTH_AMERIC	202,401,620.34	219,944
Canada	17,398,982.36	17,754
USA	185,002,637.98	202,190
⊞ ASIA_PAC	7,656,112.66	9,065
⊞ MIDDLE_EAST	1,540,410.62	2,443
Scotland	250,070.16	408
Spain	4,605,395.28	3,949

Figure 10.30 Expanded Hierarchical Data

Hierarchical Navigation in Charts

You can visually display and interact with hierarchical SAP BEx data with charts in Web Intelligence 4.1. Existing data tables containing hierarchical data can be converted to charts by right-clicking on the table and selecting TURN INTO and a chart. You can also create hierarchical charts by selecting a chart from the REPORT ELEMENT tab and then choosing a chart to insert onto the report canvas. After the chart has been added, drop a hierarchy object and measure object from the list of available objects onto the chart. Figure 10.31 shows a hierarchical data set with the top two levels displayed.

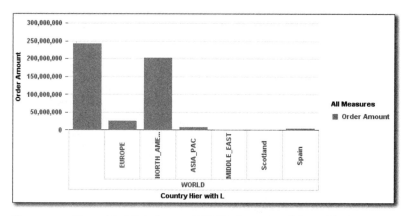

Figure 10.31 Hierarchical Data from an SAP BEx Query in a Column Chart

You can interact with hierarchical charts by clicking on the member name to drill up or down the hierarchy. You can also right-click on a chart and then mouse over the HIERARCHICAL NAVIGATION option, as shown in Figure 10.32, to expand.

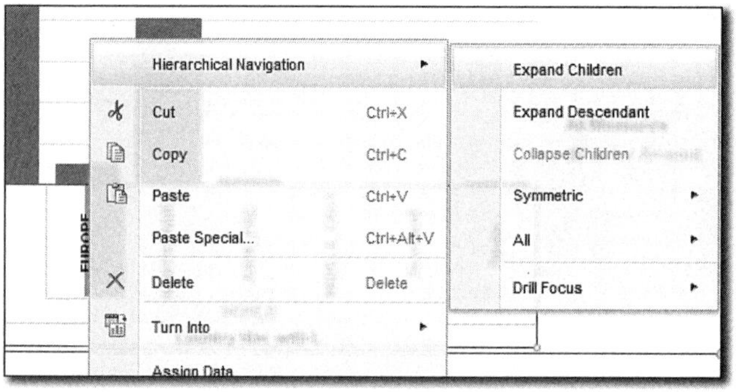

Figure 10.32 Right-Click on a Chart for Hierarchical Navigation

The HIERARCHICAL NAVIGATION menu allows you to view children, descendants, or all members at lower levels.

10.5 Summary

Filtering data in Web Intelligence 4.1 is both flexible and easy to apply. Begin filtering your documents by restricting the amount of data returned in a query by including predefined, user-defined, or prompted filters in the Query Panel.

After data is returned to the microcube in a Web Intelligence document, you can fine-tune your reports by adding element filters to precisely display subsets of data. Or you can create a series of input controls to put the power of filtering results in the hands of business users.

An extensive list of operators in both the Query Panel and Report Panel gives report developers the tools to meet any business requirement. Whether filtering the available data in your data source or limiting data from being displayed in the Report Panel, as a report developer, you have many choices for creating highly functional reporting documents.

You can use the filter bar to provide dimension and detail values in selectable dropdown lists to quickly filter entire reports, and you can conditionally hide charts, data tables and sections based on the result of a custom designed formula. This new functionality can transform the way data is delivered in a report and how users interact with reporting documents.

The next chapter will explain how the Scope of Analysis section works in the Query Panel to produce drillable hierarchies when analyzing data. This topic is important because it dictates the drill paths and interactive capabilities of report data.

Drill functionality puts the power of analysis into the end users' hands by enabling them to filter down on report tables and charts with a simple click. New features allow not only drill down, but drill up, drill by, and drill upon bars and data points in a chart, making Web Intelligence a powerful end-user reporting tool.

11   Scope of Analysis and Drill Functionality

By drilling on a report, you can see levels of data beyond your original query. For instance, let's say that you receive a monthly report summarizing sales revenue by state. Upon review of the report, you discover that sales revenue seems high for the State of Massachusetts in 2006, as shown in Figure 11.1. Exploring this anomaly further to determine its root cause would normally require running numerous additional detailed reports or even requesting a customized query to get your desired result.

Sales Revenue by State

	California	Colorado	DC	Florida	Illinois	Massachusetts
2004	$1,704,211	$448,302	$693,211	$405,985	$737,914	$238,819
2005	$2,782,680	$768,390	$1,215,158	$661,250	$1,150,659	$157,719
2006	$2,992,679	$843,584	$1,053,581	$811,924	$1,134,085	$887,169
Totals:	$7,479,569	$2,060,275	$2,961,950	$1,879,159	$3,022,658	$1,283,707

Figure 11.1 High Sales Revenue for Massachusetts in 2006

This process means that a report request is made and another query generated, which produces another report showing sales revenue results at a monthly level by state. If this still didn't answer your questions, you'd need to make another request to produce another query to further drill down the data to a lower level (perhaps city or week) in order to pinpoint the reason for the revenue results. You can see how this process could become long and cumbersome.

Here's the good news: A report developer can avoid these extra steps and, by setting scope of analysis and enable drilling on a report, put the ownership back into your hands as an end user as shown in Figure 11.2.

Sales Revenue by State

	California	Colorado	DC	Florida	Illinois	Massachusetts
2004	$1,704,211	$448,302	$693,211	$405,985	$737,914	$238,819
2005	$2,782,680	$768,390	$1,215,158	$661,250	$1,150,659	$157,719
2006	$2,992,679	$843,584	$1,053,581	$811,924	$1,134,085	$887,169
Totals:	$7,479,569	$2,060,275	$2,961,950	$1,879,159	$3,022,658	$1,283,707

Figure 11.2 Drilling on the Table to Explore the Data Further

11.1 Setting the Scope of Analysis in the Query Panel

The first step to enabling drill is to set the *scope of analysis* in the Query Panel. This tells Web Intelligence to return additional data beyond the results specified in the RESULT OBJECTS pane. The additional data returned does not appear in the initial report displayed upon execution of the query, but you can see the objects returned in the data pane of the report view, as shown in Figure 11.3.

Figure 11.3 Available Objects Pane in the Report Manager—Result Objects and Scope of Analysis Objects

Scope of analysis is the defined drill path for a data element in the universe and is only applicable for dimension objects. The default scope of analysis for a universe object is defined by the order of the objects within a class. For example, in the S𝚃𝙾𝚁𝙴 class, the objects are ordered from top to bottom as State, City, Store name, so the hierarchy for the scope of analysis would be by S𝚃𝙰𝚃𝙴, C𝙸𝚃𝚈, and S𝚃𝙾𝚁𝙴 N𝙰𝙼𝙴, as shown in Figure 11.4. The universe designer can also overwrite these defaults and define custom hierarchies in the universe. (Further detail on how to set up hierarchies in the universe is discussed in Chapter 24.)

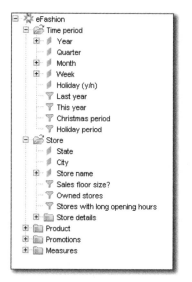

Figure 11.4 Default Object Hierarchy Defined by Order or Objects in the Universe

To view the defined hierarchies in the universe, go to the Q𝚄𝙴𝚁𝚈 P𝙰𝙽𝙴𝙻 by editing the data provider in the Web Intelligence report. In the U𝙽𝙸𝚅𝙴𝚁𝚂𝙴 𝙾𝚄𝚃𝙻𝙸𝙽𝙴 box, select the dropdown arrow next to M𝙰𝚂𝚃𝙴𝚁 P𝙴𝚁𝚂𝙿𝙴𝙲𝚃𝙸𝚅𝙴. Select the D𝙸𝚂𝙿𝙻𝙰𝚈 𝙱𝚈 N𝙰𝚅𝙸𝙶𝙰𝚃𝙸𝙾𝙽 P𝙰𝚃𝙷𝚂 radio button to view the object hierarchies for the selection universe.

From the D𝙸𝚂𝙿𝙻𝙰𝚈 𝙱𝚈 N𝙰𝚅𝙸𝙶𝙰𝚃𝙸𝙾𝙽 P𝙰𝚃𝙷𝚂 view, the report developer can see the defined hierarchies in the universe (see Figure 11.5).

To set the scope of analysis, you must first define the result objects for the query in the Query Panel. After creating the initial query by adding result objects into the R𝙴𝚂𝚄𝙻𝚃 O𝙱𝙹𝙴𝙲𝚃 pane and adding any filters into the Q𝚄𝙴𝚁𝚈 F𝙸𝙻𝚃𝙴𝚁𝚂 pane, select the S𝙲𝙾𝙿𝙴 𝙾𝙵 A𝙽𝙰𝙻𝚈𝚂𝙸𝚂 P𝙰𝙽𝙴𝙻 icon on the Q𝚄𝙴𝚁𝚈 P𝙰𝙽𝙴𝙻 toolbar, as shown in Figure 11.6. This will display the S𝙲𝙾𝙿𝙴 𝙾𝙵 𝙰𝙽𝙰𝙻𝚈𝚂𝙸𝚂 pane, as shown in Figure 11.7.

Figure 11.5 Display by Navigation View in Query Panel

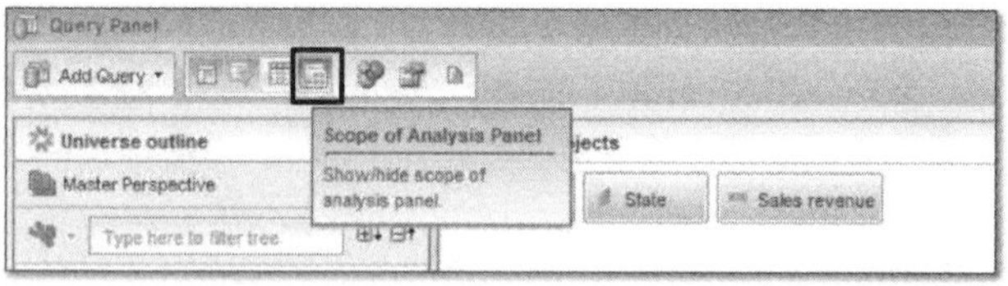

Figure 11.6 Scope of Analysis Icon on the Query Panel Menu Bar

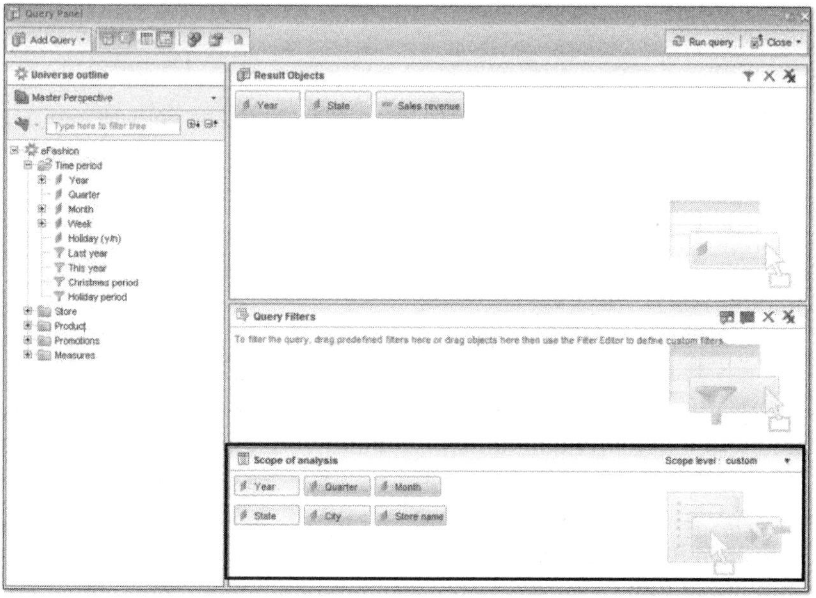

Figure 11.7 Scope of Analysis Pane

Notice that each of the dimension objects from your query appears in this pane. The additional objects shown after the result objects are the objects included in the hierarchy set up in the universe. In the SCOPE OF ANALYSIS pane, Figure 11.7 shows a hierarchy for STATE that includes STATE, CITY, and STORE NAME, and a hierarchy for YEAR that includes YEAR, QUARTER, and MONTH. These are the applicable levels of drill down that can be enabled for each dimension object included in the RESULT OBJECTS pane shown in Figure 11.8.

In the top-right corner of the SCOPE OF ANALYSIS pane is a SCOPE LEVEL list drop-down box used to define the number of levels of drill down that should be returned with the query. The options include NONE, ONE LEVEL, TWO LEVELS, THREE LEVELS, and CUSTOM.

Figure 11.8 Scope Level Options

Let's look at these options further. If NONE is selected, as it is in Figure 11.9, then only the result objects shown in the RESULT OBJECTS pane will be returned in the query results. There will be no additional objects returned with the query to enable drill down.

Figure 11.9 Scope Level: None

If ONE LEVEL is selected, then only one level of drill down will be enabled. This will return the dimension object from the RESULT OBJECTS pane as well as the next one dimension object listed in the SCOPE OF ANALYSIS. For the result object of STATE, the query would return STATE and CITY (see Figure 11.10).

Figure 11.10 Scope Level: One Level

If the TWO LEVELS option is selected, as in Figure 11.11, then two levels of drill down will be enabled. This will return the dimension object from the RESULT OBJECTS pane as well as the next two dimension objects listed in the SCOPE OF ANALYSIS.

For the result object of STATE, the query would return STATE, CITY, and STORE NAME.

Figure 11.11 Scope Level: Two Levels

If the THREE LEVELS option is selected, as in Figure 11.12, then three levels of drill down will be enabled. This will return the dimension object from the RESULT OBJECTS pane as well as the next three dimension objects listed in the SCOPE OF ANALYSIS pane. For the result object of YEAR, the query would return YEAR, QUARTER, MONTH, and WEEK.

For the STATE object, only two levels of hierarchy exist in the universe, therefore, only two will show in the SCOPE OF ANALYSIS pane.

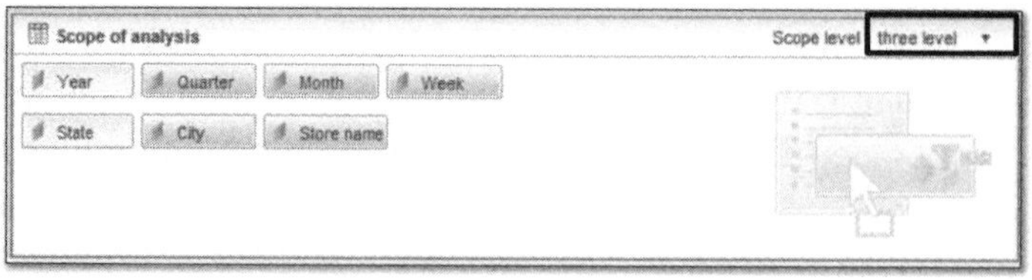

Figure 11.12 Scope Level: Three Levels

If Custom is selected, as in Figure 11.13, then all objects added manually into the Scope of analysis pane as well as those objects in the Result Objects pane are returned.

In Figure 11.13, the custom scope of analysis is defined without Quarter. Consequently, when you drill down on the report, the Year objects will drill down directly to Month, skipping the Quarter level.

This is useful if certain levels of drill are not applicable for reporting on certain business questions.

Figure 11.13 Scope Level: Custom

> **Note**
>
> When setting scope of analysis, remember that each new level of drill down increases the size of the microcube returned with the query results. The larger the microcube, the longer it will take to run the report and the larger the file size maintained in the repository.

While scope of analysis can add value to a report, it can also be a hindrance if end users must wait an unusual amount of time for their report data to populate. Report developers should gather appropriate reporting requirements to determine if drill-down capability would be a value addition for a report or whether this functionality should not be enabled. If end users will only be viewing one level of drill down, then it's important to explore the idea of creating two reports or two report tabs to achieve this result. The appropriate choice depends on each individual report based on factors such as end-user requirements, data being returned, purpose of the report, and output medium.

11.2 Drill-Down Setup in the Report Panel

After the scope of analysis has been set up in the QUERY PANEL, the query results will return the additional data required to perform drill analysis. After the data is available at the report level, the user can drill within the report against the report's microcube. No further queries are necessary to run against the database to gather more information as long as drill remains within the defined scope.

11.2.1 Enabling Drill

You can enable drill at the report level either as the report designer in the Web Intelligence report or as the end user in the BI Launch Pad toolbar.

As the Report Designer

The first step to enabling drill functionality in the Report Panel is to check that you are in drill mode. In Web Intelligence, go to design mode on the report that you want to drill on. Select the DRILL button on the ANALYSIS tab under the INTERACT section, as shown in Figure 11.14.

Figure 11.14 Drill Button on the Web Intelligence Toolbar

A DRILL icon appears on the REPORT tab. If your Web Intelligence options have been set up in BI Launch Pad to open a new report for drilling, then a duplicate report will open in a new window. We'll discuss how to personalize your drill settings later in this chapter.

As the End User

If the report designer didn't enable drill, the end user can enable drill down on a report in BI Launch Pad from the BI Launch Pad toolbar. After you've selected to view a report in BI Launch Pad, the DRILL button appears on the toolbar, as shown in Figure 11.15. When the user enables drill by clicking the button, the user's Web Intelligence preferences specify whether the report will open in a new window or whether drill will be enabled on the report in the current window.

Figure 11.15 Drill Button on BI Launch Pad Reading Toolbar

11.2.2   Drill Toolbar

The drill toolbar is enabled at the top of the report to display the drill path. Figure 11.16 shows the drill toolbar display when a user has drilled on YEAR and STATE on a table in the report. The drill toolbar shows what path has been taken. These dropdown boxes can also be used to drill back up in the hierarchy by selecting a different option from the list box.

The drill toolbar shows the filters applied to your report. You can also use the drill toolbar to filter additional data elements within your report by dragging the object from the AVAILABLE OBJECTS pane to the drill toolbar. This functionality works like a report-level filter and filters all elements in the report.

Figure 11.16 Drill Toolbar Showing State and Year Drill Filters

11.2.3   Drilling on Dimensions

When Web Intelligence projects the data elements of a query into the report, the measures are calculated based on the dimension objects placed in the same table or chart. This concept is called calculation context. Figure 11.17 shows a table where SALES REVENUE has been calculated by state and store name, because the STATE and STORE NAME objects appear in the table with the measure. State and store name is the context for this calculation.

State	Store name	Sales revenue
California	e-Fashion Los Angeles	$4,220,929
California	e-Fashion San Francisco	$3,258,641
Colorado	e-Fashion Colorado Springs	$2,060,275
DC	e-Fashion Washington Tolbooth	$2,961,950
Florida	e-Fashion Miami Sundance	$1,879,159
Illinois	e-Fashion Chicago 33rd	$3,022,658
Massachusetts	e-Fashion Boston Newbury	$1,283,707
New York	e-Fashion New York 5th	$2,960,367
New York	e-Fashion New York Magnolia	$4,621,854
Texas	e-Fashion Austin	$2,699,673
Texas	e-Fashion Dallas	$1,970,034

Figure 11.17 Table with Sales Revenue Calculated by State and Store Name

Figure 11.18 shows what happens to the calculation of a measure object when the STORE NAME dimension object is removed from the table. Now the measure recalculates and is displayed for each state.

The measure recalculates automatically based on the dimension objects contained in the table with it.

State	Sales revenue
California	$7,479,569
Colorado	$2,060,275
DC	$2,961,950
Florida	$1,879,159
Illinois	$3,022,658
Massachusetts	$1,283,707
New York	$7,582,221
Texas	$10,117,664

Figure 11.18 Table Including State and Sales Revenue Objects

This same concept exists when performing a drill on a report table. As the user drills on a dimension object in a report table or chart, the measure or measures included in that table or chart are recalculated.

Three forms of drill are available on dimension objects: drill down, drill up, and drill by. The concept of calculation context applies to each method.

Drill Down

After a report has been opened in drill mode, the objects in the tables appear with an underline. The underline indicates which objects are available for drill. To drill down on a dimension object, click on the object name in the table. The drill toolbar will appear, showing the dimension object that has been filtered. You can continue to drill down to the lowest level of grain that was set up in your scope of analysis.

Drill down can be completed by selecting the underlined data element in the report, as shown in Figure 11.19, or by right-clicking on the data element and selecting the DRILL DOWN option from the menu, as shown in Figure 11.20.

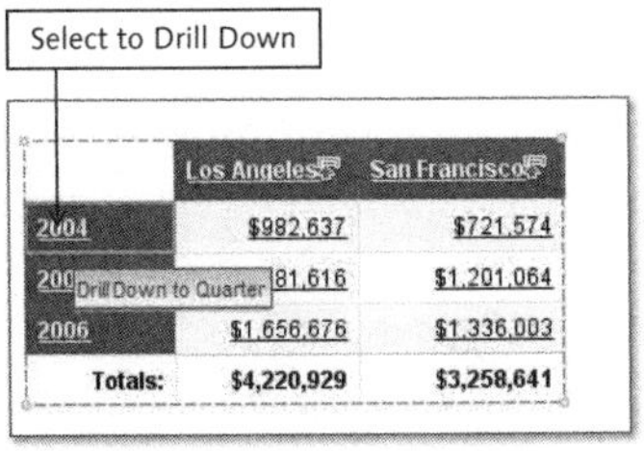

Select to Drill Down

	Los Angeles	San Francisco
2004	$982,637	$721,574
2005	81,616	$1,201,064
2006	$1,656,676	$1,336,003
Totals:	$4,220,929	$3,258,641

Drill Down to Quarter

Figure 11.19 Selecting the Underlined Data Element in a Report to Drill Down to the Next Level in the Hierarchy

To drill beyond the objects that were set up in the scope of analysis, the user must extend the scope of analysis. The right to extend a scope of analysis is set up by your SAP BusinessObjects administrator, so not all users will retain this right.

If you have the authority to extend scope of analysis, then when you hover over the object at the end of your scope of analysis, a tooltip will specify the next object that requires a new query, as shown in Figure 11.21.

If your preferences have been set to prompt before extending the scope of analysis, then a dialog box will appear allowing you to select what filters to apply to the next drill level.

In this example, the scope of analysis only included through MONTH, so WEEK is selected to include in further analysis. At this point, you can extend the scope to include HOLIDAY if you know that you will want to include another level of drill as well. As you extend to these levels, the new objects are shown in the AVAILABLE OBJECTS pane.

Figure 11.20 Right-Clicking and Selecting Drill Down to Drill Down on a Data Element

Figure 11.21 Tool Tip to Extend Scope of Analysis

Section 11.5 offers further discussion regarding setting your drill preferences.

If you select to drill on YEAR for a scope of analysis of two levels, then you would have to extend the scope of analysis when you reach the dimension of MONTH.

Figure 11.22 shows the table results of using the extend scope of analysis option in this example.

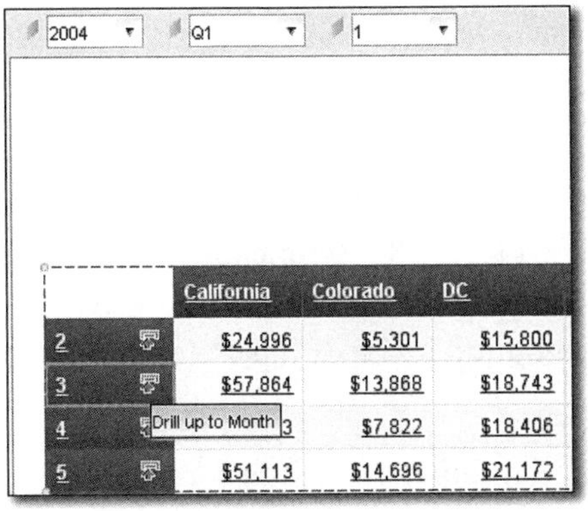

		California	Colorado	DC
2		$24,996	$5,301	$15,800
3		$57,864	$13,868	$18,743
4	Drill up to Month 3		$7,822	$18,406
5		$51,113	$14,696	$21,172

Figure 11.22 Table Results for Extended Scope of Analysis to Include Week

Drill Up

Drill up enables the user to drill from a lower level of aggregation to a higher level of aggregation. After drilling down to a lower level, you may want to drill back up to a higher grain. You can right-click on the dimension and select DRILL UP from the dropdown menu, as shown in Figure 11.23.

Drill Up to State
Drill Down to Store name
Drill By...   ▶
Stop Drill Mode

Figure 11.23 Dropdown List to Select the Drill Up Option

Another option is to click on the small arrow next to the name of the dimension that appears after you've drilled down at least one level, as shown in Figure 11.24.

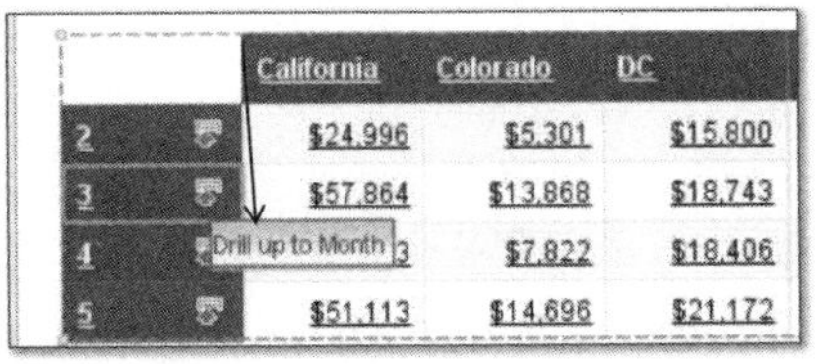

Figure 11.24 Selecting the Arrow to Drill Up in the Hierarchy

Drill By

The drill by function is found on the right-click menu when the user selects on a dimension object in a report block.

If you go back to the report example shown in Figure 11.17, you're viewing SALES REVENUE by STATE and STORE NAME. Drill down and drill up functionality will not answer your business question if your desired result is to view sales revenue for this year by STATE. In this case, YEAR is not an option in the drill path for either the STATE or STORE NAME objects.

By viewing the scope of analysis, the report developer can see that YEAR is a separate drill path. You can change from STORE NAME to YEAR by switching the drill path using the DRILL BY functionality, as shown in Figure 11.25.

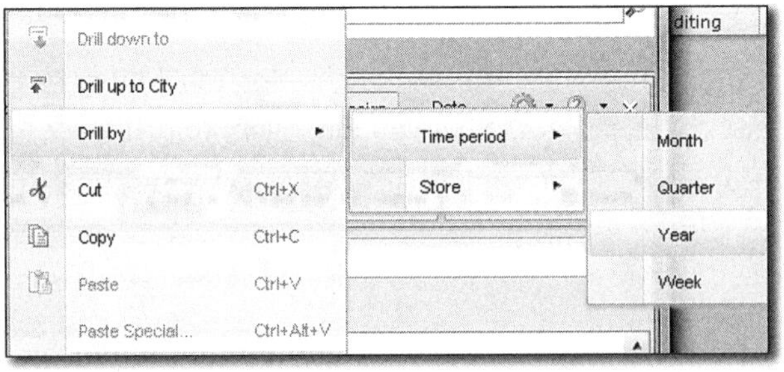

Figure 11.25 Right-Click Menu to Drill By a Dimension Object

When you right-click on STORE NAME and select DRILL BY from the menu, another menu appears with the available choices to drill by. In this example, the choices are TIME PERIOD or STORE, as shown in Figure 11.25.

After you select TIME PERIOD, another menu appears, showing the available objects in the TIME period hierarchy to drill by. Upon selection of YEAR, the measure recalculates for the new dimension object of YEAR contained within the table.

11.2.4 Drilling on Measures

There is a slight difference seen when drilling on measures. When selecting a measure to drill down or drill up in the hierarchy, Web Intelligence automatically drills all dimensions contained in the table with the measure by one level. Then the measure recalculates for the new dimension objects in the table with it.

Figure 11.26 shows a table with SALES REVENUE calculated by YEAR and STATE.

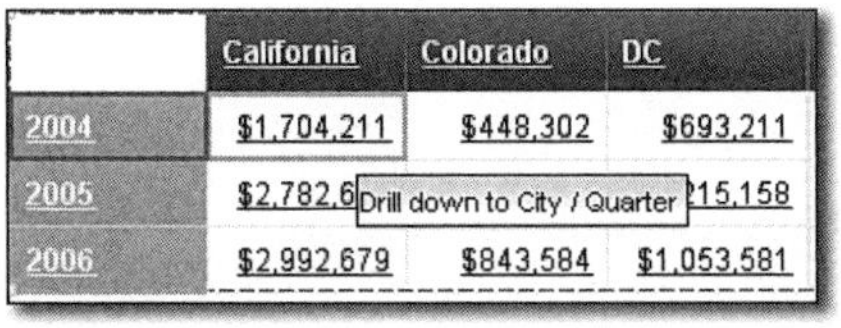

	California	Colorado	DC
2004	$1,704,211	$448,302	$693,211
2005	$2,782,6 Drill down to City / Quarter		15,158
2006	$2,992,679	$843,584	$1,053,581

Figure 11.26 Drill Down on Measure Object

When you select the measure object from the table to drill down, then both the STATE and YEAR objects are drilled down to the next level of hierarchy. Therefore, the new table appears as shown in Figure 11.27 with sales revenue calculated for city and quarter.

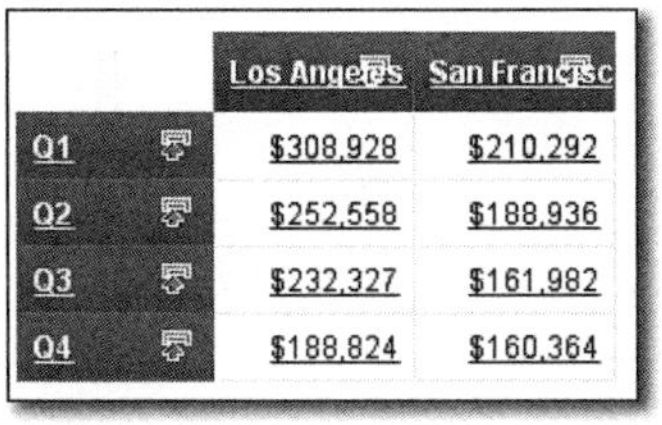

		Los Angeles	San Francisc
Q1		$308,928	$210,292
Q2		$252,558	$188,936
Q3		$232,327	$161,982
Q4		$188,824	$160,364

Figure 11.27 Table after Drill Down on Measure Object

11.2.5 Drilling on Charts

Users can drill on charts in the same ways that they can drill on tables: drill down, drill up, and drill by. Exciting chart drill features that provide a more user-friendly experience to the report consumer are available in Web Intelligence.

Dimensions on Chart Axis

Drill functionality is available on dimensions included in the chart axis. For example, a vertical bar chart containing cities along the X-axis and dollars of sales revenue along the Y-axis details the amount of sales revenue for the respective city.

The user can click on one of the cities on the X-axis to drill down to the next level in the hierarchy. A pop-up box appears showing the next level of drill available, as shown in Figure 11.28.

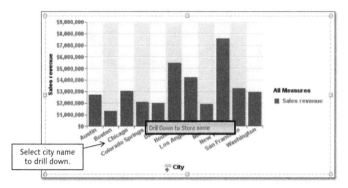

Figure 11.28 Drill Down on Chart Axis Label

The same principles for drill up apply as with the tables: You can right-click on the dimension to drill up in order to drill back to the YEAR dimension or select the up arrow. The user can also select to drill by an object by selecting the DRILL BY option from the right-click menu when selecting on a dimension. This functionality works the same as it does with a table. In some cases, the chart has multiple dimensions on the axis, as shown in Figure 11.29. In this case, DRILL BY functionality will not be available on the axis of the chart.

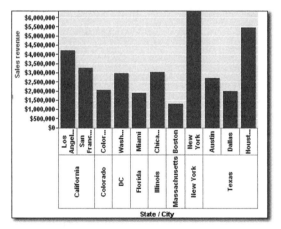

Figure 11.29 Multiple Dimensions on the Category Axis of the Chart

Dimensions on Legends

Drill functionality is also available on dimensions included in the chart legend, as long as the legend is viewable in the report. This can be especially helpful for pie charts, for which it can sometimes be difficult to determine which slice belongs to what data element, as shown in Figure 11.30.

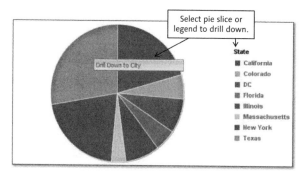

Figure 11.30 Pie Chart Showing Sales Revenue by State

In this example, the user can click on one of the states listed in the legend to drill down to the next level in the hierarchy. A pop-up box showing the next level of drill available appears.

The user can right-click on the dimension to drill up in order to drill back to the STATE dimension, as done with drill functionality on a chart axis.

The user can also select to drill by an object by selecting the DRILL BY option from the right-click menu when selecting on a dimension. This functionality works the same as it does with a table.

In some cases the chart has multiple dimensions on the axis as shown in Figure 11.29. In this case, the DRILL BY functionality won't be available on the legend of the chart.

Measures on Chart Bars and Markers

An exciting charting feature in Web Intelligence is the ability to select the bar or marker in a chart to drill up or down. This functionality is available on bar charts, pie charts, line charts, and radar charts. For bar charts, users drill on the bars. On pie charts, users drill on the pie slices. Drilling on line and radar charts is done by drilling on the line markers, as shown in Figure 11.31. The bars, slices, or markers of a chart consist of the measure data elements; therefore, the drill functionality is the same as drilling on a measure in a table.

When drilling on a measure, all dimension objects placed with it are drilled down by one level, and the measure is recalculated to match the new data elements.

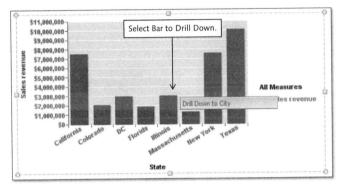

Figure 11.31 Drill on Bars of Chart

To drill down on the chart bars and markers, select the appropriate bar, and click to enable the drill down to the next level in the hierarchy. To drill up on the charts and markers, right-click on the bar or marker, and select DRILL UP to reach the next highest level in the drill hierarchy.

There are some limitations to drilling on measures in chart bars and markers. Certain chart types—such as the 2D and 3D area charts, stacked area charts, radar charts, and scatter charts—do not drill down on all dimensions included in the chart when selecting on the chart measure bars or markers. When drilling on these charts, only the dimension included in the chart legend is drilled upon, and therefore the measure object recalculates for this dimension change only.

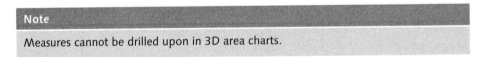

Note

Measures cannot be drilled upon in 3D area charts.

11.3 Query Drill Option

The query drill lets the user drill on a report without maintaining all the data within the data provider, thereby minimizing the refresh time and the amount of space taken up by the report.

The query drill is also essential when report measures must be calculated at the database level and cannot be calculated properly through normal drill mode. Examples of these measure calculations include ranks, percentages, distinct counts, standard deviations and variances, running aggregates, and lead and lag functions.

These measures won't recalculate correctly if recalculated at the report level during drill down. In this case, you need to use the query drill to perform the calculation correctly at the database level. This can be especially useful for databases such as Oracle 9i OLAP, which contains aggregate functions not supported at the report level in Web Intelligence.

To enable query drill, select the DOCUMENT button from the PROPERTIES menu. Select the USE QUERY DRILL checkbox, as shown in Figure 11.32.

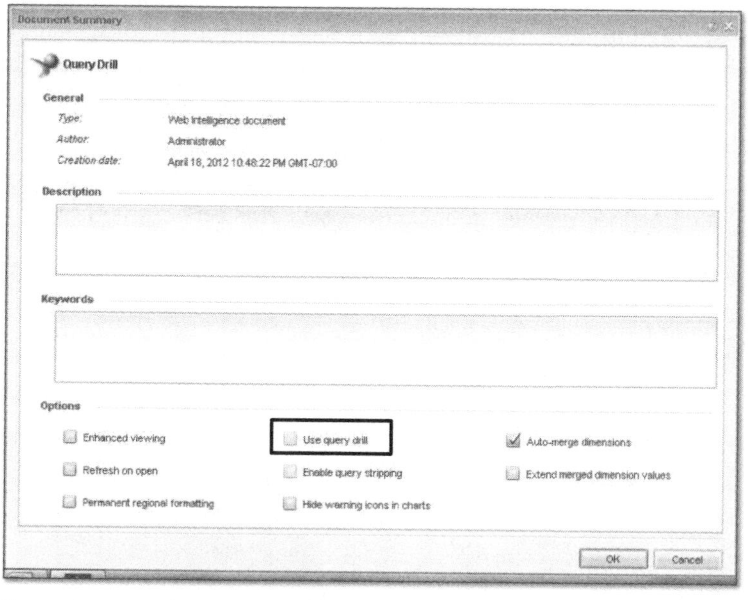

Figure 11.32 Use the Query Drill Option in the Document Properties Dialog Box

The query drill works differently from standard drill mode. When a user selects to drill down on Year and selects the year of 2001, Web Intelligence not only applies the drill filter to limit the results at the report level but also applies a query filter to limit the results at the query level. This means that the user can no longer use the dropdown boxes in the drill toolbar to change the filter because only the year 2001 exists in the report. Also, the new query filter will affect the entire report. The entire report is now filtered for only the year 2001.

> **Caution**
>
> The query drill applies the drill filter to the report query, so all report tabs will be affected by the drill.
>
> If you drill from Year to Quarter in query drill mode, then the Year object will be removed from your query and replaced with the Quarter object. Therefore, the Year object will be removed from all report tabs in your Web Intelligence report.

11.4   Taking a Snapshot

When performing on report analysis using the drill functionality, the user may need to refer to the current state of drill at a later date. Web Intelligence enables the user to take a *snapshot* of the current view of the report for future reference. After you enable the drill functionality from the INTERACT menu in the ANALYSIS ribbon, you'll find the drill menu option to select SNAPSHOT, as shown in Figure 11.33. By selecting this option, a copy of the current report at the current state of drill down is opened in a new report tab. You can save this report snapshot and reference it later.

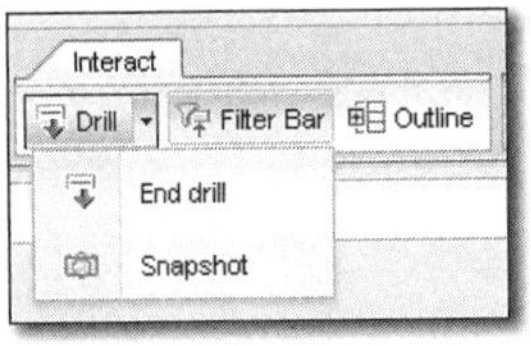

Figure 11.33 Snapshot Option

11.5   User Settings for Drill Down

Users can specify their own settings for drill in their PREFERENCES menus located on the BI Launch Pad toolbar shown in Figure 11.34.

Your drill options are found on the Web Intelligence PREFERENCES tab, as shown in Figure 11.35. Each of these options can provide a more personalized drill experience based on your drill preferences.

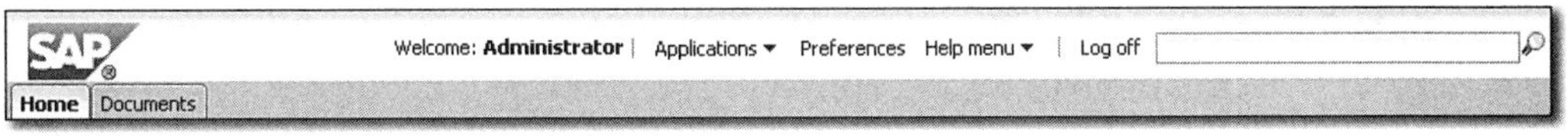

Figure 11.34 Preferences Option on the BI Launch Pad Toolbar

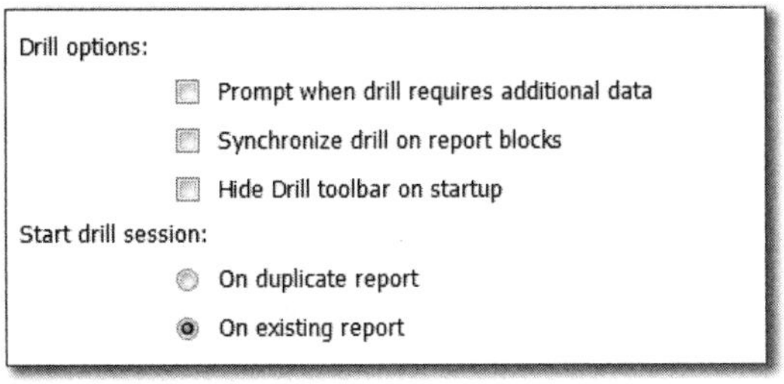

Figure 11.35 Drill Preferences

The overall capability for each of these options is determined by the administrator in the Central Management Console (CMC), so not all options may be available to use based on these user rights.

11.5.1 Prompt When Drill Requires Additional Data

When you need to extend the scope of analysis to view a higher or lower level of drill than was set up in the report scope, then you must run a query to retrieve the additional data. If the PROMPT WHEN DRILL REQUIRES ADDITIONAL DATA option is selected, then you'll be prompted to ensure that you want to run a query before the query is run. If this option is not selected, then a query will automatically be run if you choose to extend the scope of analysis by drilling beyond the designated scope.

11.5.2 Synchronize Drill on Report Blocks

The SYNCHRONIZE DRILL ON REPORT BLOCKS option lets you drill on all report blocks simultaneously. A report block can include tables or charts. If you enable synchronized drill in your Web Intelligence preferences, then when you choose to drill on an object that is contained in more than one report block, the object changes in all report blocks in which it is contained.

If the option is not enabled, then when you select to drill on an object that is contained in more than one report block, the object changes only in the block in which you selected to drill.

343

11.5.3 Hide Drill Toolbar on Startup

When drill is enabled on a report, a toolbar appears at the top of the screen that shows dropdown boxes with the selected drill filters. You can change the filters by using these boxes and see which filters you've chosen in your drill path by referencing the boxes shown in the drill toolbar.

The drill toolbar can be hidden so it doesn't show when drill is enabled. To set this option, select the HIDE DRILL TOOLBAR checkbox in the Web Intelligence PREFERENCES.

11.5.4 Start Drill Session

The START DRILL SESSION option sets whether drill is completed within the current report or whether a new report is opened in a new browser to complete drill mode. The two options are to START DRILL SESSION IN EXISTING REPORT or to START DRILL SESSION IN A DUPLICATE REPORT.

11.6 Summary

Drill functionality is an important feature that puts the power of analysis in the end user's hands. It enables users to quickly and easily answer the important business questions by performing drill down, drill up, and drill by functions, either by viewing a report in BI Launch Pad or editing a report in Web Intelligence. The report designer can set up reports to provide drill objects within the report's data cube or enable the query drill to perform live queries as drill analysis is completed by the end user.

Users can also create snapshots of their results for further analysis or distribution. It's important to know your audience and how the report will be used in order to set up the drill preferences appropriately. Chapter 12 delves further into the use of formulas and variables in your reports to provide added value to the end consumer.

Create complex calculations by using data objects retrieved from your database along with more than 160 built-in reporting functions and 40 operators in the Formula Editor. By using formulas and variables to transform data into analytical information, you'll be able to make better business decisions.

12   Using Formulas and Variables

Formulas and variables are commonly used structures that allow you to create calculations using the data retrieved from a query. Variables are used to store the calculation syntax of a formula in reusable objects that are saved in SAP Business-Objects Web Intelligence reporting documents.

Variables can be used in reports to perform a variety of tasks that display your data in different ways than when retrieved by queries. Variables can be used to insert If–Then–Else logic into a column or chart, contain complex calculations that produce precise views of information, or create analytical formulas that solve difficult business problems—all within a single object that can be used throughout a reporting document.

The *formula bar* provides the capability to quickly revise the definition of an object within a toolbar, similar to Microsoft Excel. The FORMULA EDITOR or CREATE VARIABLE windows can be used to create extensive and detailed formulas with the convenience of viewing all available data elements, functions, and operator types in the same window.

The next several sections will introduce you to the Formula Editor, explain the syntax used in creating formulas and variables, and provide examples to help you get the most out of the editor when creating unique calculations.

12.1 Formulas and Variables

The first step in creating a formula or variable or modifying the definition of an existing field is to enable either the formula bar or Formula Editor. Regardless of the viewer set in the Web Intelligence preferences, the formula bar is accessible only while in design mode. The second step is to understand the syntax used in the Web Intelligence Report Panel. We'll begin by editing an existing report and describing the various ways to access the Formula Editor, also known as the CREATE VARIABLE window.

To add a new variable to a reporting document without placing it directly in a data table, select the DATA ACCESS tab provided in the ribbon of tabs located above the report. Next, select the DATA OBJECTS tab in the second set of subtabs. Figure 12.1 shows the NEW VARIABLE icon accessible inside the DATA OBJECTS tab. The default variable type is dimension. Select the small down arrow immediately to the right of the NEW VARIABLE button to choose between NEW DIMENSION, NEW DETAIL, or NEW MEASURE as the new variable type.

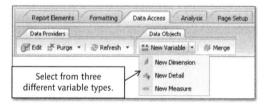

Figure 12.1 Creating a New Variable Object from the Tab Ribbon

12.1.1 Converting In-Place Objects into Formulas

Formulas are calculations created to transform data retrieved by your queries for producing results that solve business problems. These formulas can be created as variables and then used in data tables and charts throughout a Web Intelligence document rather than creating single instances of the formula.

Every object added to a table or chart in a report contains a formula definition, even if the object added comes directly from objects retrieved by the query. Figure 12.2 shows the dimension object selected in a cross table with the formula bar displayed. Notice that the formula for the selected object is =[State].

Figure 12.2 Formula of the Selected Dimension Object

The formula or definition of a selected object in a table can be edited by changing the definition in the formula bar. An example of a revision that can be applied to the selected object is displayed in Figure 12.3, in which the State object was replaced with a formula by modifying the object definition in the formula bar.

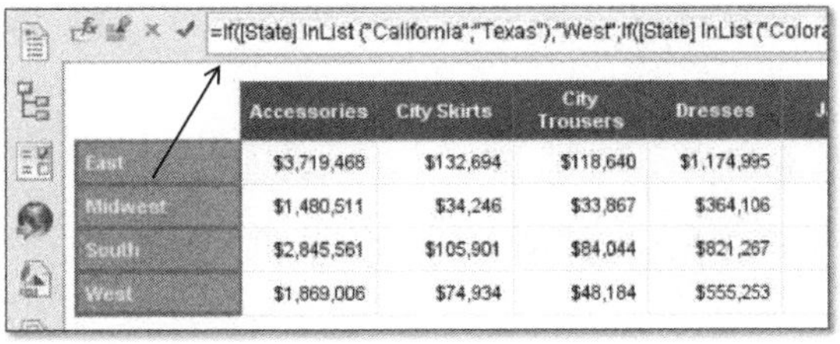

Figure 12.3 Revised Formula in the Selected Dimension Object

Editing the definition of an object in the formula bar will result only in modifying the specific instance of the object. To use the formula in other report elements within the document, click on the CREATE VARIABLE icon to transform the formula into a variable usable throughout the document.

Tip

Clicking on the CREATE VARIABLE icon located to the left of the formula bar launches the FORMULA EDITOR and gives you access to available objects, functions, and operators for creating even more complex and powerful formulas.

Figure 12.4 shows the other commands to use when editing an object definition or formula:

▶ FORMULA EDITOR
  Launch the FORMULA EDITOR by clicking on the Fx icon.

▶ CREATE VARIABLE
  Transform the existing formula into a reusable variable.

▶ CANCEL
  Cancel the revisions made to a calculation in the formula bar.

▶ VALIDATE FORMULA
  Validate the formula by clicking on the green checkmark icon.

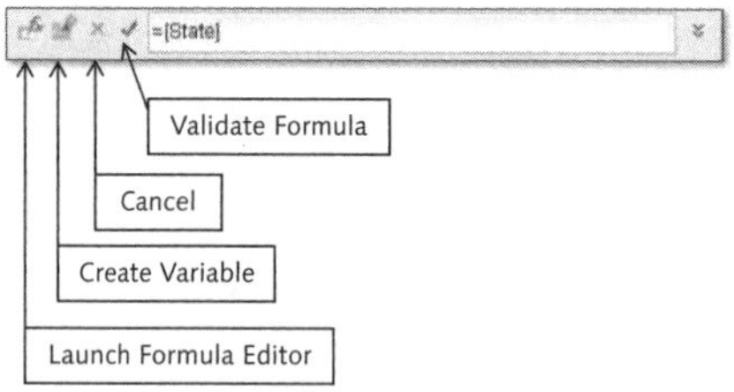

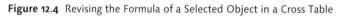

Figure 12.4 Revising the Formula of a Selected Object in a Cross Table

12.1.2 Exploring the Formula Editor

After launching the Formula Editor, you can graphically build or edit your formula by using elements from the following three categories of objects for advanced formula creation:

▶ AVAILABLE OBJECTS
  All result objects and variables that exist within the document.

▶ FUNCTIONS
  More than 140 functions are available to be used in formulas.

▶ OPERATORS
  Nearly 40 operators are available to be used in formulas.

Figure 12.5 shows the FORMULA EDITOR window, which is used for creating and editing formulas graphically, writing freehand syntax, or a combination of both.

Formulas can be edited manually, by dragging and dropping, or by double-clicking on AVAILABLE OBJECTS, FORMULAS, and OPERATORS and then placing them in the FORMULA area. To validate the syntax of the statement created in the formula, click on the green checkmark to the right of the FORMULA EDITOR window. If the formula is incorrect, the position of the first invalid identifier will be displayed.

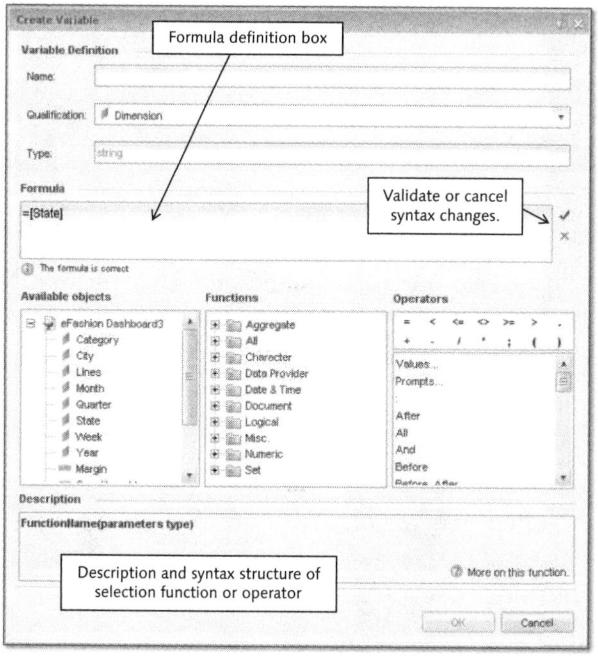

Figure 12.5 Formula Editor

For a quick example of the proper syntax to be used for a function or operator, click on the object and then view the contents of the description box located at the bottom of the Formula Editor. A brief description of the function or operator will appear, followed by the proper syntax structure of the object selected.

Functions in the Formula Editor are presented in 9 different categories. A tenth category is also provided that contains all 160+ functions. These 9 functional groups are listed here along with a few commonly used functions:

▶ AGGREGATE
Contains 24 functions, including `Average()`, `Min()`, `Max()`, `Sum()`, `Median()`, `Percentage()`, and `RunningSum()`.

▶ CHARACTER
Contains 24 functions, including `Char()`, `FormatNumber()`, `Concatenation()`, `LeftTrim()`, and `Pos()`.

▶ DATE AND TIME
Contains 18 functions, including `CurrentDate()`, `CurrentTime()`, `LastDayOf-Month()`, `Year()`, and `Month()`.

▶ DOCUMENT

Contains 13 functions, including `DocumentAuthor()`, `ReportFilter()`, `Drill-Filters()`, and `PromptSummary()`.

▶ DATA PROVIDER

Contains 17 functions, including `UserResponse()`, `Connection()`, `Universe-Name()`, and `NumberOfRows()`.

▶ MISC.

Contains 28 functions, including `If()`, `Else`, `Then`, `BlockName`, `CurrentUser()`, `ForceMerge()`, and `NameOf()`.

▶ LOGICAL

Contains 9 functions, including `Even()`, `IsDate()`, `IsNull()`, `IsNumber()`, `IsString`, `IsTime()`, and `Odd()`.

▶ NUMERIC

Contains 23 functions, including `Abs()`, `Ceil()`, `Cos()`, `Floor()`, `Power()`, `Rank()`, and `ToNumber()`.

▶ SET

Contains 7 functions, including `Ancestor()`, `Children()`, `Descendants()`, `IsLeaf()`, `Lag()`, `Parent()`, and `Siblings()`.

Section 12.2 provides examples and additional information about these formulas.

12.1.3 Creating Variables

Variables simply are in-place formulas that have been converted into reusable objects. By promoting a calculation or formula into a variable, you're creating a local result object that can be used throughout a reporting document.

To turn a formula into a variable, click on the CREATE VARIABLE icon located to the left of the formula bar, as shown in Figure 12.6.

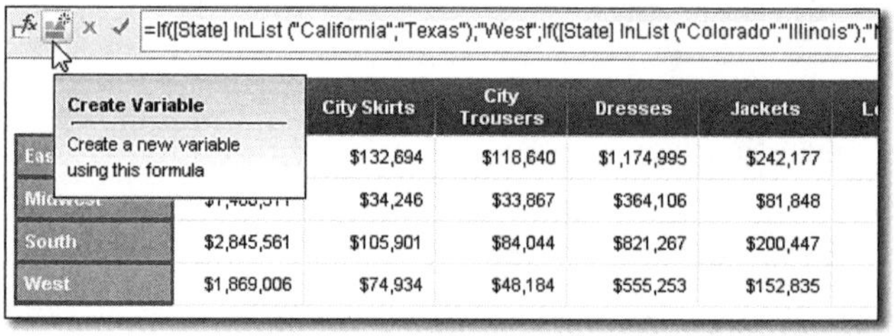

	City Skirts	City Trousers	Dresses	Jackets	L
East		$132,694	$118,640	$1,174,995	$242,177
Midwest		$34,246	$33,867	$364,106	$81,848
South	$2,845,561	$105,901	$84,044	$821,267	$200,447
West	$1,869,006	$74,934	$48,184	$555,253	$152,835

Figure 12.6 Create Variable Icon to Convert the Formula into a Variable

The CREATE VARIABLE window allows you to perform all of the same tasks as the Formula Editor, with the addition of being able to assign a name and qualification to the variable. If DETAIL is selected as the qualification type, you also have the opportunity to assign an associated dimension to the object. The following are the modifiable sections in the VARIABLE DEFINITION section of a new variable:

▶ NAME
Provide a descriptive and user-friendly term or short phrase to uniquely identify and clearly describe the variable.

▶ QUALIFICATION
Select DIMENSION, MEASURE, or DETAIL as the variable qualification type (if DETAIL is selected, choose a dimension that the new detail object should be associated with).

▶ FORMULA
Review the syntax of the formula to be used in the variable.

Figure 12.7 shows the CREATE VARIABLE window used to name and set the qualification of a new variable object being converted from a formula.

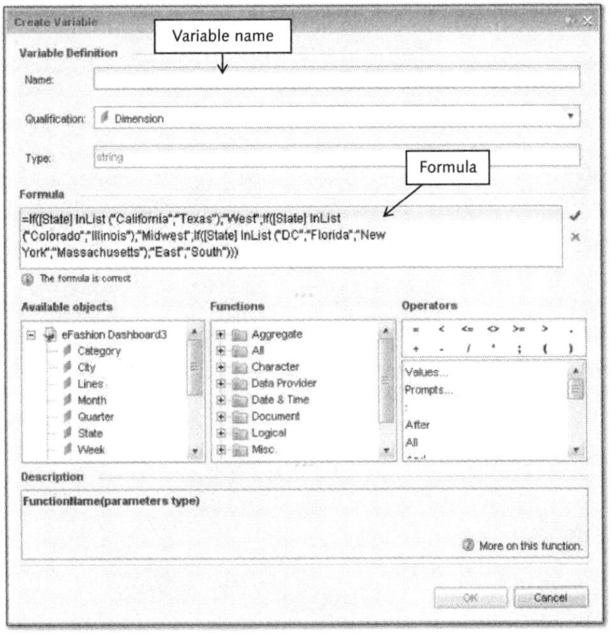

Figure 12.7 Create Variable Window

12.2   Reporting Functions and Operators

Web Intelligence 4.1 provides an even more extensive set of reporting functions with which you can create very detailed and complex formulas for producing advanced reporting documents.

This section introduces you to the full list of reporting functions available for creating formulas and variables in the Report Panel. More than 140 reporting functions can be easily located within 9 functional categories.

The broad collection of operators used in formulas and variables is also described here. With more than 40 available operators, report developers can create precise formulas that leverage the full set of built-in reporting functions.

The nine function categories for creating formulas in the Report Panel are reviewed here:

▶ **Aggregate**
  Aggregate measures.

▶ **Character**
  Functions that interact with character data.

▶ **Date and Time**
  Functions created with date data.

▶ **Document**
  Identify information about the current document.

▶ **Data Provider**
  Functions available to identify information relating to the data provider in the current document.

▶ **Misc.**
  Functions covering a variety of topics not included in the other categories.

▶ **Logical**
  Logical Boolean functions.

▶ **Numeric**
  Numerical-related functions.

▶ **Set**
  Multidimensional functions.

Let's look at each function category in more detail.

12.2.1 Aggregate Functions

Aggregate functions are used for returning numeric calculations for creating commonly used formulas with measure objects (see Table 12.1).

Function	Description
Aggregate (measure,set)	Used in a report sourced from SAP BEx queries to aggregate values by set
Average (measure;IncludeEmpty)	Returns the average value of a measure
Count (dimension|measure; IncludeEmpty;Distinct|All)	Returns the number of values in a dimension or measure
First (dimension|measure)	Returns the first value in a data set
Interpolation (measure; PointToPoint|Linear; NotOnBreak;Row|Column)	Calculates empty measure values by interpolation
Last (dimension|measure)	Returns the last value in a dimension or measure
Max (dimension|measure)	Returns the largest value in a dimension or measure
Median (measure)	Returns the median (middle value) of a measure
Min (dimension|measure)	Returns the smallest value in a dimension or measure
Mode (dimension|measure)	Returns the most frequently occurring value in a data set
Percentage (measure; break;row|col)	Expresses a measure value as a percentage of its embedding context
Percentile (measure;percentile)	Returns the *n*th percentile of a measure
Product (measure)	Multiplies the values of a measure
RunningAverage (measure; Row|Col;IncludeEmpty;reset_ dims)	Returns the running average of a measure
RunningCount (dimension| measure;Row|Col; IncludeEmpty;reset_dims)	Returns the running count of a number set

Table 12.1 Aggregate Functions

Function	Description
RunningMax (dimension| measure;Row|Col;reset_dims)	Returns the running maximum of a dimension or measure
RunningMin (dimension| measure;Row|Col;reset_dims)	Returns the running minimum of a dimension or measure
RunningProduct (dimension| measure;Row|Col;reset_dims)	Returns the running product of a measure
RunningSum (dimension| measure;Row|Col;reset_dims)	Returns the running sum of a measure
StdDev (measure)	Returns the standard deviation of a measure
StdDevP (measure)	Returns the population standard deviation of a measure
Sum (measure)	Returns the sum of a measure
Var (measure)	Returns the variance of a measure
VarP (measure)	Returns the population variance of a measure

Table 12.1 Aggregate Functions (Cont.)

12.2.2 Character Functions

Character functions are primarily used for performing tasks that manipulate dimension objects (see Table 12.2).

Function	Description
Asc (string)	Returns the ASCII value of a character
Char (ascii_code)	Returns the character associated with an ASCII code
Concatenation (first_string; second_string)	Concatenates (joins) two character strings
Fill (repeating_string; num_repeats)	Builds a string by repeating a string *n* times
FormatDate (date;format_string)	Formats a date according to a specified format

Table 12.2 Character Functions

Function	Description
FormatNumber (number; format_string)	Formats a number according to a specified format
HTMLEncode (html)	Applies HTML encoding rules to a string
InitCap (string)	Capitalizes the first letter of a string
Left (string;num_chars)	Returns the leftmost characters of a string
LeftPad (padded_string; length;left_string)	Pads a string on its left with another string
LeftTrim (trimmed_string)	Trims the leading spaces from a string
Length (string)	Returns the number of characters in a string
Lower (string)	Converts a string to lowercase
Match (string;pattern)	Determines whether a string matches a pattern
Pos (string;pattern)	Returns the starting position of a text pattern in a string
Replace (replace_in; replaced_string;replace_with)	Replaces part of a string with another string
Right (string;num_chars)	Returns the rightmost characters of a string
RightPad (padded_string; length;right_string)	Pads a string on its right with another string
RightTrim (trimmed_string)	Trims the trailing spaces from strings
Substr (string;start;length)	Returns part of a string
Trim (trimmed_string)	Trims the leading and trailing spaces from a string
Upper (string)	Converts a string to uppercase
URLEncode (html)	Applies URL encoding rules to a string
WordCap (string)	Capitalizes the first letter of all of the words in a string

Table 12.2 Character Functions (Cont.)

12.2.3 Date and Time Functions

Date and time functions allow developers to extract date elements from date objects and calculate date differences (see Table 12.3).

Function	Description
CurrentDate()	Returns the current date formatted according to the regional settings
CurrentTime()	Returns the current time formatted according to the regional settings
DayName (date)	Returns the day name from a date from the data passed to the function
DayNumberOfMonth (date)	Returns the day number in a month from the data passed to the function
DayNumberOfWeek (date)	Returns the day number in a week from the data passed to the function
DayNumberOfYear (date)	Returns the day number in a year from the data passed to the function
DaysBetween (first_date;last_date)	Returns the number of days between two dates passed into the function
LastDayOfMonth (date)	Returns the date of the last day in a month
LastDayOfWeek (date)	Returns the date of the last day in a week
Month (date)	Returns the month name in a date
MonthNumberOfYear (date)	Returns the month number in a date
MonthsBetween (first_date;last_date)	Returns the number of months between two dates
Quarter (date)	Returns the quarter number in a date
RelativeDate (start_date;num_days)	Returns a date relative to another date
TimeDim (date;period)	Completes a list of dates when the values retrieved from a query return missing dates

Table 12.3 Date and Time Functions

Function	Description
`ToDate (date_string;format)`	Returns a character string formatted according to a date format
`Week (date)`	Returns the week number in the year from the date passed to the function
`Year (date)`	Returns the year in a date from the date passed to the function

Table 12.3 Date and Time Functions (Cont.)

12.2.4 Document Functions

Document functions, which are shown in Table 12.4, let you identify various attributes of a reporting document.

Function	Description
`DocumentAuthor ()`	Returns the logon of the document creator
`DocumentCreationDate ()`	Returns the date on which a document was created
`DocumentCreationTime ()`	Returns the time when a document was created
`DocumentDate ()`	Returns the date on which a document was last saved
`DocumentName ()`	Returns the document name
`DocumentOwner ()`	Returns the logon of the user that last saved the document
`DocumentPartiallyRefreshed ()`	Determines whether a document is partially refreshed
`DocumentTime ()`	Returns the time when a document was last saved
`DrillFilters (object|separator)`	Returns the drill filters applied to a document or object in drill mode
`PromptSummary ()`	Returns the prompt text and user response of all prompts in a document

Table 12.4 Document Functions

Function	Description
QuerySummary (query_name)	Returns information about the queries in a document
ReportFilter (object)	Returns the report filters applied to an object or report
ReportFilterSummary (report_name)	Returns a summary of the report filters in a document or report

Table 12.4 Document Functions (Cont.)

12.2.5 Data Provider Functions

Data provider functions (shown in Table 12.5) let you create formulas that retrieve various details about the query, retrieved result set, and universe used to build the query.

Function	Description
Connection ([query_name])	Returns the parameters of the database connection used by a data provider
DataProvider (object)	Returns the name of the data provider containing a report object
DataProviderKeyDate ([query_name])	Returns the key date of a data provider
DataProviderKeyDateCaption ([query_name])	Returns the key date caption of a data provider
DataProviderSQL ([query_name])	Returns the SQL generated by a data provider
DataProviderType ([query_name])	Returns the type of a data provider
IsPromptAnswered ([query_name];prompt_string)	Determines whether a prompt has been answered
LastExecutionDate ([query_name])	Returns the date on which a data provider was last refreshed
LastExecutionDuration ([query_name])	Returns the time in seconds taken by the last refresh of a data provider

Table 12.5 Data Provider Functions

Function	Description
LastExecutionTime ([query_ name])	Returns the time at which a data provider was last refreshed
NumberOfDataProviders ()	Returns the number of data providers in a report
NumberOfRows ([query_name])	Returns the number of rows in a data provider
RefValueDate ()	Returns the date of the reference data used for data tracking
RefValueUserResponse ([query_ name]; prompt_string;index)	Returns the response to a prompt when the reference data was the current data
ServerValue ([measure])	Returns the value of a measure calculated by the database
UniverseName ([query_name])	Returns the name of the universe on which a data provider is based
UserResponse ([query_name]; prompt_string;index)	Returns the response to a prompt

Table 12.5 Data Provider Functions (Cont.)

12.2.6 Miscellaneous Functions

A wide variety of functions are included in the MISC. category that returns details about components and features of a report (see Table 12.6).

Function	Description
BlockName ()	Returns the block name
ColumnNumber ()	Returns the column number
CurrentUser ()	Returns the login of the current user
[member].Depth	Returns the depth of a specified member in a hierarchy
Else (false_value)	Returns a value from the If function when the test expression is false

Table 12.6 Misc. Functions

Function	Description
`ElseIf (test_value)`	Used to nest an `If` function within another `If` function
`ForceMerge (measure)`	Includes synchronized dimensions in measure calculations when the dimensions aren't in the measure's calculation context
`GetContentLocale ()`	Returns the locale of the data contained in the document (the Document Locale)
`GetDominantPreferredViewing Locale ()`	Returns the dominant locale in the user's Preferred Viewing Locale group
`GetLocale ()`	Returns the user's locale used to format the Web Intelligence interface (the Product Locale)
`GetLocalized (string;comment)`	Returns a string localized according to the user's Preferred Viewing Locale
`GetPreferredViewingLocale ()`	Returns the user's preferred locale for viewing document data (the Preferred Viewing Locale)
`If (boolean_value;true_value; false_value)`	Returns a value based on whether an expression is true or false
`[member].Key`	Returns the key of a member
`LineNumber ()`	Returns the line number in a table
`NameOf (object)`	Returns the name of an object
`NoFilter (object;all|drill)`	Ignores filters when calculating a value
`NumberOfPages ()`	Returns the number of pages in a report
`Page ()`	Returns the current page number in a report
`Previous (dimension|measure| Self; reset_dims; offset; NoNull)`	Returns a previous value of an object
`RefValue (object)`	Returns the reference value of a report object when data tracking is activated
`RelativeValue (measure|detail; slicing_dims;offset)`	Returns previous or subsequent values of an object

Table 12.6 Misc. Functions (Cont.)

Function	Description
RepFormula	Appears when a document has been converted from Desktop Intelligence and previously used a function not supported in Web Intelligence
ReportName ()	Returns the name of a report
RowIndex ()	Returns the number of a row
Then true_value	Returns a value from the If function when the test expression is true
UniqueNameOf (object)	Returns the unique name of an object
UseMerged(expression)	Forces the use of a merged dimension

Table 12.6 Misc. Functions (Cont.)

12.2.7 Logical Functions

Logical functions determine whether an object is true or false by returning either a 1 or 0 (see Table 12.7).

Function	Description
Even (number)	Determines whether a number is even
IsDate (object)	Determines whether a value is a date
IsError (object)	Determines whether an object returns an error
IsLogical (object)	Determines whether a value is Boolean
IsNull (object)	Determines whether a value is null
IsNumber (object)	Determines whether a value is a number
IsString (object)	Determines whether a value is a string
IsTime (object)	Determines whether a variable is a time variable
Odd (number)	Determines whether a number is odd

Table 12.7 Logical Functions

12.2.8 Numeric Functions

Numeric functions allow you to manipulate and measure values in a variety of ways, as shown in Table 12.8.

Function	Description
Abs (number)	Returns the absolute value of a number
Ceil (number)	Returns a number rounded up to the nearest integer
Cos (angle)	Returns the cosine of an angle
EuroConvertFrom (euro_amount; curr_code;round_level)	Converts a Euro amount to another currency
EuroConvertTo (noneuro_amount; curr_code;round_level)	Converts an amount to Euros
EuroFromRoundError (euro_amount; curr_code;round_level)	Returns the rounding error in a conversion from Euros
EuroToRoundError (noneuro_amount; curr_code;round_level)	Returns the rounding error in a conversion to Euros
Exp (power)	Returns an exponential (e raised to a power)
Fact (number)	Returns the factorial of a number
Floor (number)	Returns a number rounded down to the nearest integer
Ln (number)	Returns the natural logarithm of a number
Log (number;base)	Returns the logarithm of a number in a specified base
Log10 (number)	Returns the base 10 logarithm of a number
Mod (dividend;divisor)	Returns the remainder from the division of two numbers
Power (number;power)	Returns a number raised to a power
Rank (measure;ranking_dims; Top|Bottom;reset_dims)	Ranks a measure by dimensions
Round (number;round_level)	Rounds a number

Table 12.8 Numeric Functions

Function	Description
Sign (number)	Returns the sign of a number
Sin (angle)	Returns the sine of an angle
Sqrt (number)	Returns the square root of a number
Tan (angle)	Returns the tangent of an angle
ToNumber (string)	Returns a string as a number
Truncate (number;truncate_level)	Truncates a number

Table 12.8 Numeric Functions (Cont.)

12.2.9 Set Functions

A series of set functions have been added to the Report Panel to get more information from data retrieved by SAP BEx queries. Use these functions to identify ancestral information relating to hierarchical members, including parents, children, siblings, and ancestors of a specific member.

Many of these functions are used primarily in the input parameter in aggregate functions to specify a member to be aggregated and cannot be used as standalone functions. When using a member in a function, you need either to specify the member explicitly or provide the full hierarchical path of the member.

Table 12.9 provides a list of the set functions followed by a description of each.

Function	Description
Ancestor (member;level|distance)	Returns an ancestor member of a member by either level or distance
[member].Children	Returns the child members of a specified member or member path
Descendants (member;level | distance;desc_flag)	Returns the descendant member of a specified member by either level or distance. Optionally, in the desc_flag position, use either Self, Before, After, Self_Before, Self_After, Before_After, Self_Before_After, or Leaves

Table 12.9 Set Functions

Function	Description
[member].IsLeaf	Determines whether a member is a leaf member; returns either True or False
[member].Lag (distance)	Returns the members before or after a specified member; use a negative distance to identify the member before; use a positive number to identify the member after
[member].Parent	Returns the parent member of a specified member
[member].Siblings	Returns the sibling members of a specified member

Table 12.9 Set Functions (Cont.)

12.2.10 Operators

Operators are symbols used in formulas and variables to indicate the type of operation you want to perform. Formulas can contain several different combinations of operators, which are used to solve a variety of business problems.

Report operators are grouped into the following six categories, each of which has a corresponding table:

▶ Mathematical (see Table 12.10)

▶ Conditional (see Table 12.11)

▶ Logical (see Table 12.12)

▶ Function-specific (see Table 12.13)

▶ Extended syntax operators (see Table 12.14)

▶ Extended syntax key words (see Table 12.15)

▶ Hierarchical operators (see Table 12.16)

Operator	Description
-	Subtraction
+	Addition

Table 12.10 Mathematical Operators

Operator	Description
*	Multiplication
/	Division

Table 12.10 Mathematical Operators (Cont.)

Operator	Description
=	Equal to
>	Greater than
<	Less than
>=	Greater than or equal to
<=	Less than or equal to
<>	Not equal to

Table 12.11 Conditional Operators

Operator	Description
And	Links Boolean values, commonly used in IF statements
Or	Links Boolean values, commonly used in IF statements
Not	Returns the opposite of a Boolean value
Between	Determines whether a value is between two values
InList	Determines whether a value is within a list of values

Table 12.12 Logical Operators

Operator	Description
All	Used as an optional parameter in many functions to calculate all or distinct values
Drill	Used with the NoFilter function to ignore report filters
Bottom	Ranks values in ascending order

Table 12.13 Function-Specific Operators

Operator	Description
Break	Forces the `Percentage` function to calculate within table breaks
Col	Optionally used to set the calculation direction in the following functions: `Percentage`, `RunningAverage`, `RunningCount`, `RunningMax`, `RunningMin`, `RunningProduct`, `RunningSum`
Distinct	Used as an optional parameter in many functions to calculate distinct or all values
IncludeEmpty	Optionally used to tell an aggregate function to include empty values
Index	Used by the `UserResponse` and `RefValueUserResponse` functions to return the database primary key of a prompt response
Linear	Used by the `Interpolation` function to use linear regression
NoNull	Tells the `Previous` function to ignore null values
NotOnBreak	Optionally used by the `Interpolation` function to ignore section and block breaks
PointToPoint	Used by the `Interpolation` function to use point-to-point to account for missing values
Row	Optionally used to set the calculation direction in the following functions: `Percentage`, `RunningAverage`, `RunningCount`, `RunningMax`, `RunningMin`, `RunningProduct`, `RunningSum`
Self	Refers the `Previous` function to the previous cell when it doesn't contain a report object
Top	Ranks values in descending order
Where	Restricts the data to calculate a measure

Table 12.13 Function-Specific Operators (Cont.)

Operator	Description
In	Specifies an explicit list of dimensions to use in the context
ForAll	Removes dimensions from the default context
ForEach	Adds dimensions to the default

Table 12.14 Extended Syntax Operators

Operator	Description
Block	Refers to data within an entire block, ignores breaks, respects filters: `Sum([Revenue]) In Block`
Body	Displays the value of the data presented in a block and can be used in a footer, header, or body: `Sum([Revenue]) In Body`
Break	Calculates the total for the dimension used in a break: `Sum([Revenue]) In Break`
Report	Displays all report data: `Sum([Revenue]) In Report`
Section	Calculates the section total of a measure when a section has been set in a report: `Sum([Revenue]) in Section`

Table 12.15 Extended Syntax Key Words

The hierarchical operators are used in place of the `desc_flag` keyword in the `Descendants` function to specify the distance of the descendant in relation to the specified member.

Operator	Description
After	Returns the descendants *after* the level or distance is specified in the `Descendants` function
Before	Returns the descendants *before* the level or distance is specified in the `Descendants` function
Before_After	Returns the current member and all descendants except those specified by the `level|distance` parameter in the `Descendants` function
Leaves	Returns all members between the current member and the level or distance specified for members that do not have child members
Range (:)	Returns a set of members at the same level existing between the two members specified
Self_After	Returns the current member and all descendants at and *after* the level or distance specified in the `Descendants` function
Self_Before	Returns the current member and all descendants at and *before* the level or distance specified in the `Descendants` function
Self_Before_After	Returns the current member and all descendants

Table 12.16 Hierarchical Operators

12.3 Formula Syntax

The first step in writing formulas and creating variables is to understand the Web Intelligence formula syntax. You must follow a few basic rules to create a valid formula. After you understand how to apply these basic rules, the task of writing a formula will no longer be a challenge. You can then focus your efforts on writing formulas and building analytical Web Intelligence reports that provide the greatest value to your client.

12.3.1 Primary Formula Syntax Rules

Consider these primary rules:

1. Each formula must begin with the equals symbol (=).
2. Data objects used in a formula must be encapsulated by brackets ([ ]).
3. Use a semicolon to represent Else in an If-Then-Else statement (;).
4. Use a semicolon to represent Then in an If-Then-Else statement (;).
5. Every statement with an open parenthesis must also include a closing parenthesis.
6. Click on the green checkmark button to validate the syntax of the formula or variable.
7. Change the qualification type when creating a measure or detail variable.
8. Assign a commonly used business term or phrase with the proper naming convention as the variable name.

12.3.2 If – Then – Else Syntax

Figure 12.8 shows a simple formula entered into the FORMULA EDITOR window. Several key areas of the formula are labeled in the screenshot, including three of the most important rules:

1. Begin a formula with the equals symbol (=).
2. Use a semicolon for THEN (;).
3. Use a semicolon for ELSE (;).

(You'll notice that these rules are repeated from the list of primary syntax rules.)

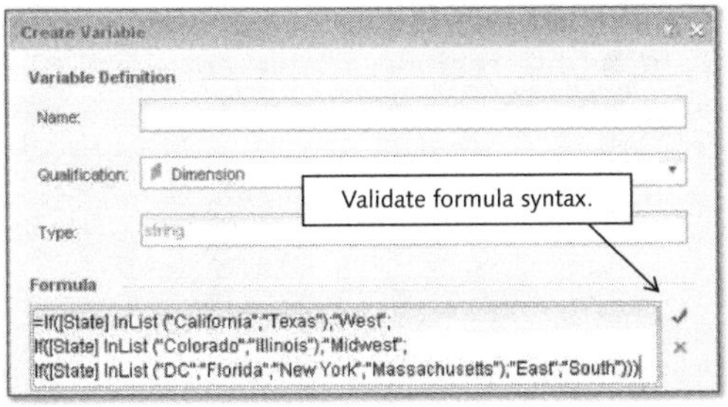

Figure 12.8 Example of Variable Syntax in a Formula

The formula shown in the FORMULA box in Figure 12.8 is translated into English as the following:

> *If the State data object contains values of California or Texas, then assign the value to West. If the State data object contains values of Colorado or Illinois, then assign the value to Midwest. If the State data object contains values of DC, Florida, New York, or Massachusetts, then assign the value to East. If the State data object contains any other values, then return the word South.*

12.3.3 Saving a Variable

Before clicking on OK in the FORMULA EDITOR and saving a formula, click on the green checkmark button located to the right of the formula. This button validates the syntax in the formula.

If the syntax is valid, a small statement beneath the formula will appear that reads, THE FORMULA IS CORRECT. Click on OK to at the bottom of the FORMULA EDITOR to proceed.

If there's an error in the syntax, the formula can't be validated. To close the Formula Editor, all modifications will either have to be discarded or revised to include the correct syntax. If an error in the formula is present, the position of the first occurrence will be displayed beneath the formula when the syntax is validated.

12.3.4 Modifying a Variable

When a variable is created in a Web Intelligence report, the new object will be added to the AVAILABLE OBJECTS section for use in report elements throughout the document. The variable will appear along with all of the existing result objects returned from the query. Figure 12.9 shows the region variable created in the previous section.

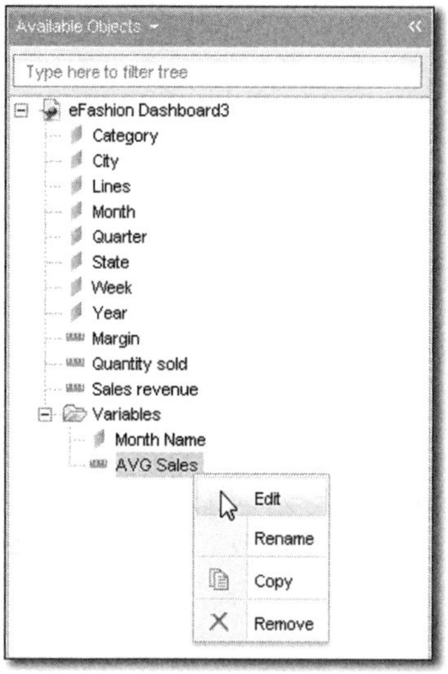

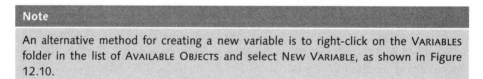

Figure 12.9 Right-Clicking on a Variable to Edit, Rename, or Remove

All variables created in a document are easily identified because they're automatically added to a VARIABLES folder. To modify a variable, right-click on the object and select EDIT. Editing a variable will launch the VARIABLE EDITOR, in which you can modify the formula, name, or qualification of the object.

> **Note**
>
> An alternative method for creating a new variable is to right-click on the VARIABLES folder in the list of AVAILABLE OBJECTS and select NEW VARIABLE, as shown in Figure 12.10.

The next section will describe the differences between input and output context formula types that can be created in the WebI Report Panel.

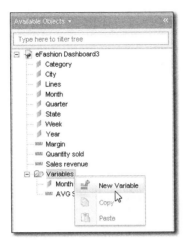

Figure 12.10 Adding a New Variable by Right-Clicking on the Variables Folder

12.4 Input, Output, and Calculation Contexts

Calculation contexts can be a sticky wicket to master, but if you're successful, the data in your reports can be transformed from just data returned by a query to truly analytical information. We'll begin this coverage of calculation contexts by discussing how SAP BusinessObjects aggregates data by default and then show how the values can be changed to meet different requirements with the addition of certain operators and key words to your formulas.

The default aggregation behavior in Web Intelligence is to sum a measure by the dimensions in the table. These values automatically update anytime the dimensions or contexts are changed. Whether simple filters or input controls are selected or new dimensions are added to the table, the summed measure column(s) update immediately. An example of this functionality is shown in Figure 12.11 with a vertical table that contains two objects: Lines and Sales revenue.

By default, the dimensions are automatically aggregated to show the sales revenue total for each distinct value. Also by default, the values are being displayed in both the block and report. As we'll learn later, these two keywords can be used to further restrict or specify the calculation.

> **Note**
>
> This example is based on the projection function of the measure objects being set to the
> Sum function in the object's definition at the universe level.

Lines	Sales revenue
Accessories	$9,914,546
City Skirts	$347,775
City Trousers	$284,734
Dresses	$2,915,620
Jackets	$677,307
Leather	$187,413
Outerwear	$1,183,083

Figure 12.11 Default Aggregation of a Single Dimension and Measure Object

When another dimension is added to the data block, the SALES REVENUE measure will summarize the values based on the dimensions added to the block (see Figure 12.12).

Lines	Year	Sales revenue
Accessories	2004	$2,546,222
Accessories	2005	$5,468,919
Accessories	2006	$1,899,405
City Skirts	2004	$48,774
City Skirts	2005	$102,716
City Skirts	2006	$196,285

Figure 12.12 Default Aggregation with Two Dimensions and a Measure Object

To override the YEAR column that was added to the block and continue displaying the values aggregated at the LINES dimension, use the In operator as illustrated in the formula bar in Figure 12.13.

Next, we'll look at the different aggregation types and how you can use them together with context operators and key words to further transform calculations.

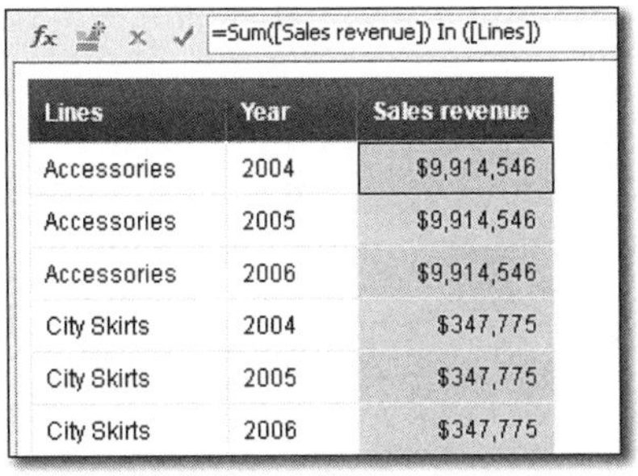

Figure 12.13 Using the IN Operator to Aggregate Values for a Specified Dimension

12.4.1 Aggregates in Context Formulas

Input and output contexts are generally used to produce values at different dimensional levels to calculate maximums, minimums, averages, sums, and percentages. One of the most common requirements is to calculate the percentage of each dimension value's contribution to the whole. To do this, we need each row to be divided by the whole within the block.

Figure 12.14 shows the data table with a new column added to aggregate the total Sales revenue for the entire block. This formula uses the In Block operator and key word to bypass the default calculation behavior and providing the values at the block level rather than dimensional row level.

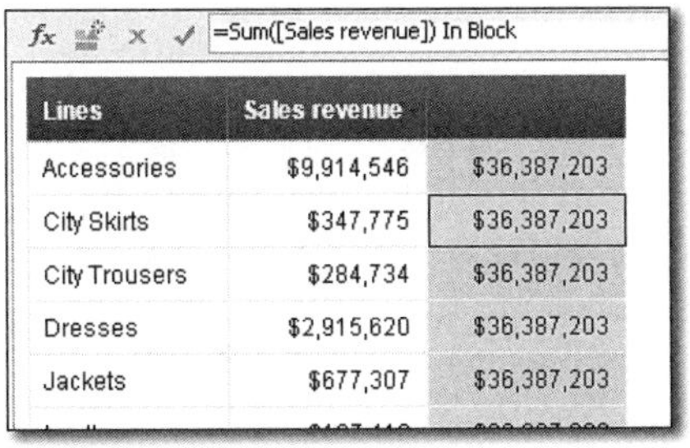

Figure 12.14 Calculating a Total within the Block

Click the CREATE VARIABLE icon on the formula bar to convert the formula into a variable that can be used throughout the report (see Figure 12.15).

From the CREATE VARIABLE window, enter a unique NAME for your variable, and click OK to proceed. In Figure 12.16, the variable is named "Sales Rev Totals".

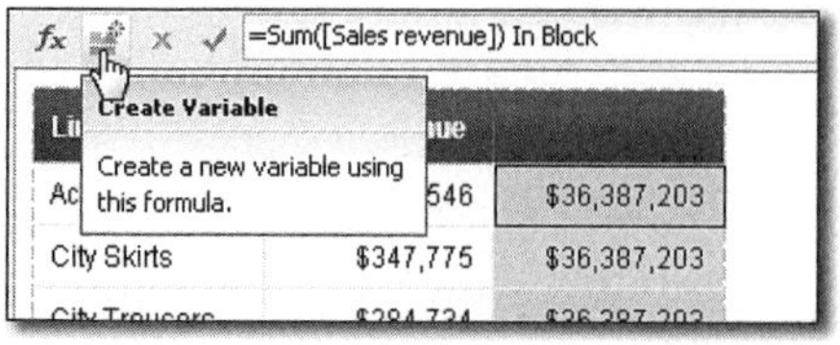

Figure 12.15 Converting a Formula into a Reusable Variable

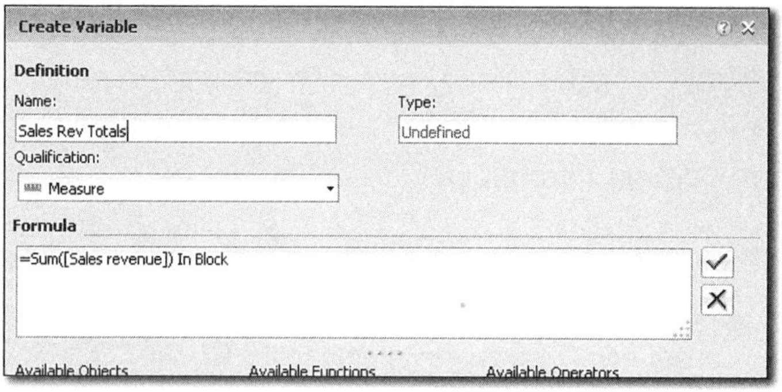

Figure 12.16 Giving a Name to a Formula

Now that we have a variable that calculates the Sales Revenue Totals within the block, let's divide it by the `Sales revenue` object, as shown in Figure 12.17. This new column now shows each row's percentage of the total value. Just as we did in the preceding step, this formula can also be converted to a variable.

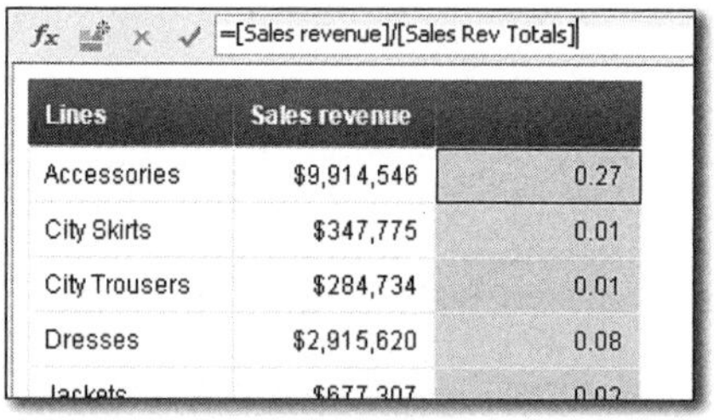

Figure 12.17 Sales Revenue Totals Divided by Sales Revenue

> **Note**
>
> To format the new percentage column to show values in a percentage format, right-click on the column, select FORMAT NUMBER, and then navigate to the PERCENTAGE grouping. The new method of formatting percentages introduced in SAP BusinessObjects BI 4.1 is discussed next.

New in SAP BusinessObjects BI 4.1 is a single-click icon used for applying the percentage format to a column. Figure 12.18 shows this icon and percentage column after clicking the icon. It's located in the FORMATTING tab and NUMBERS subtab.

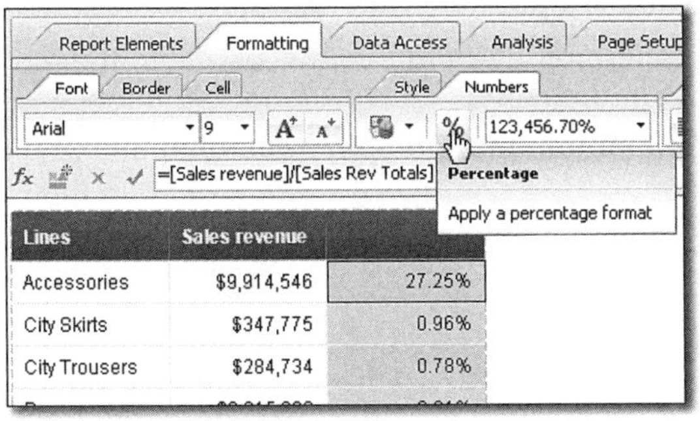

Figure 12.18 Formatting a Column to Percentage Format with Icon

Because we created the new Sales Rev Totals variable to include the In Block operator and keyword, we'll now describe the four report structure operator and key word combinations that can be used in formulas. If no keyword is provided, the implicit level of aggregation will be In Body.

12.4.2 Report Structure Operator and Keyword Combinations

Following are the four report structure operator and keyword combinations:

▶ In Report
This combination is used to set the formula to display at the report total level to produce a grand total for the visible and nonfiltered data objects on the report.

▶ In Block
This combination is used to set the context of the formula to the data table. If a section is applied in the report, this operator will function within each section individually. If a section has been added, and values at the entire block are needed rather than aggregates at the section level, the In Report operator should be used.

▶ In Section
This combination works exactly the same as In Block when applied to a data block within a section on a report.

▶ In Body

This combination is the implicit default operator of a formula. For instance, these two formulas produce the same result:

▶ `Max([Sales revenue]) In Body`

▶ `Max([Sales revenue])`

12.4.3 Context Operators

We've already discussed the `IN` operator, so now let's examine the `Where`, `ForEach`, and `ForAll` context operators. These two context operators are commonly used in conjunction with an aggregation function such as `max()` and `min()`. Following are definitions of the context operators that describe how they're used in formulas:

▶ `Where`

This operator can be used in formulas to restrict calculations to specific values.

▶ `ForEach`

This operator is used to explicitly add additional dimensions to a context. Existing dimensions in the block continue to impact the formula. This is considered an input context operator because it requires explicitly named dimensional objects to be included in the calculation.

▶ `ForAll`

This operator is used to remove dimensions from a context. Dimensions as part of the `ForAll` construct will be removed, but other dimensions within the block will continue to have a bearing on the formula. This is considered an output context operator because it aggregates out at the dimensional level.

The ForEach Operator

This context operator should be used to add a dimensional break to a calculation even when the dimension is not assigned to the same data block. An example of this operator can be used to calculate the maximum sales revenue by quarter for each year.

In this example, the data table contains a single dimension—`Year`—but needs to display the highest quarterly revenue for each year. This is shown in Figure 12.19, along with the total annual sales revenue.

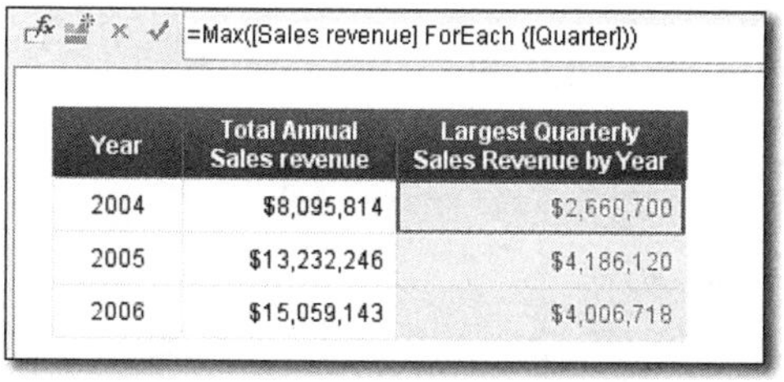
=Max([Sales revenue] ForEach ([Quarter]))

Year	Total Annual Sales revenue	Largest Quarterly Sales Revenue by Year
2004	$8,095,814	$2,660,700
2005	$13,232,246	$4,186,120
2006	$15,059,143	$4,006,718

Figure 12.19 Highest Sales Revenue for each Quarter

We can add to this formula to get even more information by using the `ForEach` operator. Let's say that you need to know the highest revenue producing categories by quarter and by year. This can be accomplished by adding the `Category` object to the formula after the `Quarter` object as in Figure 12.20.

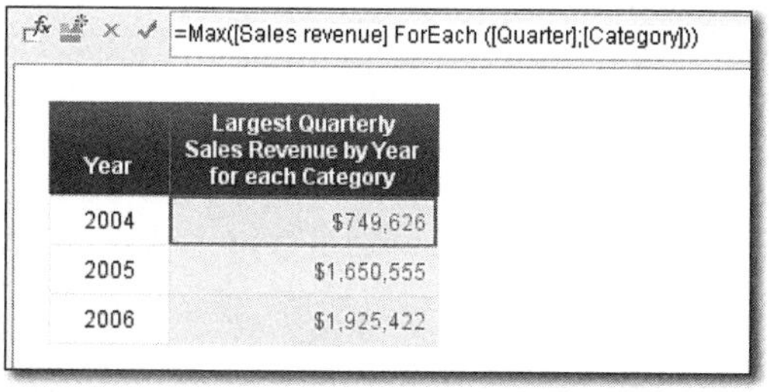
=Max([Sales revenue] ForEach ([Quarter];[Category]))

Year	Largest Quarterly Sales Revenue by Year for each Category
2004	$749,626
2005	$1,650,555
2006	$1,925,422

Figure 12.20 Calculating the Maximum Sales Revenue for Each Category Quarterly and within Each Year

The ForAll Operator

This operator is used to calculate a value after removing a dimension from a context. In this example, we have a data table with two dimensions—`Year` and `Quarter`. Our calculation uses the `ForAll` operator to aggregate `Sales revenue` by `Year` and remove the `Quarter` dimension from the calculation. We can also calculate the maximum `Sales revenue` for all quarters within each year. These columns are shown in Figure 12.21.

The formulas used in these calculations are the following:

- `=Sum([Sales revenue]) ForAll ([Quarter])`
- `=Max([Sales revenue]) ForAll ([Quarter])`

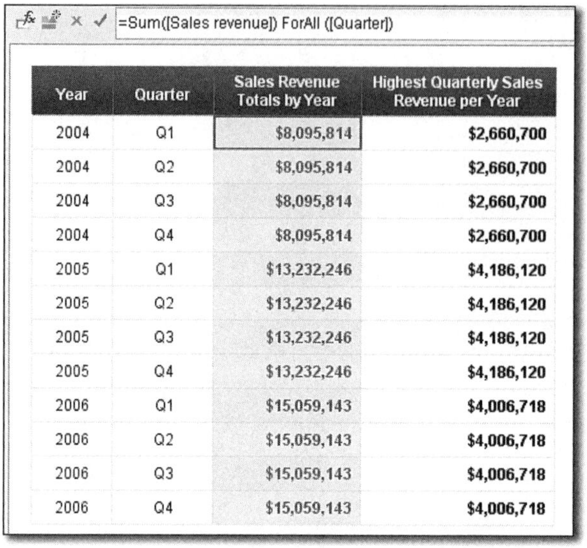

=Sum([Sales revenue]) ForAll ([Quarter])

Year	Quarter	Sales Revenue Totals by Year	Highest Quarterly Sales Revenue per Year
2004	Q1	$8,095,814	$2,660,700
2004	Q2	$8,095,814	$2,660,700
2004	Q3	$8,095,814	$2,660,700
2004	Q4	$8,095,814	$2,660,700
2005	Q1	$13,232,246	$4,186,120
2005	Q2	$13,232,246	$4,186,120
2005	Q3	$13,232,246	$4,186,120
2005	Q4	$13,232,246	$4,186,120
2006	Q1	$15,059,143	$4,006,718
2006	Q2	$15,059,143	$4,006,718
2006	Q3	$15,059,143	$4,006,718
2006	Q4	$15,059,143	$4,006,718

Figure 12.21 Using the ForAll Operator to Remove the Quarter Dimension from the Calculation

12.5 Summary

Functions and variables allow report developers to provide valuable analytical insight by using business data to create calculations. Data retrieved by a Web Intelligence query can be used in combination with more than 160 functions and almost 40 operators to create complex and precise formulas.

Formulas can be converted into variables, used throughout an entire reporting document, and saved within a document to provide ongoing and maintenance-free analysis.

You can use result objects returned by your queries to create functions that aggregate data, extract information from dates, or dissect string values by using character functions.

You can create formulas and variables to calculate data at an even more detailed level of analysis by using a unique set of operators. Examples of these operators include filtering values with the Where operator and aggregating values by block, section, or report.

Chapter 13 discusses how to extend Query Panel functionalities.

You can apply complex filtering strategies when retrieving data to create reports with highly customized and refined data sets. Use advanced querying techniques to produce tightly focused reporting documents. And connect to your SAP HANA data sources to leverage its powerful in-memory and real-time capabilities.

13   Extending Query Panel Functionality

All reporting requirements begin with a business question and end with a refined set of data displayed in a report that delivers a clear business answer. You can achieve your reporting objectives and make more informed decisions when data is transformed into actionable information. Web Intelligence allows report consumers and report developers to achieve these goals by providing several different query filtering options for producing highly constrained data sets.

You can retrieve data and create powerful and interactive reports by using many advanced techniques in the Query Panel. These techniques include modifying the generated SQL with freehand SQL, creating complex and nested filters, building subqueries, and prompting users for input with optional filters.

When queries are refreshed and data is returned, each Web Intelligence document stores the data in its own microcube. After data has made it to the microcube, you can create reports by adding result objects to a variety of available components. Chapters 3 through 10 provided very detailed information on creating and filtering reports after successfully querying a data source.

Visually tracking data changes in a report is discussed later in this chapter. You can use data tracking to assist users with identifying revised or updated data from the most recent refresh compared to the previously refreshed instance.

We'll start the discussion of extending the Query Panel with information on the complex filtering options available, and then move to cascading prompts, tracking data changes, and previewing a sample of data before running the query.

13.1   Complex Filtering Options

Several techniques can be employed in the Query Panel to filter data retrieved by a query. Chapter 3 discussed the use of combined queries and subqueries in the Query Panel. This section covers additional methods of filtering queries to produce reports that contain the data needed for solving specific business problems.

13.1.1   Filtering with Wild Cards

You can use wild cards to help you filter an object when the entire value isn't known, such as when the exact spelling of the intended filter is uncertain.

Wild cards are created by using the Matches pattern operator. Figure 13.1 shows the State object using the Matches pattern operator and % wild card to return all states that begin with C.

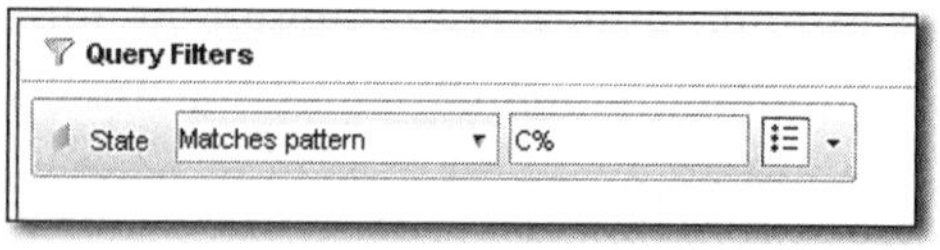

Figure 13.1 Query Filter Using Matches Pattern and the % Wild Card

Use the underscore character for each character to be represented in a filtered value. For example, if you want to filter an object to return the color beige, use both wild cards in combination with the known characters.

Figure 13.2 shows two different wild cards with the Color object, in which a percentage sign is used to represent any number of characters, and an underscore is used to represent a single character.

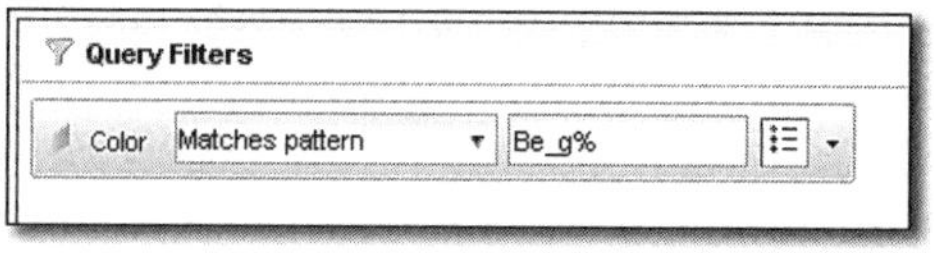

Figure 13.2 Custom Filter Containing the Wild Cards _ and %

The Matches pattern operator is converted to LIKE when the SQL statement is generated. Figure 13.3 shows the SQL translation of the operator in combination with the % wild card.

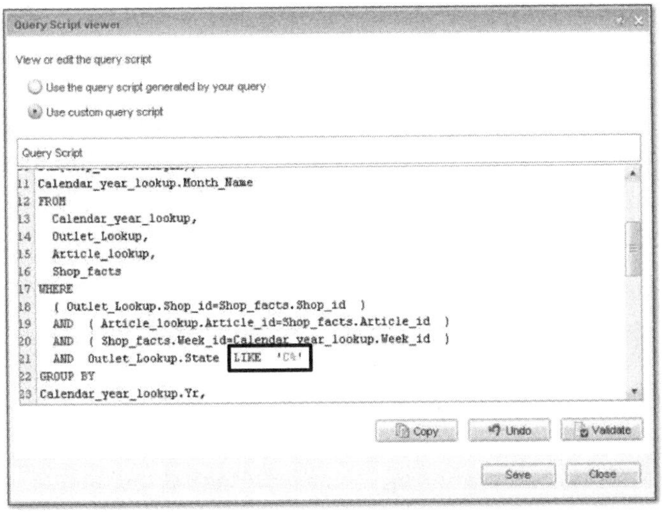

Figure 13.3 Matches Pattern Converted to LIKE in Generated SQL

Figure 13.4 shows the SQL generated by the `Matches pattern` operator that includes an underscore wild card and a % wild card.

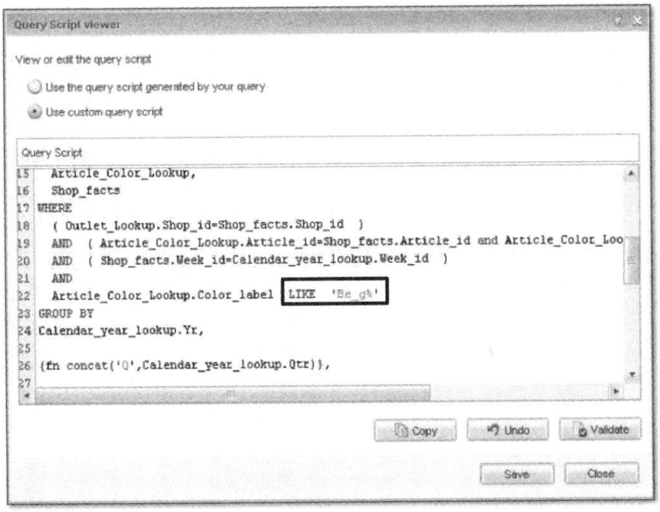

Figure 13.4 SQL Generated by the Matches Pattern Operator

13.1.2 Nested Query Filters

You can use nested query filters to group a series of targeted constraints that return a precise data set. When you nest filters, dimensions and measures can be grouped into several combinations by using the AND or OR operators. Nested filters can be applied to many layers of grouped objects with the AND or OR operator. This method of filtering is very easy to set up.

Adding and Nesting Query Filters

To add and nest query filters, follow these steps:

1. Drag and drop predefined filters, prompted objects, or standard results objects into the QUERY PANEL.

2. Drop the filter directly on top of an existing filter object to nest the filter.

3. Drop the filter immediately beneath an existing filter to apply filtering outside of a nested relationship.

4. Double-click on the AND and OR operator located immediately to the left of the nested group to toggle the operator type.

Figure 13.5 shows several query filters included at the same level in a Web Intelligence document grouped by default with the AND operator. If a query containing the filters in the screenshot were executed, the result would include only results from the current year's CHRISTMAS PERIOD, OWNED STORES only, and for color lines that begin with "Be". The results must meet all criteria for results to be returned.

But if the filters were grouped using the OR operator for the collection of filters, the SQL statement would be generated differently and results would be returned relating to *any* of the four filters rather than *all* four.

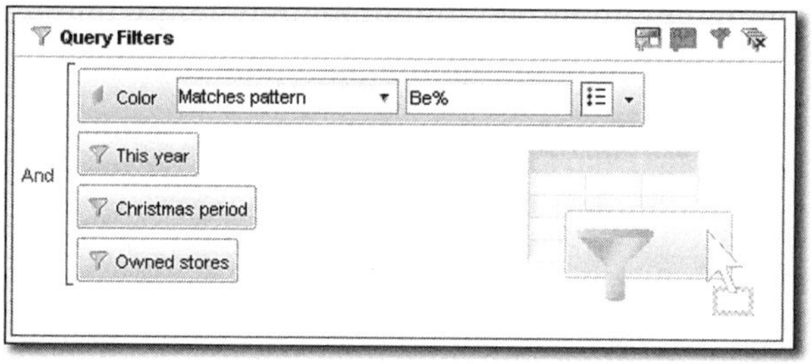

Figure 13.5 Query Filters Grouped by the AND Operator

> **Note**
>
> The default group operator is AND. Double-click on it to change it to OR. Query filters can be grouped by both AND and OR in the same document.

Nesting Filters

Figure 13.6 shows the exact same filters listed in the previous screenshot, but the results from the two queries are quite different. The SQL statement generated with this set of query filters returns rows that meet the criteria from two pairs of filters separated by the OR operator. Results from THIS YEAR or when the COLOR object begins with "Be" make up the first pair of filters; the second pair limits the results to either OWNED STORES or CHRISTMAS PERIOD.

Figure 13.6 Nested Query Filters

Query filters can be added to a nested group with objects that have already been added to the Query Filters pane or by dragging and dropping new custom or pre-defined filter objects into the Query Filters pane.

Creating a Nested Group

To create a nested group, drop an object on top of an existing filter in the Query Panel. A thin vertical line will be displayed to the left of two or more filters to denote that a nested group has been created with the filters. Double-click on AND to the left of the thin vertical line to switch the nested group to the OR operator.

This can also be achieved with existing filters by dragging and dropping an object on top of another filter to add it to an existing group. Figure 13.7 shows the pre-defined CHRISTMAS PERIOD filter being dropped onto the OWNED STORES filter to create a new nested filter group.

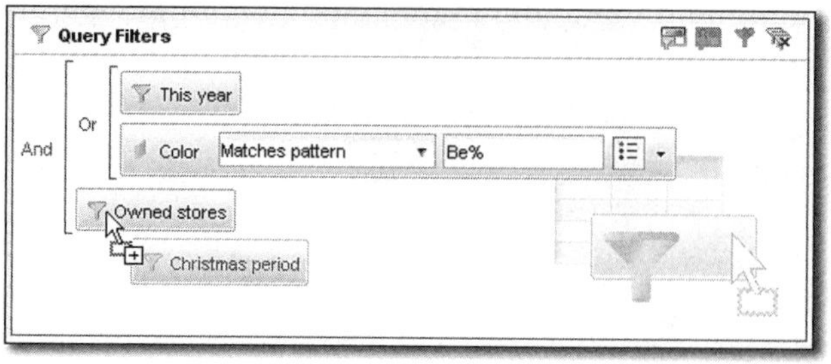

Figure 13.7 Creating a New Nested Group with Existing Query Filters

Removing Query Filters from a Nest

To remove a query filter from a nested group, drag and drop it to a different location. This can mean moving it to a different nested group, moving it to the bottom of the list of query filters to be outside of all filter groups, or dropping it back into the AVAILABLE OBJECTS section to completely remove it from the query.

Figure 13.8 shows the This year object being moved from a nested group and dropped to the bottom of the query filters.

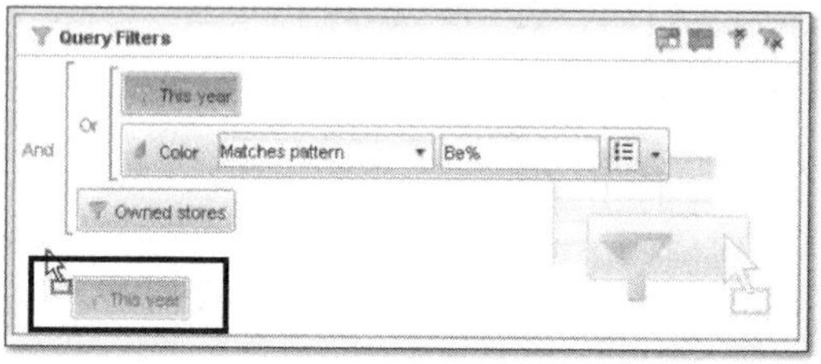

Figure 13.8 Removing a Query Filter from a Nested Group

13.1.3   Database Ranking

Database ranking is used in a reporting document to return only the rows meeting the ranking criteria. By pushing ranking onto the database instead of performing ranking locally, you can significantly minimize the amount of data retrieved in a Web Intelligence document.

However, you can use database ranking only if your database supports it. The addition of a database ranking shortcut icon will be disabled if your database doesn't support ranking.

Adding Database Ranking

You can add database ranking to a document by clicking on the ADD A DATABASE RANKING button located in the upper-right corner of the QUERY FILTERS pane, as shown in Figure 13.9. Click this icon to configure the database ranking parameters. The default setup is arranged to return the Top 10 <dimensions> based on a <measure>. Following are details about the options available when adding a database ranking:

▶ **Rank direction**
The default ranking number is set to 10 but can be adjusted up or down:

  ▶ TOP: Returns the top 10 <dimension> object values based on the <measure>, with the number 10 being adjustable.

  ▶ BOTTOM: Returns the bottom 10 <dimension> object values based on the <measure>, with the number 10 being adjustable.

  ▶ % TOP: Returns the top 10% of the <dimension> object based on the <measure>, with 10 being adjustable.

  ▶ % BOTTOM: Returns the bottom 10% of the <dimension> object based on the <measure>, with 10 being adjustable.

▶ **Ranked number**
Use the default number of 10, change to a different constant value, or prompt the user for a value.

▶ **Context for ranking**
Insert a dimension object to be used in the ranking by dragging and dropping it into the database ranking structure.

▶ **Ranking based on**
Drop a measure object as the basis for the ranking.

▶ **Optional rank**
Add another dimension object to rank by.

▶ **Ranking filtering**
Drop predefined filters or objects for custom filters to restrict the data set returned by the ranking query.

Figure 13.9 Adding Database Ranking in the Query Panel

The DATABASE RANKING PARAMETERS filter will be added to the QUERY FILTERS pane when ADD A DATABASE RANKING is clicked. Figure 13.10 shows the database ranking parameter filter object.

Figure 13.10 Database Ranking Parameters

Enabling Database Ranking

To complete the parameters for database ranking, follow these steps:

1. Select a ranking direction (TOP or BOTTOM).

2. Enter the number of records to be ranked, or click on the small down arrow beside the value box to select PROMPT. The default value is CONSTANT.

3. Drop a dimension object for the context of the ranking.

4. Drop a measure object to be ranked in the BASED ON box.

5. (Optional) Specify additional calculation context by clicking the small arrow to the right of the BASED ON measure to expand the RANKING PARAMETERS box and display a FOR EACH (dimension) option.

Whenever possible, apply complex filtering options at the query level rather than at the report level to produce a result set that already meets the business requirements. Simple filters added in the Report Panel can be easily removed and can potentially misrepresent the information. By restricting the results at the query level, only the needed information is returned.

Filters can also be added at the query level that prompt users for input when the report is opened or refreshed. The next section describes how to set up optional prompts that present users with a list of available values to select from.

13.2   Cascading and Optional Prompts

Cascading prompts are used to assist users with selecting values in prompted Web Intelligence reports. Use the Universe Design Tool to create and modify cascading prompts for dimension objects by creating a cascading list of values (LOV). Figure 13.11 shows the steps for opening the CREATE A CASCADING LIST OF VALUES window. Choose TOOLS • LISTS OF VALUES • CREATE CASCADING LISTS OF VALUES to begin setting up cascading LOVs.

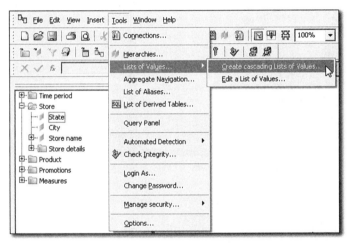

Figure 13.11 Create Cascading Lists of Values in the Universe Design Tool

13.2.1   Defining a Cascading List of Values in the Universe Design Tool

You can use this utility to provide users with a hierarchical structure for selecting values in prompted reports. By providing a functional context of the dimensional values, users have a better understanding of the data in a report that uses a cascading LOV in the prompted filter.

To add dimensional objects to a cascading list, double-click on dimension objects or select them from the list of AVAILABLE OBJECTS, and click the > icon. LOVs should be created from logical hierarchies previously set up in the universe.

Figure 13.12 shows the CREATE CASCADING LIST OF VALUES window launched from the step described previously with three objects added to create a cascading list of dimensional values.

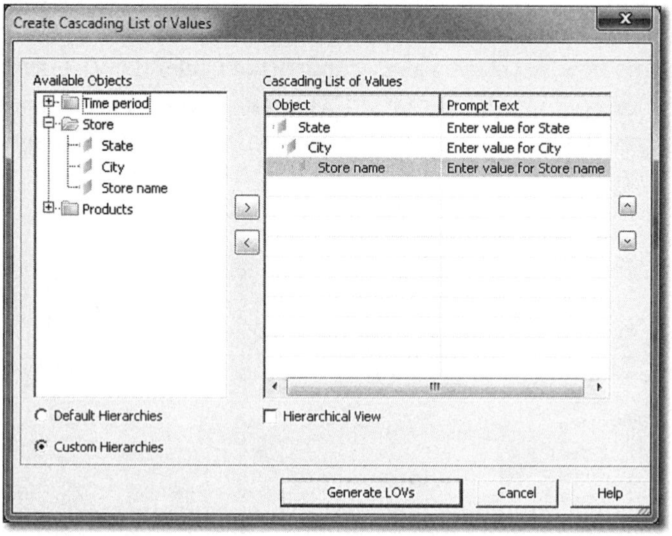

Figure 13.12 Cascading Lists of Values Window

To create a cascading LOV, follow these steps:

1. Select objects to generate a cascading LOV.

2. Click the > symbol to add objects to the CASCADING LIST OF VALUES section.

3. Revise the prompt text of each object (optional).

4. Click GENERATE LOVs to accept the selections and create the cascading list.

Note

Be sure to save and export your universe to the repository after creating the LOV.

13.2.2 Using a Cascading List of Values Object as a Prompted Filter in a Report

After you create a cascading LOV in the universe, you can use any object in the LOV as a prompted filter by following these steps:

1. Drop the object onto the QUERY FILTERS pane.

2. Select PROMPT as the filter type (see Figure 13.13).

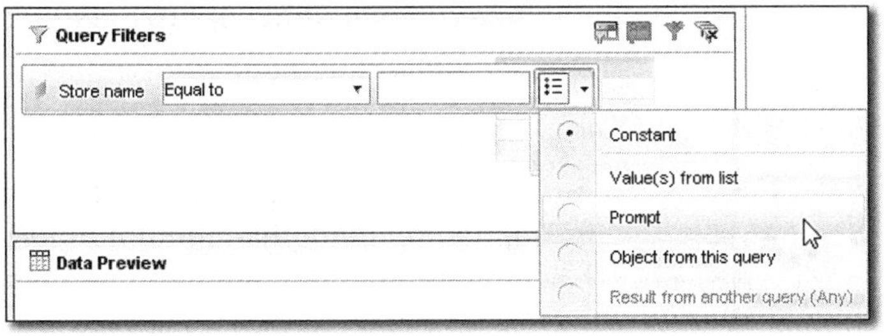

Figure 13.13 Using Cascading Objects as a Prompted Filter

3. Click the SETTINGS button to view the prompt settings.

4. Be sure to check the PROMPT WITH LIST OF VALUES checkbox, as shown in Figure 13.14.

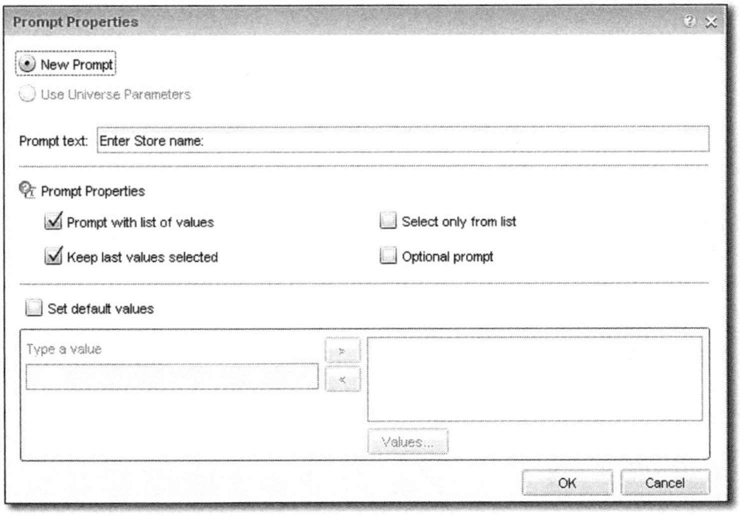

Figure 13.14 Prompt Properties

> **Note**
>
> Although KEEP LAST VALUES SELECTED is checked by default, it's optional and can be unchecked.

13.2.3 Refreshing a Report with a Prompted List of Values Object Filter

Cascading prompted filters become useful when refreshing reports. All objects in the cascading list will appear in the prompted values list in tree form. Navigate into the tree to select the values you want.

As an example, Figure 13.15 shows the order of the cascading list of objects that we set up at the universal level in the previous step. Notice that the STORE NAME object is at the bottom of the hierarchy, the `City` object is one level up, and the `State` object is at the top of the hierarchy.

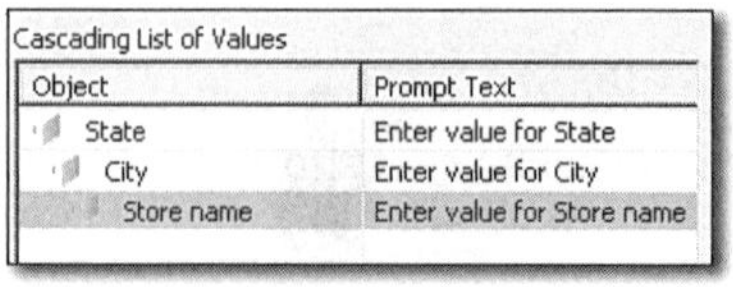

Figure 13.15 Hierarchy of Cascading List of Values

When the STORE NAME object is added as a prompted filter, and the report is refreshed, you'll be prompted to select a value from the list of available customer objects.

When the object being filtered is at the bottom of the hierarchy in a cascading LOV, you need to expand the object values above it in the hierarchy until you get down to the level of the object.

In this example, the `Store name` object prompts the user to expand a STATE value, followed by expanding a CITY within the state selected, and finally selecting the STORE NAME value (see Figure 13.16). Click on the > symbol to add the value to the list, and then click RUN QUERY.

The RUN QUERY button becomes enabled when at least one value is added.

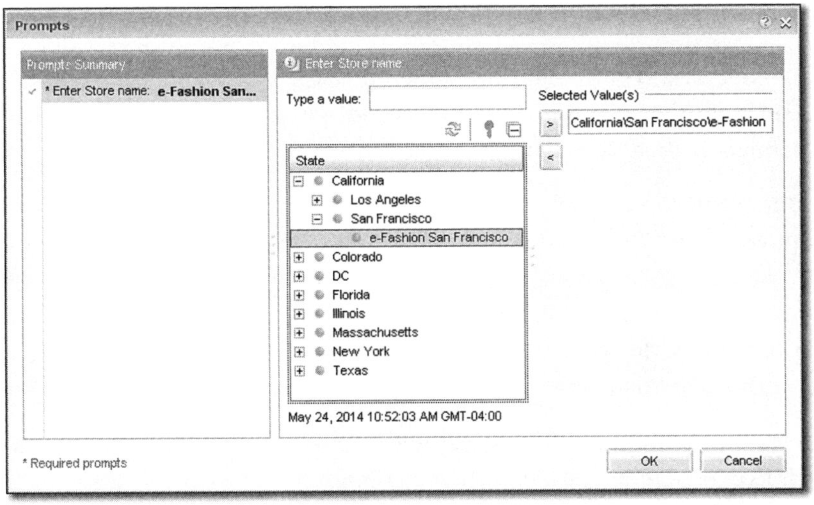

Figure 13.16 Prompted Filter of Cascading List of Values Object

13.2.4 Optional Prompts

Check the OPTIONAL PROMPT checkbox in the PROMPT PROPERTIES section of the PARAMETER PROPERTIES window to make a prompted filter object optional when answering prompts rather than requiring the user to select or enter a value (Figure 13.17). To access this setting, set the filter type to PROMPT in the QUERY FILTERS pane, and then launch the PROMPT PROPERTIES dialog box.

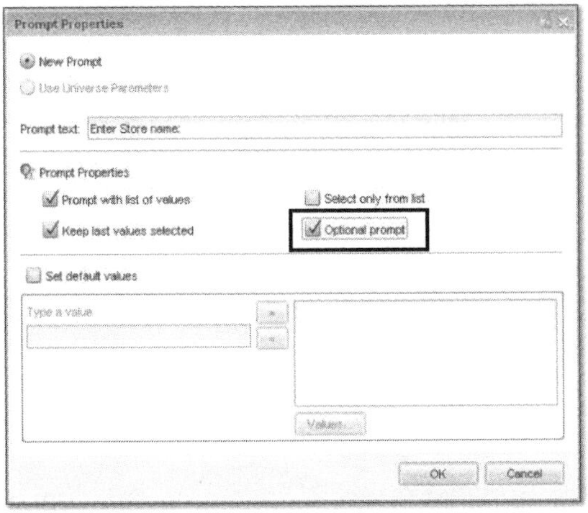

Figure 13.17 Making a Prompt Filter Optional

13.3   Editing Auto-Generated SQL Scripts

To executive queries, Web Intelligence generates SQL statements based on the join paths set up at the universe level, objects added to the RESULT OBJECTS pane, and user-defined or predefined conditions added to the QUERY FILTERS pane.

On occasion, report developers might encounter a need to make minor changes to the script generated by Web Intelligence, and this capability is available in the QUERY SCRIPT VIEWER of the Query Panel. Although it gives the appearance of free-hand SQL, a couple of very specific rules must be followed when editing and overriding the SQL script generated by the Web Intelligence engine, making it more of a script editor than an option to write completely freehand SQL.

We'll cover these rules and describe the simple steps for customizing and overriding the script generated by your queries in the coming sections.

Figure 13.18 shows the icon in the QUERY PANEL used for viewing and editing the script generated by Web Intelligence.

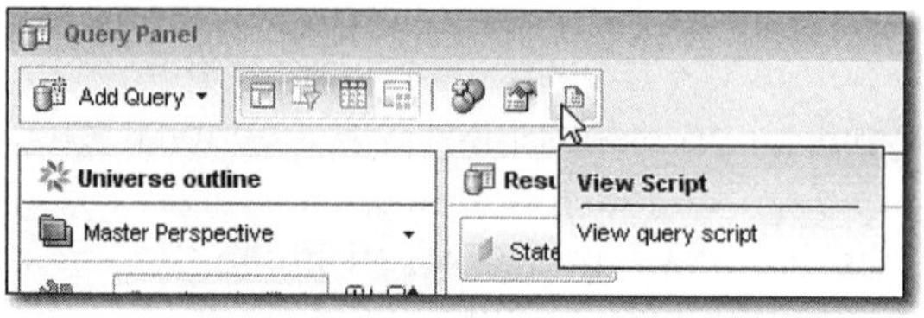

Figure 13.18 Viewing SQL Button in the Query Toolbar

Viewing a Generated Query Script

As previously mentioned, the QUERY SCRIPT VIEWER is used to display the SQL generated by the objects in your query. The SQL syntax is displayed in light gray lettering until the USE CUSTOM QUERY SCRIPT option is selected.

Figure 13.19 shows the QUERY SCRIPT VIEWER with the generated SQL syntax displayed. The UNDO and VALIDATE buttons are disabled unless changes are made to the SQL generated by Web Intelligence.

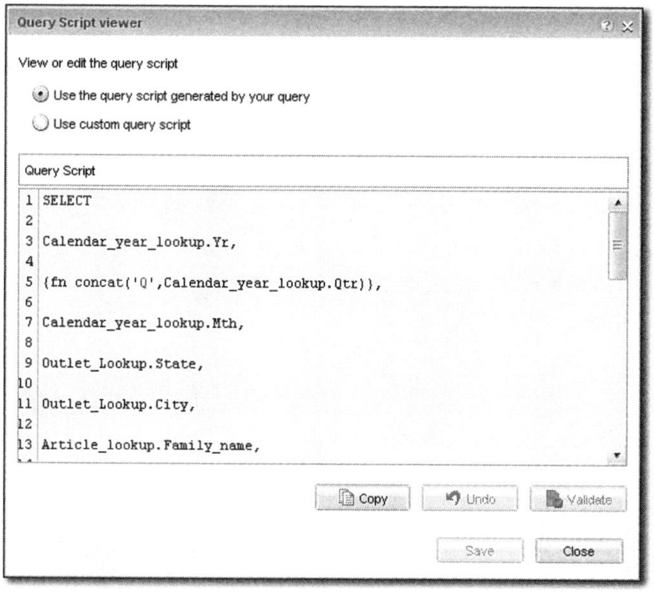

Figure 13.19 SQL Viewer Displaying Generated SQL

Use Custom Query Script

Select the USE CUSTOM QUERY SCRIPT option to enable the text area that displays the generated SQL statement. The code is then displayed in black lettering and is editable.

Figure 13.20 shows the QUERY SCRIPT VIEWER with a customizable SQL statement. Modify or replace the existing SQL, and then click on VALIDATE to test the syntax of your changes. The image shows a change made to the Outlet_Lookup.State object. Instead of returning only the state, the edited line combines the City and State object into a single field.

If no errors were found after validating the syntax, click on SAVE to overwrite the SQL generated by the QUERY PANEL.

Requirements for Using Custom Query Scripts

▶ The number of items in the Select section of the edited SQL statement must match the number of result objects originally placed in the query.

▶ The data type of the objects in the edited Query Script viewer must match the data type of the result objects originally placed in the query.

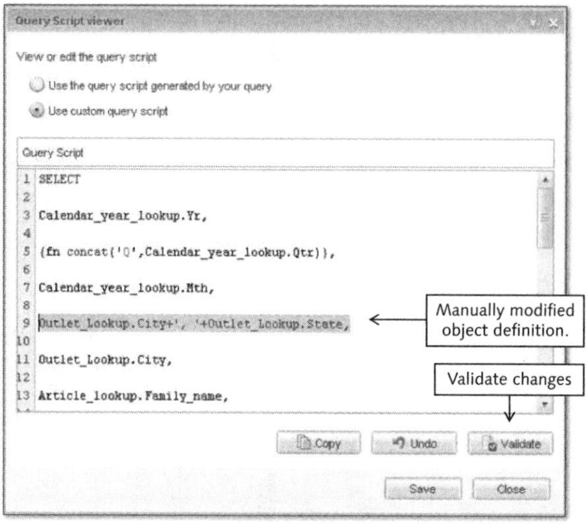

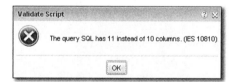

Figure 13.20 SQL Viewer with Custom SQL

Figure 13.21 shows an error message received when attempting to add an additional object to the Select section in the query script generated by the Query Panel. Because the number of objects being returned is now different than in the RESULT OBJECTS pane, an error message will be displayed when validating the script.

Figure 13.21 Error When Modifying Generated SQL

13.4 Visually Tracking Data Changes in the Report Panel

Tracking data changes allows you to visually identify data changes at a glance when a query is refreshed. Many viewing options can be modified to customize the appearance of data values that have changed when a report is refreshed.

To compare the changes in data, you must first set a reference point. Two options are available when setting the reference point:

▶ COMPARE WITH LAST DATA REFRESH (default)

▶ COMPARE WITH DATA REFRESH FROM (select from several recent refresh dates from a dropdown menu)

Data tracking is toggled on or off by clicking the TRACK button located on the DATA TRACKING subtab, which is found on the ANALYSIS tab in the REPORT PANEL (see Figure 13.22).

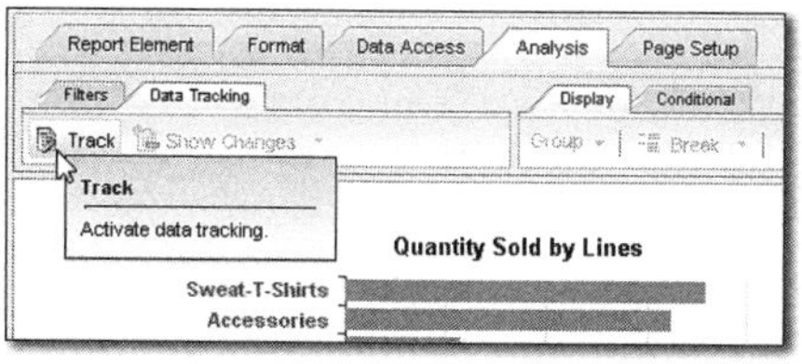

Figure 13.22 Track Data Changes Button

Let's examine a few other actions that relate to data changes.

13.4.1 Showing and Hiding Data Changes

After clicking on TRACK and toggling data tracking on, you'll see that a SHOW CHANGES button becomes enabled. This button allows you to either show or hide the data changes found by the data tracking tool without deactivating tracking. After tracking has been deactivated, you won't be able to compare the current data with the reference data.

Figure 13.23 shows the default data tracking formatting when values from the reference point are different from the values in the latest refresh. Different background colors, font colors, and font types can be configured to represent increased values, decreased values, insertions, deletions, or changes.

City	Sales revenue	Quantity sold	Margin
Austin	$7,173	44	$3,209
Chicago	$3,698	20	$1,583
Colorado Springs	$3,264	21	$910
Dallas	$2,489	17	$926
Los Angeles	$10,973	65	$3,580
Miami	$2,655	17	$882
New York	$23,855	136	$10,342
San Francisco	$7,462	46	$1,985
Washington	$3,765	25	$910

Figure 13.23 Visible Changes When Tracking Data Changes

13.4.2 Data Tracking Options

You can launch the DATA TRACKING OPTIONS dialog box by clicking on the button to the right of the HIDE/SHOW CHANGES tracking button on the default toolbar in the REPORT PANEL. Formatting can be applied to modify a variety of font- and background-related attributes. Figure 13.24 shows the five options to visually display data changes: INSERTIONS, DELETIONS, CHANGES, INCREASED VALUES, and DECREASED VALUES.

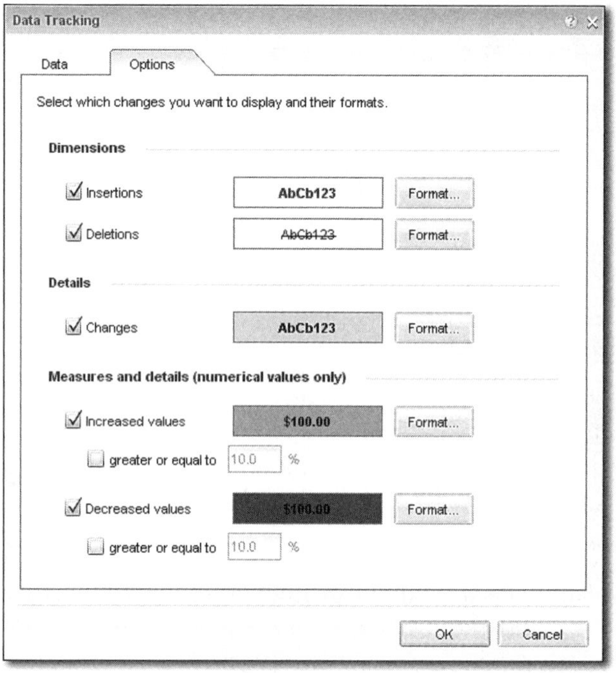

Figure 13.24 Data Tracking Options

Data tracking can be applied to every report in a Web Intelligence document or to only specific report tabs. Click on the DATA tab when configuring data tracking to select the context for comparing the refreshed data and also for selecting which reports to include data tracking.

It's common for one tab to have data tracking enabled, but all other tabs to have data tracking disabled. Other scenarios require that all tabs have data tracking enabled. Figure 13.25 shows the DATA tab in the DATA TRACKING screen. Use this screen to define the instance to compare data against and also which reports should show data tracking. Check REFRESH DATA NOW to refresh the query immediately after clicking on OK.

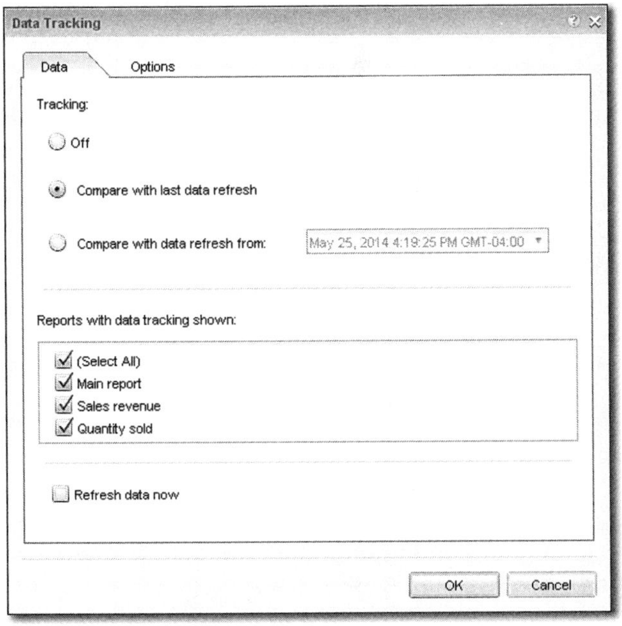

Figure 13.25 Data Tracking Settings

13.4.3 Purging Data

The option to purge data is commonly used before publishing Web Intelligence reports to the server that may contain restricted information. You can purge data in the Query Panel and Report Panel. Figure 13.26 shows the PURGE icon located on the default toolbar in the REPORT PANEL.

Figure 13.26 Purge Data

13.4.4 Identify and Modify Partial Results

If a query refreshes successfully but returns partial results, the bottom-right corner of the report will display a yellow icon containing an exclamation point, as shown in Figure 13.27. This icon indicates that only partial results have been retrieved.

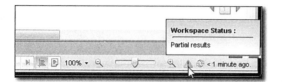

Figure 13.27 Yellow Icon Indicating Partial Results

Partial results leave reporting documents incomplete and should be resolved before publishing, printing, or exporting a report locally or to the SAP Business-Objects BI platform.

The following are the three most common scenarios that cause partial results:

▶ MAX ROWS RETRIEVED setting in the LIMITS category of the QUERY PROPERTIES window in the QUERY PANEL, as shown in Figure 13.28

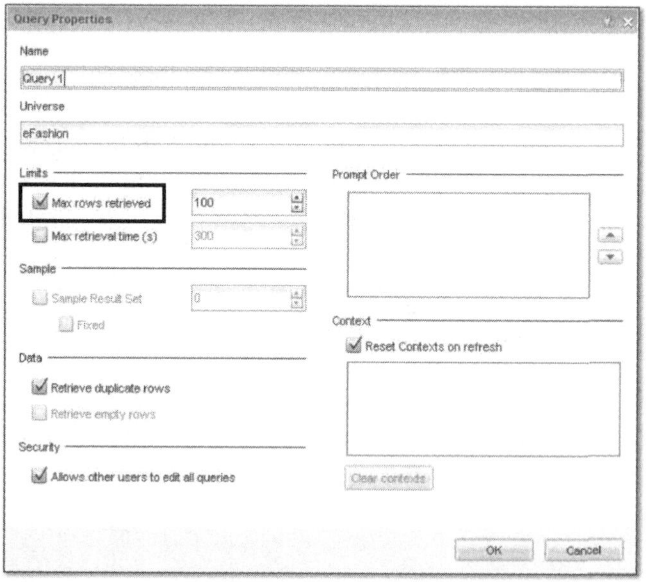

Figure 13.28 Max Rows Retrieved and Max Retrieval Time Settings

▶ MAX RETRIEVAL TIME setting in the LIMITS category of the QUERY PROPERTIES window

▶ CONTROLS tab in the UNIVERSE PARAMETERS dialog box, as shown in Figure 13.29

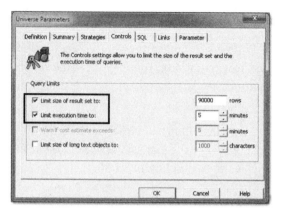

Figure 13.29 Controls Tab in the Universe Parameters

To modify the maximum number of rows retrieved in the query, follow these steps:

1. From the REPORT PANEL, click the DATA ACCESS tab to enter the QUERY PANEL.

2. Click the QUERY PROPERTIES shortcut icon located at the top of the screen.

3. Check or uncheck the MAX ROWS RETRIEVED setting. If checked, modify the number of rows.

4. Check or uncheck the MAX RETRIEVAL TIME setting. If checked, modify the time value.

Use the following steps to modify the maximum number of retrievable rows at the universe level:

1. Launch the UNIVERSE DESIGN TOOL.

2. Open the UNIVERSE PARAMETERS dialog box.

3. Click on the CONTROLS tab.

4. Check or uncheck the LIMIT SIZE OF RESULT SET TO, and then modify the maximum number of rows to be retrieved.

The capability to visually track the changes from a previous report instance to a recently refreshed instance enables users to quickly spot increases or decreases that otherwise may not be as easy to spot. Before running a new query or rerunning an existing one, preview the data while you're still in the Query Panel.

13.5 Data Preview

The DATA PREVIEW panel is a relatively new addition to the Query Panel in Web Intelligence as it was first introduced in version 4.0. This panel can be helpful because it lets you preview a sample of the data based on the existing result objects and query filters before actually running a query.

To view a preview of the data, open the DATA PREVIEW panel, and click on the REFRESH icon located in the upper-right corner of the panel. A sample of the result data will be displayed inside the panel, as shown in Figure 13.30.

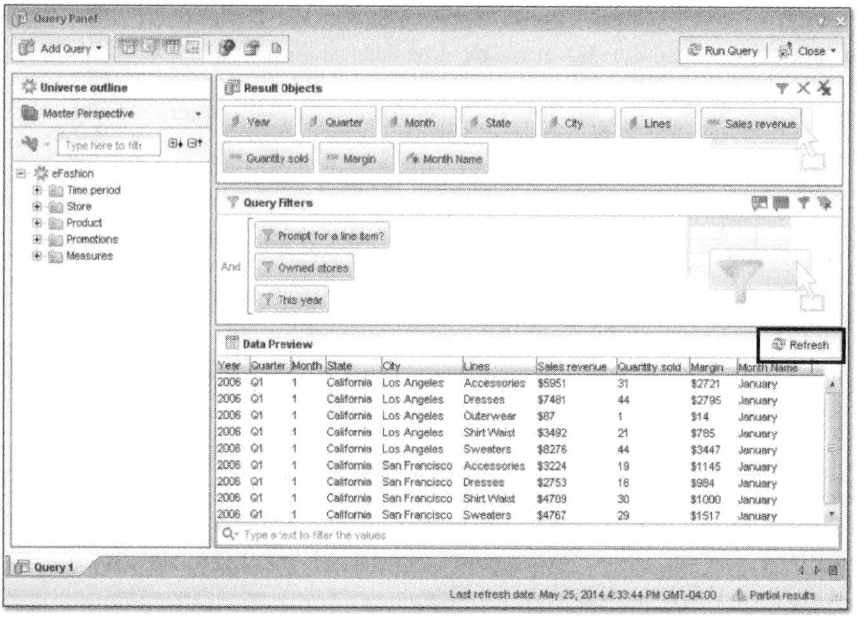

Figure 13.30 Data Preview

13.5.1 Filter Preview Data

While reviewing data in the DATA PREVIEW panel, you have the option to further restrict the result set by creating a query filter for a specific value. To do this, right-click on a value in the panel and select CREATE SIMPLE FILTER. This selection will add the object and value to the QUERY FILTERS panel. Click on REFRESH in the DATA PREVIEW panel again to preview the updated data set.

Figure 13.31 shows the DATA PREVIEW panel if you right-clicked on LOS ANGELES in the CITY column. Select the CREATE SIMPLE FILTER: CITY EQUAL TO LOS ANGELES option to dynamically create a custom filter object in the QUERY FILTERS panel.

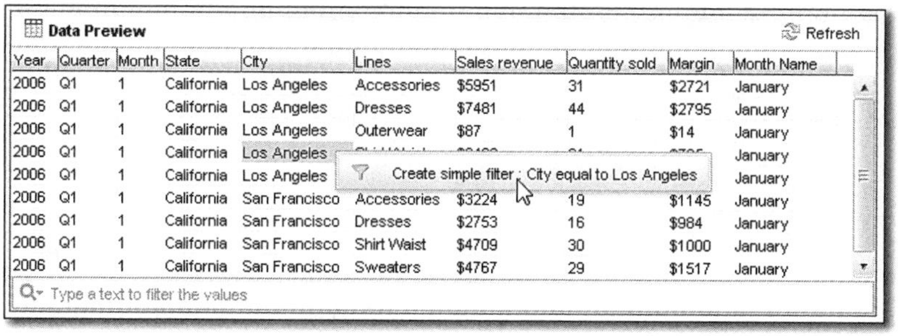
Data Preview
Refresh
Year Quarter Month State City Lines Sales revenue Quantity sold Margin Month Name
2006 Q1 1 California Los Angeles Accessories $5951 31 $2721 January
2006 Q1 1 California Los Angeles Dresses $7481 44 $2795 January
2006 Q1 1 California Los Angeles Outerwear $87 1 $14 January
2006 Q1 1 California Los Angeles January
2006 Q1 1 California Los Angeles January
Create simple filter : City equal to Los Angeles
2006 Q1 1 California San Francisco Accessories $3224 19 $1145 January
2006 Q1 1 California San Francisco Dresses $2753 16 $984 January
2006 Q1 1 California San Francisco Shirt Waist $4709 30 $1000 January
2006 Q1 1 California San Francisco Sweaters $4767 29 $1517 January
Type a text to filter the values

Figure 13.31 Creating Simple Filters from the Data Preview Section

13.5.2 Using Search to Filter Data Preview Values

If you're looking for a specific value in a data set but are unable to locate it in the DATA PREVIEW panel, click in the search window located beneath the panel, and begin entering your term or phrase. The box will search through every row in the panel and immediately filter the results. Searching begins when a single letter or number is entered, and every column in each row is searched.

Figure 13.32 shows the letters "Sw" entered in the search bar with the LINES column selected. The data in the DATA PREVIEW panel filters the results immediately, and the rows with sweaters are easily located.

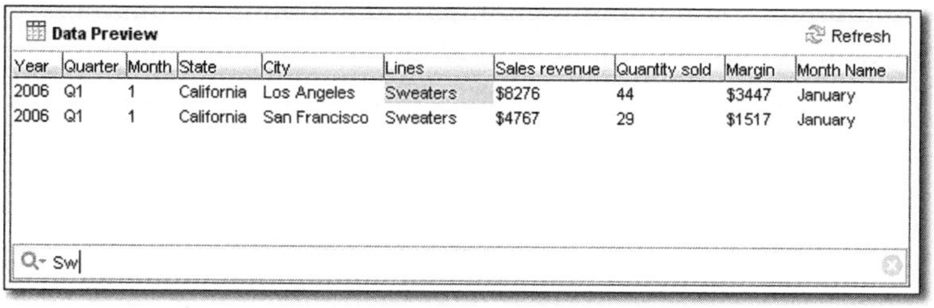
Data Preview
Refresh
Year Quarter Month State City Lines Sales revenue Quantity sold Margin Month Name
2006 Q1 1 California Los Angeles Sweaters $8276 44 $3447 January
2006 Q1 1 California San Francisco Sweaters $4767 29 $1517 January
Sw

Figure 13.32 Dynamically Filtering Preview Data

By previewing a sample of the data set, you can identify areas to improve the query and further refine the information set to be retrieved from the data source.

13.6   Additional Queries and New Data Providers

Adding additional queries to a Web Intelligence document while working in the BI Launch Pad offers four different data source types:

▶ FROM UNIVERSE

▶ FROM EXCEL

▶ FROM BEX

▶ FROM ANALYSIS VIEW

These data source types are accessed by selecting NEW DATA PROVIDER from the DATA ACCESS tab and DATA PROVIDERS subtab in the REPORT PANEL, as shown in Figure 13.33.

Figure 13.33 Adding a New Data Provider from the Report Panel

These same data source types are also available when ADD QUERY is selected from the QUERY PANEL, as shown in Figure 13.34.

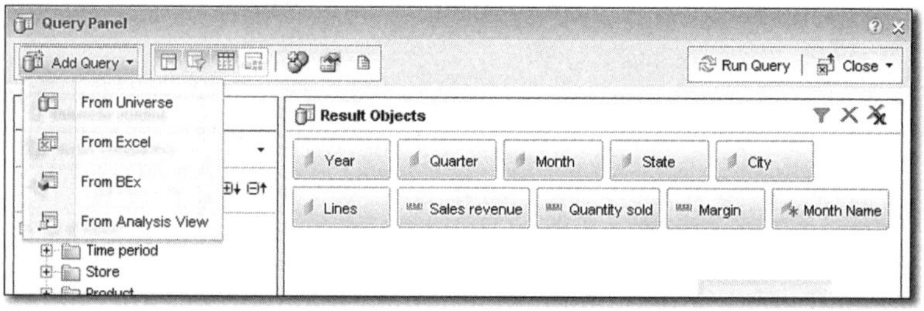

Figure 13.34 Adding a New Query from the Query Panel

In addition to the four primary sources, two additional data sources can be used to create Web Intelligence documents while working in the Web Intelligence Rich Client application: Text and Web Services.

When Web Intelligence Rich Client is launched, users can create reporting documents from six different source types (see Figure 13.35):

► UNIVERSE

► MICROSOFT EXCEL

► BEX

► ANALYSIS VIEW

► TEXT

► WEB SERVICES

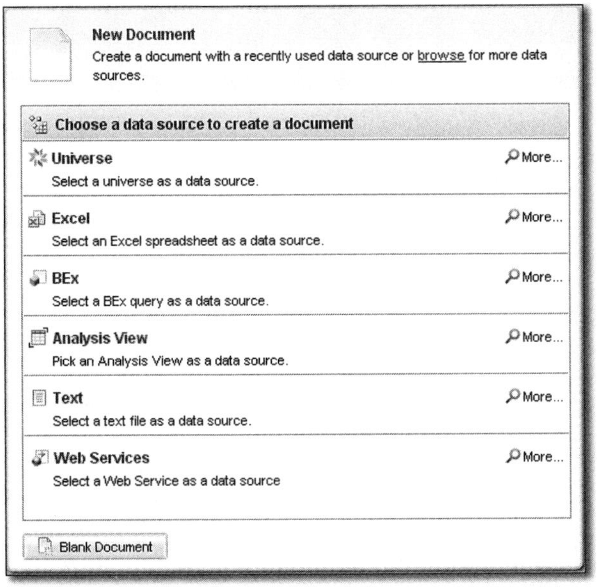

Figure 13.35 Data Source Types Available in Web Intelligence Rich Client

13.6.1 Text Files as a Data Source

When TEXT is selected as the data source, the CUSTOM DATA PROVIDER – TEXT window is launched and provides a BROWSE button for searching for local text files in the .TXT format (see Figure 13.36). Options are provided for the DATA SEPARATOR and TEXT DELIMITER of the source text file. Other options include assigning the first row of the file as column names, and selecting the LOCALE, CHARSET, and DATE FORMAT.

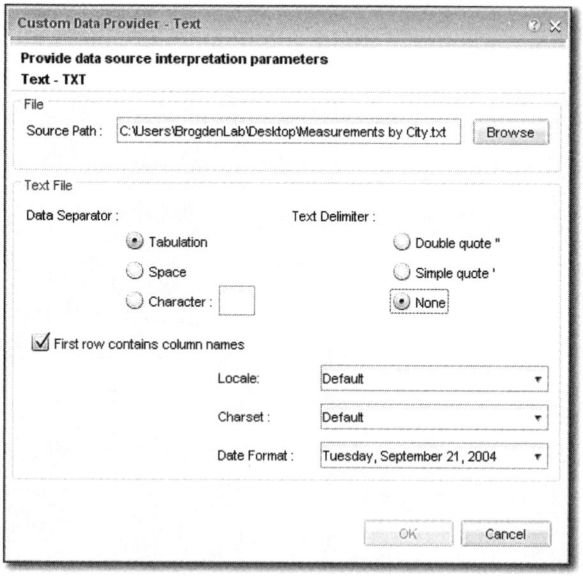

Figure 13.36 Creating a New Variable Object from the Tab Ribbon

13.6.2 Web Services as a Data Source

You can also create Web Intelligence documents using web services as the data source. These web services can be created from Query as a Web Service, data blocks published as web services from other Web Intelligence documents, or generic web services.

After selecting web services as the data source, the CUSTOM DATA PROVIDER – WEB SERVICES window will be launched, as shown in Figure 13.37. To get started, paste your web service URL into the SOURCE URL box and click on SUBMIT. Selections should be made in the SERVICE NAME, PORT NAME, and OPERATION NAME settings located in the SERVICE DETAILS group.

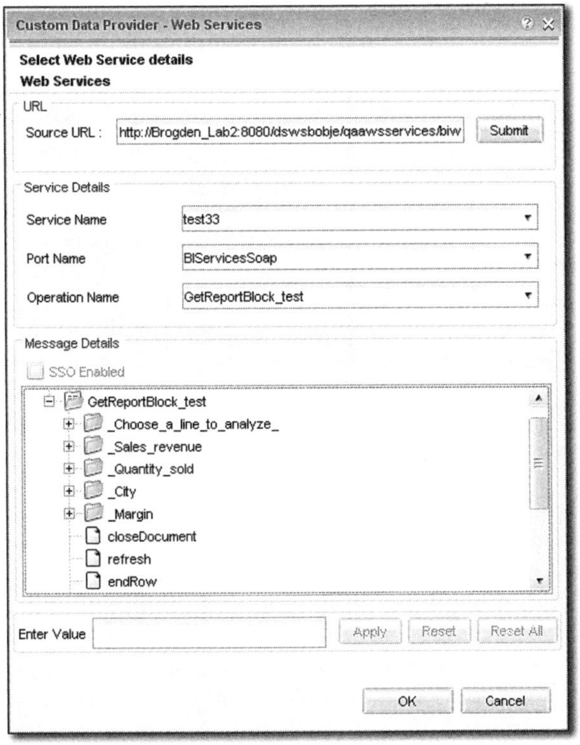

Figure 13.37 Options for Using a Web Service as a Data Source

13.6.3 Microsoft Excel Files as a Data Source

Web Intelligence documents can be sourced from Excel files when working in Web Intelligence Rich Client. Figure 13.38 shows the CUSTOM DATA PROVIDER – EXCEL window opened when creating a document with Excel as the data source. Click on BROWSE to locate a local .XLS file, and then select the sheet name that contains the data. Next choose from using ALL FIELDS, DEFINING A RANGE DEFINITION, or SELECTING A RANGE NAME. Additionally, you can check or uncheck the option to accept the first row in the spreadsheet as column names.

Custom data providers let business users leverage the extensive capabilities of Web Intelligence to display data found in Excel files, text files, and web services in unique and powerful ways.

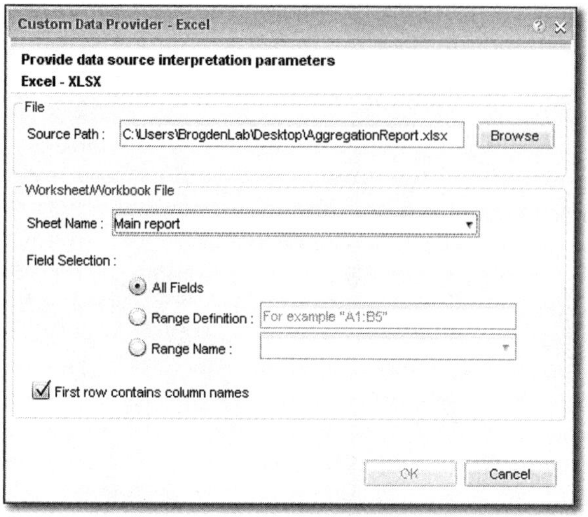

Figure 13.38 Options for Using an Excel File as a Data Source

Next, we'll discuss using the in-memory data platform SAP HANA.

13.7 SAP HANA as a Data Source

You can get the best of both worlds by connecting Web Intelligence, the market's premier data analysis and reporting tool, to the most disruptive and revolutionary business technology introduced in recent memory—SAP HANA. This high-powered, in-memory data platform fulfills the promise of real-time analytics and enables businesses to create competitive advantages and make more agile decisions with very large volumes of transactional and analytical data. The use cases for SAP HANA are impressive and countless.

From SAP HANA to Web Intelligence Reports

SAP BusinessObjects BI 4.1 and Web Intelligence provide the ideal solution and technology fit for accessing and delivering data from SAP HANA. Setting up a connection to SAP HANA is as simple as setting up a new relational connection. The first step is to install the SAP HANA middleware from the SAP Service Marketplace. After that is in place, you'll be able to create an Open Database Connectivity (ODBC) connection using the SAP HANA driver.

ODBC and JDBC (Java Database Connectivity) connections are set up by adding a new system data source name (DSN) by launching the ODBC data source administrator located at CONTROL PANEL • ALL CONTROL PANEL ITEMS • ADMINISTRATIVE TOOLS – DATA SOURCES (ODBC). Click the SYSTEM DSN tab to select the SAP HANA driver needed for setting up the data source.

Leveraging the Information Design Tool

With a system DSN in place, you're ready to launch the Information Design Tool (IDT) and create a new relational connection to your SAP HANA environment. After opening the IDT, click FILE • NEW • RELATIONAL CONNECTION to set up a relational connection to SAP HANA (see Figure 13.39).

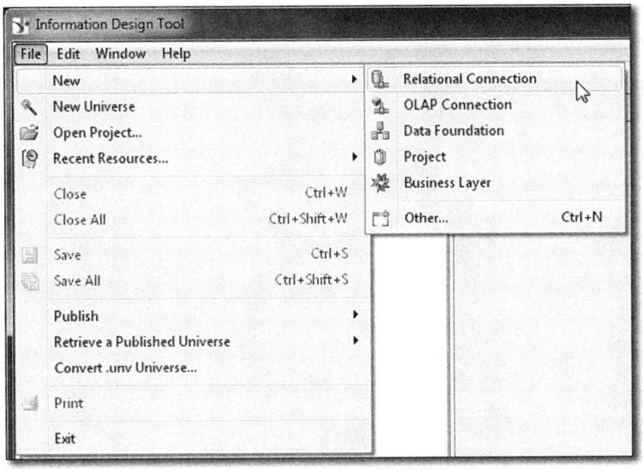

Figure 13.39 Creating a New Relational Connection in the IDT

Select a local project, and then enter a RESOURCE NAME for the new relational connection (see Figure 13.40).

Expand the list of database middleware drivers and expand SAP. Next, expand the SAP HANA database 1.0 selection, and click on ODBC DRIVERS (see Figure 13.41).

After making this selection, log on to the SAP HANA database, and click NEXT to proceed. Notice that in SAP BusinessObjects BI 4.1 SP3, the default ARRAY FETCH SIZE has been set to 1000. This setting allows for optimal query performance from columnar SAP HANA tables.

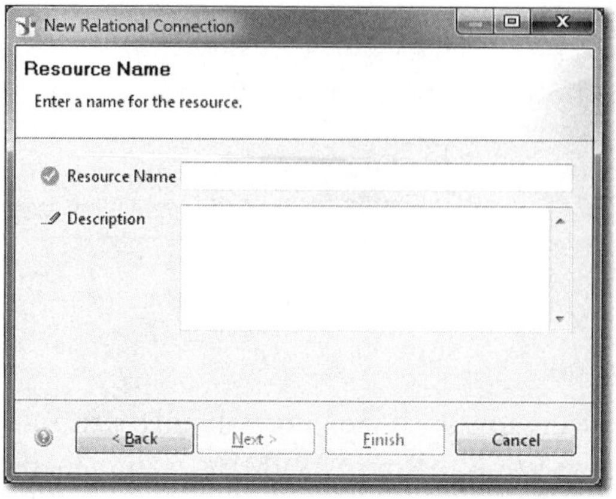

Figure 13.40 Defining a New Relational Connection

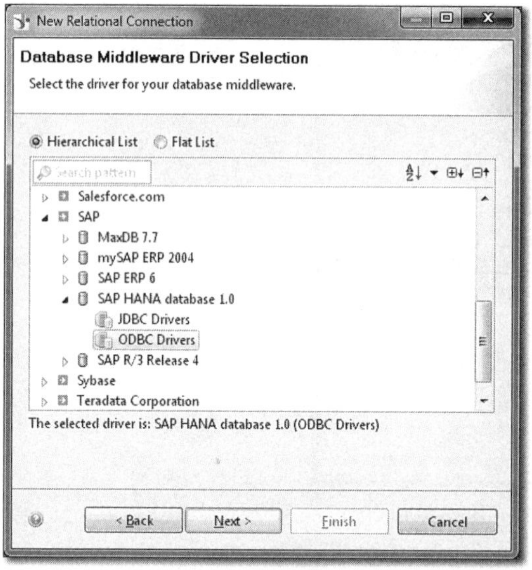

Figure 13.41 Selecting the SAP HANA ODBC Driver

Data Foundation Layer

The next step is to create a relational connection shortcut on the SAP Business-Objects BI 4.1 repository. This is required to create the data foundation layer in your SAP HANA project in the IDT. To accomplish this, click on your connection under REPOSITORY RESOURCES, and select CREATE RELATIONAL CONNECTION SHORT-CUT. The next step is to select your SAP HANA project to complete the shortcut creation. After you've completed these steps, a DFX file will appear under the project, and you can begin creating the business layer to expose the tables and views.

Business Layer

With the data foundation layer in place in your project in the IDT, you're ready to proceed with creating the business layer. This is the layer that exposes the SAP HANA tables and views to the user to access in Web Intelligence.

With the business layer in place, you'll be able to perform the following actions in your relational SAP HANA universe to optimize the way the data will be retrieved by Web Intelligence:

▶ Utilize SAP HANA columnar tables.

▶ Generate custom SQL in derived tables.

SAP HANA universes can be created from either tables or *information views* (also known as information models). These information model types include the following:

▶ **Attribute view**
Provides descriptions of dimensions and details.

▶ **Analytic view**
Describes the facts or measures that relate to dimension objects.

▶ **Calculation view**
Can be defined with custom SQL on database tables or attribute and analytic views.

For a deeper look at integrating SAP HANA and the SAP BusinessObjects reporting tools, please see *Implementing SAP HANA* (SAP PRESS, 2013), by Don Loden, Jonathan Haun, Chris Hickman, and Roy Wells.

13.8   Summary

You can get the most out of your queries by including complex nested filters, prompted filters with cascading LOVs, database ranking, and custom SQL in a Web Intelligence report. You can produce the most accurate, valuable, and actionable reports possible for your clients by using the extensive features available in the Query Panel.

Use a variety of data tracking features in a report to easily identify changes in company data compared to values from a specified reference point. With the addition of the DATA PREVIEW panel, you can catch a glimpse of a data set before running a query. And while you're reviewing preview data, custom query filters can be created with just two clicks. Then you can move on to Web Intelligence Rich Client and create documents from Excel files, text files, and web services to leverage all the strengths of the Web Intelligence application.

Chapter 14 explains how to use multiple data sources and merge dimensions in a Web Intelligence document. Reports created with multiple queries sourced from different data sources can produce highly actionable information in areas such as cost analysis, variance analysis, and other analytical comparisons that is only possible when combining data from disparate sources.

Integrate data from multiple sources into a single Web Intelligence document to produce powerful and analytical reports. You can join unrelated results by merging compatible dimension objects from disparate sources.

14   Using Multiple Data Sources

Web Intelligence 4.1 lets you combine data retrieved from separate queries into a single reporting document. Several different queries can be added to a single document by querying the same universe, querying different universes, or accessing other data sources such as text files, Microsoft Excel files, SAP BEx queries, Analysis workspaces, or web services.

Chapter 2 briefly discussed the improvements in SAP BusinessObjects BI 4.1 for merging dimensions in a report. This chapter will take you deeper into the processes of working with multiple queries, synchronizing data by merging dimensions, and using local data providers to bring data into a document with Web Intelligence in BI Launch Pad or Web Intelligence Rich Client. First, we'll explain how you can create a Web Intelligence document with multiple queries from the same universe. Next, we'll explain how to create a Web Intelligence document using multiple queries from different universes. In both cases, common dimensions are required for synchronization. Finally, we'll discuss how to create a Web Intelligence document that combines data from a universe with a portable Microsoft Excel spreadsheet.

14.1   Combining Multiple Queries from the Same Data Source

Our first example involves combining two data providers, both from the same eFashion universe, using Web Intelligence in the BI Launch Pad. This can also be done using the Web Intelligence Rich Client.

For the first data provider, we'll create a query using the Store name, Sales revenue, and Margin objects. The results should appear similar to Figure 14.1.

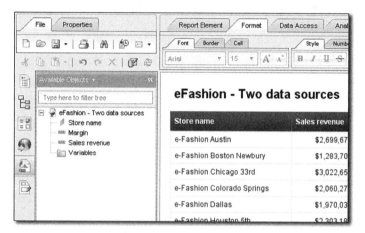

Figure 14.1 Single Query from the eFashion Universe

Next, we'll add a second data provider to the Web Intelligence document. Two methods are available for adding additional queries:

▶ **Option 1**
Click the Data Access tab and then select the New Data Provider button from the Data Providers subtab. Note that this option is only available when using the Applet viewer.

▶ **Option 2**
Return to the Query Panel and then click the Add Query button in the top-left corner as shown in Figure 14.2. Note that the options in this image are also only available in the Applet viewer. When working in the HTML viewer, the only data source option is From Universe. With the Applet viewer the data sources options include From Universe, From Excel, From BEx, and From Analysis View.

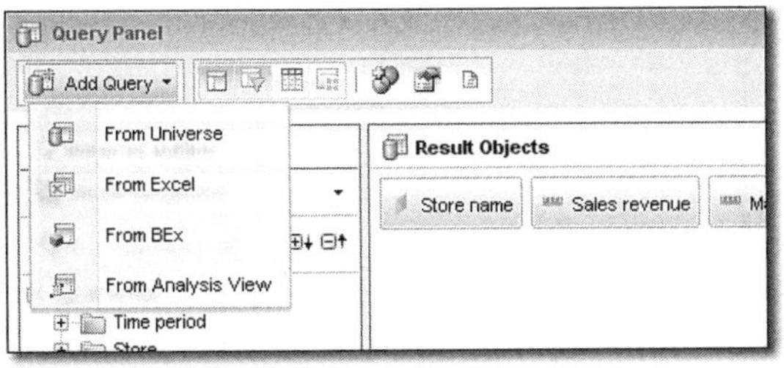

Figure 14.2 Adding a Query from the Web Intelligence Query Panel

As an alternative method, choose NEW DATA PROVIDER directly from the DATA PRO-VIDERS subtab with the Applet viewer as shown in Figure 14.3.

Figure 14.3 Adding a New Data Provider from the Report Panel

Adding a query using this method will add the result objects in a new table and onto the current report. Adding a new query from the Query Panel will prompt you for how you'd like to include the data from the new query.

In either case, choose the eFashion universe again for the second data provider. Add the Store name and Quantity sold objects to the Query Panel.

Notice that the RUN QUERY button now reads RUN QUERIES, indicating that multiple queries exist in the Web Intelligence document, as shown in Figure 14.4. To run both or all queries, click the RUN QUERIES button.

New in SAP BusinessObjects BI 4.1, click the down arrow to the right of the RUN QUERIES button to select and run a single query rather than the requirement in SAP BusinessObjects BI 4.0 of having to run all the queries within the document.

As new data providers are added to the Web Intelligence document from the Query Panel, you'll be prompted to instruct Web Intelligence where to place the data from the new query, as shown in Figure 14.5.

Figure 14.4 Running Both Queries

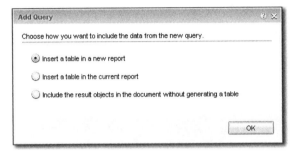

Figure 14.5 Options for Placement of Query Data

There are the three possibilities:

▶ INSERT A TABLE IN A NEW REPORT
Creates a new report tab with data shown in a standard vertical table.

▶ INSERT A TABLE IN THE CURRENT REPORT
Adds a new table on the currently active report tab, alongside any existing tables and charts on the report.

▶ INCLUDE THE RESULT OBJECTS IN THE DOCUMENT WITHOUT GENERATING A TABLE
Projects data from the Report Manager later in the report.

To continue our example, you should choose the third option, INCLUDE THE RESULT OBJECTS IN THE DOCUMENT WITHOUT GENERATING A TABLE.

Available objects are displayed in alphabetical order by default, as shown in Figure 14.6.

When working with multiple data providers, it's often helpful to display available objects by query, as shown in Figure 14.7. This is an extremely simple example, but in actual practice, you may encounter queries with 5 to 10 queries and more than 100 objects. In these scenarios, it's very helpful to arrange the objects by query.

Figure 14.6 Available Objects Arranged by Alphabetical Order

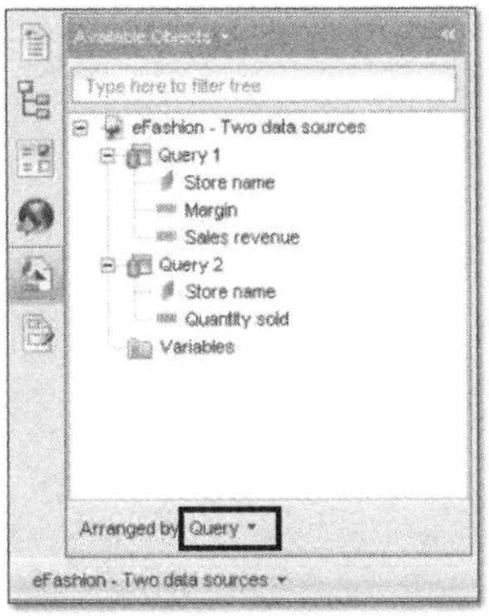

Figure 14.7 Available Objects Arranged by Query

Because both data providers included the Store Name object, Web Intelligence automatically merges the dimensions of objects with matching names and data types if Auto-merge dimensions has been enabled.

A special icon showing two overlapping dimension objects is used to indicate a merged dimension (see Figure 14.8).

By default, the Auto-merge dimensions setting is disabled. To access it, click the Properties tab in the upper-left corner of the control panel, and select the Document button (see Figure 14.9).

The Auto-merge dimension setting was enabled before running the second query. This allows the Quantity sold measure from the second query to be added to the table containing objects from the first query, as shown in Figure 14.10.

415

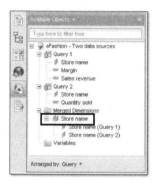

Figure 14.8 Symbol Indicating Merged Dimensions

Figure 14.9 Document Summary Options to Enable Auto-Merge Dimensions

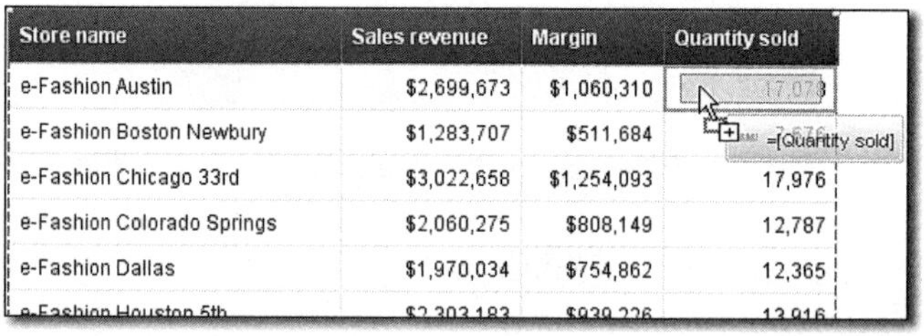

Store name	Sales revenue	Margin	Quantity sold
e-Fashion Austin	$2,699,673	$1,060,310	17,073
e-Fashion Boston Newbury	$1,283,707	$511,684	=[Quantity sold]
e-Fashion Chicago 33rd	$3,022,658	$1,254,093	17,976
e-Fashion Colorado Springs	$2,060,275	$808,149	12,787
e-Fashion Dallas	$1,970,034	$754,862	12,365
e-Fashion Houston 5th	$2,303,183	$939,226	13,916

Figure 14.10 Combining Measures from Two Queries into a Single Table

The options in the DOCUMENT SUMMARY are shown in Figure 14.11.

Let's turn our attention to how automatic merging of dimensions works.

Data synchronization allows a report developer to combine measures from multiple queries into a single table without worrying about data accuracy. For example, the total sales revenue for the eFashion Austin store is perfectly synchronized with the quantity sold for eFashion Austin, even though it came from a separate query.

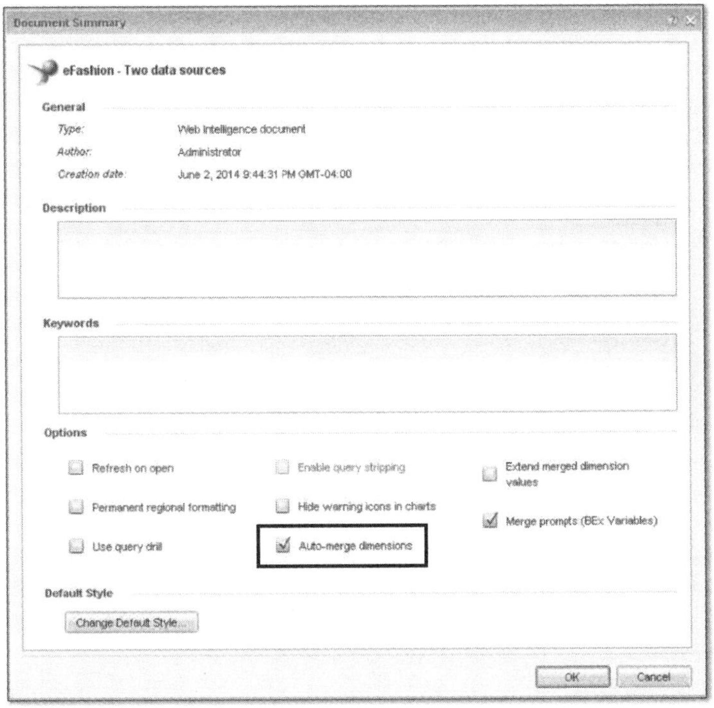

Figure 14.11 Document Summary with Auto-Merge Dimensions Option

Two requirements govern merging dimensions:

▶ The result objects to be merged must have the same data type.

▶ The result objects to be merged must contain compatible and related data.

In the next section, you'll learn how to manually merge dimensions when the queries come from different sources or when the AUTO-MERGE DIMENSIONS option remains disabled.

14.2 Combining Data from Different Universes

In this section, we'll explain how to combine data from two or more queries. Figure 14.12 shows a Web Intelligence document with data from two queries. Because data from two different sources isn't automatically synchronized, data from both queries can't accurately be used in the same table.

Notice that each row in the table shows 223,229 for the quantity sold, the total for all stores. Because the data providers aren't synchronized, Web Intelligence doesn't understand how to take the sales revenue from the eFashion Austin store and combine it with the quantity sold for the Austin store. Therefore, it combines a single store's revenue with the employee count for all stores, which is incorrect.

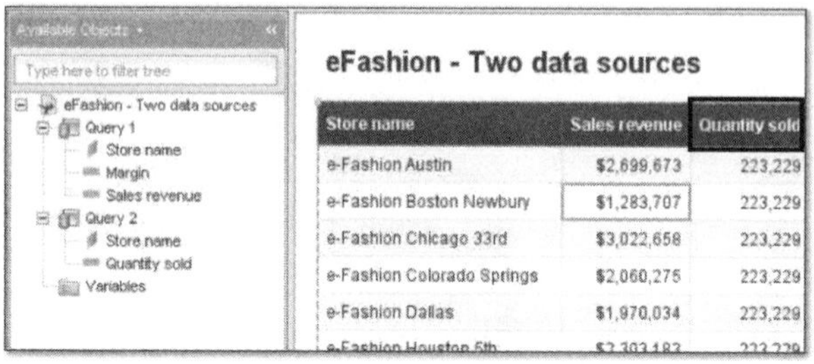

eFashion - Two data sources

Store name	Sales revenue	Quantity sold
e-Fashion Austin	$2,699,673	223,229
e-Fashion Boston Newbury	$1,283,707	223,229
e-Fashion Chicago 33rd	$3,022,658	223,229
e-Fashion Colorado Springs	$2,060,275	223,229
e-Fashion Dallas	$1,970,034	223,229
e-Fashion Houston 5th	$2,303,183	223,229

Figure 14.12 Objects in a Table from Two Unsynchronized Queries

> **Note**
>
> When working with multiple queries, it's worth the extra effort to rename them with useful and descriptive names.

The Store Name dimension object from both queries meets the two requirements to be merged into a single dimension:

▸ The result objects to be merged have the same data type (character).

▸ The result objects to be merged contain compatible and related data (eFashion Austin, eFashion Boston Newbury, etc.).

Merging Dimensions—Method 1

New to SAP BusinessObjects BI 4.1, there are two different methods for creating merged dimensions.

The first approach to manually synchronizing data providers and merge their dimensions is to select the DATA ACCESS tab and then click on the MERGE button on the DATA OBJECTS subtab, as shown in Figure 14.13.

From the list of AVAILABLE OBJECTS, shown in Figure 14.14, choose the desired dimension, Store name, from QUERY 1.

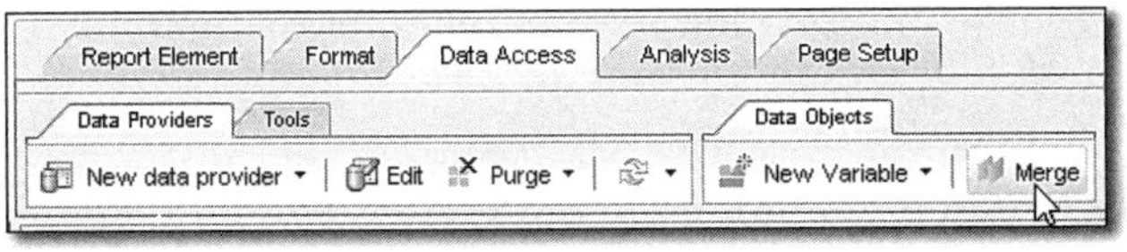

Figure 14.13 Merge Data Providers Button on Toolbar

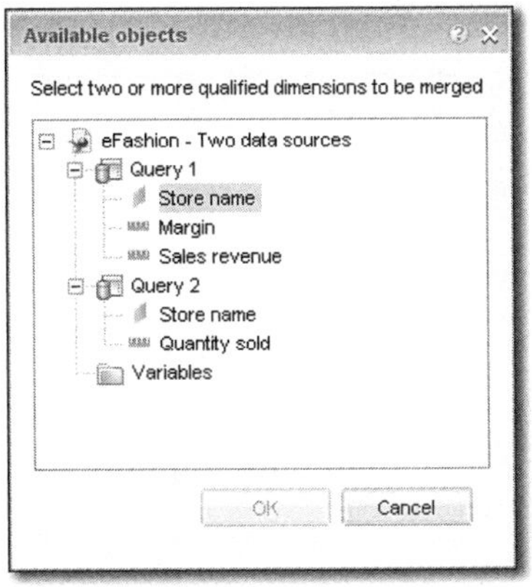

Figure 14.14 Choosing the First Dimension to Be Merged

While holding down the `Ctrl` key, choose the `Store name` dimension from QUERY 2, as shown in Figure 14.15. Then choose OK.

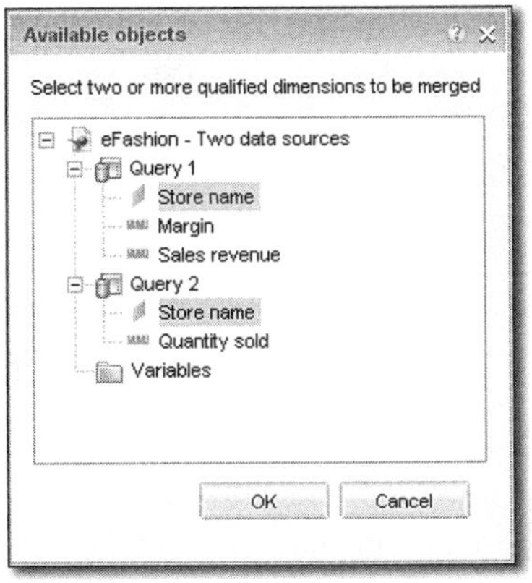

Figure 14.15 Choosing the Second Dimension to Be Merged

The appropriate dimensions in both queries have been merged, and the data is properly synchronized. Now `Quantity sold` values from QUERY 2 display the correct results when placed in the same table as the objects from QUERY 1, as shown in Figure 14.16.

Note

Be sure to add the new merged instance of the Store name object to the data table rather than assigning it directly from one of the queries.

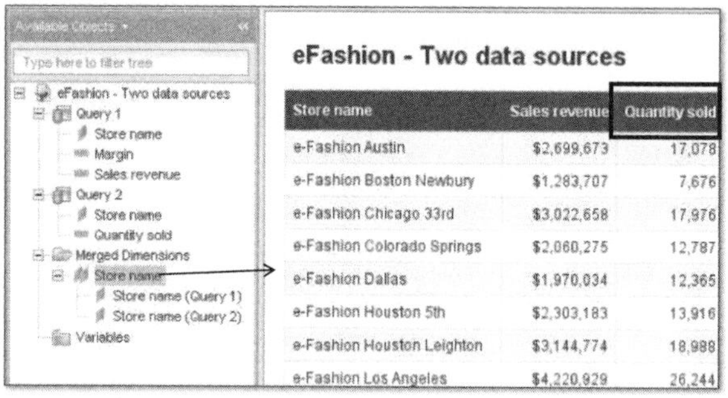

Figure 14.16 Data Providers Synchronized

In this simple example, only a single pair of dimensions needed to be merged. In practice, additional dimensions shared among multiple data providers must be merged by repeating this technique.

Merging Dimensions—Method 2

Now in SAP BusinessObjects BI 4.1, an additional workflow has been added for merging dimensions. This method is extremely helpful because if new queries are added to a document with existing merged dimensions, it's easy to add compatible objects to a merged dimension without having to completely re-create it.

In this method, the MERGE button in the toolbar isn't required. Select compatible objects from the AVAILABLE OBJECTS pane and right-click. An option to merge the dimensions will appear as shown in Figure 14.17.

Follow these steps if new queries are added to a document that contains objects that should be merged to an existing merged dimension:

1. Select the merged instance of the object.

2. Holding down the Ctrl key, select the compatible object from the new query.

3. Right-click and select MERGE.

Figure 14.17 Merging Dimensions from the Available Objects Pane

Additional Options for Merged Dimensions

After objects have been merged, they aren't permanently merged. You can unmerge them by right-clicking on the merged instance and selecting UNMERGE (see Figure 14.18).

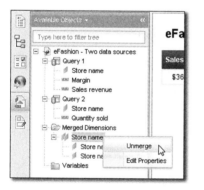

Figure 14.18 Unmerging a Merged Dimension

Another option is to edit a merged dimension's properties (see Figure 14.19). This is a useful property if you need to rename a merged dimension object's name.

By selecting the dropdown under SOURCE DIMENSION, you'll see a list of the objects that have been merged along with the query name of each object instance.

From this window, you can edit the MERGED DIMENSION NAME and provide a DESCRIPTION for the merged object.

Figure 14.19 Merged Dimension Properties

14.3 Data Synchronization Recommendations

Keep the following guidelines in mind when merging dimensions:

- ▶ Multiple queries from the same universe can be added to a single document that include results with different result objects and query filters.
- ▶ Multiple queries from different universes can be inserted into a single Web Intelligence document.
- ▶ Dimensions to be merged must have the same data type.
- ▶ When manually merging dimensions, only the data type of the selected objects is required to create the merged dimension. Both objects should, however, contain compatible data. The object name has no bearing.
- ▶ An unlimited number of data sources can exist within a single document.
- ▶ An unlimited number of data source dimensions can be merged.

You can use the EXTEND MERGED DIMENSION VALUES setting in the document properties to perform a full outer join of merged dimension objects. This setting allows for all of the values from both data sources to be merged into the newly created merged dimension object.

You can use the `forceMerge()` formula to provide synchronization to data providers with different aggregation levels. The `forceMerge()` formula works to display accurate results when the dimensions merged have objects above it in the hierarchy.

> **Note**
>
> Filtering in reports can't be applied to merged dimension objects. The premerged dimension objects must be used when adding report filters. When a filter is added to a report that was used to create a merged dimension, the filter is applied to all synchronized data providers.

14.4 Summary

This chapter builds on the information presented in Chapter 2 to provide you with advanced techniques for creating Web Intelligence documents with multiple queries. You can use multiple data sources in a single document to expand the capabilities of your reports by combining data from a variety of sources. Report writers and developers can include the results from multiple queries sourced from the same universe, different universes, and other data sources such as SAP BEx queries, Analysis workspaces, Excel files, various text formats, and web services.

Data synchronization is the key to combining the results from multiple data sources. This is achieved by auto-merging dimensions or manually merging dimension objects through the Merge Dimensions options.

Next, in Chapter 15, we'll talk about creating report links in reports.

Embed hyperlinks into Web Intelligence reports to connect to multiple document types. You can add element links to create interactivity between reporting components or to create hyperlinks to pass variables to prompted reports using the OpenDocument() function and associated syntax.

15 Linking in Web Intelligence 4.1 Reports

Hyperlinks enable report developers to create comprehensive and cohesive reporting solutions that connect SAP BusinessObjects documents with single-click navigation. This feature can be used to provide business users with a form of guided analysis by connecting to reports and dashboards that tell a different story with the data. Strategically inserted links in Web Intelligence reports expand on the data being viewed by opening and refreshing other related reporting documents.

Hyperlinks allow reports to be connected for a variety of purposes. They can launch reports to open in a printer-friendly PDF format, connect to SAP Business-Objects Dashboards for interactive visualizations, or provide additional information in detailed reports associated by specified parameters in prompted documents.

One of the most significant benefits of hyperlinking is opening and refreshing reports that pass values to prompted Web Intelligence documents. This feature gives business users access to the most current data possible by refreshing target reports at the moment the link is clicked. Links can also go outside of the SAP BusinessObjects BI 4.1 platform to intranet or public-facing websites.

Element linking provides more control than ever before in a Web Intelligence report. This feature allows report designers to add interactivity between individual components or groups of report elements to create a more cohesive and guided analytical solution.

This chapter describes how to link to other reports graphically while working in the HTML viewer or by configuring them manually in the Applet viewer. We'll explain the relative advantages and disadvantages of setting up links in each viewer and describe the detailed steps for manually building hyperlinks.

15.1 Linking to Documents with the HTML Viewer

You can easily add hyperlinks to existing Web Intelligence documents when in design mode and when you've selected the HTML viewer in the Web Intelligence preferences. This viewer provides an additional feature that's not available when the view and modify preferences are set to the Applet viewer. The ADD DOCUMENT LINK option provides the ability to link to a document published to the SAP BusinessObjects BI 4.1 platform.

The next several sections discuss how to add hyperlinks to reports and how to customize and add additional parameters to hyperlinks using both the HTML viewer and Applet viewer.

15.1.1 Adding Hyperlinks to Published SAP BusinessObjects BI 4.1 Web Intelligence Documents

To add a hyperlink to a document published to the SAP BusinessObjects BI 4.1 platform with the HTML viewer, right-click on a row, column, or cell in a data table, and then select the LINKING option from the menu. From this menu, you can add a hyperlink, document link, or element link to an existing reporting document.

Figure 15.1 shows the menu that appears when you right-click on a column in a data table while in design mode. The same hyperlink options appear when right-clicking on a freestanding cell. Mouse over LINKING and then select ADD DOCUMENT LINK to create a connection to another document published to the SAP BusinessObjects BI 4.1 platform.

After you click on ADD DOCUMENT LINK, the CREATE HYPERLINK window opens with options divided into two tabs:

▶ LINK TO WEB PAGE

▶ LINK TO DOCUMENT

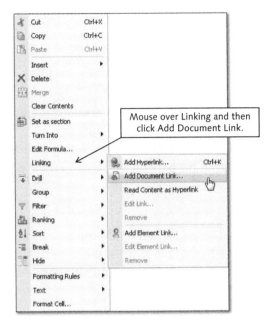

Figure 15.1 Adding a Hyperlink While Designing a Report in the HTML Viewer

If you right-click on a cell or column that already contains a hyperlink, the ADD HYPERLINK and ADD DOCUMENT LINK options will be disabled, and the options to EDIT LINK and REMOVE will be enabled so that you can make changes to an existing hyperlink.

After a hyperlink has been created, the READ CONTENTS AS HYPERLINK setting will be checked, indicating that the cell contains an enabled link. Unchecking this option will disable the link but not get rid of the link completely. Use the REMOVE option to completely disable and delete a hyperlink.

Another Method for Adding Hyperlinks

When using the HTML viewer, begin by selecting a row, column, or cell in a data table or freestanding cell, and then locate the linking icons in the tabbed ribbon running across the top of the report.

To do this, click on the REPORT ELEMENTS tab, followed by the LINKING tab in the third set of subtabs. Notice that the icon to add a document link is available while working within the HTML viewer, as shown in Figure 15.2.

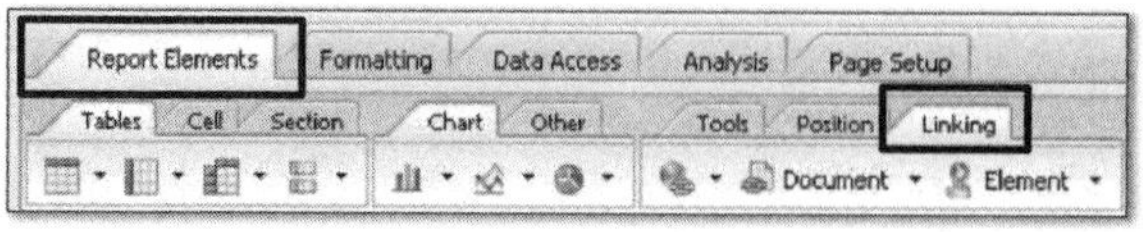

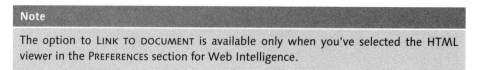

Figure 15.2 Linking Options in the HTML Viewer

The three linking icons you see enable you to create hyperlinks, document links, and element links. Each link provides an option to create a new link and edit or remove an existing link. The same options are also available when you right-click on a report element to be used as the source of the hyperlink.

Browsing for Documents

With the LINK TO DOCUMENT tab selected, click on BROWSE to choose an existing document on the SAP BusinessObjects BI 4.1 platform to set as the target document of the hyperlink. Figure 15.3 shows the CREATE HYPERLINK window displayed when linking to a document.

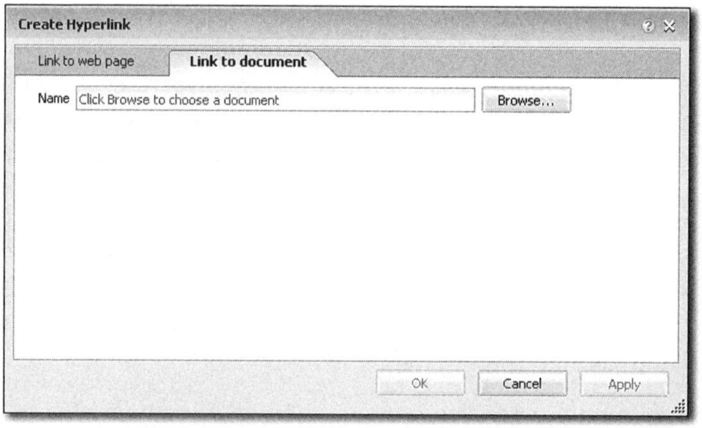

Figure 15.3 Linking to a Document in the HTML Viewer

> **Note**
>
> The option to LINK TO DOCUMENT is available only when you've selected the HTML viewer in the PREFERENCES section for Web Intelligence.

Clicking on BROWSE launches the CHOOSE A DOCUMENT window, where you'll see a full list of reporting documents that you have the rights to access and link to:

- Web Intelligence documents
- SAP Crystal Reports
- SAP BusinessObjects BI workspaces
- Analysis workspaces
- SAP BusinessObjects Dashboards

Figure 15.4 shows the window opened when browsing for a document. Follow these steps to select a document to link to while viewing a report:

1. From the left side of the window, select the storage location of the target document. Options include the following:

   - MY DOCUMENTS
   - PUBLIC FOLDERS

2. From the right side of the window, select the document to link to, and then click on OPEN to confirm.

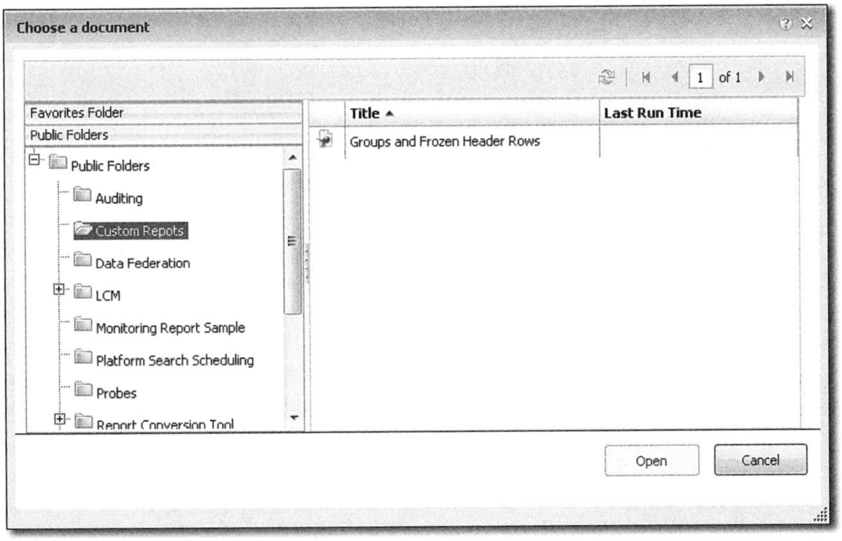

Figure 15.4 Choosing a Document to Link To

Setting Hyperlink Properties

After selecting a document, you have the opportunity to revise four properties and three or four settings depending on whether the target document contains a prompted filter. Figure 15.5 shows the available hyperlink properties after a document has been created. Properties of the new hyperlink are broken down into three categories:

▶ HYPERLINK PROPERTIES

▶ DOCUMENT PROMPTS (displayed only when linking to a report that contains a prompted filter)

▶ CUSTOMIZE THE LOOK AND BEHAVIOR OF THE HYPERLINK

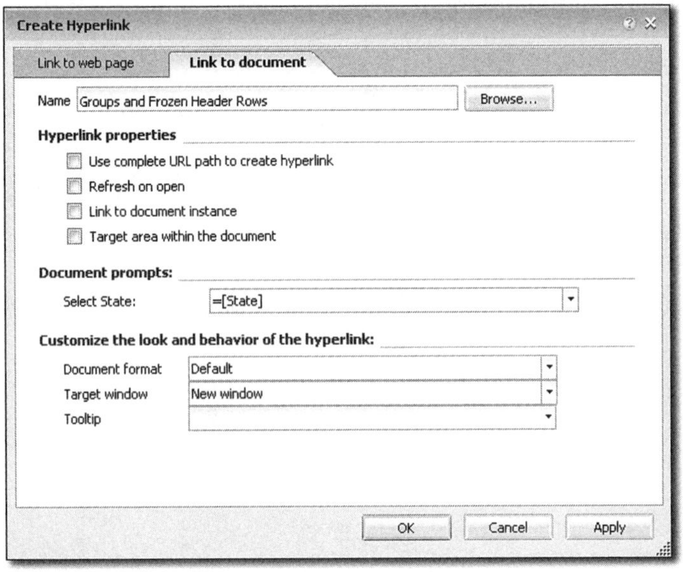

Figure 15.5 Configuring Properties of a New Hyperlink

Any of the four hyperlink properties can be selected to provide the following types of functionality. All four are unchecked by default:

▶ USE COMPLETE URL PATH TO CREATE HYPERLINK
Includes the web server name and port number in the hyperlink.

▶ REFRESH ON OPEN
Sets the linked report to refresh on open (recommended when connected to a prompted document).

▶ LINK TO DOCUMENT INSTANCE
Used when linking to a scheduled instance.

▶ TARGET AREA WITHIN THE DOCUMENT

Provides the option to link to a specific report tab if multiple reports exist in the linked document as well as the capability to link to a report part.

Figure 15.6 shows the options available when the TARGET AREAS WITHIN THE DOCUMENT property is selected. Set the target document to open to a specific REPORT NAME or select the REPORT PART option to target a specific chart or data table within a report. Both options are helpful for creating connections that guide users directly to the information needed for specific scenarios.

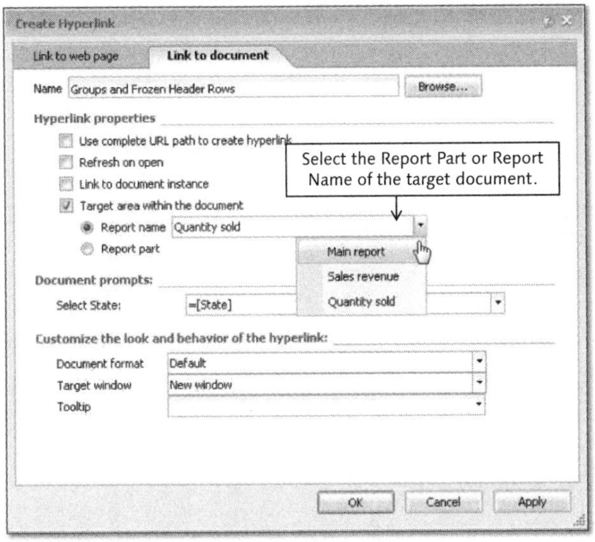

Figure 15.6 Linking to a Target Area or Report Part

If a target document contains a prompted filter, a document prompt property will be presented in the list of LINK TO DOCUMENT properties. Use this entry to define what is passed to the prompted filter in the linked document.

The best practice for linking to a prompted report is to set the hyperlink on a column or value that contains the same object as the prompted filter. You can use one of the following five choices to pass values to a prompt:

▶ Select object

▶ Build formula

▶ Enter a constant

▶ Prompt user at runtime

▶ Use document default

Three settings are provided to customize the look and behavior of the target document:

▶ Document Format
  Choose from Default, HTML, PDF, Excel, and Word.

▶ Target Window
  Open documents in the CURRENT or NEW WINDOW.

▶ Tooltip
  Type a message for the tooltip, and choose SELECT OBJECT or BUILD A FORMULA to display specific information when a user hovers above an active link.

We'll discuss document prompts shortly.

Note

After checking property boxes and making selections from the behavior dropdowns, click on APPLY and then OK to accept the changes and set the hyperlink.

When a hyperlink has been applied to a cell or column in a data table, the values will be displayed with a blue text color and underlined by default.

15.1.2   Insert a Hyperlink to a Web Page

The second type of hyperlinking that can be added to a Web Intelligence report is to a web page. This setting allows you to create and embed hyperlinks to your company websites, blogs, or other types of web pages.

Figure 15.7 shows the LINK TO WEB PAGE selection in the CREATE HYPERLINK window. Click on PARSE after adding the URL to view the components of the link and any dynamic elements in the URL.

The URL properties are broken down into three parts on the LINK TO WEB PAGE tab:

▶ ADDRESS

▶ CUSTOMIZE URL PARAMETERS

▶ CUSTOMIZE THE LOOK AND BEHAVIOR OF THE HYPERLINK

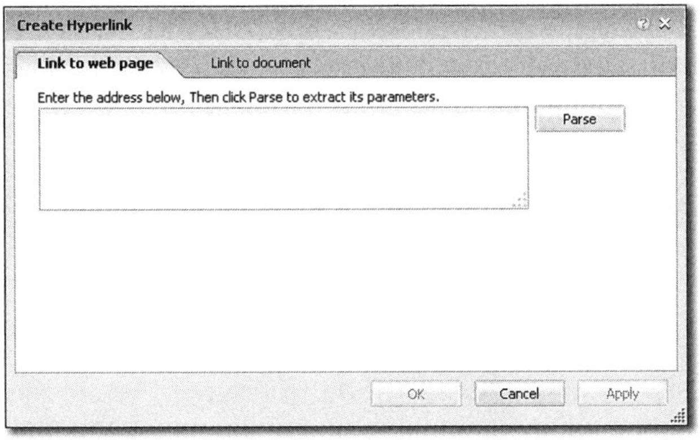

Figure 15.7 Adding a Hyperlink to a Web Page

Figure 15.8 shows the expanded CREATE HYPERLINK window that enables you to modify two default link behavior settings:

▶ TARGET WINDOW
Specify whether documents are to be opened in a new window or the current window.

▶ TOOLTIP
Enter a tooltip to be displayed when you mouse over the hyperlink, and use dropdown options to assign a formula or object as the tooltip.

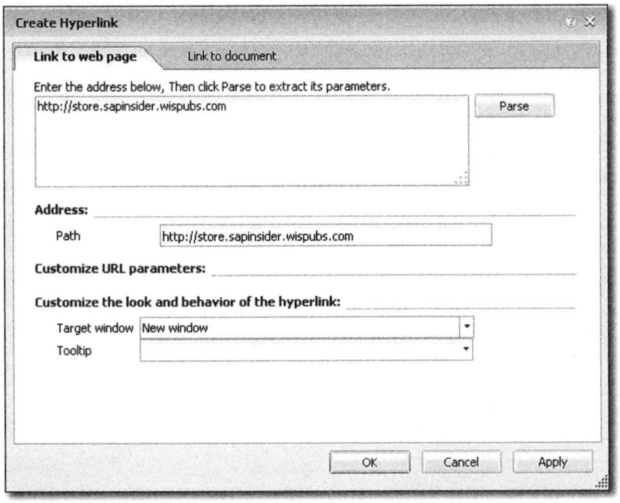

Figure 15.8 Customize the Look and Behavior of Web Page Links

15.1.3 Adding Hyperlinks to Prompted Documents

When a prompted Web Intelligence document is selected in the CHOOSE A DOCU-MENT window, an additional set of options are displayed for Document prompts. This section allows you to pass values to a prompted filter in the linked document.

The DOCUMENT PROMPTS section of the link properties displays a list of all prompted filters listed by the prompt text for each filter in the linked document.

By default, the object in the column or cell that contains the link will be passed to the prompted filter. Additionally, five options (shown in Figure 15.9) are provided to allow different ways of dynamically passing values to a prompted filter in the linked document:

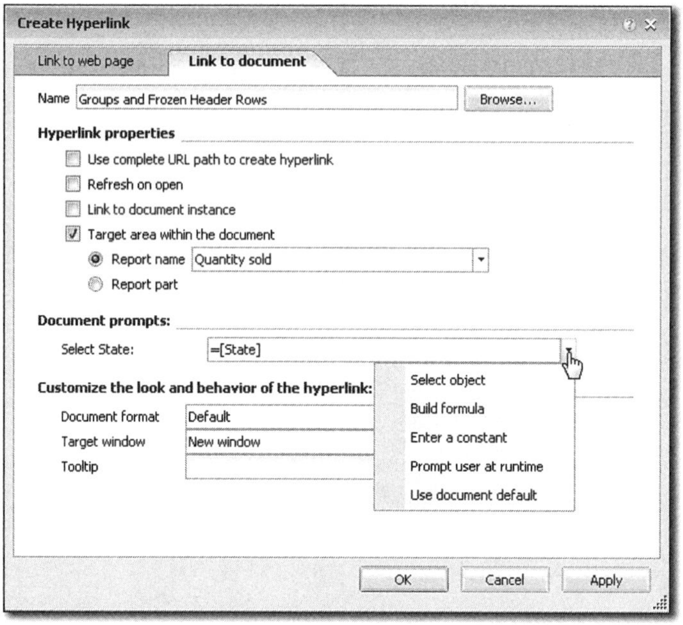

Figure 15.9 Creating a Hyperlink to a Prompted Web Intelligence Report

▶ SELECT OBJECT
Selects an object or variable from the source document.

▶ BUILD FORMULA
Opens the FORMULA EDITOR for custom formula creation.

► ENTER A CONSTANT
Allows manually entered values.

► PROMPT USER AT RUNTIME
Prompts the user at runtime.

► USE DOCUMENT DEFAULT
Uses the default prompt value selection type.

> **Note**
>
> If a prompted document contains two or more prompted filters and is selected as the linked document, a SELECT PROMPTS window will present you with both prompted filters, allowing you to choose which object will receive the value.

Figure 15.10 shows the SELECT PROMPTS window when a new hyperlink has been created based on the State object in a data table and linked to a document containing two prompted filters. Choose the prompt filter to receive the value.

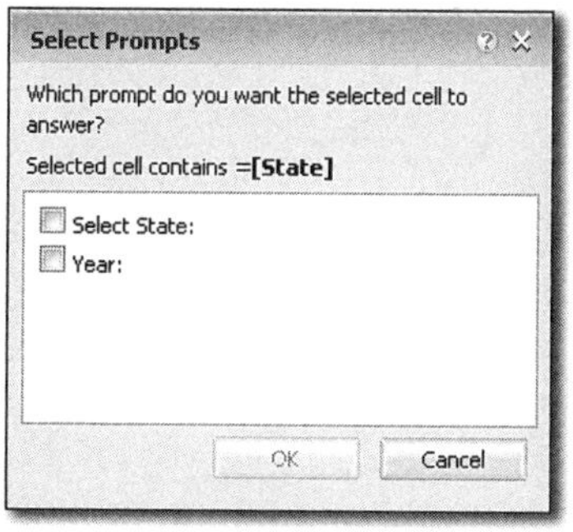

Figure 15.10 Select Prompts Window

Passing a Selected Object to a Prompted Report

An excellent way of linking Web Intelligence reports is to create a hyperlink based on the value of a selected object. This type of linking works best when the target report contains a single prompted filter that contains compatible values. This is most commonly used when creating a hyperlink on a dimension object when the same object serves as the prompted filter in another document.

An example of this type of linking is shown in Figure 15.11, in which you right-click on a column in a vertical table that contains the State object as the basis for the hyperlink. Mouse over the Linking option to display the available linking choices, and then select Add Document Link to create a connection to another document. The selected value in the `State` object will be used as the basis for the new link. If the target document contains a prompted filter, then by default the value selected will be passed to the prompted filter in the linked document.

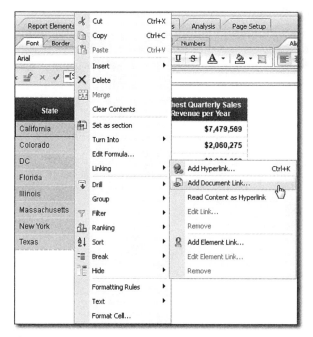

Figure 15.11 Creating a Hyperlink Based on the State Object

Note
The result of setting up a hyperlink containing this parameter-passing feature is that any `[State]` value selected in the data table is dynamically passed as part of the hyperlink to the target document when the value is clicked.

15.2   Linking with the Applet Viewer

You can also add hyperlinks to reports while designing documents in the Applet viewer. With this viewer, you'll notice that the right-click menu and the overall look and feel of creating a hyperlink are slightly different. Similar to adding links to reports using the HTML viewer, you must be in design mode to add hyperlinks.

When adding hyperlinks using the Applet viewer, it's important to note that the ADD DOCUMENT LINK option isn't available. Adding hyperlinks to other documents published to the SAP BusinessObjects BI 4.1 platform is much more of a manual process than in the HTML viewer and requires writing the full URL to create a link to another document. Figure 15.12 shows the linking options available when right-clicking on a report element while in the Applet viewer and in design mode. Right-click on a dimension column in a table, and then select LINKING from the available options. Next, select ADD HYPERLINK to launch the HYPERLINKS window.

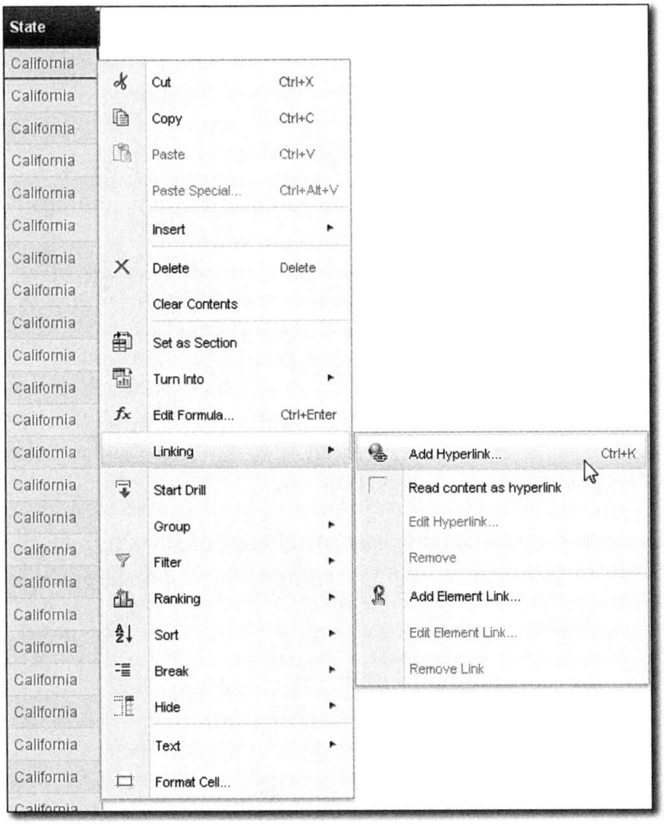

Figure 15.12 Adding a New Hyperlink While Editing a Report

Clicking on ADD HYPERLINK provides the capability of linking to another document or web page. The result of this selection is shown in Figure 15.13.

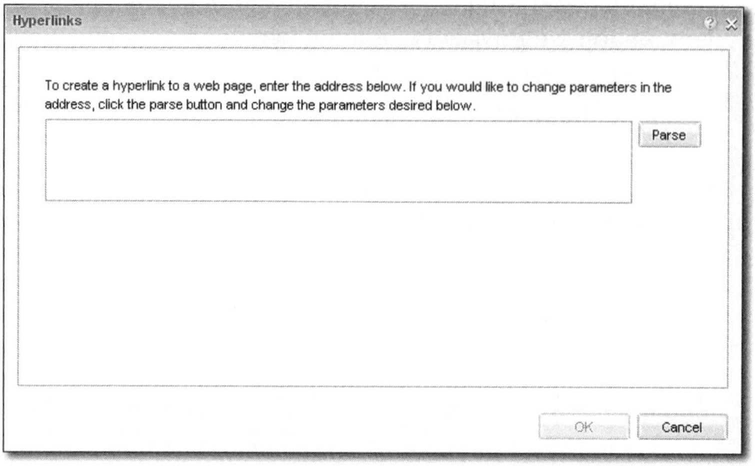

Hyperlinks

To create a hyperlink to a web page, enter the address below. If you would like to change parameters in the address, click the parse button and change the parameters desired below.

Parse

OK   Cancel

Figure 15.13 Adding a New Hyperlink in the Applet viewer

Paste or type a URL, and then click on PARSE to display the dynamic elements of the URL entered in the provided text area.

Alternative Method of Adding Hyperlinks

Another way of adding hyperlinks is with the shortcut icons provided in the multilayer tabbed ribbon located across the top of the report. To add a hyperlink using these icons, begin by selecting a report element, freestanding cell, or value in a data table and then click on the REPORT ELEMENT tab.

Next, select the LINKING tab located in the third set of subtabs, as shown in Figure 15.14. Finally, click the HYPERLINK icon to begin creating a document/hyperlink.

Figure 15.14 Adding Hyperlinks Using Icons in the Ribbon

Notice that only the icons for creating a hyperlink and element link are available in the Applet viewer.

To link to a web page while using the Applet viewer, use the standard URL structure. An example of this format is *www.sap.com*.

Linking to Documents Published to the SAP BusinessObjects BI 4.1 Platform

To link to documents published to the SAP BusinessObjects BI 4.1 platform, use this basic format below for constructing your URL and using the OpenDocument syntax:

```
http://<server>:<port>/BOE/OpenDocument/opendoc/openDocument.jsp?
```

Unlike SAP BusinessObjects Enterprise XI 3.x, SAP BusinessObjects BI 4.1 supports only a Java deployment. This means you'll need to use openDocument.jsp when creating document hyperlinks.

One of the easiest ways to become familiar with the structure of a hyperlink URL is to analyze the syntax generated when the HTML viewer is used to add a document link. To do this, follow these steps:

1. Add a document link using the HTML viewer, and check the option to USE THE COMPLETE URL PATH TO CREATE THE HYPERLINK.
2. Select the cell or column that contains the new hyperlink, and view it in the formula bar while in design mode.
3. Copy the full URL beginning with http:// and ending at the final double-quote symbol located before the title parameter.
4. Change the viewer to RICH INTERNET APPLICATION, and add a new hyperlink.
5. Paste the full URL retrieved from the previous step into the hyperlink box, and click on PARSE.

Consider this example of the full URL created when a link to another Web Intelligence document is added:

```
="<a href=\"http://localhost:8080/BOE/OpenDocument/opendoc/openDocu-
ment.jsp?iDocID=AUDaOIxRp3dNq09Yg.MSyyE&sIDType=CUID&sType=wid&sRefresh
=N&lsSSelect%20State%3A="+URLEncode(""+[State])+"\" title=\"\" target=\
"_blank\" nav=\"doc\">"+[State]+"</a>"
```

Recognize that the URL within the statement begins with `http://` and ends with the final slash before the quotation mark and `title` parameter. To use this URL to link to another document, switch to the Applet viewer, and create a new hyperlink. Paste the URL into the hyperlink box, and click on PARSE.

Figure 15.15 shows the dynamic elements of the URL after adding it to the hyperlinks box and clicking on PARSE. The syntax used in the URL is broken into three different groupings:

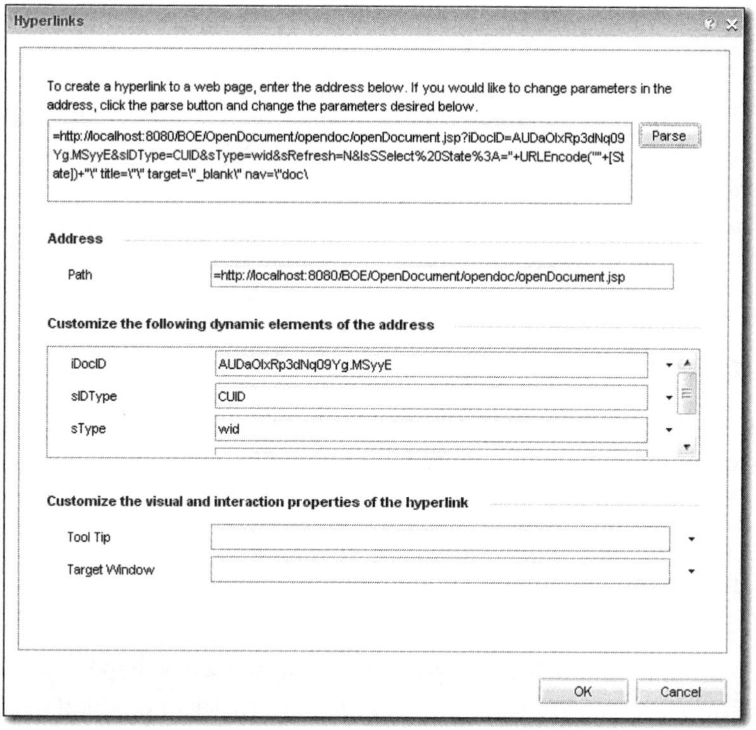

Figure 15.15 Hyperlink Parsed in the Applet Viewer

▶ ADDRESS

Uses the `openDocument.jsp application`.

▶ CUSTOMIZE THE FOLLOWING DYNAMIC ELEMENTS OF THE URL

Contains the dynamic identifier parameters of the target document:

- ▶ iDocID
- ▶ sIDTYPE
- ▶ sTYPE

▶ CUSTOMIZE THE VISUAL AND INTERACTION PROPERTIES OF THE HYPERLINK

- ▶ TOOL TIP: Manually enter a constant, select an object, or build a formula to provide a tooltip or mouse over message to the user.
- ▶ TARGET WINDOW: Specify where to open the target window (e.g., current window or new window).

15.2.1 Manually Creating Links Using the OpenDocument Syntax Structure

Let's focus our attention briefly on the parameters used in the URL displayed in Figure 15.15. By understanding the syntax generated in a link to another report, you'll be able to manually create your own links or edit existing ones.

Although the sType and sRefresh parameters were included in the URL, neither element is required.

▶ **Full OpenDocument URL example**

```
=http://localhost:8080/BOE/OpenDocument/opendoc/openDocument.jsp?
iDocID=AUDaOIxRp3dNq09Yg.MSyyE&sIDType=CUID&sType=wid&sRefresh=N&
lsSSelect%20State%3A="+URLEncode(""+[State])+"\" title=\"\" target=
\"_blank\" nav=\"doc\
```

▶ **Main URL**

```
http://localhost:8080/BOE/OpenDocument/opendoc/openDocument.jsp?
```

▶ **Document ID**

```
iDocID= AUDaOIxRp3dNq09Yg.MSyyE
```

> **Note**
>
> The /BOE/ entry is a new addition to the main OpenDocument syntax in SAP Business-Objects BI 4.x. Be sure to update your hyperlinks if you've migrated reports from SAP BusinessObjects BI.

Figure 15.16 shows the document ID of the hyperlink's target document. This property is used in conjunction with the sIDType parameter and CUID value. The document ID can be found by right-clicking on a published document's name in the BI Launch Pad and then selecting PROPERTIES.

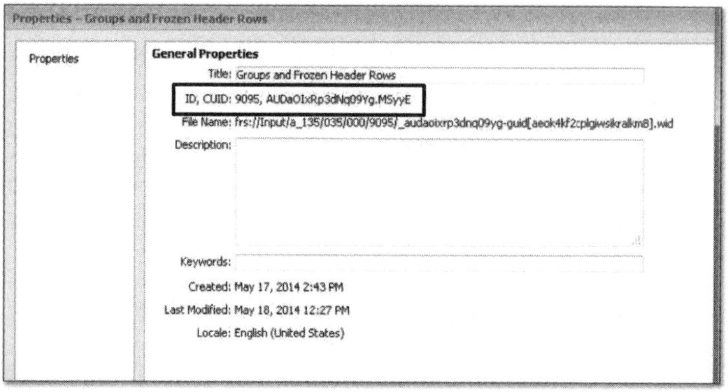

Figure 15.16 Locating the iDocID or CUID of a Web Intelligence Document

▶ **Document Type:** sType=wid
This is an optional parameter that's still generated when adding Web Intelligence document links while working in the HTML viewer.

▶ **Refresh:** sRefresh=N
Include a Y to force the target Web Intelligence document to refresh when opened. The use of N to open the target document without refreshing is optional.

15.2.2 Adding a Hyperlink to an SAP BusinessObjects Dashboard

Hyperlinks to dashboards can be created by adding as few as a single parameter to the end of the main URL. This can be achieved by using the sDocName parameter, followed by the name of the target document.

Use a plus (+) symbol to represent spaces between words in the document title, as in this working URL that links to a dashboard:

```
http://localhost:8080/BOE/OpenDocument/opendoc/openDocument.jsp?
sDocName=Simple+Dashboard
```

Whether linking to a report by using the HTML viewer or Applet viewer, understanding the syntax of document linking is crucial to being able to edit it and expand on it. The next section introduces the various parameters available for customizing a document link using the OpenDocument syntax.

> **Tip**
>
> Using a single parameter in a document link provides a very easy way of connecting to a dashboard, but it could also lead to problems if multiple instances of the same document name exist in different folders on the SAP BusinessObjects BI 4.1 platform.
>
> The ideal solution for linking to another document is to use these two linking parameters: `iDocID=<document ID>` and `sIDType=CUID`.

15.3   OpenDocument Syntax

The OpenDocument syntax can be used to pass a wide variety of parameters to the document being opened with the OpenDocument URL hyperlink.

Parameters are grouped into three different categories:

▶ Document identifier parameters

▶ Input parameters

▶ Output parameters

15.3.1   Document Identifier Parameters

The platform parameters are described in Table 15.1.

Parameter	Description	Mandatory	Additional Information
`iDocID`	Document identifier	Yes*	Document ID located in document properties.
`sDocName`	Document name	Yes*	Use the plus symbol to represent spaces between words.
`sIDType`	CMS Object ID type	Yes*	Values: `CUID`, `ParentID`, `InfoObjectID`.

Table 15.1 Document Identifier Parameters

Parameter	Description	Mandatory	Additional Information
sType	File type of target document	No	Values: `wid`, `rpt`, `car`, `flash`.
sInstance	Opens the latest instance owned by the current user, latest instance of the report, or latest instance of report with matching parameter values	No	Values: `user`, `last`, `param`.

Table 15.1 Document Identifier Parameters (Cont.)

▶ `*iDocID` is required if the `sDocName` parameter isn't used.

▶ `*sDocName` is required if the `iDocID` parameter isn't used.

▶ `*sIDType` is required in conjunction with the `iDocID` parameter.

15.3.2 Input Parameters

The input parameters are described in Table 15.2.

Parameter	Description	Additional Information
lsC	Specifies a contextual prompt if there is an ambiguity during SQL generation (SAP BusinessObjects and Web Intelligence documents only).	Resolves ambiguity of generated SQL by providing a prompt value.
lsM[Name]	Specifies multiple values for a prompt. [NAME] is the text of the prompt.	Allows multiple prompt values to be passed to a prompt filter. Values are separated by commas.
lsI[Name]	Specifies index or key values. This parameter must be associated with one of these parameters: `lsS[Name]`, `lsM[Name]`, or `lsR[Name]`.	Used for index aware prompts. Can be used to pass technical name of the variable setup in the SAP BEx Query Designer. URL encoding is required.

Table 15.2 Input Parameters

Parameter	Description	Additional Information
lsR[Name]	Specifies a range of values for a prompt. [NAME] is the text of the prompt.	A range of values are passed to the prompt, separated by a double period (. .). Use no_value to ignore an optional prompt.
lsS[Name]	Specifies a value for a single prompt. [NAME] is the text of the prompt.	Pass single values using the lsS parameter; pass multiple values using lsM.
sPartContext	Used when linking to an SAP Crystal Report. Use with sReportPart.	Data context of report part.
sRefresh	Indicates whether a refresh should be forced when the target document is opened.	Use Y to force the document to refresh on open.
sReportMode	For SAP Crystal Report targets only, indicates whether the link should open the full target report or just the report part specified in sReportPart.	Use Full or Part as the report mode.
sReportName	Identifies the report to open if the target document contains multiple reports.	Use the report name in a Web Intelligence document.
sReportPart	Indicates which specific part of the target SAP Crystal Report to open.	Name of the report part. Easily selected when creating a hyperlink and selecting a report part while viewing a report in BI Launch Pad.

Table 15.2 Input Parameters (Cont.)

The only required input parameter is for sPartContext when a sReportPart parameter has been included in a URL.

15.3.3 Output Parameters

The output parameters are described in Table 15.3.

Parameter	Description	Additional Information
NAII	Forces the display of the prompt selection page. Web Intelligence only.	Document ID located in document properties.
sOutputFormat	Defines the format of target document.	H (HTML), P (PDF), E (Excel), W (Word).
sWindow	Specifies window of target report.	Same (current window), New (new window).
sViewer	Specifies the selected report viewer.	Available viewer types: html, part.
sViewer	Forces Web Intelligence target documents to open in design mode.	Use the value of true to force the report to open in design mode.

Table 15.3 Output Parameters

By knowing the available parameters that can be used with the OpenDocument function and the syntax required for using them, you can create complex links to meet unique business requirements. Links can contain several input parameters, output parameters, and document identifier parameters. Remember to separate every parameter and value combination with an ampersand (&) symbol.

Passing SAP BEx Prompt Variables

Technical names for SAP BEx variables, not the more readable name aliases, must be used in OpenDocument URLs. These technical names can be obtained using the multidimensional expressions (MDX) test editor. A technical name has no spaces, uses only uppercase letters, and must be encoded in square brackets.

The next section introduces a capability new in Web Intelligence 4.1 known as element linking. Use this feature to link charts and tables and create a cohesive and interactive experience for report consumers.

15.4   Element Linking

Element linking lets you create an interaction between a chart or data table and one or more report elements. This new functionality allows report designers to produce a form of guided navigation by using a chart value or object in a data table to filter other report elements.

This form of linking bears a similarity to drilling and also resembles the type of interaction experienced with input controls. But element linking performs much differently by allowing a component to pass filters to other elements on a report. This new functionality leads to the creation report/dashboard hybrids and can be accomplished within the HTML viewer or Applet viewer.

15.4.1   Adding Element Linking

Two methods for adding element links are available. The first step in both methods is to enter design mode and select the source element to be used as the basis for the document link. This can be a chart or object in a data table. The first method requires the following steps:

1. Right-click on the element to be used as the source of the element link.

2. Select LINKING from the menu, and then select ADD ELEMENT LINKING.

The second method of adding element links is by selecting the ADD ELEMENT LINK icon from the tabbed property ribbon. Click on the REPORT ELEMENT tab, followed by selecting the LINKING subtab to reveal the icons for the available linking types (see Figure 15.17).

After clicking ADD ELEMENT LINK, the DEFINE INPUT CONTROL window will open. Use this window to select the report objects to be used for filtering data in the dependency elements. When a chart is used as an element link source that contains multiple dimensions, a unique value from each dimension can be passed to its dependency objects.

To only pass a single value, change the default selection from ALL OBJECTS to SINGLE OBJECT, and a value from a single object will be passed to filter the dependency report elements.

The next step is to select the object to filter data in the dependency elements and then click on NEXT to proceed.

🗃	Set as Section	
🗃	Turn Into	►
fx	Edit Formula...	Ctrl+Enter
	Linking	►
🗑	Start Drill	
	Group	►
🔽	Filter	►
🗃	Ranking	►
↕↓	Sort	►
⬛	Break	►
▤	Hide	►
	Text	►
▭	Format Cell...	

🔗	Add Hyperlink...	Ctrl+K
☐	Read content as hyperlink	
	Edit Hyperlink...	
	Remove	
⚡	Add Element Link...	
	Edit Element Link...	
	Remove Link	

Figure 15.17 Adding Element Linking

Figure 15.18 shows the DEFINE INPUT CONTROL window, which you'll use to select the report objects that filter and connect data to the dependency components.

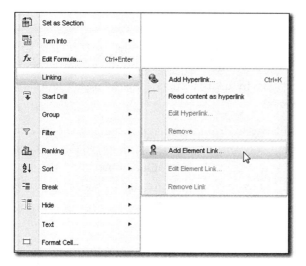

Figure 15.18 Selecting Objects Used to Filter Data in Element Linking

After choosing the report object used to filter data, you can make changes to the label name or add a description to the source component of the element link in the next window. Updates to this screen are optional.

Figure 15.19 shows the SET CONTROL PROPERTIES window as it appears after you've selected the report object to be used in adding an element link.

A best practice is to change the default label value to a more meaningful and descriptive term or phrase for the benefit of users.

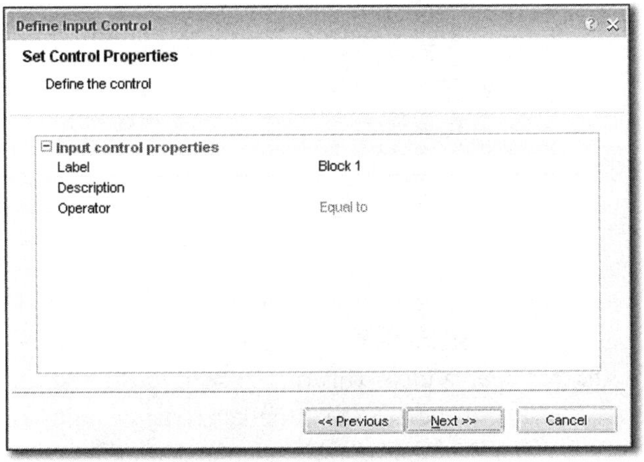

Figure 15.19 Setting Control Properties of Element Link

The final screen in the process is where you'll assign the report elements to be filtered by the selections made in the element link. These report elements, shown in Figure 15.20, are also known as dependency objects. Notice that only one object is unavailable for selection. That's because block 5 is the object that the element link is based on in this example.

Report elements that can be dependencies of an element link include the following:

▶ Page body
▶ Sections
▶ Charts
▶ Data tables

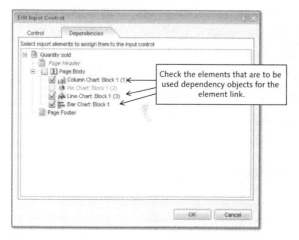

Figure 15.20 Selecting Report Elements as Dependencies of Element Link

15.4.2   The Impact of Element Linking

After an element link has been added to an object in a report, the chart or table containing the link will display a small icon in the upper-right corner of the object to indicate that an element link has been added. This can be seen in the chart in the upper-left corner in Figure 15.21. In the example, the bar chart contains an element link, and all three of the other elements display data related to the selection made by the user.

Valid and accurate labeling is very import when developing dynamic and interactive reports. Because of the filtering capabilities of element links, we recommend that you label dependency charts with the filtered value used in the link.

As an example, use the following steps to add the filtered value to a dependency chart's title:

1. Right-click on a dependency chart object, and select FORMAT CHART.

2. Navigate to the TITLE section in the FORMAT CHART window.

3. Edit the TITLE label to include the dynamic filtered value.

4. Click on the green checkmark icon to validate the syntax.

5. Click on APPLY, and then click OK.

Figure 15.22 shows the edited title of a dependency chart with the [Lines] object used as the filter object.

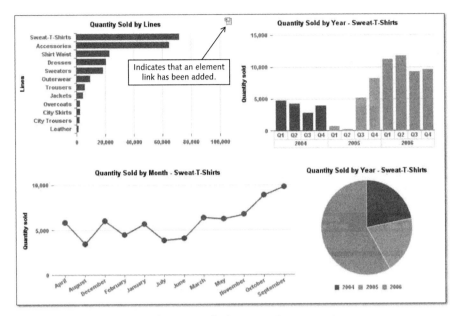

Figure 15.21 Series of Report Elements with Element Linking

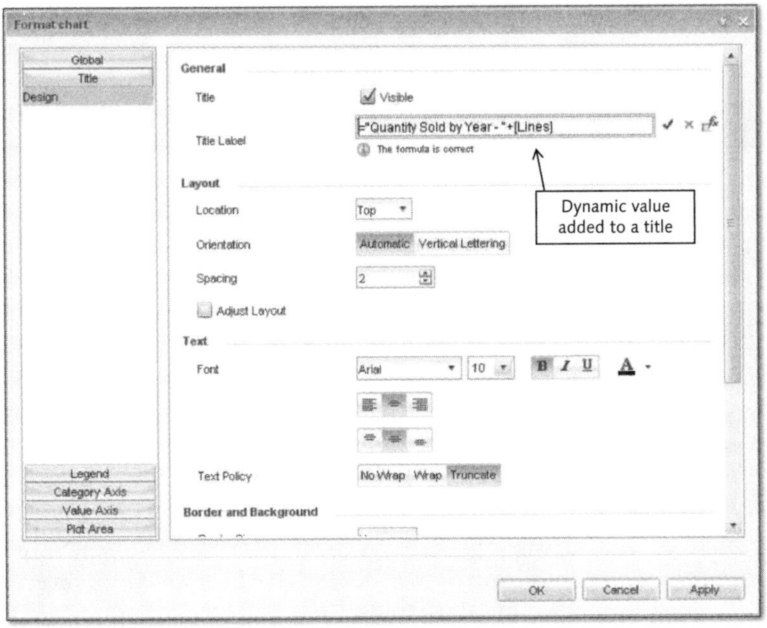

Figure 15.22 Adding a Dynamic Value to a Chart Title

Adding the filtered object used in creating the element link to the title of a dependency chart will provide a better context for users viewing the report. An example of a dynamic title can be seen in Figure 15.23 using the following formula in the title label:

```
="Quantity Sold by Year - "+[Lines]
```

Use this formula to produce a valid title when the lines object is used as a simple filter. The purpose of this formula is to display QUANTITY SOLD BY YEAR – ALL LINES if a value has not been selected and QUANTITY SOLD BY YEAR – ACCESSORIES if the value selected in the [Lines] filter object is accessories:

```
="Quantity Sold by Year"+If(Count([Lines])=1;" - "+[Lines];" - All Lines")
```

In Figure 15.23, the bar chart contains an element link. The values being charted in the column chart are associated with the line selected in the bar chart. The Lines object has also been included in the title of the column chart.

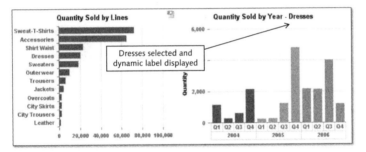

Figure 15.23 Dynamic Chart Title Resulting from an Element Link

Resetting a Chart with an Element Link Selected

If you need to reset an element link value to remove the filters from the dependency charts, right-click on the INPUT CONTROL icon located in the upper-right corner of the chart and select RESET.

This action will release the filter and return the dependency charts to their original state. The RESET button is shown in Figure 15.24. From this menu, you can also click HIGHLIGHT DEPENDENCIES to see which charts have been set up to receive the element value from the source element.

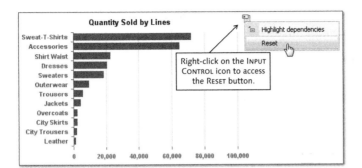

Figure 15.24 Clearing Element Link Filters

> **Note**
>
> Element linking can't be used when it's added to a chart that contains a dimension object that's part of a hierarchy and when drill mode has been enabled. This is because drill mode will force the chart either to drill up or to drill down the hierarchy rather than functioning as an element link. Disabling drill mode will allow the element link to function as designed.

15.5 Summary

Hyperlinks are useful additions to Web Intelligence reports. They allow report developers to embed links to other reporting documents or to web pages. Links can be added to documents while working in the HTML viewer through document linking or with the Applet viewer and Web Intelligence Rich Client using the OpenDocument syntax.

Guided analysis to deeper information can be easily added to reports by strategically inserting hyperlinks and element links that contain related data at different hierarchy levels and featuring different dimension objects. Use element linking to produce a cohesive collection of report elements that encourage interaction. This new feature allows developers to produce reports that function similar to dashboards.

One of the biggest benefits of inserting hyperlinks in reports is the capability of passing dynamic values to prompted filters. This feature allows entire columns to serve as hyperlinks that pass only the selected value to a prompted filter in a Web

Intelligence document. Reporting documents can also be refreshed and opened to display up-to-date data with a single click.

An extensive list of input, output, and document identifier parameters are available for passing values to linked reports published to the SAP BusinessObjects BI 4.1 platform. These parameters are appended to URLs created with the OpenDocument syntax structure that connect to target documents.

Chapter 16 provides details on working within the BI Launch Pad.

The BI Launch Pad web portal used to access Web Intelligence documents provides a fully integrated interface for organizing, viewing, analyzing, and sharing business intelligence content. The added functionality and ease of use of the interface make BI Launch Pad a powerful tool for end users and report writers alike.

16 Working in the BI Launch Pad

Web Intelligence reports are accessed using the SAP BusinessObjects BI platform web portal called *BI Launch Pad* (formerly InfoView). The BI Launch Pad portal gives you access to a variety of business content outside of Web Intelligence reports including SAP Crystal Reports, dashboards, Microsoft Office documents, and so on. This gives business users one secure location to view business intelligence content. You can also publish and distribute content to other users in Web Intelligence, Excel, PDF, SAP StreamWork, and MIME HTML (MHTML) format from within BI Launch Pad.

16.1 Navigating in BI Launch Pad

Figure 16.1 shows the default view after you log in to BI Launch Pad. The initial view shows the HOME tab, which can be customized in GENERAL PREFERENCES. The screen is divided into three sections by default: header panel, tabs, and HOME tab view. The header panel includes the BI Launch Pad toolbar with menu options applicable across the BI Launch Pad. The tabs display the default HOME and DOCUMENTS tabs as well as any tabs pinned to the BI Launch Pad interface. Additional tabs may be available by default depending on your configuration. If your environment is integrated with SAP StreamWork, you may see a tab for the feeds.

Let's begin by focusing on the header panel.

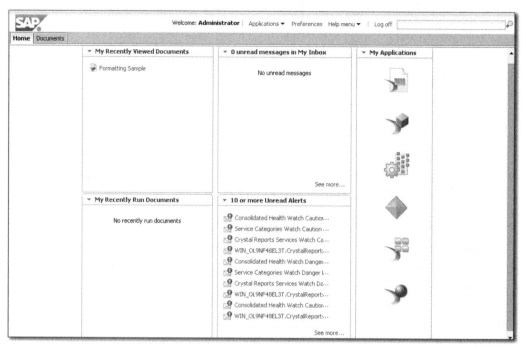

Figure 16.1 BI Launch Pad Initial View

16.1.1 Header Panel

The header panel menu options may vary dependent on any customization that may have been applied to your environment or security group (see Figure 16.2).

Figure 16.2 Header Panel

The header panel includes the customizable top header section with the company logo and the header panel menus. A number of menu options are available by default, although availability of these options depends on your access rights. The header also displays the name of the user account that is currently logged in.

The following are various menus and tabs found in the header panel:

▶ HOME tab

  Selecting the HOME tab brings you back to the initial view shown in Figure

16.1. Your Home tab can be customized in your General Preferences as discussed in Section 16.2. Administrators can also create custom Home tabs for users or groups.

▶ Documents tab
Selecting the Documents tab option enables you to view the drawers with the folders and categories organization structure as well as the documents available within these folders and categories.

▶ Applications menu
Upon selecting the Applications menu from the header panel, a dropdown list appears of the available types of applications that can be opened within BI Launch Pad, as shown in Figure 16.3. These options will vary based on the settings in your environment as well as your user rights.

Figure 16.3 Applications Menu on Header Panel

▶ Preferences menu
Selecting the Preferences menu opens the personal preferences available to customize BI Launch Pad and Web Intelligence for your user account. Further discussion regarding setting preferences is contained in Section 16.2.

▶ Help menu
Selecting the Help menu opens the About page with the specific product information about your environment as well as access to additional help resources.

▶ Log Off option
Selecting the Log Off option will end your current SAP BusinessObjects BI platform session. It's important to log out of BI Launch Pad rather than closing the browser because your session will remain open until the default timeout period set up by your system administrator. Depending on your company's licensing structure, numerous open sessions may restrict your access to BI Launch Pad. If you experience this problem, contact your system administrator to re-enable your access.

Home Tab

The default HOME tab (refer to Figure 16.1) features icons for quick access to applications as well as five panels:

▶ MY RECENTLY VIEWED DOCUMENTS
The first quadrant includes links to the 10 last viewed documents sorted by view date with the most recent at the top of the list.

▶ UNREAD MESSAGES IN MY INBOX
The second quadrant displays the 10 most recent unread messages in your BI Inbox. Selecting the SEE MORE... link at the bottom right of the box will bring you to your BI Inbox to view the unread messages.

▶ MY RECENTLY RUN DOCUMENTS
The third quadrant lists the last 10 documents that you scheduled or ran. It also includes the status of each instance. You may select the document name to open the instance.

▶ UNREAD ALERTS
The fourth quadrant includes a listing of unread alert messages that you are subscribed to in your alert subscriptions. Selecting the SEE MORE link at the bottom right of the box will bring you to your alerts to view the unread messages.

▶ MY APPLICATIONS
This area provides links to the applications that you have access to within the BI Launch Pad.

Documents Tab

The second default tab in the initial workspace is the DOCUMENTS tab, shown in Figure 16.4, which contains the drawer menus and objects such as folders, categories, Web Intelligence documents, and publications for your use in BI Launch Pad.

The expandable panes on the left of the screen in the DOCUMENTS tab are called *drawers*. Depending on your access rights, not all objects in the drawers may be visible to you. The following drawer menus are available:

▶ MY DOCUMENTS
The items included in the MY DOCUMENTS drawer include objects that are visible only to you. It also has a MY FAVORITES folder, in which you can store your

personal documents as well as temporary files saved from a timeout. You can create additional folder hierarchies within your MY FAVORITES folder to further personalize and organize your documents. Other folders include your BI INBOX, MY ALERTS, SUBSCRIBED ALERTS, and PERSONAL CATEGORIES.

▶ FOLDERS
The FOLDERS drawer includes the public folders visible to all users although which specific folders are available is dependent on access rights.

▶ CATEGORIES
The CATEGORIES drawer includes the categories available for public consumption. These will be discussed later in Section 16.3.

▶ SEARCH
The SEARCH drawer includes the search box discussed in further detail in Chapter 18.

Figure 16.4 Documents Tab

If you select the DOCUMENTS tab instead of the HOME tab, you'll see the drawers for navigation, the folders, or categories set up within BI Launch Pad.

Figure 16.5 shows a sample NAVIGATION PANEL structure within the FOLDERS drawer. The Navigation Panel within each organization will be customized to their needs, so your navigation panel will be different from this view. Along with the folder hierarchy in the NAVIGATION PANEL, you will see the list of documents in the LIST PANEL as well as the toolbar and DETAILS PANEL. Figure 16.5 shows a sample view of the LIST PANEL after selection of PUBLIC FOLDERS from the FOLDERS drawer.

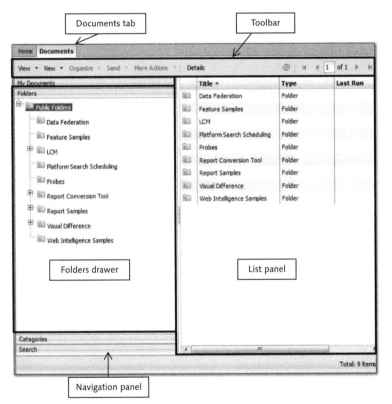

Figure 16.5 Folders Drawer

When you've selected the DOCUMENTS tab from the BI Launch Pad, you can access the documents toolbar, as shown in Figure 16.6.

Figure 16.6 Toolbar

This toolbar includes the following items:

▶ VIEW

As shown in Figure 16.7, you have several options when you select the VIEW menu: VIEW the document, VIEW LATEST INSTANCE, or PROPERTIES. To activate the menu options, you must first select a document from the LIST PANEL. The VIEW option will open the document in reading mode within BI Launch Pad. The VIEW LATEST INSTANCE option will open the latest scheduled instances in the reading mode. If there are no saved instances, then this option won't show active in the menu options. The PROPERTIES option displays the document properties with specific information regarding the selected report.

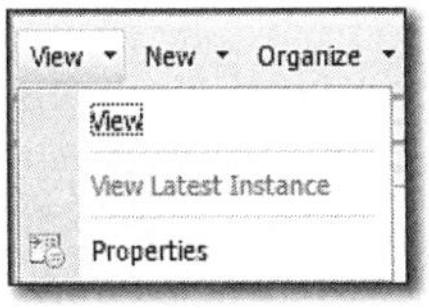

Figure 16.7 View Menu

▶ NEW

When you select the NEW menu from the toolbar, a dropdown list displays the available options as shown in Figure 16.8. The available options will depend on your environment and user settings.

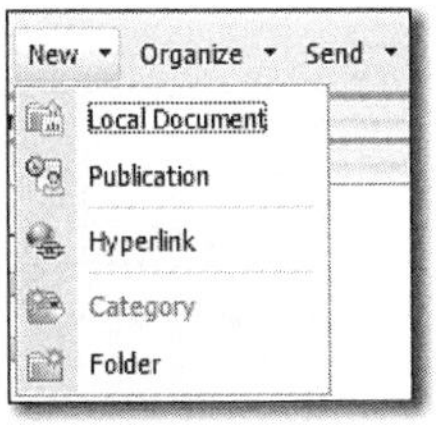

Figure 16.8 New Menu

▶ ORGANIZE

The ORGANIZE menu contains options that are standard in a number of programs, such as CUT, COPY, COPY SHORTCUT, PASTE, and DELETE, as shown in Figure 16.9. The ORGANIZE button will only become enabled when selecting a folder where your rights allow you to perform this action. When selected on a document in the LIST PANEL, it also contains the option to CREATE SHORTCUT IN MY FAVORITES.

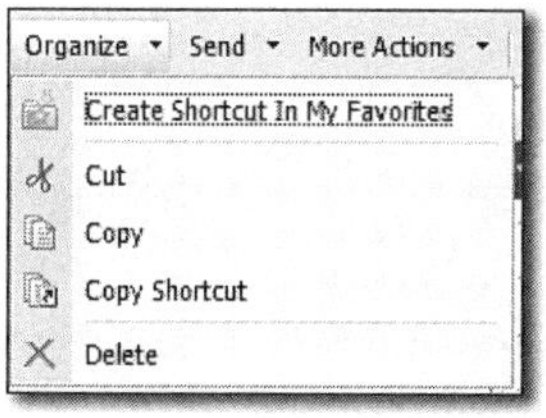

Figure 16.9 Organize Menu

▶ SEND

The SEND menu contains options for sending a document to other users across the enterprise, including to another user's BI Inbox.

▶ MORE ACTIONS

The MORE ACTIONS menu displays only after you select an object from the WORKSPACE PANEL. This menu contains a number of actions you can perform on a Web Intelligence document from within BI Launch Pad (see Figure 16.10).

> ▷ MODIFY: Allows you to modify the object. For a Web Intelligence report, selecting the MODIFY option will open the report in Web Intelligence in design mode to make any necessary changes.

> ▷ SCHEDULE: Allows you to schedule to a designated distribution. Refer to Chapter 19 for detailed information on scheduling reports.

> ▷ HISTORY: Displays the schedule history. Refer to Chapter 19 for detailed information on scheduling reports.

> ▷ CATEGORIES: Allows you to select which categories an object should display in.

> ▷ DOCUMENT LINK: Provides the OpenDocument hyperlink information. Chapter 15 provides further information on utilizing document linking. You also have the ability to create a URL link to a public folder or category.

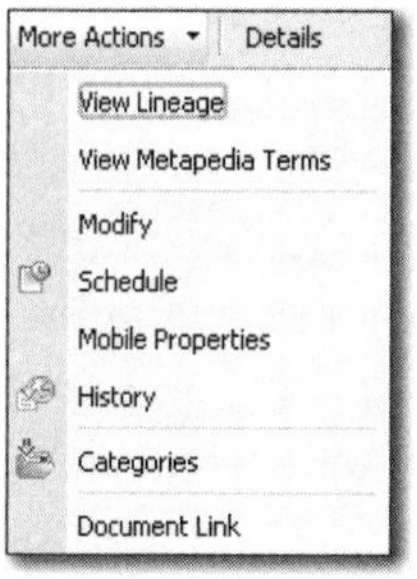

Figure 16.10 More Actions Menu

► DETAILS

The DETAILS button opens the DETAILS panel (as shown in Figure 16.11), which provides information about the document. A drawer menu is also available on the DETAILS tab, including SUMMARY, COLLABORATION, and DISCUSSIONS drawers. The SUMMARY drawer displays information about your current selection. The COLLABORATION drawer is available based on your settings. This drawer exposes the collaboration options available with SAP StreamWork or SAP Jam. The third drawer is the DISCUSSION PANEL, which is reviewed in further detail in Chapter 18.

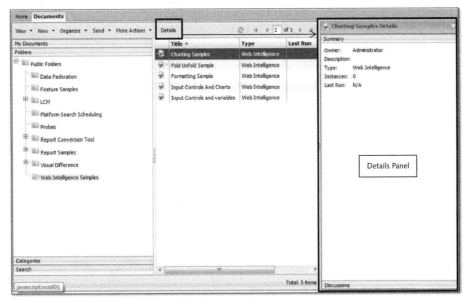

Figure 16.11 Details Panel

► REFRESH

Selecting the REFRESH button refreshes the DOCUMENTS tab. This can be helpful when a new report is added to BI Launch Pad or after creating a new folder or category.

► PAGE NAVIGATION

The PAGE NAVIGATION includes the current page number of the NAVIGATION PANEL with arrows allowing you to quickly navigate between pages. The default number of items displayed per page is set in the GENERAL PREFERENCES, as discussed in Section 16.2.

16.1.2 List Panel

The List Panel, as shown previously in Figure 16.5, displays the objects selected in the Navigation Panel.

16.1.3 Tabs

Additional tabs may be available to you, depending on your environment. The system administrator can designate specific default tabs for your organization. Also, if your implementation includes integration with SAP StreamWork or SAP Jam, you may see a tab for COLLABORATION. You can also select the PIN THIS TAB option to pin a selected document to your initial view, as shown in Figure 16.12.

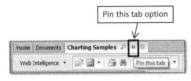

Figure 16.12 Pin This Tab Option

16.2 Setting BI Launch Pad Preferences

The majority of user settings are set by the system administrator in the Central Management Console (CMC), but there are some preferences that the user can set. These include preferences for BI Launch Pad, Web Intelligence, and possibly SAP Crystal Reports or SAP BusinessObjects BI workplace. Refer to Chapter 1 for a more substantial discussion on Web Intelligence preferences. Settings that are specific to the BI Launch Pad environment are defined in the general preferences.

16.2.1 General Preferences

General preferences includes settings for your BI Launch Pad environment. The USE DEFAULT SETTINGS (ADMINISTRATOR DEFINED) checkbox—which enables you to naturally inherit default settings—is selected by default. You can define your own custom preferences if you uncheck this box.

The first setting allows you to define the BI Launch Pad start page, whose options are shown in Table 16.1.

Home	The HOME tab is the default setting as shown earlier in Figure 16.1. You can select the default HOME tab or browse the repository for a custom HOME tab.
Documents tab	
My Documents • My Favorites	The MY FAVORITES option opens BI Launch Pad with the NAVIGATION PANEL selected on your FAVORITES folder and the LIST PANEL showing the contents of your FAVORITES folder.
My Documents • Personal Categories	The PERSONAL CATEGORIES option opens BI Launch Pad with the NAVIGATION PANEL selected on your personal categories and the LIST PANEL showing the contents of your categories.
My Documents • My Inbox	The MY INBOX option opens BI Launch Pad with the NAVIGATION PANEL selected on your BI Inbox and the LIST PANEL showing the contents of your BI Inbox.
Folders	The FOLDERS option shows the tree view set to the folder you specify in the BROWSE FOLDER box and the WORKSPACE DETAIL PANEL showing the contents of the selected folder.
Categories	The CATEGORY option shows the tree view set to the category you specify in the BROWSE CATEGORY box and the WORKSPACE DETAIL PANEL showing the contents of the selected category.

Table 16.1 BI Launch Pad Start Page Options

The DOCUMENTS tab preferences allow you to select the default view of either folder or categories that will display in your workspace. We'll discuss the differences between folders and categories in further detail in the next section.

The DOCUMENTS tab display option allows you to select which columns will be displayed by default when viewing the DOCUMENTS tab in the LIST PANEL. Select the checkbox to display the property according to your preference. Options include: TYPE, LAST RUN, INSTANCES, DESCRIPTION, CREATED BY, CREATED ON, LOCATION (CATEGORIES), RECEIVED ON (INBOX), and FROM (INBOX).

The DOCUMENT VIEWING LOCATION property specifies how you'll view documents upon selection of VIEW from toolbar in the BI Launch Pad. The available options include the following:

▸ In the BI Launch Pad portal as tabs
▸ In multiple full screen browser windows, one window for each document

The final option on the general preferences allows you to set the maximum number of objects to show at one time per page in the Workspace Details panel of BI Launch Pad. The default setting is set to 50 items per page. Increasing the number of objects shown per page can have an impact on performance, so exercise caution when changing these settings.

16.2.2   Locales and Time Zone Preferences

Additional properties specific to your locale are shown in Figure 16.13. Locale-specific properties are usually defined in the CMC by your system administrator. If you prefer to use customized personal properties, then the option is available in PREFERENCES.

The following are locale-specific properties:

► PRODUCT LOCALE
The default setting uses the locale of your browser.

► PREFERRED VIEWING LOCALE
The default setting uses the locale of your browser.

► CURRENT TIME ZONE
The default setting uses the time zone of the web server used by SAP Business-Objects.

Figure 16.13 Preferences for Locales and Time Zone

16.2.3 Changing your Password

The ability to change your password will depend on your authentication type. If you are set to enterprise authentication, and the administrator has enabled this right, then you can change your password. The CHANGE PASSWORD preferences are shown in Figure 16.14.

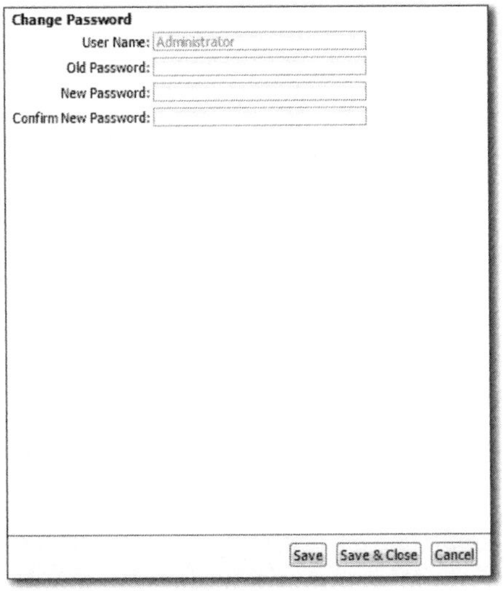

Figure 16.14 Change Password Preferences

> **Note**
>
> The options that are available to you in the PREFERENCES may be different depending on the settings in the CMC set by your SAP BusinessObjects administrator as well as your specific SAP BusinessObjects deployment.

16.3 Organizing in Folders and Categories

There are two ways to organize your documents within BI Launch Pad: folders and categories. The key difference between folders and categories is that every document must belong to a folder, but a document doesn't have to belong to a category. Categories are a way to organize your documents into logical groupings without having to create copies or shortcuts of your documents. The documents contained within categories are not duplicates, but the same original document organized in a different way. For example, your public folders may be organized by region so that each region is restricted to see their folder alone. The category structure could be organized by logical grouping of time when reports are normally viewed or run: yearly, monthly, weekly, or daily. This helps the users quickly see which reports to view using categories but also lets them navigate through the folders based on their company structure.

16.3.1 Folders

There are two types of folders: public and personal. Public folders are usually set up by the SAP BusinessObjects administrator and restricted on who can set up new public folders. They also can be restricted on who can publish documents to the public folders in order to maintain a system of testing and quality assurance before reports are published for public consumption. They are contained in the FOLDERS drawer.

In contrast, only you or users with administrative access can view documents contained in personal folders. Each user has his own personal folders to organize documents for his own personal use. These documents are not available for public consumption. They are found in the My Documents drawer.

Personal folders include the My Favorites documents and the user's BI Inbox. Users across an organization can share documents by sending them to each other's BI Inbox. More detail on sharing documents is discussed in Chapter 19. My Favorites consists of personal documents for the user's own consumption. You can create additional personal folders within your My Favorites to further organize your documents provided you've been given the appropriate rights. Refer to Figure 16.5, which shows a sample folder structure in BI Launch Pad.

16.3.2 Categories

Categories are created to help organize documents in a way that is different from the folder view. A report can belong to only one folder, but it can belong to numerous categories. But like folders, categories can include both personal and corporate. Corporate categories are available across an organization, while personal categories are only available to the specific user. Figure 16.15 shows a sample category view in BI Launch Pad available in the CATEGORIES drawer in the DOCUMENTS tab. You can access personal categories from the MY DOCUMENTS drawer.

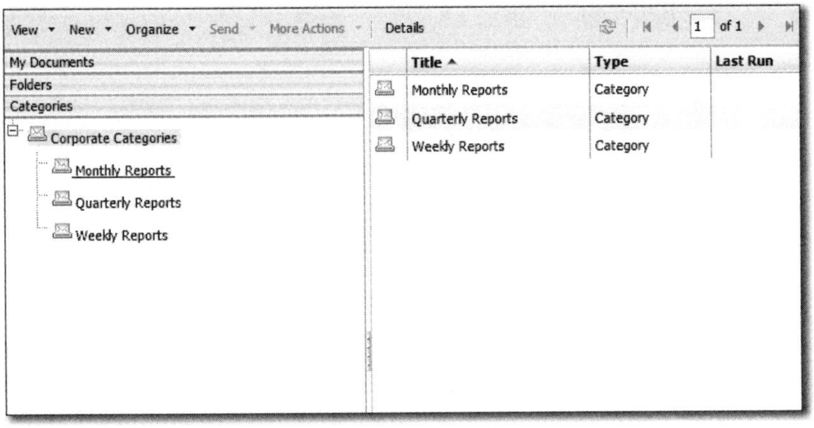

Figure 16.15 Sample Category View

16.3.3 Organizing Objects

Objects such as Web Intelligence documents are organized in BI Launch Pad using folders and categories. Depending on your user rights, you can create new folders and categories, move and copy existing folders and categories, sort objects within folders and categories, delete unneeded folders and categories, and set folder and category preferences. Let's explore all of these options further.

Creating New Folders and Categories

To create a new folder, it's necessary to be in the folder drawer or selected in MY FAVORITES in the MY DOCUMENTS drawer. Select NEW from the BI Launch Pad workspace toolbar, and choose FOLDER from the dropdown list.

To create a new category, it's necessary to be in the CATEGORIES drawer or selected on PERSONAL CATEGORIES in the MY DOCUMENTS drawer. Select NEW from the BI Launch Pad workspace toolbar, and choose CATEGORY from the dropdown list.

Moving Objects in Folders and Categories

Use the CUT • PASTE option from the ORGANIZE menu to move an object in a folder or category. First, select the object to be moved. Then select the ORGANIZE menu from the BI Launch Pad workspace toolbar, and choose CUT. This will remove the object from its current location and allow you to paste it into the new location.

Navigate to the new folder or category location, and select PASTE from the ORGA-
NIZE menu.

> **Note**
>
> Any shortcuts that have been applied to an object will be maintained when copying and
> pasting objects to a new location.

Copying Objects in Folders and Categories

To copy an object in a folder or category to another location, highlight the object
to be copied, and select COPY from the ORGANIZE menu on the DOCUMENTS tab
toolbar. Then navigate to the new folder or category to add the object to the new
location, and select PASTE from the ORGANIZE menu. This will create another
instance of this object in the new location. If you make changes to one object, you
also need to make them to the other object to maintain consistency. If you want
the second instance to automatically reflect any changes made to the original
object, then you should use the shortcut function discussed in Chapter 18.

Sorting and Filtering Objects in Folders and Categories

You can sort objects from within folders and categories into ascending or
descending order by selecting the heading of the column of the workspace panel.
The default setting is to sort objects from A to Z by title. When hovering over the
title bar, a funnel icon will appear. Select this icon to filter content in the list, as
shown in Figure 16.16. Reselect the FILTER icon, and select the CLEAR FILTER
checkbox to remove the content filter.

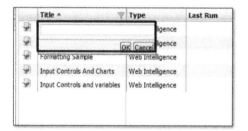

Figure 16.16 Column Filters Option

Deleting Objects in Folders and Categories

To delete an object in a folder or category, select the object and choose the DELETE option from the ORGANIZE menu. Whether you're authorized to delete objects will be dependent upon your user rights. Usually users are only authorized to delete objects in their personal folders or categories unless they have administrative level access.

Setting Object Properties

To set object properties, highlight the object in the WORKSPACE PANEL and select PROPERTIES from the VIEW menu. The PROPERTIES box allows you to define the object title, description, and key words.

16.4 Viewing, Printing, and Saving Objects in BI Launch Pad

You can view, print, and save Web Intelligence documents within the BI Launch Pad without having to edit them in Web Intelligence. From within the LIST PANEL, select the Web Intelligence document that you want to view within BI Launch Pad, and select VIEW from the ACTIONS menu on the BI Launch Pad workspace toolbar. You can also double-click on the name of a report to open it in reading mode, or select VIEW from the right-click menu when selected on a document. (The VIEW option also opens the Web Intelligence document in reading mode. How the document opens within reading mode will be dependent on your preferences, as discussed in Section 16.3.) When viewing a Web Intelligence document within BI Launch Pad, the Web Intelligence viewer toolbar, shown in Figure 16.17, will appear with the options available to you.

Figure 16.17 Web Intelligence Viewer Toolbar in Reading Mode

Let's examine this toolbar closely.

16.4.1 Web Intelligence Viewer Toolbar

The first menu on the Web Intelligence viewer toolbar is the WEB INTELLIGENCE menu, where you can select options for your toolbar views. This includes toggling on or off the filter bar, outline view, side panel, report tabs, and status bar.

The following toolbar options are shown in Figure 16.17:

▶ NEW
Creates a new Web Intelligence document.

▶ OPEN
Enables you to select from the DOCUMENTS tab to open another Web Intelligence report in reading mode.

▶ SAVE MENU
Two options are available:

  ▷ The SAVE option saves any changes made to the report.

  ▷ The SAVE AS option saves any changes made to the report as a new name and/or to a new location.

▶ PRINT
Exports the report to PDF format for printing. Web Intelligence documents must first be exported to PDF before they can be printed. After you select the EXPORT TO PDF button, you will be prompted to open the PDF or save it. You don't need to save the PDF to create a printed copy, but you may want to save the PDF for further reference.

▶ FIND
Searches for text in tables and cells on the page being viewed of the report.

▶ HISTORY
Lists dates corresponding with the history of the scheduled instances of the document.

▶ EXPORT
Enables you to export a document in PDF, Excel, Excel 2007, CSV Archive, or Text format.

▶ SEND TO
Allows you to send to email, BI Inbox, or FTP location, depending on your access rights.

▶ UNDO
Undoes the previous action.

▶ REDO
Redoes the previous action.

▶ REFRESH
Refreshes selected queries or all queries used by the report.

▶ TRACK
Activates or deactivates the data tracking mode (to be discussed shortly).

▶ DRILL
Enables drill mode, as discussed in Chapter 11.

▶ FILTER BAR
Displays the filter bar on the report.

▶ FREEZE
Provides the ability to freeze headers or columns in tables to keep them displayed as you scroll through data. This is a new menu option.

▶ OUTLINE
Shows or hides the outline providing the ability to use fold/unfold features on the report.

▶ READING MENU
Lets you switch between different modes such as HTML and PDF for viewing the document.

▶ DESIGN MENU
Lets you edit the document in Web Intelligence by selecting to DESIGN WITH DATA or STRUCTURE ONLY.

▶ HELP
Opens the online help.

Other menu options extend Web Intelligence viewer functionality, as described next.

16.4.2 Additional Menu Options

The left side panel includes additional toggle menu options, including Document Summary, Navigation Map, Input Controls, and User Prompt Input. Document

Summary details the properties of the Web Intelligence document. The Navigation Map shows the sections of the document, including the content on each report tab. The Input Controls (which were discussed in Chapter 10) let you specify values or move selectors to change the content of the report. This option is only available if this feature has been enabled and set up by the report designer. The USER PROMPT INPUT box, which is shown in Figure 16.18, shows the prompt values and enables you to change the prompt values to refresh a report.

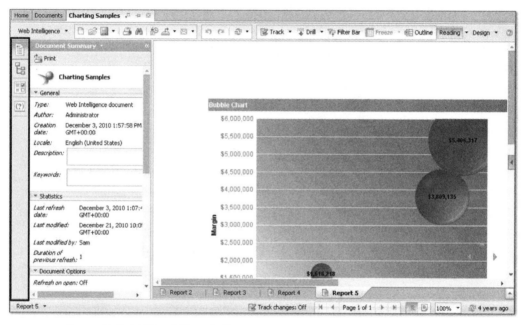

Figure 16.18 Additional Menu Options

16.5   Summary

The BI Launch Pad portal provides a multifunctional interface for the casual user to organize, view, print, and share Web Intelligence documents. Additional features discussed in Chapter 18 (such as tracking data changes and robust search capabilities) make the SAP BusinessObjects BI platform interface a powerful tool for collaboration across the business. Chapter 17 discusses the use of the SAP BusinessObjects BI workspaces in creating custom pages for viewing your report content.

Using BI workspaces, users can create multitabbed dashboards that combine multiple types of SAP BusinessObjects BI content.

17 Using Web Intelligence with SAP BusinessObjects BI Workspaces

The BI workspaces web application allows users to define multitabbed workspaces to organize related objects from the SAP BusinessObjects BI platform for an integrated viewing experience. BI workspaces can combine SAP Crystal Reports, SAP BusinessObjects Analysis, OLAP edition workspaces, Web Intelligence documents, and dashboards with agnostic content such as static text, HTML, or web pages external to the SAP BusinessObjects BI platform. You can also integrate existing BI workspaces into new BI workspaces. Once created, BI workspaces can be accessed on demand or set as the default HOME tab to be seen when users log on to the BI Launch Pad.

In this chapter, we'll explore the BI workspaces application and learn how to combine Web Intelligence documents and report parts into a single, cohesive BI workspace.

> **Note**
>
> In versions prior to SAP BusinessObjects BI 4.x, the BI workspaces application was known as Dashboard Builder.

17.1 Introducing BI Workspaces

The BI workspaces application can be launched from the APPLICATIONS menu in the BI Launch Pad, as shown in Figure 17.1.

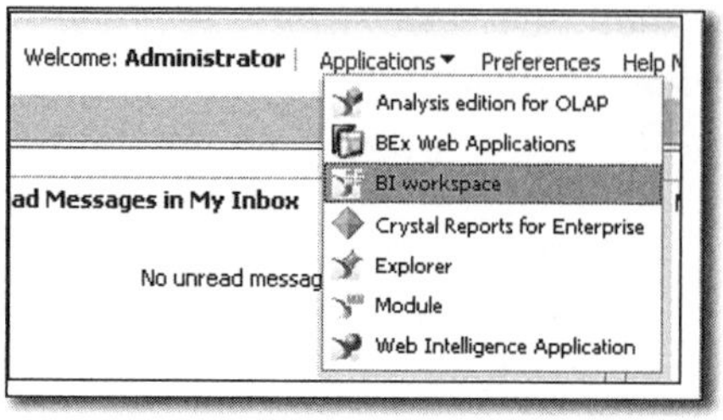

Figure 17.1 BI Workspace on the BI Launch Pad Applications Menu

Within the BI workspaces application, there is a large canvas for laying out the design of the workspace. At the top of the canvas, you'll find the BI workspaces toolbar. On its left side is the MODULE LIBRARY. In the next sections, we'll explore how to use the BI workspaces toolbar and the Module Library to add content to the workspace canvas.

17.1.1 BI Workspaces Toolbar

The BI workspaces toolbar appears across the top of the BI workspaces application, as shown in Figure 17.2 and includes the following options:

▶ NEW
Creates a new BI workspace.

▶ OPEN
Opens an existing BI workspace.

▶ SAVE
Updates the repository with the latest BI workspace changes.

▶ SAVE AS
Saves a new BI workspace with a different name or location than the original.

▶ SHOW MODULE LIBRARY
Opens the MODULE LIBRARY sidebar.

▶ REVERT CHANGES
Returns BI workspace to the last saved revision.

▶ CONTENT LINKING
Enables content linking between different modules in the BI workspace.

▶ LAYOUT
Organizes the canvas by columns, template, or freeform layout.

▶ EXIT EDIT MODE
Exits the edit mode (any unsaved changes will be lost).

Note

Other options appear on the toolbar depending on which layout (column, template, or freeform) is chosen.

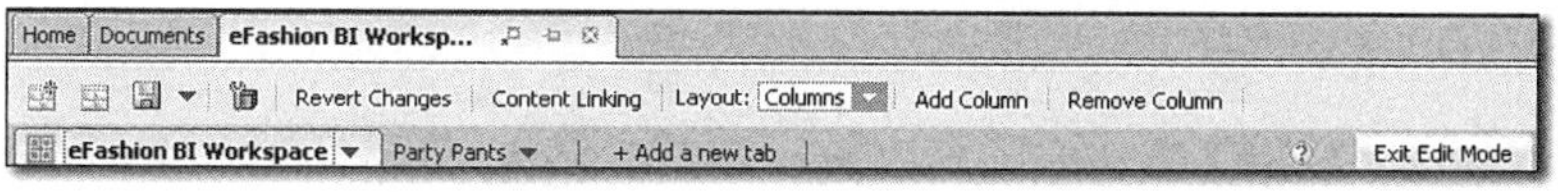

Figure 17.2 BI Workspaces Toolbar

A BI workspace consists of a primary, or HOME, tab. This HOME tab can be extended with a series of tabs and subtabs, permitting a two-layer hierarchy to be constructed, as shown in Figure 17.3.

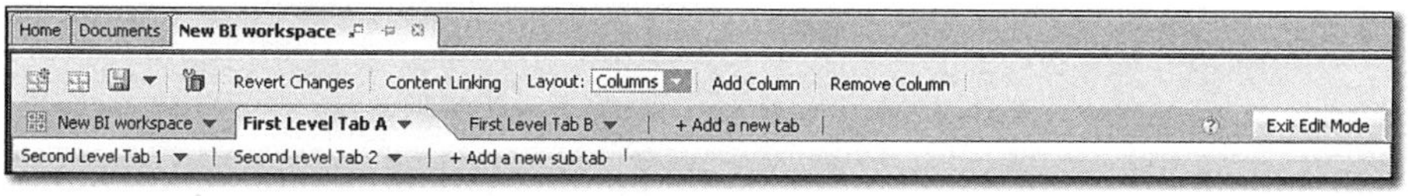

Figure 17.3 Two-Layer Hierarchy

The options for each tab or subtab can be modified by right-clicking on the desired tab or subtab. There are five options, as shown in Figure 17.4:

▶ RENAME
Renames the current tab or subtab.

▶ DUPLICATE
Duplicates the current tab or subtab.

▶ DELETE
Deletes the current tab or subtab.

▶ PROPERTIES
Modifies the properties of the current tab or subtab.

▶ SET AS DEFAULT
Sets the current tab or subtab as the default, meaning it will appear first when the user selects BI WORKSPACE.

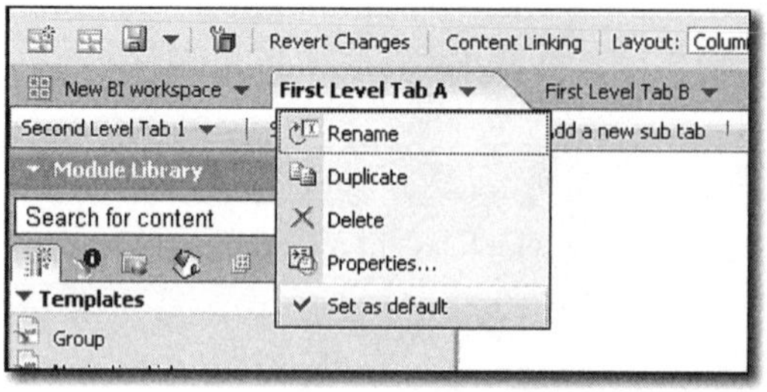

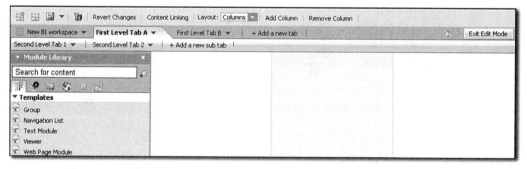

Figure 17.4 Tab Options

Each tab or subtab can display multiple objects from the SAP BusinessObjects BI platform. Three different layout options are available from the BI workspaces toolbar: Column layout, Template layout, and Freeform layout.

Column layout, shown in Figure 17.5, organizes the content into multiple columns for an orderly appearance.

Figure 17.5 Column Layout

Template layout, shown in Figure 17.6, provides several predefined templates with options for either rows or columns.

Freeform layout, shown in Figure 17.7, offers the most flexibility of the three layout options. BI workspace authors can choose a visible grid to assist with module placement and can even choose to snap modules to the grid lines for better organization.

The BI workspaces Module Library is a left-hand pane found underneath the BI workspaces toolbar.

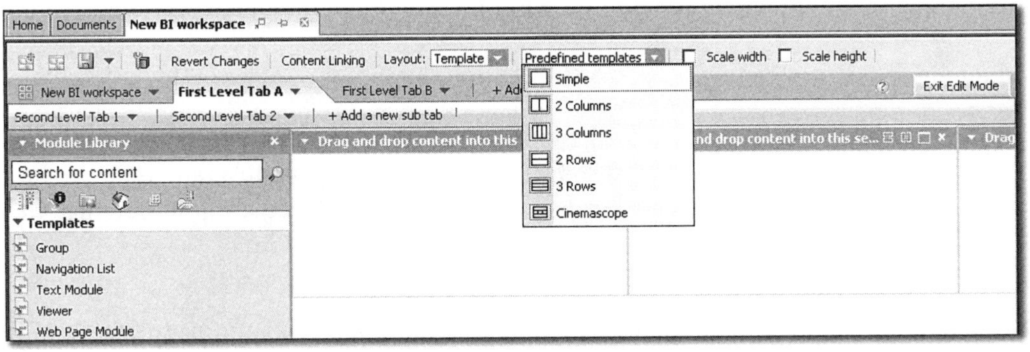

Figure 17.6 Template Layout

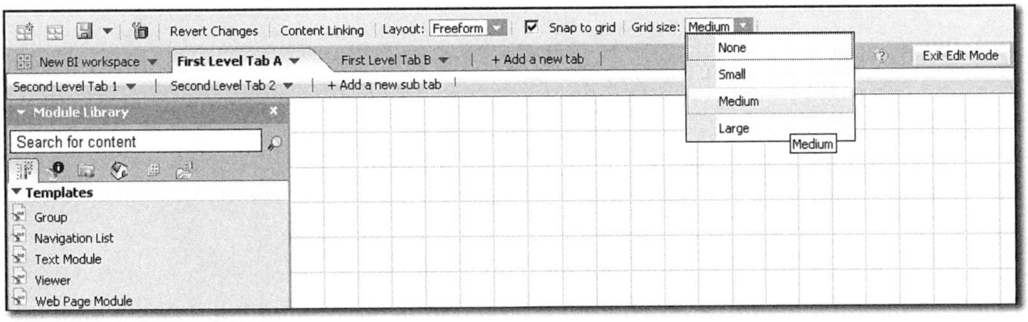

Figure 17.7 Freeform Layout

17.1.2   BI Workspaces Module Library

The Module Library offers six different sources of business intelligence content: templates, BI Launch Pad modules, public modules, private modules, BI workspaces, and Document Explorer. Let's explore each of these now.

Template Modules

The five types of templates that can be used with BI workspace are shown in Figure 17.8:

▶ GROUP
Provides a box outline. This outline can improve the appearance of other modules.

► NAVIGATION LIST

Can be used as a table of contents. It can be paired with a VIEWER module using module variables.

► TEXT MODULE

Displays either plain text or formatted HTML. Text modules are useful for documentation or navigation when neither presently exist on an external web page.

► VIEWER

Displays content from the SAP BusinessObjects BI platform, such as a Web Intelligence document. Content can also be selected using the PUBLIC and PRIVATE modules, which are covered later in this chapter.

► WEB PAGE MODULE

Displays the contents of a web page. An example is the contents of a corporate intranet such as a help page.

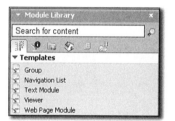

Figure 17.8 Template Modules in the Module Library

BI Launch Pad Modules

The modules available from the BI LAUNCH PAD MODULES tab should be familiar to even the most casual SAP BusinessObjects user, as they appear on the default HOME page tab in the BI Launch Pad. The following modules are shown in Figure 17.9:

► MY ALERTS

Displays alerts from the SAP BusinessObjects BI platform.

► MY APPLICATIONS

Displays icons for applications if the user has rights to access them.

► MY INBOX

Displays the contents of the user's BI Inbox.

▶ MY RECENTLY RUN DOCUMENTS

Displays documents recently run (or, in other words, scheduled) by the user.

▶ MY RECENTLY VIEWED DOCUMENTS

Displays documents recently viewed by the user.

▶ SAP STREAMWORK FEED

Displays the user's SAP StreamWork feed (requires SAP StreamWork to be integrated with the SAP BusinessObjects BI platform).

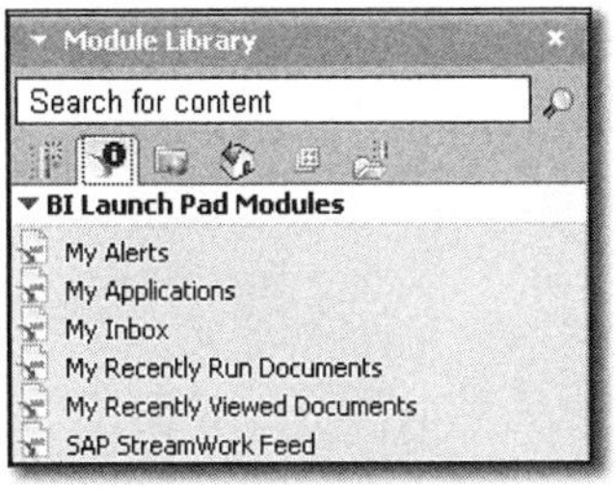

Figure 17.9 BI Launch Pad Modules in the Module Library

Public Modules

As shown in Figure 17.10, the PUBLIC MODULES tab displays all of the business intelligence content available from the public folders. To access them, simply navigate to the desired public folder, identify the desired module, such as a Web Intelligence document, and drag it to the BI workspace canvas.

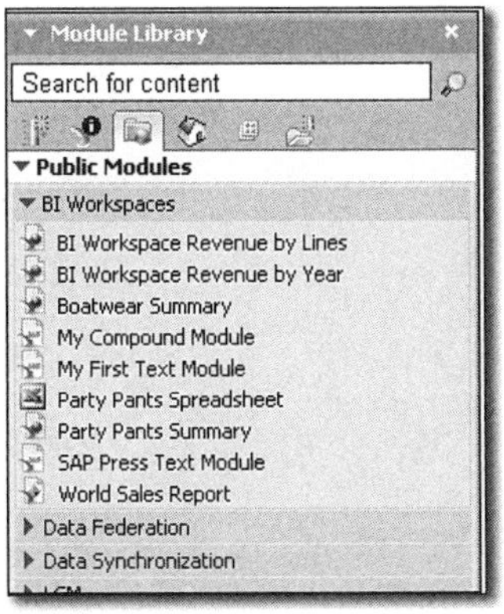

Figure 17.10 Public Modules in the Module Library

Private Modules

The PRIVATE MODULES tab of the Module Library, shown in Figure 17.11, displays the modules present in the BI workspace author's personal folders, such as EFASHION AND ESTAFF and eFASHION EXPERT EXCEL. These modules can only be used for personal BI workspaces that will be saved in the user's personal folders because other users don't have sufficient rights to private modules to use them.

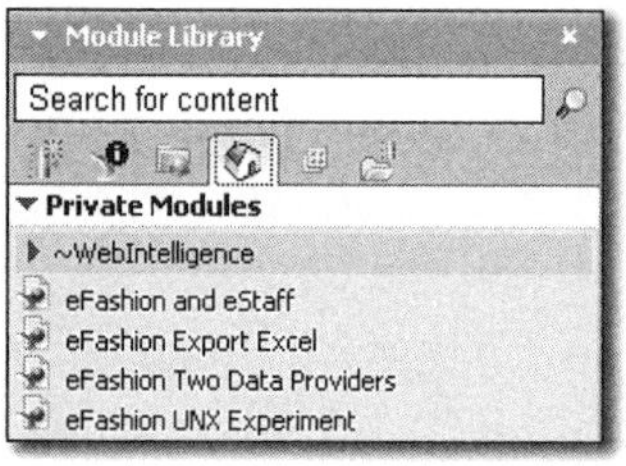

Figure 17.11 Private Modules in the Module Library

BI Workspaces

Tabs and subtabs from other BI workspaces can be reused by choosing them from the BI WORKSPACES tab in the Module Library, as shown in Figure 17.12. In our example, you can see that a single BI workspace, named CATEGORY, exists in the repository. That BI workspace contains three tabs (CATEGORY SUMMARY, CATEGORY DETAIL, and CATEGORY CHART), which can be added to the currently open BI workspace canvas.

Figure 17.12 BI Workspaces in the Module Library

Document Explorer

The DOCUMENT EXPLORER tab in the Module Library, shown in Figure 17.13, provides an easy way to add an entire public folder to a BI WORKSPACES tab or subtab. Document explorers for personal lists, such as the BI Inbox or Query Panel, are also available.

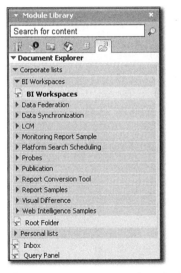

Figure 17.13 Document Explorer in the Module Library

17.1.3 Setting BI Workspaces Preferences in the BI Launch Pad

Only a single setting, default style, is available in the BI Launch Pad preferences, as shown in Figure 17.14. Several of these styles are carried over from previous versions of the SAP BusinessObjects BI platform for backwards compatibility, so the appearance is outdated. You might prefer the newer BI Launch Pad style for new BI workspaces.

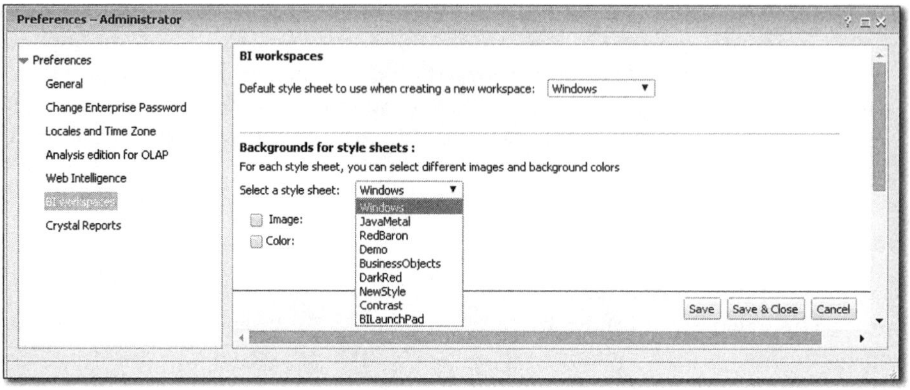

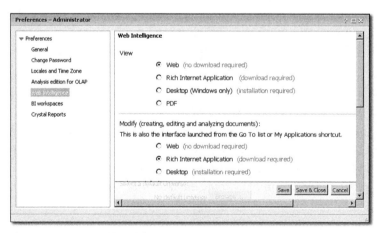

Figure 17.14 BI Workspaces Preferences in the BI Launch Pad

17.1.4 Setting Web Intelligence Preferences in the BI Launch Pad

The ability to include a single report part from a Web Intelligence document is a useful feature of Web Intelligence 4.0 that will be explored later on in the chapter. It's important to choose the WEB viewer (VIEW setting) in the Web Intelligence preferences because the Java-based Rich Internet Application viewer doesn't permit the selection of report parts, but it makes no difference to the BI workspaces application which version of Web Intelligence is used to create and modify Web Intelligence documents (MODIFY setting). For example, in Figure 17.15, the WEB application has been specified for viewing, but the Rich Internet Application has been specified for modification.

Figure 17.15 View and Modify Options

17.2 Working with Modules

The BI Launch Pad application menu also offers an application to create modules; this MODULE application is shown in Figure 17.16.

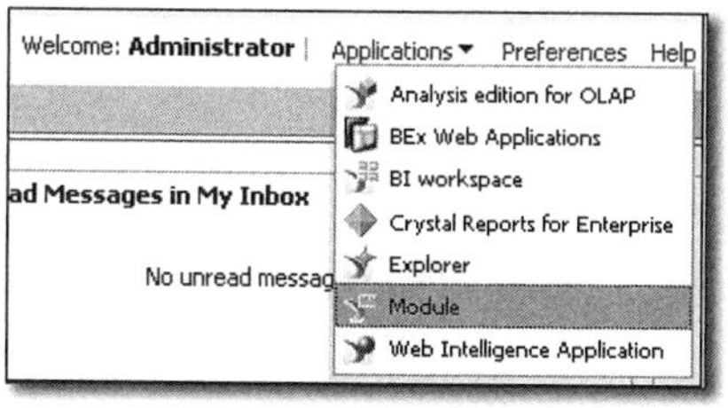

Welcome: Administrator
Applications
Preferences
Help
Analysis edition for OLAP
BEx Web Applications
BI workspace
ad Messages in My Inbox
Crystal Reports for Enterprise
Explorer
No unread messag
Module
Web Intelligence Application

Figure 17.16 BI Launch Pad Module Application

Two types of modules can be created in this manner: text modules and compound modules. Let's take a closer look at both of these.

Text Modules

Text modules can contain either plain text or formatted HTML. They can be useful for annotating BI workspaces with simple documentation or hyperlinks to locations outside of the SAP BusinessObjects BI platform when a preexisting web page that performs those functions doesn't exist.

To begin, chose TEXT MODULE from the NEW MODULE tab, as shown in Figure 17.17.

Welcome: Administrator
Applications
Preferences
Help menu
Log off
Home
Documents
New Module
Select the module type:
Tools
To add text to a BI workspace, select:
• Text Module
To create a group of modules, select:
• Compound Module
Text Module
Compound Module

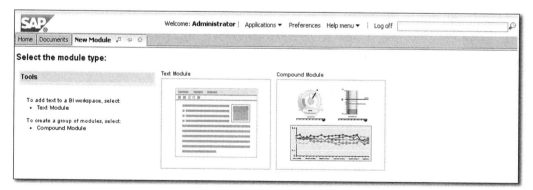

Figure 17.17 Text Modules and Compound Modules

Next, choose either REGULAR (plain) or HTML text, which has been selected in Figure 17.18.

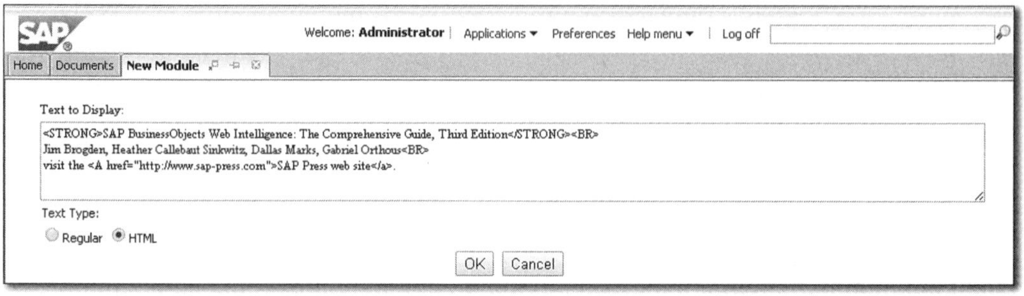

Figure 17.18 Creating a Text Module Using HTML

The formatted HTML, shown in Figure 17.19, can be saved as a module in a personal or public folder.

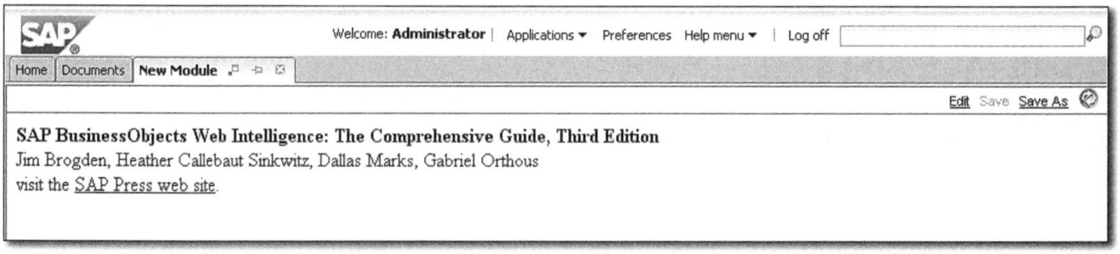

Figure 17.19 Viewing a Text Module Using HTML

Compound Modules

In contrast to text modules, a compound module is a simplified BI workspace that doesn't contain tabs and subtabs. Compound modules are useful for reusing content in multiple tabs or subtabs of the same BI workspace or even across multiple BI workspaces. For example, it may be beneficial to create a compound module containing corporate branding elements for BI workspaces.

17.3   Working with Web Intelligence Report Parts

Although entire Web Intelligence documents can be placed inside a viewer on a BI workspace, it can be more effective to place a single report part (either a table or chart) on a single tab or subtab. In this section, we'll place a tag cloud chart from a Web Intelligence 4.0 document on a subtab of an existing BI workspace (see Figure 17.20).

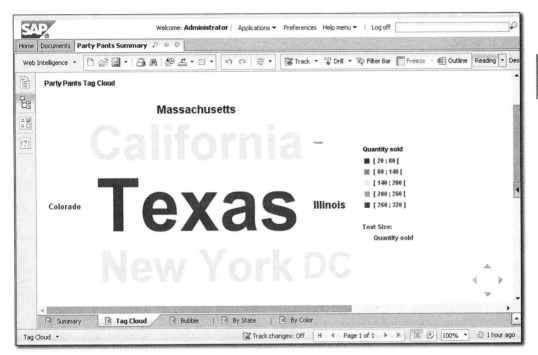

Figure 17.20 Web Intelligence Document with a Tag Cloud Chart

The existing BI workspace is called eFashion BI Workspace. As shown in Figure 17.21, it already contains a tab named Party Pants with a subtab named Bubble, which is where the bubble chart report is found. To begin editing an existing BI workspace, click on the Edit BI Workspace button in the top-right corner.

Next, add a new subtab next to the Bubble subtab by clicking on + Add a new subtab, as shown in Figure 17.22.

Next, assign the subtab a name by replacing the default text "New subtab," shown in Figure 17.23. In our example, the new subtab is named "Tag Cloud."

The next step is to choose the layout of your new subtab. In our example, we've selected the Freeform layout, as shown in Figure 17.24.

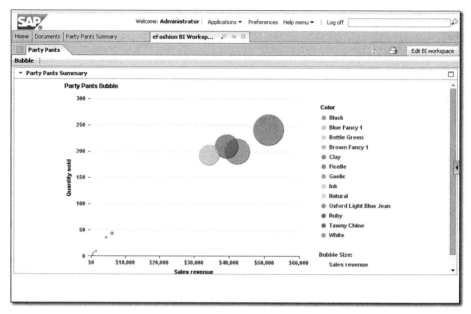

Figure 17.21 Editing an Existing BI Workspace

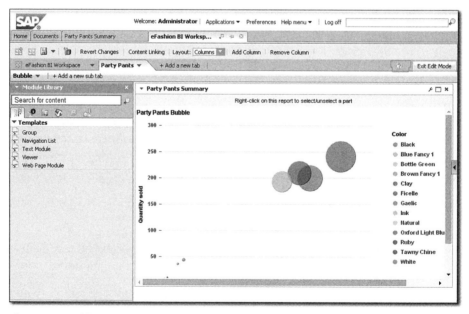

Figure 17.22 Adding a New Subtab

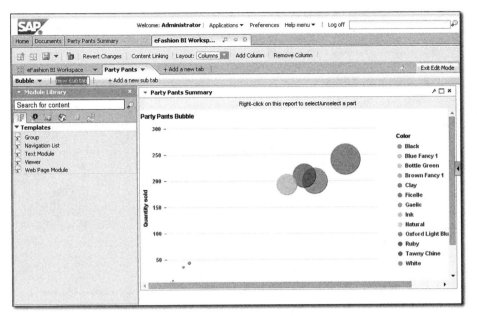

Figure 17.23 Naming the New Subtab

Figure 17.24 Choosing the Layout

Next, you need to choose the PUBLIC MODULES tab from the MODULE LIBRARY. In our example, we navigate to the public folder BI WORKSPACES and drag the PARTY PANTS SUMMARY Web Intelligence document from the MODULE LIBRARY to the BI workspace canvas, as shown in Figure 17.25.

By default, the entire Web Intelligence document is placed on the subtab. However, we prefer to select a single report part (a tag cloud chart), which is located on a Web Intelligence report tab named TAG CLOUD. Right-click on the desired chart, and choose SELECT THIS REPORT PART from the menu, as shown in Figure 17.26.

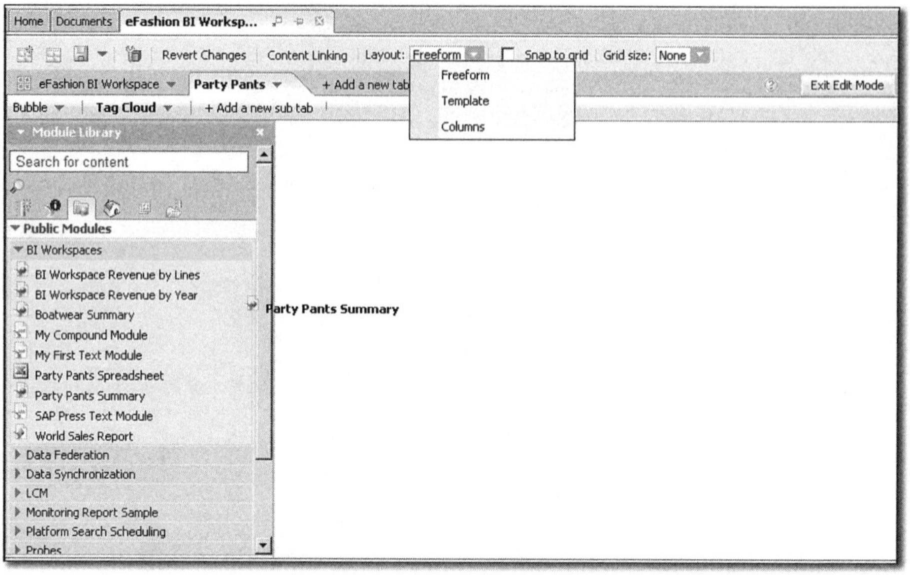

Figure 17.25 Dragging Desired Web Intelligence Document to BI Workspaces Tab

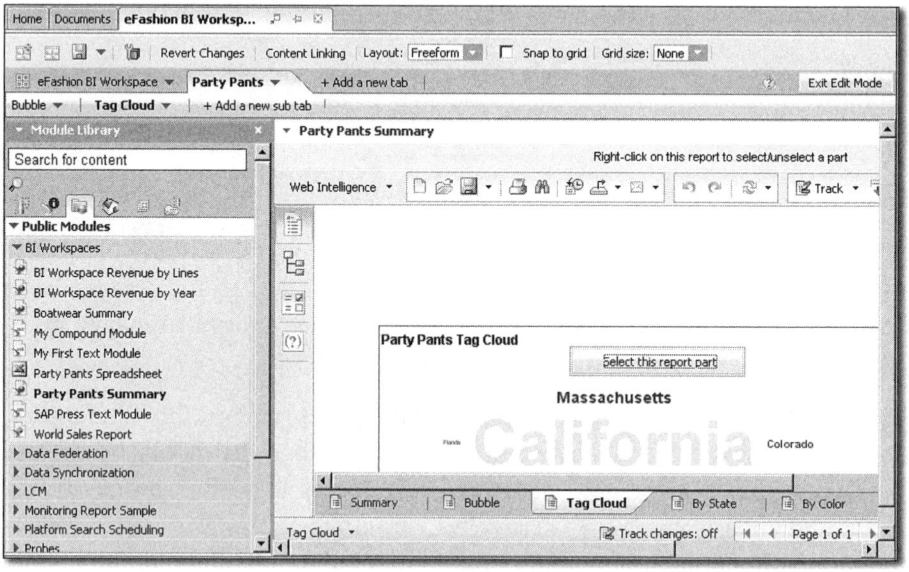

Figure 17.26 Right-Clicking on the Desired Report Part

The report part is now part of the BI WORKSPACES subtab. Notice that, by default, the subtab is labeled with the name of the Web Intelligence document, PARTY PANTS SUMMARY, as shown in Figure 17.27. To modify this label and other properties, click on the EDIT (wrench) icon in the top-right corner of the subtab.

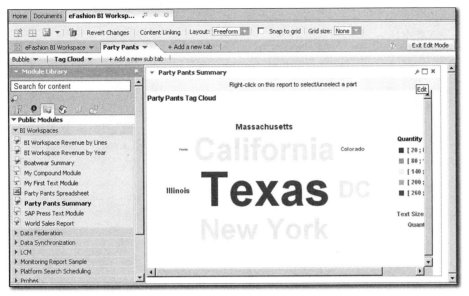

Figure 17.27 Editing the Report Part

When you edit the report part, you'll find that module properties are located on two tabs: CONTENT and LAYOUT (see Figure 17.28). On the CONTENT tab, notice that the DISPLAY MODE is set to SELECTED REPORT PART. Notice that the report content can be loaded on demand, from the latest instance (selected), or from the latest instance of a specific user. This functionality allows the BI workspace designer to take advantage of Web Intelligence documents that were previously scheduled— a useful feature particularly for long-running Web Intelligence documents.

On the LAYOUT tab, you can change the default title (the NAME of the Web Intelligence document). In the example shown in Figure 17.29, we have changed the title to "My Tag Cloud."

After all modifications are complete, click on EXIT EDIT MODE in the top-right corner of the BI WORKSPACES subtab, as shown in Figure 17.30.

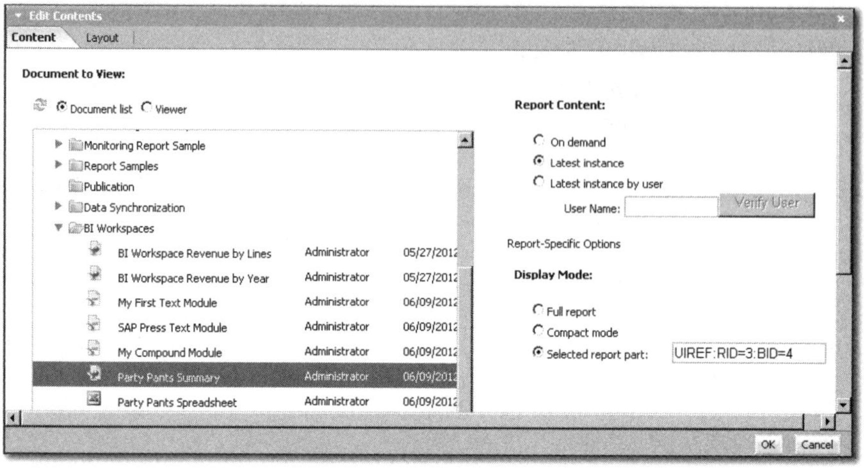

Figure 17.28 Review Properties on Content Tab

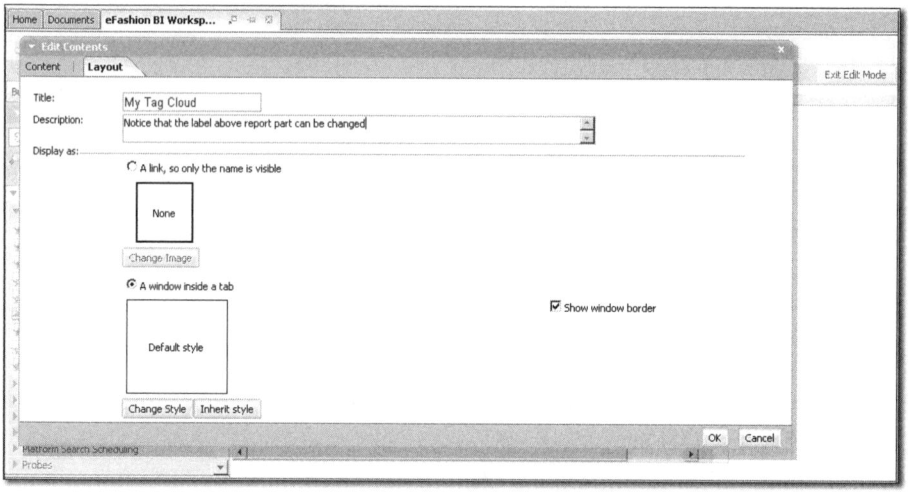

Figure 17.29 Modify Properties on Layout Tab

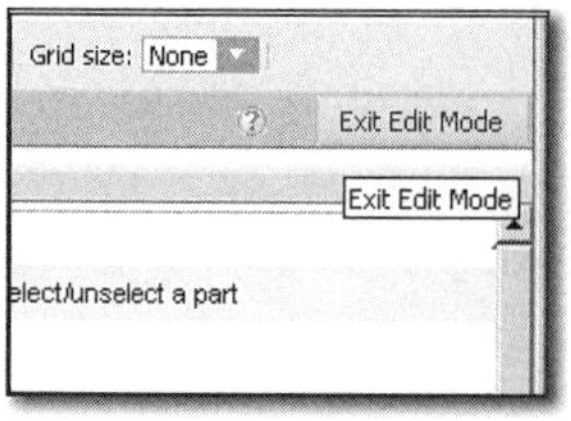

Figure 17.30 Exit Edit Mode

To finish, click on the SAVE icon on the BI workspaces toolbar to update the BI workspace with all modifications, as shown in Figure 17.31.

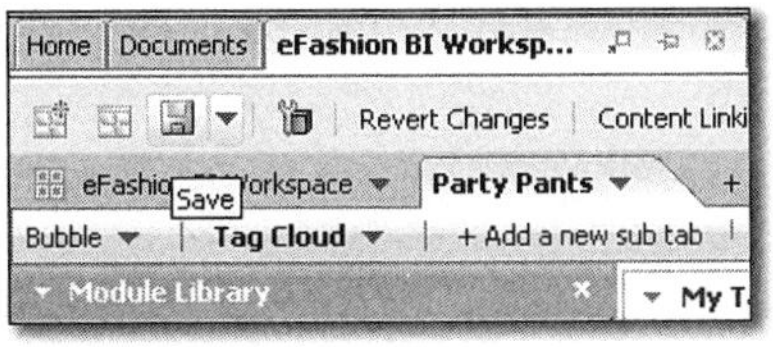

Figure 17.31 Saving Changes on the BI Workspaces Toolbar

You'll receive a message indicating that the BI workspace was saved, such as the one shown in Figure 17.32.

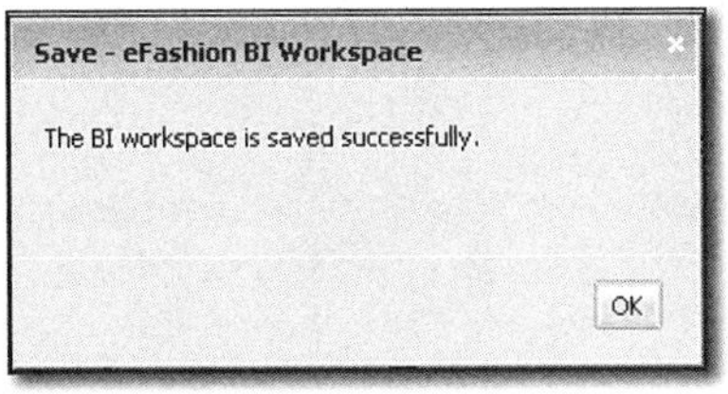

Figure 17.32 Saved BI Workspace

17.4 Using a BI Workspace as the Default Home Tab

If desired, you can replace your default HOME tab with a custom BI workspaces tab. To begin, open the BI Launch Pad Preferences. The GENERAL tab is active by default. Uncheck the USE DEFAULT SETTINGS (ADMINISTRATOR DEFINED) box, and choose SELECT HOME TAB from the HOME TAB menu. Next, click on the BROWSE HOME TAB button, as shown in Figure 17.33.

Next, browse to the folder containing the desired BI workspace. For our example, we've selected the EFASHION BI WORKSPACE from the public folder BI WORKSPACE, as shown in Figure 17.34.

Notice that the selected BI workspace appears in the GENERAL PREFERENCES screen, as shown in Figure 17.35. Save and close the BI Launch Pad Preferences.

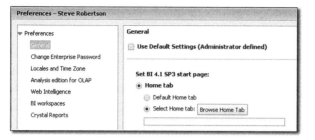

Figure 17.33 Setting a Custom Home Tab in BI Launch Pad General Preferences

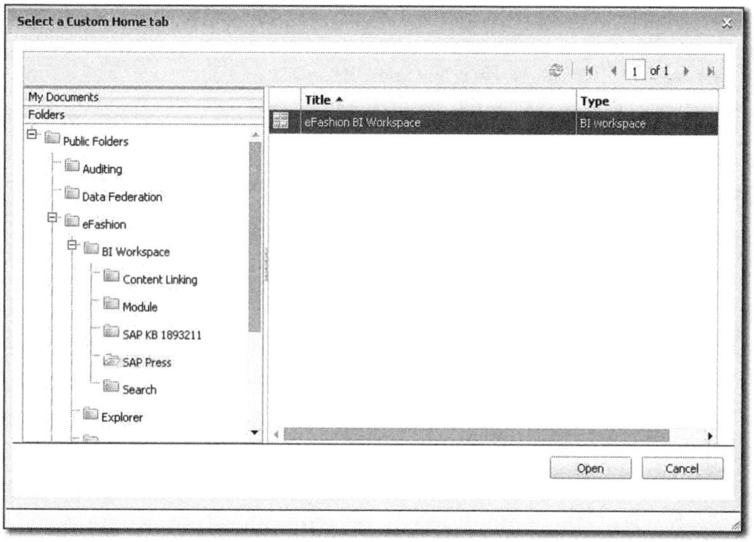

Figure 17.34 Selecting Content for a Custom Home Tab

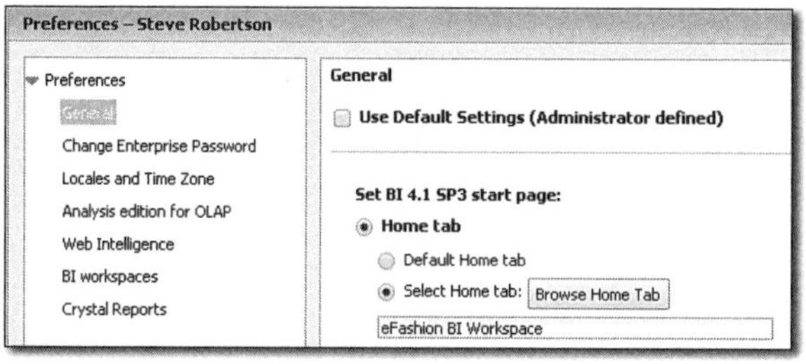

Figure 17.35 Workspace Selected as a Custom Home Tab

The user will see the customized HOME tab the next time he logs on to the BI Launch Pad, as shown in Figure 17.36.

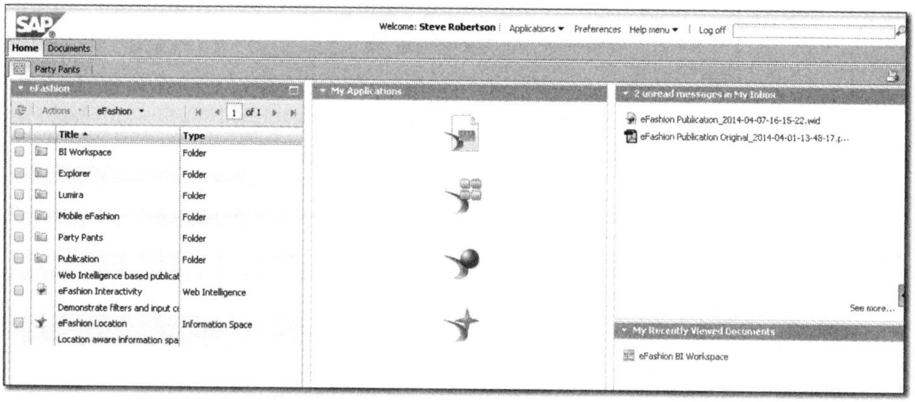

Figure 17.36 BI Workspace as the New Default Home Tab

17.5 Printing BI Workspaces

BI workspaces can now be printed using SAP BusinessObjects BI 4.1. Simply click on the PRINTER icon in the top-right corner of a BI workspace (see Figure 17.37).

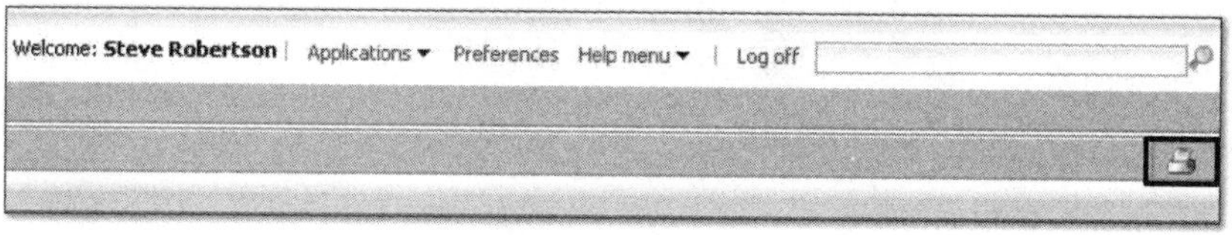

Figure 17.37 Printing BI Workspaces

Choose whether to print the current tab or all tabs of the BI workspace (see Figure 17.38). Change your printer settings to LANDSCAPE.

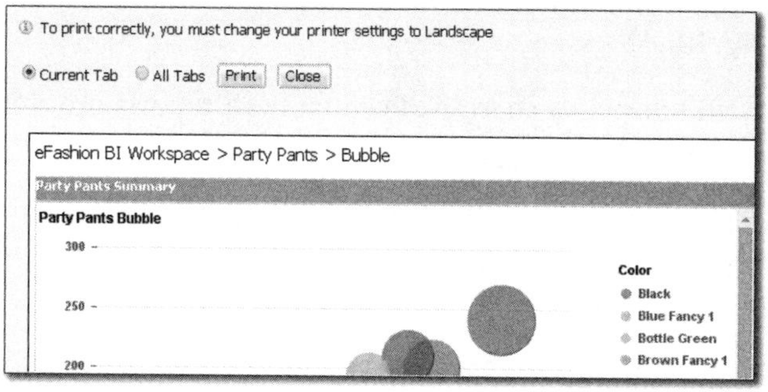

Figure 17.38 Printing Options

17.6   Content Linking

Using a feature called *content linking*, we can allow modules in our BI workspace to communicate. In this example, we'll create three Web Intelligence reports and link them together in a single BI workspace.

The first report, CATEGORY SUMMARY, will display a list of categories and will be the source content (see Figure 17.39).

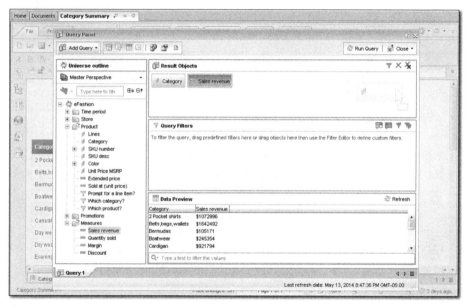

Figure 17.39 Creating a Source Document

The next two Web Intelligence documents will define prompts so they can receive a user selection from the source report. The CATEGORY DETAIL report will display a table (see Figure 17.40).

The CATEGORY CHART report will display a chart. Notice that both reports prompt on the CATEGORY object (see Figure 17.41).

We will define a two-column layout, placing the CATEGORY SOURCE report part in the left column, and the CATEGORY DETAIL and CATEGORY CHART report parts in the right column (see Figure 17.42).

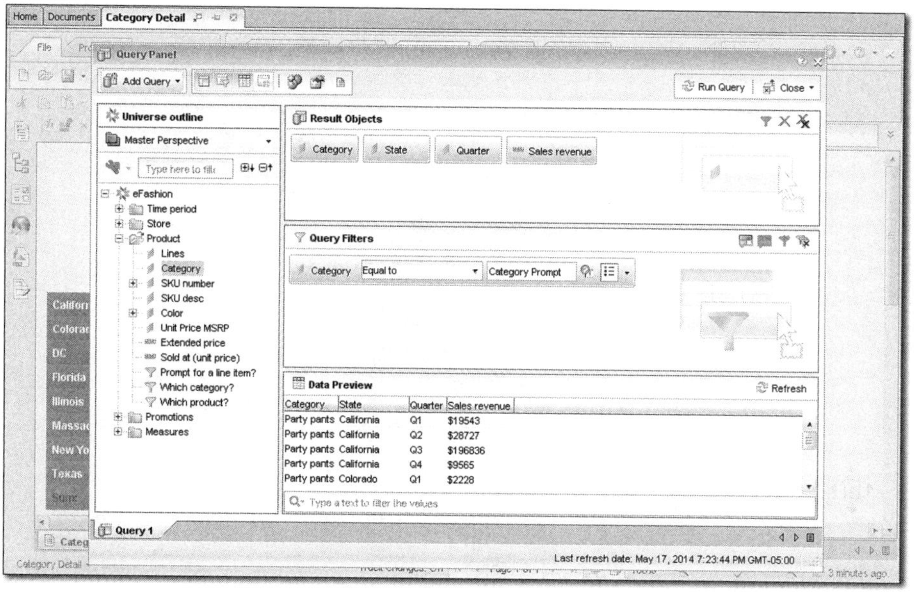

Figure 17.40 Creating a Target Document with a Prompt

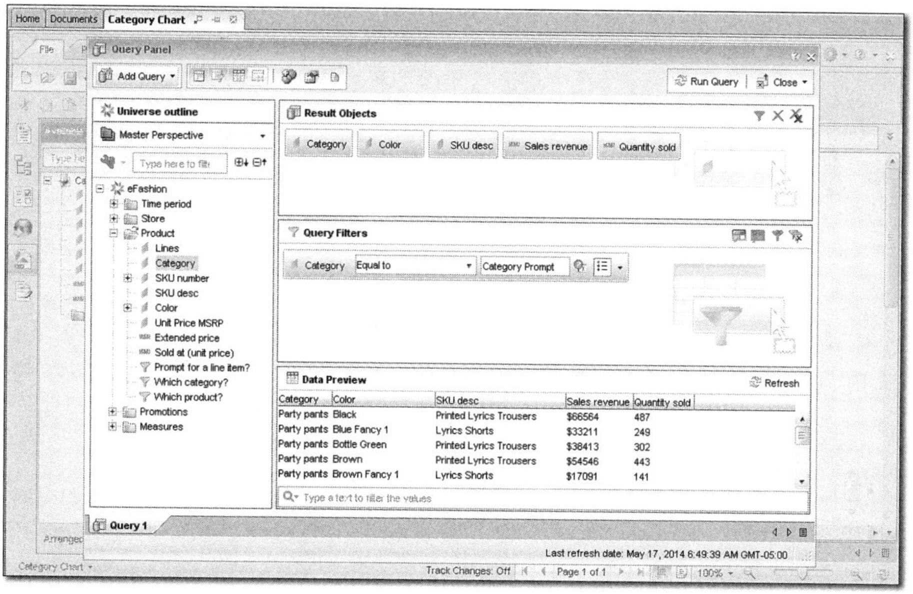

Figure 17.41 Creating a Second Target with a Prompt

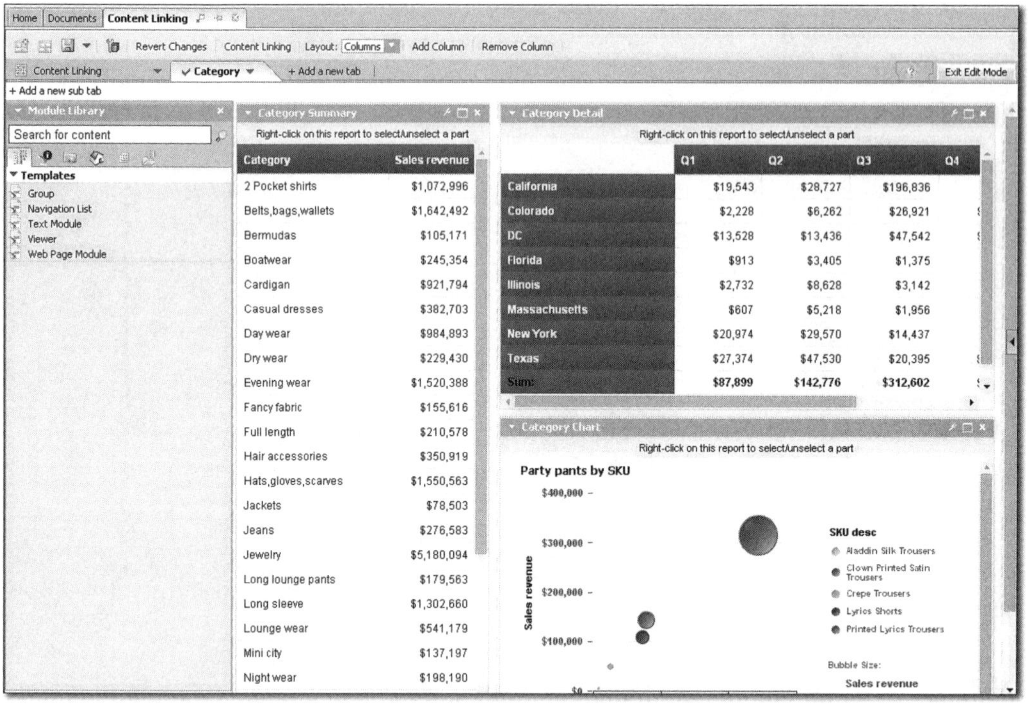

Figure 17.42 A Two-Column Layout with All Three Web Intelligence Reports

To connect these three Web Intelligence reports, click on the CONTENT LINKING button on the toolbar. A pop-up window showing a graphical representation of the reports will appear at the top of the window. Using the mouse, connect the output (PARAMETERS_OUT) of the CATEGORY SOURCE report to the inputs (PROMPT_IN) of the CATEGORY DETAIL and CATEGORY CHART reports.

Next, at the bottom of the screen for each source/target combination, map the parameters by selecting the Web Intelligence prompts as TARGET parameters for the SOURCE parameter (CATEGORY) in the CATEGORY SOURCE REPORT (see Figure 17.43).

Close the CONTENT LINKING pop-up window, save the BI workspace, and choose EXIT EDIT MODE. Clicking a desired category in the CATEGORY SOURCE report will cause both the CATEGORY DETAIL and CATEGORY CHART report parts to refresh using that category as their prompt values. Choosing CASUAL DRESSES (see Figure 17.44) and PARTY PANTS (see Figure 17.45) will show different results.

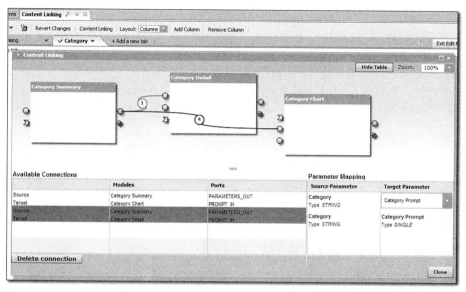

Figure 17.43 Content Linking Pop-up

Category	Sales revenue
2 Pocket shirts	$1,072,996
Belts,bags,wallets	$1,642,492
Bermudas	$105,171
Boatwear	$245,354
Cardigan	$921,794
Casual dresses	$382,703
Day wear	$984,893
Dry wear	$229,430
Evening wear	$1,520,388
Fancy fabric	$155,616
Full length	$210,578
Hair accessories	$350,919
Hats,gloves,scarves	$1,550,563
Jackets	$78,503
Jeans	$276,583
Jewelry	$5,180,094
Long lounge pants	$179,563
Long sleeve	$1,302,660
Lounge wear	$541,179
Mini city	$137,197
Night wear	$198,190
Outdoor	$276,646
Pants	$40,555
Party pants	$626,737

Category Detail

	Q1	Q2	Q3	Q4	Sum:
California	$7,520	$14,862	$26,720	$16,127	$65,229
Colorado	$1,563	$4,309	$8,391	$1,358	$15,621
DC	$4,457	$6,371	$11,294	$8,322	$30,443
Florida	$2,406	$4,645	$11,300	$380	$18,731
Illinois	$2,428	$6,616	$10,267	$5,888	$25,198
Massachusetts	Discontinued	$1,763	$7,113	$1,129	$10,005
New York	$11,092	$27,522	$47,912	$17,585	$104,110
Texas	$16,724	$32,473	$54,444	$9,724	$113,365
Sum:	$46,189	$98,560	$177,441	$60,513	$382,703

Figure 17.44 A Selection in the Category Summary Updates the Category Detail and Category Chart (Casual Dresses)

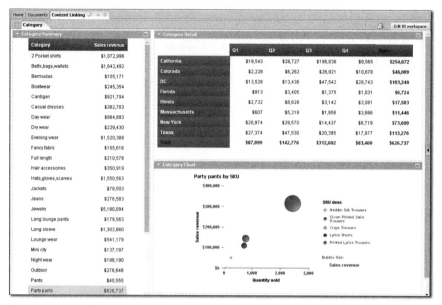

Figure 17.45 A Selection in the Category Summary Updates the Category Detail and Category Chart (Party Pants)

The content linking feature is not limited to Web Intelligence, and can be used to link SAP Crystal Reports and dashboards, too.

17.7   Summary

The BI workspaces application provides you with a powerful way to mash up multiple types of content into a cohesive user experience within the BI Launch Pad. Although this book focuses on Web Intelligence, BI workspaces can additionally contain SAP Crystal Reports, SAP BusinessObjects Analysis, OLAP edition workspaces, dashboards, and content such as web pages from outside the SAP BusinessObjects BI platform. In SAP BusinessObjects BI 4.1, BI workspaces can now be printed.

You can customize the login experience for BI Launch Pad users and replace the default HOME tab with a BI workspace.

By using content linking, you can create interactive BI workspaces that accept input choices that update the data displayed by various BI workspace modules. The next chapter will explore interaction from a user's perspective.

Many features and functionalities are available for navigation within the BI Launch Pad, making it a powerful tool for end-user report consumption. Report consumers use this interface to implement powerful reporting capabilities, including hyperlinks, tracking data changes, sorting, filtering, discussions, and alerts.

18   Interaction from a User's Perspective

The casual user navigates within the BI Launch Pad to consume Web Intelligence documents and other content. These users usually don't develop their own documents but refresh canned reports already created and contained within the SAP BusinessObjects BI platform. Report consumers can create shortcuts and hyperlinks, track data changes within reports, complete powerful searches, sort and filter content, leverage discussions regarding reports, and manage alerts. In this chapter, we'll explore these functions.

18.1   Creating Shortcuts and Hyperlinks

One method of organizing content within BI Launch Pad is to create a hyperlink or a shortcut to another location or document. This enables quick collaboration and ease of updating a report without having to update numerous copies of the same report.

18.1.1   Shortcuts

Creating a shortcut can help organize documents that are viewed by different security profiles without having to maintain numerous copies of the same report.

To create one, you can select the report and then select COPY SHORTCUT from the ORGANIZE menu on the BI Launch Pad toolbar, as shown in Figure 18.1. You can then navigate to the folder location to paste the shortcut. Another option is to select CREATE SHORTCUT IN MY FAVORITES from the ORGANIZE menu when selected on a document. This will automatically create a shortcut to the selected document in your MY FAVORITES folder. Both of these options are also available from the right-click menu when the report name in the workspace is selected.

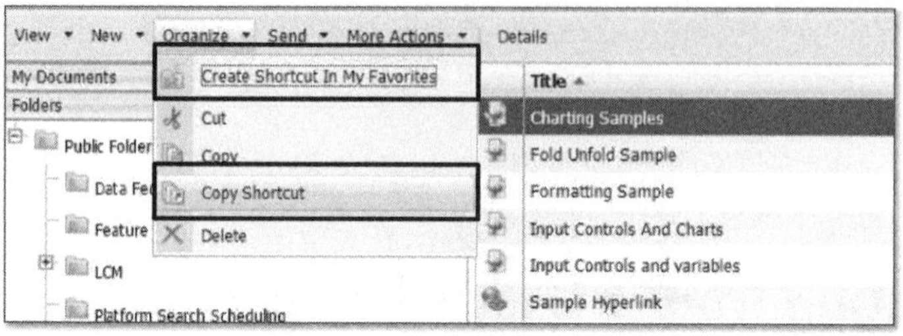

Figure 18.1 Shortcut Options from the Organize Menu

18.1.2 Hyperlinks

Hyperlinks can be helpful in sharing online help resources or internal help resources for quick reference. You can create hyperlinks within BI Launch Pad to reference other important web pages or information resources. To create a hyperlink, select the NEW button on the BI Launch Pad toolbar, and choose the HYPERLINK option from the dropdown menu, as shown in Figure 18.2.

Figure 18.2 Hyperlink from the New Menu on the BI Launch Pad Toolbar

A box will appear to enter the properties, URL address, and categories for the hyperlink, as shown in Figure 18.3. The hyperlink will appear as an object in the designated folder, categories, or both.

Shortcuts and hyperlinks provide enhanced functionality for organizing content within the BI Launch Pad. Additional features are available within this environment to enable more robust data analysis for the report customer.

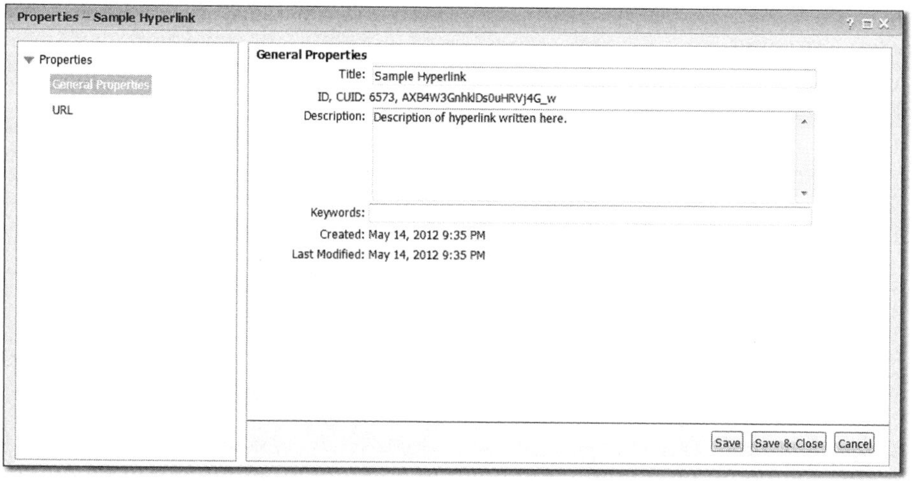

Figure 18.3 Hyperlink Properties

18.2 Tracking Data Changes

The ability to track data changes is an exciting feature in Web Intelligence. This functionality enables you to easily pinpoint changes to data to make informed decisions in a timely manner. Reference data is chosen during setup and used to base the changes; these are highlighted in your reports based on your selections. You can also use formulas and functions within Web Intelligence and build custom alerts to highlight changed data.

The following data changes can be tracked within a Web Intelligence report, as shown in Figure 18.4:

▶ INSERTED DATA

▶ REMOVED DATA

▶ MODIFIED DATA

▶ INCREASED DATA

▶ DECREASED DATA

The setup of the reference data and display of the changes is completed from within Web Intelligence.

	Q1	Q2	Q3	Q4	Sum
Increased					
Decreased					
Changed					
Inserted					
~~Removed~~		Product Line Sales for 2006			
Sweat-T-Shirts	1,967,328.20	2,121,860.20	1,506,478.90	1,863,826.20	7,459,493.50
Accessories	357,834.80	526,371.10	645,054.70	370,144.10	1,899,404.70
Sweaters	337,200.70	426,442.70	525,878.30	370,518.60	1,660,040.30
Shirt Waist	495,577.90	377,973.70	391,807.80	388,999.10	1,654,358.50
Dresses	295,717.80	355,629.50	564,570.30	192,677.30	1,408,594.90
Jackets	109,943.30	51,513.60	70,667.70	72,555.80	304,680.40
Trousers	60,114.60	87,518.50	71,101.20	53,702.00	272,436.30
City Skirts	19,634.30	55,353.90	103,390.20	17,906.60	196,285.00
Overcoats	40,269.40	518.20	22,308.70	7,915.60	71,011.90

Figure 18.4 Sample Report with Data Tracking

18.2.1 Setting Reference Data

When you enable tracking of data changes, you select a particular data refresh as your reference point. This data is known as your *reference data*. If you make changes to your data provider, the reference data is lost, and consequently, data tracking won't be available. These actions enact changes that will cause the current version of the document to be incompatible with the reference data, making data tracking misleading.

> **Note**
>
> An asterisk appears on the report tab when changed data tracking is activated on the report.

The following actions are incompatible with data tracking:

▸ Drilling out of scope

▸ Query drilling

▸ Deleting a query

▸ Making any changes to the SQL generated by the data provider

- Modifying security rights that will affect the SQL generated
- Purging the document data
- Refreshing on open (prior data is purged when the document is refreshed on open)

Reference data is set in Web Intelligence. To set reference data, select the DATA TRACKING tab from the ANALYSIS menu on the Web Intelligence document. There are two options available for the selection of reference data, as shown in Table 18.1.

COMPARE WITH LAST DATA REFRESH	The data existing before the refresh data button is selected becomes the reference data, and the new data after the refresh is tracked against this prior refresh.
COMPARE WITH DATA REFRESH FROM [SELECT DATE]	The data selected becomes the reference data and remains the reference data after each refresh regardless of the number of times the data is refreshed. The newly refreshed data is tracked against the fixed reference data.

Table 18.1 Data Tracking Options

Select the TRACK button on the BI Launch Pad viewer toolbar to activate data tracking from within BI Launch Pad. From within Web Intelligence, select the TRACK button on the DATA TRACKING tab of the ANALYSIS ribbon in design mode. This displays the DATA TRACKING dialog box, which displays the options to either compare with last data refresh or compare with a specific refresh date instance.

18.2.2 Formatting Changed Data

The default setting for the formatting of changed data is defined by the SAP BusinessObjects administrator in the Central Management Console (CMC). You can overwrite these defaults by setting your formatting within the DATA TRACKING options dialog box. Select the FORMAT tab to specify your formatting dependent on the type of changed data. Figure 18.5 shows the options available in the DATA TRACKING dialog box.

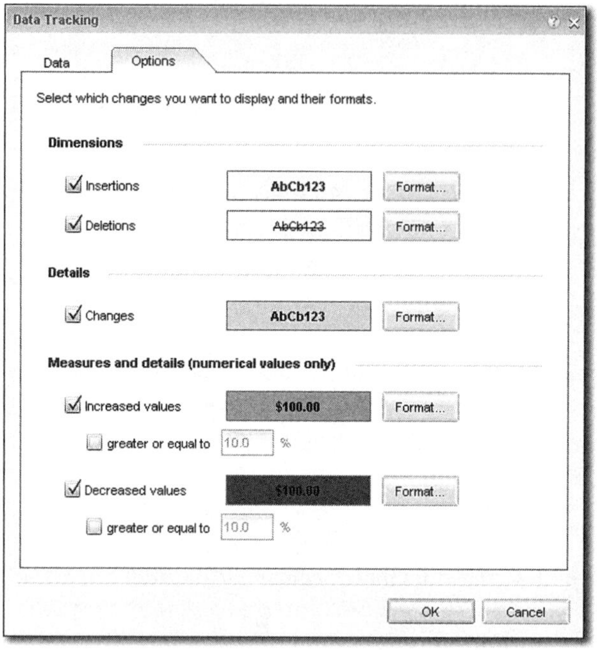

Figure 18.5 Data Tracking Options Dialog Box

The following changes are available for configuration of formatting:

▶ Inserted dimension and detail values

▶ Deleted dimension and detail values

▶ Changed dimension and detail values

▶ Increased measure values

▶ Decreased measure values

Changed data is displayed differently in blocks, sections, breaks, charts, and reports with merged dimensions.

Displayed Data in Blocks

If data is removed from a row in a block, deleted data formatting is applied to all cells as defined in the DATA TRACKING properties. If a measure increases for a row, increased data formatting is applied to the Measure cell. If a measure has decreased, decreased data formatting will be applied to the Measure cell. New data appearing in a block will show inserted data formatting on all cells.

Let's take a look at an example that details how these formatting changes will appear given a block of sample data. The sample reference data in Table 18.2 shows sales revenue by year and by state.

Year	State	Sales Revenue
2013	Arizona	$1,100,000
2014	Arizona	$1,200,000
2012	California	$1,100,000
2012	New York	$1,150,000

Table 18.2 Example Reference Data

The changed data in Table 18.3 shows the comparison data used for the data tracking.

Year	State	Sales Revenue
2014	Arizona	$1,300,000
2013	California	$1,900,000
2012	New York	$1,000,000
2014	Washington	$1,700,000

Table 18.3 Example Changed Data

When data tracking is enabled, the reference and changed data are compared, and formatting is applied to the resulting data block as per the options selected in the DATA TRACKING dialog box (see Table 18.4).

Year	State	Sales Revenue	Formatting
2013	Arizona	$1,100,000	[deleted data formatting on all cells]
2014	Arizona	$1,300,000	[increased data formatting on Revenue cell]
2012	California	$1,300,000	[deleted data formatting on all cells]
2013	California	$1,900,000	[inserted data formatting on all cells]

Table 18.4 Example with Data Tracking Activated and Results Displayed

Year	State	Sales Revenue	Formatting
2012	New York	$1,150,000	[decreased data formatting on Revenue cell]
2014	Washington	$1,700,000	[inserted data formatting on all cells]

Table 18.4 Example with Data Tracking Activated and Results Displayed (Cont.)

Displayed Data in Sections

The data in the section header can be displayed in two ways, depending on whether the entire section data changed or just some of the rows within in the section:

▸ If all rows in the section have changed in the same way, the section header format will be the same as all the rows.

▸ If only some rows in a section have changed or the rows have changed in different ways, the section header will stay in its default format.

Displayed Data in Breaks

If the CENTER VALUE ACROSS BREAK option is applied to the break in the properties, the same formatting rules apply as with sections:

▸ If all rows in the break for the centered value have changed in the same way, the centered break value format will be the same as all the rows.

▸ If only some rows in a centered break section have changed or the rows have changed in different ways, the centered break value will stay in its default format.

Displayed Data in Charts

Tracked data isn't displayed within a chart. When data tracking is applied to a chart, an icon will appear above the chart. Select the icon to display the tracked data changes. The chart will be converted to a table to allow you to see the detailed tracked data changes.

Displayed Data in Reports with Merged Dimensions

When using merged dimensions, Web Intelligence doesn't display that a new data element was added to a block unless the data element has been added to all dimensions participating in the merge.

18.2.3 Displaying Tracked Data

Select the HIDE CHANGES/SHOW CHANGES button to the right of the TRACK button on the toolbar in report mode or the BI Launch Pad viewer toolbar to display tracked data.

18.2.4 Advanced Tracking Techniques

Several formulas are available for use within Web Intelligence to perform advanced techniques with the data tracking functionality. Two are shown in Table 18.5.

`RefValue`	`RefValue` returns the value of the reference data.
`RefValueDate`	`RefValueDate` returns the date of the reference data.

Table 18.5 Web Intelligence Functions for Data Tracking

These functions can be used in a formula to find the difference between changed data and reference data. For example:

```
=[Sales Revenue] – RefValue([Sales Revenue])
```

If the current refresh returned sales revenue equal to $2.5 million, and the reference data showed sales revenue equal to $1.5 million, then this difference formula would return a result of $1 million.

18.3 Searching within the BI Launch Pad

Web Intelligence documents, SAP Crystal reports, Microsoft Excel, Word, Power-Point, RTF, PDF, and text files are all searchable if they are contained within the BI Launch Pad environment. The metadata of additional object types are also searchable. The files that you can search depend on your access rights. The data regarded by a search is different for each document type.

Searches are performed within BI Launch Pad from the DOCUMENTS tab in the SEARCH drawer, as shown in Figure 18.6. You can type the words to locate in the search box. If you pause while typing in the search box, the quick search functionality is prompted, and the top six matches are displayed.

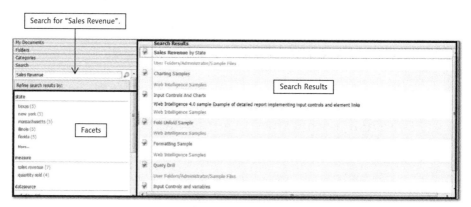

Figure 18.6 Search Drawer

When you finish typing your search criteria, select the SEARCH icon. The search results are shown in the LIST PANEL, and additional facets appear in the SEARCH drawer, as shown in Figure 18.7.

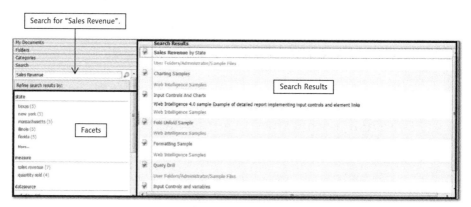

Figure 18.7 Search Drawer Results Sample

To view a result, double-click the object link in the LIST PANEL, or click on a facet in the SEARCH drawer, and double-click the generated object link. When the document opens, the viewer will scroll to the location of the first match to your search criteria.

18.3.1   Search Facets

Facets are different attributes about your documents that help to provide further filtering of your search content. These appear in the Search drawer, as shown previously in Figure 18.7. The following facet categories may appear:

▶ Location

▶ Type

▶ Refresh Time

▶ Author

▶ Data sources

18.3.2   Searchable Object Types

A large number of object types are available for search within the BI Launch Pad. There are also a number of attributes that are searched within your commonly consumed document types, which enables thorough search capabilities:

▶ Web Intelligence documents

  ▶ Report title

  ▶ Report description (as defined in report properties)

  ▶ Universe filter names

  ▶ Universe object names

  ▶ Data contained in the report as saved data

  ▶ Constants in filter conditions that are defined in a document

  ▶ Static text contained within the report

▶ SAP Crystal Reports

  ▶ Report title

  ▶ Report description (as defined in report properties)

  ▶ Selection formulas

- ▶ Data contained in the report as saved data
- ▶ Text fields
- ▶ Parameter values
- ▶ Subreports
- ▶ Microsoft Excel and Word documents
  - ▶ Data
  - ▶ Document properties
  - ▶ Header and footer text
  - ▶ Numerical values
  - ▶ Calculation or formula values (Excel only)
  - ▶ Date/time values (Excel only)
- ▶ Document types with text-only searchable content
  - ▶ Rich Text Format (RTF)
  - ▶ Portable Document Format (PDF)
  - ▶ Microsoft PowerPoint
  - ▶ Text files (TXT)
- ▶ Document types with metadata-only searchable content
  - ▶ Agnostic objects
  - ▶ Analysis views
  - ▶ BI workspaces
  - ▶ Dashboards objects
  - ▶ Discussions
  - ▶ Events
  - ▶ Adobe Flash objects
  - ▶ Hyperlinks
  - ▶ Lifecycle management console jobs
  - ▶ Metadata from Information Designer
  - ▶ Modules
  - ▶ Object packages
  - ▶ Profiles

- Program objects
- Publications
- Queries from Query as a Web Service
- Universes
- Widgets
- Workspaces created in SAP BusinessObjects Analysis, OLAP edition

18.3.3 Search Techniques

There are certain recommended techniques to use when searching content within the BI Launch Pad. For example, separate search terms using spaces, which implies the AND separator. Table 18.6 defines key techniques.

Technique	Description
Space	Space between words implies the AND separator (e.g., sales revenue).
Asterisk *	Asterisk returns results with any number of characters in its place (e.g., 19*).
Question Mark	Question mark represents a single character (e.g., Sm?th).
Quotation marks	Quotation marks are used to indicate an exact phrase that should be found in the documents returned by the results (e.g., "sales revenue").
Plus sign +	Plus sign forces the inclusion of a search term (e.g., sales + revenue).
Minus sign -	Minus sign removes results that have the indicated term (e.g., sales – revenue).
OR	OR returns results when the word before or after the word "or" are found in the document (e.g., income OR profit statement).

Table 18.6 Search Techniques

You can perform attribute searches by typing the name of the attribute with a colon and then the term to be searched. You may also combine search techniques from the preceding table for more specific results.

18.4 Sorting and Filtering Content

Objects within BI Launch Pad are sorted alphabetically by title. Of course, your access to the content depends on whether you have the appropriate rights to view in each folder or category. It may be useful to customize these views to sort by different criteria or filter for your desired results.

Selecting the column heading re-sorts the list by that heading in ascending order. Selecting the heading again sorts the list in descending order. When you hover over a column heading, you'll notice that the FILTER icon (a yellow funnel) appears, as shown in Figure 18.8.

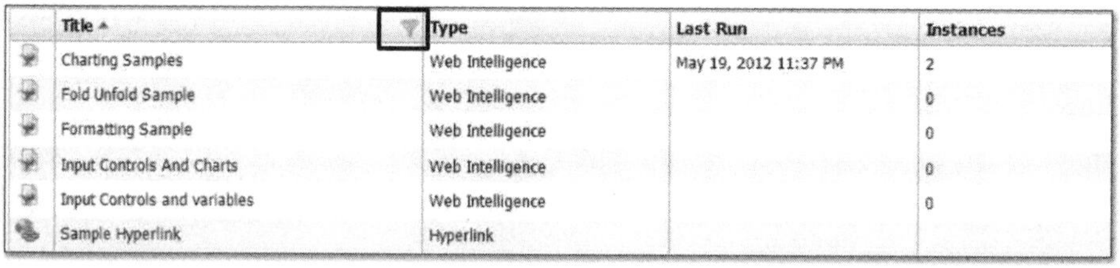

Title ▲	Type	Last Run	Instances
Charting Samples	Web Intelligence	May 19, 2012 11:37 PM	2
Fold Unfold Sample	Web Intelligence		0
Formatting Sample	Web Intelligence		0
Input Controls And Charts	Web Intelligence		0
Input Controls and variables	Web Intelligence		0
Sample Hyperlink	Hyperlink		

Figure 18.8 Filter Icon on the Column Heading

Click the icon to filter the content in the list. After applying the filter, the filtered results will only display in the list view, as shown in Figure 18.9.

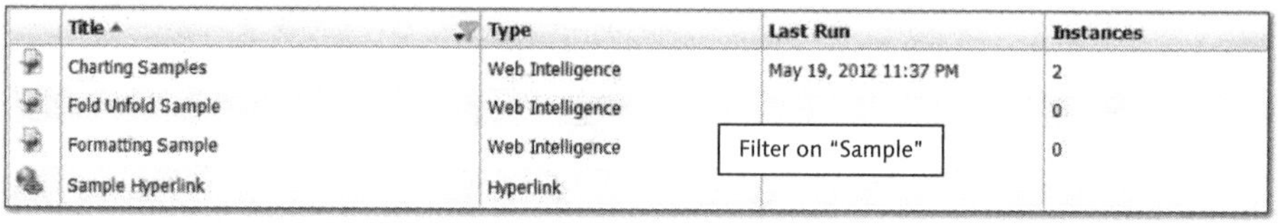

Title ▲	Type	Last Run	Instances
Charting Samples	Web Intelligence	May 19, 2012 11:37 PM	2
Fold Unfold Sample	Web Intelligence		0
Formatting Sample	Web Intelligence	Filter on "Sample"	0
Sample Hyperlink	Hyperlink		

Figure 18.9 Filters Results in List View

To remove the filter, select the title bar again, and select the CLEAR FILTER checkbox.

18.5 Creating Discussions

Users can create *discussions* for SAP BusinessObjects BI platform documents to post document-relevant information. These discussions can be organized in threads or as notes in a document. Figure 18.10 shows a sample discussion.

Figure 18.10 Discussion Sample

Discussions must first be enabled by your SAP BusinessObjects administrator for them to be created against your Web Intelligence documents in the BI Launch Pad. If you're integrated with SAP StreamWork or SAP Jam, you can post comments and participate in online discussions with other SAP StreamWork or SAP Jam users from within BI Launch Pad.

Discussions are located within the Details Panel of the selected document. Select the DISCUSSIONS drawer at the bottom of the DETAILS PANEL to view the notes and discussion threads.

18.5.1 Notes

To add a *note*, select the NEW MESSAGE icon, and type the SUBJECT and MESSAGE as relevant. You may also change the level of importance to HIGH or LOW, which will create a flag indicator on the note as shown in Figure 18.11.

You can edit notes you've created by selecting an already existing note and making any modifications to the previous text as necessary. If a note has replies in a discussion thread, then you may no longer modify it unless you have administrative rights. The same is true for deleting a note, which you would do by clicking the DELETE icon.

Figure 18.11 Note with High Importance Flag

18.5.2 Discussion Threads

You can create a *discussion thread* by replying to an existing note, as shown in Figure 18.12. After selecting a note, you have the option to reply to group or reply to sender. The REPLY TO GROUP option makes your response visible to everyone, while the REPLY TO SENDER displays your comments to only the sender of the note. After completing your comments and selecting POST, the note will display in the hierarchy of the conversation. The plus sign (+) indicates that there is a discussion thread associated with a note.

Figure 18.12 Discussion Thread

18.6 Summary

A variety of functionalities are available to the end user within the BI Launch Pad portal to customize the user experience. Creating hyperlinks, tracking data changes, searching within the environment, and managing discussions provide extra features to go above and beyond the capability of only reviewing a static report.

Chapter 19 discusses methods of sharing your Web Intelligence document with other users inside and outside the organization. From basic copy and paste functionality to robust scheduling, the BI Launch Pad offers a variety of options to answer the need for collaboration.

The core functionality of Web Intelligence involves querying, reporting, analyzing, and sharing information across the enterprise. The ability to share information quickly and easily is vital to successful business intelligence reporting. Web Intelligence 4.x provides enhanced sharing capabilities to schedule, publish, and burst your information to your internal and external audience.

19   Sharing a Web Intelligence Report

So far, you've learned how to create a Web Intelligence report, use advanced query techniques and multiple data providers, create unique charts, and format your report to create the most meaningful output for your audience. Now that your report design is complete, it's time to share your results with others.

Web Intelligence provides a variety of ways to distribute and share your reports across an organization, including many new features to enhance the publishing capabilities. From the enhanced ability to copy and paste data between Web Intelligence reports to the capability to create publications and burst them out for end-user consumption, you have a wide variety of options for sharing reports from within Web Intelligence or BI Launch Pad. We'll review each of these methods within this chapter to give you a thorough understanding of each of the options available to you.

19.1   Copying and Pasting

The most basic way to share a Web Intelligence report is a method used often in numerous tools: *copy* and *paste*. This powerful tool for sharing reports enables the end user to bring report parts into other applications and between Web Intelligence documents.

19.1.1 Copying and Pasting between Applications

Report parts can be pasted into spreadsheets, presentations, and word processing documents to integrate with additional business content.

From within the Report Panel on a Web Intelligence document, right-click on the report part that should be copied to display the menu options as shown in Figure 19.1. Select to either CUT or COPY your content.

Figure 19.1 Copy Options in Web Intelligence

Copying will copy the data contained within the report block in the format as it appears on your screen. When pasting into your destination application, you can select to paste with or without formatting. This is useful when copying the report part into a Word document or within a PowerPoint presentation so it will maintain its formatting.

Pasting as text will convert all elements to a text format. PASTE is helpful to copy the data itself into the columns in the spreadsheet without the formatting to perform further manipulation of the data within Excel. Figure 19.2 displays the COPY options in Excel.

Paste without
Formatting

⊿	A	B	C	D	E	F	G	H	I
1									
2		California	Colorado	DC	Florida	Illinois	Massachu	New York	Texas
3	2	$24,996	$5,301	$15,800	$6,040	$11,438	$13,296	$32,548	$30,692
4	3	$57,864	$13,868	$18,743	$21,166	$38,487	$7,398	$79,263	$100,268
5	4	$44,213	$7,822	$18,406	$8,576	$28,620	$8,849	$61,589	$92,043
6	5	$51,113	$14,696	$21,172	$19,949	$23,440	$9,255	$49,074	$67,557
7	Totals:	$178,186	$41,687	$74,120	$55,732	$101,985	$38,798	$222,474	$290,560
8									
9									
10									
11		California	Colorado	DC	Florida	Illinois	Massachu setts	New York	Texas
12	2	$24,996	$5,301	$15,800	$6,040	$11,438	$13,296	$32,548	$30,692
13	3	$57,864	$13,868	$18,743	$21,166	$38,487	$7,398	$79,263	$100,268
14	4	$44,213	$7,822	$18,406	$8,576	$28,620	$8,849	$61,589	$92,043
15	5	$51,113	$14,696	$21,172	$19,949	$23,440	$9,255	$49,074	$67,557
16	Totals:	$178,186	$41,687	$74,120	$55,732	$101,985	$38,798	$222,474	$290,560
17									
18									
19									
20									

Sheet1　Sheet2　Sheet3

Paste with
Formatting

Figure 19.2 Copy Options to Microsoft Excel

19.1.2 Copying and Pasting between Web Intelligence Documents

New capabilities in Web Intelligence allow you to copy and paste report parts between Web Intelligence documents. Select the report content that you want to copy into a new or existing report, and then select COPY from the right-click menu. Figure 19.3 shows the initial chart before it's copied into a new document using the NO DATA SOURCE option.

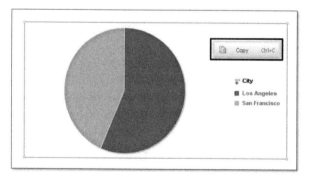

Figure 19.3 Copy on Right-Click Menu

After creating your new Web Intelligence document or navigating to an existing document, select PASTE from the right-click menu on your report canvas to paste your copied content. Figure 19.4 shows the copied results, including the objects available in the data pane when pasting the initial chart from Figure 19.3. In this example, additional data is shown because drill was enabled on the original report.

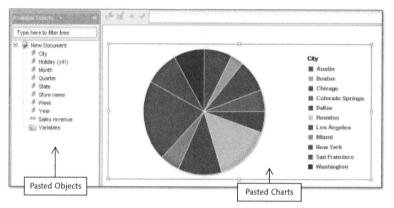

Figure 19.4 Pasted Chart and Result Objects

The query used in the report block is also brought over with the content as shown in Figure 19.5. This is a powerful tool for leveraging current content among different reports and expediting report creation.

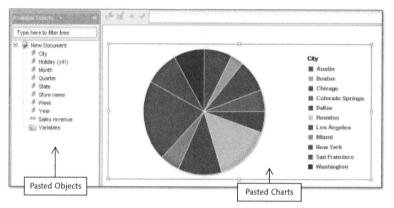

Figure 19.5 Query Results Copied between Web Intelligence Documents

The copy and paste functionality available in Web Intelligence 4.x provides a wealth of time-savings for the report designer.

19.2   Using the Send Feature in BI Launch Pad

You can easily share reports from within the BI Launch Pad portal provided that you've been given the rights by the system administrator. Another option available in BI Launch Pad is the ability to send Web Intelligence reports.

> **Note**
>
> Chapter 15 discusses how to view a Web Intelligence report in BI Launch Pad; refer to it for a review of this and other features within BI Launch Pad.

To activate the SEND option on the BI Launch Pad toolbar, you must first select the report to be sent so that it's highlighted in the Workspace Panel. The SEND button will become active.

Select the SEND button to display the dropdown list options shown for sending a document: BI Inbox, mail, FTP Location, File Location, or SAP StreamWork. The options available will depend on your configuration, so we'll examine them further.

19.2.1   BI Platform Inbox

You can send a Web Intelligence document to another SAP BusinessObjects BI platform user's inbox. The report will be displayed in his MY DOCUMENTS drawer in the inbox, as shown in Figure 19.6. The new report will be listed in the UNREAD MESSAGES IN MY INBOX panel on the HOME tab.

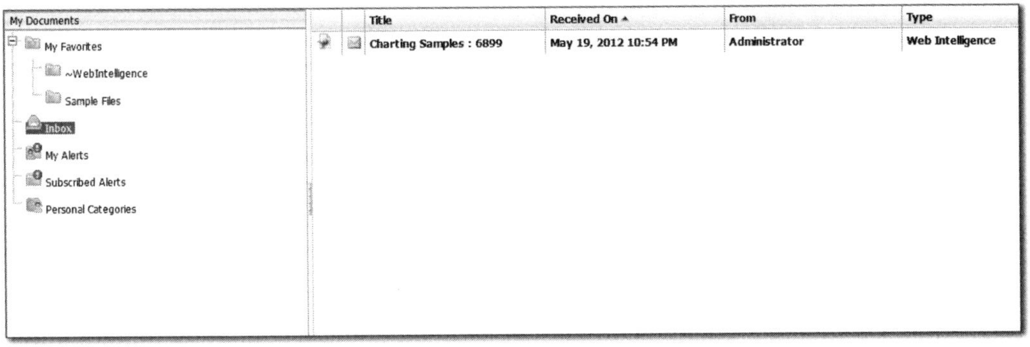

My Documents		Title	Received On ▲	From	Type
⊟ 📁 My Favorites		📄 **Charting Samples : 6899**	**May 19, 2012 10:54 PM**	**Administrator**	**Web Intelligence**
📁 ~WebIntelligence					
📁 Sample Files					
📁 Inbox					
📁 My Alerts					
📁 Subscribed Alerts					
📁 Personal Categories					

Figure 19.6 BI Inbox

Upon selecting the option to send a report to a BI Inbox, a dialog box appears to indicate the SEND options, as shown in Figure 19.7. When marking the USE DEFAULT SETTINGS checkbox at the top of the dialog box, the user won't be able to complete any custom settings. The default settings for distribution will be used as defined by the system administrator. To select personalized settings for the report destination, proceed to the settings discussed next.

Figure 19.7 shows the selection of users and SEND TO inbox settings.

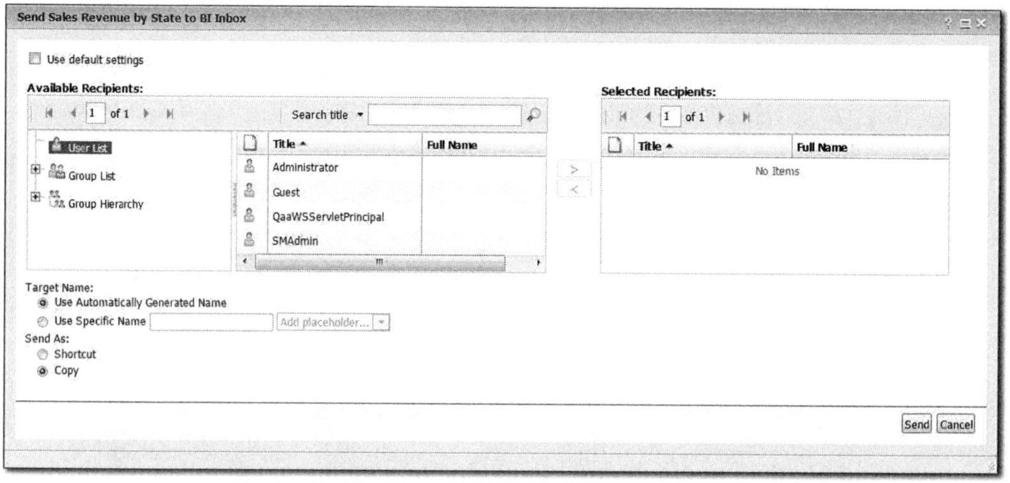

Figure 19.7 Send to BI Inbox Settings

You'll be prompted to select the destination BI Inbox from the USER LIST or from the GROUP LIST. Selecting from the GROUP LIST will enable you to select all members of a group to receive the same report in his BI Inbox. A search box is also available to aid in finding the appropriate name from the USER LIST or GROUP LIST. Select the arrows to move the names into the SELECTED RECIPIENTS box.

The next option is to designate a TARGET NAME by selecting one of the options:

▶ USE AUTOMATICALLY GENERATED NAME
This will use the current name of the document selected as the name of the report as it appears in the recipient's inbox.

▶ USE SPECIFIC NAME
This will enable you to generate a unique name to use for the report name as it will appear in the inbox. There is also a dropdown list to add placeholder values, which are shown in Table 19.1.

TITLE	Inserts the title as it exists when the report is sent
ID	Inserts the unique identifier number for the report as it exists in the system at the time the report is sent
OWNER	Inserts the name of the owner of the document as it appears in the properties
DATETIME	Inserts the current date and time when the report is sent
EMAIL ADDRESS	Inserts the email address the report is being sent to
USER FULL NAME	Inserts the user's full name
DOCUMENT NAME	Inserts the document name as it exists when the document is sent
FILE EXTENSION	Inserts the file extension of the document type

Table 19.1 Placeholder Values

Finally, the SEND AS option enables you to select whether the recipient will receive a shortcut or copy of the report. After these options have been marked, select SUBMIT to send your document to the recipient's BI Inbox.

Note

Use caution when sending a shortcut. If the recipient doesn't have the right to view reports in the folder where the original report resides, then he will be unable to view the report.

For example, if you send a report to another user that resides in your MY DOCUMENTS drawer (i.e., FAVORITES or INBOX) the recipient won't have the right to view these reports unless he has administrative level access to this location, which is unlikely.

19.2.2 Email

A Web Intelligence report can be sent to an email address for the user to view outside of BI Launch Pad. If Web Intelligence format is sent by email, the user must have an SAP BusinessObjects BI platform user account to view the Web Intelligence report because he'll need to enter his credentials to log on to the SAP BusinessObjects BI platform.

There is an additional placeholder in the list for the message body from those mentioned in Section 19.2.1. The placeholder of Viewer Hyperlink allows you to insert a hyperlink to the report within the BI Launch Pad environment. The user would select the hyperlink and log in to the SAP BusinessObjects BI platform environment to view the report. Figure 19.8 provides a view of the SEND TO email options.

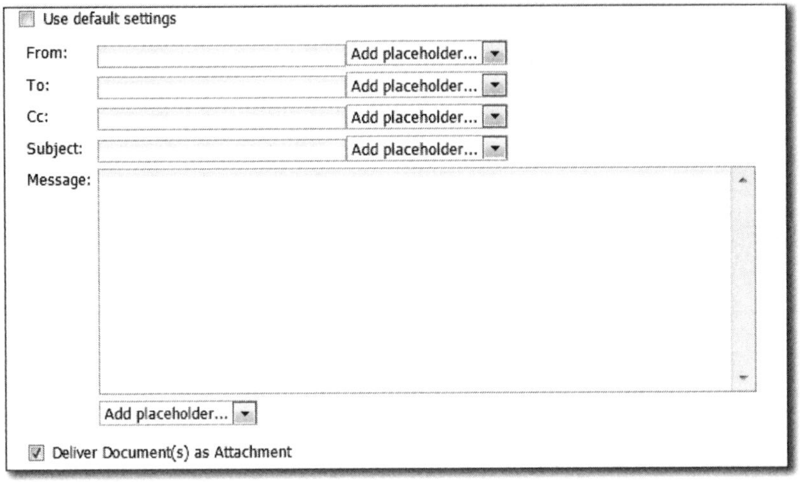

Figure 19.8 Send To Email Options

19.2.3 FTP Location

SEND TO FTP LOCATION enables the user to send the Web Intelligence document to a File Transfer Protocol (FTP) location. An FTP location is a standard network protocol location used to exchange files over a network.

Specific information regarding the FTP location must be specified in the options box, including HOST, PORT, USER NAME, PASSWORD, ACCOUNT, and DIRECTORY. This information will be specific to the FTP location the document is being sent to.

After the FTP-specific properties are set, the FILE NAME properties are specified, including whether the report is automatically generated or uses a specific name with placeholder options. Figure 19.9 shows the options for sending documents to FTP locations.

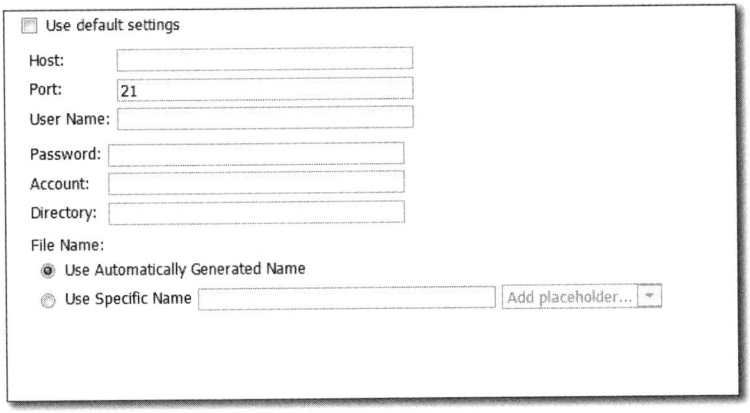

Figure 19.9 Send to FTP Location Options

19.2.4 File Location

The final possible location to send a report is a *file location*. Sometimes the best option may be to send PDF or Excel versions of Web Intelligence documents to a location on a shared drive that can be viewed by numerous users for collaborative purposes and ease of access.

When specifying a file location, the directory path must be specified as well as a USER NAME and PASSWORD for that directory if applicable. Then the file name property can be set to use an automatically generated name or a specific name with placeholder options. Figure 19.10 shows the file location options when scheduling a report.

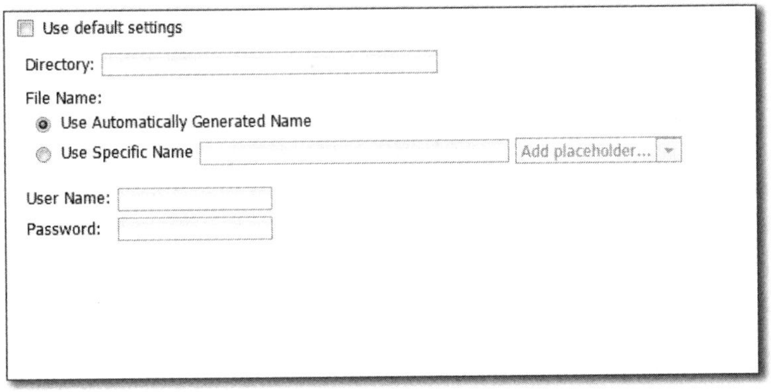

Figure 19.10 File Location Options

527

19.3   Exporting a Web Intelligence Report

Business users are often faced with the requirement of analyzing company data in Excel for even more detailed analysis or distributing reports in PDF format. Web Intelligence enables report consumers to export report data retrieved from the universe and database into one of the following file formats: Excel, PDF, CSV, or text.

19.3.1   Export Options in BI Launch Pad

The export options available to you within BI Launch Pad will depend on your user settings created by the SAP BusinessObjects administrator. There are drop-down menu options on the BI Launch Pad viewer toolbar when viewing a Web Intelligence report in BI Launch Pad. The EXPORT menu, as shown in Figure 19.11, includes the export options of PDF, Excel 2007, Excel, CSV Archive, and PDF in the dropdown list, as shown in Figure 19.12.

Figure 19.11 Export Button on the BI Launch Pad Viewer Toolbar

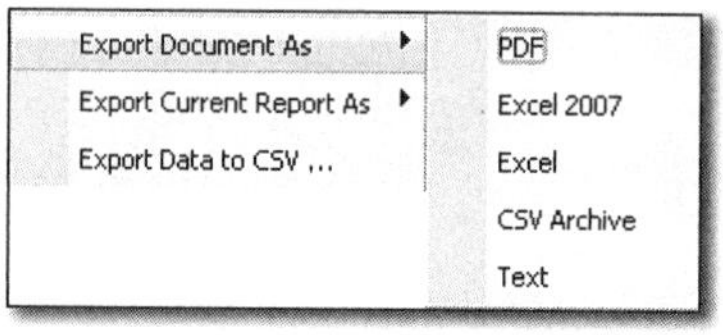

Figure 19.12 Export Options

Microsoft Excel

Saving with the Excel option will convert the Web Intelligence report into Excel format and allow you to open or save the report. The data in the tables of the Web Intelligence document will drop into the columns and rows of the Excel spreadsheet, as you saw with the Paste without Formatting option. Further manipulation of the data is then available in this format.

Microsoft Excel 2007

The Microsoft Excel 2007 option allows the user to save the document into the .XLSX format—effectively enabling up to one million rows of data to export into the spreadsheet. The previously mentioned EXCEL option saves the report into .XLS format, which limits the resulting rows to 65,000.

PDF

Selecting to save with the PDF option will convert the Web Intelligence report into PDF format and allow you to open or save the report. The report will appear similar to a picture, so further manipulation of the data will not be available. This is a preferable format to use when you want to maintain the report formatting and ensure that the data can't be manually changed in the future.

CSV Archive

The CSV Archive export option saves the Web Intelligence report as a compressed .zip file with a compilation of comma-separated value format files. It creates a separate CSV file for each report tab in your document. This enables you to import the report into a number of different programs outside of Excel. The CSV format gives you additional options for customizing the format of your CSV output file, letting you designate the specific format to make the CSV file compatible with the end program where you may be importing your data.

19.3.2 Export Options in Web Intelligence

The same options for export are also available within Web Intelligence. From the REPORT PANEL, select the EXPORT icon on the REPORT toolbar. Upon selecting the EXPORT option, a menu will display the options of PDF, EXCEL 2007, EXCEL, CSV ARCHIVE, and TEXT as your file output format for export, as shown in Figure 19.13.

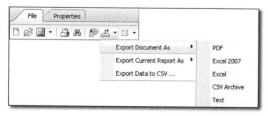

Figure 19.13 Export Options in the Web Intelligence Report Panel Toolbar

19.4   Scheduling a Web Intelligence Report

The processes discussed so far included manually generated methods of sharing Web Intelligence reports. A document can also be scheduled to be distributed out to recipients in a variety of formats and methods. This scheduling ability is available within BI Launch Pad from which you can schedule a report, view the latest instance of a scheduled report, and view the scheduling history of the report.

19.4.1   Scheduling in BI Launch Pad

After selecting the report to be scheduled in the Workspace panel, navigate to the MORE ACTIONS menu on the BI Launch Pad toolbar as shown in Figure 19.14. Select the SCHEDULE option to set the scheduling properties.

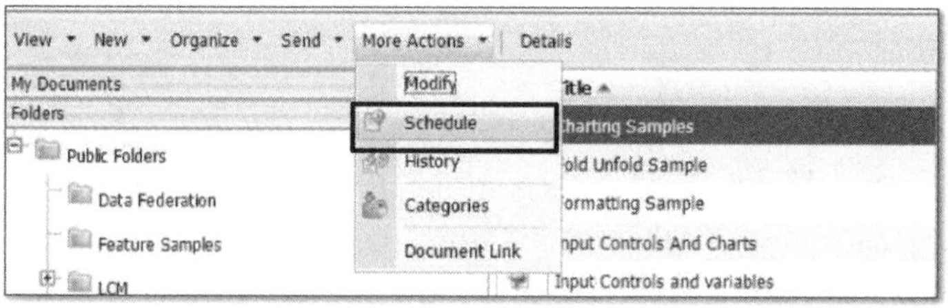

Figure 19.14 Selecting Schedule from the Actions Menu on the BI Launch Pad Toolbar

You'll be prompted to complete the following items:

▶ INSTANCE TITLE
Type in the title for this instance of the report, or use the default title already entered.

▶ RECURRENCE
Numerous options are available in the dropdown menu for selection dependent upon your report distribution requirements:

  ▶ Now: The Now option runs your report schedule immediately upon completion of your scheduling properties and selecting the SUBMIT button.

  ▶ ONCE: The ONCE option runs your report schedule once during the time frame specified in the RECURRENCE properties box, as shown in Figure 19.15.

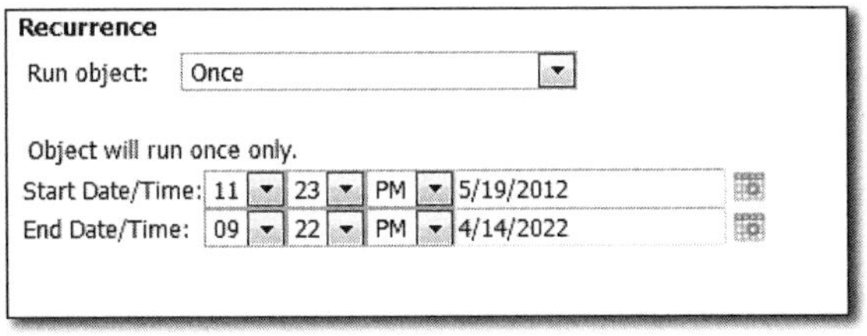

Figure 19.15 Once View

▶ HOURLY: The HOURLY option shown in Figure 19.16 runs the report at the hourly increments specified in the HOURS and MINUTES boxes in the RECURRENCE properties. The START and END DATE/TIMES are also specified.

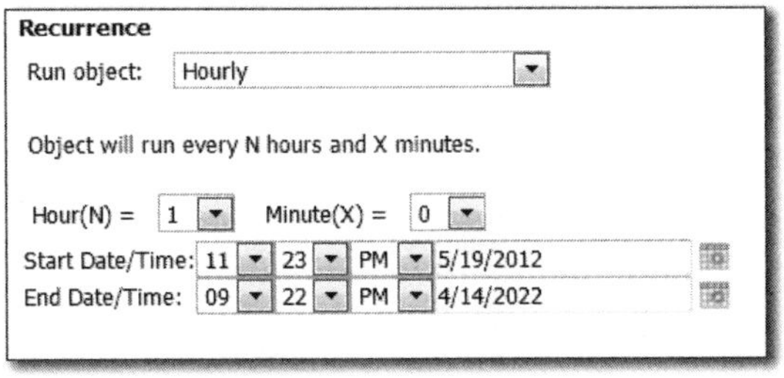

Figure 19.16 Hourly View

▶ DAILY: The DAILY option shown in Figure 19.17 runs the report daily for *N* number of days as specified in the RECURRENCE properties. The START and END DATE/TIMES are also specified.

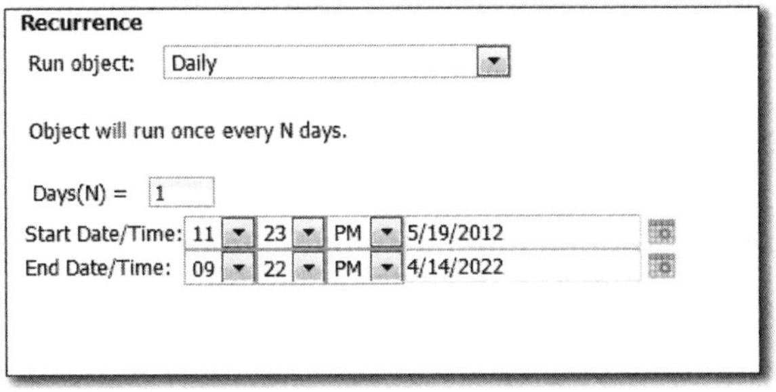

Figure 19.17 Daily View

▶ WEEKLY: The WEEKLY option shown in Figure 19.18 runs the report weekly on the day or days specified by the checkboxes. You also specify the START and END DATE/TIMES for when the schedule will start and end.

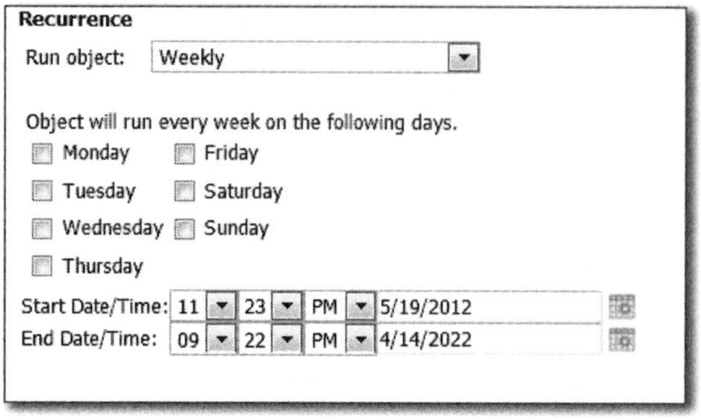

Recurrence

Run object: Weekly ▼

Object will run every week on the following days.
☐ Monday   ☐ Friday
☐ Tuesday   ☐ Saturday
☐ Wednesday ☐ Sunday
☐ Thursday

Start Date/Time: 11 ▼ 23 ▼ PM ▼ 5/19/2012
End Date/Time: 09 ▼ 22 ▼ PM ▼ 4/14/2022

Figure 19.18 Weekly View

▶ MONTHLY: The MONTHLY option shown in Figure 19.19 will run the report monthly EVERY N MONTHS as specified. A START and END DATE/TIME are also specified for this schedule.

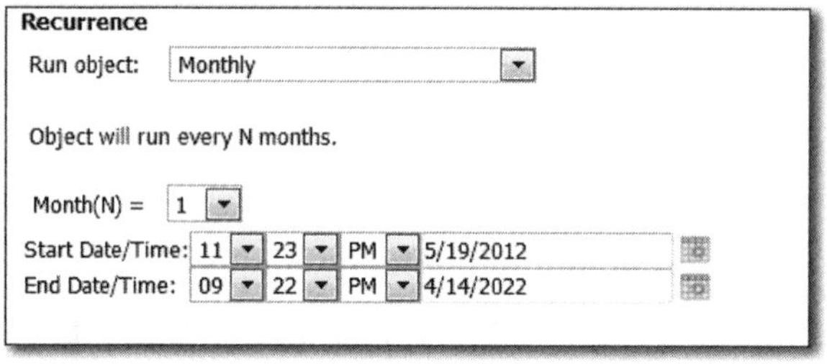

Recurrence

Run object: Monthly ▼

Object will run every N months.

Month(N) = 1 ▼
Start Date/Time: 11 ▼ 23 ▼ PM ▼ 5/19/2012
End Date/Time: 09 ▼ 22 ▼ PM ▼ 4/14/2022

Figure 19.19 Monthly View

▶ NTH DAY OF MONTH: The NTH DAY OF MONTH schedule shown in Figure 19.20 allows you to specify the exact day of the month to run the schedule. This can be especially useful for financial reports run for month-end reporting. A START and End DATE/TIME is also specified for the schedule.

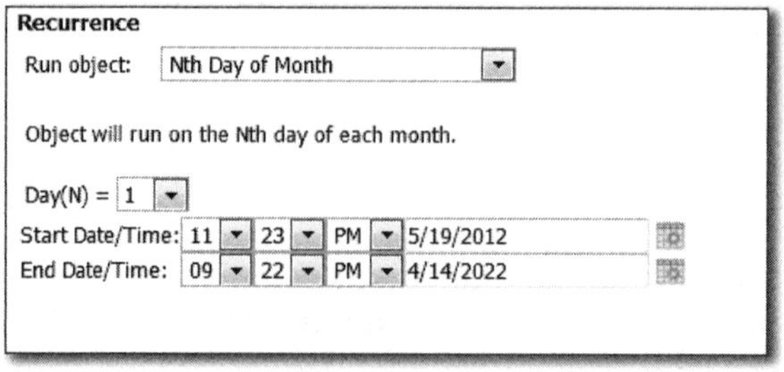

Recurrence

Run object: Nth Day of Month ▼

Object will run on the Nth day of each month.

Day(N) = 1 ▼
Start Date/Time: 11 ▼ 23 ▼ PM ▼ 5/19/2012
End Date/Time: 09 ▼ 22 ▼ PM ▼ 4/14/2022

Figure 19.20 Nth Day of Month View

▶ 1ST MONDAY OF MONTH: This schedule allows you to run the report on the first Monday of every month. This can be useful for monthly reports to maintain consistency in the run date. You'll also specify the schedule START and END DATE/TIME, as shown in Figure 19.21.

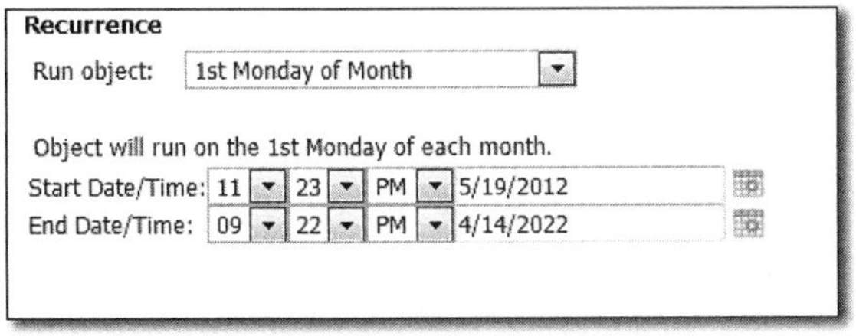

Figure 19.21 1st Monday of Month View

▶ LAST DAY OF MONTH: The LAST DAY OF MONTH option will run the report on the final day of each month. You'll specify the schedule START and END DATE/TIME. Figure 19.22 shows the options available when selecting the Last Day of Month recurrence option.

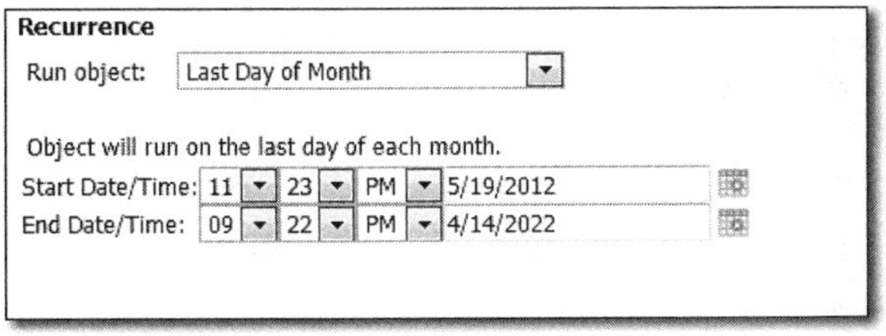

Figure 19.22 Last Day of Month View

▶ X DAY OF NTH WEEK OF THE MONTH: This schedule, as shown in Figure 19.23, enables you to specify the week and day of each month that the schedule should be run. For example, you can specify to run the report on the third Thursday of each month. In this case, you would specify week number 3 and the day of Thursday. You'll also specify the schedule START and END DATE/TIME.

▶ CALENDAR: Calendars need to be set up in the CMC by the system administrator for them to be seen here. If a customized calendar is set up, you can specify to use them here, as shown in Figure 19.24. These enable you to have more specific options on dates to run the report.

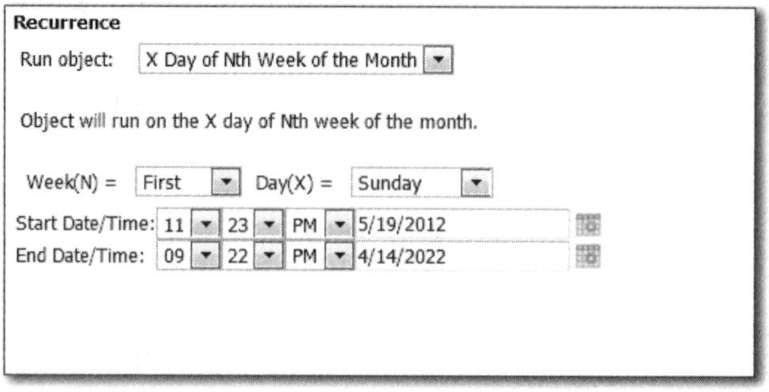

Figure 19.23 X Day of Nth Week of the Month View

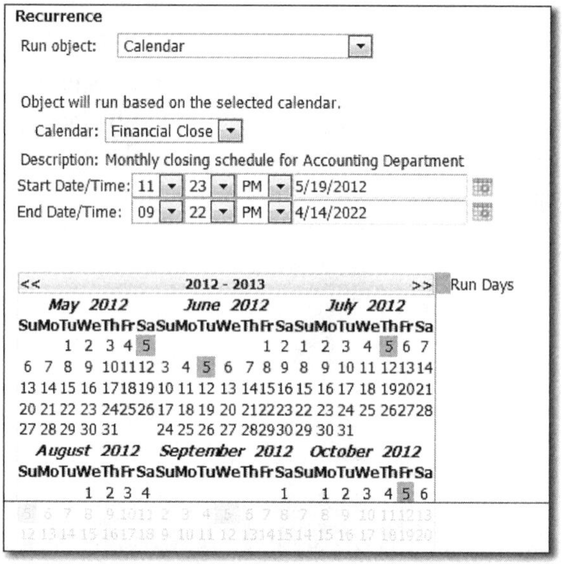

Figure 19.24 Calendar View

▶ FORMATS AND DESTINATIONS

Output formats include Web Intelligence, Excel, and Adobe Acrobat. Available destinations include BI Inbox, file locations, FTP server, and email recipients.

Destination options and settings change depending on the OUTPUT FORMAT DETAILS selected in the OUTPUT FORMAT AND DESTINATION section. These settings are the same as discussed in Section 19.2.

When you check the CLEANUP INSTANCE AFTER SCHEDULING box, the instance will be removed from the history after it has been sent out to the selected recipients. This removes unnecessary extra copies of the report to maximize disk space.

▶ CACHING

Select the formats to be used to pre-load the cache when scheduling (only applicable if scheduling in Web Intelligence format). Available formats to cache include: Excel, standard HTML, and Adobe Acrobat. Select the formatting locales to be used to pre-load the cache when scheduling. The available locales will show in the left box. You must select the arrow to move to the SELECTED LOCALES box to specify your selection.

▶ EVENTS

Events are set up by your system administrator in the CMC. Available events are listed in the box on the left. Select the arrows to move your selections to the EVENTS TO WAIT FOR box. You may also select the event in the AVAILABLE SCHEDULE EVENTS box to move to the EVENTS TO TRIGGER on completion. This will specify which events must occur for the job to be triggered. This can be useful to ensure a nightly data load job has completed loading the new data before the report is run.

▶ SCHEDULING SERVER GROUP

This option enables you to specify a specific server group to use when scheduling your document. The usual setting is to use the first available server. Note that if a specified server is busy, your job will likely fail. The SCHEDULING SERVER GROUP options are detailed in Figure 19.25.

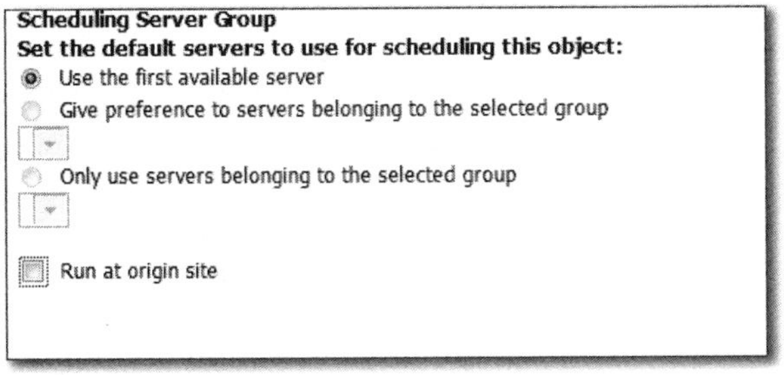

Figure 19.25 Scheduling Server Group Box

19.4.2   Viewing Latest Instance

After scheduling a report, you can view the latest instance of the report. After selecting the report name in the WORKSPACE PANEL, select the MORE ACTIONS menu on the BI Launch Pad toolbar to view the dropdown list options. Figure 19.26 displays the actions available when viewing a report.

If a report has been scheduled previously, then the VIEW LATEST INSTANCE option will appear in the menu. The latest instance shows you the last scheduled version of the report as distributed to your selected recipients.

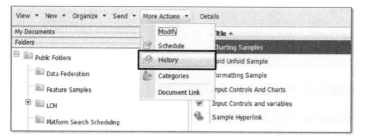

Figure 19.26 Action Menu Options

19.4.3 Viewing History

You are also able to see the history of all instances scheduled for a report by selecting HISTORY from the ACTIONS dropdown list. The HISTORY view will show a listing of all scheduled reports, including the date/time of the instance, title, run by, parameters (if applicable), format, and status.

In Figure 19.27, the instance in the HISTORY view is showing a status of RUNNING. This indicates that the report schedule is currently running and not yet complete to view. Additional radio buttons and checkboxes at the top of the HISTORY view can aid you in filtering a longer list of instances to customize your view. These options include SHOW ALL, SHOW COMPLETED, SHOW ONLY INSTANCES OWNED BY ME, and FILTER INSTANCES BY TYPE.

History – Charting Samples					
View ▾	Organize ▾	Send ▾	More Actions ▾		⟳ ⟼ ◀ 1 of 1 ▶ ⟻

Instance Time ▾	Title	Status	Created By	Type	Parameters
May 19, 2012 11:37 PM	Charting Samples	Running	Administrator	Microsoft Excel	
May 19, 2012 11:35 PM	Charting Samples	Success	Administrator	Microsoft Excel	

Figure 19.27 History View

19.5 Summary

The collaboration features available in Web Intelligence 4.x make it a powerful business intelligence reporting tool. The manual sharing capabilities of copy and paste, or sending to a user or group, enable quick and easy collaboration. Scheduling enables the user to automate the process.

Chapter 20 discusses another exciting feature available for sharing report content called publications. Publications provide a powerful tool for creating robust, customized distributions of documents contained within the SAP BusinessObjects BI platform.

The SAP BusinessObjects platform can be harnessed to distribute personalized reports, known as publications, to subscribers, either inside or outside of your organization.

20 Report Scheduling and Distribution with Publications

The primary strength of Web Intelligence is that it allows business users to query and manipulate corporate data with minimal assistance from corporate IT. However, the SAP BusinessObjects BI platform also includes powerful capabilities for automatically distributing data to business users using a feature called *publications* and known more generically in the business intelligence industry as *report bursting*.

A *publication* is a collection of documents intended for distribution to a mass audience, often personalized to target this group specifically. You can define the publication metadata surrounding these documents, such as document sources, recipients, and personalization rules, from either the BI Launch Pad or the Central Management Console (CMC). Publication subscribers can view publications through the secure BI Launch Pad portal or via email.

Publications have been part of the SAP BusinessObjects platform since an add-on product named Broadcast Agent Publisher was introduced on the classic (pre-SAP BusinessObjects Enterprise XI) SAP BusinessObjects platform. Beginning with SAP BusinessObjects Enterprise XI Release 2, when Desktop Intelligence was reintroduced to the platform (SAP BusinessObjects Enterprise XI Release 1 did not include Desktop Intelligence), publications could be created only in the Desktop Intelligence format. Additionally, a recipient required an SAP BusinessObjects BI license to receive a publication.

SAP BusinessObjects Enterprise XI 3.0 added significant new capabilities to publications. For the first time, publications could be created using SAP Crystal

Reports or Web Intelligence, in addition to Desktop Intelligence. Also, a new feature called dynamic recipients permitted organizations to schedule and distribute publications via email for users who weren't license holders on the SAP BusinessObjects BI platform. This enhancement was particularly useful for distributing publications to customers outside the traditional walls of the organization. Dynamic recipients also made the distribution of publications more cost effective, as no user license was required.

The SAP BusinessObjects BI 4 platform continues the features introduced in SAP BusinessObjects Enterprise XI 3.0, but no longer supports publications based on Desktop Intelligence. Desktop Intelligence documents can be converted to the Web Intelligence format using the Report Conversion Tool (see Appendix A).

The focus of this chapter is on publications created using SAP BusinessObjects Web Intelligence. For publications that use SAP Crystal Reports, refer to *100 Things You Should Know about Reporting with SAP Crystal Reports* (SAP PRESS, 2012) by Coy W. Yonce, III.

Publications allow critical business information such as corporate sales figures to be pushed directly to recipients and complement the self-service features of the SAP BusinessObjects BI platform. As necessary, each recipient can receive a personalized version of the publication that displays only data of interest to him; this personalization can also serve as a security measure, limiting access to sensitive data. For example, employees in the Asia Pacific region will receive a publication with only their data; data for the Americas and EMEA regions will not appear in their copy of the publication.

One of the key features of publications is its efficient use of database resources during personalization, known as single-pass report bursting. Instead of executing unique database queries for each publication recipient, the publication executes nonpersonalized database queries. By applying one or more report filters to the source document, you can make sure that the data is personalized after it's retrieved from the database. Publications use Web Intelligence report filters, so one popular practice is to distribute publications in a neutral format such as Adobe PDF or Microsoft Excel because a savvy user could potentially remove the report filtering from the original document and view sensitive corporate data.

As we look ahead to the publication creation process, let's begin by understanding the various roles that are involved.

20.1   Publication Roles

Four roles are involved in the creation and consumption of a publication: administrator, report designer, publisher, and recipient. The first three roles can be filled by a single person with access to both the BI Launch Pad and CMC. In larger organizations, these roles are often divided among multiple people:

▶ **Administrator**
The SAP BusinessObjects administrator ensures that the SAP BusinessObjects BI environment is functioning, that security roles are defined, and that desired destinations such as Simple Mail Transfer Protocol (SMTP) email or mobile devices are configured. These tasks are performed in the CMC.

▶ **Report designer**
This individual will use the techniques outlined in this book to create one or more Web Intelligence documents to form the foundation of a publication. These Web Intelligence documents can be created using either Web Intelligence from the BI Launch Pad or the Web Intelligence Rich Client.

▶ **Publisher**
This individual creates the publication and configures its metadata, including the personalization information. Publications can be created by users from the BI Launch Pad or administrators from the CMC.

▶ **Recipient**
This individual receives the publication, typically via email, although the BI Launch Pad Inbox can also be used for both desktop and mobile access.

Let's examine each of the four roles in greater detail.

20.1.1   The SAP BusinessObjects Administrator

The SAP BusinessObjects administrator has several important tasks. First, he is responsible for ensuring that the user account used to schedule the publication has access to the public folders containing the publication source documents, universes, and connections on which those documents are based. He must also ensure that the desired destination (inbox, email, FTP, file system) is properly configured on the publication job server. Lastly, the administrator will create and manage profiles that are used to personalize publications for enterprise recipients. Each of these administrative tasks requires access to various management areas of the CMC.

20.1.2 The Web Intelligence Report Designer

The Web Intelligence report designer is responsible for creating one or more source documents for the publication.

All documents in the publications must be of a single type—in other words, they must all be Web Intelligence documents—because it isn't possible to combine Web Intelligence documents and SAP Crystal Reports into the same publication.

Although the report designer doesn't need to understand the inner mechanics of the publication mechanism, the report designer must understand the reporting requirements and the personalization requirements. Personalization is applied by the publication server to documents as report filters, which are presented in Chapter 10 of this book.

20.1.3 The Publication Designer

The publication designer uses either the CMC or the BI Launch Pad to build a new publication. This chapter focuses mainly on this role.

20.1.4 The Recipient

The publication recipient has the easiest responsibilities of the four roles. The recipient simply checks his BI Inbox or corporate email inbox to see whether a publication has been sent. A recipient can also subscribe or unsubscribe to a publication from the BI Launch Pad.

20.2 Creating a Publication

We'll use a single Web Intelligence document based on the eFashion universe as the basis of our publication. The sample document is shown in Figure 20.1.

The query in the publication source will retrieve all eFashion stores; however, the publication's metadata will ensure that each recipient only receives data for one store by applying a report filter to the store name object in the report section.

To begin creating a new publication, open the BI Launch Pad, and choose PUBLICATION from the NEW menu on the main toolbar, as shown in Figure 20.2.

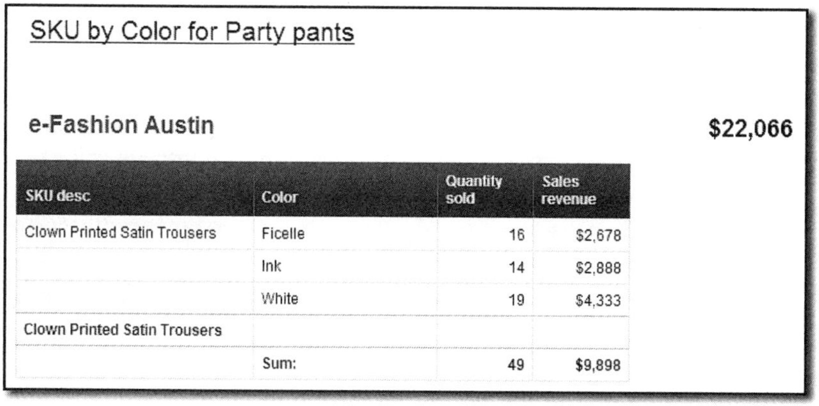

SKU by Color for Party pants

e-Fashion Austin			$22,066
SKU desc	**Color**	**Quantity sold**	**Sales revenue**
Clown Printed Satin Trousers	Ficelle	16	$2,678
	Ink	14	$2,888
	White	19	$4,333
Clown Printed Satin Trousers			
	Sum:	49	$9,898

Figure 20.1 Sample eFashion Publication

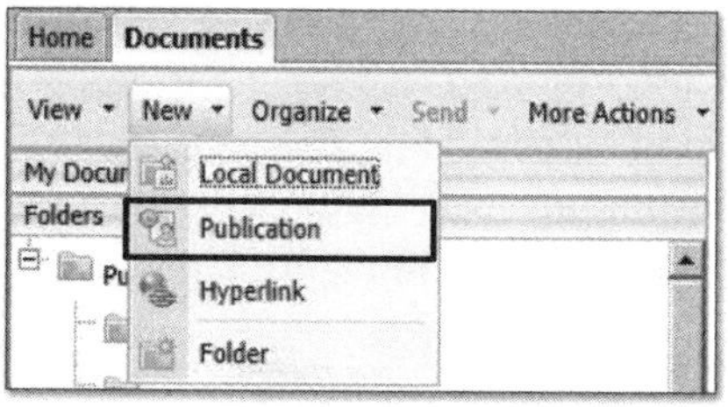

Figure 20.2 Select Publication from the New Shortcut Icon in BI Launch Pad

20.2.1 Naming the Publication

First you must give the publication a name. The sample publication is called "eFashion Publication Dynamic", as shown in Figure 20.3. Adding a DESCRIPTION and KEYWORDS that help identify the publication is optional.

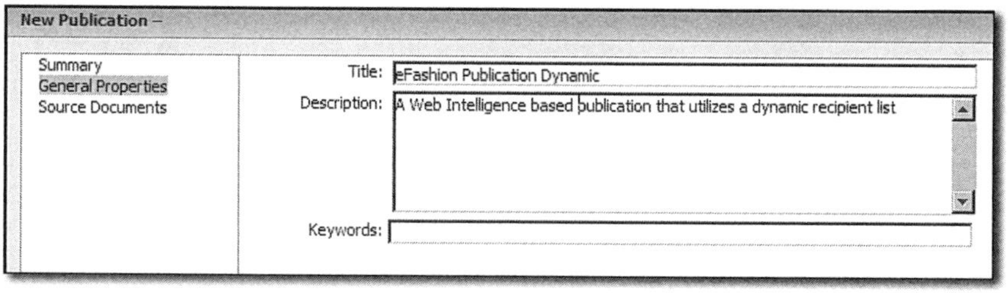

Figure 20.3 Publication General Properties

543

20.2.2 Choosing the Source Documents

Choose one or more source documents from the SOURCE DOCUMENTS box, as shown in Figure 20.4.

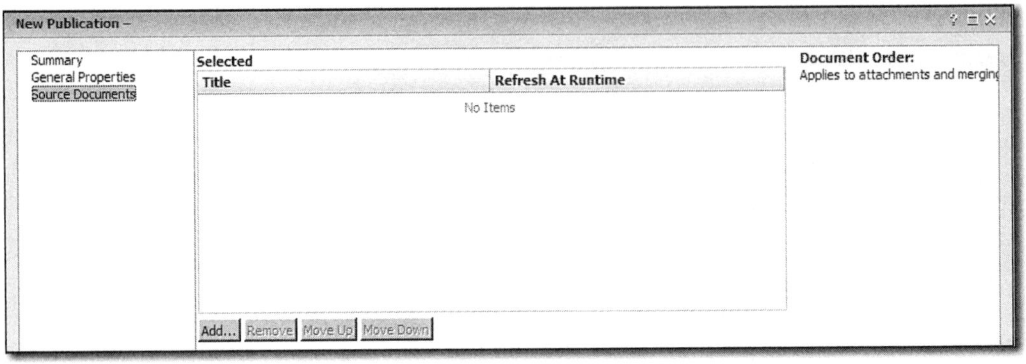

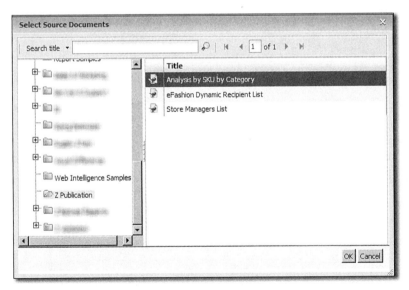

Figure 20.4 Source Documents

Now choose one or more Web Intelligence documents. Our example uses a single document named ANALYSIS BY SKU BY CATEGORY, as shown in Figure 20.5.

Figure 20.5 Source Document Selection

After you've entered the general properties and source documents, you'll see additional menus on the left side of the screen, as shown in Figure 20.6.

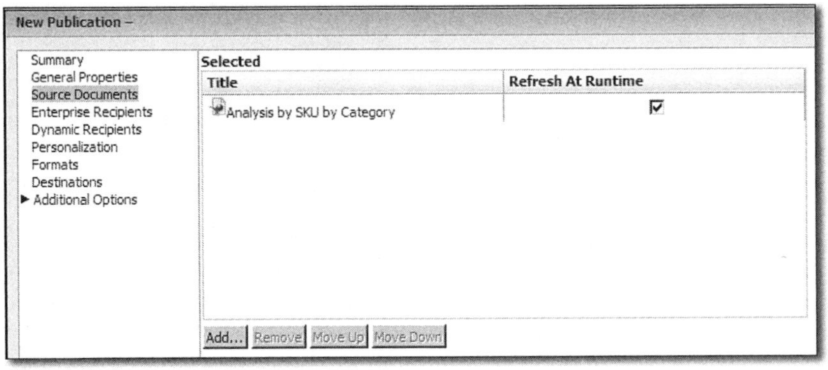

Figure 20.6 Source Documents

20.2.3 Choosing Enterprise Recipients

A publication may have enterprise recipients, dynamic recipients, or both. You can add enterprise recipients as individual users or as groups using the selection box, as shown in Figure 20.7. In our example, a group named eFashion has been chosen.

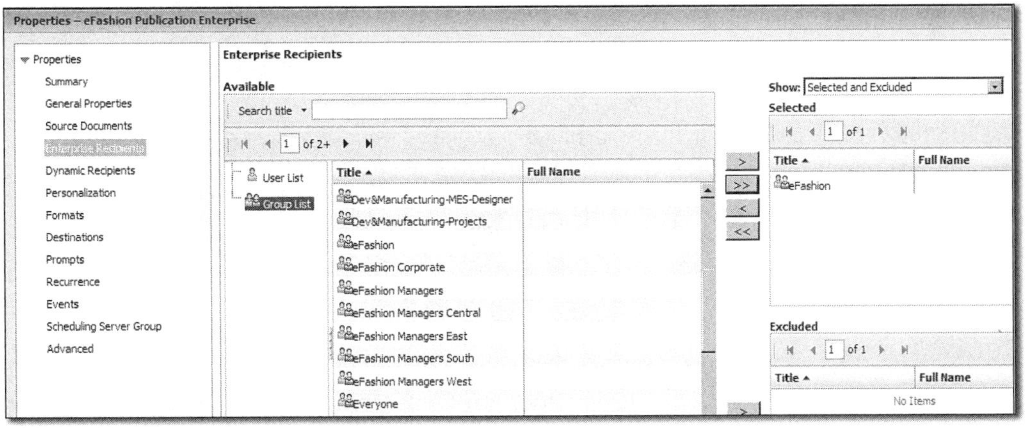

Figure 20.7 Enterprise Recipients

545

> **Note**
>
> Keep in mind that users with access to the folder containing the publication can sub-scribe or unsubscribe themselves via the BI Launch Pad, which will be described later in the chapter.

Personalization with a Global Profile

If the SAP BusinessObjects administrator has created a suitable profile in the CMC, it may be applied to the publication. The administrator must grant viewing rights to the profile to the publication author; otherwise, the profile will not appear in the author's dropdown list. In Figure 20.8, the profile EFASHION MAN-AGER PROFILE is used to personalize the publication.

The inner workings of the profile and which universes and objects it filters can only be examined using the CMC.

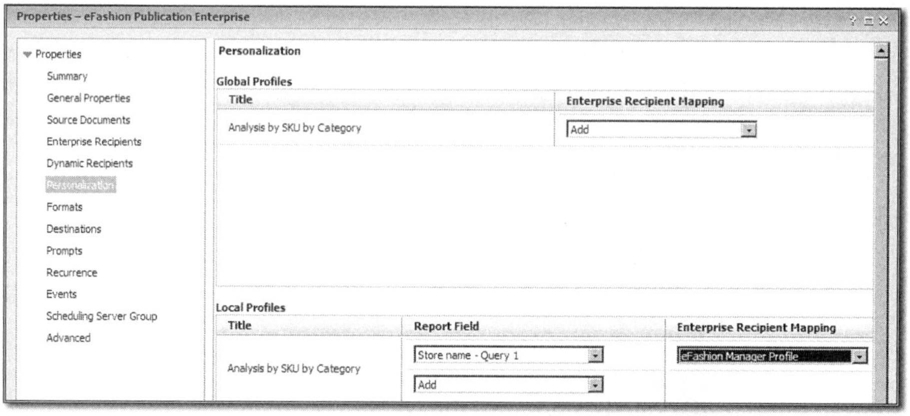

Figure 20.8 Personalization with a Global Profile

Personalization Using a Local Profile

Personalization for enterprise recipients can also be accomplished by a local pro-file, as shown in Figure 20.9. A local profile filters a report field in the Web Intel-ligence source document. Although local profile filters can be used to filter universe objects, they are typically employed when the source document con-tains a report variable to be filtered that isn't present in the universe.

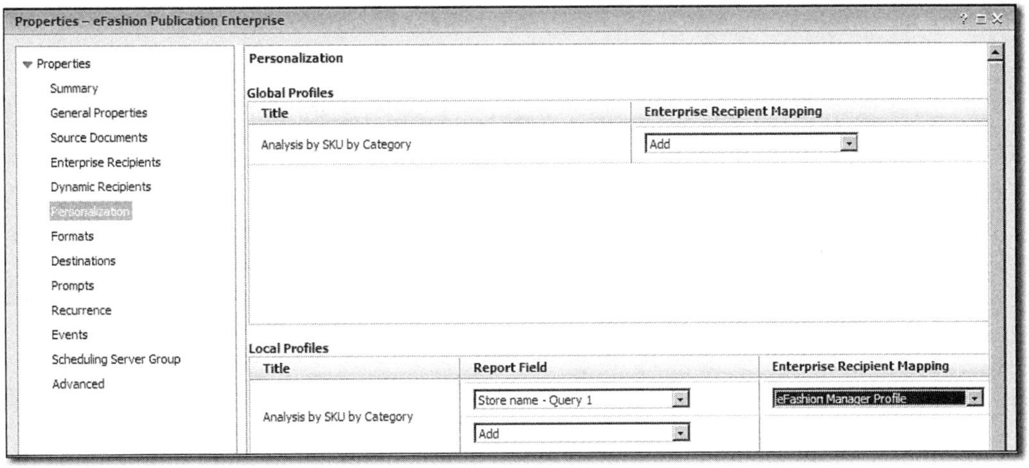

Figure 20.9 Personalization with a Local Profile

20.2.4 Choosing Dynamic Recipients

Dynamic recipients are specified using a dynamic recipient provider, which is a report authored using either SAP Crystal Reports or Web Intelligence. In this example, we've selected Web Intelligence as the WEB INTELLIGENCE REPORT DYNAMIC RECIPIENT PROVIDER, as shown in Figure 20.10.

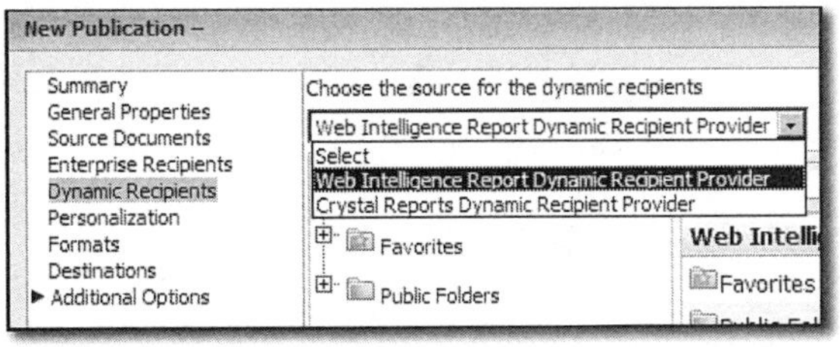

Figure 20.10 Web Intelligence Report Dynamic Recipient Provider

Next, you need to select the desired Web Intelligence report. Figure 20.11 shows eFASHION DYNAMIC RECIPIENT LIST as our selection.

After the dynamic recipient provider report is selected, choose the data provider containing the dynamic recipient list, as shown in Figure 20.12. In our example, the default QUERY 1 contains the dynamic recipient list.

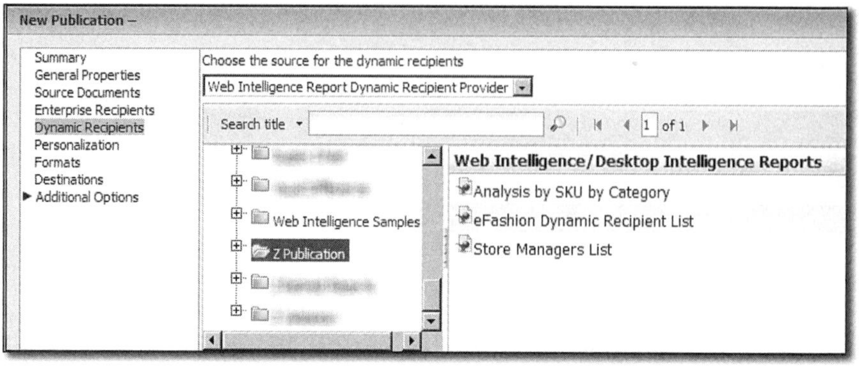

Figure 20.11 Choosing eFashion Dynamic Recipient List Report

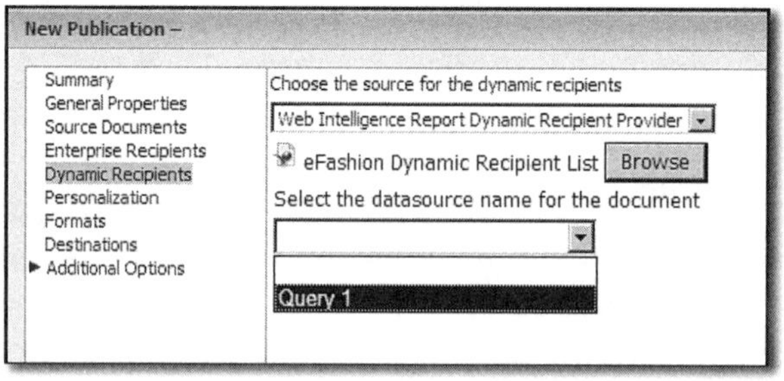

Figure 20.12 Selecting the Data Source Name for the Document

After the data provider is chosen, three fields appear for the RECIPIENT IDENTIFIER, FULL NAME, and EMAIL of the recipients. These fields should be mapped to the proper objects in the data provider, as shown in Figure 20.13.

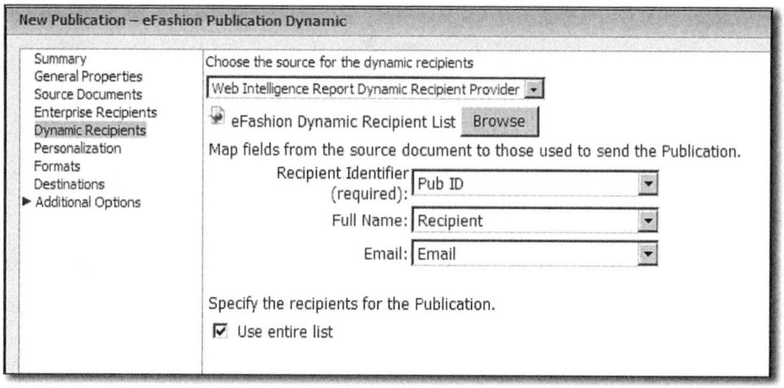

Figure 20.13 Map Fields from the Source Document

Personalization with a Local Profile

After the dynamic recipients are specified, the publication can be personalized for each recipient using additional fields in the Dynamic Recipient Provider report, as shown in Figure 20.14. In our example, each recipient will receive a publication for a single store name.

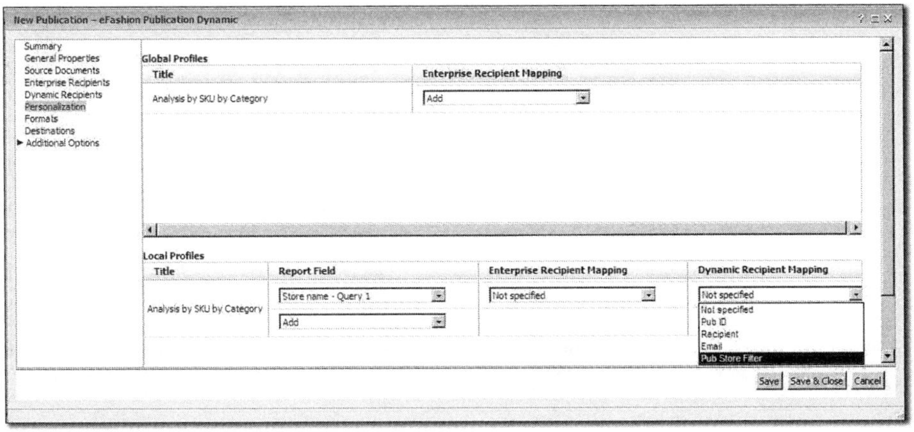

Figure 20.14 Personalizing Dynamic Recipients with Local Profile

20.2.5 Setting Publication Properties

A variety of settings are available to format your publication with your audience in mind.

Formats

Publications can be delivered in four formats: Web Intelligence, Microsoft Excel, Adobe Acrobat (PDF), and MIME HTML (MHTML), as shown in Figure 20.15.

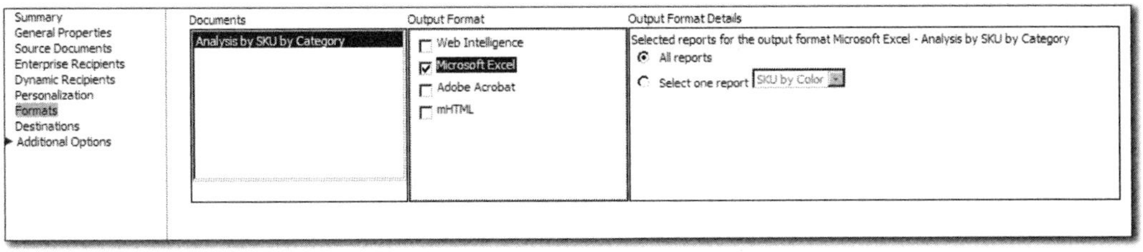

Figure 20.15 Formats

Destinations

As with any scheduled job, you can send publications to the five standard destinations: DEFAULT ENTERPRISE LOCATION, BI INBOX, EMAIL, FTP SERVER, and FILE SYSTEM, as shown in Figure 20.16. Except for the DEFAULT ENTERPRISE LOCATION, the other destinations may require additional configuration by the SAP Business-Objects administrator.

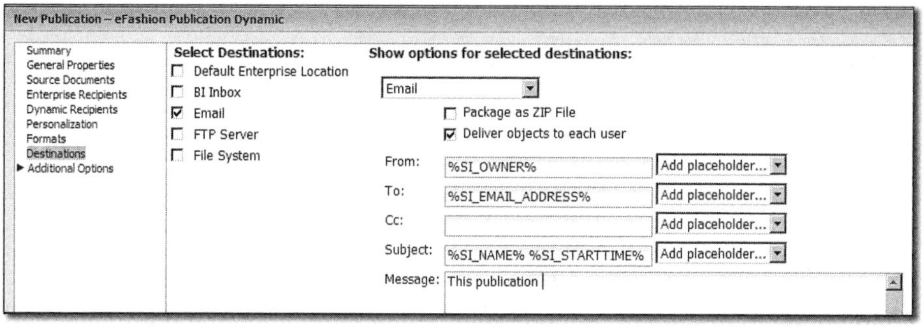

Figure 20.16 Destinations

Prompts

If any of the source documents contain prompts, they can be modified. Figure 20.17 shows a default value of PARTY PANTS for the publication source document.

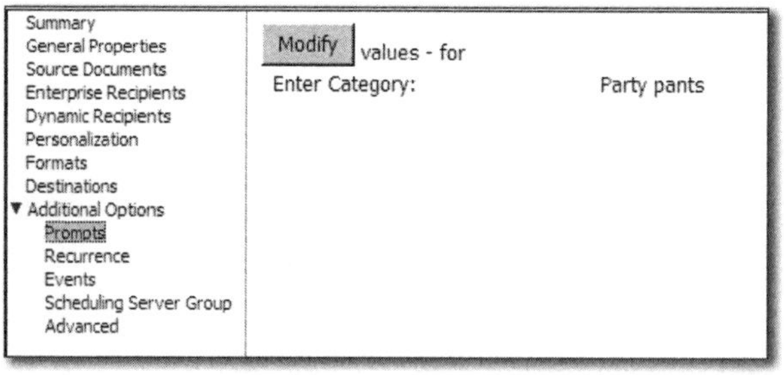

Figure 20.17 Prompts

Recurrence

Publications support all of the standard recurrence intervals of the SAP Business-Objects BI platform, as shown in Figure 20.18. For more information about scheduling recurrence options, see Chapter 19.

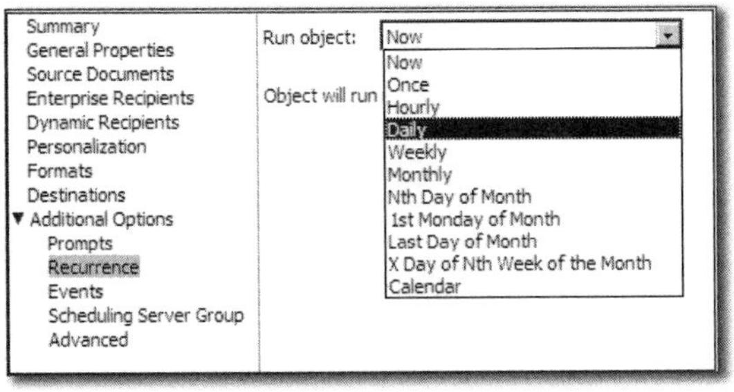

Figure 20.18 Recurrence

Events

Publications support all of the standard event types (file, schedule, and custom) of the SAP BusinessObjects BI platform, as shown in Figure 20.19. Again, see Chapter 19 for more information.

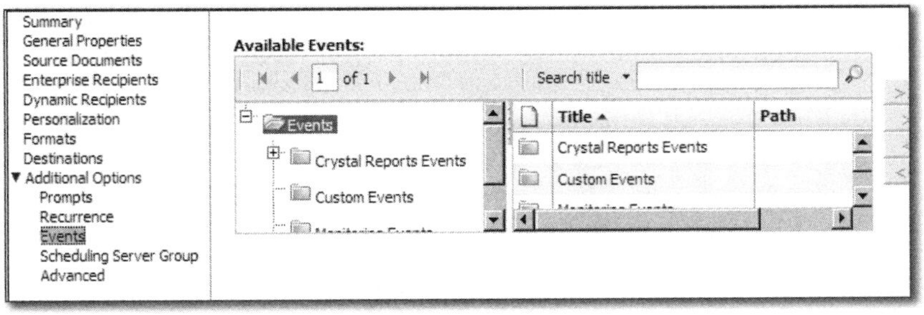

Figure 20.19 Events

Scheduling Server Group

Server groups are created and managed by the SAP BusinessObjects administrator to specify specific resources in the SAP BusinessObjects BI platform cluster, as shown in Figure 20.20. Ask your SAP BusinessObjects administrator if your publication should use a server group that assigns long-running jobs to the largest, fastest machines in the SAP BusinessObjects BI server cluster.

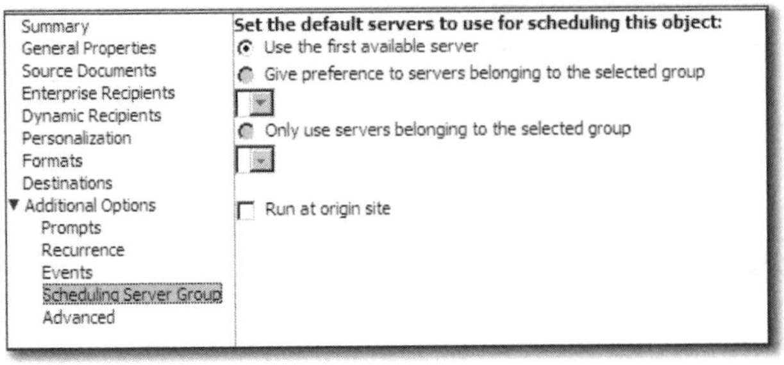

Figure 20.20 Scheduling Server Group

Advanced Options

Advanced options is where you control profile resolution, display of users who have no personalization applied, and the method for report bursting, as shown in Figure 20.21.

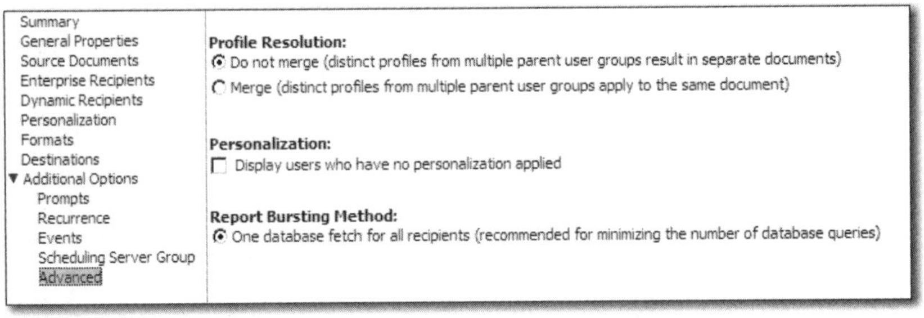

Figure 20.21 Advanced Options

Let's examine these options.

Profile Resolution

In certain cases, an enterprise recipient may be defined in more than one profile. The profile resolution specifies how the publication should behave for these recipients. If Do not merge is chosen, the recipient will receive multiple distinct documents for each profile in which the recipient is defined. If Merge is chosen, the distinct profiles will be combined, and the recipient will receive a single document.

Personalization

By selecting the DISPLAY USERS WHO HAVE NO PERSONALIZATION APPLIED box, publishers can see which subscribed recipients have no personalization applied, meaning that those recipients will see the entire unfiltered source documents. Depending on business requirements, it may be totally appropriate for corporate executives and senior managers to appear on this list, as their role in the organization dictates that they should have visibility to all corporate operations.

Report Bursting Method

Publications based on Web Intelligence can only have the option of one database fetch for all recipients. Additional report bursting methods exist for publications based on SAP Crystal Reports.

Summary Screen

After the publisher has completed the publication setup, it's helpful to return to the SUMMARY screen, shown in Figure 20.22, to review all options you've selected.

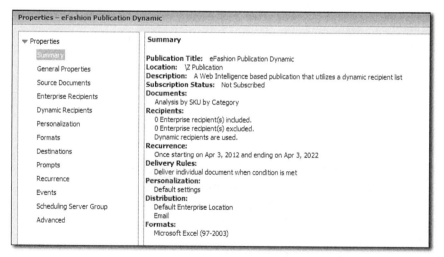

Figure 20.22 Summary Screen

20.2.6 Testing the Publication

Test mode, shown in Figure 20.23, allows the publisher to validate a publication before sending it to actual recipients. All instances of the publication will be sent to the publisher—not the actual recipients—so the publication behavior can be tested. Testing the publication is an important step to ensure that sensitive corporate data is not inadvertently revealed by the publication.

Figure 20.23 Test Mode

20.3 Mobile Publications

Using the latest version of SAP BusinessObjects Mobile BI (available for iOS and Android devices), publications scheduled to the BI Inbox can be viewed on a mobile device, allowing you to deliver personalized analytics nearly anywhere (see Figure 20.24).

Figure 20.24 BI Inbox in the SAP BusinessObjects Mobile BI Application (iOS Shown)

To demonstrate, we loaded a Desktop Intelligence XI R2 document from an old Business Intelligence Archive Resource (BIAR) file into SAP BusinessObjects BI 4.1, which can host Desktop Intelligence documents as part of the Desktop Intelligence Compatibility Pack. Next, we converted the document to Web Intelligence using the Report Conversion Tool. Finally, we created a personalized publication to enterprise recipients using the techniques covered in this chapter, scheduling to the BI Inbox. The result is shown in Figure 20.25.

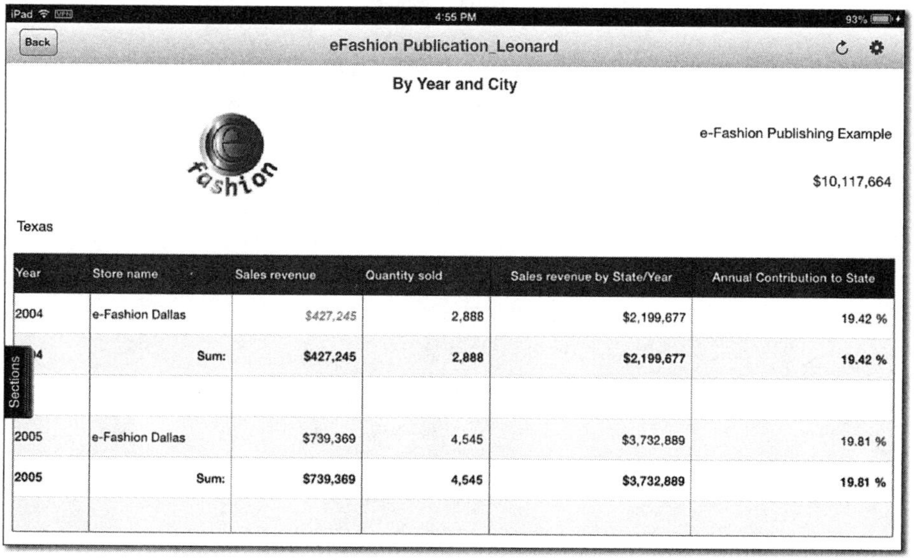

Figure 20.25 Web Intelligence-Based Publication Delivered to the SAP BusinessObjects Mobile BI Inbox (iOS Shown)

20.4 Summary

Publications allow organizations to complement self-service reporting by publishing personalized content directly to users, both inside (enterprise recipients) and outside (dynamic recipients) the organization.

Of the four roles involved in publications (administrator, report designer, publication designer, and recipient), this chapter has focused on the role of the publication designer. The publication designer builds a publication using one or more Web Intelligence documents and assigns personalization through either a global profile (a reusable profile managed in the CMC) or a local profile (unique to a single publication).

Publications use the same destinations and scheduling options available to other document types on the SAP BusinessObjects BI platform. The most common destination is email, as it allows publications to serve customers outside the walls of an organization. However, new capabilities in the SAP BusinessObjects Mobile app allow you to send personalized content to the BI Inbox to view almost anywhere using supported phone and tablet devices.

In the next chapter, we'll cover Web Intelligence Rich Client, which enables the use of local data providers to create reports.

Web Intelligence Rich Client puts the power of Web Intelligence reporting on the user's local machine. It provides all the same capabilities while working in offline or standalone mode — with no Central Management Server required!

21 Web Intelligence Rich Client

Prior to the release of Web Intelligence 3.x, Web Intelligence reporting existed over the web only. Users were required to log into the web portal of BI Launch Pad to view, create, modify, and share Web Intelligence report content. With the introduction of this thin client version, Web Intelligence 3.x provided you with the ability to use all the functionality of Web Intelligence from your local PC, completely unconnected from the Central Management Server (CMS). Web Intelligence documents can be stored locally, which provides you with another means for backing up your reports. Local data providers can be used to create reports with Web Intelligence Rich Client.

There are two ways to install Web Intelligence Rich Client: using the SAP BusinessObjects BI Platform CD to install Web Intelligence Rich Client as part of a client installation, or by selecting INSTALL Now in the Web Intelligence preferences to easily install Web Intelligence Rich Client from BI Launch Pad.

This chapter will explore the unique functionality available within Web Intelligence Rich Client as well as differences in navigation when working in the desktop product as compared to the online version.

21.1 How Web Intelligence Rich Client Is Different

Web Intelligence Rich Client enables you to access Web Intelligence from a Windows-based application installed on your local computer. The familiar interface of Web Intelligence Rich Client, which is shown in Figure 21.1, makes it a favorite destination for report writers. Access to the Central Management Console (CMC) isn't required. Documents can be saved to your local computer, and you can use local data providers when building queries. Timeouts or web-based issues won't create interruptions to your Web Intelligence report writing and viewing. These features provide exciting new capabilities for the Web Intelligence report consumer.

Figure 21.1 Web Intelligence Rich Client Interface

Compelling reasons for users to turn to Web Intelligence Rich Client for their reporting needs include the following:

▶ Web Intelligence Rich Client can work offline without a connection to the CMS.

▶ Web Intelligence Rich Client performs calculations locally—rather than on the server—for improved performance.

▶ Web Intelligence Rich Client can be used in standalone mode when there is no CMS or application server installed.

▶ When the data source is contained in Excel, CSV, text, or web services, you can use Web Intelligence Rich Client as a local data source.

Note that all of the features of Web Intelligence via BI Launch Pad are available in Web Intelligence Rich Client. Additional available features will be discussed in further detail in this chapter, though for the purposes of this chapter, we won't duplicate our discussions in other chapters on the core functionality of Web Intelligence. Instead, we'll discuss only the differences found when using Web Intelligence Rich Client for your Web Intelligence reporting needs.

There are two ways to access Web Intelligence Rich Client: locally or through the BI Launch Pad. After Web Intelligence Rich Client is installed in your local machine, you can access it through the PROGRAMS menu. Go to START • PROGRAMS • SAP BUSINESS INTELLIGENCE • SAP BUSINESSOBJECTS WEB INTELLIGENCE • SAP BUSINESSOBJECTS WEB INTELLIGENCE, as shown in Figure 21.2. To launch Web Intelligence Rich Client from BI Launch Pad, set your Web Intelligence preferences to use DESKTOP as your default creation/editing tool.

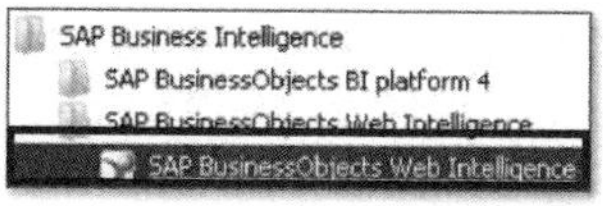

Figure 21.2 Web Intelligence Rich Client Program Path

When opening Web Intelligence Rich Client, you are presented with the initial screen to create a new document or open an existing document. At the bottom left of the screen is the BLANK DOCUMENT option, shown in Figure 21.3. Selecting this option opens Web Intelligence Rich Client without establishing a connection to the repository; therefore, a logon screen doesn't appear. With this option, you default to enter Web Intelligence Rich Client in offline mode. You may begin working with a blank Web Intelligence document now and add queries and connections at a later time.

After selecting a connected option, the login screen will appear. At this point, you may select to log on to the repository or log on in standalone mode. You have three options when accessing Web Intelligence Rich Client: offline, connected, and standalone.

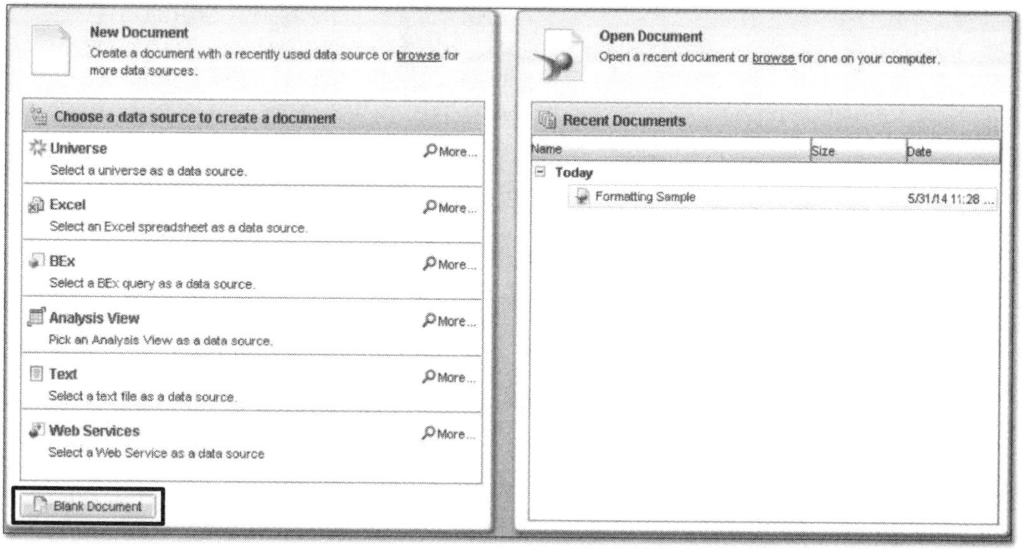

Figure 21.3 Initial Options When Opening Web Intelligence Rich Client

21.1.1 Working in Offline Mode

The first new option available is the OFFLINE MODE checkbox, as shown in Figure 21.4. Offline mode uses the security of the CMS stored on your local machine. The first time you log in to Web Intelligence Rich Client, you have to log in using connected mode in order for the CMS security information to be downloaded to your local machine. Every document and universe stored locally on your machine carries an access control list that stores the groups and users that have access rights to the object. Therefore, when working in offline mode, you aren't connected to the CMS, but CMS security is applied. You have the ability to work with secured or unsecured local documents and universes. When creating or refreshing documents, you'll will need a local universe and local connection server.

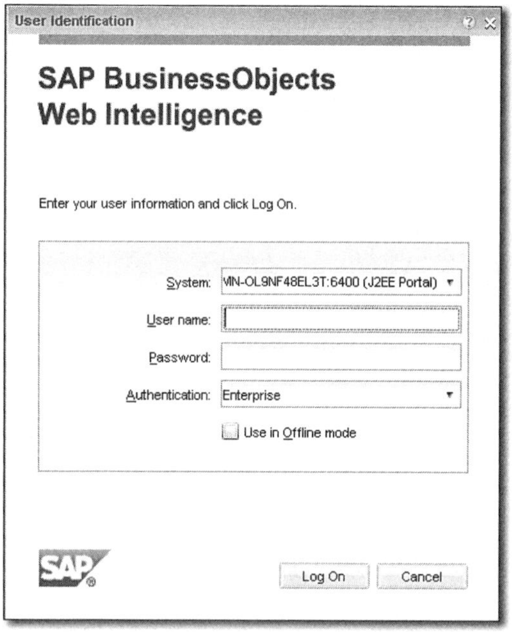

Figure 21.4 Offline Mode

21.1.2 Working in Connected Mode

Working in *connected mode* enables you to import documents and universes from the CMS as well as export Web Intelligence documents back to the CMS. This capability isn't available in offline or standalone modes. There are two options to log in to connected mode. From within BI Launch Pad, set your Web Intelligence preferences to use DESKTOP as your default creation/editing tool. When you select to edit an existing Web Intelligence document in or create a new Web Intelligence document form BI Launch Pad, Web Intelligence Rich Client is launched on your local computer. When you use this method, Web Intelligence connects to the CMS in client-server mode, and database middleware is needed on your local machine.

Another method involves logging in to Web Intelligence Rich Client by launching Web Intelligence Rich Client from your PROGRAMS on your local machine. When presented with the login dialog box, select the CMS, and then select the same authentication type used when logging in to BI Launch Pad.

21.1.3 Working in Standalone Mode

To log in using *standalone mode*, select STANDALONE from the SYSTEM list when entering your login credentials, as shown in Figure 21.5. Standalone mode doesn't connect to the CMS, and security isn't enforced as in offline mode. While in connected and offline mode, you could work with secured or unsecured documents and universes; in standalone mode, you can work with secured documents and universes only. This requires the appropriate database connection middleware to enable you to create and refresh documents with local universes.

Figure 21.5 Standalone Mode

21.2   Data Provider Options

Multiple types of data sources are available in Web Intelligence Rich Client: universe, Excel, SAP BEx, Analysis View, text, and web services. The universe data source includes all universes stored within the CMC as discussed in previous chapters. When you select the TEXT and EXCEL options, the personal data provider dialog box opens. Personal data providers include the following file types:

- ▶ *.TXT
- ▶ *.CSV
- ▶ *.PRN
- ▶ *.ASC
- ▶ *.XLS

After selecting the file type, you're prompted to define further options for selection of your data source.

Another data source available is the use of a web service. When selecting these options from the OTHER DATA SOURCES menu, you are prompted to enter your source URL as well as additional pertinent information about your web service. This functionality can be used to bring in real-time information to your Web Intelligence document. Data from Query as a Web Service or SAP BusinessObjects BI Services can be integrated into your Web Intelligence Rich Client document. Refer to Chapter 13 for further details on using a web service as your custom data provider.

21.2.1   Import a Universe from the CMS

When creating a new Web Intelligence report in Web Intelligence Rich Client, you are prompted to select your data source. When selecting a universe as a data source, you have the option to choose a local universe or a universe saved in the CMS. Note that you can only use a universe in the CMS if you're working in connected mode. If you want to store additional universes locally for use in unconnected sessions, you can use TOOLS • IMPORT UNIVERSE to import universes from the CMS. Upon selecting UNIVERSES from the TOOLS menu, you'll receive a list of available universes as shown in Figure 21.6. Select the universe to be imported locally, and choose the IMPORT button.

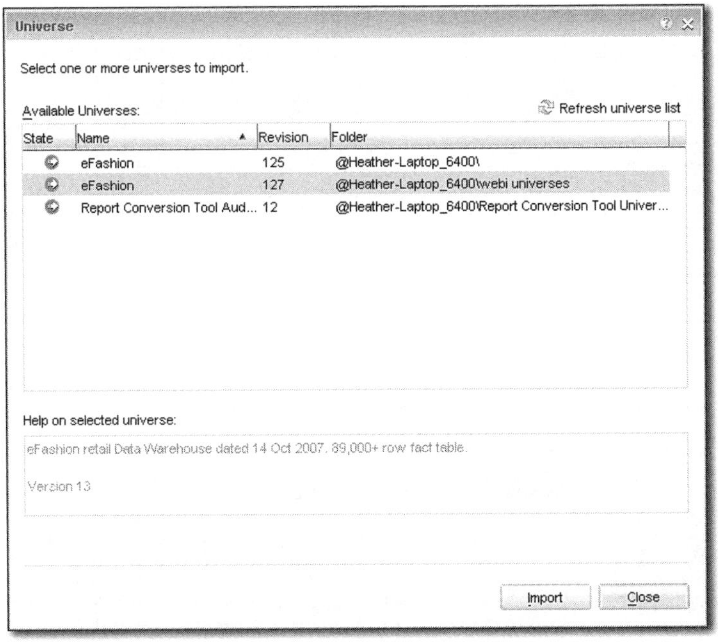

Figure 21.6 Universe Dialog Box: Importing

> **Note**
>
> Universes showing a green checkmark have already been imported locally.

21.2.2 Query Panel in Web Intelligence Rich Client

Within Web Intelligence Rich Client, select EDIT from the DATA ACCESS menu to view the QUERY PANEL. This is the same workflow as operating from within the web-based interface. Upon selecting EDIT, the QUERY PANEL dialog box appears. Make any appropriate changes to the query from this panel, and then click RUN QUERY to see your changes reflected in your report. This functionality works the same as within web-based Web Intelligence.

21.3 Working with Web Intelligence Reports

When working in Web Intelligence Rich Client, the same ribbon and menu exist as seen when working with Web Intelligence reports over the web. This provides a familiar source of organization for the options available for use when designing Web Intelligence reports. Figure 21.7 shows the menu options as seen in Web Intelligence Rich Client.

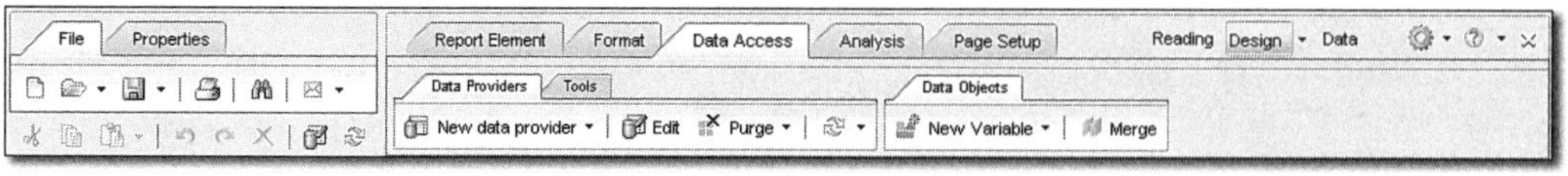

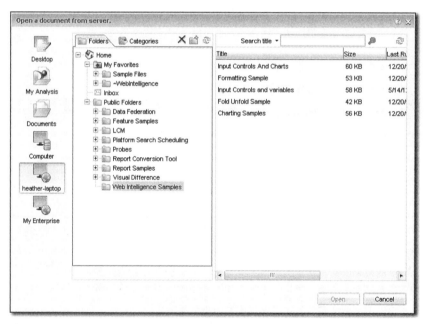

Figure 21.7 Web Intelligence Rich Client Menu

21.3.1 Opening Documents from the CMS

To import a report from the CMS, you first must be in connected mode. Select OPEN from the FILE menu. (You may also select the OPEN FROM option.) The OPEN A DOCUMENT FROM SERVER dialog box appears as shown in Figure 21.8.

Figure 21.8 Open Documents from Server Dialog Box

Select the name on your SAP BusinessObjects BI platform from the left panel. Navigate through your personal and public folders or categories to select the name of the document from the document list. You may also search for the document by using the SEARCH TITLE box at the top of the dialog box. These search options are similar to those in BI Launch Pad. You can select one or many documents to be opened on your local machine. After selecting a document, click the ADD button to move the document to your list of documents to be imported locally. When complete, select the OPEN button at the bottom of the dialog box.

The new document opens by default in a new window in reading mode.

21.3.2 Saving Reports Locally

To save a Web Intelligence Rich Client document locally, you can select SAVE or SAVE As from the FILE menu. SAVE will save the document as its original name to its original location. SAVE As has a number of options, including: Web Intelligence Document, Excel, or PDF. These documents won't be viewable in BI Launch Pad. The next step is dependent on which file type you save the document as; these file types are located in the dropdown menu at the bottom of the dialog box.

The SAVE AS A WEB INTELLIGENCE DOCUMENT option opens another dialog box, which is shown in Figure 21.9.

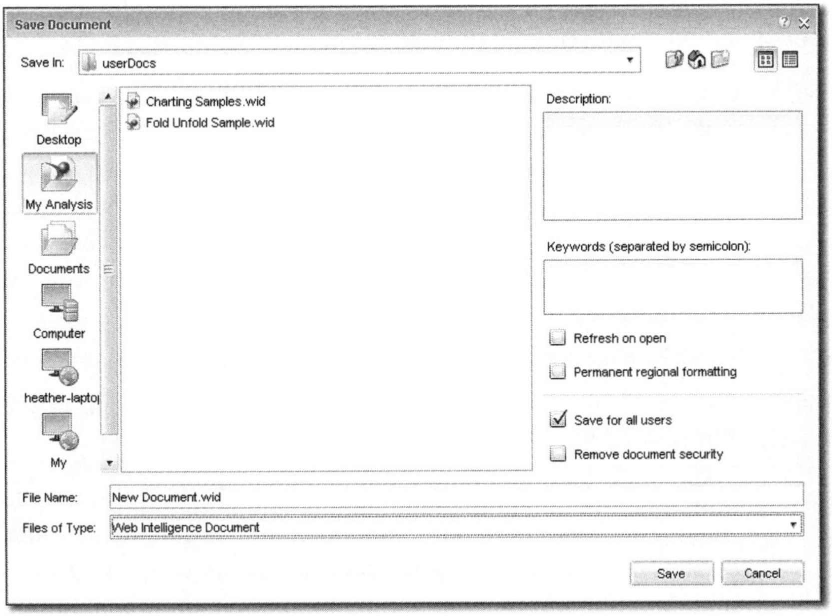

Figure 21.9 Web Intelligence Document Dialog Box

Enter the Web Intelligence document FILE NAME, DESCRIPTION, and KEYWORDS as you would like them to appear within BI Launch Pad. You also can indicate whether to refresh the document upon open by selecting the REFRESH ON OPEN checkbox. the PERMANENT REGIONAL FORMATTING checkbox indicates that it will maintain permanent regional formatting rather than adjusting per the user's settings. The new options that are available when saving a Web Intelligence document within Web Intelligence Rich Client include:

▶ SAVE FOR ALL USERS
Saves the document for all users to view and enables the Web Intelligence report to be moved between environments.

▶ REMOVE DOCUMENT SECURITY
Saves the document as unsecured so it can be viewed in standalone or offline mode.

After selecting available options and indicating the report FILE NAME, DESCRIPTION, and KEYWORDS, you can select a location to save the document outside of the SAP BusinessObjects BI platform environment. The default location is to save to your *userDocs* folder. The path for this folder is defined in your Web Intelligence Rich Client options as discussed in Section 21.4.

The SAVE AS EXCEL or EXCEL 2007 option changes the dialog box properties as shown in Figure 21.10. When saving a Web Intelligence document as an Excel file, you have the option to convert all report tabs to Excel or select only certain report tabs for export. You can also select the option on how to prioritize the processing of the Excel document. The default setting for these preferences are defined in the RICH CLIENT OPTIONS in the TOOLS menu. Further information on these options is discussed in previous chapters.

The SAVE AS PDF option opens another dialog box as shown in Figure 21.11. When saving as a PDF, you are given the option to define which reports and pages to include in your PDF.

The SAVE AS CSV (DATA ONLY) option opens another dialog box where you can define the text qualifier, column delimiter, and character set for the CSV file. There is also the option to save as CSV ARCHIVE, as discussed in Chapter 19.

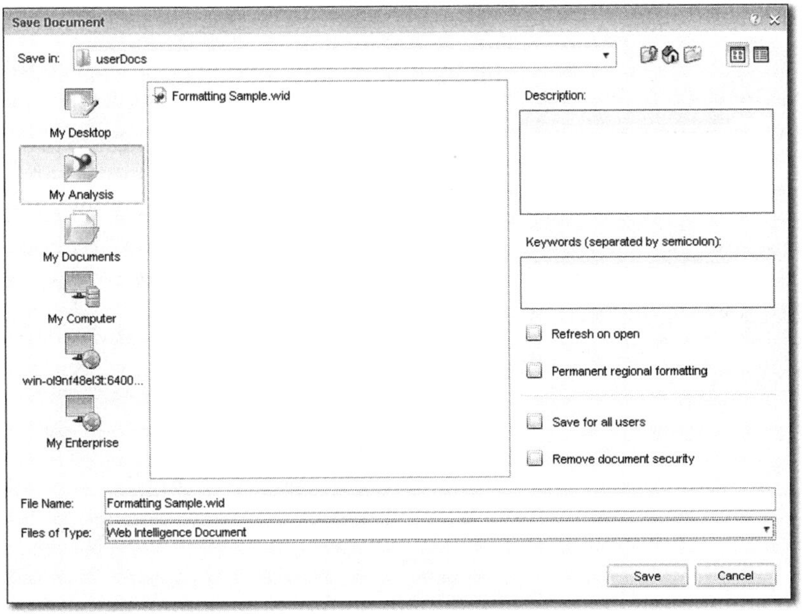

Figure 21.10 Save as Excel

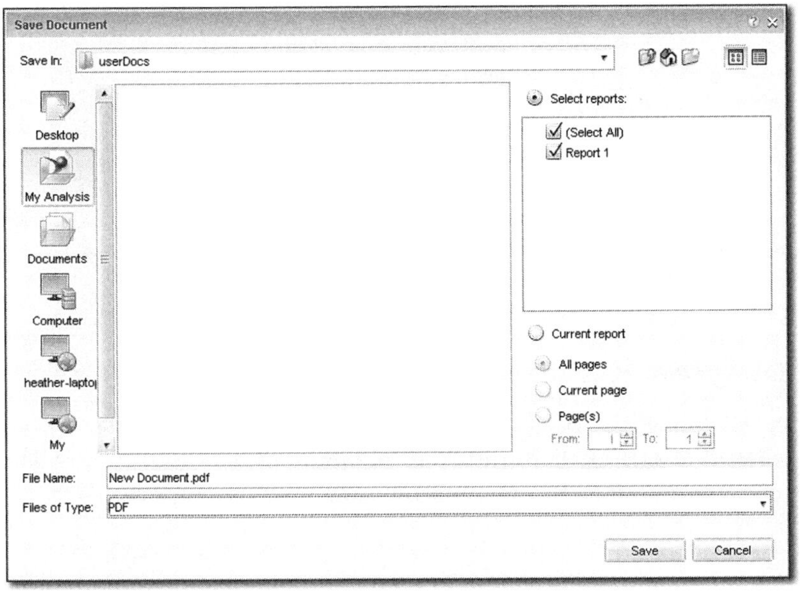

Figure 21.11 Save as PDF

21.3.3 Exporting Reports to CMS

To view these documents within BI Launch Pad and share with other users in the web portal, you have to save your report to the CMS. To export your document to the CMS, you must first be in connected mode. Then select PUBLISH TO CMS from the SAVE dropdown list. Select the folder and categories to export your document to for viewing within BI Launch Pad, and then select the SAVE button as shown in Figure 21.12. Additional export options are available by selecting the ADVANCED button in the dialog box. This enables options to SAVE FOR ALL USERS or REMOVE DOCUMENT SECURITY as mentioned earlier.

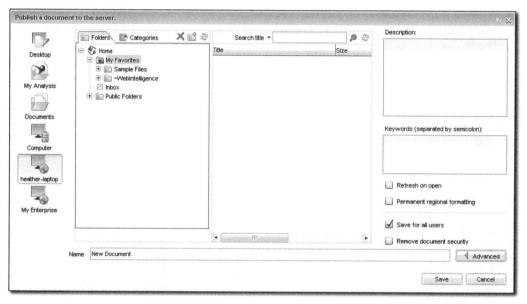

Figure 21.12 Publish Document Dialog Box

21.3.4 Printing from Web Intelligence Rich Client

To print from Web Intelligence Rich Client, select PRINT from the FILE menu. You are presented with print options, as shown in Figure 21.13. The document will be sent to the printer without having to open within the PDF format first.

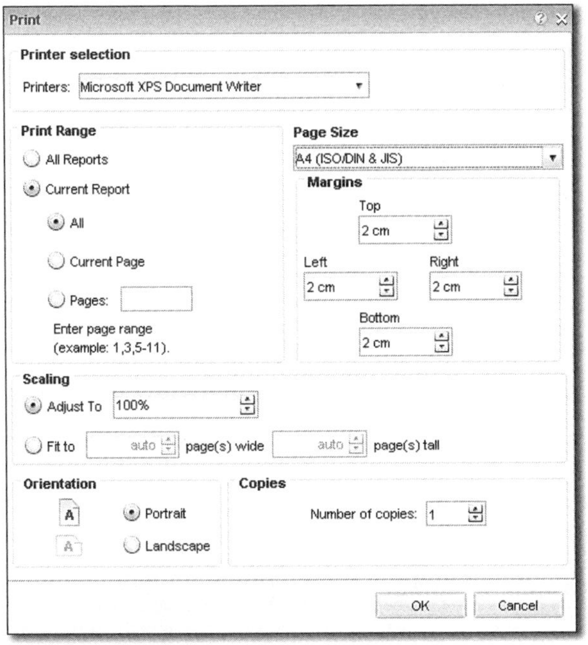

Figure 21.13 Print Dialog Box

21.3.5 Sending Reports as Email Attachments

Another option available in Web Intelligence Rich Client is to send a report as an email attachment. From the FILE menu, select SEND BY EMAIL ATTACHMENT. You have the choice to send the document in a number of formats, including Web Intelligence document, unsecured Web Intelligence document, Excel, PDF, and CSV.

21.4 Setting Preferences in Web Intelligence Rich Client

Preferences are available in Web Intelligence Rich Client as shown in the Web Intelligence preferences in BI Launch Pad. These options are available from the PROPERTIES ribbon under APPLICATION or from the TOOLS menu under OPTIONS. Preferences can be defined for DRILLING, LOCALES, VIEWING, and GENERAL PREFERENCES. These are defined separately in Web Intelligence Rich Client from what is defined for Web Intelligence documents viewed in BI Launch Pad.

21.5 Summary

Web Intelligence Rich Client brings the features of web-based Web Intelligence onto your desktop by opening up new features that are instrumental to the report writer. Former SAP BusinessObjects Desktop Intelligence users will appreciate the new thin client capabilities of Web Intelligence provided within Web Intelligence 4.x. The ability to work whether connected or disconnected from the CMS, save universes and documents locally, and use local data providers provides additional capabilities to aid the report designer in the report creation, consumption, and sharing processes.

Chapter 22 discusses the ability to bring Web Intelligence report content into Microsoft Office documents using another tool called SAP BusinessObjects Live Office. This provides another familiar interface for report writers and consumers alike to work with data within the easy-to-use environment of programs such as Excel.

SAP BusinessObjects Live Office is a powerful tool to enable the use of business intelligence content within Microsoft Office documents. SAP BusinessObjects Live Office allows a larger audience to consume, query, analyze, and visualize Web Intelligence content in a familiar interface.

22 Connecting SAP BusinessObjects Live Office to Web Intelligence

With SAP BusinessObjects Live Office, you can work with your business intelligence content within Microsoft Office applications such as Word, Excel, Power-Point and Outlook. This functionality allows you to quickly and easily collaborate with other users across your organization. It also empowers users of different skill sets or comfort levels to manipulate their Web Intelligence query results within other mediums. This chapter reviews the core functionality, basic settings, and usage of the SAP BusinessObjects Live Office product with Web Intelligence documents. SAP BusinessObjects Live Office 4.x is compatible with Office 2003, 2007, and 2010. The menu options may appear different in the different versions as compared to those shown in this chapter.

22.1 Introduction to SAP BusinessObjects Live Office

SAP BusinessObjects Live Office is an Excel plug-in that can be installed on a client machine. After SAP BusinessObjects Live Office has been installed on your machine, a new LIVE OFFICE ribbon will appear on your toolbar when you are in Microsoft Office applications (Word, Excel, PowerPoint or Outlook), as shown in Figure 22.1. SAP BusinessObjects Live Office allows you to bring report data from Web Intelligence reports, SAP Crystal Reports, and universe queries to do further manipulation within the Office applications. Excel is frequently used with SAP BusinessObjects Live Office because it lets users perform further analysis of the data in a familiar place. Users in finance departments are often very familiar with Excel, and SAP BusinessObjects Live Office gives them a tool that works within their comfort zone and requires little additional training.

Figure 22.1 Live Office Ribbon from within Excel

> **Note**
>
> SAP BusinessObjects Live Office 4.0 supports Web Intelligence documents created with .UNV universes created with the Universe Design Tool and universe queries from .UNV universes. Reports created with the new .UNX universe from the Information Design Tool and universe queries from this tool are *not* supported; neither are Web Intelligence reports created from SAP BEx query data and SAP Crystal Reports for Enterprise.

22.1.1 Integration with Web Intelligence Reports

SAP BusinessObjects Live Office enables you to insert Web Intelligence report content into your Office documents as tables, charts or freestanding cells.

> **Tip**
>
> Consider the format of the application you're adding content to. If using PowerPoint, for example, make sure you have adequate space available for your content to display.

Excel is the most common destination for Web Intelligence content because it uses a tabular interface and enables further manipulation of the data. A user who is not fully trained in how to use Web Intelligence can easily create a report using Web Intelligence content from within SAP BusinessObjects Live Office.

Web Intelligence content involves report objects, report instances, and reports parts:

▶ *Report objects* are the actual Web Intelligence reports contained within SAP BusinessObjects BI.

▶ *Report instances* are the versions of reports created when a report is scheduled. RA report instances will contain data from a specified report refresh with the prompt values used at the time of that refresh.

▶ *Report parts* are the various elements of the report (such as the tables and charts) contained within the report.

It's important to understand each of these elements when using the Live Office Insert Wizard for specification of the Web Intelligence content to integrate in your Office document.

22.1.2 Live Office Ribbon Menu

The *Live Office* ribbon menu is available from within your Word, Excel, Power-Point, or Outlook documents beginning with Office 2007. In Office 2003, these options appear in the toolbar. The ribbon menu, as shown earlier in Figure 22.1, enables quick access to the most commonly used functions available within SAP BusinessObjects Live Office.

The following options are available on the Live Office ribbon menu, are organized by pane:

▶ INSERT

  ▶ CRYSTAL REPORTS: This option opens the Live Office Insert Wizard to define the options available for inserting content from an SAP Crystal Report.

  ▶ INTERACTIVE ANALYSIS: This option opens the Live Office Insert Wizard to define the options available for inserting content from a Web Intelligence report.

  ▶ UNIVERSE QUERY:This option opens the Live Office Insert Wizard to define the options available for creating a universe query to insert results into your destination Office document.

▶ OBJECT ACTIONS

  ▶ GO TO OBJECT: This option enables you to go to a specific object in your SAP BusinessObjects Live Office document.

  ▶ MODIFY OBJECT: This option allows you to modify the properties for a specific object.

  ▶ REFRESH OBJECT: This option enables you to refresh a specific object only.

► REFRESH ALL OBJECTS: This option lets you refresh all objects contained in your SAP BusinessObjects Live Office document.

► EXPLORE

   ► SELECTION: This enables you to export a selection in your SAP BusinessObjects Live Office document to SAP BusinessObjects Explorer for further analysis.

   ► SHEET: This feature enables you to export an entire sheet in your document to SAP BusinessObjects Explorer for further analysis.

► PUBLISHING

   ► CREATE SNAPSHOT: This option enables you to create a snapshot of the document in the current state to save for further reference. More information on snapshots is discussed in Chapter 11.

   ► SAVE: This option saves the SAP BusinessObjects Live Office document to the SAP BusinessObjects BI platform to share and collaborate with others in your organization.

   ► SAVE AS NEW TO REPOSITORY: This option allows you to save as a different name or to a different location for an SAP BusinessObjects Live Office document existing in the SAP BusinessObjects BI platform.

   ► OPEN FROM REPOSITORY: This option allows you to open an SAP BusinessObjects Live Office document saved to the Business Objects Repository (BOR).

► SETTINGS

   ► OBJECT PROPERTIES: This option allows you to define object-specific properties.

   ► REFRESH OPTIONS: This option allows you to define refresh options for the SAP BusinessObjects Live Office document.

   ► APPLICATION OPTIONS: This option allows you to define SAP BusinessObjects Live Office application options.

► VIEW

   ► OBJECT IN BROWSER: This option opens the object in a browser window.

   ► HELP: This option opens the SAP BusinessObjects Live Office HELP dialog box.

   ► ABOUT SAP BUSINESSOBJECTS LIVE OFFICE: This option shows the version information for your current SAP BusinessObjects Live Office installation.

Now that you're familiar with the SAP BusinessObjects Live Office basics, let's shift our attention to how to create documents in this tool that contain valuable Web Intelligence information.

22.2 Creating SAP BusinessObjects Live Office Documents with Web Intelligence Content

The integration of Web Intelligence content within SAP BusinessObjects Live Office provides a powerful tool for the end user and report writer alike. To integrate Web Intelligence content, a Web Intelligence report must already exist in the repository for access within SAP BusinessObjects Live Office. This report content can be brought into Word, Excel, PowerPoint, or Outlook. For the purpose of this section, we'll use Excel to integrate our Web Intelligence content.

22.2.1 Accessing the Live Office Insert Wizard

Navigate to the appropriate cell where you want the content to be dropped in your Excel worksheet. From the LIVE OFFICE ribbon menu, select the INSERT WEB INTELLIGENCE/INTERACTIVE ANALYSIS CONTENT button. If you haven't already logged on or selected auto-authentication, then the login dialog box will appear. After authentication, the LIVE OFFICE INSERT WIZARD will display.

22.2.2 Selecting the Web Intelligence Document

The first option in the Live Office Insert Wizard is to select the Web Intelligence document to use for content in your Excel document. Figure 22.2 shows the CHOOSE DOCUMENT screen in the LIVE OFFICE INSERT WIZARD.

The screen displays the Web Intelligence documents available for integration within the repository. This view displays the folders and categories in the BI Launch Pad. You can navigate by folders or categories by selecting the icons at the top. You can also search by title, keyword, content, or all fields to find a document, and you can include Web Intelligence objects, instances, or publications in SAP BusinessObjects Live Office. Highlight the name of your chosen document, and select NEXT.

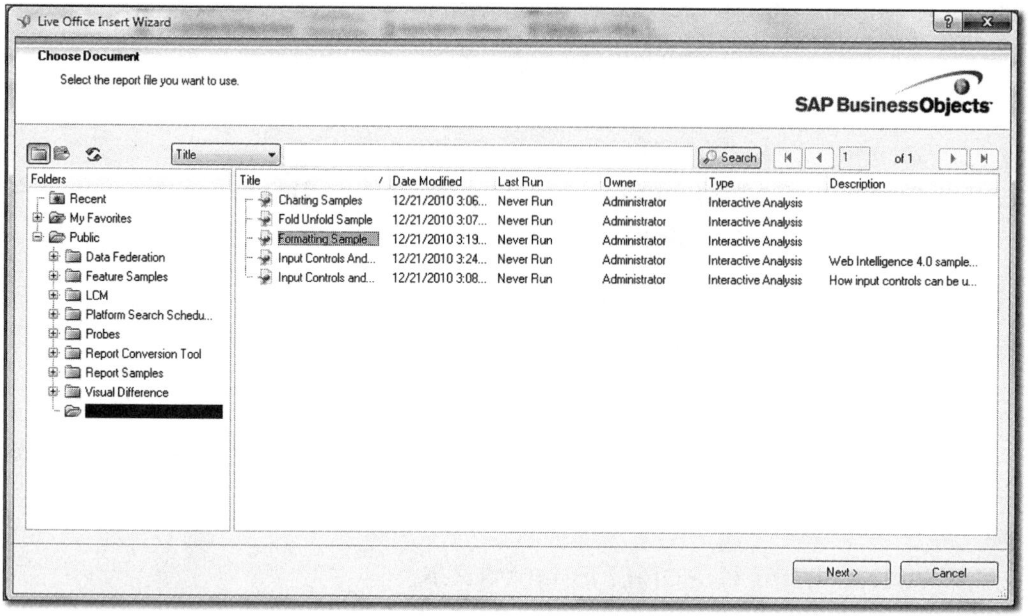

Figure 22.2 Choosing a Document in the Live Office Insert Wizard

22.2.3 Setting Context

If more than one context exists for the Web Intelligence report, you'll be prompted to set context as part of the Live Office Insert Wizard. After choosing the appropriate context, select NEXT.

22.2.4 Configuring Prompt Values

The option to configure prompt values will appear only if prompts are set up on the Web Intelligence report. If no prompts exist, then this option won't appear. The prompt properties allow you to select the prompt value from a list or set to be prompted to enter the prompt value each time the data is refreshed. After specifying prompt values, select NEXT.

22.2.5 Selecting Report Content

After choosing the Web Intelligence document, you need to select the report content to be included in the SAP BusinessObjects Live Office document. Select each report block to include it in the report. All selected blocks will be brought into your SAP BusinessObjects Live Office document starting at the cell where you placed your cursor. See Figure 22.3 for the CHOOSE DATA dialog box. After making all selections of relevant report parts, select NEXT.

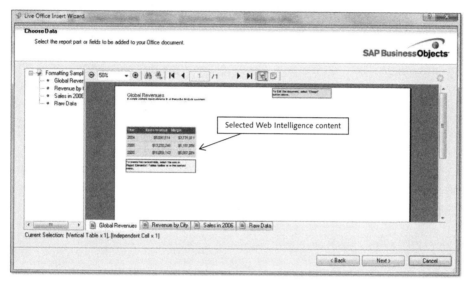

Figure 22.3 Choose Data in the Live Office Insert Wizard

22.2.6 Creating the Summary

Upon selection of the report parts to be included in your SAP BusinessObjects Live Office document, you are shown the SUMMARY. At this time, you'll give a name to your particular SAP BusinessObjects Live Office content before selecting FINISH. Figure 22.4 shows Web Intelligence report content in an Excel document using SAP BusinessObjects Live Office.

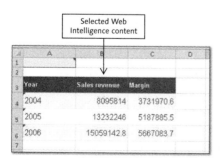

Figure 22.4 Web Intelligence Content in Excel Using SAP BusinessObjects Live Office

22.2.7 Adding More Content

After your selected report content is displayed within Excel, you may want to add in more report blocks from the same report. To add additional content, right-click on the report content within Excel and then select the LIVE OFFICE option to view the available options as shown in Figure 22.5.

You'll have the option to insert or remove rows and columns within your SAP BusinessObjects Live Office object. Using these menu items ensures that you don't use your object mapping. You can refresh or set options from the right-click menu as well. To add more content from the same report, select the NEW OBJECT FROM SAME REPORT option. The LIVE OFFICE INSERT WIZARD will appear to select the relevant options using the same Web Intelligence document.

To insert new content from a new Web Intelligence document, select the INSERT WEB INTELLIGENCE DOCUMENT from the LIVE OFFICE toolbar and select the appropriate new report in the LIVE OFFICE INSERT WIZARD.

Figure 22.5 Live Office Menu Options

22.3 Setting Preferences

You can customize your session using a number of preferences within SAP BusinessObjects Live Office. Preferences apply to application options, refresh options, object properties, and prompt binding options.

22.3.1 Application Options

The Application Options enables you to define default settings for all your SAP BusinessObjects Live Office documents within the application. To define application options, select APPLICATION OPTIONS from the LIVE OFFICE ribbon menu. The dialog box tabs define three types of application options: GENERAL, VIEW, and ENTERPRISE.

General

GENERAL tab properties will vary depending on the Office application. In the GENERAL tab from Excel (shown in Figure 22.6), you can define the SHORTCUT MENU options. In addition, options for the treatment of SAP BusinessObjects Live Office cells and refresh options are available. If you selected the option to PROMPT BEFORE OVERWRITING LIVE OFFICE CELLS, you will be prompted before you can type over content that is being fed by your business intelligence content. If you select the option to REFRESH LIVE OFFICE OBJECT WHEN BINDING CELL CHANGES, the content will refresh when you bind your business intelligence content to cells in your Excel spreadsheet. If you select REFRESH LIVE OFFICE OBJECT ON DOCUMENT OPEN, then SAP BusinessObjects Live Office will go to the BOR and return the most recent results for your specified content. The COPY AND PASTE WITH LIVE OFFICE CONNECTIVITY option enables you to move bound ranges without losing the connectivity to SAP BusinessObjects Live Office. If this is disabled, then only the results will move, and the copied content won't be refreshed when the SAP BusinessObjects Live Office content is refreshed.

Figure 22.6 General Application Options

View

The VIEW tab options apply to how the data will be displayed in your SAP BusinessObjects Live Office document. The APPEARANCE options are set to determine whether the formatting from the original report should be maintained. The APPEARANCE options also allow you to set whether to show filters as comments in the SAP BusinessObjects Live Office document and to alert you when a time-consuming operation occurs that will affect a defined number of cells.

The VIEW tab options also define how cells will display for default cell values of NO DATA, DATA ERROR, and CONCEALED DATA. You can also define column headings to be set to the FIELD NAME, FIELD DESCRIPTION, or BOTH by default, as shown in Figure 22.7.

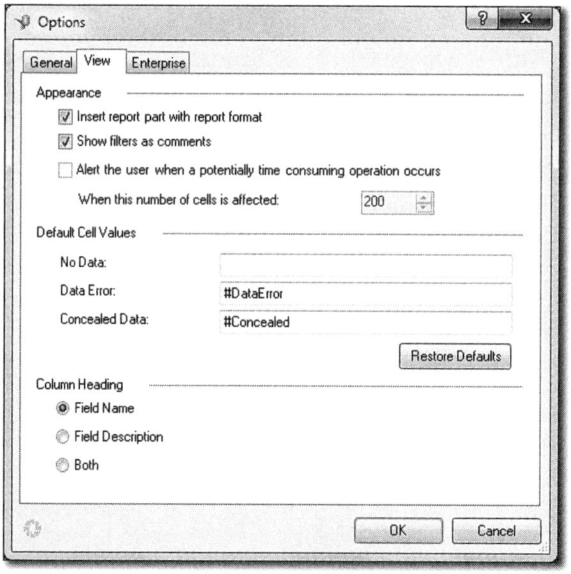

Figure 22.7 View Application Options

Enterprise

The ENTERPRISE tab options allow you to define your login criteria, as shown in Figure 22.8. The appropriate criteria should be given by your SAP BusinessObjects administrator. The USER NAME and PASSWORD will be your SAP BusinessObjects BI user name and password. The AUTHENTICATION and SYSTEM will be the same as well. The WEB SERVICES URL is defined as follows: *http://webserver:port-number/dswsbobje/services/session. Web server* and *port number* should be replaced with the appropriate information for your SAP BusinessObjects deployment. The last setting in this tab allows you to define the OpenDocument URL for viewing content in a web browser.

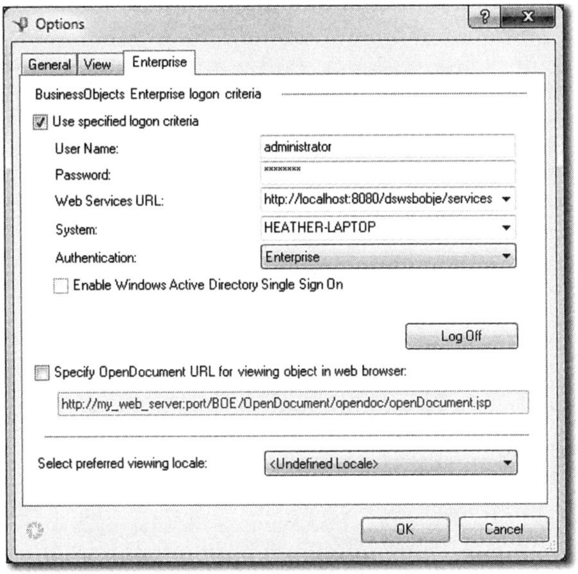

Figure 22.8 Enterprise Application Options

22.3.2 Data Refresh Options

The data in a report can be set to refresh based on the original report, an instance, or on demand. The following options are available for refreshing data:

▶ LATEST INSTANCE
The first option in the REFRESH OPTIONS box shown in Figure 22.9 is to refresh data based on the latest instance of a scheduled report. Therefore, the SAP BusinessObjects Live Office data will refresh as the scheduled report data refreshes. The SAP BusinessObjects Live Office object will use the latest instance of the report for its data.

▶ ON DEMAND
This option enables you to manually refresh the SAP BusinessObjects Live Office document when you want updated data. The source of the update will

come from the database rather than the original Web Intelligence report or instance.

► USE REPORT SAVED DATA

This option refreshes the SAP BusinessObjects Live Office objects with the data saved in the original Web Intelligence report contained in the SAP BusinessObjects BI platform environment.

► SPECIFIC INSTANCE

This option enables you to use one of the scheduled instances of a Web Intelligence report as the source data for the SAP BusinessObjects Live Office report.

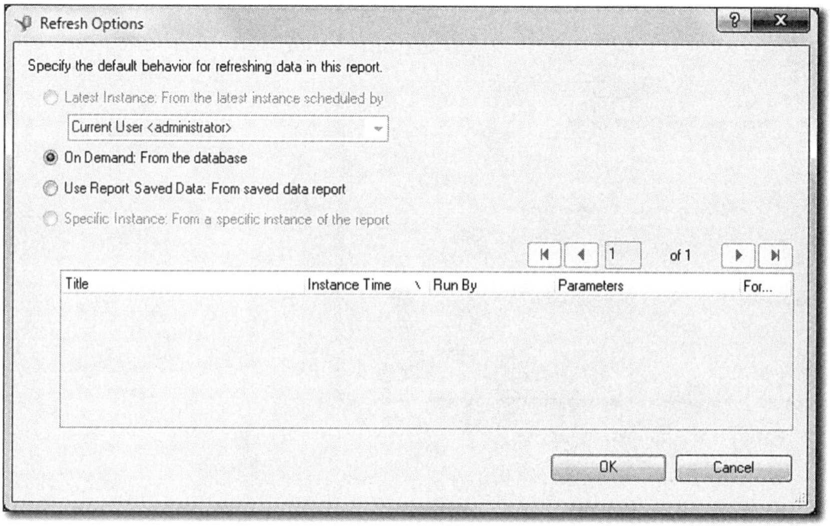

Figure 22.9 Refresh Options Box

22.3.3 Object Properties

The LIVE OFFICE OBJECT PROPERTIES screen shown in Figure 22.10 allows you to specify properties that are specific to an object contained in your SAP BusinessObjects Live Office document. An object is defined as one of the report parts from the Web Intelligence report. In the sample report, there are two report objects as shown in the OBJECTS OF THE REPORT box. When you click on each object, detailed information about the object is shown on the right of the box. Specific details on the Web Intelligence report used in the SAP BusinessObjects Live Office document are also contained within the OBJECTS/REPORTS box at the top. By clicking on each of these objects, you can see the properties display to the right.

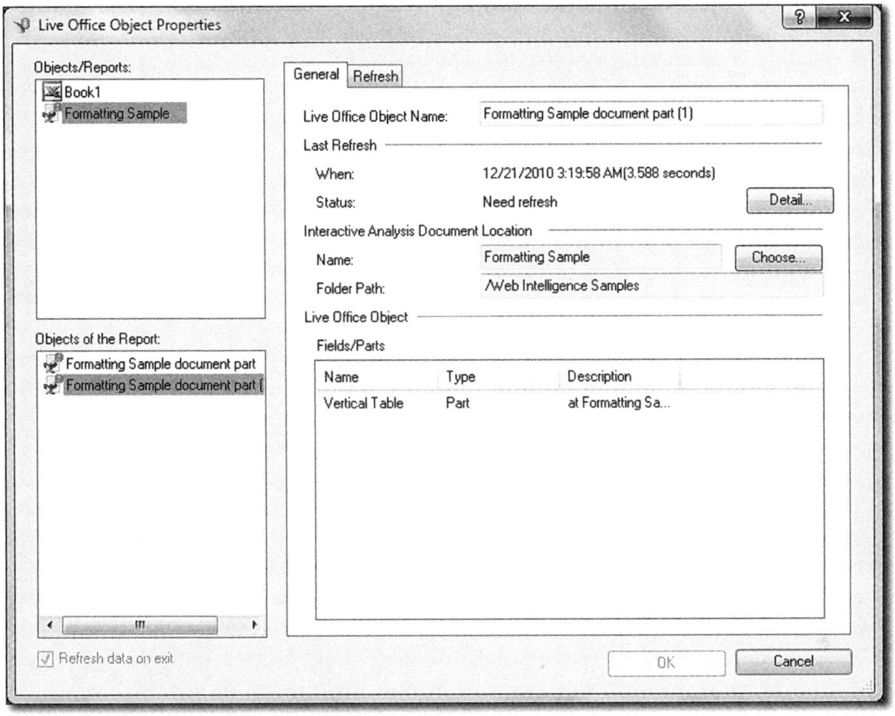

Figure 22.10 General Object Properties Box

To set refresh properties for the object, select the object from the OBJECTS OF THE REPORT box on the bottom left, and then select the appropriate properties in the REFRESH tab (see Figure 22.11). Available properties include whether to APPLY REPORT FORMAT WHEN REFRESHING, CONCEAL DATA ON SAVING, and REFRESH SETTING. CONCEAL DATA ON SAVING enables you to secure the data so that a refresh must be made before a user can view the data. This will ensure that the user is seeing only the data that he is allowed to access, given his security settings.

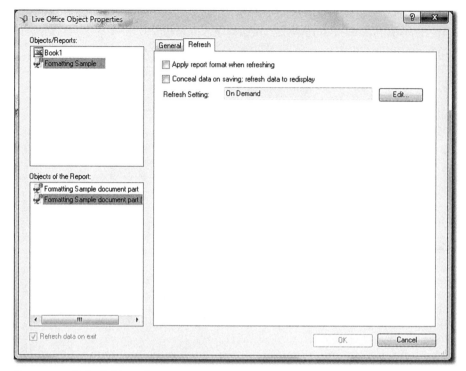

Figure 22.11 Refresh Object Properties Box

22.4 Summary

SAP BusinessObjects Live Office is a powerful tool that enables the consumption of Web Intelligence report content within Office documents. This combines the power of business intelligence queries in a comfortable, familiar setting for end users and report writers alike.

The next chapter will discuss another powerful tool to customize your Web Intelligence reporting experience. SAP BusinessObjects Mobile allows users to create customized mobile reporting to be shared on mobile devices, which is one more step toward a completely integrated business intelligence reporting experience.

Because the mobile landscape has changed significantly in recent years, business intelligence must respond accordingly to provide advanced analytics available on mobile devices. Web Intelligence answered this need through on-device mobile integration with SAP BusinessObjects Mobile.

23   Mobile Business Intelligence

The ability to quickly and easily view, analyze, and interact with key metrics while performing day-to-day activities is a requirement for today's organizations. For everyone from executives to operational employees, business analytics provide a consumable source of data on the current status of the company, enabling them to respond quickly to business needs. Web Intelligence documents can be easily created for mobile consumption and made available on a variety of mobile devices. Mobile business intelligence can be deployed in a range of form factors and from tablets to phones that use the BlackBerry OS, Apple iOS (iPad and iPhone), and Android OS. The SAP BusinessObjects Mobile application integrates with your SAP Crystal Reports, SAP BusinessObjects Dashboards, SAP BusinessObjects Explorer, and SAP Lumira applications in addition to SAP BusinessObjects Web Intelligence. The SAP BusinessObjects Mobile BI application provides powerful functionality to answer the call for on-device analytics for today's increasingly mobile workplace.

23.1   New Features in SAP BusinessObjects Mobile

SAP BusinessObjects Mobile has experienced some dramatic changes since we discussed the topic in the second edition of this book. With the development of SAP BusinessObjects Mobile 6.0, several features have been enhanced.

On the server side, the Vaultus Authentication Server (VAS) and Vaultus Messaging Server (VMS) were replaced starting with SAP BusinessObjects Business Intelligence 4.0 SP4, with a much easier to deploy web application based on the Sybase Unwired Platform (now rebranded simply as the SAP Mobile Platform).

On the device side, enterprises have standardized by an overwhelming margin on devices based on Apple iOS such as the iPhone and iPad, with Android phones and tablets coming in second. SAP has followed its customers' lead by introducing new innovations on iOS and later incorporating into Android. BlackBerry devices are still supported by SAP BusinessObjects BI 4.1 SP3 on which this chapter is based, but we'll focus our attention on the SAP BusinessObjects Mobile for iOS application. As of this writing, SAP BusinessObjects Mobile 6.0 for iOS (available from the Apple iTunes App Store), SAP BusinessObjects Mobile 5.1 for Android (available from the Google Play store), and SAP BusinessObjects Mobile 5.0 for BlackBerry (downloaded OTA from the SAP BusinessObjects BI platform) are the most recent versions.

The current version of SAP BusinessObjects Mobile for iOS supports content from all the major SAP business intelligence applications, including SAP Crystal Reports, SAP BusinessObjects Dashboards, SAP BusinessObjects Design Studio, SAP BusinessObjects Explorer, SAP Lumira, and SAP BusinessObjects Web Intelligence. SAP introduces new features on iOS first and later adds them to the Android edition. Expect innovation to continue at a breakneck pace, realizing that new mobile features typically require the software on both the business intelligence platform as well as the mobile device to be upgraded to the latest versions.

Note

New mobile features are frequently dependent on changes to the business intelligence platform. Be sure to review the release notes when new versions of mobile applications are released, taking note if server-side patches are required to use new features.

Let's now focus our attention on how best to mobilize your existing Web Intelligence documents by taking advantage of mobile-online visualization techniques, beginning with designing your reports for mobile viewing.

23.2 Designing Reports for Mobile Viewing

Unlike previous generations of mobile devices with small screens, limited memory, and slow connection speeds, today's mobile devices provide high-resolution displays, operating systems that support application development, and high-speed 4G and Wi-Fi connectivity. Although screen resolution on an Apple iPad is significantly greater than a BlackBerry phone, report designers must still consider readability on a mobile device. Additionally, some features available on desktop- and browser-based Web Intelligence remain unsupported on the mobile application. When viewing reports in tables, charts, and other visual representations, it's important to consider whether the information is still coming across as clear. Report designers must consider this when constructing information on supported views.

In Figure 23.1, all three table types (vertical, horizontal, and crosstab) are supported. However, there are limits to how many rows these tables may contain.

Table Formats

Lines	Category	Sales revenue
	Belts,bags,wallets	$1,642,492
	Hair accessories	$350,919
	Hats,gloves,scarves	$1,550,563
Accessories	Jewelry	$5,180,094
	Lounge wear	$541,179
	Samples	$649,298
	Sum:	**$9,914,546**

	2004	2005	2006	Sum:
Belts,bags,wallets	$389,699	$492,931	$759,861	**$1,642,492**
Hair accessories	$83,923	$119,953	$147,043	**$350,919**
Hats,gloves,scarves	$459,394	$1,053,580	$37,588	**$1,550,563**
Jewelry	$1,521,327	$3,600,207	$58,560	**$5,180,094**
Lounge wear	$91,880	$202,247	$247,053	**$541,179**
Samples	Discontinued	Discontinued	$649,298	**$649,298**
Sum:	**$2,546,222**	**$5,468,919**	**$1,899,405**	**$9,914,546**

Category	Belts,bags,wallets	Hair accessories	Hats,gloves,scarves	Jewelry	Lounge wear	Samples	Sum:
Sales revenue	$1,642,492	$350,919	$1,550,563	$5,180,094	$541,179	$649,298	**$9,914,546**

Figure 23.1 Tables Viewed in the BI Launch Pad

In contrast, Web Intelligence tables viewed from SAP BusinessObjects Mobile have a high degree of fidelity when compared to those same tables viewed from the BI Launch Pad (see Figure 23.2).

Lines	Category	Sales revenue
	Belts,bags,wallets	$1,642,492
	Hair accessories	$350,919
Accessories	Hats,gloves,scarves	$1,550,563
	Jewelry	$5,180,094

	2004	2005	2006	Sum:
Belts,bags,wallets	$389,699	$492,931	$759,861	$1,642,492
Hair accessories	$83,923	$119,953	$147,043	$350,919
Hats,gloves,scarves	$459,394	$1,053,580	$37,588	$1,550,563
Jewelry	$1,521,327	$3,600,207	$58,560	$5,180,094
Lounge wear	$91,880	$202,247	$247,053	$541,179
Samples	Discontinued	Discontinued	$649,298	$649,298
Sum:	$2,546,222	$5,468,919	$1,899,405	$9,914,546

Category	Belts,bags,wallets	Hair accessories	Hats,gloves,scarves	Jewelry	Lounge wear	Samples	Sum:
Sales revenue	$1,642,492	$350,919	$1,550,563	$5,180,094	$541,179	$649,298	$9,914,546

Figure 23.2 Tables Viewed on SAP BusinessObjects Mobile

Web Intelligence has many more chart types than previous versions; however, not all of these charts can be viewed on mobile devices. For example, Figure 23.3 shows what a 3D pie chart would look like if viewed in the BI Launch Pad.

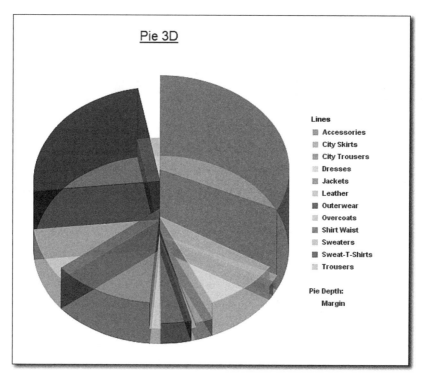

Figure 23.3 Three-Dimensional Pie Chart in BI Launch Pad

However, the three-dimensional pie chart is currently not supported by the SAP BusinessObjects Mobile application. When the SAP BusinessObjects Mobile application can't render content, a CONTENT NOT SUPPORTED error is displayed, as shown in Figure 23.4.

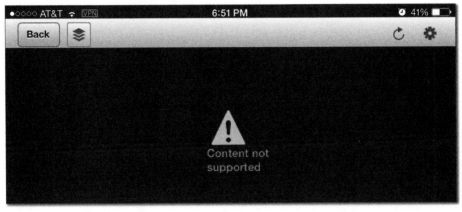

Figure 23.4 Three-Dimensional Pie Chart Viewed in SAP BusinessObjects Mobile

Because not every Web Intelligence document renders properly on a mobile device, SAP leverages corporate categories to control whether a Web Intelligence document is available to mobile devices.

23.2.1 Mobile Categories

The SAP BusinessObjects BI platform uses categories to control which Web Intelligence documents will display correctly on mobile devices, as explained in Table 23.1. These categories can either be created in the BI Launch Pad or the Central Management Console (CMC).

Category	Description
MOBILE	Acts as a control switch to determine if a Web Intelligence document should be displayed on a mobile device. Renders reports on mobile devices using a "card" layout.
CONFIDENTIAL	Prevents users from saving Web Intelligence documents tagged with the category on their mobile device, even if the SAP BusinessObjects BI platform settings allow users to save documents.

Table 23.1 Mobile Device Web Intelligence Document Displays

Category	Description
MOBILEDESIGNED	Formats mobile documents as closely as possible to their original layout; also known as "page layout."

Table 23.1 Mobile Device Web Intelligence Document Displays (Cont.)

These categories can be created side-by-side at the top level, although you may find them easier to work within a hierarchy (see Figure 23.5). Create the MOBILE category at the top level, and then create CONFIDENTIAL and MOBILEDESIGNED as subcategories. In this arrangement, a Web Intelligence document tagged as CON-FIDENTIAL or MOBILEDESIGNED is already tagged as MOBILE due to inheritance.

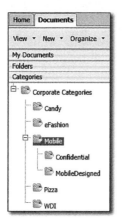

Figure 23.5 Mobile Categories in the BI Launch Pad

Note

Always test Web Intelligence documents in a nonproduction environment for mobile compatibility. If the document doesn't display properly, don't tag it with the MOBILE category in the production environment, or users may see the CONTENT NOT SUPPORTED message and assume the document is defective.

The Mobile, Confidential, and MobileDesigned categories are used by the SAP BusinessObjects Mobile application but never seen by an SAP BusinessObjects Mobile user. However, other categories are visible to mobile users and can be used to organize mobile content such as CANDY, PIZZA, WDI, and EFASHION (see Figure 23.6).

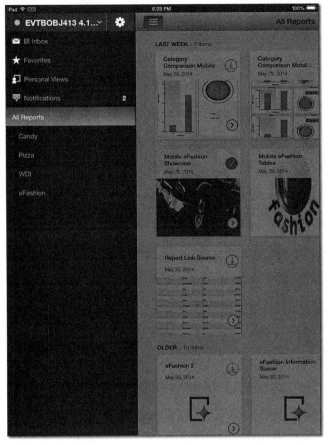

Figure 23.6 Categories in an SAP BusinessObjects Mobile Application

23.2.2 Mobile versus MobileDesigned

Mobile report designers will need to evaluate on a case-by-case basis whether to tag a Web Intelligence document with only the Mobile category (card layout) or whether to tag with both the Mobile and MobileDesigned categories (page layout). This section illustrates how documents appear with each layout scheme. To illustrate, we've created a document that shows a 2 × 3 grid of charts on one report tab and a 3 × 3 grid of charts on another report tab. Figure 23.7 and Figure 23.8, respectively, show how these charts, also known as report parts, appear when viewed from the BI Launch Pad.

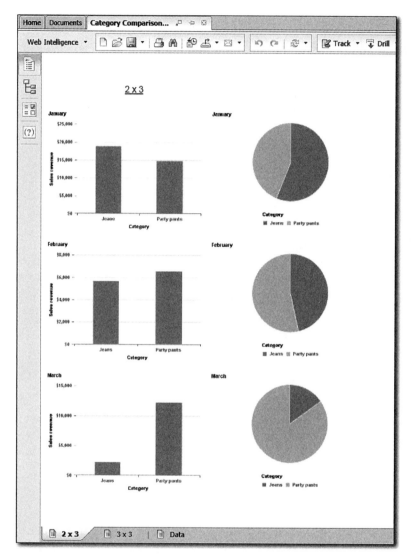

Figure 23.7 The 2 × 3 Grid Viewed in the BI Launch Pad

Let's first look at using the Mobile category, which instructs the mobile device to use a card layout. If the mobile application can't fit all of the report parts on a single screen of the device, it will distribute the report parts across multiple screens, which a user can view by swiping.

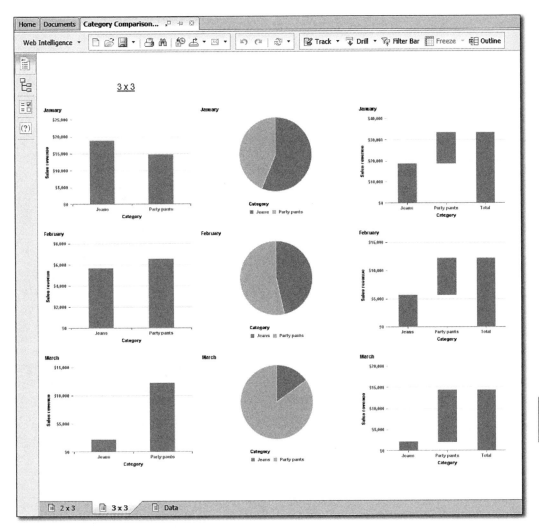

Figure 23.8 The 3 × 3 Grid Viewed in the BI Launch Pad

In Figure 23.9, the 2 × 3 grid is displayed using the MOBILE category, or card layout. Notice that only four of the six report parts are shown, and the remaining two report parts are displayed on a separate screen, not visible.

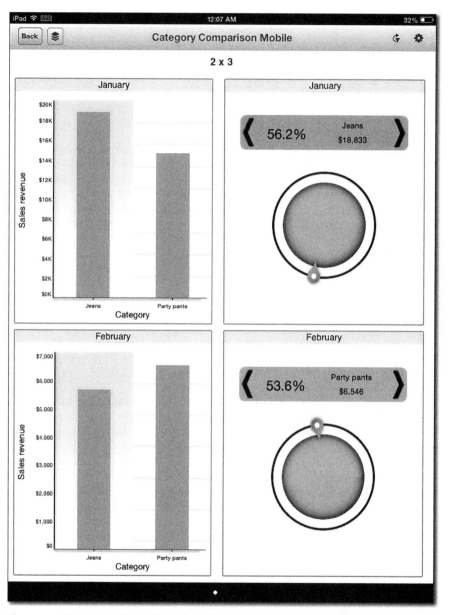

Figure 23.9 The 2 × 3 Grid in SAP BusinessObjects Mobile with the Mobile Category

When the Web Intelligence document is additionally tagged with the MOBILEDE-SIGNED category, the mobile app renders it using page layout, not card layout.

Therefore, all six report parts are rendered on a single screen, as shown in Figure 23.10.

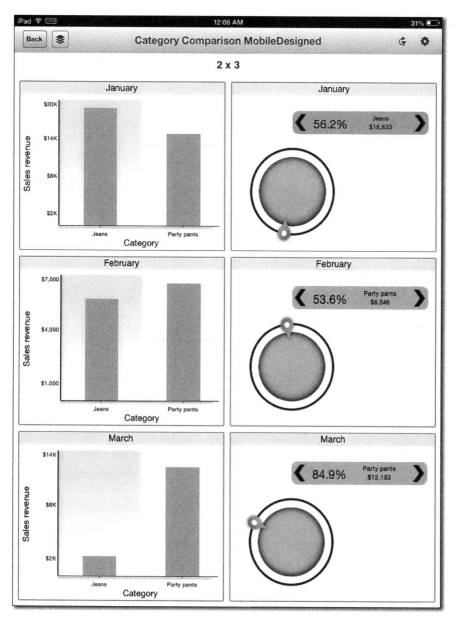

Figure 23.10 The 2 × 3 Grid in SAP BusinessObjects Mobile with the MobileDesigned Category (Portrait Orientation)

MOBILEDESIGNED also displays all six report parts when the tablet is in a landscape position, as shown in Figure 23.11.

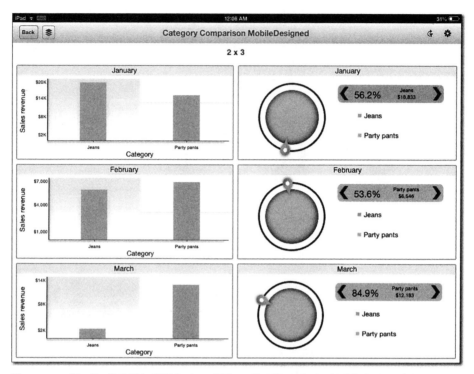

Figure 23.11 The 2 × 3 Grid in SAP BusinessObjects Mobile with the MobileDesigned Category (Landscape Orientation)

Next, we'll consider the 3 × 3 grid of Web Intelligence report parts. Using only the MOBILE category, the mobile device is unable to display all nine report parts using card layout. Only three report parts are rendered per screen, with the other six report parts organized on two additional screens (see Figure 23.12).

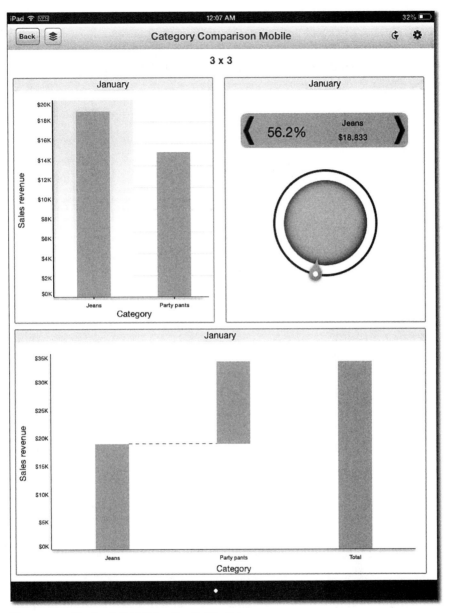

Figure 23.12 The 3 × 3 Grid Using the Mobile Category

But when the document is also tagged with the MobileDesigned category, the SAP BusinessObjects Mobile app is able to render all nine report parts on a single screen without the need to swipe to additional screens. Figure 23.13 shows how the MOBILEDESIGNED report will appear in portrait orientation.

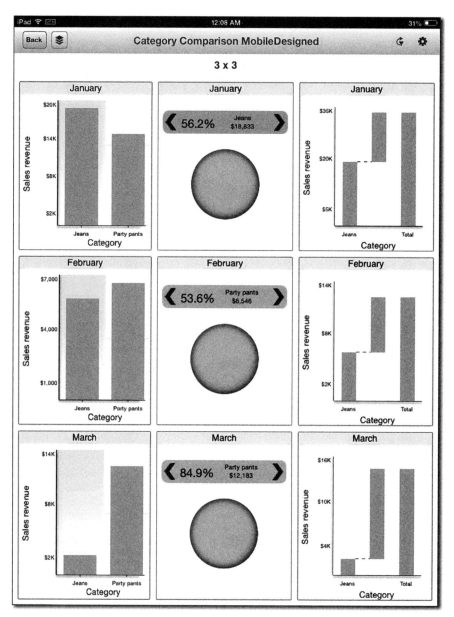

Figure 23.13 The 3 × 3 Grid Using the MobileDesigned Category (Portrait Orientation)

Figure 23.14 shows how the MOBILEDESIGNED report will appear in landscape orientation.

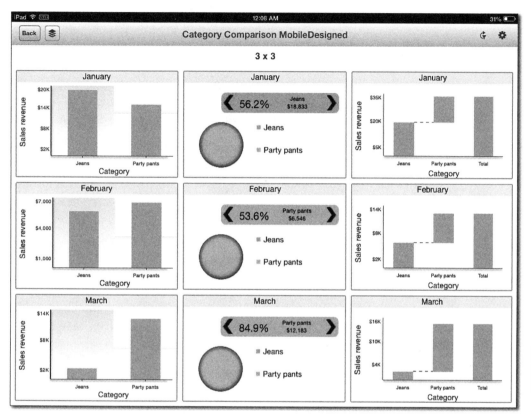

Figure 23.14 The 3 × 3 Grid Using the MobileDesigned Category (Landscape Orientation)

The MOBILEDESIGNED category and page mode allow the SAP BusinessObjects Mobile app to more closely observe the layout of the original Web Intelligence document, although the importance of fidelity in layout must be weighed against the size of the report parts. However, mobile users can zoom in on any report part simply by double-tapping on it.

> **Note**
>
> The behavior of the card layout model and page layout model depend on the version and patch level of the SAP BusinessObjects BI platform as well as the version and patch level of the SAP BusinessObjects Mobile app. You may notice slight changes in rendering when either is updated to a new version or patch level.

23.3   Mobile-Only Analytic Types

In the previous section, you learned how the SAP BusinessObjects Mobile app renders Web Intelligence tables and charts. In this section, you'll learn how to create additional visualizations such as sparklines, bullet graphs, and scorecards that are unique to the mobile experience.

These visualizations are created by assigning a formula to the name property of a table block. These formulas always begin with a semicolon (;) and use a combination of alphanumeric codes and column numbers to inform the SAP BusinessObjects Mobile app how to render the visualization.

Although you can't see the visualization at design time from either the Web Intelligence Rich Client or the browser-based edition of Web Intelligence, this formula is interpreted by the SAP BusinessObjects Mobile BI app, which renders the visualization. To develop these visualizations, you'll want to keep your tablet close at hand so you can immediately test changes to the formulas.

23.3.1   Query and Formula Design

All of the examples in this section can be created in a single Web Intelligence document that uses the following objects from the eFashion universe: YEAR, MONTH, MONTH NAME, STATE, CITY, CATEGORY, LINES, SALES REVENUE, QUANTITY SOLD, MARGIN, and DISCOUNT (see Figure 23.15).

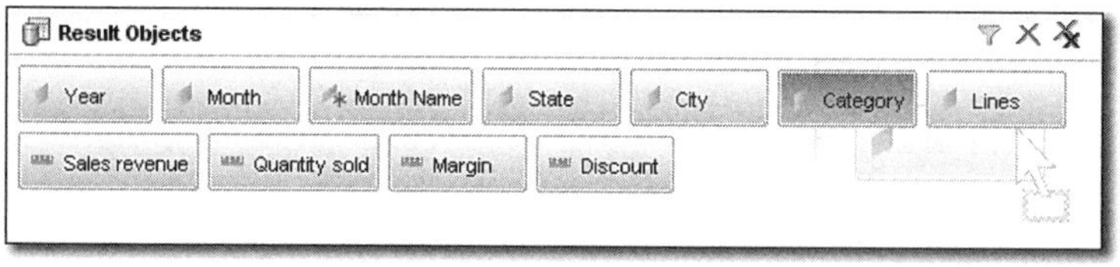

Figure 23.15 Exploration of Mobile-Only Analytic Types in the eFashion Query

The eFashion universe contains three years of data. Using output contexts, you can create variables for the current year (2006) and previous year (2005).

To calculate the current year's revenue, create a variable named "Revenue CY" with the following FORMULA (see Figure 23.16):

```
=Sum([Sales revenue] Where ([Year]="2006"))
```

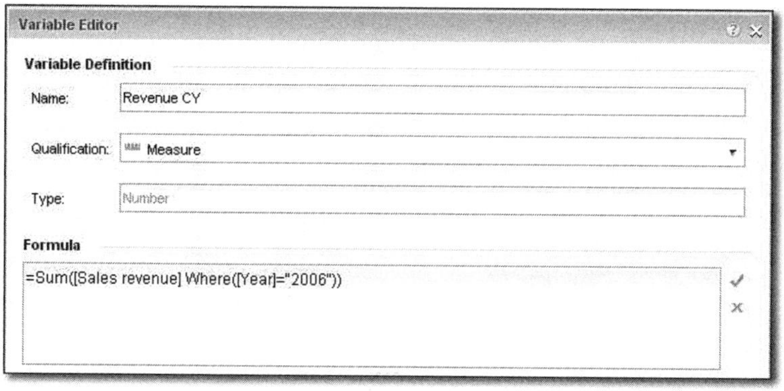

Figure 23.16 Formula for Current Year's Revenue

To calculate the previous year's revenue, create a variable named "Revenue LY" with the following FORMULA (see Figure 23.17):

```
=Sum([Sales revenue] Where ([Year]= "2005"))
```

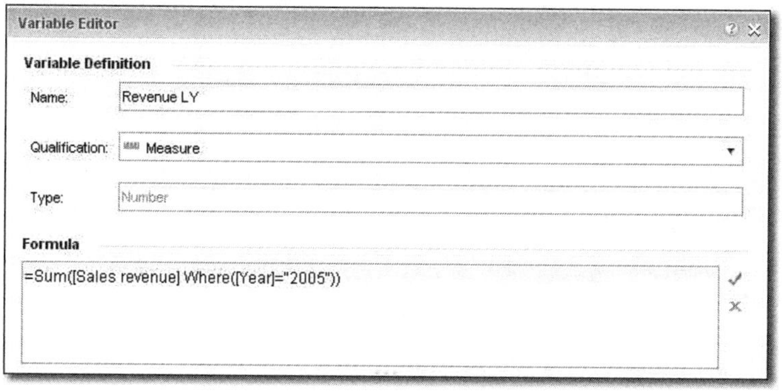

Figure 23.17 Formula for Previous Year's Revenue

You can also compute the minimum revenue amount, average revenue amount, and maximum revenue amount.

The minimum yearly revenue for a particular state can be computed by the following variable (see Figure 23.18):

```
=Min([Sales revenue] Where([Year]="2006")) ForAll([State]; [Year])
```

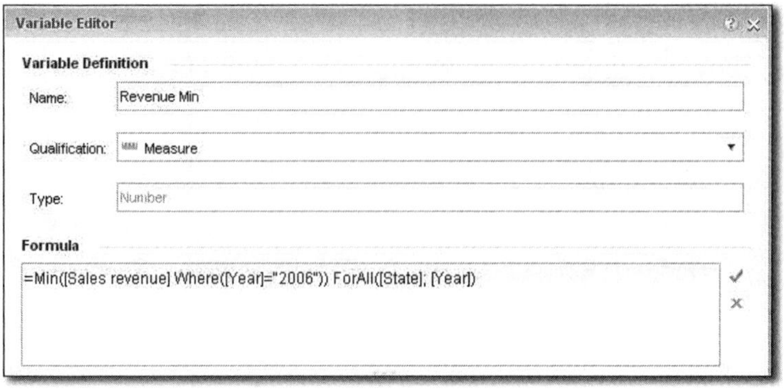

Figure 23.18 Formula for Lowest Annual Revenue

The maximum yearly revenue for a particular state can be computed by the following variable (see Figure 23.19):

```
=Max([Sales revenue] Where([Year="2006")) ForAll([State]; [Year])
```

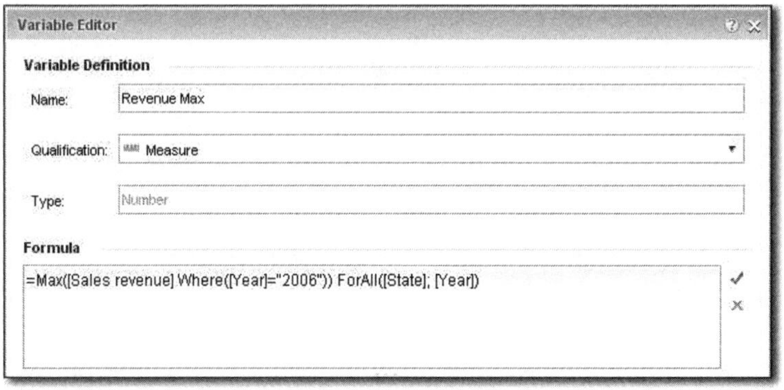

Figure 23.19 Formula for Highest Annual Revenue

The average yearly revenue for all states in a given year can be computed by the following variable (see Figure 23.20):

```
=Avg([Sales revenue] Where([Year="2006")) ForAll([State]; [Year])
```

Lastly, to create a variable for year-over-year percentage growth, which can be used with scorecards (see Figure 23.21), use this formula:

```
=([Revenue CY]-[Revenue LY])/[Revenue LY]
```

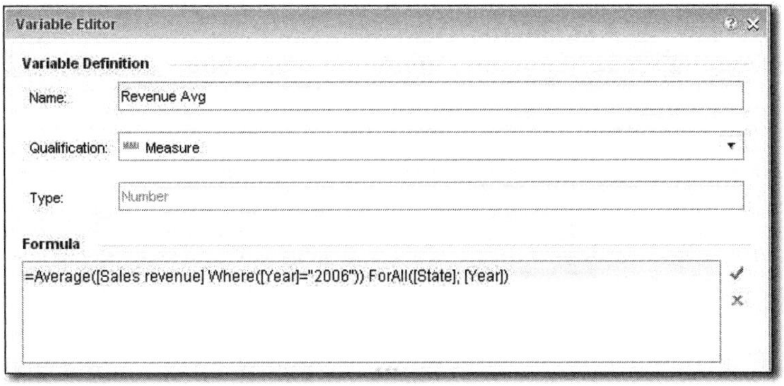

Variable Editor

Variable Definition

Name: Revenue Avg

Qualification: Measure

Type: Number

Formula

=Average([Sales revenue] Where([Year]="2006")) ForAll([State]; [Year])

Figure 23.20 Formula for Average Yearly Revenue

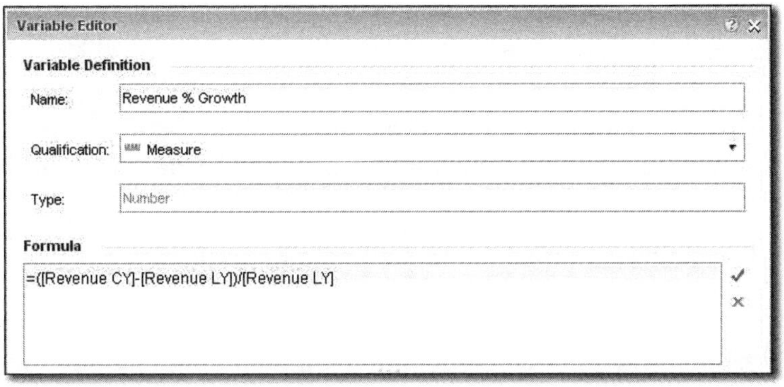

Variable Editor

Variable Definition

Name: Revenue % Growth

Qualification: Measure

Type: Number

Formula

=([Revenue CY]-[Revenue LY])/[Revenue LY]

Figure 23.21 Formula for Revenue Percentage Growth

Next, let's investigate the benefits of sparklines.

23.3.2 Creating Sparklines

A *sparkline* is a line chart that is small enough to be embedded alongside text, such as a table. The term sparkline is attributed to data visualization pioneer Edward Tufte.

Create a crosstab table that shows monthly sales revenue by state. Add total calculations for both the rows and columns. Then add the variables for last year's sales revenue and this year's sales revenue to the right of the state column. The results are shown in Figure 23.22.

Spark Line (Area)														
	Last Year	This Year	January	February	March	April	May	June	July	August	September	October	November	December	TOTAL
California	$2,782,680	$2,992,679	$288,260	$161,506	$279,979	$260,420	$327,341	$201,638	$250,330	$156,525	$368,911	$298,918	$202,128	$196,726	$2,992,679
Colorado	$768,390	$843,584	$82,188	$49,653	$72,912	$71,550	$81,342	$60,770	$64,338	$49,775	$118,776	$80,313	$59,011	$52,954	$843,584
DC	$1,215,158	$1,053,581	$108,675	$73,420	$96,913	$94,272	$98,438	$70,388	$91,387	$47,496	$132,762	$102,744	$84,697	$52,389	$1,053,581
Florida	$661,250	$811,924	$85,677	$42,192	$76,014	$64,080	$86,731	$70,658	$67,346	$45,600	$102,623	$73,109	$49,372	$48,523	$811,924
Illinois	$1,150,659	$1,134,085	$116,260	$53,410	$85,989	$90,183	$170,066	$94,476	$71,733	$54,915	$146,539	$81,115	$91,693	$77,709	$1,134,085
Massachusetts	$157,719	$887,169	$83,637	$60,773	$75,890	$71,267	$86,464	$62,797	$72,316	$53,530	$111,618	$95,671	$61,474	$51,732	$887,169
New York	$2,763,503	$3,151,022	$320,715	$163,063	$263,382	$215,974	$355,162	$284,480	$313,186	$170,350	$430,711	$282,432	$188,334	$163,232	$3,151,022
Texas	$3,732,889	$4,185,098	$415,955	$259,434	$427,091	$354,584	$408,604	$325,034	$316,677	$231,174	$484,778	$416,000	$306,390	$239,377	$4,185,098
TOTAL	$13,232,246	$13,232,246	$1,501,367	$863,452	$1,378,170	$1,222,329	$1,614,147	$1,170,241	$1,247,314	$809,365	$1,896,716	$1,430,300	$1,043,099	$882,642	$15,059,143

Figure 23.22 Sparkline Table Design

To create a sparkline for the monthly sales figures, change the name of the table block to the following formula:

```
;SL_GF_[column name for MicroChart]_C_[starting number of column]_[End-
ing number of column]
```

Because January revenue figures appear in column 4 and December revenue figures appear in column 15, the final formula should look like this (see Figure 23.23):

```
;SL_GF_Revenue_C_4_15
```

Format Table		? ×
General	Name	;SL_GF_Revenue_C_4_15
Border	**Display**	
Appearance	☐ Avoid duplicate row aggregation	☐ Show object name
Layout		

Figure 23.23 Sparkline Formula – Area

When viewed on the mobile device, all other columns will appear in a table. But instead of 12 months of sales revenue figures, the mobile user will see an inline sparkline, as shown in Figure 23.24.

If desired, the sparkline can be displayed as a line chart instead of an area chart by replacing the "GF" in the block name with an "L" (see Figure 23.25). The revised sparkline is shown in Figure 23.26.

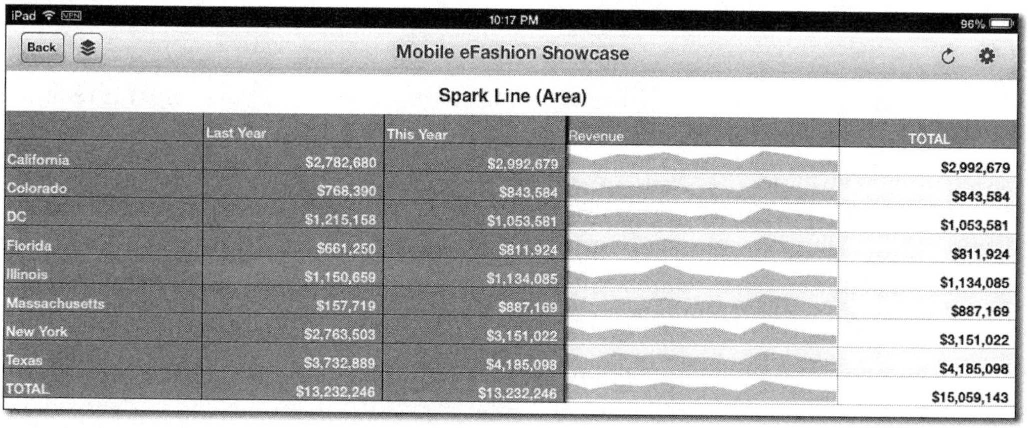

iPad
10:17 PM
96%
Back
Mobile eFashion Showcase
Spark Line (Area)
Last Year
This Year
Revenue
TOTAL
California $2,782,680 $2,992,679 $2,992,679
Colorado $768,390 $843,584 $843,584
DC $1,215,158 $1,053,581 $1,053,581
Florida $661,250 $811,924 $811,924
Illinois $1,150,659 $1,134,085 $1,134,085
Massachusetts $157,719 $887,169 $887,169
New York $2,763,503 $3,151,022 $3,151,022
Texas $3,732,889 $4,185,098 $4,185,098
TOTAL $13,232,246 $13,232,246 $15,059,143

Figure 23.24 Sparkline (Area) Displayed on a Mobile Device

Format Table
General
Border
Appearance
Layout
Name
;SL_L_Revenue_C_4_15
Display
Avoid duplicate row aggregation
Show object name

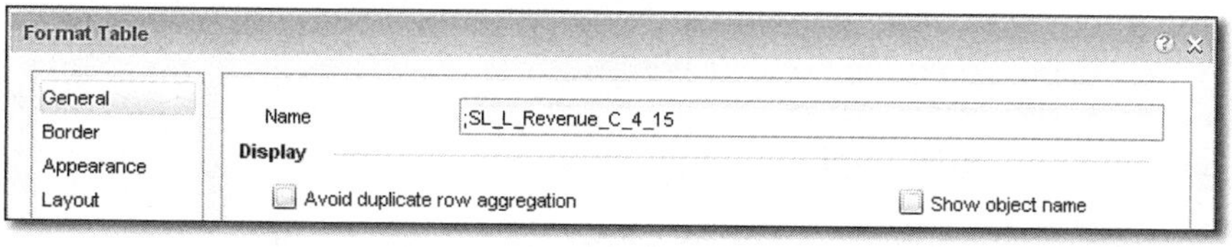

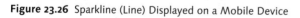

Figure 23.25 Sparkline (Line) Formula

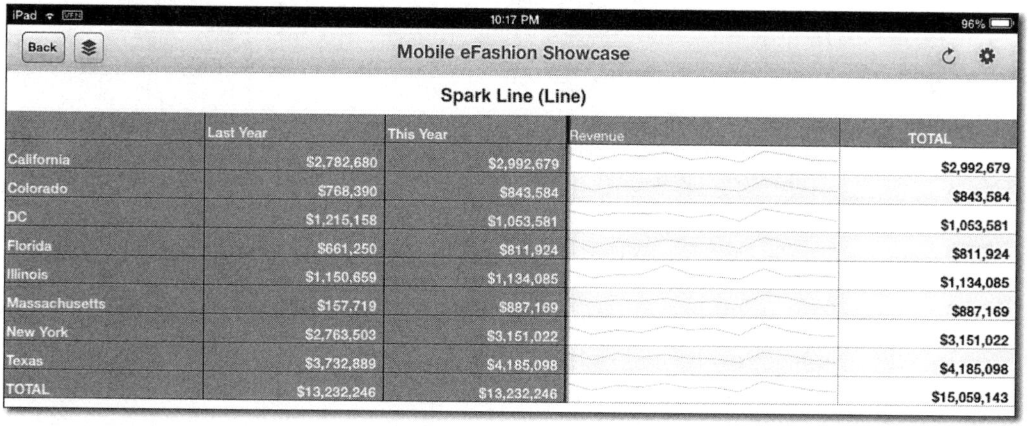

iPad
10:17 PM
96%
Back
Mobile eFashion Showcase
Spark Line (Line)
Last Year
This Year
Revenue
TOTAL
California $2,782,680 $2,992,679 $2,992,679
Colorado $768,390 $843,584 $843,584
DC $1,215,158 $1,053,581 $1,053,581
Florida $661,250 $811,924 $811,924
Illinois $1,150,659 $1,134,085 $1,134,085
Massachusetts $157,719 $887,169 $887,169
New York $2,763,503 $3,151,022 $3,151,022
Texas $3,732,889 $4,185,098 $4,185,098
TOTAL $13,232,246 $13,232,246 $15,059,143

Figure 23.26 Sparkline (Line) Displayed on a Mobile Device

23.3.3 Creating Bullet Graphs

The *bullet graph* was designed by Stephen Few. The goal of a bullet graph is to display a single metric in a bar format using much less space than what is required for other visualization types, such as gauges. To provide context, a bullet graph also displays a comparison value (e.g., last year's sales in comparison to this year's) and a qualitative scale to help the SAP BusinessObjects Mobile user determine if the metric displayed by the bullet graph is good, bad, or ugly. Lastly, the bullet chart has a quantitative scale that helps the user determine the value of the metric. Let's attempt this now.

Create a vertical table that displays STATE and YEARLY REVENUE for the current year (the Revenue CY variable created earlier in this chapter). These values will be displayed in table format on the mobile device. Next, add the REVENUE CY, REVENUE LY, REVENUE MIN, REVENUE AVG, and REVENUE MAX variables to the table, as shown in Figure 23.27.

| | Bullet Graph | | | | | |
State	Yearly Revenue	Revenue CY	Revenue LY	Revenue Min	Revenue Avg	Revenue Max
California	$2,992,679	$2,992,679	$2,782,680	$811,924	$1,882,393	$4,185,098
Colorado	$843,584	$843,584	$768,390	$811,924	$1,882,393	$4,185,098
DC	$1,053,581	$1,053,581	$1,215,158	$811,924	$1,882,393	$4,185,098
Florida	$811,924	$811,924	$661,250	$811,924	$1,882,393	$4,185,098
Illinois	$1,134,085	$1,134,085	$1,150,659	$811,924	$1,882,393	$4,185,098
Massachuset	$887,169	$887,169	$157,719	$811,924	$1,882,393	$4,185,098
New York	$3,151,022	$3,151,022	$2,763,503	$811,924	$1,882,393	$4,185,098
Texas	$4,185,098	$4,185,098	$3,732,889	$811,924	$1,882,393	$4,185,098

Figure 23.27 Bullet Graph Table Design

A Web Intelligence bullet graph requires an actual value, a comparative value, three (min, mid, and max) qualitative values, and an optional title. The formula is represented generically as:

```
;BC_[Graph Name]_C_[Starting Column]_[Ending Column]_tl_[Title]
```

For the data represented in Figure 23.27, the formula should be (see Figure 23.28):

```
;BC_State Comparison_C_3_7_tl_1
```

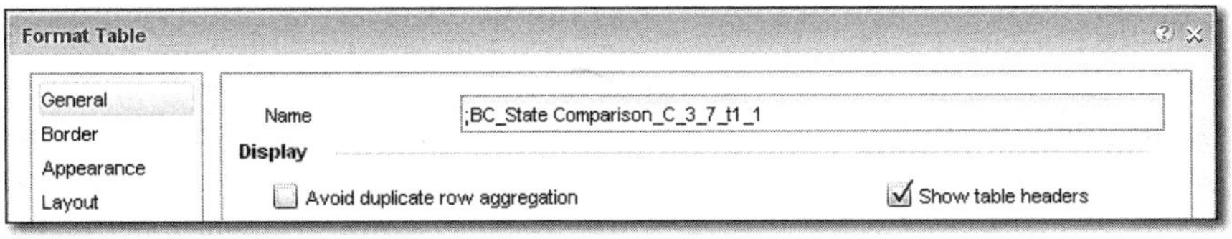

Figure 23.28 Bullet Graph Block Name

The bullet graph is rendered on a tablet, as shown in Figure 23.29.

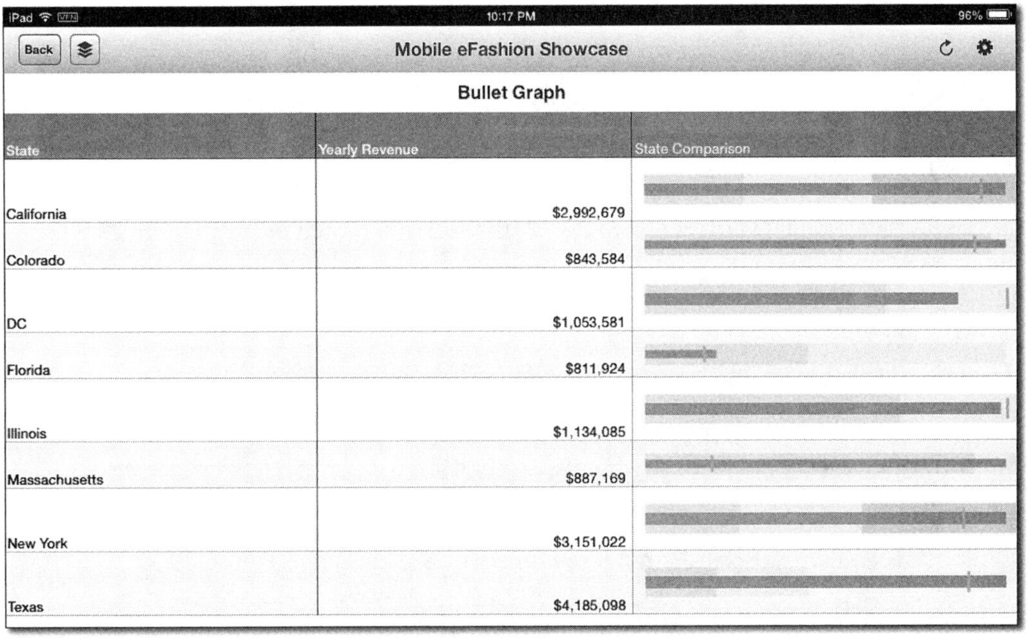

Figure 23.29 Bullet Graph Displayed in SAP BusinessObjects Mobile

On an iPhone 5 display, SAP BusinessObjects Mobile can show up to eight bullet graphs.

23.3.4 Creating Micro Bar Charts

A *micro bar chart* is similar to a sparkline in that it's displayed inline with text. But unlike a sparkline, it uses discrete bars rather than a continuous line to display its values. Use the same table design that was used in the earlier sparkline example, which is shown in Figure 23.30.

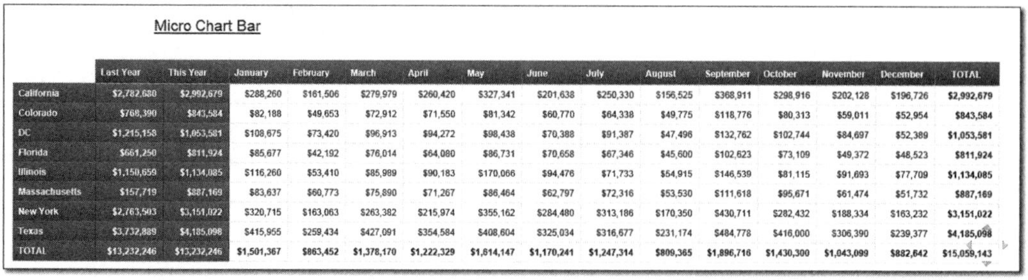

Figure 23.30 Micro Bar Chart Design

The formula to render a micro bar chart is:

```
;MBC_TYPE_< micro bar chart name >_C_<starting_column_number>_<ending_
column_number>
```

Using the table from Figure 23.30, the formula should be (see Figure 23.31):

```
;MBC_TYPE_Monthly_Sales_C_4_15
```

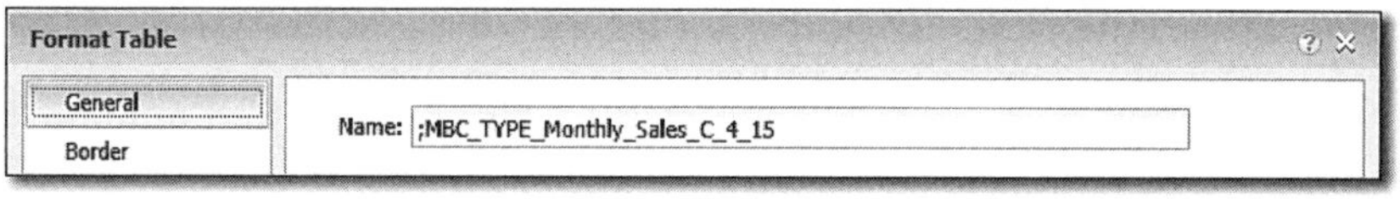

Figure 23.31 Micro Bar Chart block name

The micro bar chart is rendered on a tablet as shown in Figure 23.32.

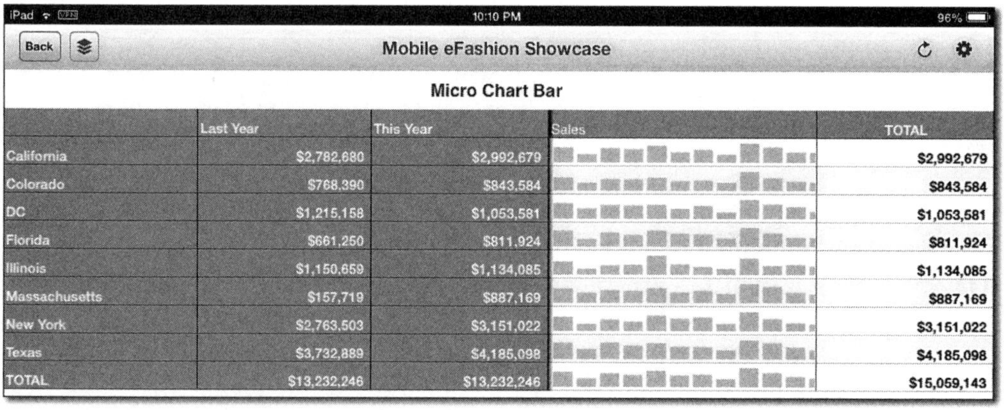

Figure 23.32 Micro Bar Chart Displayed on an SAP BusinessObjects Mobile Tablet

23.3.5 Creating Scorecards

The last type of mobile analytic is the *scorecard*. Scorecards focus on displaying a trend going up or down with an at-a-glance indicator rather than displaying discrete values as with other analytic types. An example of a trend is year-over-year percent revenue growth, as it's either going up (positive numbers) or down (negative numbers). The SAP BusinessObjects Mobile app can display the trend in three different visual formats: glossy icon, button, or arrow.

Create a scorecard using STATE, REVENUE LY (last year's revenue), REVENUE CY (current year's revenue), and REVENUE % GROWTH, as shown in Figure 23.33. The trend icon is displayed using the text color of the trend metric. Therefore, if desired, create conditional formatting (known as an alerter in previous versions of Web Intelligence) for REVENUE % GROWTH, displaying positive revenue growth with the color green, and negative revenue growth with the color red.

State	Revenue LY	Revenue CY	Revenue % Growth
California	$2,782,680	$2,992,679	7.55%
Colorado	$768,390	$843,584	9.79%
DC	$1,215,158	$1,053,581	-13.30%
Florida	$661,250	$811,924	22.79%
Illinois	$1,150,659	$1,134,085	-1.44%
Massachusetts	$157,719	$887,169	462.50%
New York	$2,763,503	$3,151,022	14.02%
Texas	$3,732,889	$4,185,098	12.11%

Figure 23.33 Scorecard Table Design

Create a scorecard using the trend icon (see Figure 23.34), which uses the following generic formula:

```
;SC_TT_C_[Column number of trend]_[Position of the icon to be displayed]
```

or

```
;SC_TT_C_4_R
```

The table appears with the TREND icon to the right of the TREND METRIC (revenue percent growth), as shown in Figure 23.35.

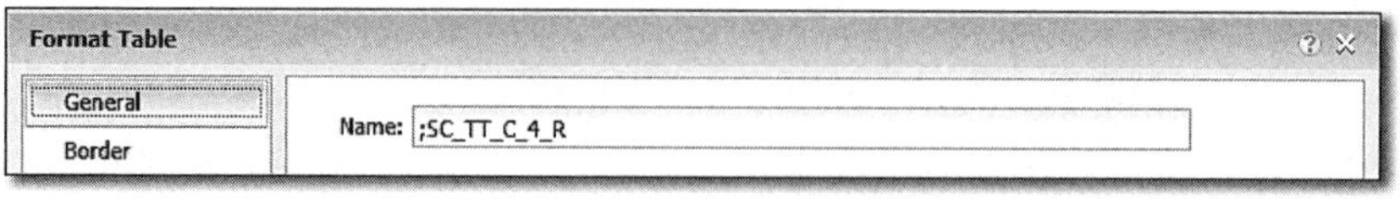

Figure 23.34 Scorecard with Trend Icon Block Name

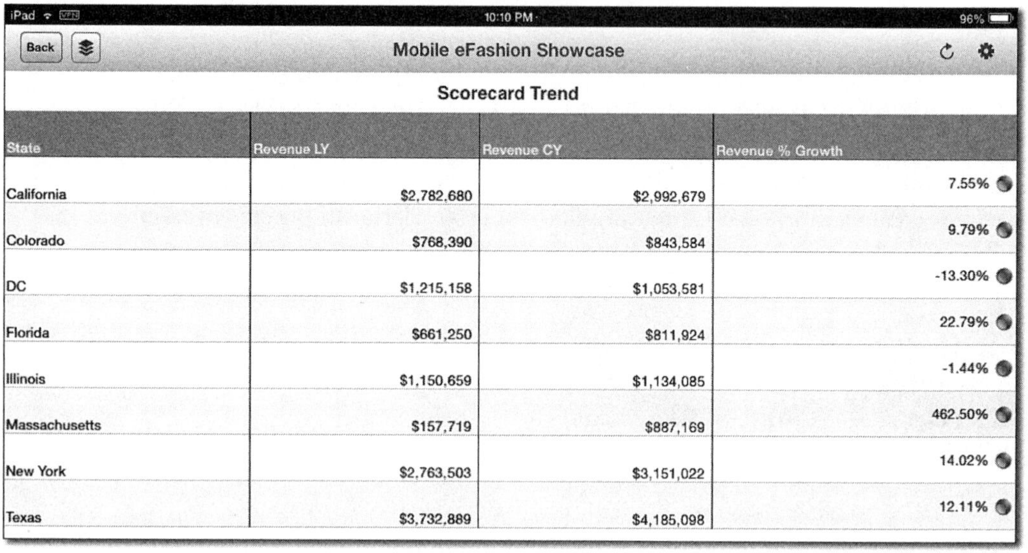

Figure 23.35 Scorecard with Trend Icon

The icon can be changed to an arrow by changing the "TT" in the formula to "TA" (see Figure 23.36). For example,

```
;SC_TA_C_[Column number of trend]_[Position of the icon to be displayed]
```

or

```
;SC_TA_C_4_L
```

Figure 23.36 Scorecard with Arrow Block Name

The arrow appears to the left of the trend metric, as shown in Figure 23.37.

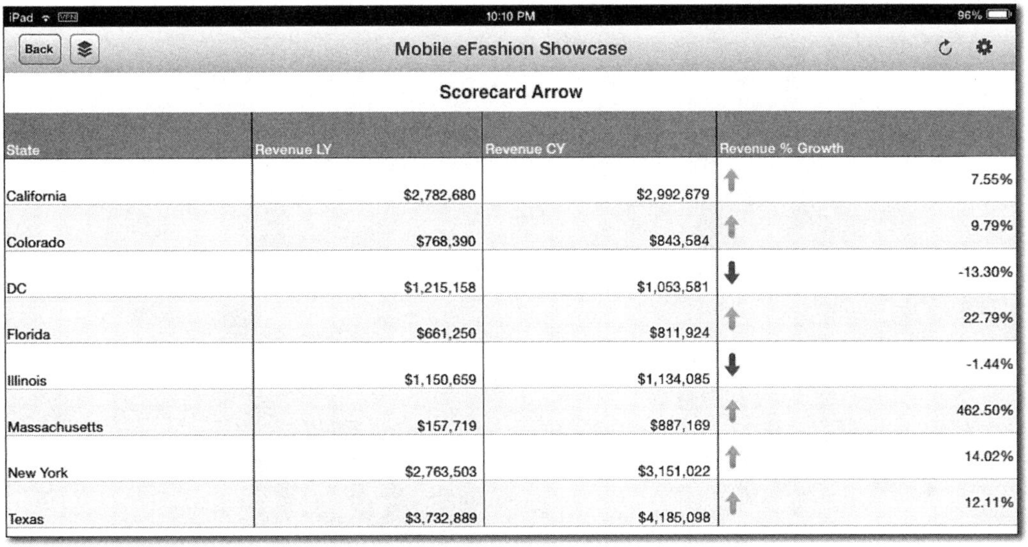

Figure 23.37 Scorecard with Arrow Displayed on SAP BusinessObjects Mobile

The third and final scorecard indicator is a button. The formula to generate a trend button is the following (see Figure 23.38):

```
;SC_GF_C_[Column number of trend]_[Position of the icon to be displayed]
```

or

```
;SC_TT_C_4
```

Figure 23.38 Scorecard with Button Block Name

Notice that there isn't an "R" or "L" for right or left because the trend button is displayed as a bar chart behind the trend value. The scorecard with the button indicator appears in Figure 23.39. Notice that it doesn't display negative values, so in certain circumstances, the icon or arrow may be a more effective trend indicator.

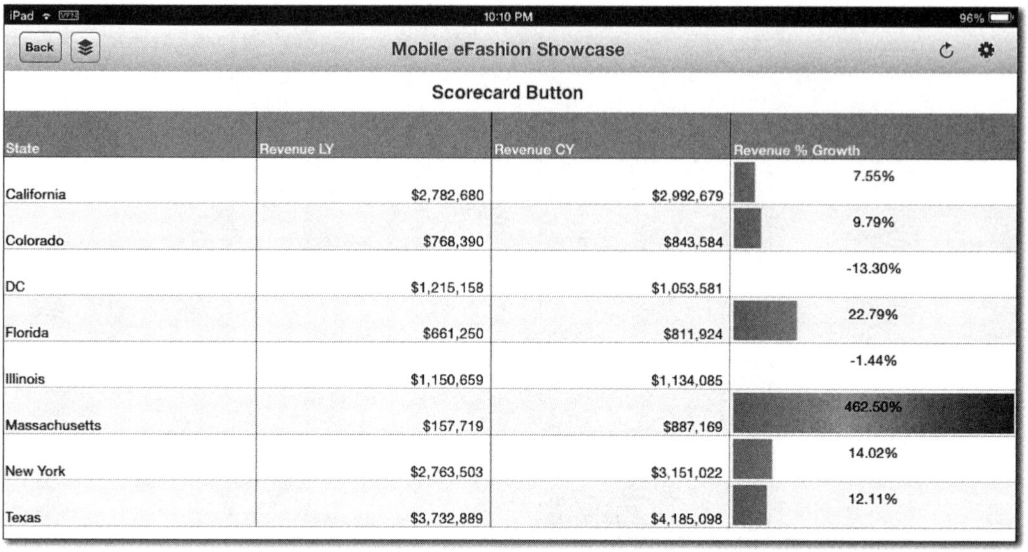

Figure 23.39 Scorecard with Button Displayed in SAP BusinessObjects Mobile

23.4 Report Linking

Mobile Web Intelligence reports can support *report linking* just like their browser-based counterparts. For example, a store name can be configured to link to a details report. The linked column appears in a different color, as shown in Figure 23.40. Report linking is configured using the HTML viewer.

Navigate to the linked detail report by clicking on the store name. The detail report is shown in Figure 23.41.

To return to the master report, simply click on the BACK button in the top-left corner.

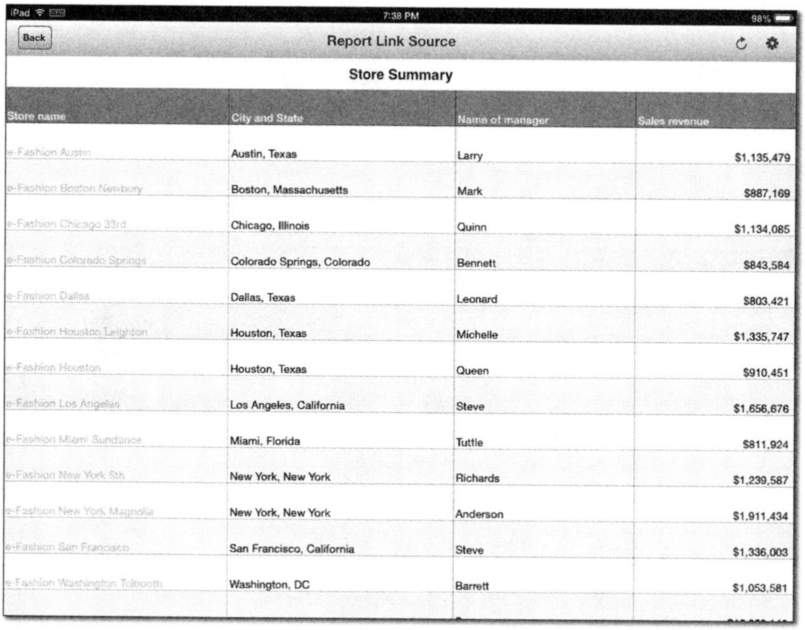

Figure 23.40 Report Linking – Hyperlinks in Source Report

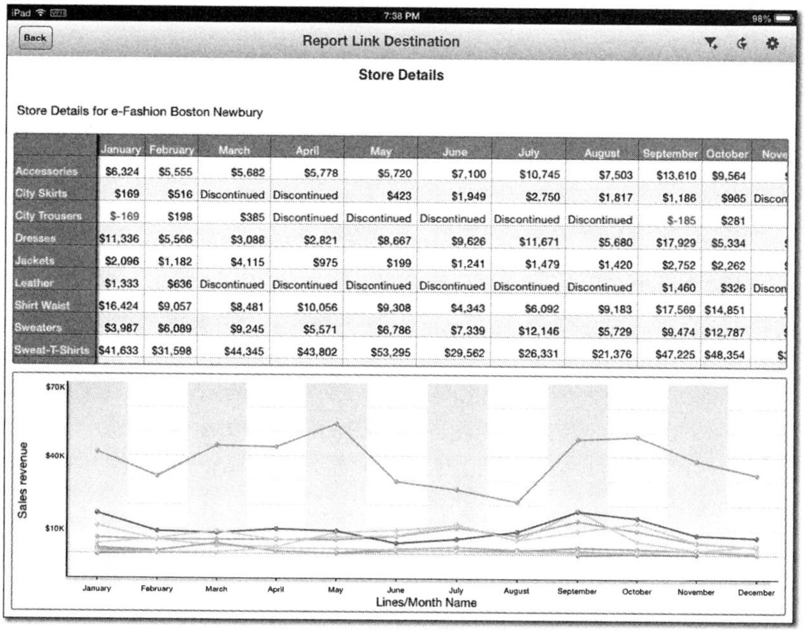

Figure 23.41 Report Linking – Prompted Destination Report

23.5   Input Controls

Mobile Web Intelligence documents can use *input controls*, which can be invoked by clicking on the FILTER icon in the top-right corner of the Web Intelligence document. Figure 23.42 shows a document that has an input control for the eFashion Lines object.

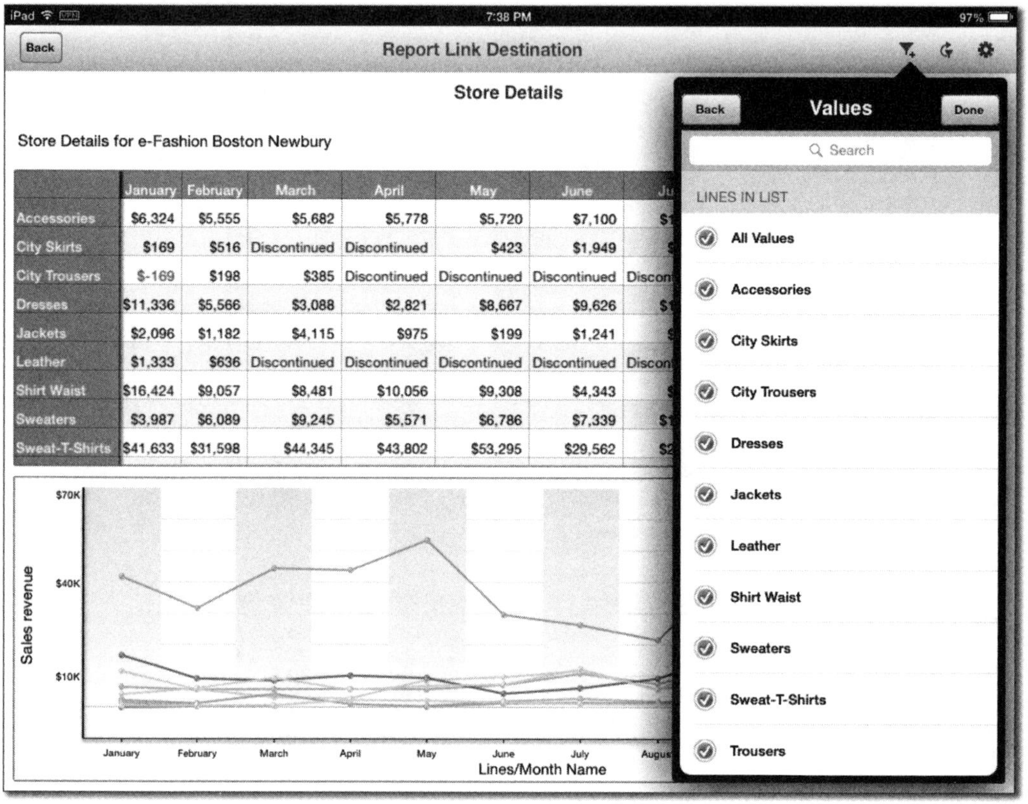

Figure 23.42 Mobile Input Controls

Because the input controls were configured to filter the entire report, choosing only the lines of CITY TROUSERS and TROUSERS filters both the table and the chart, as shown in Figure 23.43.

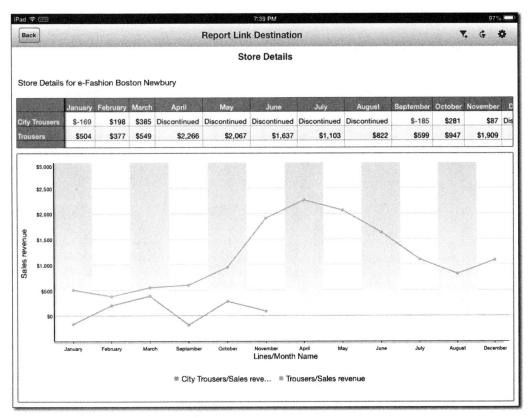

Figure 23.43 Report Filtered Using Input Control

23.6 Mobile Thumbnails

You can give your mobile reports a professional appearance by creating *thumbnail* images. These images should be 208 × 208 pixels square, in either JPEG or PNG format with .JPG, .JPEG, or .tif file extensions. These images should be stored on a publically available web server. Some examples of thumbnail images are shown in Figure 23.44.

To specify the thumbnail image, edit the Web Intelligence document properties from either the BI Launch Pad or CMC, and place the URL for the image in the KEYWORDS field, as shown in Figure 23.45.

Figure 23.44 Sample Mobile Thumbnails

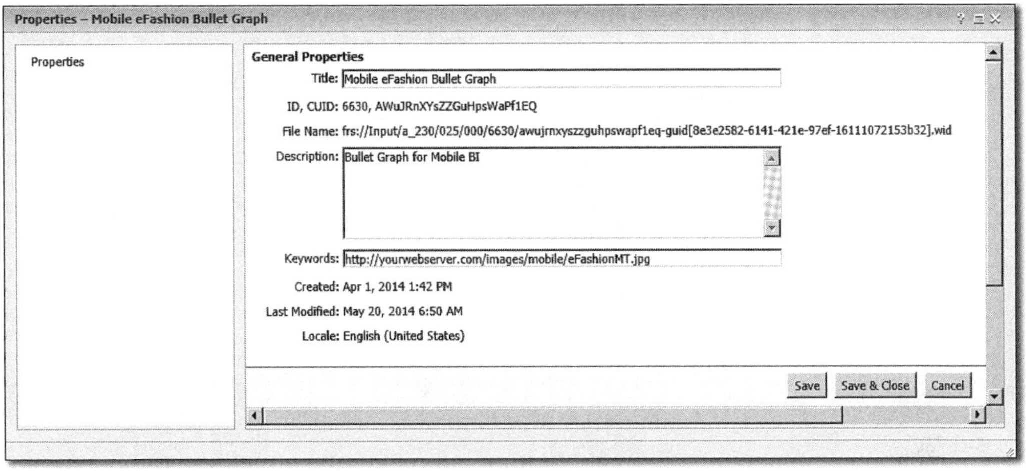

Figure 23.45 URL for Mobile Thumbnail Image in Keywords Field

23.7 Summary

The on-device mobile integration capabilities of Web Intelligence with the SAP BusinessObjects Mobile app provide a powerful tool for collaboration and analysis. The functionality extends the reach of your Web Intelligence reports to key audiences and organizations, providing the means for informed decision making in a fast-paced, ever-changing market.

Chapter 24 delves into the features of the new Information Design Tool used for universe design. From basic design of the data layer to integration of multidimensional data sources to utilization of multiple database connections, the Information Design Tool provides an integrated source for creation of robust semantic layers for report design.

The SAP BusinessObjects universe plays a key role in solving business problems and creating a successful SAP BusinessObjects BI solution.

24   Universe Basics: The Information Design Tool

In the previous edition of this book, we wrote:

"Universe design is a topic worthy of its own book because of the wide range of capabilities available when connecting to data sources and designing robust semantic layers for reporting."

Today, we can heartily recommend *Universe Design with SAP BusinessObjects BI: The Comprehensive Guide* by Christian Ah-Soon, Didier Mazoué, and Pierpaolo Vezzosi (SAP PRESS, 2013). In its 724 pages, you'll find a thorough treatment of the Information Design Tool (IDT). Our goal for this chapter is much more modest—to provide you with an introduction to the basic concepts of universe design and describe the product at the core of an SAP BusinessObjects BI solution.

The SAP BusinessObjects universe is the secure semantic layer that shields business users from the complexities of the database and provides a reliable and consistent data retrieval experience across many of the SAP BusinessObjects tools. The universe is a secure window into the database or data warehouse in your organization.

Universes allow you to graphically visualize selected database tables and views and then create joins to match table relationships in the database schema. You can create objects and categorize them for the fields that business users need to solve business problems. Universes also allow you to incorporate business logic into objects with case statements and other types of calculations.

24.1 Universe Basics

The SAP BusinessObjects universe is the common semantic layer that allows report designers to access the database without having to know any information about the underlying data structure. Being able to query corporate data sources without writing SQL or MDX statements highlights the ease of use of the SAP BusinessObjects suite of business intelligence tools.

> **The Importance of the Universe**
>
> Each universe is a single file that contains a connection to your database and business "objects" aliases to database fields. An unlimited number of SAP BusinessObjects Web Intelligence reports are then sourced from a single universe. As the database evolves and structures change, updates flow through seamlessly to reports by making corrections in one place: the universe.

The success of your business intelligence projects depends heavily on the careful creation of this foundational layer. It's important to note that universes should be created by experienced developers with extensive knowledge of the business and the SQL language. Understanding the structure of the database schema and table relationships is critical in developing a functional universe.

Although the concepts are fairly simple and straightforward, your universes should be carefully designed and tested. Errors in universe design can have profound negative effects on reports, leading to long-running queries and, worst of all, inaccurate results.

24.1.1 Introducing the Information Design Tool

In versions prior to SAP BusinessObjects BI 4.0, universes were created and maintained using a tool called Designer, which was renamed in the 4.0 platform as the Universe Design Tool. Universes created with this legacy tool have a .UNV file extension. Although originally designed for use with query and analysis tools such as Web Intelligence and its now-retired predecessor, Desktop Intelligence, universes constructed with the Universe Design Tool can also power enterprise reports created with SAP Crystal Reports 2011, dashboards created with SAP Crystal Dashboard Design, and SAP BusinessObjects Live Office.

SAP BusinessObjects BI 4.1 introduced a new universe creation tool called the Information Design Tool (IDT). Universes created with the IDT have a .UNX rather than the .UNV extension. In addition to Web Intelligence, universes constructed with the IDT can also power enterprise reports created with SAP Crystal Reports for Enterprise, dashboards created with SAP Crystal Dashboard Design, and SAP BusinessObjects Explorer.

Converting from Classic UNV Universes to New UNX Universes

Classic UNV universes can be loaded from previous versions of SAP BusinessObjects using the Upgrade Management Tool and continue to be used in Web Intelligence without modification. However, to use new tools such as SAP Crystal Reports for BI or new product features such as the Query Browser in SAP BusinessObjects Dashboards, classic universes must be converted to the new .UNX format. This procedure will be covered later in Section 24.8.

Although the IDT will ultimately replace the Universe Design Tool in an undetermined future version of SAP BusinessObjects BI, both are installed with the other client tools such as the Web Intelligence Rich Client, Query as a Web Service (QaaWS) Designer, and Translation Management Tool.

The IDT supports a wide array of both relational and OLAP data sources, making Web Intelligence ideal for nearly any reporting situation. These platforms are supported by SAP BusinessObjects BI 4.1 SP3:

- Amazon EMR Hive
- Apache Derby and Hadoop
- Generic ODBC, JDBC, OLEDB, and text files
- Greenplumb
- HP Neoview and Vertica
- HyperSQL (HSQLDB)
- IBM DB2 and Informix
- Ingres
- Microsoft Access, Excel, and SQL Server
- Netezza
- Oracle RDBMS, Hyperion, mySQL, EBS, and Exadata
- PostgreSQL

- ▶ Progress

- ▶ SalesForce.com

- ▶ SAP ERP, MaxDB, SAP Business Warehouse (SAP BW), and SAP HANA

- ▶ SAS

- ▶ Sybase APS, SQL Anywhere, and Sybase IQ

- ▶ Teradata

- ▶ WSDL 1.1 web services

- ▶ XML files

You should always consult the Product Availability Matrix (PAM) to confirm that the vendor and version of the desired data source is supported by the version of the SAP BusinessObjects BI platform you are deploying. PAM is available from the SAP Service Marketplace at *http://service.sap.com/*.

24.1.2 Components of a Universe

The traditional Universe Design Tool has two main panels in its interface, as shown in Figure 24.1. On the right is the schema panel, where the designer defines a data foundation, the tables, and joins in the underlying relational struc-ture. On the left is the universe panel, where the designer creates a business layer of classes and objects that users see when creating Web Intelligence documents. The universe specifies the universe connection, which defines where the data is physically located, but the connection is managed separately.

The IDT organizes universes into projects. A common relational database uni-verse project will contain three separate files:

- ▶ A connection (.CNX) or connection shortcut (.CNS) that defines the properties of the data source

- ▶ A data foundation (.DLX) that defines the tables and joins

- ▶ A business layer (.BLX) that defines the folders (formerly known as classes) and objects, and a universe connection shortcut that points to a defined universe connection in the repository

These three files are "compiled" by the IDT to generate a universe file (.UNX) that is stored in the Business Objects Repository (BOR). Figure 24.2 shows a view of the IDT.

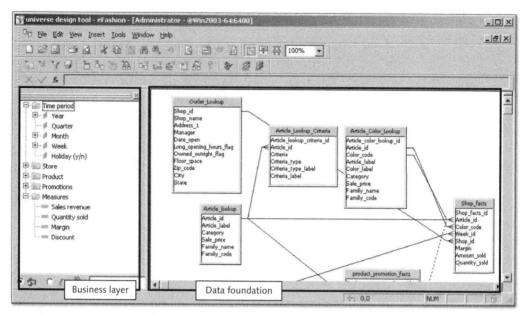

Figure 24.1 Business Layer and Data Foundation of the Classic Universe Design Tool (Formerly Designer)

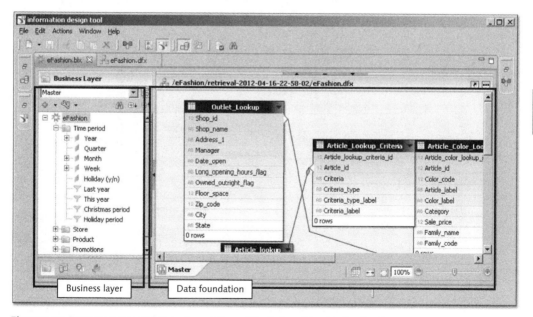

Figure 24.2 Business Layer and Data Foundation of the Information Design Tool

24.2   Creating a New Universe Project

To begin, launch the IDT from the Microsoft Windows START menu. Select NEW •
PROJECT, as shown in Figure 24.3.

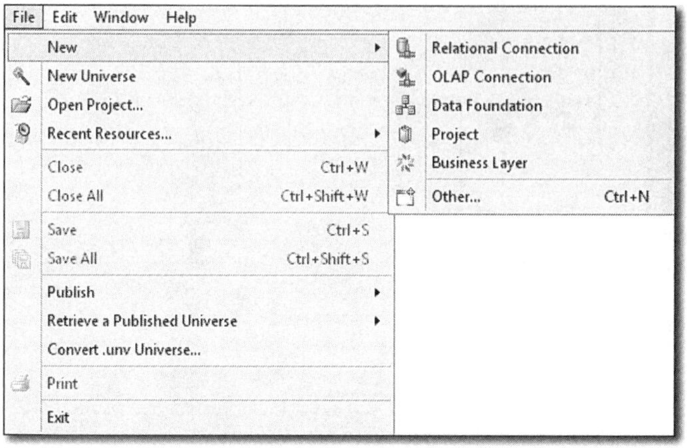

Figure 24.3 Creating a New Project from the File Menu

Next, assign a useful name for your universe project, as shown in Figure 24.4.
Note that the PROJECT NAME doesn't need to match the universe name.

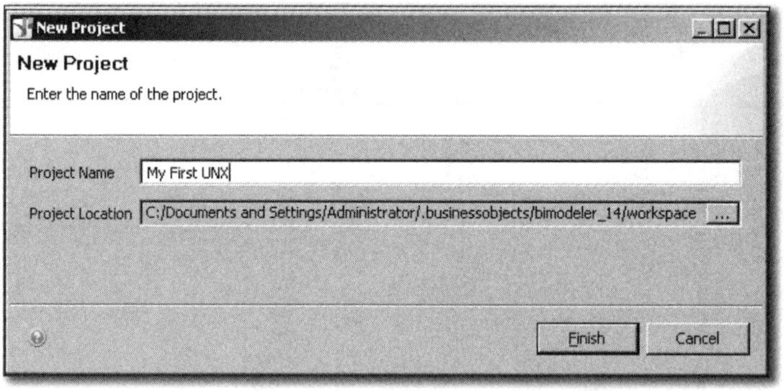

Figure 24.4 Assigning a Name to a New Information Design Tool Project

The project is now ready to accept connection shortcuts, data foundations, and
business layers.

24.3   Creating Connections

Two types of connections can be created in the IDT: local and secured. A local connection can be used when working locally with the Web Intelligence Rich Client. However, a secured connection is required for connections that need to be accessible to users of the SAP BusinessObjects BI platform. Secured connections are stored remotely in the BOR. Once created, secured connections can be referenced in universe projects by creating connection shortcuts, which have .CNS file extensions instead of the .CNX extension used for local connections or secured connections stored in the repository.

Both relational and OLAP secure connections are created in the REPOSITORY RESOURCES window. You'll need to create a session to the desired SAP Business-Objects system by providing your user credentials. Make sure that the SAP BusinessObjects administrator has given you privileges to create and manage connections. Starting with SAP BusinessObjects BI 4.0, connections can be organized into folders. Choose the desired folder, and use either the INSERT button at the top of the REPOSITORY RESOURCES window or the right-click menu of the folder. From either menu, choose INSERT RELATIONAL CONNECTION, as shown in Figure 24.5. OLAP connections are similarly created by choosing INSERT OLAP CONNECTION (not shown).

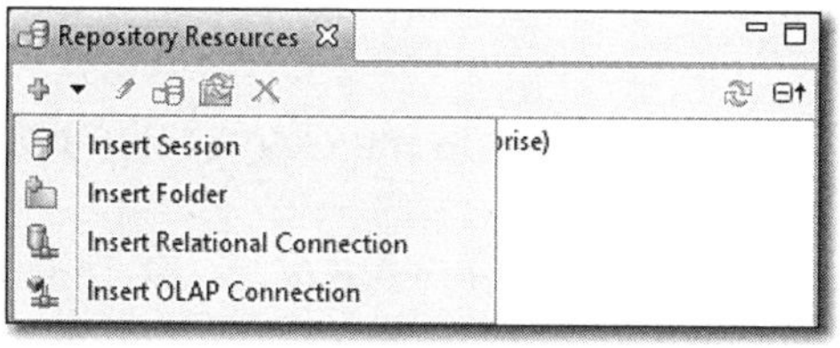

Figure 24.5 Inserting a New Relation Connection into the Repository Resources

Continue to define the connection using the NEW RELATIONAL CONNECTION wizard.

Best Practices for Connections

The following are recommended best practices and settings for connections. These settings are recommended, but they may not be the best solutions for every environment. Each setting should be tested on the developer's own network and database:

▶ **Set the universe connection to disconnect after each transaction**
This can help to avoid having long-running queries bog down the connections.

▶ **Set the Array Fetch Size parameter to the appropriate size for each database environment**
This is the setting that determines how many rows are fetched at a time from the database. A larger fetch size reduces the number of fetches required but has a direct effect on system memory. There is no magic size, so it may need to be set differently depending on the database platform and its characteristics. Consult with your organization's database administrators to determine the best value.

▶ **Manage connection rights globally in the Central Management Console (CMC) to simplify the security**
Except for rare occurrences, it will be sufficient to assign identical rights to all connections regardless of data source because user access is also controlled at the universe level. The typical exception to managing rights globally is when a connection points to sensitive data (such as employee salary) that should not be seen by all universe designers.

▶ **SAP BusinessObjects BI 4.x connections can now be organized into folders, just like reports and universes**
Consider creating a top-level folder for each database platform (SQL Server, SAP Sybase, SAP HANA, Teradata, etc.) to help document the source of data connections.

▶ **Create useful descriptions for universe connections in the CMC as self-documentation**
By default, a new connection will have no description, but one can be added later via the CMC. It's also beneficial to document connections and their parameters outside of the SAP BusinessObjects BI platform using Excel or a wiki.

▶ **Use restraint when creating connections**
Connections are deliberately separate from the data foundation to encourage reuse. It isn't necessary or advisable to create separate connections for each universe, although there are exceptions when certain universes require different access rights to the database than is provided by an existing connection. To avoid redundant connections, it may be desirable to limit the number of users

who have the security privileges required to create connections. These rights are managed in the CONNECTIONS MANAGEMENT area in the CMC.

Now that the connection is created and tested, you can turn your attention to the development of the universe data foundation, which is covered in the next section.

24.4 Creating Data Foundations

A data foundation describes a collection of relational database tables and joins that can be used by one or more business layers. OLAP data sources don't have data foundations because the cube metadata serves as the data foundation. To begin creating a relational data foundation, right-click in the project and choose NEW • DATA FOUNDATION, as shown in Figure 24.6.

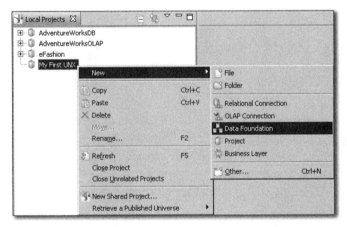

Figure 24.6 Adding a New Data Foundation to a Local Project

24.4.1 Inserting Tables into a Data Foundation

You begin creating a data foundation by inserting tables. A list of available tables can be invoked from the ACTIONS menu (shown in Figure 24.7), the INSERT button at the top of the data foundation layer, or from the right-click menu in the SCHEMA window.

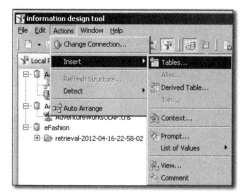

Figure 24.7 Inserting Tables into the Data Foundation

24.4.2 Inserting Joins into the Data Foundation

Traditional join types are inner join, outer join, left join, right join, and full outer join. Other joins include the following:

▶ **Equi-joins**
Two tables are linked when the values in both fields are equal. This type of join is also considered a simple join.

▶ **Theta joins**
Theta joins are most commonly used in warehouses that don't contain keys and when an equivalent field doesn't exist in both the fact and dimension table. The operator can be anything except equal.

> **Note**
>
> It's important that you understand the data before applying these types of joins. Outer joins can have a significant impact on the speed at which a query is returned. This is especially true when views are used.

To create a join, begin by selecting the field in the first table, and then drag the mouse while holding the left button, as shown in Figure 24.8.

Next, attach the join to the desired field in the second table, as shown in Figure 24.9. The default join is an equi-join. The question marks indicate that cardinality is not set. Join cardinality is an important topic that will be discussed later in this chapter.

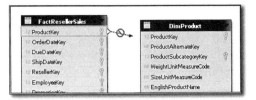

Figure 24.8 Connecting Two Tables with a Join

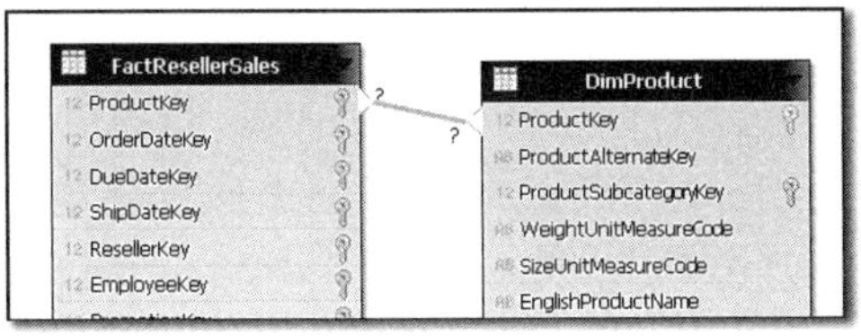

Figure 24.9 Completed Join

After the initial join is created, double-click on the join to edit its properties, as shown in Figure 24.10.

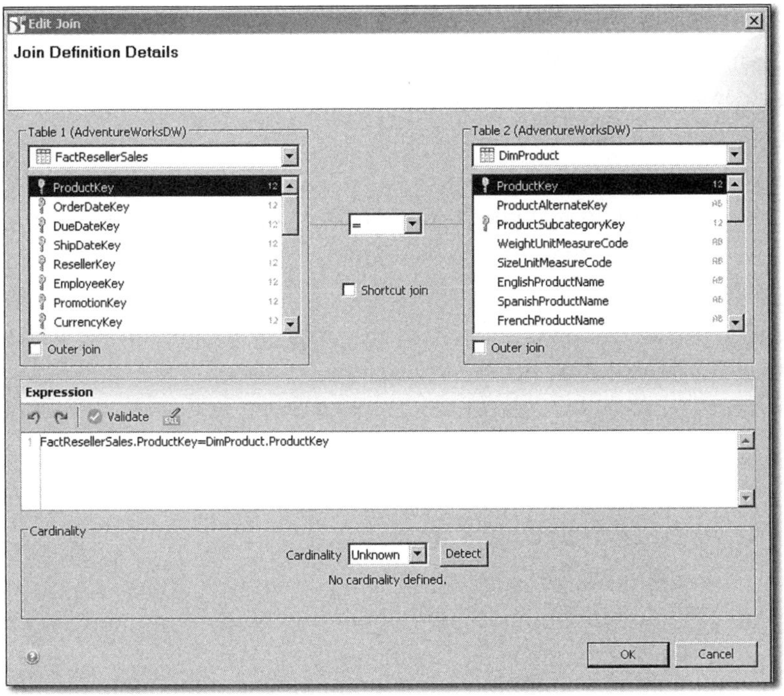

Figure 24.10 Editing Join Properties

In this window, you can revise a variety of join settings:

► **Cardinality**

This setting explicitly forces the join to a one-to-one, one-to-many, or many-to-many relationship. By selecting a one-to-many or many-to-many relationship, a crow's-foot is added to the join line connecting the two tables.

► **Detect cardinality**

This setting is used to detect the type of relationship that exists between the two tables.

► **Set outer joins**

Two checkboxes labeled Outer join are located just beneath each table. Check the box just beneath the table that requires all fields to be returned. If both boxes are checked, a full outer join will be created.

► **Setting join conditions**

Six default conditions are available in a simple equi-join: =, !=, >, <, >=, and <=.

► **Between condition**

If two fields are selected from one of the tables, then the between condition is set by default. This is very useful when joining to a table that doesn't contain a key or field to join to with an equi-join. An example of this type of join is available in the demo Island Resorts Marketing universe connecting the Customer table to the Age_group table.

► **Complex join condition**

If your join requires additional modification to duplicate the business rules in the universe, a complex condition can be used to further customize the join.

► **Shortcut join**

A shortcut join is an optional path that can be taken depending on which objects a user chooses in his query. Its purpose is to reduce the number of tables required in an SQL statement with the goal of improving query performance.

24.4.3 The Importance of Setting Cardinality

When creating joins in the data foundation, it's important to set cardinality. The cardinality setting has no effect on how SQL is generated. However, it does affect the behavior of the loop detection and resolution tools in the IDT.

Cardinality can be set automatically in the IDT but is best set manually after careful consideration of the relationships between tables. Cardinality is based on logic, but cardinality detection is based on data. Whether populated with sample data or production data, the actual data present may be too sparse. In such cases, the automatic cardinality detection may generate an inaccurate result. If the cardinality is inaccurate, the results of the loop detection tools such as DETECT LOOPS, DETECT ALIASES, and DETECT CONTEXTS will be inaccurate also.

24.4.4 Detecting Loops

Loops are inherent in universes because a small number of tables are used to define a large number of potential queries. This creates a problem that rarely exists in a hand-crafted SQL statement: loops. An unresolved loop will result in an inaccurate SQL statement where too few rows of data are returned. Fortunately, the IDT, just like its Universe Design Tool predecessor, has built-in tools to help the designer resolve loops. Depending on the join cardinality of the tables involved, a loop can be resolved with either an alias or a context, both of which are covered in the next section.

24.4.5 Detecting Aliases

Aliases are required when a single table performs multiple roles in the data model. For example, a calendar dimension may be used to represent order date, due date, and ship date. If only a single copy of the dimension table is used, multiple loops are created.

If the loop is unresolved, the universe will generate inappropriate SQL that returns fewer rows than expected, as shown in Figure 24.11. That is because the only rows returned by the query will be those where all three dates have the same value—an unlikely coincidence.

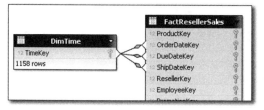

Figure 24.11 Unresolved Loop Requiring Aliases

The solution is to resolve the loop using aliased tables, either inserted manually or by the DETECT ALIASES feature, which is available from the menu at the top of the DATA FOUNDATION window, as shown in Figure 24.12.

Figure 24.12 Detect Aliases Tool

The DETECT ALIASES feature studies the joins in the data foundation and identifies tables that are on the "one" end of multiple one-to-many joins. In our example of three date dimensions, the DETECT ALIASES feature will insert two new aliased tables and keep the original one in place (see Figure 24.13).

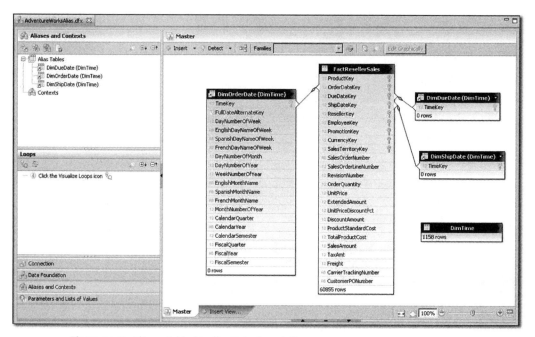

Figure 24.13 Aliases Added to the Data Foundation

Best Practices for Aliases

After the loop is resolved, take care to ensure that any existing objects in the business layer use the correct aliased version of the table. For example, check that sale date dimension objects use the sale date alias.

One drawback to aliased tables is that the aliases are deleted from the data foundation if the original table is deleted. To prevent this, a best practice is not to create objects on any original tables that have been aliased; instead, use aliased tables exclusively in the data foundation. In the preceding example, notice that the original DIMTIME table is never used, only its aliases. Place the original table in an isolated corner of the data foundation canvas. These original tables should be clearly labeled with a comment, warning other universe designers of the consequences of deleting the tables, as shown in Figure 24.14.

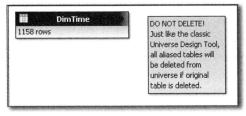

Figure 24.14 Warning about Deleting Tables

24.4.6 Detecting Contexts

Contexts are required when a single table retains its meaning in the data model but must be joined to multiple other tables in the data foundation. A common example is a dimension table that must be shared by multiple fact tables. When all of the joins are created, a loop is formed, as shown in Figure 24.15. Without resolution, the SQL generated will result in the desired fact table being joined to other fact tables. The most obvious effect of unresolved loops that require contexts is inflated numerical values in measure objects, as the number of rows returned by the query is higher than it should be.

Like aliases, the loop conditions need to be resolved by the universe designer, either visually or by using the built-in DETECT CONTEXTS feature, as shown in Figure 24.16.

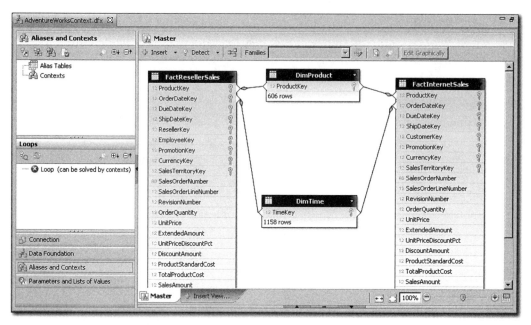

Figure 24.15 Loop Condition Created by Shared Dimension Tables

Figure 24.16 Detect Contexts Button in Aliases and Contexts Area

In our example, two contexts have been identified by the DETECT CONTEXTS feature, as shown in Figure 24.17. The default context name is the name of the table containing only the many ends of a set of one-to-many joins. These names can be changed, if desired, by clicking on the default name.

Unlike aliases, the loop remains present in the data foundation; however, context definitions instruct the SQL generator to create multiple SQL statements, one for each context. Figure 24.18 highlights one of the two contexts that were created in our example.

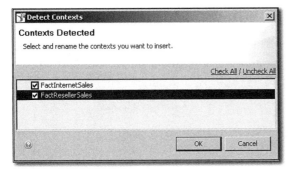

Figure 24.17 Detect Contexts Panel

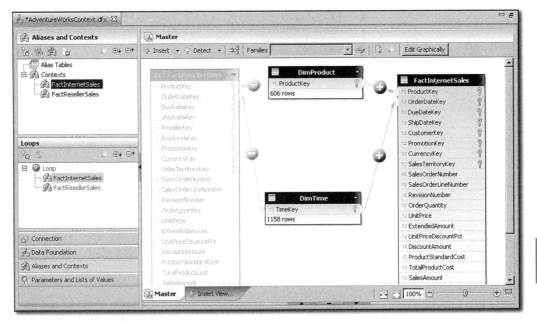

Figure 24.18 One Context in the Data Foundation Layer

Using this information will help you create the data foundation layers in your universes. The next step in the universe design process is to create a business layer of business objects organized into folders, which is covered in the next section.

24.5 Creating Business Layers

After the data foundation is established, you can focus on creating the business layer, which is the view of the universe that a user will see in Web Intelligence. The business layer consists of folders, objects, and filters, as shown in Figure 24.19.

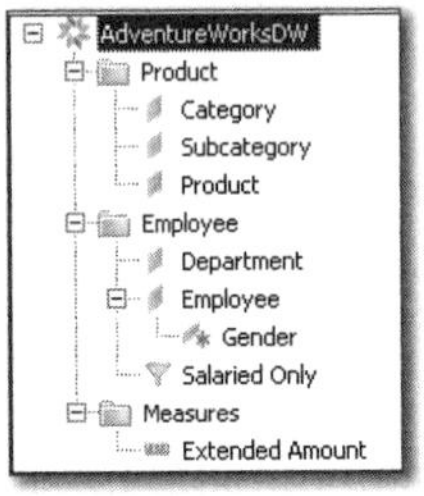

Figure 24.19 Unique Shapes for Each Object Type and Filter

Let's look at each separately.

Folders

Folders allow the universe designer to organize related objects into grouping related by the business user. The folder structure of the business layer should be organized according to how a business user visualizes the data model, not how a universe designer or data architect visualizes the data model. For example, customer data might exist in three separate database tables in the data foundation. Resist the temptation to automatically create three folders, one per table. Instead, organize the objects into a folder structure that makes it easy for business users to quickly find what they're looking for.

> **Note**
>
> Folders are known as classes in the Universe Design Tool.

Objects

An object exposes data in the data source to users. In a relational universe, an object can be a single database field, multiple database fields, or database functions. Any SQL that is valid in the database platform's `Select` clause can be used as the basis for an object.

There are three types of objects in a relational universe: dimension, attribute, and measure. In addition to those three object types, universes based on OLAP data foundations may have the following additional objects types:

▶ Hierarchies

▶ Analysis dimensions

▶ Named member sets

▶ Calculated members

> **Note**
>
> Attributes are known as details in the Universe Design Tool.

Dimension Objects

A dimension, like the one shown in Figure 24.20, is an object that maps to one or more table columns or a function in a database and represents an axis of analysis in a query. For example, Product, Customer, Geography, and Time are common dimensions.

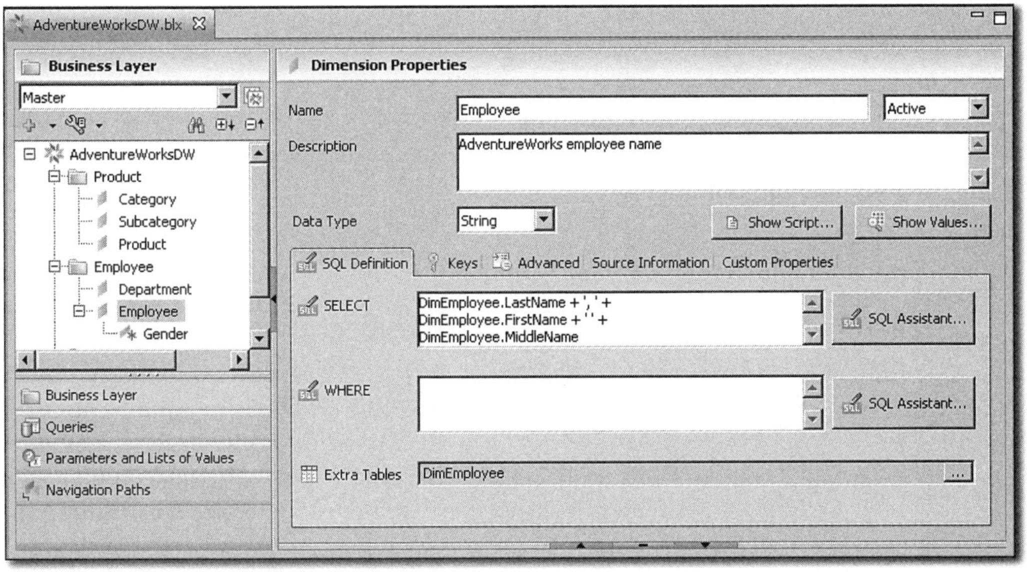

Figure 24.20 Dimension Object

Attribute Objects

An attribute is an object that provides additional information about another object in the universe, as shown in Figure 24.21. Attributes are generally specified when an object doesn't make sense on its own. For example, an object such as a telephone number can be ambiguous but has greater clarity when associated with a parent object such as a customer or employee dimension. Attributes can be defined for dimensions, hierarchies, and levels.

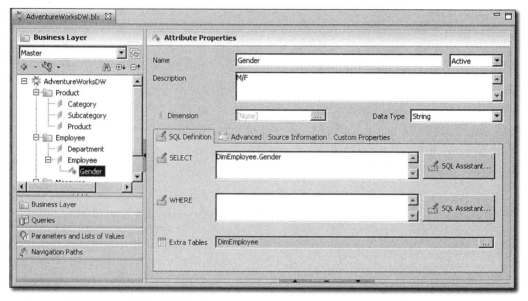

Figure 24.21 Attribute Objects

Measure Objects

As their name indicates, measures are objects that measure aggregate data such as revenue, expenses, and quantity, as shown in Figure 24.22. It's important that measure objects specify both a database aggregate function (SUM, COUNT, MIN, MAX, and AVERAGE) as well as a projection function. Omitting the database aggregate may still deliver accurate results if the correct projection aggregate is used. But the resulting SQL statement will not have an appropriate GROUP BY clause. The SQL query will return a much larger result set than necessary, often with a dramatic negative impact to query performance.

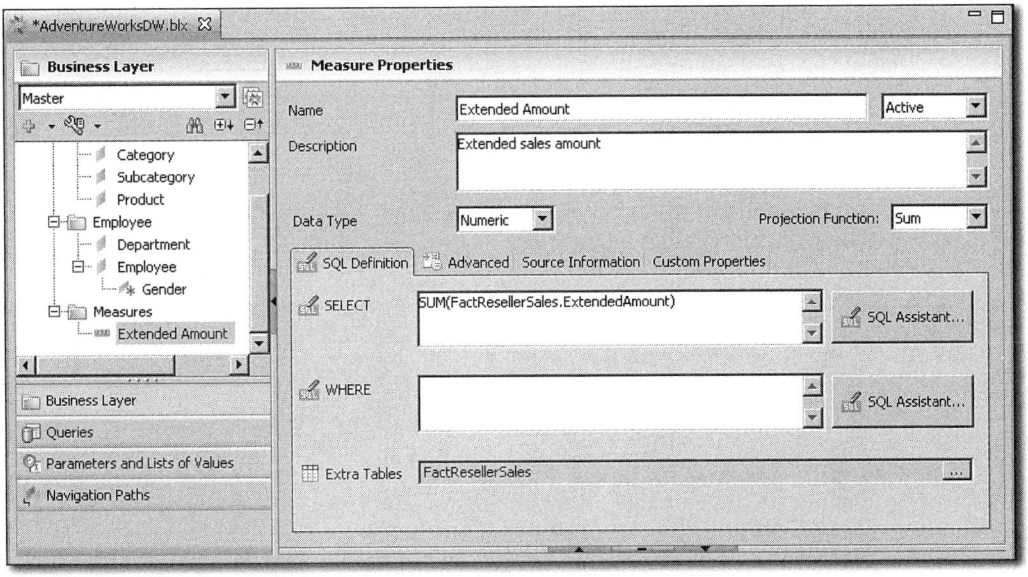

Figure 24.22 Measure Objects

Filters

Filters are predefined optional conditions that users can add to queries to restrict the data returned, as shown in Figure 24.23. Users can create their own filters in the Web Intelligence Query Panel based on other objects. However, universe designers should provide filters for users for commonly used conditions or situations where filter logic is complex. Keeping the filter logic centralized in the universe instead of in multiple Web Intelligence documents makes maintenance easier should the logic for the condition change.

> **Note**
>
> Filters are known as conditions in the Universe Design Tool.

Various universe parameters can be set for the business layer:

▶ LIMIT SIZE OF RESULT SET TO X ROWS
Limits the amount of data that a query can return to avoid performance penalties.

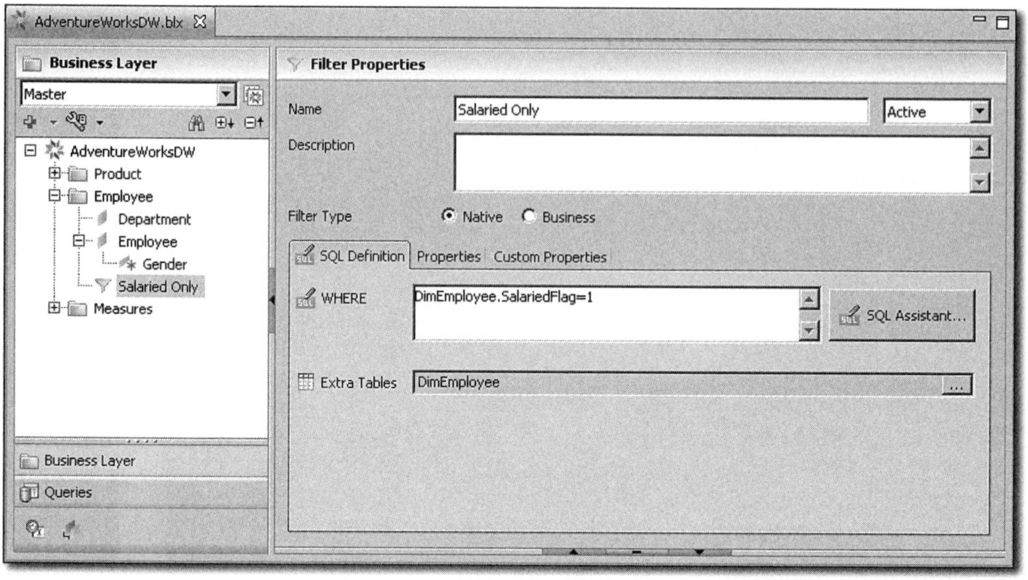

Figure 24.23 Filter Object

- ▶ LIMIT EXECUTION TIME TO *X* MINUTES
  Limits the amount of time a query may execute to avoid performance penalties.

- ▶ WARN IF COST ESTIMATE EXCEEDS *X* MINUTES
  For data sources that provide cost estimates, notifies the user if a query will exceed this threshold.

- ▶ ALLOW USE OF SUBQUERIES
  Controls whether a user can create a subquery in the Web Intelligence Query Panel.

- ▶ ALLOW COMPLEX OPERANDS IN QUERY PANEL
  Controls whether a user can use complex operands such as BOTH and EXCEPT in the Web Intelligence Query Panel.

- ▶ ALLOW USE OF UNION, INTERSECT, AND MINUS OPERATORS
  Controls whether a user can create a combined query.

- ▶ MULTIPLE SQL STATEMENTS FOR EACH MEASURE
  Generates separate SQL statements for each table that contains measure objects.

These parameters are shown in Figure 24.24.

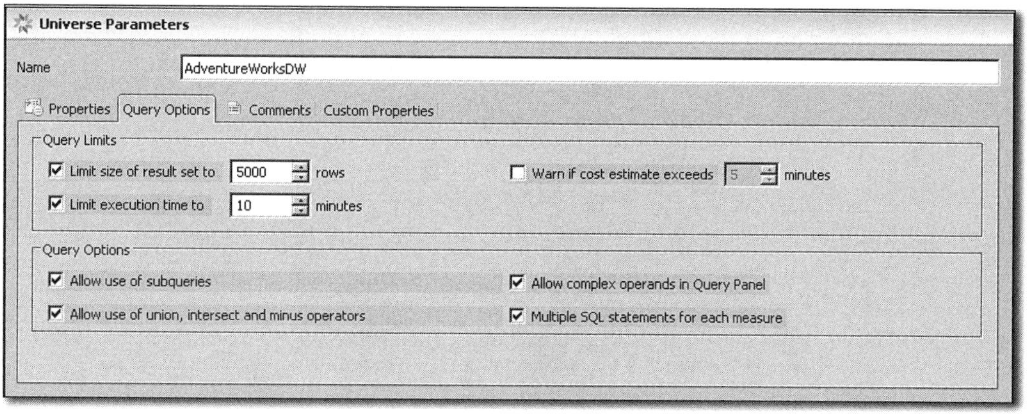
Universe Parameters
Name
AdventureWorksDW
Properties
Query Options
Comments
Custom Properties
Query Limits
Limit size of result set to
5000
rows
Warn if cost estimate exceeds
5
minutes
Limit execution time to
10
minutes
Query Options
Allow use of subqueries
Allow complex operands in Query Panel
Allow use of union, intersect and minus operators
Multiple SQL statements for each measure

Figure 24.24 Universe Parameters

24.6 Creating Multisource Universes

The ability to create multisource universes is a new capability unique to the IDT and isn't present in the classic Universe Design Tool. Using a subset of SAP Data Federator technology located on the SAP BusinessObjects BI platform, you can create universes that combine data from multiple disparate data sources. Data federation, also known as Enterprise Information Integration (EII), allows data to be queried in its original location without the need to use extract, transform, and load (ETL) tools such as SAP Data Services to integrate the data in a data store such as a data mart or data warehouse.

To begin, create a universe project in the IDT that contains multiple connections, as shown in Figure 24.25.

SAP Press MultiSource
eFashionMSSQL.cns
eStaffMSSQL.cns

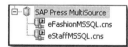

Figure 24.25 Information Design Tool Project with Multiple Connections

Next, add a data foundation to the project, as shown in Figure 24.26.

Figure 24.26 New Data Foundation

Assign the data foundation to a local project, as shown in Figure 24.27.

Figure 24.27 Selecting a Local Project

Choose MULTISOURCE-ENABLED as the data foundation type, as shown in Figure 24.28.

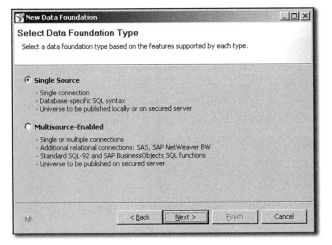

Figure 24.28 Selecting a Data Foundation Type

You are asked to authenticate to a CMS repository where the secured connections are stored, as shown in Figure 24.29.

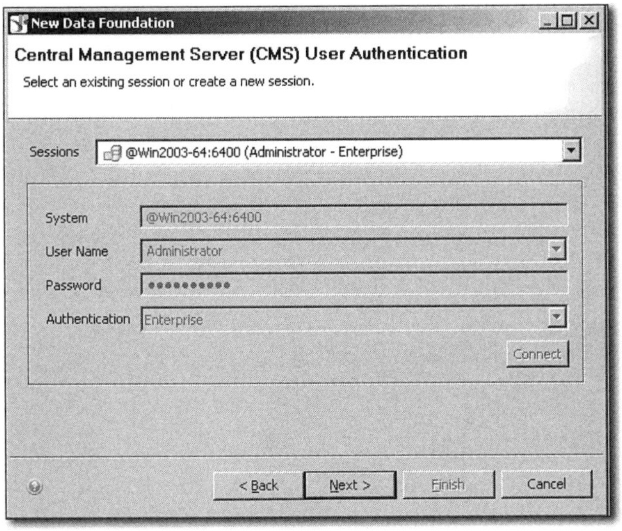

Figure 24.29 Creating a New Session

Choose which connection shortcuts currently in the project will be used for the data foundation, as shown in Figure 24.30.

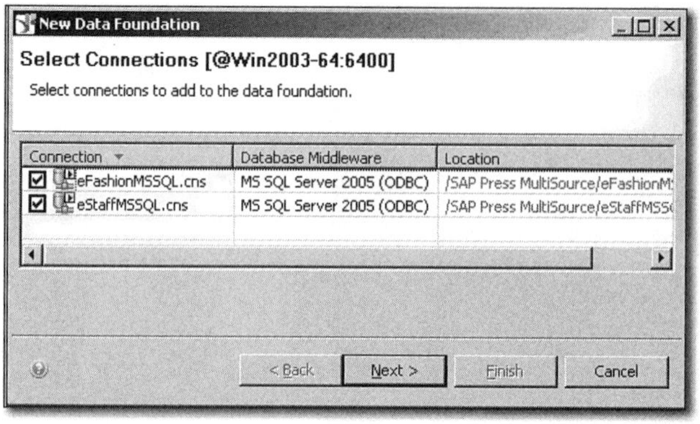

Figure 24.30 Selecting Connections to Add to the Data Foundation

Define the connection properties for each connection in the data foundation. In our example, we'll give the connection a more human-readable short name and assign a color to its table headers, as shown in Figure 24.31.

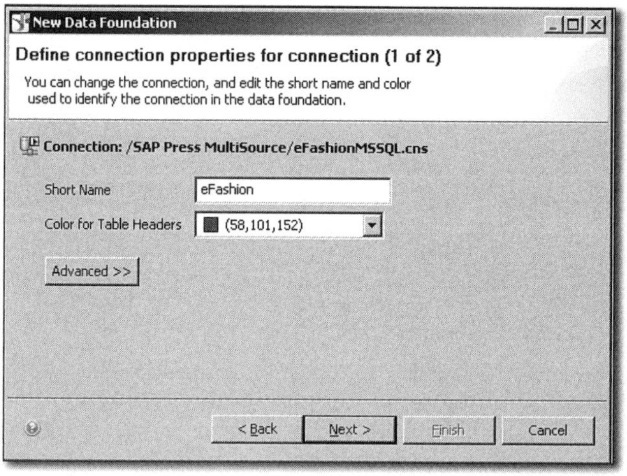

Figure 24.31 Defining Connection Properties for eFashion Connection

Next, define a short name and table header color for the second connection, as shown in Figure 24.32.

Next, add a data foundation on top of the multisource data foundation, as shown in Figure 24.33. Notice that the unique table header colors make it easy to identify the data source used by each table.

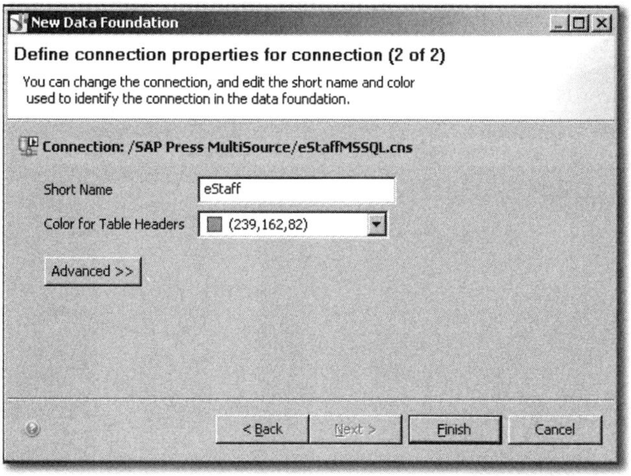

Figure 24.32 Defining Connection Properties for eStaff Connection

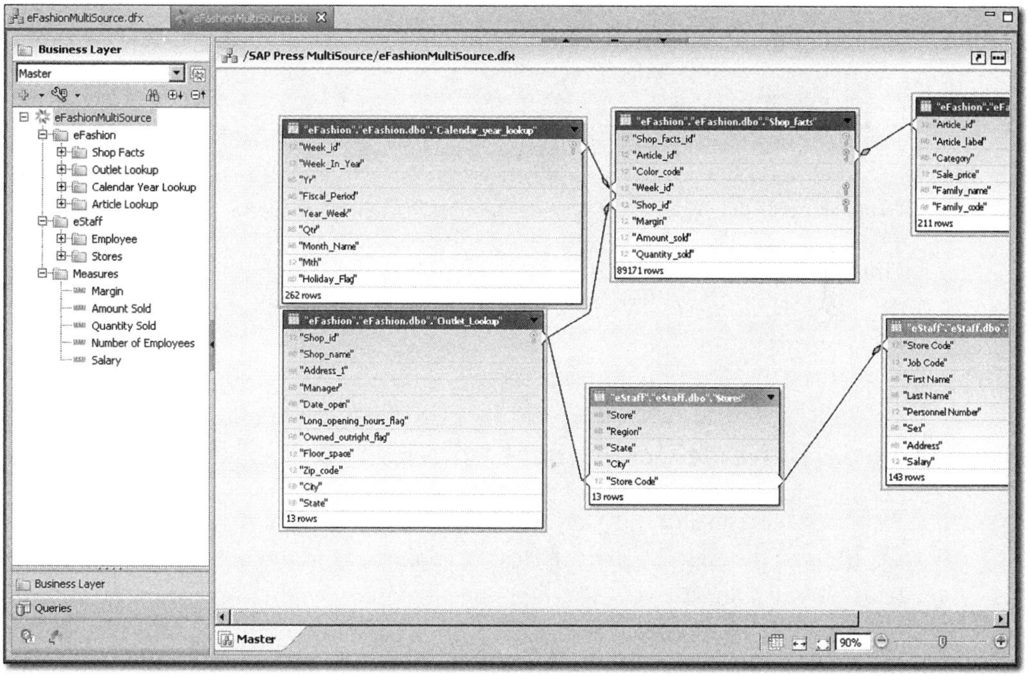

Figure 24.33 eFashion and eStaff Combined in the Same Universe

After the universe is published, confirm that the multisource joins return desired results, as shown in Figure 24.34.

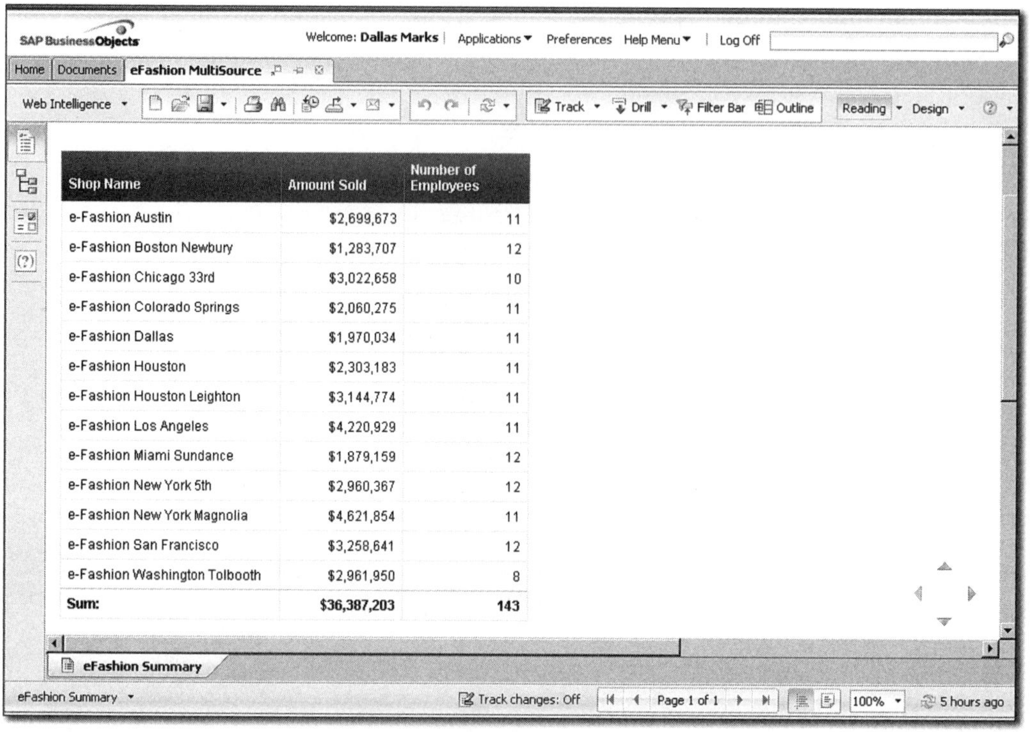

Shop Name	Amount Sold	Number of Employees
e-Fashion Austin	$2,699,673	11
e-Fashion Boston Newbury	$1,283,707	12
e-Fashion Chicago 33rd	$3,022,658	10
e-Fashion Colorado Springs	$2,060,275	11
e-Fashion Dallas	$1,970,034	11
e-Fashion Houston	$2,303,183	11
e-Fashion Houston Leighton	$3,144,774	11
e-Fashion Los Angeles	$4,220,929	11
e-Fashion Miami Sundance	$1,879,159	12
e-Fashion New York 5th	$2,960,367	12
e-Fashion New York Magnolia	$4,621,854	11
e-Fashion San Francisco	$3,258,641	12
e-Fashion Washington Tolbooth	$2,961,950	8
Sum:	**$36,387,203**	**143**

Figure 24.34 eFashion and eStaff Data Retrieved Using a Single Universe

This section explored how to create universes that combine data from multiple disparate data sources. We'll cover general best practices for designing universes in the next section.

24.7 Universe Design Best Practices

Although the user interface and workflows for creating universes differ between the IDT and the classic Universe Design Tool, many of the best practices are identical.

24.7.1 Design with the Business User in Mind

The most important best practice is to design with the business user in mind. Database field names are often quite different from business terms and should always be translated to appropriate object names with commonly known business terminology. In addition to having useful names, each object in the universe should have a clear description. Consider partnering with a subject matter expert (SME) from the user team that can assist with appropriate terminology and definitions.

We recommend that you organize objects into folders according to how an end user might draw the data model on a cocktail napkin, not how it's actually modeled. Use subfolders where appropriate, rather than a single folder that has too many objects to be easily understood.

For multinational organizations, a single universe can be translated into multiple languages using the Translation Management Tool.

Incorporate business logic into universe objects whenever possible to facilitate consistent report development by reducing the need for report-level variables. Business logic such as complex case statements or filter conditions can be centrally maintained in the universe. Changing the business logic in one universe is much easier than adjusting it in dozens or even hundreds of reports.

Keep universes as small and simple as possible by keeping the number of objects to a reasonable amount. The definition of "reasonable" is subjective, but we recommend that you limit your universe to fewer than 200 or 300 objects as a rule of thumb. Let the reporting requirements—rather than the complexity of the data source—determine the appropriate size of the universe. Larger universes are technically feasible but not user-friendly. If users are confronted with a large universe with complex folder structures and thousands of objects, they are likely to send reporting requirements back to the business intelligence team, defeating any corporate self-service reporting strategy. By limiting the universe size, you tend to reduce future maintenance costs and increase end-user productivity.

Because the IDT separates the data foundation from the business layer, an appropriate solution may be a single expansive data foundation that is shared by multiple business layers, each generating a universe for a logical subset of the data source.

24.7.2 Design for Performance

Universes can be constructed on a wide variety of relational and OLAP database platforms. Although they can be constructed on nearly any data model, creating universes directly on transactional systems isn't recommended due to the complex SQL required for analytical reporting. Transforming the data into a star or snowflake schema or OLAP cube will result in better-performing universes.

24.7.3 Design for Maintainability

The requirements for a universe will change over time and therefore require maintenance. Frequently, the universe designer performing the maintenance is not the original universe author, who may no longer be part of the organization. Arrange the tables visually in a logical manner, so the universe is easy to navigate. And take advantage of the new families feature to add color coding to related tables.

Designers should plan for evolution. This includes setting expectations with users for an iterative (which has multiple phases), rather than waterfall (one big deliverable after a long wait), approach to universe design. It may be possible to give users a simple universe that is easy to create and delivered in a short time frame. The first version of the universe may not answer all of the business questions, but it can address a substantial number of them while the business intelligence team refines the second, more extensive, version of the universe.

24.7.4 Design for Governance

Develop your organization's own standards for universe design and development. This is particularly important if universe designers are distributed throughout the organization, outsourced resources, or both. Create governance processes that ensure corporate standards are followed prior to promoting a universe to the production environment.

24.8 Converting an Existing Universe to a .UNX Universe

Universes created by the classic Universe Design Tool or migrated from earlier versions of the SAP BusinessObjects BI platform can be used as-is without modifications. However, SAP Crystal Reports for BI and some of the new query capabilities of SAP BusinessObjects Dashboards can only be used with the new universe format.

The IDT can convert classic universes in the .UNV file format to universes in the .UNX format. In this section, we'll cover the steps necessary to convert the sample eFashion.unv universe to eFashion.unx.

The original eFashion universe in the Universe Design Tool is shown in Figure 24.35.

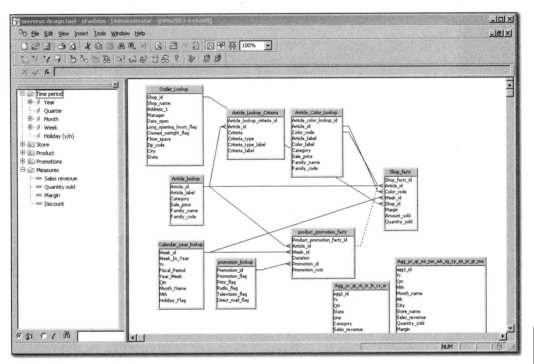

Figure 24.35 Original Universe in Universe Design Tool

To begin, select CONVERT .UNV UNIVERSE from the Information Design Tool FILE menu, as shown in Figure 24.36.

Next, browse to the location of the original .UNV universe, as shown in Figure 24.37. Notice that this file can be retrieved from either the local file system or from the BOR.

File	Edit	Window	Help

New ▶
New Universe
Open Project...
Recent Resources... ▶

Close   Ctrl+W
Close All   Ctrl+Shift+W

Save   Ctrl+S
Save All   Ctrl+Shift+S

Publish ▶
Retrieve a Published Universe ▶
Convert .unv Universe...

Print

Exit

Figure 24.36 Converting the .UNV Universe

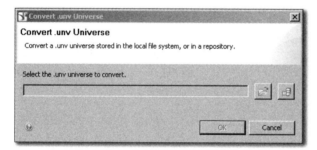

Figure 24.37 Specifying the Original .UNV Universe to Convert

If you choose a universe from the repository, you'll be asked to provide valid credentials, as shown in Figure 24.38.

Browse through the universe folder structure and identify the desired .UNV universe to convert. In this example, the eFashion.unv is being retrieved from the WEBI UNIVERSES folder, as shown in Figure 24.39.

Next, choose the DESTINATION REPOSITORY FOLDER, which can be identical to the source, shown in Figure 24.40. You can also choose to add the converted .UNX to an existing local project, convert @prompt expressions into universe-named parameters, or save the local project copy for all users, as shown in Figure 24.40.

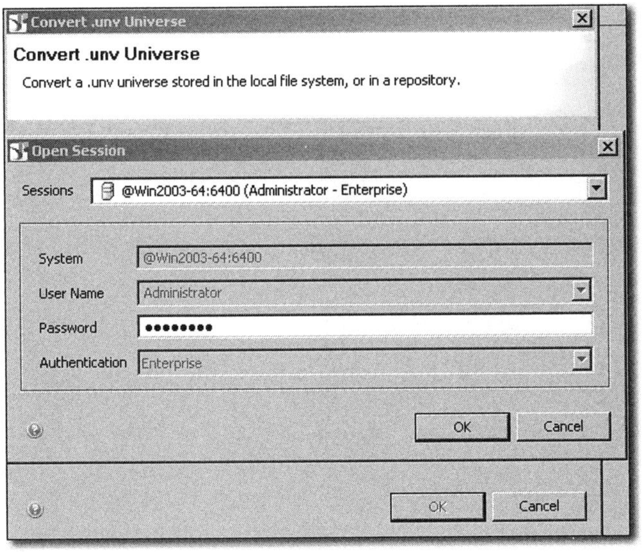

Figure 24.38 Open Session to CMS

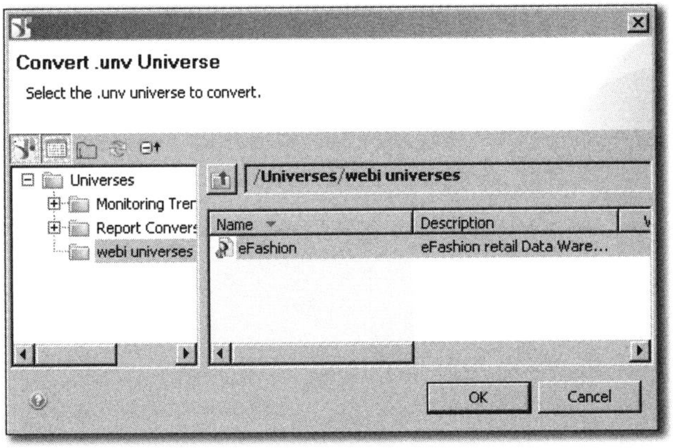

Figure 24.39 Choosing the .UNV Universe

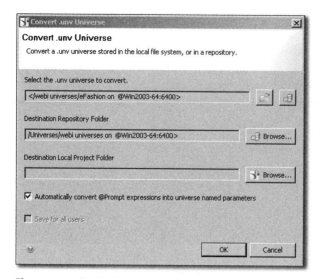

Figure 24.40 Setting Destination Repository Folder and (Optional) Local Project Folder

The IDT will convert the .UNV, publish the corresponding .UNX, and notify you of its success, as shown in Figure 24.41.

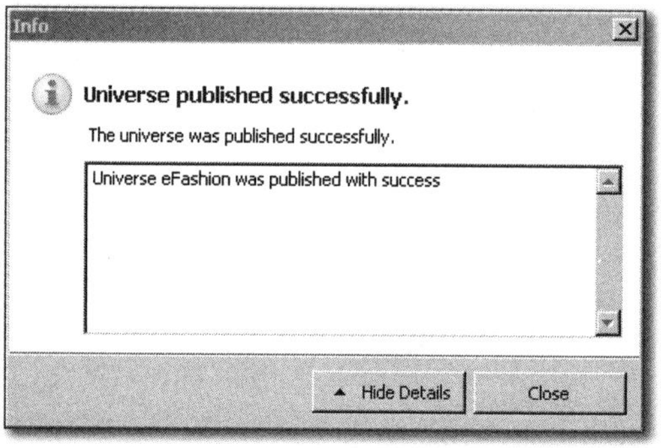

Figure 24.41 Universe Published Successfully

You can confirm that the universe was published to the desired folder by confirming using the CMC, as shown in Figure 24.42. Notice the converted universe has an explicit .UNX suffix in its name.

The converted universe can now be viewed and modified from the IDT, as shown in Figure 24.43.

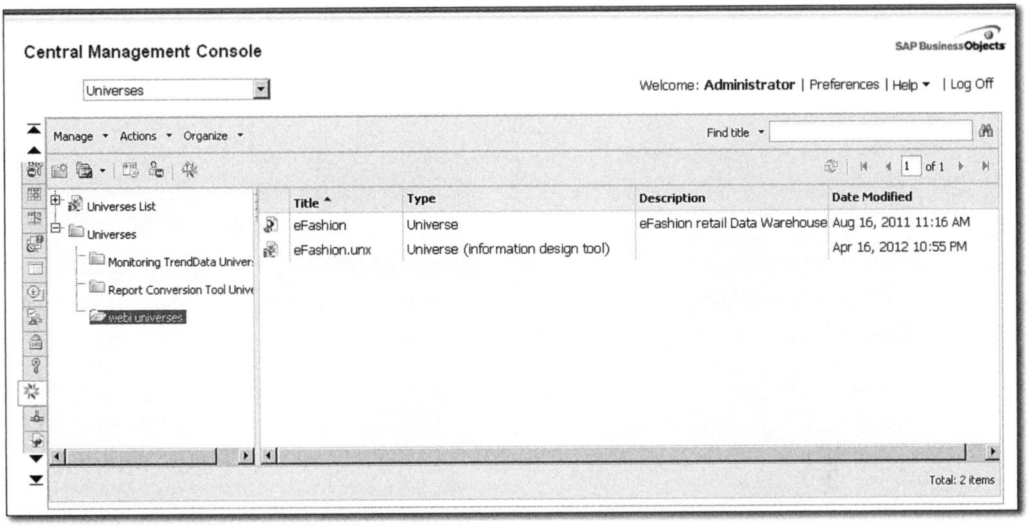

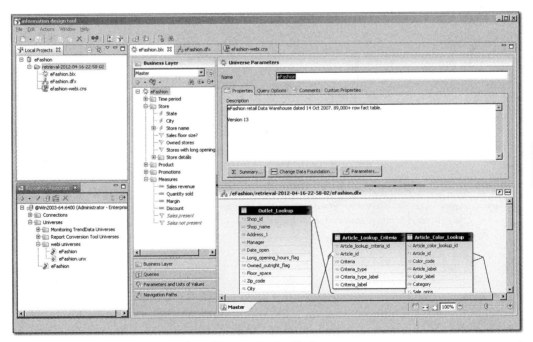

Figure 24.42 Verifying the .UNX Universe in CMC

Figure 24.43 Converted Universe in the Information Design Tool

24.9   Summary

The universe is SAP's patented semantic layer that allows nontechnical business users to access and analyze corporate data sources. Universe design is a topic robust enough for its own book. In this chapter, we provided a basic understanding of how the IDT is used to create universes and how it varies from the classic Universe Design Tool. Universes created with the IDT consist of three distinct components that are assembled into a universe: the connection, data foundation, and business layer. The resulting universe is then published to the BOR with a .UNX file extension.

Although universes created by the classic Universe Design Tool can be used by Web Intelligence without modification, the desire to use other tools in the SAP BusinessObjects BI suite may make it necessary or desirable to convert these universes to the new .UNX format using the IDT.

More information is available from the Information Design Tool's HELP menu, which includes links to online tutorials, as shown in Figure 24.44.

Figure 24.44 Information Design Tool Help Menu

Readers looking for more comprehensive coverage about universes should pick up a copy of *Universe Design with SAP BusinessObjects BI: The Comprehensive Guide* by Christian Ah-Soon, Didier Mazoué, and Pierpaolo Vezzosi (SAP PRESS, 2013).

Appendices

You can convert Desktop Intelligence reports from SAP BusinessObjects BI XI 3.x or XI R2 (once known as Enterprise) to Web Intelligence to be used in SAP BusinessObjects BI 4.1. Follow our checklist of best practices for a methodical conversion that produces a highly functioning series of Web Intelligence reports in SAP BusinessObjects BI 4.1 that were once Desktop Intelligence reports.

A Converting Desktop Intelligence Reports to Web Intelligence Documents

Now that SAP BusinessObjects Desktop Intelligence (commonly known as DeskI) has reached its end-of-life stage with the release of the SAP BusinessObjects BI 4.x platform, the conversion of Desktop Intelligence reports to Web Intelligence is an important topic for customers still using the classic desktop reporting tool. As the product known to many as the original SAP BusinessObjects full-client reporting tool, Desktop Intelligence offered advanced functional capabilities that set it apart from other reporting tools in the market. Many of these were so valuable to business users that many clients opted to continue to use the product.

In fact, even when its successor, Web Intelligence, began to receive an influx of enhancements and improved functionality, many customers found it difficult to trade in the classic desktop client for its zero-client reporting tool successor. Functional differences and the pervasiveness of locally saved documents have continually been cited as leading reasons for continued use of Desktop Intelligence.

By offering a greatly enhanced product that far exceeds the capabilities delivered in Desktop Intelligence, Web Intelligence 4.1 has made a big leap in minimizing the functional differences between the two products. But even with all the enhancements, there are still capabilities in the last version of Desktop Intelligence that aren't yet available in Web Intelligence 4.1, such as Freehand SQL, custom VBA code, and the capability to export a report to HTML. These features and a few others can present challenges in migration and conversion efforts when upgrading from SAP BusinessObjects BI XI R2 or XI 3.1 to SAP BusinessObjects BI 4.1.

A.1 Report Conversion Tool (RCT)

The Report Conversion Tool (RCT) is an easy and effective tool for converting .REP (Desktop Intelligence) files to .WID (Web Intelligence document) files. Outside of a few complex scenarios, described in the coming section, this tool will convert the majority of Deski files to Webi.

New to SAP BusinessObjects BI 4.1 in SP2, the RCT can now convert local and secure .REP files in an authenticated nonstandalone mode.

A.2 Conversion to Web Intelligence

This section focuses on the major steps in performing a successful conversion from Desktop Intelligence to Web Intelligence. The conversion process checklist contains nine general key steps for completing an effective report conversion from Desktop Intelligence to Web Intelligence.

Conversion Checklist: Desktop Intelligence to Web Intelligence
▶ Analyze existing Desktop Intelligence report usage.
▶ Identify users with Desktop Intelligence installed.
▶ Publish locally saved Desktop Intelligence reports to the repository.
▶ Prioritize, consolidate, and eliminate reports that are no longer needed.
▶ Customize the conversion plan and roadmap.
▶ Perform report conversion.
▶ Perform post-conversion analysis and validation.
▶ Manually create unconverted reports.
▶ Educate users on Web Intelligence 4.1.

The steps outlined in the checklist describe general best practices for any Desktop Intelligence to Web Intelligence conversion project. The RCT is used to perform these types of conversions. It's important to know that even though a tool exists specifically for performing conversions, almost every conversion will require some level of manual rework to achieve 100% success.

A.2.1 Analyze Existing Desktop Intelligence Report Usage

Before you create an in-depth conversion plan or rely on a cookie-cutter roadmap to conversion, it's critical to understand what you're dealing with in terms of Desktop Intelligence report existence and usage. We recommend that you perform a comprehensive review of the reporting documents published to the repository to begin creating an inventory of DeskI reports currently in use.

You can determine actual usage by enabling auditing in the source system to audit the events of the Desktop Intelligence application. Usage statistics are a very powerful indicator of the value of a report. Because Desktop Intelligence is a legacy reporting tool, it's possible that many reports in production have a very small viewership and can be consolidated or eliminated rather than converted. On the other hand, you may discover that a number of published DeskI reports are still frequently viewed by business users and very valuable to organizations. The priority to convert these reports to Web Intelligence is high.

The goal of this step is to determine the number of high-value and high-visibility reports to convert to Web Intelligence. It's also important to determine which reports can be eliminated. Take this opportunity to perform some clean-up before attempting to convert every Desktop Intelligence report to Web Intelligence 4.1.

Note
The number of existing Desktop Intelligence reports is an important statistic to the system administrator. The number of Web Intelligence Services will likely need to be increased to accommodate the increased number of Web Intelligence reports after conversion.

A.2.2 Identify Users with Desktop Intelligence Installed

Over the course of the past several years, Desktop Intelligence may have been installed on several hundred or even several thousand PCs, depending on the size of the organization. Inevitably, each user will have a number of DeskI reports saved locally.

Even though all important reports should exist on the server, to comply with most corporate policies, some reports will exist locally. This is often the case simply because the tool lends itself to working offline and provides the capability of storing .REP files locally.

A.2.3 Publish Locally Saved Desktop Intelligence Reports to the Repository

After you've identified the users and report developers who are still using Desktop Intelligence, ask them to publish all important personal DeskI files and locally saved reports to the repository. This step puts potentially valuable reports onto the repository so that the migration team can review, analyze, and then convert them to Web Intelligence.

It's important to get every useful Desk Intelligence report published to the repository so they can be converted to Web Intelligence and be used in the SAP BusinessObjects BI 4.1 system after migration. Insist that your users make every effort to only retain necessary DeskI files to minimize the buildup of unneeded or duplicate reports.

A.2.4 Prioritize, Consolidate, and Eliminate

Before converting every single Desktop Intelligence document ever created at your organization, take this opportunity to archive or completely eliminate documents that are no longer being used. As companies evolve and data sources change, it's likely that a large number of locally saved Desktop Intelligence reports are no longer needed. You'll recognize the distinction between ad hoc reports and valuable reports that are used by business users.

When you're prioritizing reports, create categories or buckets to differentiate reports based on the frequency of use and the visibility of the data presented in the reports.

A.2.5 Customize the Conversion Plan and Roadmap

After completing the first four steps, you'll understand the scope of the project and conversion effort. The volume of reports to be migrated plays a major role in developing the roadmap and conversion plan. There are two common approaches to conversion:

▸ **Single-pass conversion**
The entire repository is converted in one pass.

▸ **Staged conversion**
Conversion is segmented by business area or departmental group.

The decision regarding which approach to select depends on the following factors:

▸ Number of DeskI reports to convert

▸ Complexity of DeskI reports

▸ Amount of rework required to fully convert to Web Intelligence

▸ 64-bit server architecture of the SAP BusinessObjects BI 4.1 system

▸ Combination of any of the first four potential scenarios

When you're preparing the conversion plan, you should also determine report complexity. The difficulty level of conversion can be anticipated after evaluating the DeskI reports in the source environment. Any DeskI report containing Freehand SQL should be placed into a category of its own.

Detailed analysis of reports containing Freehand SQL can lead to best practices for discontinuing the use of Freehand SQL. The goal is to find patterns in the SQL and common fact tables from the same databases and schemas.

These scenarios provide the greatest opportunity to create a small number of new universes that can be used by a much larger number of DeskI reports; therefore, these universes should include several objects and predefined filters to increase their usefulness. Changing the data source of DeskI reports from Freehand SQL to a universe will simplify the conversion process and increase the likelihood of converting to Web Intelligence.

Depending on the practices of DeskI report designers, it's possible that you'll need to manually create some reports in Web Intelligence. These reports should be identified and placed into their own groups. These are the three most common reasons for known conversion problems:

▸ Reports with Freehand SQL

▸ Reports containing VBA

▸ Reports with personal data providers

Reports with any of these three features should be manually revised before converting.

> **Note**
>
> It's possible to convert reports containing Freehand SQL to Web Intelligence, but the conversion will generate a new universe containing a derived table for each report. This scenario could produce hundreds or potentially thousands of single-use universes.
>
> Every effort should be made to consolidate the source SQL into a much smaller number of universes that can be used by multiple reports.

After you complete a thorough analysis on the source system and group reports by business area, the likelihood of conversion success, and the need for manual rework, it's time to proceed to conversion.

You can help stay on track by setting milestones and time lines. Customizing a project time line will help guide you through the conversion process and ensure that every aspect of the conversion is completed and in the correct order.

Other critical decisions must be made and conveyed to users, such as the following:

▸ Well-communicated end date for development of DeskI reports in the source system

▸ Documented deadline for refreshing existing DeskI reports

▸ Go-live date to begin using reports converted to Web Intelligence in the new system

A.2.6 Perform Report Conversion

Launch the RCT as an administrator, and perform the type of conversion:

▸ **Single-pass conversion**
Convert all reports.

▸ **Staged conversion**
Convert only a portion of reports.

As a result, there are two possible conversion paths:

▸ Convert Desktop Intelligence documents to Web Intelligence with the SAP BusinessObjects BI XI 3.1 RCT.

▸ Convert Desktop Intelligence documents to Web Intelligence with the SAP BusinessObjects BI 4.1 RCT.

Select the appropriate conversion path based on your organization's hardware capabilities in a test environment. Converting DeskI documents using the Web Intelligence 4.1 RCT will fully convert a greater number of documents.

After completing a conversion, reports are grouped into three categories:

▸ Fully converted

▸ Partially converted

▸ Not converted

The seventh conversion step leads you to performing a post-conversion analysis. Partially converted reports can be evaluated to determine the reason that it wasn't fully converted. In many cases, minor manual modifications can be made to fully convert reports. This can be a labor-intensive exercise depending on the volume of partially converted reports.

Reports that aren't converted will often need even more manual corrections or will need to be recreated in Web Intelligence rather than converted with the RCT.

A.2.7 Execute Post-Conversion Analysis and Validation

Perform validation on reports that were fully converted. Verify that all data sources, formulas, and report functions continue to work properly in Web Intelligence as they did in Desktop Intelligence.

You need to identify the reason that partially converted documents weren't fully completed by reviewing log files. In many cases, these reports can be quickly edited. In other cases, it can be easier to recreate partially converted documents in Web Intelligence rather than making the necessary corrections.

A.2.8   Manually Create Unconverted Reports

As mentioned in the seventh step, it's common that unconverted reports will need to be manually recreated in Web Intelligence if resources permit. Even though Web Intelligence now contains almost all of the function capabilities of Desktop Intelligence, a number of features will still cause DeskI reports to not be converted.

You should create a focused strategy for handling reports that remain unconverted even after running them through the RCT. It's possible that the reason reports aren't converted can be removed or modified. After making changes, run the RCT again for a second attempt at converting the DeskI reports to Web Intelligence.

A.2.9   Educate Users on Web Intelligence 4.1

Invest in user training for all users and report designers who will be using Web Intelligence in an SAP BusinessObjects BI 4.1 environment. Training comes in many different forms, including text books, blogs, webinars, e-learning sessions, and official training from SAP and from vendors specializing in providing SAP BusinessObjects training.

We recommend the following resources for learning Web Intelligence 4.1:

► Join ASUG and attend webinars, conferences, and explore online content at *www.ASUG.com.*

► Explore content at the SAP Community Network (SCN) at *http://scn.sap.com/community/businessobjects-web-intelligence.*

► Attend official SAP training courses at *www.sap.com/training-education/overview.html.*

► Obtain training from private vendors specialized in providing SAP BusinessObjects and Web Intelligence training courses.

A.3   Desktop Intelligence Compatibility Pack (DCP)

The last commercial release of Desktop Intelligence came in SAP BusinessObjects BI XI 3.1 and will be supported with mainstream maintenance until 2015 and with priority-one support until 2017. With these dates in mind, remaining customers still using Desktop Intelligence will need to plan their conversions to Web Intelligence accordingly to remain in support.

The tool delivered to help with migrations from SAP BusinessObjects BI (formerly known as Enterprise) XI 3.1 and conversions of DeskI documents to WebI reports is the Desktop Intelligence Compatibility Pack (DCP). This tool was introduced in SAP BusinessObjects BI 4.1 to allow Desktop Intelligence reports to connect to an SAP BusinessObjects BI 4.1 Central Management Server (CMS).

> **Note**
>
> It's important to note that for Desktop Intelligence .REP files to be reachable in SAP BusinessObjects BI 4.1, the SAP BusinessObjects BI XI 3.1 client tools must be upgraded to at least Fix Pack 6.1 (FP6.1) on SP6.

The following details outline the features provided by the DCP in SAP Business-Objects BI 4.1:

▶ Desktop Intelligence documents can be moved to SAP BusinessObjects BI 4.1 using the Upgrade Management Tool.

▶ The RCT can now access .REP files in an SAP BusinessObjects BI 4.1 CMS for conversion to Web Intelligence.

▶ Scheduling functionality is provided using the Windows Task Scheduler.

▶ Desktop Intelligence documents are only accessible through the CMC.

▶ Users accessing DeskI reports from the BI Launch Pad will receive data in the following formats: PDF, XLS, or TXT.

▶ The recommended sequence for installing the DCP is described here:

  ▷ Upgrade your SAP BusinessObjects BI XI 3.1 client tools, or more specifically, Desktop Intelligence, to SP6. The SAP BusinessObjects BI must also be on SP6.

  ▷ Install the SAP BusinessObjects BI 4.1 client tools in a side-by-side installation. Be sure to select Web Intelligence Rich Client and the RCT when installing the client tools.

  ▷ Install FP6.1 or higher for the client tools.

> **Note**
>
> It's strongly recommended to install FP6.1 for your SAP BusinessObjects BI (formerly known as Enterprise) XI 3.1 client tools after installing the latest SAP BusinessObjects 4.1 client tools.

A.4 Summary

A step-by-step methodical approach to report conversion produces the safest and most effective way to move away from Desktop Intelligence reports in SAP BusinessObjects BI XI R2 or XI 3.1 and begin using Web Intelligence 4.1 for reporting with all of your data sources.

Collaboration among users, designers, and the conversion/migration team is essential to success. In addition, clearly communicating deadlines and the importance of publishing locally saved Desktop Intelligence reports to the repository is an important part of the conversion process. After you analyze all of the existing Deski reports in an environment, you'll need to determine which reports continue to deliver relevant and valuable information to users while also identifying reports that can be retired.

Review the last save date and last refresh date of reports to help identify obsolete content rather than converting unneeded reports. You should also look for ways to consolidate redundant reports that may have been repeated many times over.

After a complete analysis, prepare a customized roadmap for converting existing Desktop Intelligence reports. You can perform the conversion in a staged multi-pass approach or single-pass approach depending on the number of documents to convert and the level of complexity.

Group all reports containing Freehand SQL, and evaluate the syntax of the SQL statements in use. Create new robust universes to replace Freehand SQL data sources with derived tables and produce a semantic layer that can be used by many reports rather than generating a new derived universe for every report containing Freehand SQL.

Third-party tools fill a valuable niche by extending SAP BusinessObjects BI 4.1 platform implementations with very powerful and exciting functionalities. By using the tools from any of these vendors, you'll be able to maximize your return on investment of SAP BusinessObjects 4.1 with very innovative products that offer creative and highly useful capabilities.

B   Third-Party Vendors and SAP Partners

Several SAP partners and third-party vendors offer software products that integrate with Web Intelligence and the SAP BusinessObjects BI 4.1 platform. These products present many exciting capabilities that extend and complement SAP BusinessObjects BI 4.1 implementations. From capacity planning and monitoring to BI on BI, mobile deployment monitoring, advanced bursting, and enhanced auditing, third-party vendors fill a valuable function to organizations around the world.

This appendix will alphabetically introduce seven third-party vendors and provide a brief description of their product offerings and key features.

> **Note**
>
> This appendix includes third-party vendors that integrate with the SAP BusinessObjects BI 4.1 version of Web Intelligence that the authors were aware of at the time of publication. There may be others that were not included. The inclusion or omission of a vendor from this appendix should not be seen as an endorsement or critique of their products and services.

We'll discuss the following third-party vendors:

▶ Antivia—*www.antivia.com*

▶ APOS Systems—*www.apos.com*

▶ Centigon Solutions—*www.centigonsolutions.com*

▶ EV Technologies—*www.evtechnologies.com*

▶ GB & Smith—*www.gbandsmith.com*

▶ InfoSol—*www.infosol.com*

▶ LaunchWorks—*www.launchworks.com*

B.1 Antivia

Antivia (*www.antivia.com*) is an SAP partner and currently offers a powerful product that seamlessly integrates with SAP BusinessObjects BI 4.1 called XWIS DecisionPoint™. DecisionPoint allows you to create next-generation engaging dashboards and reports for both desktop and mobile devices. Antivia also offers a tool called XWIS Advantage Express Edition to leverage Web Intelligence reports for creating new dashboards.

▶ **XWIS DecisionPoint**

  ▶ Connects quickly to a wide range of data sources, including SAP BusinessObjects content and local data sources

  ▶ Implements a client-side data cube to store data locally for delivering high-performing dashboards online or offline

  ▶ Delivers BI content using HTML5 technology

▶ **XWIS Advantage Express Edition**

  ▶ Leverages Web Intelligence reports to be used as a data source

  ▶ Reengineers high maintenance and poorly performing dashboards

  ▶ Easily transitions to DecisionPoint

B.2 APOS Systems

APOS Systems (*www.apos.com*) is an SAP BusinessObjects solution provider in the SAP PartnerEdge™ program. The company has been named SAP BusinessObjects "Technology Partner of the Year" numerous times due to its in-depth platform knowledge and expertise in extending SAP BusinessObjects.

APOS provides several tools in extending the functionality of existing SAP BusinessObjects enterprise installations and are SAP-certified for integration with SAP BusinessObjects. APOS offers several products that integrate with SAP BusinessObjects and cover a wide variety of functionality:

▶ **APOS Administrator**
Agile BI platform management for SAP BusinessObjects

▶ **APOS Insight**
System metrics, performance analytics, system planning

▶ **APOS Insight Elements**
SAP BusinessObjects system metrics

▶ **APOS IDAC**
Monitor, manage, and audit BI data connectivity

▶ **APOS Storage Center**
Backup, archive, selective restore

▶ **APOS Publisher**
Complete SAP BusinessObjects publishing solution

▶ **APOS BI Mobile App for iPad and iPhone**

▶ **APOS Security Manager**
Simplified security management for SAP BusinessObjects

B.3   Centigon Solutions

Centigon Solutions Inc. (*www.centigonsolutions.com*) provides a premier location intelligence solution that integrates with Web Intelligence while producing the most widely adopted mapping integration for SAP Dashboards (GMaps Plugin and GMaps Mobile). Now branded CMaps Analytics, Centigon Solutions' new location intelligence suite will expand the availability and consumption of location intelligence to new on-premise and cloud solutions.

▶ **CMaps Analytics**

▶ CMaps Analytics Extension V1 serves as a bridge between the SAP Dashboards CMaps plug-in and Web Intelligence.

▶ The dashboard files containing CMaps plug in inside of Web Intelligence to allow for data from WebI to flow directly inside the dashboard object to provide mapping capabilities.

- **CMaps Analytics Extension for Web Intelligence**
  - CMaps Analytics Extension for Web Intelligence version 1 allows designers to import a map into Web Intelligence by leveraging the CMaps plug-in.
  - Allows designers to configure and secure a custom mapping experience.
  - Configures dashboards to receive data from Web Intelligence report parts and then imports CMaps Analytics to configure designers' own custom mapping styles and workflows.
  - Publishes dashboards directly to the SAP BusinessObjects BI 4.1 platform.

B.4   EV Technologies

EV Technologies (*www.evtechnologies.com*) is a business intelligence consultancy based in Australia and the United States. With experience as an SAP Gold Partner and an SAP Authorized Education Partner, customers leverage EV Technologies for strategic business intelligence architecture, systems administration, and application development requirements.

EV Technologies' roots are deep in the BusinessObjects community, with experience going back as far as the original SAP BusinessObjects 4. EV not only employs several SAP Certified Associates but also 3 members of its team are SAP Mentors (3 of approximately 120 individuals in the entire world). Further, EV Technologies is an active community member, and team members are regular presenters at SAP events around the world.

The company's flagship product is Sherlock 3 for "Better Management of SAP BusinessObjects Platforms." The company's other current products include the following:

- **Sherlock for SAP BusinessObjects**
  A powerful product that exposes a great deal of metadata about your SAP BusinessObjects analytics, data sources, and how they fit together. It comes with the ability to report on data in a near-real-time fashion and captures history.

- **Sherlock for SAP Crystal Server**
  Allows SAP Crystal Server customers to receive the same actionable information available to larger SAP BusinessObjects BI customers.

▶ **Sherlock System Metrics**
A near-real-time inspector aimed at providing up-to-date information on the performance and use of your SAP BusinessObjects environment.

▶ **Sherlock Mobile**
Provides your IT organization with the ability to monitor the health and capacity of your SAP BusinessObjects deployment while on the go.

▶ **Sherlock Quick Sizer**
Analyzes your current SAP BusinessObjects environment to help with sizing your SAP BusinessObjects BI 4.1 platform.

B.5 GB & Smith

GB & Smith (*www.gbandsmith.com*) currently offers five tools to implement, manage, and document the security rights in your SAP BusinessObjects BI 4.x deployments. These tools provide easy-to-use interfaces for managing complex SAP BusinessObjects deployments and enable you to see the entire 360-degree view of the security configuration.

GB & Smith has the following current product offerings:

▶ **360View**
BOE security solution.

▶ **360Cast**
Report bursting solution.

▶ **360Plus**
SAP BusinessObjects backup solution for versioning.

▶ **Integrity**
License compliance solution.

▶ **360Eyes**
Compliance and auditing.

▶ **360Gate**
Customized portals.

B.6   InfoSol

InfoSol (*www.infosol.com*) has been an SAP BusinessObjects partner for more than 15 years and offers end-to-end design, implementation, and development services, in addition to the full suite of SAP BusinessObjects tools.

InfoSol, a provider of information systems solutions, delivers compelling and effective business intelligence and custom applications. Following are the company's current product offerings:

▸ **InfoBurst Enterprise**
A state-of-the-art BI publishing system that schedules, refreshes, bursts, and delivers reports and dashboards to your users, customers, and partners. InfoBurst Apps creates stunning HTML5 apps for deployment on mobile and desktop systems.

  ▸ InfoBurst Report Bursting

  ▸ InfoBurst Publishing

  ▸ InfoBurst Delivery and Dashboard Delivery

  ▸ InfoBurst Actions & Alerts

  ▸ InfoBurst Scheduling

▸ **360Suite:**

  ▸ **360View:** Offers simplified and flexible management, implementation, and documentation of SAP BusinessObjects BI XI security.

  ▸ **360Plus:** Provides simple and logical backup and recovery of your SAP BusinessObjects content.

  ▸ **360Eyes:** Facilitates auditing and impact analysis of your SAP BusinessObjects environment.

B.7   LaunchWorks

LaunchWorks (*www.launchworks.com*) is an SAP-certified partner for integration with SAP BusinessObjects and a specialized provider of embedded BI solutions. Embedded BI—analytics embedded directly into operational applications and processes that, in turn, more effectively drive the business—has always occupied a central position in the LaunchWorks portfolio.

LaunchWorks supports its customers with solutions, multiple competencies, and extensive expertise architecting and delivering Embedded BI projects. The LaunchWorks product portfolio has multiple business applications, including CRM integration/enhancement. LaunchWorks has the following current product offerings:

▸ **LaunchPortal for SAP BusinessObjects**
  A turnkey secure external reporting panel.

▸ **Report Launch**
  Export, embed, refresh, simplify, and integrate reports.

▸ **Dashboard Launch**
  Share, embed, diversify, and manage dashboards. Also translates Web Intelligence dashboards into SAP Crystal dashboards.

▸ **Activity Launch**
  Real-time, data-driven, and analyzes alerts.

▸ **LaunchPages**
  Dynamic pages, supports embeddable owner-controlled content with widget applications.

B.8   Summary

Many third-party vendors and SAP solution partners such as those listed in this appendix exist in the market today to help users extend the functionality of their SAP BusinessObjects BI 4.1 deployments, while getting the most out of their SAP investment.

The purpose of this appendix was to introduce and briefly describe the product offerings of the known third-party vendors that integrate with SAP BusinessObjects. Using these third-party vendors, you can increase your return on investment with SAP BusinessObjects and provide new functionality that goes beyond a standard deployment.

Please explore the websites of each of these vendors for more in-depth descriptions and up-to-the-minute products and features.

C   The Authors

Jim Brogden is an award-winning technical author and dashboard designer, and a Senior Data Warehouse Developer for Intercontinental Exchange (ICE) in Atlanta, Georgia. He combines a master's degree in Information Technology with nearly ten years of business intelligence consulting experience and a proven track record for delivering BI solutions in a variety of industries. He's the lead author of all three official textbooks dedicated to Web Intelligence, and is an active contributor to SAP's Idea Place (*http://ideas.sap.com*). A happily married father of sons Jamie and Hunter, in his off time Jim proclaims himself an avid (beginner) cricket player on the ICE Storm cricket team, a passionate hacker of the golf ball, and a runner (jogger/walker) of frequent (annual) 10Ks in Atlanta.

Heather Callebaut Sinkwitz gained her expertise while working as a business intelligence consultant, specializing as a certified SAP BusinessObjects instructor and solution provider. She currently dedicates herself to building innovative Business Intelligence solutions using a variety of technologies. A data junkie, she enjoys presenting meaningful information in new and unique ways to aid customers in making informed decisions. She remains actively involved in the BI community through participation in user groups and speaking engagements, both locally in her home state of Arizona or nationally. Currently, Heather is the Analytics and Reporting Product Manager for Trax Technologies (*www.traxtech.com*).

Dallas Marks is a principal technical architect and trainer for EV Technologies and an SAP Certified Application Associate for SAP BusinessObjects Web Intelligence and the Business Intelligence platform. Dallas has worked with SAP BusinessObjects BI tools since 2003 and has implemented solutions for a number of industries, including retail, energy, health care, and manufacturing. He is a frequent speaker at local ASUG chapters, national ASUG, and SAPinsider conferences, and independent SAP BusinessObjects user groups. Dallas holds a master's degree in computer engineering from the University of Cincinnati. Dallas blogs about various business intelligence topics at *http://www.dallasmarks.org/*. You can follow him on Twitter at *@dallasmarks*. Photo by Morgan Noble.

Gabriel Orthous is a population health management and healthcare analytics expert, and a senior consultant to Wellcentive. Gabe has more than 15 years of business analytics managerial and software engineering experience with extensive expertise around business intelligence, financial reporting, and decision analytics. Gabe graduated from Mercer University with a master's degree in Business Administration and was inducted to the International Honor Society Beta Gamma Sigma in 2008. In addition, Gabe is chair for the Dashboarding and Visualization Special Interest Group for ASUG, co-chair for ASUG's Business Objects' Strategic SIG, and an active member of the Customer Advisory Council, as well as a renowned international speaker.

Index

D

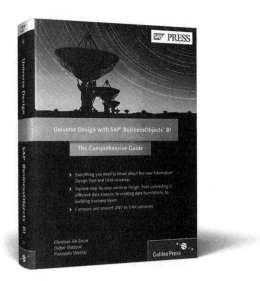

- Everything about the new Information Design Tool and UNX universes

- Explore step-by-step universe design

- Compare and convert UNV to UNX universes

Christian Ah-Soon, Didier Mazoué, Pierpaolo Vezzosi

Universe Design with SAP BusinessObjects BI

The Comprehensive Guide

Are you the master of your UNX universes? This comprehensive resource spans universe creation to universe publication. You'll learn to build single- and multi-source data foundations and business layers and to convert UNV to UNX using the new Information Design Tool. Up to date for SAP BusinessObjects BI 4.1, this book offers the step-by-step instructions and screenshots you need to design universes for the world.

729 pp., 79,95 Euro / US$ 79.95
ISBN 978-1-59229-901-0, Nov 2013
www.sap-press.com/3412

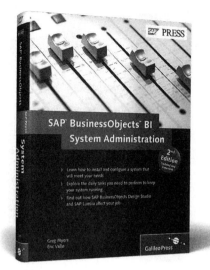

- Get your system up: sizing, installation, configuration

- Get your system running: security, monitoring, mobility

- Get your system current: SAP BusinessObjects Design Studio, SAP Lumira

Greg Myers, Eric Vallo

SAP BusinessObjects BI System Administration

Users keeping you on your toes? Stay one step ahead with this guide to BOBJ administration. From sizing to troubleshooting, get the background you need to administer a system that does what it's supposed to do. Revised for release 4.1 and offering new coverage of Design Studio and Lumira, this book will help you keep your system up to snuff.

approx. 550 pp., 69,95 Euro / US$ 69.95
ISBN 978-1-4932-1000-8, 2. edition, Nov 2014
www.sap-press.com/3605

■ Get up to speed on the next generation of SAP business intelligence

■ Learn how to model and visualize data to tell a story

■ Find out about options for desktop, mobile, and cloud deployment

Christian Ah-Soon, Peter Snowdon

Getting Started with SAP Lumira

What story does your data tell? See what SAP Lumira can do and how to identify trends and find hidden insights in your business data. Get the details on progressing from data acquisitions to data manipulation to data visualization so you can add some color to your data. See how SAP Lumira fits into existing BI landscapes and which administration options are best for each setup. This introduction to SAP Lumira will help make each picture—or chart—worth a thousand words.

approx. 565 pp., 69,95 Euro / US$ 69.95
ISBN 978-1-4932-1033-6, Dec 2014
www.sap-press.com/3645

- Implement SAP HANA as a standalone data warehouse

- Integrate SAP Data Services and the SAP BusinessObjects BI tools with SAP HANA

- Benefit from step-by-step instructions, technical details, and downloadable data for every step

Jonathan Haun, Chris Hickman, Don Loden, Roy Wells

Implementing SAP HANA

You know what SAP HANA is—now you need to see it in action. Look no further than this book, which will steer you through a real-life implementation of the standalone version of SAP HANA. You'll find step-by-step instructions and screenshots that show you how to implement real data in a real system, from concept to go-live.

837 pp., 69,95 Euro / US$ 69.95
ISBN 978-1-59229-856-3, Sep 2013
www.sap-press.com/3342

Interested in reading more?

Please visit our website for all new
book and e-book releases from SAP PRESS.

www.sap-press.com